SERVICES MARKETING

INTEGRATING CUSTOMER FOCUS ACROSS THE FIRM

ALAN WILSON, VALARIE A. ZEITHAML, MARY JO BITNER AND DWAYNE D. GREMLER

THIRD EUROPEAN EDITION

SERVICES MARKETING

INTEGRATING CUSTOMER FOCUS ACROSS THE FIRM

THIRD EUROPEAN EDITION

London Boston Burr Ridge, IL Dubuque, IA Madison, WI New York San Francisco St. Louis Bangkok Bogotá Caracas Kuala Lumpur Lisbon Madrid Mexico City Milan Montreal New Delhi Santiago Seoul Singapore Sydney Taipei Toronto

Services Marketing, Third European Edition
Alan Wilson, Valarie A. Zeithaml, Mary Jo Bitner and Dwayne D. Gremler
ISBN-13 9780077169312
ISBN-10 007716931X

Published by McGraw-Hill Education
Shoppenhangers Road
Maidenhead
Berkshire
SL6 2QL
Telephone: 44 (0) 1628 502 500
Fax: 44 (0) 1628 770 224
Website: www.mheducation.co.uk

British Library Cataloguing in Publication Data
A catalogue record for this book is available from the British Library
Library of Congress Cataloguing in Publication Data
The Library of Congress data for this book has been applied for from the Library of Congress

Programme Manager: Natalie Jacobs / Leiah Norcott
Product Developer: Mark Sapwell
Content Product Manager: Ben Wilcox
Marketing Manager: Geeta Kumar

Text Design by Kamae Design, Oxford
Cover design by Adam Renvoize
Printed and bound in Great Britain by Ashford Colour Press Ltd.

Brief Table of Contents

Detailed Table of Contents

About the Authors

Alan Wilson is Professor of Marketing and was previous Head of the Marketing Department within the University of Strathclyde Business School. Before joining the university, he was a senior consultant and executive trainer within the services division of a London-based marketing consultancy practice and prior to that an Associate Director of a leading London-based marketing research agency. He specializes in the marketing of services and has a PhD in the subject. He is a Fellow of both the Chartered Institute of Marketing and the Market Research Society. His book, *Marketing Research: An Integrated Approach*, is in its third edition and he has published in a wide range of marketing and service management journals, for which he has won a number of awards and prizes. Professor Wilson has delivered high-level executive training to a wide range of service organizations in the banking, hospitality, professional service and business-to-business service sectors and has been invited to deliver lectures and seminars on both services marketing and marketing research in a variety of countries throughout the world.

Valarie A. Zeithaml is the David S. Van Pelt Professor of Marketing at the Kenan-Flagler Business School at the University of North Carolina at Chapel Hill. Since receiving her MBA and PhD in Marketing from the Robert H. Smith School of Business at the University of Maryland, Dr. Zeithaml has devoted her career to researching and teaching the topics of service quality and services management. She is the co-author of *Delivering Quality Service: Balancing Customer Perceptions and Expectations* (The Free Press, 1990), now in its 20th printing, and *Driving Customer Equity: How Customer Lifetime Value Is Reshaping Corporate Strategy* (The Free Press, 2000). In 2002, *Driving Customer Equity* won the first Berry–American Marketing Association Book Prize for the best marketing book of the past three years.

Mary Jo Bitner is the executive director of the Center for Services Leadership, PetSmart Chair in Services Leadership, and Professor of Marketing at the W. P. Carey School of Business, Arizona State University (ASU). In her career as a professor and researcher, Dr. Bitner has been recognized as one of the founders and pioneers in the field of service marketing and management worldwide. At ASU she was a founding faculty member of the Center for Services Leadership and has been a leader in its emergence as the premier university-based centre for the study of services marketing and management.

Dwayne D. Gremler is Professor of marketing at Bowling Green State University (BGSU). He received his MBA and PhD degrees from the W. P. Carey School of Business at Arizona State University. Throughout his academic career, Dr. Gremler has been a passionate advocate for the research and instruction of services marketing issues. He has served as chair of the American Marketing Association's Services Marketing Special Interest Group and has helped organize services marketing conferences in Australia, The Netherlands, France, Portugal, Finland and the United States.

Preface

This third European edition of this highly successful *Services Marketing* text is for students and business people who recognize the vital role that services play in the economy and our lives. European economies are now dominated by services, and virtually all companies view service as critical to retaining their customers today and in the future. Even manufacturing companies that, in the past, have depended on physical products for their livelihood now recognize that service provides one of their few sustainable competitive advantages.

This third European edition takes the theories, concepts and frameworks that exist in the original American version of the text and applies them to the European context. European examples, cases and readings are used to provide a true European flavour to the material. The material in this third edition has also been updated and restructured to reflect the latest services marketing thinking.

The foundation of the text is the recognition that services present special challenges that must be identified and addressed. Issues commonly encountered in service organizations – the inability to inventory, the difficulty in synchronizing demand and supply, and challenges in controlling the performance quality of human interactions – need to be articulated and tackled by managers. This text aims to help students and managers understand and address these special challenges of services marketing.

The development of strong customer relationships through quality service (and services) are at the heart of the book's content. The topics covered are equally applicable to organizations whose core product is service (such as banks, transportation companies, hotels, hospitals, educational institutions, professional services, telecommunication) and to organizations that depend on service excellence for competitive advantage (high-technology manufacturers, automotive and industrial products, and so on).

The book's content focuses on the knowledge needed to implement service strategies for competitive advantage across industries. Included are frameworks for customer-focused management, and strategies for increasing customer satisfaction and retention through service. In addition to standard marketing topics (such as pricing), this text introduces students to topics that include management and measurement of service quality, service recovery, the linking of customer measurement to performance measurement, service blueprinting, customer co-production, and cross-functional treatment of issues through integration of marketing with disciplines such as operations and human resources. Each of these topics represents pivotal content for tomorrow's businesses as they structure around process rather than task, engage in digital marketing, mass customize their offerings, deliver services using mobile and digital platforms, and attempt to build strong relationships with their customers.

DISTINGUISHING CONTENT FEATURES

The distinguishing features of the text, some of which are new to this third European edition, include the following:

1 **Cross-functional treatment** of issues through integration of marketing with other disciplines such as operations and human resources management.
2 A focus on understanding **the foundations of services marketing** and the customer before introducing the conceptual framework of the remainder of the book based on the **gaps model**.
3 Greater emphasis on the topic of **service quality** than existing marketing and service marketing texts.

4 Increased focus on **customer expectations and perceptions** and what they imply for marketers.

5 Increased **technology, social media and digital coverage** throughout the text.

6 A chapter on **service recovery** that includes a conceptual framework for understanding the topic.

7 An improved chapter on **listening to customers through research and social media**.

8 A chapter on **customer-defined service standards**.

9 Consumer-based pricing and **value pricing strategies**.

10 A chapter on **integrated services marketing communications**.

11 Increased focus on **customer relationships and relationship marketing strategies**.

12 An entire chapter that recognizes **human resource challenges and human resource strategies** for delivering customer-focused services.

13 Coverage of new service development processes and a detailed and complete introduction to **service blueprinting** – a tool for describing, designing and positioning services.

14 Coverage of the customer's role in service delivery and strategies for **co-production**.

15 A chapter on the role of **physical evidence**, particularly the physical environment or 'servicescape'.

16 A chapter on the **financial impact** of service quality.

To support these topics, there are:

1 **European cases and vignettes**.

2 **'Service Spotlights'** in each chapter providing short **European examples** to illustrate services marketing in action.

3 **Discussion questions** and **exercises** appropriate to the **European context** in each chapter.

4 **Up-to-date Suggestions for further reading** (particularly **European reading**) in each chapter.

5 Short revision lists of **Key concepts** provided at the end of each chapter.

The framework of the book continues to be managerially focused, with every chapter presenting company examples and strategies for addressing key issues. There are integrating frameworks in most chapters. For example, there are frameworks for understanding service recovery strategies, service pricing, integrated marketing communications, customer relationships, customer roles and internal marketing.

UNIQUE STRUCTURE

The text features a structure completely different from the standard 4P (marketing mix) structure of introductory marketing texts. The text starts by introducing the reader to the key foundations for service marketing by introducing services (Chapter 1) and understanding the customer, in terms of behaviour (Chapter 2), expectations (Chapter 3) and perceptions (Chapter 4). The remainder of the text is organized around the gaps model of service quality, which is described fully in Chapter 5. Beginning with Chapter 6, the text is organized into parts around the provider gaps in the gaps model. For example, Chapters 6 and 7 deal with understanding customer requirements; Chapters 8, 9 and 10 with aligning service design and standards; Chapters 11 through to 15 address delivering and performing services; and Chapters 16 and 17 managing service promises. Chapter 18 then focuses on the total picture of service and the bottom line.

WHAT COURSES AND WHICH STUDENTS SHOULD USE THIS TEXT?

Students need to have completed at least a basic marketing course as a prerequisite to using this text. The primary target audience for the text is services marketing classes at the undergraduate, postgraduate (both masters and doctoral courses), and executive education levels. Other target audiences are (1) service management classes at both the undergraduate and postgraduate levels and (2) postgraduate level marketing management classes in which a lecturer wishes to provide a more comprehensive teaching of services than is possible with a standard marketing management text. A subset of chapters would also provide a more concise text for use in a specialized mini-semester course. A further reduced set of chapters may be used to supplement undergraduate and graduate basic marketing courses to enhance the treatment of services.

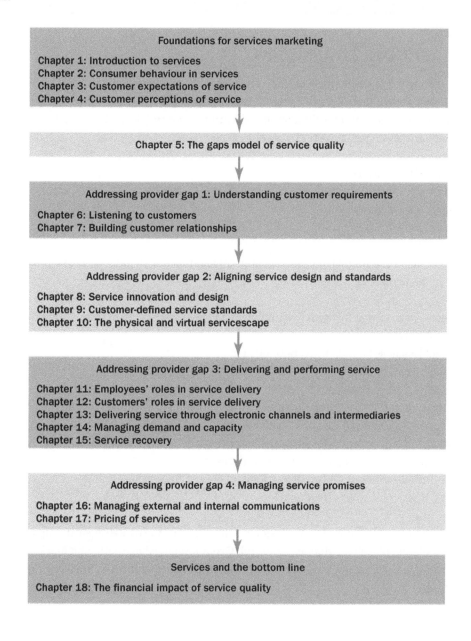

Foundations for services marketing

Chapter 1: Introduction to services
Chapter 2: Consumer behaviour in services
Chapter 3: Customer expectations of service
Chapter 4: Customer perceptions of service

Chapter 5: The gaps model of service quality

Addressing provider gap 1: Understanding customer requirements

Chapter 6: Listening to customers
Chapter 7: Building customer relationships

Addressing provider gap 2: Aligning service design and standards

Chapter 8: Service innovation and design
Chapter 9: Customer-defined service standards
Chapter 10: The physical and virtual servicescape

Addressing provider gap 3: Delivering and performing service

Chapter 11: Employees' roles in service delivery
Chapter 12: Customers' roles in service delivery
Chapter 13: Delivering service through electronic channels and intermediaries
Chapter 14: Managing demand and capacity
Chapter 15: Service recovery

Addressing provider gap 4: Managing service promises

Chapter 16: Managing external and internal communications
Chapter 17: Pricing of services

Services and the bottom line

Chapter 18: The financial impact of service quality

Acknowledgements

AUTHOR'S ACKNOWLEDGEMENTS

I would like to acknowledge the suggestions for improvements made by the reviewers of the book. Their feedback on the book and on the stages of the draft manuscript has helped us to improve the third European edition for academics' teaching and for their students' learning. Our thanks go to the following reviewers for their comments at various stages in the text's development:

Raphael K Akamavi, Hull University
Panayiota Alevizou, Sheffield University
Line Lervik-Olsen, Oslo University
Ghasem Zaefarian, Leeds University

I would also like to thank the following case contributors and those who gave permission for material to be reproduced within the textbook:

Jean-Pierre Balliot, International Institute for Management Development, Lausanne, Switzerland
Fran Baylis, Case Centre
Luke Fletcher, Kent Business School, University of Kent
Monali Hota, Iéseg School of Management
Marie-Catherine Mars, Edhec Business School
Stefan Michel, International Institute for Management Development, Lausanne, Switzerland
Suchitra Mohanty, Amity Research Centers Headquarters
Debapratim Purkayastha, IBS Center for Management Research
Syeda Maseeha Qumer, IBS Center for Management Research
Katie Truss, Kent Business School, University of Kent
Vasudha M, Amity Research Centers Headquarters

I would further like to acknowledge the professional efforts of the McGraw-Hill staff. My sincere thanks to Leiah Norcott, Natalie Jacobs, Peter Hooper, Tom Hill, Geeta Kumar, Nina Smith, and Mark Sapwell.

Finally I would like to thank my wife and family, Sandra, Duncan and Kirsty for keeping me sane whilst writing this edition.

PICTURE ACKNOWLEDGEMENTS

The authors and publishers would like to extend thanks to the following for the reproduction of company advertising and/or logos:

Part 1: Thanks to AGE Fotostock; Chapter 1: Thanks to Stockfood; Chapter Opening Example: Thanks to Alamy Images; Chapter 2: Thanks to iStockphoto; Chapter 2 Opening Example: Thanks to Erica Simone Leeds; Chapter 3: Thanks to Ingram Publishing/SuperStock; Chapter 3 Opening Example: Thanks to AGE Fotostock; Chapter 4: Thanks to Alamy Images; Chapter 4 Opening Example: Thanks to Virgin Money Manchester Lounge/Cloudbound 2012; Chapter 5: Thanks to Alamy Images; Chapter 5 Opening Example: Thanks to Blend Images; Part 2: Thanks to Gregg Vignal/Alamy Images; Chapter 6: Thanks to Superstock; Chapter 6 Opening Example: Thanks to McGraw-Hill Companies Chapter 7: Thanks to

Costa Coffee; Chapter 7 Opening Example: Thanks to Brian Zhang; Part 3: Thanks to Caia Image/Glow Images; Chapter 8: Thanks to AGE Fotostock; Chapter 8 Opening Example: McGraw-Hill Companies; Chapter 9: Thanks to Superstock; Chapter 9 Opening Example: Thanks to Dave Moyer; Chapter 10: Thanks to Alamy Images; Chapter 10 Opening Example: Thanks to McDonald's; Part 4: Thanks to iStockphoto; Chapter 11: Thanks to Alamy Images; Chapter 11 Opening Example: Chapter 12: Thanks to Campus Life; Chapter 12 Opening Example: Thanks to Blend Images; Thanks to Holger Ellgaard 2009; Chapter 13: Thanks to Superstock; Chapter 13 Opening Example: Thanks to Schlaier; Thanks to Andreas Praefcke 2011; Chapter 14: Thanks to iStockphoto; Chapter 14 Opening Example: Thanks to Darcy VanWyck; Chapter 15: Thanks to Twitter/Alamy Images; Chapter 15 Opening Example: Thanks to Hermann Mock; Part 5: Thanks to iStockphoto; Chapter 16: Thanks to iStockphoto; Chapter 16 Opening Example: Thanks to Santander press office; Chapter 17: Thanks to Alamy Images; Chapter 17 Opening Example: Thanks to airberlin media centre; Part 6: Thanks to iStockphoto; Chapter 18: Thanks to AGE Fotostock; Chapter 18 Opening Example: Thanks to Jeffrey Friedl 2013. Case 1: Thanks to Illene MacDonald/ Alamy Images; Case 2: Thanks to Adrian Pingstone; Case 3: Thanks to Glow Images; Case 4: Thanks to Nandaro; Case 5: Thanks to McDonald's; Case 6: Thanks to Jill Braaten; Case 7: Thanks to Mark-making; Case 8: Thanks to AXA.

Every effort has been made to trace and acknowledge ownership of copyright and to clear permission for material reproduced in this book. The publishers will be pleased to make suitable arrangements to clear permission with any copyright holders whom it has not been possible to contact.

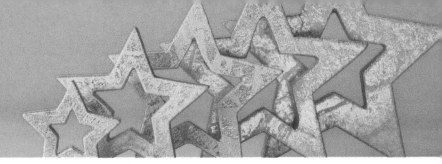

LEARNING OBJECTIVES

This chapter's objectives are to:

1. Explain what services are and identify important trends in services.
2. Explain the need for special services marketing concepts and practices and why the need has developed and is accelerating.
3. Explore the profound impact of technology on service.
4. Outline the basic differences between goods and services and the resulting challenges and opportunities for service businesses.
5. Introduce the expanded marketing mix for services and the philosophy of customer focus, as powerful frameworks and themes that are fundamental to the rest of the text.
6. Introduce the servuction system model and the concept of the services triangle.

Changing Perceptions – Virgin Money

As part of its expansion into the UK retail banking sector, Virgin Money are attempting to change customers' perceptions of the service delivered by bank branches through the opening of five Virgin Money Lounges in major cities. These lounges do have areas where customers can do their online banking or receive service relating to their Virgin Money products, but they are about more than money and banking. They are designed to be places where customers can relax and local communities come together.

They provide free hot and cold drinks, fruit and snacks as well as free Wi-Fi and access to free iPads. Television is available all day as well as newspapers and a selection of magazines. Children are welcomed; there is a dedicated children's area in every Lounge, complete with toys, books and games

PHYSICAL EVIDENCE

WHAT IS PHYSICAL EVIDENCE?

Customers often rely on tangible cues, or physical evidence, to evaluate the service before its purchase and to assess their satisfaction with the service during and after consumption. Effective design of physical, tangible evidence is important for closing provider gap 2.

General elements of physical evidence are shown in Table 10.1. They include all aspects of the organization's physical facility (the servicescape) as well as other forms of tangible communication. Elements of the servicescape that affect customers include both exterior attributes (such as signage, parking, and the landscape) and interior attributes (such as design, layout, equipment and decor). Note that web pages and virtual servicescapes conveyed over the Internet are more recent forms of physical evidence that companies can use to communicate about the service experience, making services more tangible for customers both before and after purchase. For example, travellers can now preview destinations, tour natural environments and 'experience' entertainment venues online before booking their trips or even deciding where to travel. Virtual tours and 360-degree views of hotels and their rooms allow potential guests to view the facilities in and out before booking.

SERVICE SPOTLIGHT

Omega Bank, a private bank with branches across Greece, has designed its branch interiors to communicate a feeling of 'understated quality', avoiding ostentation and short-lived trendiness. Instead of using Greek marble and granite flooring, they imported honed green slate from the Lake District in the UK which better matched the 'understated quality' image. The teller desks were designed in etched glass and steel, with maple timber slab ends. Aesthetically, they are meant to be very open and welcoming in appearance, accentuated by 'floating' all the surface planes on stainless steel spacers, so that none of the major elements actually touch each other.

The same design system is incorporated into graphic and print items such as banking and ATM cards, promotional leaflets and private banking communication and print items.[10]

The design of a physical setting can also differentiate one area of a service organization from another. For example, in the hotel industry, one large hotel may have several levels of dining possibilities, each signalled by differences in design. Price differentiation is also often partly achieved through variations in physical setting. Bigger rooms with more physical amenities cost more, just as larger seats with more leg room (generally in first class) are more expensive on an airline.

SUMMARY

This chapter discussed the discrepancy between company perceptions of customer expectations and the standards they set to deliver to these expectations. Among the major causes for provider gap 2 are inadequate standardization of service behaviours and actions, absence of formal processes for setting service quality goals, and lack of customer-defined standards. These problems were discussed and detailed, along with strategies to close the gap.

Customer-defined standards are at the heart of delivery of service that customers expect; they are the link between customers' expressed expectations and company actions to deliver to those expectations. Creating these service standards is not always done by service organizations. Doing so requires that companies' marketing and operations departments work together by using the marketing research as input for operations design. Unless the operations standards are defined by customer priorities, they are not likely to have an impact on customer perceptions of service.

LEARNING OBJECTIVES

Each chapter opens with a set of learning objectives, summarizing what knowledge, skills or understanding readers should acquire from each chapter.

OPENING EXAMPLES

Each chapter opens with an example of service marketing in action or a services marketing issue that helps you to understand how the theory explored in the chapter is relevant to real practice. Examples include Airbnb, Skyscanner, Starbucks, and Amazon.

SOCIAL MEDIA AND DIGITAL MARKETING

Icons highlight materials that focus on issues involving social media and digital marketing in each chapter, to help you explore how recent technological innovations and behaviours affect established service marketing theories.

SERVICE SPOTLIGHTS

Each chapter is interspersed with numerous short service spotlights that tie theory to practice and show how companies bring services to their customers. Examples come from a variety of customer and business-to-business servers, and include Amex, FSA, Hilton and IKEA.

CHAPTER SUMMARY

This briefly reviews and reinforces the main topics covered in each chapter to ensure that you have developed a solid understanding of the key topics. Use it in conjunction with the learning objectives as a quick reference.

KEY CONCEPTS

An ideal tool for revision or to check definitions as you read, key concepts are highlighted in bold, with page number references at the end of each chapter so they can be found easily.

FURTHER READING

Berry, L.L. and Parasuraman, A. (1993). Building a new academic *Journal of Retailing*, 69(1), 13–60.

Grönroos, C. (2011). Value co-creation in service logic: A critical analy

Grönroos, C. and Gummerus, J. (2014). The service revolution ar logic vs service-dominant logic. *Managing Service Quality*, 24(3), 206

IfM and IBM (2008). *Succeeding through Service Innovation: A Research, Business and Government*. Cambridge, United Kingdom: Manufacturing.

Lovelock, C. and Gummesson, E. (2004). Whither services marketi fresh perspectives. *Journal of Service Research*, 7(1), 20–41.

FURTHER READING

Each chapter ends with a list of suggested reading, listing international research in services marketing.

DISCUSSION QUESTIONS

1. Using your own personal examples, discuss the general importance of customers in the successful creation and delivery of service experiences.

2. Why might customer actions and attitudes cause the service performance gap to occur? Use your own examples to illustrate your understanding.

3. Using Table 12.1, think of specific services you have experienced that fall within each of the three levels of customer participation: low, medium and high. Describe specifically what you did as a customer in each case. How did your involvement vary across the three types of service situations?

4. Describe a time when your satisfaction in a particular situation was *increased* because of something another customer did. Could (or does) the organization do anything to ensure that this experience happens routinely? What does it do? Should it try to make this situation a routine occurrence?

5. Describe a time when your satisfaction in a particular situation was *decreased* because of something another customer did. Could the organization have done anything to manage this situation more effectively? If so, what?

6. Discuss the customer's role as a *productive resource* for the firm. Describe a time when you

DISCUSSION QUESTIONS AND EXERCISES

Discussion questions encourage you to review and apply the knowledge you have developed from each chapter. Exercises require a little more time and thought, and can be used as group assignments or exam practice.

CASE 1   DISNEY'S MAGIC BANDS: ENHANCING CUSTOMER EXPE

This case was written by Vasudha M, Amity Research Centers Headquar © 2014, Amity Research Centers Headquarters, Bangalore.

More than a y announcement ab of the MagicBanc The MagicBands among guests sta hotels were als

CASE STUDIES

The book includes a case study section designed to test how well you can apply the main ideas presented throughout the book to real company examples. The cases integrate a number of service ideas into a fuller example that needs deeper analysis and understanding. Each case study has its own set of questions. Cases include Disneyland, McDonald's, Ryanair, Starbucks and Uniqlo.

connect®

Mc Graw Hill Education

McGraw-Hill Connect Marketing is a learning and teaching environment that improves student performance and outcomes whilst promoting engagement and comprehension of content.

You can utilize publisher-provided materials, or add your own content to design a complete course to help your students achieve higher outcomes.

PROVEN EFFECTIVE

With Connect / Without Connect

MORE As and Bs WITH CONNECT

A   B   C   D

INSTRUCTORS

With McGraw-Hill Connect Marketing, instructors get:

- Simple **assignment management,** allowing you to spend more time teaching.
- **Auto-graded** assignments, quizzes and tests.
- **Detailed visual reporting** where students and section results can be viewed and analysed.
- Sophisticated **online testing** capability.
- A **filtering and reporting** function that allows you to easily assign and report on materials that are correlated to a range of categories. Reports can be accessed for individual students or the whole class, as well as offering the ability to drill into individual assignments, questions or categories.
- **Instructor materials** to help supplement your course.

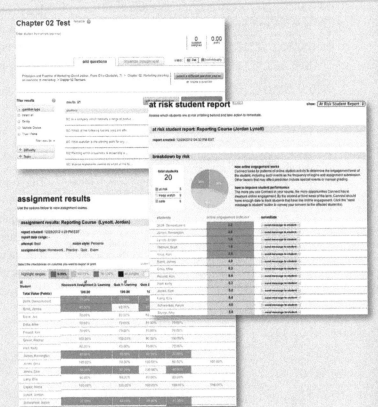

Get Connected. Get Results.

Available online via Connect we have a range of instructor support materials:

- Lecturer manual to support your module preparation, with case notes, guide answers, teaching tips and more;

- PowerPoint presentations including artwork;

- Image library

- Video links

STUDENTS

With McGraw-Hill Connect Marketing, students get:

Assigned content

- Easy **online access** to homework, tests and quizzes.

- **Immediate feedback** and 24-hour tech support.

With McGraw-Hill SmartBook, students can:

- Take control of your own learning with a personalized and adaptive reading experience

- Understand what you know and don't know; SmartBook takes you through the stages of reading and practice, prompting you to recharge your knowledge throughout the course for maximum retention.

- Achieve the most efficient and productive study time by adapting to what you do and don't know.

- Hone in on concepts you are most likely to forget, to ensure knowledge of key concept is learnt and retained.

FEATURES

Videos

Videos featuring interviews with marketing managers and directors from a wide range of companies will engage students with the idea of marketing as a career and how the concepts they learn relate to a real world context. Autogradable questions encourage them to analyse and assess the content in the videos.

Multiple Choice Questions

Check students knowledge and conceptual understanding

Quick to answer, these questions can provide students with feedback immediately. MCQs are available via our quiz content and also the testbank.

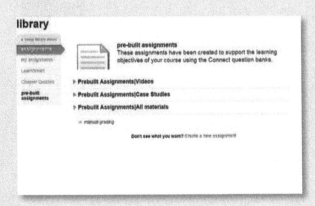

Pre-built assignments

Assign autogradable material as a ready-made assignment with the simple click of a button.

SmartBook™

Fueled by LearnSmart—the most widely used and intelligent adaptive learning resource—SmartBook is the first and only adaptive reading experience available today. Distinguishing what a student knows from what they don't, and honing in on concepts they are most likely to forget, SmartBook personalizes content for each student in a continuously adapting reading experience. Valuable reports provide instructors insight as to how students are progressing through textbook content, and are useful for shaping in-class time or assessment.

LearnSmart™

McGraw-Hill LearnSmart is an adaptive learning program that identifies what an individual student knows and doesn't know. LearnSmart's adaptive learning path helps students learn faster, study more efficiently, and retain more knowledge. Now with integrated learning resources which present topics and concepts in different and engaging formats increases student engagement and promotes additional practice of key concepts. Reports available for both students and instructors indicate where students need to study more and assess their success rate in retaining knowledge.

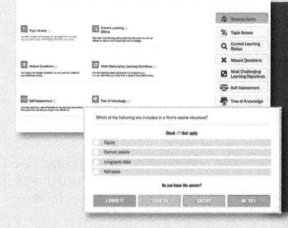

Let us help make our **content** your **solution**

At McGraw-Hill Education our aim is to help lecturers to find the most suitable content for their needs delivered to their students in the most appropriate way. Our custom publishing solutions offer the ideal combination of content delivered in the way which best suits lecturer and students.

Our custom publishing programme offers lecturers the opportunity to select just the chapters or sections of material they wish to deliver to their students from a database called CREATE™ at

http://create.mheducation.com/uk/

CREATE™ contains over two million pages of content from:
- textbooks
- professional books
- case books - Harvard Articles, Insead, Ivey, Darden, Thunderbird and BusinessWeek
- Taking Sides - debate materials

Across the following imprints:
- McGraw-Hill Education
- Open University Press
- Harvard Business Publishing
- US and European material

There is also the option to include additional material authored by lecturers in the custom product – this does not necessarily have to be in English.

We will take care of everything from start to finish in the process of developing and delivering a custom product to ensure that lecturers and students receive exactly the material needed in the most suitable way.

With a Custom Publishing Solution, students enjoy the best selection of material deemed to be the most suitable for learning everything they need for their courses – something of real value to support their learning. Teachers are able to use exactly the material they want, in the way they want, to support their teaching on the course.

Please contact your local McGraw-Hill Education representative with any questions or alternatively contact Warren Eels e: warren.eels@mheducation.com.

PART 1

Foundations for Services Marketing

This first part of the text provides you with the foundations needed to begin your study of services marketing. The first chapter identifies up-to-date trends, issues, and opportunities in services as a backdrop for the strategies addressed in the remaining chapters. Knowing what customers want and how they assess what they receive is the foundation for designing effective services. Therefore, Chapter 2 focuses on what is known about customer behaviour for services, Chapter 3 looks at customer expectations and Chapter 4 considers customer perceptions. Chapter 5 introduces the gaps model of service quality, the framework that provides the structure for the rest of the text. The remaining parts of the book will include information and strategies to address the specific gaps identified by this model, giving you the tools and knowledge to become a services marketing leader.

CHAPTER 1

Introduction to Services

CHAPTER OUTLINE

LEARNING OBJECTIVES

This chapter's objectives are to:

1 Explain what services are and identify important trends in services.
2 Explain the need for special services marketing concepts and practices and why the need has developed and is accelerating.
3 Explore the profound impact of technology on service.
4 Outline the basic differences between goods and services and the resulting challenges and opportunities for service businesses.
5 Introduce the expanded marketing mix for services and the philosophy of customer focus, as powerful frameworks and themes that are fundamental to the rest of the text.
6 Introduce the servuction system model and the concept of the services triangle.

OPENING EXAMPLE
Europe's Position as a Global Services Provider

Each year the US magazine *Forbes* produces a comprehensive list of the world's biggest and most powerful companies as measured by a composite ranking for sales, profits, assets and market value. In 2014 there were 29 European companies within the world's top 100 organizations. Of these, 14 of the companies were directly involved in the provision of services such as banking/financial services (HSBC Group, BNP Paribas, Banco Santander, UBS, Credit Agricole and ING Group), insurance (Allianz, AXA Group, Zurich Insurance Group and Munich Re), energy and utilities (EDF), and telecommunication services (Vodafone and Telefonica).

These organizations operate in the sectors that are traditionally associated with, and classified as, services. However, almost all of the other European companies that appear in the top 100 rely on service and services to sell their products. For example, Siemens offers consultancy services to develop and sell their product solutions to their customers. Volkswagen and BMW provide after-sales service, warranties, breakdown cover and financial packages as part of their offering and rely on the service provided by their dealers to attract custom. Shell and the other large oil companies in the top 100 aim to improve their corporate customers' business performance by providing leading-edge energy consulting supported by innovative technology.

Services are therefore critical to today's economy and although the organizations in the top 100 organizations only represent the tip of the iceberg of the European service sector, they clearly demonstrate Europe's position as a key global player in the provision of services and highlight the need to study and understand services marketing.

Source: Extracted from www.forbes.com.[1]

WHAT ARE SERVICES?

Put in the simplest terms, *services are deeds, processes and performances*. Our opening vignette illustrates what is traditionally meant by this definition. The services offered by HSBC, AXA Group and Vodafone are not tangible things that can be touched, seen and felt, but are rather intangible deeds and performances. This may be obvious for banking, insurance and telecommunication organizations, but even a product-based organization such as IBM offers client solutions that may include a range of service offerings such as a repair and maintenance service for its equipment, consulting services for information technology (IT) and e-commerce applications, training services, Web design and hosting, and other services. These services may include a final, tangible report, a website or, in the case of training, tangible instructional materials. However, for the most part, the entire service is represented to the client through problem analysis activities, meetings with the client, follow-up calls and reporting – a series of deeds, processes and performances.

Although we will rely on the simple, broad definition of *services*, you should be aware that over time *services* and the *service sector of the economy* have been defined in subtly different ways. The variety of definitions can often explain the confusion or disagreements people have when discussing services and when

Figure 1.1   Lovelock's classification of services[2]

	People as Recipients	Possessions as Recipients
Tangible Actions	Services Directed at People's Bodies Passenger Transportation Healthcare Spa Treatments	Services Directed at People's Tangible Possessions Courier Services Car Repair Laundry and Dry Cleaning
Intangible Actions	Services Directed at People's Minds Education Entertainment Psychotherapy	Services Directed at Intangible Assets/Possessions Accounting Banking Legal Services

describing industries that comprise the service sector of the economy. Compatible with our simple, broad definition is one that defines services to include:

> *all economic activities whose output is not a physical product or construction, is generally consumed at the time it is produced, and provides added value in forms (such as convenience, amusement, timeliness, comfort, or health) that are essentially intangible concerns of its first purchaser.*[3]

The size of the service sector is evident from the fact that services account for around 72 per cent of all European employment and 73 per cent of European gross domestic product (CIA, 2014 *The World Factbook 2014*). The breadth of industries making up the service sector is large, and many attempts have been made to classify them into different categories. The best-known classification was developed by Lovelock[4] in 1983 and is shown in Figure 1.1. This classifies services into four broad categories from a process perspective relating to whether the service performance was enacted on a person or their possessions and the extent to which performance was more or less tangible. Although the categories share similar process-related characteristics, they also have distinctive implications for marketing, operations and human resource management.

SERVICES DIRECTED AT PEOPLE'S BODIES

Services in this category require the recipient to be physically present within the service system. You need to sit on the train, visit the dentist's surgery, lie on the massage table in order to receive the service. Sometimes it is possible for the service provider to come to you: for example, you could get your hair cut at home or the doctor could visit you, but more commonly you have to go to them. You are, therefore, a key part of the delivery of this service as you have to be present at the correct time and enact your role in the service experience. If you don't sit still in the dentist's chair and open and close your mouth at the right time, it will be very difficult for the dentist to deliver the service. The airline cannot provide the service properly unless you check in on time, get through security, turn up at the boarding gate and put on your seat belt when told. Managers need to think through the information that the customer requires in order to carry out the correct actions and behaviour. The premises or transportation vehicles in which the service is performed have to be inviting and attractive to potential customers and generally need to be located in a place that is convenient. Expanding into overseas markets requires premises, equipment and employees to be located in the new markets.

SERVICES DIRECTED AT PEOPLE'S TANGIBLE POSSESSIONS

Services in this category do not require the customer to be present when the service is being delivered, although they may need to be present at the start and end of the service – for example, when dropping off and collecting a car from a car repair centre. Some services such as laundry and dry cleaning may collect the clothes from the customer and the customer may never see the service premises. The attractiveness of the design of the premises and the convenience of their location is less important for such services, since the emphasis is more likely to be on operational issues rather than customer ones. Expanding overseas is still likely to require investment in people, premises and equipment in the new markets, although some services such as ship repair may require the owner to take the ship to a neighbouring country for repair.

SERVICES DIRECTED AT PEOPLE'S MINDS

Services directed at people's minds include services such as education, the arts, professional advice, news and information. Although customers may go to physical premises such as universities and theatres, these premises may not be needed as technology such as the Internet and other broadcasting technologies can deliver the service at a distance without the customer being present in the place where the service is produced. Sports events and orchestral concerts can be transmitted by a satellite television broadcaster to a country, or distance learning can be offered in a country, even if the broadcaster or supplier has no physical presence in the receiving country. Unlike many other services, the service can be produced, then stored for delayed use through the digital recording of the performance. This means the service provider and the customer don't necessarily need to be active at the same time.

SERVICES DIRECTED AT PEOPLE'S INTANGIBLE POSSESSIONS

Services such as banking, insurance, and accountancy can be delivered with very little direct interaction between the customer and the organization. The processing of transactions on your bank account may be fully automated and may be undertaken in a location that is distant from the customer – it may even be in a different continent. Products such as insurance may involve no ongoing production activity after purchase unless there is a claim. As the customer sees very little that is tangible, it is often difficult to differentiate such services and to communicate their true value.

TANGIBILITY SPECTRUM

The broad definition of services implies that intangibility is a key determinant of whether an offering is a service. Although this is true, it is also true that very few products are purely intangible or totally tangible. Instead, services tend to be *more intangible* than manufactured products, and manufactured products tend to be *more tangible* than services. For example, the fast-food industry, while classified as a service, also has many tangible components such as the food, the packaging, and so on. Cars, while classified within the manufacturing sector, also supply many intangibles, such as transportation and navigation services. The tangibility spectrum shown in Figure 1.2 captures this idea. Throughout this text, when we refer to services we will be assuming the broad definition of services and acknowledging that there are very few 'pure services' or 'pure goods'. Although issues and approaches we discuss are directed more toward those offerings that lie on the right-hand side, the intangible side, of the spectrum.

SERVICE DOMINANT LOGIC

Service dominant logic is another way to look at what service means. In an article in the *Journal of Marketing*, Steve Vargo and Bob Lusch argue for a new dominant logic for marketing that suggests that all products and physical goods are valued for the services they provide.[5] Drawing on the work of respected economists, marketers and philosophers, the two authors suggest that the value derived from physical goods is really the service provided by the good, not the good itself. For example, they suggest that a pharmaceutical product provides medical services, a razor provides shaving services, and computers provide information and data manipulation services. Although this view is somewhat abstract, it suggests an even broader, more inclusive, view of the meaning of service. Their argument is that companies provide service solutions for

Figure 1.2   Tangibility spectrum

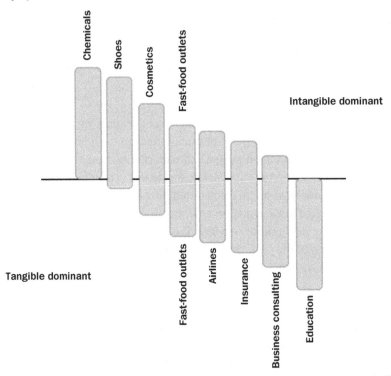

Source: Adapted from G. Lynn Shostack, 'Breaking free from product marketing', *Journal of Marketing* 41 (April 1977), pp. 73–80.

customers and should therefore offer the best combinations of service and products to create that solution. The over-arching concept is that it is the knowledge and competencies of the providers and the customers that represent the essential source of value creation rather than the products on their own. In the traditional view of goods, a product is delivered to a customer who uses and consumes it. The thinking behind service dominant logic is that value is not something that is simply created and delivered to the customer; the value is co-created in a process that requires the active participation of the producer, its customers and possibly other stakeholders (of the producer and the customer).

Value is created not at the time of the exchange between the producer and the customer but when the customer integrates, applies and uses the resources of a particular producer. A car has limited value unless it can provide a way of getting people to work; or it can provide a way of communicating a person's self-image; or it provides a sense of freedom for some. This is termed 'value in use' and is supported by warranties, advertising, branding, finance schemes as well as the physical product itself. It is also co-created by the customer, as the customer is expected to perform in certain ways in order to ensure their optimum achievement of the 'value in use'. It will depend on their driving skills, their knowledge of cars, roads and destinations as well as the manner in which they display the car (how clean they keep it, the accessories they use and the manner in which they drive). The value also varies contextually in relation to time and place dimensions. This 'value-in-context'[6] concept takes account of external influences and other stakeholders covering government-imposed laws and restrictions; traffic congestion, fuel prices; ecological and social pressures relating to emissions or fast driving and fuel consumption. Producers and customers may work together to influence these external forces in order to co-create better value for each other. This may mean that in the future, car manufacturers do not simply develop and sell electric cars but also work with customers and other stakeholders to provide solutions that allow householders to generate sufficient power for the cars, as well as charging points in city centres, or better road layouts in addition to education programmes on energy conservation.

To fully understand service dominant logic, it is also important to consider the role of interaction in creating value. This was highlighted by Christian Grönroos[7] but also stems from the traditional view of

Figure 1.3   A value-in-use creation model

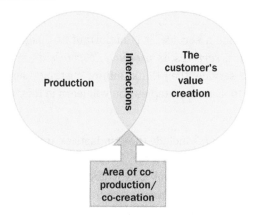

services (see servuction system on **page 24**) that a service involves interaction between a service provider and a customer.

A company is producing an offering of potential value to the customer through product development, design, manufacture and delivery. This may happen with or without direct interaction with the customer. The customers, in turn, are responsible for the value-creating processes, where value is created or emerges as value in use. Where customers interact through being engaged with the company in product design or with the company's personnel in delivery, installation or customer service activities, co-production of the resources can occur and/or co-creation of value in use is made possible (see Figure 1.3). If there are no direct interactions, customers are engaged in independent value creation with products or resources obtained from the independent activities undertaken by the company aimed at facilitating the customer's future value creation.

In many markets, the Internet and other technologies have enabled the complexity and dynamism of these interactions and inter-relationships to evolve further with websites, online forums, review sites, real-time data, mobile applications and location-based services, all adding to the value created for the customer and the producer. Therefore service dominant logic moves thinking away from the fallacy that products are different from services because they only create value in a linear, sequential creation, exchange and consumption set of stages. Instead it puts forward a much more complex and dynamic system of stakeholders, communications and technology that creates value and the context in which it is obtained.[8]

SERVICE SPOTLIGHT

Ford along with other car manufacturers has added value to their cars by adding the service provided by their Ford's Sync Emergency Assistance technology. This technology can potentially reduce the time taken to respond to accidents by assisting vehicle occupants to place a direct emergency call with location details in the correct local language. It helps notify the emergency services in that vital 'golden hour' after a serious crash when rapid medical attention can be the difference between life and death.

The vehicle's SYNC system initiates an emergency call through the occupant's Bluetooth-connected mobile phone following the deployment of an airbag. The system plays an introductory message and then relays the accident location co-ordinates using the on-board GPS unit, map and mobile network information. Emergency Assist saves crucial seconds by placing a call directly to emergency service operators rather than first routing through a third-party call centre. The value is co-created through a network of the car manufacturer, the driver switching on the Bluetooth function, the mobile phone manufacturer and the emergency services.

Source: **www.euroncap.com/rewards/ford_sync_emergency_assistance.aspx.**

SERVICES INDUSTRIES, SERVICES AS PRODUCTS, SERVICES AS EXPERIENCES AND CUSTOMER SERVICE

However broad or narrow we define a service, it is important at this point to draw distinctions between *service industries and companies, services as products, services as experiences* and *customer service*. Sometimes when people think of service, they think only of customer service, but service can be divided into four distinct categories. The tools and strategies you will learn in this text can be applied to any of these categories.

1 *Service industries and companies* include those industries and companies typically classified within the service sector whose core product is a service. All of the following companies can be considered pure service companies: Accor (hotels such as Novotel and Ibis), Lufthansa (transportation) and HSBC (banking). The total services sector comprises a wide range of service organizations, as suggested by Figure 1.2. Organizations in these sectors provide or sell services as their core offering.

The service sector is estimated to represent 73 per cent (CIA, 2014) of the gross domestic product (GDP) of the European Union (the data for individual European countries are set out in Table 1.1). Almost all the absolute growth in numbers of jobs and the fastest growth rates in job formation are in service-dominant industries.

There is a growing market for services and increasing dominance of services in economies worldwide, and not just in Europe. The tremendous growth and economic contributions of the service sector have drawn increasing attention to the issues and challenges of service sector industries worldwide.

Specific demand for services marketing concepts has come from the deregulated industries and professional services as both these groups have gone through rapid changes in the ways they do business. In recent decades many very large service industries, including airlines, banking, telecommunications and energy supply, have been deregulated by European governments. As a result, marketing decisions that used to be tightly controlled by the government are now partially, and in some cases totally, within the control of individual firms.[9]

For example, until the late 1990s all UK electricity supply pricing was determined and monitored by the government. A householder could only buy electricity from the one designated local supplier. Since that time electricity companies have been free to set their own pricing structures and bundle the purchase of electricity with the supply of other utilities such as gas and telephony. Similar changes have happened across other countries in Europe such as Sweden, Finland, Germany, Spain, Netherlands, Austria and Denmark. Needless to say, deregulation initially creates turmoil in the electricity generation and supply industry, accelerating the need for more sophisticated, customer-based and competition-sensitive marketing.

⭐ SERVICE SPOTLIGHT

One company to take advantage of deregulation in energy markets is EDF Energy. It is now one of the UK's largest energy companies providing generation, trading, transmission, distribution, supply and other energy services. It is a wholly owned subsidiary of the EDF Group, headquartered in France, and as one of Europe's largest energy groups, it generates around one-fifth of the UK's electricity and employs around 15,000 people. It supplies electricity and gas to around 6 million residential and business customers, making it the biggest supplier of electricity by volume. Elsewhere in Europe it has over 39 million customers, with over 28 million of these in France. It has over 158,000 employees worldwide and offers services in 26 countries (12 of these in Europe).

Source: **www.edfenergy.com.**

Table 1.1 Percentage of GDP attributable to services, 2013

Country	GDP attributed to services
Luxembourg	87
Cyprus	82
Greece	80
France	79
United Kingdom	79
Belgium	78
Denmark	77
Finland	77
Portugal	74
Italy	74
Netherlands	74
Sweden	74
Malta	73
Iceland	73
Spain	72
Switzerland	72
Ireland	71
Austria	70
Latvia	69
Germany	69
Hungary	69
Croatia	69
Lithuania	68
Slovenia	68
Estonia	67
Turkey	64
Bulgaria	63
Poland	63
Czech Republic	60
Norway	58
Romania	50
Slovakia	47

Sources: *The World Factbook 2014* published by the Central Intelligence Agency (CIA), www.cia.gov/library/publications/the-world-factbook and *The World Databank* 2014 published by the World Bank, http://databank.worldbank.org.

Providers of professional services (such as dentists, lawyers, accountants, engineers and architects) have also demanded new concepts and approaches for their businesses as these industries have become increasingly competitive and as professional standards have been modified to allow advertising. Whereas traditionally the professions avoided even using the word *marketing*, they are now seeking better ways to understand and segment their customers, to ensure the delivery of quality services, and to strengthen their position amid a growing number of competitors.

2 *Services as products* represent a wide range of intangible product offerings that customers value and pay for in the marketplace. Service products are sold by service companies and by non-service companies such as manufacturers and technology companies. For example, IBM and Hewlett-Packard offer information technology consulting services to the marketplace, competing with firms such as Accenture and Capita, which are traditional pure services firms. Other industry examples include retailers, like Tesco, that sell services such as insurance and photograph processing.

Early in the development of the field of services marketing and management, most of the impetus came from service industries such as banking, transportation and retailing. As these traditional service industries evolve and become more competitive, the need for effective services management and marketing strategies continues. Now, along with the growth in service-dominant logic thinking, manufacturing and technology industries such as cars, computers and software are also recognizing the need to provide quality service and revenue-producing services in order to compete worldwide.

From Ericsson and Apple to Hewlett-Packard and Siemens, companies are recognizing the opportunity to grow and profit through services.[10] Why? Because the quick pace of developing technologies and increasing competition make it difficult to gain strategic competitive advantage through physical products alone. Moreover, customers are more demanding. Not only do they expect excellent, high-quality goods and technology, they also expect high levels of customer service and total service solutions along with them.

★ SERVICE SPOTLIGHT

Siemens design and manufacture products and systems ranging from traffic lights, gas turbines and turbine spares to the superconducting magnets used in medical scanners and the drives that are behind many of Europe's manufacturing plants. In the UK more than half of Siemens's turnover comes from the provision of services. For example, the industry solutions division is the systems and solutions integrator for processing plant business. It provides services ranging from planning and construction to operation and maintenance over a plant's entire life-cycle. The division aims to use its process know-how for increasing the productivity and competitiveness of enterprises in various industries.

Other divisions of Siemens generate around 40 per cent of the UK's wind energy; install, maintain and read meters in nearly 9 million homes and businesses; maintain a fleet of electric trains; and repair and maintain traffic lights in towns and cities. This service portfolio is aimed at supporting technology (including non-Siemens technology) to provide solutions for customers.

Source: **www.siemens.com.**

As manufacturers such as Siemens and IT companies such as IBM move to become services organizations, the need for special concepts and approaches for managing and marketing services is becoming increasingly apparent.[11]

3 *Services as experiences* The term 'Experience Economy' was first described in an article published in 1998 by Pine and Gilmore.[12] The article argued that service companies would evolve from simply providing a service to creating memorable events for their customers, with the memory of the

experience becoming the product. Rather than the service company charging for the activities it performs, it would be charging for the feelings that customers derive from engaging in the service. Many organizations in the hospitality (boutique hotels) and entertainment sectors (Disneyland Paris) have focused on experiences for many years. However, we are now seeing other services including retailers (Nike Stores) and Airlines (Virgin Atlantic) doing likewise.

4 *Customer service* is also a critical aspect of what we mean by 'service'. Customer service is the service provided in support of a company's core products. Companies typically do not charge for customer service. Customer service can occur on-site (as when a retail employee helps a customer find a desired item or answers a question), or it can occur over the telephone or via the Internet (e.g. Dell computer provides real-time chat sessions to help customers diagnose hardware problems). Many companies operate customer service call centres or helplines, often staffed around the clock. Quality customer service is essential to building customer relationships. It should not, however, be confused with the services provided for sale by the company.

WHY SERVICES MARKETING?

Why is it important to learn about services marketing, service quality and service management? What are the differences in services versus product marketing that have led to the demand for books and courses on services? Many forces have led to the growth of services marketing, and many industries, companies and individuals have defined the scope of the concepts, frameworks and strategies that define the field. The field of services marketing and management has evolved as a result of these combined forces.

SERVICES MARKETING IS DIFFERENT

Over time, business people have realized that marketing and managing services presents issues and challenges not faced in the marketing of products. As service businesses began to turn to marketing and decided to employ marketing people, they naturally recruited from the best marketers in the world – Procter & Gamble, General Foods and Kodak. People who moved from marketing in packaged goods industries to marketing in airlines, banking and other service industries found that their skills and experiences were not directly transferable. They faced issues and dilemmas in marketing services that their experiences in packaged goods and manufacturing had not prepared them for. These people realized the need for new concepts and approaches for marketing and managing service businesses.

Service marketers responded to these forces and began to work across disciplines and with academics and business practitioners from around the world to develop and document marketing practices for services. As the field evolved, it expanded to address the concerns and needs of *any* business in which service is an integral part of the offering. Frameworks, concepts and strategies have been developed to address the fact that 'services marketing is different'. As the field continues to evolve in the twenty-first century, new trends will shape it and accelerate the need for services marketing concepts and tools.

In the final decades of the twentieth century, many firms jumped on the service bandwagon, investing in service initiatives and promoting service quality as ways to differentiate themselves and create competitive advantage. Many of these investments were based on faith and intuition by managers who believed in serving customers well and who believed in their hearts that quality service made good business sense. Indeed, a dedication to quality service has been the foundation for success for many firms, across industries. In his book *Discovering the Soul of Service*, Leonard Berry describes in detail 14 such companies.[13] The companies featured in his book had been in business an average of 31 years in 1999 when the book was written. These companies had been profitable in all but five of their combined 407 years of existence. Dr Berry discovered through his research that these successful businesses share devotion to nine common service themes.

Among these are values-driven leadership, commitment to investment in employee success, and trust-based relationships with customers and other partners at the foundation of the organization.

Since the mid-1990s firms have demanded hard evidence of the bottom-line effectiveness of service strategies, and researchers are building a convincing case that service strategies, implemented appropriately, can be very profitable. Work sponsored by the Marketing Science Institute suggests that corporate strategies focused on customer satisfaction, revenue generation, and service quality may actually be more profitable than strategies focused on cost-cutting or strategies that attempt to do both simultaneously.[14] Research from the Harvard Business School builds a case for the 'service–profit chain', linking internal service and employee satisfaction to customer value and ultimately to profits.[15] Also, considerable research shows linkages from customer satisfaction (often driven by service outcomes) to profits.[16]

An important key to these successes is that the right strategies are chosen and that these strategies are implemented appropriately and well. Much of what you learn from this text will guide you in making such correct choices and in providing superior implementation. Throughout the text we will point out the profit implications and trade-offs to be made with service strategies.

SERVICE AND TECHNOLOGY

The preceding sections examined the roots of services marketing and the reasons why the field exists. Another major trend – technology, specifically information technology – is currently shaping the field and profoundly influencing the practice of services marketing. In this section we explore trends in technology (positive *and* negative) to set the stage for topics that will be discussed throughout this text. Together with globalization, the influence of technology is the most profound trend affecting services marketing today.

POTENTIAL FOR NEW SERVICE OFFERINGS

Looking to the recent past, it is apparent how technology has been the basic force behind service innovations now taken for granted. Automated voice mail, interactive voice response systems, mobile phone apps, location-based services, automated teller machines (ATMs) and other common services only became possible because of new technologies. Just think how dramatically different your world would be without these basic technology services.

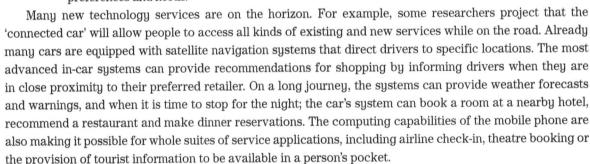

The Internet has also resulted in a host of new services. Internet-based companies like Amazon, Facebook and eBay offer services previously unheard of. And established companies find that the Internet provides a way to offer new services as well.[17] For example, the *Financial Times* offers an interactive edition that allows customers to organize the newspaper's content to suit their individual preferences and needs.

Many new technology services are on the horizon. For example, some researchers project that the 'connected car' will allow people to access all kinds of existing and new services while on the road. Already many cars are equipped with satellite navigation systems that direct drivers to specific locations. The most advanced in-car systems can provide recommendations for shopping by informing drivers when they are in close proximity to their preferred retailer. On a long journey, the systems can provide weather forecasts and warnings, and when it is time to stop for the night; the car's system can book a room at a nearby hotel, recommend a restaurant and make dinner reservations. The computing capabilities of the mobile phone are also making it possible for whole suites of service applications, including airline check-in, theatre booking or the provision of tourist information to be available in a person's pocket.

Other technological advances are making it possible for medical professionals to monitor patients' conditions remotely and even to provide medical diagnoses, treatment, and surgery guidance via technology interfaces. Similarly, a company such as Rolls-Royce can now remotely monitor and adjust jet engines on commercial aeroplanes, as well as provide sophisticated information and data about each engine to the airlines remotely through the Internet.

NEW WAYS TO DELIVER SERVICE

In addition to providing opportunities for new service offerings, technology is providing vehicles for delivering existing services in more accessible, convenient, productive ways. Technology facilitates basic customer service functions (bill-paying, questions, bank account records, tracking orders), transactions (both retail and business to business) and learning or information seeking. Companies have moved from face-to-face service to telephone-based service to widespread use of interactive voice response systems to Internet-based customer service and now to mobile services. Interestingly, many companies are coming full circle and now offer human contact as the ultimate form of customer service!

Technology also facilitates transactions by offering a direct vehicle for making purchases. Technology giant Dell offers virtually all its customer service and ordering functions to its business customers via technology. Over 90 per cent of its transactions with customers are completed online. On the consumer side, online shopping and transactions have already revolutionized the music and book businesses. Predictions suggest that online ordering will also rewrite the rules for purchasing jewellery, real estate, hotel rooms and software.

Finally, technology, specifically the Internet, provides an easy way for customers to learn and research. Access to information has never been easier. For example, health-related websites are now among the most frequently accessed sites on the Internet with current estimates indicating that there are now over 100,000 sites offering health-related information.[18] There can be dangers with this, as the public is often unsure as to which sites are providing accurate information and which are providing spurious cures for serious health conditions.

★ SERVICE SPOTLIGHT

As there are so many online sites and mobile applications addressing health and medicines. The NHS in the UK has set up an online site to help people easily find safe and trusted mobile apps. The NHS Choices Health Apps Library (http://apps.nhs.uk) provides access to a range of applications aimed at assisting patients manage their health and medical conditions through mobile phones and tablet computers. The apps range from those addressing certain conditions, treatments, body parts, to those supporting healthy living and providing health information. All the apps in the Health Apps Library are reviewed to ensure that they are clinically safe.

Source: **http://apps.nhs.uk.**

ENABLING BOTH CUSTOMERS AND EMPLOYEES

Technology enables both customers and employees to be more effective in getting and providing service.[19] Through self-service technologies, customers can serve themselves more effectively. Via online or mobile phone banking, customers can access their accounts, check balances, apply for loans, shift money between accounts and take care of just about any banking need they might have – all without the assistance of the bank's employees. These online and mobile banking services are just one example of the types of self-service technologies that are proliferating across industries.

For employees, technology can provide tremendous support in making them more effective and efficient in delivering service. Customer relationship management and sales support software are broad categories of technology that can aid frontline employees in providing better service. By having immediate access to information about their product and service offerings as well as about particular customers, employees are better able to serve them. This type of information allows employees to customize services to fit the customer's needs. They can also be much more efficient and timely than in the old days when most customer and product information was in paper files or in the heads of sales and customer service representatives.

EXTENDING THE GLOBAL REACH OF SERVICES

Technology infusion results in the potential for reaching out to customers around the globe in ways not possible before. The Internet itself knows no boundaries, and therefore information, customer service and transactions can move across countries and across continents, reaching any customer who has access to the Web.

SERVICE SPOTLIGHT

easyJet offers an online flight tracker service for all of its flights in Europe. It is possible to track any of their flights in real time on a map allowing friends, relatives or business partners picking up passengers from an airport to check the most up to date status of a flight using a tablet or smart phone. This enhances the service for the customer and increases consumer confidence in the easyJet brand and the quality of their operations.

Technology also allows employees of international companies to stay in touch easily – to share information, to ask questions, to serve on virtual teams together. All this technology facilitates the global reach as well as the effectiveness of service businesses.

THE INTERNET *IS* A SERVICE

An interesting way to look at the influence of technology is to realize that the Internet is just 'one big service'. All businesses and organizations that operate on the Internet are essentially providing a service – whether they are giving information, performing basic customer service functions or facilitating transactions. Thus, all the tools, concepts and strategies you learn in studying services marketing and management have direct application in an Internet or e-business world. Although technology and the Internet are profoundly changing how people do business and what offerings are possible, it is clear that customers still want basic service. They want what they have always wanted: dependable outcomes, easy access, responsive systems, flexibility, apologies and compensation when things go wrong. But now they expect these same outcomes from technology-based businesses and from e-commerce solutions.[20] With hindsight it is obvious that many dot-com start-ups suffered and even failed because of lack of basic customer knowledge and failure of implementation, logistics, and service follow-up.[21]

THE PARADOXES AND DARK SIDE OF TECHNOLOGY AND SERVICE

Although there is clearly great potential for technology to support and enhance services, there are potential negative outcomes as well. Customer concerns about privacy and confidentiality raise major issues for firms as they seek to learn about and interact directly with customers through the Internet. These types of concerns are what have stymied and precluded many efforts to advance technology applications in the healthcare industry, for example. Nor are all customers equally interested in using technology as a means of interacting with companies. Research exploring 'customer technology readiness' suggests that some customers are simply not interested in, or ready to use, technology.[22] Employees can also be reluctant to accept and integrate technology into their work lives – especially when they perceive, rightly or wrongly, that the technology will become a substitute for human labour and perhaps eliminate their jobs.

With technology infusion comes a loss of human contact, which many people believe is detrimental purely from quality of life and human relationships perspectives. Parents may lament that their children spend hours in front of computer screens, interacting with games, seeking information and relating to their friends only through instant messaging without any face-to-face human contact. And workers in organizations become more and more reliant on communicating through technology – even communicating via email with the person in the next office!

Finally, the payback in technology investments is often uncertain. It may take a long time for an investment to result in productivity or customer satisfaction gains. Airlines such as British Airways and KLM originally had to use ticket discounting to get passengers to migrate to Internet booking services.

CHARACTERISTICS OF SERVICES IMPACTING ON MARKETING ACTIVITIES

There is general agreement that the distinctive characteristics discussed in this section result in challenges (as well as advantages) for managers of services.[23] It is also important to realize that each of these characteristics could be arranged on a continuum similar to the tangibility spectrum shown in Figure 1.2. That is, services tend to be more heterogeneous, more intangible and more difficult to evaluate than goods, but the differences between goods and services are not black and white by any means.[24]

Table 1.2 summarizes the traditional view of the differences between goods and services and the implications of these characteristics. Many of the strategies, tools and frameworks in this text were developed to address these characteristics. It has been suggested that these distinctive characteristics should not be viewed as unique to services but that they are also relevant to goods, as all products are simply tools or objects used to provide a service to the customer and that 'economic exchange is fundamentally about service provision'.[25] This is complicated by the fact there is a growing diversity of activities within the service sector,

Table 1.2 Goods versus services

Goods	Services	Resulting implications
Tangible	Intangible	Services cannot be inventoried
		Services cannot be easily patented
		Services cannot be readily displayed or communicated
		Pricing is difficult
Standardized	Heterogeneous	Service delivery and customer satisfaction depend on employee and customer actions
		Service quality depends on many uncontrollable factors
		There is no sure knowledge that the service delivered matches what was planned and promoted
Production separate from consumption	Inseparability – simultaneous production and consumption	Customers participate in and affect the transaction
		Customers affect each other
		Employees affect the service outcome
		Decentralization may be essential
		Mass production is difficult
Non-perishable	Perishable	It is difficult to synchronize supply and demand with services
		Services cannot be returned or resold

Source: A. Parasuraman, V.A. Zeithaml and L.L. Berry, 'A conceptual model of service quality and its implications for future research', *Journal of Marketing* 49 (Fall 1985) pp. 41–50.

many of which involve a combination of goods and services within the offering. However, the continuing importance of understanding these differences can be explained as follows:[26]

1 The identification of these characteristics provided the impetus and legitimacy necessary to launch the new field of services marketing and the related academic research.
2 The characteristics identified enabled service researchers to recognize that achieving quality in manufacturing requires a different approach to that required for a service quality improvement.
3 Each of the characteristics taken separately or in combination continues to inform research and management in specific service industries, categories and situations.

INTANGIBILITY

The most basic distinguishing characteristic of services is intangibility. Because services are performances or actions rather than objects, they cannot be seen, felt, tasted or touched in the same manner as tangible goods. For example, healthcare services are actions (such as surgery, diagnosis, examination and treatment) performed by providers and directed towards patients and their families. These services cannot actually be seen or touched by the patient, although the patient may be able to see and touch certain tangible components of the service (such as the equipment or hospital room). In fact, many services such as healthcare are difficult for the consumer to grasp even mentally. Even after a diagnosis or surgery has been completed, the patient may not fully comprehend the service performed, although tangible evidence of the service (e.g. incision, bandaging, pain) may be quite apparent.

RESULTING MARKETING IMPLICATIONS

Intangibility presents several marketing challenges. Services cannot be patented easily, and new service concepts can therefore easily be copied by competitors. Services cannot be readily displayed or easily communicated to customers, so quality may be difficult for consumers to assess. Decisions about what to include in advertising and other promotional materials are challenging, as is pricing. The actual costs of a 'unit of service' are hard to determine, and the price–quality relationship is complex.

HETEROGENEITY

Because services are performances, frequently produced by humans, no two services will be precisely alike. The employees delivering the service frequently *are* the service in the customer's eyes, and people may differ in their performance from day to day or even hour to hour. Heterogeneity also results because no two customers are precisely alike: each will have unique demands or experience the service in a unique way. Thus, the heterogeneity connected with services is largely the result of human interaction (between and among employees and customers) and all of the vagaries that accompany it. For example, a tax accountant may provide a different service experience to two different customers on the same day, depending on their individual needs and personalities and on whether the accountant is interviewing them when he or she is fresh in the morning or tired at the end of a long day of meetings.

RESULTING MARKETING IMPLICATIONS

Because services are heterogeneous across time, organizations and people, ensuring consistent service quality is challenging. Quality actually depends on many factors that cannot be fully controlled by the service supplier, such as the ability of the consumer to articulate his or her needs, the ability and willingness of personnel to satisfy those needs, the presence (or absence) of other customers and the level of demand for the service. Because of these complicating factors, the service manager cannot always know for sure that the service is being delivered in a manner consistent with what was originally planned and promoted. This can be a particular challenge for service brands such as hotels and restaurants that attempt to deliver a consistent brand offering throughout the world in each of their locations. If customers receive inconsistent service that doesn't match the brand promise, this may impact on their future brand choice. Sometimes services may be provided by a third party (for example baggage handling agents and check-in agents for an airline), further increasing the potential heterogeneity of the offering. Some of the variation can be reduced by replacing human inputs by automation (automated teller machines and self-service check-in facilities) or through the adoption of rigorous quality control improvement procedures.

INSEPARABILITY

Whereas most goods are produced first, then sold and consumed, most services are sold first and then produced and consumed simultaneously. For example, a car can be manufactured in Japan, shipped to Paris, sold four months later and consumed over a period of years. By contrast, restaurant services cannot be provided until they have been sold, and the dining experience is essentially produced and consumed at the same time. Frequently this situation also means that the customer is present while the service is being produced, and thus views and may even take part in the production process. Inseparability also means that customers will frequently interact with each other during the service production process and thus may affect each other's experiences. For example, strangers seated next to each other in an aeroplane may well affect the nature of the service experience for each other. That passengers understand this fact is clearly apparent in the way business travellers will often go to great lengths to be sure they are not seated next to families with small children. Another outcome of simultaneous production and consumption is that service producers find themselves playing a role as part of the product itself and as an essential ingredient in the service experience for the consumer.

RESULTING MARKETING IMPLICATIONS

Because services are often produced and consumed at the same time, mass production is difficult. The quality of service and customer satisfaction will be highly dependent on what happens in 'real time', including actions of employees and the interactions between employees and customers. Clearly the real-time nature of services also results in advantages in terms of opportunities to customize offerings for individual consumers. Simultaneous production and consumption also means that it is not usually possible to gain significant economies of scale through centralization. Often, operations need to be relatively decentralized so that the service can be delivered directly to the consumer in a convenient location, although the growth of technology-delivered services is changing this requirement for many services. Also, because of simultaneous production and consumption, the customer is involved in, and observes, the production process and thus may affect (positively or negatively) the outcome of the service transaction. However, advances in the Internet and telecommunications have made it possible in some information-based sectors to separate customers in both time and space from production.

PERISHABILITY

Perishability refers to the fact that services cannot be saved, stored, resold or returned. A seat on a flight or in a restaurant, an hour of a lawyer's time or telephone line capacity not used cannot be reclaimed and used or resold at a later time. Perishability is in contrast to goods (with the exception of fresh food products) that can be stored in inventory or resold another day, or even returned if the consumer is unhappy. Would it not be nice if a bad haircut could be returned or resold to another consumer? Perishability makes this action an unlikely possibility for most services, although it should be noted that there are services such as education and entertainment where performances can be captured and replayed or rebroadcast time and time again.

RESULTING MARKETING IMPLICATIONS

A primary issue that marketers face in relation to service perishability is the inability to hold stock. Demand forecasting and creative planning for capacity utilization are therefore important and challenging decision areas. For example, there is tremendous demand for resort accommodation in the French Alps for skiing in February, but much less demand in July. Yet hotel and chalet owners have the same number of rooms to sell all year round. The fact that services cannot typically be returned or resold also implies a need for strong recovery strategies when things do go wrong. For example, although a bad haircut cannot be returned, the hairdresser can and should have strategies for recovering the customer's goodwill if and when such a problem occurs.

CHALLENGES AND QUESTIONS FOR SERVICE MARKETERS

Because of the basic characteristics of services, marketers of services face some very real and quite distinctive challenges. Answers to questions such as those listed here still elude managers of services:

- *How can service quality be defined and improved* when the product is intangible and non-standardized?
- *How can new services be designed and tested effectively* when the service is essentially an intangible process?
- *How can the firm be certain it is communicating a consistent and relevant image* when so many elements of the marketing mix communicate to customers and some of these elements are the service providers themselves?
- *How does the firm accommodate fluctuating demand* when capacity is fixed and the service itself is perishable?
- *How can the firm best motivate and select service employees* who, because the service is delivered in real time, become a critical part of the product itself?
- *How should prices be set* when it is difficult to determine actual costs of production and price may be inextricably intertwined with perceptions of quality?
- *How should the firm be organized so that good strategic and tactical decisions are made* when a decision in any of the functional areas of marketing, operations and human resources may have significant impact on the other two areas?
- *How can the balance between standardization and personalization be determined* to maximize both the efficiency of the organization and the satisfaction of its customers?
- *How can the organization protect new service concepts from competitors* when service processes cannot be readily patented?
- *How does the firm communicate quality and value to consumers* when the offering is intangible and cannot be readily tried or displayed?
- *How can the organization ensure the delivery of consistent quality service* when both the organization's employees and the customers themselves can affect the service outcome?

THE SERVICES TRIANGLE

To answer some of these questions, it is important to understand that services marketing is about promises – promises made and promises kept to customers. A strategic framework known as the *services marketing triangle* (illustrated in Figure 1.4) shows the three interlinked groups that work together to develop, promote and deliver these service promises. These key players are labelled on the points of the triangle: the *company* (or strategic business unit (SBU) or department or 'management'), the *customers* and the *employees/technology*. This last group can be the firm's employees and subcontractors that deliver the company's services or it can be the technology such as automated teller machines that supply the service. Between these three points on the triangle, three types of marketing must be successfully carried out for a service to succeed: external marketing, interactive marketing, and internal marketing.

On the right-hand side of the triangle are the *external marketing* efforts that the firm engages in to set up its customers' expectations and promise them what is to be delivered. Anything or anyone that communicates to the customer before service delivery can be viewed as part of this external marketing function. But external

Figure 1.4   The services marketing triangle

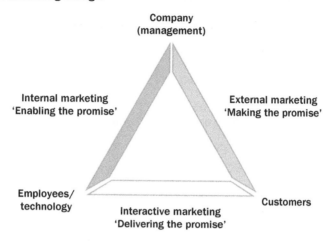

Source: Adapted from M.J. Bitner, 'Building service relationships: it's all about promises', *Journal of the Academy of Marketing Science* 23, no. 4 (1995), pp. 246–51; C. Grönroos, *Service Management and Marketing* (Lexington, MA: Lexington Books, 1990); and P. Kotler, *Marketing Management: Analysis, Planning, Implementation, and Control*, 8th edn (Englewood Cliffs, NJ: Prentice Hall, 1994), p. 470.

marketing is just the beginning for services marketers: promises made must be kept. On the bottom of the triangle is what has been termed *interactive marketing* or *real-time marketing*. Here is where promises are kept or broken by the firm's employees, technology, subcontractors or agents. If promises are not kept, customers become dissatisfied and eventually leave. The left-hand side of the triangle suggests the critical role played by *internal marketing*. Management engages in these activities to aid the providers in their ability to deliver on the service promise: recruiting, training, motivating, rewarding, and providing equipment and technology. Unless service employees are able and willing to deliver on the promises made, the firm will not be successful, and the services triangle will collapse.

All three sides of the triangle are essential to complete the whole, and the sides of the triangle should be aligned – that is, what is promised through external marketing should be the same as what is delivered; and the enabling activities inside the organization should be aligned with what is expected of service providers and employees.

SERVICES MARKETING MIX

One of the most basic concepts in marketing is the marketing mix, defined as the elements an organization controls that can be used to satisfy or communicate with customers. The traditional marketing mix is composed of the four Ps: *product, price, place* (distribution) and *promotion*.[27] These elements appear as core decision variables in any marketing text or marketing plan. The notion of a mix implies that all the variables are interrelated and depend on each other to some extent. Further, the marketing mix philosophy implies an optimal mix of the four factors for a given market segment at a given point in time.

Key strategy decision areas for each of the four Ps are captured in the four columns in Table 1.3. Careful management of product, place, promotion and price will clearly be essential to the successful marketing of services. However, the strategies for the four Ps require some modifications when applied to services. For example, traditionally promotion is thought of as involving decisions related to sales, advertising, sales promotions and publicity. In services these factors are also important, but because services are produced and consumed simultaneously, service delivery people (such as checkout operators, ticket collectors, nurses and telephone personnel) are involved in real-time promotion of the service even if their jobs are typically defined in terms of the operational function they perform.

Table 1.3 Expanded marketing mix for services

Product	Place	Promotion	Price
Physical good features	Channel type	Promotion blend	Flexibility
Quality level	Exposure	Salespeople	Price level
Accessories	Intermediaries	Selection	Terms
Packaging	Outlet locations	Training	Differentiation
Warranties	Transportation	Incentives	Discounts
Product lines	Storage	Advertising	Allowances
Branding	Managing channels	Media types	
		Types of ads	
		Sales promotion	
		Publicity	
		Digital Media	

People	Physical Evidence	Process	
Employees	Facility design	Flow of activities	
Recruiting	Equipment	Standardized	
Training	Signage	Customized	
Motivation	Employee dress	Number of steps	
Rewards	Other tangibles	Simple	
Teamwork	Reports	Complex	
Customers	Business cards	Customer involvement	
Education	Statements		
Training	Guarantees		
	Web page design		

Because services are usually produced and consumed simultaneously, customers are often present in the firm's factory, interact directly with the firm's personnel and are actually part of the service production process. Also, because services are intangible, customers will often be looking for any tangible cue to help them understand the nature of the service experience. For example, in the hotel industry the design and decor of the hotel as well as the appearance and attitudes of its employees will influence customer perceptions and experiences.

Acknowledgement of the importance of these additional variables has led services marketers to adopt the concept of an expanded marketing mix for services. In addition to the traditional four Ps, the services marketing mix includes people, physical evidence and process, as shown in the bottom section of Table 1.3.[28]

> *People* All human actors who play a part in service delivery and thus influence the buyer's perceptions: namely, the firm's personnel, the customer, and other customers in the service environment.

All the human actors participating in the delivery of a service provide cues to the customer regarding the nature of the service itself. How these people are dressed, their personal appearance, and their attitudes and behaviours all influence the customer's perceptions of the service. The service provider or contact person can be very important. In fact, for some services, such as consulting, counselling, teaching and other professional relationship-based services, the provider *is* the service. In other cases the contact person may play what appears to be a relatively small part in service delivery – for instance, a telephone installer, an airline baggage handler or an equipment delivery dispatcher. Yet research suggests that even these providers may be the focal point of service encounters that can prove critical for the organization.

In many service situations, customers themselves can also influence service delivery, thus affecting service quality and their own satisfaction. For example, a client of a consulting company can influence the quality of service received by providing needed and timely information and by implementing recommendations provided by the consultant. Similarly, healthcare patients greatly affect the quality of service they receive when they either comply or do not comply with health regimes prescribed by the provider.

Customers not only influence their own service outcomes, but they can influence other customers as well. In a theatre, at a football match or in a classroom, customers can influence the quality of service received by others – either enhancing or detracting from other customers' experiences.

Physical evidence The environment in which the service is delivered and where the firm and customer interact, and any tangible components that facilitate performance or communication of the service.

The physical evidence of service includes all the tangible representations of the service such as brochures, letterhead, business cards, report formats, signage and equipment. In some cases it includes the physical facility where the service is offered – the 'servicescape' – for example, the retail bank branch facility. In other cases, such as telecommunication services, the physical facility may be irrelevant. In this case other tangibles such as billing statements and appearance of the telephone engineer's van may be important indicators of quality. Especially when consumers have little on which to judge the actual quality of service, they will rely on these cues, just as they rely on the cues provided by the people and the service process. Physical evidence cues provide excellent opportunities for the firm to send consistent and strong messages regarding the organization's purpose, the intended market segments and the nature of the service.

Process The actual procedures, mechanisms, and flow of activities by which the service is delivered – the service delivery and operating systems.

The actual delivery steps that the customer experiences, or the operational flow of the service, also give customers evidence on which to judge the service. Some services are very complex, requiring the customer to follow a complicated and extensive series of actions to complete the process. Highly bureaucratized services frequently follow this pattern, and the logic of the steps involved often escapes the customer. Another distinguishing characteristic of the process that can provide evidence to the customer is whether the service follows a production line/standardized approach or whether the process is an empowered/customized one. None of these characteristics of the service is inherently better or worse than another. Rather, the point is that these process characteristics are another form of evidence used by the consumer to judge service. For example, two successful airline companies, easyJet and Singapore Airlines, follow extremely different process models. easyJet is a no-frills (no food, no assigned seats), low-priced airline that offers frequent, relatively short flights within Europe. All the evidence it provides is consistent with its vision and market position. Singapore Airlines, on the other hand, focuses on the business traveller and is concerned with meeting individual traveller needs. Thus, its process is highly customized to the individual, and employees are empowered to provide non-standard service when needed. Both airlines have been very successful.

The three new marketing mix elements (people, physical evidence, and process) are included in the marketing mix as separate elements because they are within the control of the firm *and* because any or all of them may influence the customer's initial decision to purchase a service as well as the customer's level of satisfaction and repurchase decisions. Their impact is evident in the servuction system model (Figure 1.5),

Figure 1.5   The servuction system model[29]

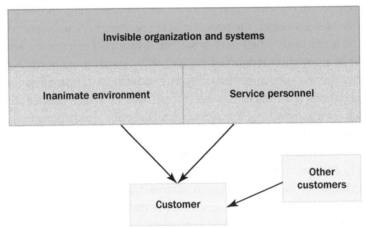

developed by two French academics.[30] This model breaks the service delivery process that a customer receives into two parts: that which is visible to the customer and that which is not. The invisible part is the process element from the extended marketing mix consisting of systems, backroom procedures and the technology or equipment needed to produce the service. In a restaurant this would involve the ordering of ingredients, the cooking facilities and the procedures involved in preparing the food.

The visible part is broken into the inanimate environment (physical evidence) and the service providers or the individuals (people) who interact with the customer during the service experience. The inanimate environment consists of the physical design elements that the customer comes into contact with. This could include aspects such as the lighting, place settings, colour schemes, staff uniforms and the final bill. The model also suggests that customers interact with each other. Their behaviour and characteristics impact on each other's experience. Therefore the benefits derived by customer A come from the interaction with the physical environment and the people (service providers and other customers). Each of these elements is supported and influenced by the process, much of which may be invisible to the customer.

These new marketing mix elements as well as the traditional elements are explored in depth in future chapters.

STAYING FOCUSED ON THE CUSTOMER

A critical theme running throughout this text is *customer focus*. In fact, the subtitle of the book is 'Integrating customer focus across the firm'. From the firm's point of view, all strategies are developed with an eye on the customer, and all implementations are carried out with an understanding of their impact on the customer. From a practical perspective, decisions regarding new services and communication plans will integrate the customer's point of view; operations and human resource decisions will be considered in terms of their impact on customers. All the tools, strategies and frameworks included in this text have customers at their foundation. The services marketing mix just described is clearly an important tool that addresses the uniqueness of services, keeping the customer at the centre.

In this text we also view customers as assets to be valued, developed and retained. The strategies and tools we offer thus focus on customer relationship-building and loyalty as opposed to a more transactional focus in which customers are viewed as one-time revenue producers. This text looks at customer relationship management not as a software program but as an entire architecture or business philosophy. Every chapter in the text can be considered a component needed to build a complete customer relationship management approach.

SUMMARY

This chapter has set the stage for further learning about services marketing by presenting information on changes in the world economy and business practice that have driven the focus on service: the fact that services dominate the modern economies of the world; the focus on service as a competitive business imperative; specific needs of the deregulated and professional service industries; the role of new service concepts growing from technological advances; and the realization that the characteristics of services result in unique challenges and opportunities. The chapter presented a broad definition of services as deeds, processes and performances, and it drew distinctions among pure services, value-added services, service experiences and customer service. It also introduced the concept of service dominant logic.

Building on this fundamental understanding of the service economy, the chapter went on to present the key characteristics of services that underlie the need for distinct strategies and concepts for managing service businesses. These basic characteristics are that services are intangible, heterogeneous, produced and consumed simultaneously, and perishable. Because of these characteristics, service managers face a number of challenges in marketing, including the complex problem of how to deliver quality services consistently.

The chapter described two themes that provide the foundation for future chapters: the expanded marketing mix for services; and customer focus as a unifying theme. It also introduced the concept of the services triangle and the servuction system. The remainder of the text focuses on exploring the unique opportunities and challenges faced by organizations that sell and deliver services, and on developing solutions that will help you become an effective services champion and manager.

KEY CONCEPTS

Heterogeneity	18	Self-service technologies	15
Inseparability	19	Service dominant logic	7
Intangibility	7	Services marketing mix	22
People	22	Services marketing triangle	20
Perishability	19	Servuction system	23
Physical evidence	23	Tangibility spectrum	7
Process	23		

EXERCISES

1   Roughly calculate your budget for an average month. What percentage of your budget goes for services versus goods? Do the services you purchase have value? In what sense? If you had to cut back on your expenses, what would you cut out?

2   Visit two local retail service providers that you believe are positioned very differently (such as IKEA and a local family-owned furniture store, or Burger King and a fine restaurant). From your own observations, compare their strategies on the elements of the services marketing mix.

3   Try a service you have never tried before on the Internet. Analyse the benefits of this service. Was enough information provided to make it easy to use? How would you compare this service to other methods of obtaining the same benefits?

4   Select a service and use the servuction system model to highlight the key components and interactions impacting on the customer during service delivery.

DISCUSSION QUESTIONS

1   What distinguishes service offerings from customer service? Provide specific examples.

2   How is technology changing the nature of customer service and service offerings?

3   What are the basic characteristics of services v. goods? What are the implications of these characteristics for Accenture or for easyJet?

4   One of the underlying frameworks for the text is the services marketing mix. Discuss why each of the three new mix elements (process, people and physical evidence) is included. How might each of these communicate with or help to satisfy an organization's customers?

5   Think of a service job you have had or currently have. How effective, in your opinion, was or is the organization in managing the elements of the services marketing mix?

6   Think of a service and examine how technology is used or could be used to improve its delivery.

7   How can quality service be used in a manufacturing context for competitive advantage? Think of your answer in the context of cars or computers or some other manufactured product that you have actually purchased.

8   Discuss the concept that the value a customer derives from a physical good such as a vacuum cleaner is really the cleaning service provided by the good, not the good itself.

FURTHER READING

Berry, L.L. and Parasuraman, A. (1993). Building a new academic field: the case of services marketing. *Journal of Retailing*, 69(1), 13–60.

Grönroos, C. (2011). Value co-creation in service logic: A critical analysis. *Marketing Theory*, 11(3), 279–301.

Grönroos, C. and Gummerus, J. (2014). The service revolution and its marketing implications: service logic vs service-dominant logic. *Managing Service Quality*, 24(3), 206–29.

IfM and IBM (2008). *Succeeding through Service Innovation: A Service Perspective for Education, Research, Business and Government*. Cambridge, United Kingdom: University of Cambridge Institute for Manufacturing.

Lovelock, C. and Gummesson, E. (2004). Whither services marketing? In search of a new paradigm and fresh perspectives. *Journal of Service Research*, 7(1), 20–41.

Lusch, R. and Vargo, S. (2006). Service Dominant Logic: Reactions, Reflections, and Refinements. *Marketing Theory*, 6 (3), 281–88.

Shostack, G.L. (1977). Breaking free from product marketing. *Journal of Marketing*, 41(April), 73–80.

Vargo, S.L. and Lusch, R.F. (2004). The four service marketing myths: remnants of a goods-based, manufacturing model. *Journal of Service Research*, 6(4), 324–35.

Vargo, S.L. and Lusch, R.F. (2008). Service-dominant logic: continuing the evolution. *Journal of the Academy of Marketing Science*, 36(1), 1–10.

CHAPTER 2

Consumer Behaviour in Services

LEARNING OBJECTIVES

The chapter's objectives are to:

1 Enhance understanding of how consumers choose and evaluate services, through focusing on factors that are particularly relevant for services.
2 Describe how consumers judge goods versus services in terms of search, experience and credence criteria.
3 Develop the elements of consumer behaviour that a services marketer must understand: choice behaviour, consumer experiences and post-experience evaluation.
4 Examine attitudes towards the use of self-service technologies.
5 Explore how differences among consumers (cultural differences, group decision-making) affect consumer behaviour and influence services marketing strategies.

OPENING EXAMPLE
The Travelling Millenniums and their Buying Behaviour

TripAdvisor, the world's largest travel website, regularly undertakes research to gain insight into the attitudes and behaviours of consumers in the travel industry. The research is based upon an online survey, the TripBarometer, which in 2015 had 34,016 respondents from 26 countries.

One research theme has highlighted some of the unique characteristics of the millennial traveller. This generation of travellers born between the early 1980s and early 2000s is two to three times more likely than older travellers to leave booking their trips until less than two weeks before departure. Also compared to earlier generations, millennials are two to three times more likely to leave the booking of their accommodation until they arrive at their destination. The most common reasons for booking in this manner primarily revolve around convenience and spontaneity. This also means that they can change travel plans at the last minute in response to their friends' postings on social media. Millenial travellers are connected 24/7.

They are more willing than other generations to sacrifice nights out, entertainment and even grocery budgets in order to travel. Tourist attractions and activities are a huge draw for them, and steadily become less influential for older travellers. Online reviews are an important factor for this group when choosing where to travel and if they do book in advance, they are more likely to book through a travel review site than through the property's own website.

Although price is important, compared to the prior generation millennials are more influenced by special offers, proximity to transportation options and sustainable travel. They are less likely to care about brand name or proximity to the beach.

However, although this connected generation are more likely to book via mobile apps and bring their tablets when travelling, they are also more likely to want their accommodation providers to have printed tourism information available within their hotel. This may be indicative of how their last-minute booking habit prevents them from doing any advance planning.

Once checked in, millennials are more likely to indulge in hotel services such as massages, spa treatments and dry cleaning. They also value upgrades and elite membership status more than their older counterparts.

In comparison with those in older age ranges, millenials were more likely in 2014 to travel to North America and Asia.

Sources: www.tripadvisor.com/tripadvisorinsights; Daily Mail (13 June 2014).

The primary objectives of services producers and marketers are identical to those of all marketers: to develop and provide offerings that satisfy consumer needs and expectations, thereby ensuring their own economic survival. To achieve these objectives, service providers need to understand how consumers choose, experience and evaluate their service offerings. However, most of what is known about consumer evaluation processes pertains specifically to goods. The assumption appears to be that services, if not identical to goods, are at least similar enough in the consumer's mind that they are chosen, experienced and evaluated in the same manner.

This chapter challenges that assumption and shows that services' characteristics result in some differences in consumer evaluation processes compared with those used in assessing goods. Recognizing these differences and thoroughly understanding consumer evaluation processes are critical for the customer focus on which effective services marketing is based. Because the premise of this text is that the customer is at the heart of effective services marketing, we begin with the customer and maintain this focus throughout the text.

Consumers have a more difficult time evaluating and choosing among services than they have choosing between goods. In part this is because services are intangible and non-standardized, but also because consumption is so closely intertwined with production. These characteristics lead to differences in consumer evaluation processes for goods and services in all stages of the buying and consumption process.

SEARCH, EXPERIENCE AND CREDENCE PROPERTIES

One framework for isolating differences in evaluation processes between goods and services is a classification of properties of offerings proposed by economists.[1] Economists first distinguished between two categories of properties of consumer products: search qualities, attributes that a consumer can determine before purchasing a product; and experience qualities, attributes that can be discerned only after purchase or during consumption. Search qualities include colour, style, price, fit, feel, hardness and smell; experience qualities include taste and wearability. Products such as cars, clothing, furniture, and jewellery are high in search qualities because their attributes can be almost completely determined and evaluated before purchase. Products such as vacations and restaurant meals are high in experience qualities, because their attributes cannot be fully known or assessed until they have been purchased and are being consumed. A third category, credence qualities, includes characteristics that the consumer may find impossible to evaluate even after purchase and consumption.[2] Examples of offerings high in credence qualities are insurance and brake replacement on cars. Few consumers possess sufficient knowledge of risk or the mechanical skills required to evaluate whether these services are necessary or are performed properly, even after they have been prescribed and produced by the seller.

Figure 2.1 arrays products high in search, experience, or credence qualities along a continuum of evaluation ranging from easy to evaluate to difficult to evaluate. Products high in search qualities are

Figure 2.1   Continuum of evaluation for different types of products

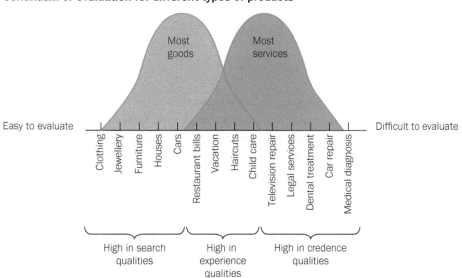

Figure 2.2   Stages in consumer decision-making and evaluation of services

- Need recognition
- Information search
- Evaluation of alternatives
- Purchase
- Consumer experience
- Post-purchase evaluation

the easiest to evaluate (left-hand end of the continuum). Products high in experience qualities are more difficult to evaluate, because they must be purchased and consumed before assessment is possible (centre of continuum). Products high in credence qualities are the most difficult to evaluate, because the consumer may be unaware of or may lack sufficient knowledge to appraise whether the offerings satisfy given wants or needs even after consumption (right-hand end of the continuum). The major premise of this chapter is that most goods fall to the left of the continuum, whereas most services fall to the right because of the distinguishing characteristics described in Chapter 1. These characteristics make services more difficult to evaluate than goods, particularly in advance of purchase. Difficulty in evaluation, in turn, forces consumers to rely on different cues and processes when assessing services.

The following sections of this chapter build from these basic differences to explore the stages of consumer decision-making and evaluation for services. This discussion is organized around three broad stages of consumer behaviour, as shown in Figure 2.2: consumer choice (linking in to the stages of the buying behaviour process: need recognition, information search, evaluation of alternatives and purchase), consumer experience of the service while it is being delivered, and post-experience evaluation. Within each of these stages, you will see similarities and differences between goods and services.

CONSUMER CHOICE

The first important area of consumer behaviour that marketers are concerned with is how customers choose and make decisions and the steps that lead to the purchase of a particular service. This process is similar to that used for goods in some ways and different in others. Customers follow a logical sequence, including need recognition, information search, evaluation of alternatives, and purchase. The following sections discuss this sequence, particularly focusing on the ways in which services decision-making is different from goods decision-making.

NEED RECOGNITION

The process of buying a service begins with the recognition that a need or want exists. Although there are many different ways to characterize needs, the most widely known is Maslow's hierarchy, which specifies five need categories arranged in a sequence from basic lower-level needs to higher-level needs. Services can fill all these needs, and they become increasingly important for higher-level social, ego and self-actualization needs.

1   *Physiological needs are biological needs such as food, water and sleep.* The recognition of these basic needs is fairly straightforward. Recall the last time you were on vacation, perhaps sightseeing in a new place. At some point around lunchtime you recognized that you were thirsty and hungry and needed to stop and have lunch. Restaurants, coffee shops, bistros and other service establishments that provided food and water were more likely to become noticeable at this point.

2   *Safety and security needs* include *shelter, protection and security.* When visiting cities, people will seek accommodation in safe areas. They will travel with airlines that have good safety records. They seek bank accounts that provide security for their money as well as insurance products to protect them from future negative events. They seek reliable suppliers of electricity, gas and telecommunications. Organizations will promote reassurance, trust and professionalism to address these needs. For example, Vodafone emphasize coverage, reliability and business continuity.

3   *Social needs* are for *affection, friendship and acceptance.* Social needs are critical to all cultures but are particularly important in the East. In countries like Japan and China, consumers place a great deal of value on social and belonging needs. They spend more time with their families and work colleagues than do those in the West and therefore consume more services that can be shared. The Japanese spend more annually per capita in restaurants, than people from any other country. Consumers in all cultures use many types of services to address social needs, including health and dance clubs, dating services and packaged holidays (like Club Med) in which socializing is encouraged.

4   *Ego needs* are for *prestige, success, accomplishment and self-esteem.* Food, safety and belonging are not enough for many consumers. Individuals also seek to look good to others and to feel good about themselves because of what they have accomplished. Needs to improve oneself and achieve success are responsible for the growth of education, training and other services that increase the skills and prestige of consumers. Personal services such as spa services, plastic surgery, teeth-whitening and gym membership also satisfy these needs.

5   *Self-actualization* involves *self-fulfilment and enriching experiences.* Consumers desire to live up to their full potential and enjoy themselves. Some consumers purchase experiences such as skydiving, jungle safaris and bungee-jumping for the pure thrill of the experience, a need quite different from the others in Maslow's hierarchy. Other people self-actualize through classes in oil painting or poetry-writing, thereby expressing feelings and meanings that are unrelated to the basic needs of day-to-day living.

The hierarchical nature of Maslow's need categorization has been disputed, and evidence exists that people with unfilled basic needs can be motivated to self-actualize. We are not concerned with the hierarchy of needs in this section; we use it only as a way to discuss different drivers that lead customers to the next stages of consumer behaviour in services.

INFORMATION SEARCH

Once they recognize a need, consumers obtain information about goods and services that might satisfy this need. Seeking information may be an extensive, formalized process if the service or good is important to the consumer or it represents a major investment (for example, an Australian vacation package or a professional landscape service). In other cases the information search may be quick and relatively automatic (for example, a restaurant for a quick lunch or a service station for fuel). Consumers use both customer opinion sources (such as friends or online customer review sites) and promotional sources (such as advertising and corporate websites) to gain information about goods and services. Seeking information is a way of reducing risk, helping consumers feel more confident about their choices.

CUSTOMER OPINION, SOCIAL MEDIA AND ONLINE REVIEW SITES

When purchasing goods, consumers make use of both customer opinion and promotional sources because both effectively convey information about search qualities. When purchasing services, on the other hand, consumers seek and rely to a greater extent on online review sites and talking to friends and family directly or through social media. There are a number of reasons for this.

First, promotional sources can convey information about search qualities but can communicate far less about experience qualities. Checking online customer review sites or asking friends directly or through social media can provide consumers with information about the experience qualities of a service. Review sites such as Tripadvisor are used extensively by consumers when they are choosing hotels, restaurants and visitor attractions. This type of site allows users to post 'content' online in a number of formats from text reviews to images and pictures. Based on this content, other consumers are likely to avoid a service provider with too many negative comments and choose a provider with positive comments. When Jeff Bezos, the founder and CEO of Amazon, was asked why he allowed negative reviews about products on his site, as this may impact on sales, he stated: 'We don't make money when we sell things. We make money when we help customers make purchase decisions.' As such, customers are more likely to find a helpful site with reviews and detailed information more appealing than a site that may simply push the manufacturer's view of a product.

A second reason for greater use of customer opinion sources of information for services is that many types of promotional sources of information are not as readily available for services. Many service providers are local, independent merchants with neither the experience nor the funds to advertise. If you want to choose a hairdresser in your local area, you are more likely to ask friends and work colleagues directly or through social media rather than relying on local advertisements or web-pages. Furthermore, cooperative advertising (advertising funded jointly by the retailer and the manufacturer) is used infrequently with services because most local providers are both producer and retailer of the service. And, because professional associations representing lawyers, architects, etc. banned advertising for so long, both professionals and consumers tend to resist its use even though it is now permitted.

Finally, because consumers can assess few attributes before purchase of a service, they may feel there is a greater risk in selecting a little-known alternative. Personal influence becomes pivotal as product complexity increases and when objective standards by which to evaluate a product decrease (that is, when experience qualities are high).[3] Managers in service industries clearly recognize the strong influence of word-of-mouth communication.

⭐ **SERVICE SPOTLIGHT**

The Crowne Plaza Hotel in London Docklands recognizes the importance of word of mouth. The Guest Services Manager responds to every comment about the hotel posted by guests on TripAdvisor. It makes no difference whether the comment is positive or negative, a reply is provided. Guests are thanked for their comment and if there has been a specific problem, information is provided regarding how the problem will be rectified either for the dissatisfied customer or for future guests. This demonstrates that the hotel is listening to its customers and that it is concerned about providing an appropriate service level for their guests. Potential customers may look more positively on an organization that is seen to be willing to address problems and satisfy its guests.

PERCEIVED RISK

Although some degree of perceived risk probably accompanies all purchase transactions, more risk appears to be involved in the purchase of services than in the purchase of goods because services are typically more intangible, variable and perishable. Risk can come in various forms: financial, time, performance, social or psychological, any of which may be greater for services.

The intangible nature of services and their high level of experience qualities imply that services generally must be selected on the basis of less pre-purchase information than is the case for goods. There is clear evidence that greater intangibility (whether for goods or services) increases perceptions of risk.[4] Also, because services are non-standardized, the consumer will feel some uncertainty about the outcome and consequences each time a service is purchased. In addition, services purchases may involve more perceived risk than other purchases because, with some exceptions, services are not accompanied by warranties or guarantees. Dissatisfied customers can rarely 'return' a service; they have already consumed it by the time they realize their dissatisfaction. Finally, many services are so technical or specialized (healthcare or legal services) that consumers possess neither the knowledge nor the experience to evaluate whether they are satisfied, even after they have consumed the service.

The increase in perceived risk in purchasing services suggests the use of strategies to reduce risk. Risk reduction can be accomplished through tactics that reduce risk directly (e.g. guarantees) or by addressing the factors that contribute to the perception of risk (e.g. making the service more tangible).[5] For example, DHL provides tracking numbers for customers so they can follow their shipments online and know exactly where a package is. This system helps reduce the risk for consumers. Offering a free or reduced-cost trial period for a service would be another means to reduce risk. For example, gyms and health clubs often encourage a free trial day for prospective clients to reduce the sense of risk in this important decision. To the extent that it is possible, service providers should emphasize employee training and other procedures to standardize their offerings so that consumers learn to expect a given level of quality, again reducing perceived risk.

EVALUATION OF SERVICE ALTERNATIVES

The evoked set of alternatives – that group of products that a consumer considers acceptable options in a given product category – has traditionally been smaller with services than with goods. One reason involved differences in retailing between goods and services. To purchase goods, consumers generally shop in retail stores that display competing products in close proximity, clearly demonstrating the possible alternatives. To purchase services, on the other hand, the consumer had to visit an establishment (such as a bank, a dry cleaner or a hair salon) that almost always offered only a single 'brand' for sale. A second reason for the smaller evoked set was that consumers were unlikely to find more than one or two businesses providing the same services in a given geographic area, whereas they may find numerous retail stores carrying the identical manufacturer's product. A third reason for a smaller evoked set was the difficulty of obtaining adequate pre-purchase information about services. The Internet is changing this as it widens the set of alternatives. This trend is most notable in areas such as insurance, airlines and hotels with comparison websites where a wide range of information on suppliers and prices can be accessed in one place.

For non-professional services, consumers' decisions often entail the choice between performing the services for themselves or hiring someone to perform them.[6] Working people may choose between cleaning their own homes or hiring housekeepers, between altering their families' clothes or taking them to a tailor, even between staying home to take care of their children or engaging a nursery to provide child care. Consumers may consider themselves as sources of supply for many services, including lawn care, tax preparation and preparing meals. Thus, the customer's evoked set frequently includes self-provision of the service. Self-service via technology is also a viable alternative for many services.

EXAMPLE
Evaluating Self-Service

One of the major recent changes in consumer behaviour is the growing tendency for consumers to interact with technology to create services instead of interacting with a live service firm employee. Self-service technologies (SSTs) are technological interfaces that allow customers to produce services independent of direct service employee involvement. Examples that you are probably very familiar with are bank ATM machines, pay-at-the-pump terminals at service stations and automated airline check-in. All forms of services over the Internet are also self-service technologies, many of which are very innovative. In the UK, for example, users can complete their tax return online rather than use the usual paper forms. Electronic self-ordering is being developed at fast-food chains, and self-scanning at grocery stores is available in Tesco stores and many other supermarkets.

Table 2.1 Categories and examples of self-service technologies

Interface Purpose	Telephone/interactive voice response	Online/Internet	Interactive
Customer service	• Telephone banking • Flight information • Order status	• Package tracking • Account information	• ATMs • Hotel checkout
Transactions	• Telephone banking • Prescription refills	• Retail purchasing • Financial transactions	• Pay at the pump • Hotel checkout • Car rental
Self-help	• Information telephone lines	• Internet information search • Distance learning	• Blood pressure machines • Tourist information

Table 2.1 shows a comprehensive set of categories and examples of self-service technologies in use today. The columns of the matrix represent the types of technologies that companies are using to interface with customers in self-service encounters, and the rows show purposes of the technologies from the customer perspective. As you can see, customers use the technologies to provide customer service (deal with questions about accounts, bill-paying and delivery-tracking), to conduct transactions (order, buy and exchange resources with companies without direct interaction), and to provide self-help (learn, receive information, train themselves and provide their own services).

Customers may have strong feelings about self-service technologies,[7] they love them when:

- *They bail them out of difficult situations*. A single parent with a sleeping child in the car needs to get fuel and a fast meal. Using a pay-at-the-pump service station and drive-up fast-food restaurant allows the parent to accomplish these tasks without leaving the sleeping child.
- *They are better than the interpersonal alternative*. Self-service technology has the potential to save customers time, money and psychological costs. The Internet, in particular, allows customers to shop at any time and complete transactions more quickly than they could in person. Internet loans and finance also allow customers to avoid the anxiety of meeting a banker in person and feeling judged.
- *They work as they are supposed to*. When self-service technologies work as they are supposed to, customers are impressed. Many of you have had the experience of using one-click ordering at Amazon. When these transactions work smoothly, as they usually do after the proper setup, they are satisfying.

On the other hand, customers hate self-service technology when the following problems occur:

- *They fail to work*. Broken machines, failed PIN numbers, websites that are down and items not shipped as promised all frustrate consumers.
- *They are poorly designed*. Poorly designed technologies that are difficult to use or understand create hassles for customers, making them feel as though the technology is not worth using. Websites that are difficult to navigate are particularly troublesome. If customers cannot reach information they need within a few clicks (some researchers say that two clicks are all that customers will tolerate), then they shun the website.
- *The customer messes up*. Customers dislike technologies that they don't feel they can use adequately. Even though they feel partially responsible, they will avoid using them in the future. A common frustration is having various user names and passwords for different websites. When

confronted with a screen requiring this information – and not recalling it accurately – many customers will give up and go elsewhere.

* ***There is no service recovery***. When the process or technology fails, self-service technologies rarely provide ways to recover on the spot. For example, a vending machine may take a customer's money but fail to deliver the product requested. In these cases customers must then call or visit the company, precisely what they were trying to avoid by using the self-service technology.

It is increasingly evident that these technological innovations are a critical component of many customer–firm interactions. If these technologies are to succeed, they must become more reliable, be better than the interpersonal alternatives and have recovery systems in place when they fail.

SERVICE PURCHASE

Following consideration of alternatives (whether an extensive process or more automatic), consumers make the decision to purchase a particular service or to do it themselves. One of the most interesting differences between goods and services is that many goods are fully produced (at the factory) prior to being purchased by consumers. Thus, consumers, prior to making their final purchase decision, can see and frequently try the exact object that they will buy. For services much is still unknown at the point of purchase. In many cases, the service is purchased and produced almost simultaneously – as with a restaurant meal or live entertainment. In other cases consumers pay all or part of the purchase price up front for a service they will not fully experience until it is produced for them much later. This situation arises with services such as packaged holidays or kitchen design, or ongoing services such as health club memberships or university education. In business-to-business situations, long-term contracts for services (such as payroll, network integration or landscaping) may be signed prior to anything being produced at all.

Because of the inherent risk in the purchase decision for services, some providers offer 'free' (or 'deeply discounted') initial trials or extensive tours of their facilities (for example, prospective student and parent tours at universities) in order to reduce risk in the final purchase decision. In business-to-business situations, trust in the provider is paramount when customers sign long-term service contracts, and frequently the contracts themselves spell out in detail the service level agreements and penalties for non-performance.

SERVICE SPOTLIGHT

Virgin Active, which operates health clubs in Italy, Spain, Portugal and the UK offers a free workout or free temporary memberships to enable potential new members to try out the facilities before taking out a full membership. This is aimed at reducing the perceived risk to the consumer by allowing them to see the facilities, talk to existing members and ask questions of the staff.

CONSUMER EXPERIENCE

Because the choice process for services is inherently risky with many unknowns, the experience itself often dominates the evaluation process. As noted, services are high in experience and credence qualities relative to goods; thus, how consumers evaluate the actual experience of the service is critical in their evaluation process and their decision to repurchase later. In fact, noted customer experience experts have stated that 'the experience is the marketing'.[8]

Much has been written recently about customer experiences and their important role in influencing consumer behaviour. Goods and services companies alike are being urged to create 'memorable experiences for their customers'.[9]

In this section we describe elements of consumer behaviour that are relevant to understanding service experiences and how customers evaluate them. We do not limit our discussion to fun, exciting or memorable experiences only. Instead, we use the term *customer experience* to encompass service processes that span the mundane to the spectacular. Customers purchasing building maintenance and dry-cleaning services still have experiences, albeit less exciting ones than customers of entertainment or travel services. All services *are* experiences – some are long in duration and some are short; some are complex and others are simple; some are mundane, whereas others are exciting and unique. Creating and managing effective processes and experiences are always essential management tasks for service organizations. Many subsequent chapters in this book will provide you with tools and approaches for managing specific elements of the customer experience – the heart of services marketing and management.

SERVICES AS PROCESSES

Because services are actions or performances done for and with customers, they typically involve a sequence of steps, actions and activities. Consider medical services. Some of the steps in medical care involve customers interacting with providers (e.g. patients interacting with their doctor), other steps may be carried out by the customers themselves (e.g. 'following the doctor's orders', taking medications) and other steps may involve third parties (e.g. going to a hospital for tests). The combination of these steps, and many others along the way, constitute a process, a service experience that is evaluated by the consumer. It is the combination of steps, the flow of the activities or the 'experience' that is evaluated by the customer. In many cases, the customer's experience comprises interactions with multiple, interconnected organizations, as in the case of medical services, car insurance or home buying. Diverse sets of experiences across the network of firms (e.g. a doctor's office, a pharmacy, hospital and physiotherapy clinic) will likely influence consumers' overall impressions of their experience. Whether or not the provider acknowledges it or seeks to control this experience in a particular way, it is inevitable that the customer will have an experience – good, bad or indifferent.

SERVICE PROVISION AS DRAMA

The metaphor of service as theatre is a useful framework for describing and analysing service performances. Both the theatre and service organizations aim to create and maintain a desirable impression before an audience and recognize that the way to accomplish this is by carefully managing the actors and the physical setting of their behaviour.[10] The service marketer must play many drama-related roles – including director, choreographer and writer – to be sure the performances of the actors are pleasing to the audience. The Walt Disney Company explicitly considers its service provision a 'performance', even using show business terms such as *cast member, onstage* and *show* to describe the operations at Disneyland Paris.[11]

The skill of the service *actors* in performing their routines, the way they appear and their commitment to the 'show' are all essential to service delivery. Although service actors are present in most service performances, their importance increases in three conditions. First, service actors are critical when the degree of direct personal contact is high. Consider the difference between a visit to see a lawyer in comparison to a visit to a fast-food restaurant. The second condition in which service actors' skills are critical is when the services involve repeat contact. Nurses in hospitals, favourite waiters or tennis coaches in resorts or captains on cruises are essential characters in service theatre, and their individual performances can make or break the success of the services. The third condition in which contact personnel are critical is when they have discretion in determining the nature of the service and how it is delivered. When you consider the quality of the education you are receiving in university, you are certain to focus much of your evaluation on your lecturers' delivery of classes. In education, as in other services such as medical and legal services, the professional is the key actor in the performance.[12]

Ray Fisk and Steve Grove, two experts in the area of service dramaturgy, point out that service actors' performances can be characterized as sincere or cynical.[13] A sincere performance occurs when an actor becomes one with the role that he or she is playing, whereas a cynical performance occurs when an actor views a performance only as a means to an end, such as getting paid for doing the job. When a service employee takes the time to listen and help, the performance is sincere and often noteworthy. Unfortunately, too many examples of cynical performances exist in which front-line 'actors' seem to care little about the 'audience' of customers. As Grove and Fisk point out, a single employee can ruin the service experience by ridiculing other cast members' efforts, failing to perform his or her role correctly or projecting the wrong image. To create the right impression, three characteristics are necessary: loyalty, discipline and circumspection.[14]

The physical setting of the service can be likened to the staging of a theatrical production, including scenery, props and other physical cues to create desired impressions. Among a setting's features that may influence the character of a service are the colours or brightness of the service's surroundings; the volume and pitch of sounds in the setting; the smells, movement, freshness and temperature of the air; the use of space; the style and comfort of the furnishings; and the setting's design and cleanliness.[15] As an example, the service provided by a cruise ship features its layout (cabins and entertainment/eating areas), decor and comfort (large, cushioned deckchairs), furnishings (lots of polished wood and brass) and cleanliness ('shipshape'). The setting increases in importance when the environment distinguishes the service. Consider how critical the setting is for a city-centre law firm, which must appear professional, capable, even imposing.[16] In essence, the delivery of service can be conceived as drama, where service personnel are the actors, service customers are the audience, physical evidence of the service is the setting and the process of service assembly is the performance. The drama metaphor offers a useful way to improve service performances.[17] Selection of personnel can be viewed as auditioning the actors. An actor's personal appearance, manner, facial expression, gestures, personality and demographic profile can be determined in large part in the interview or audition. Training of personnel can become rehearsing. Clearly defining the role can be seen as scripting the performance. Creation of the service environment involves setting the stage. Finally, deciding which aspects of the service should be performed in the presence of the customer (onstage) and which should be performed in the back room (backstage) helps define the performances the customer experiences.

SERVICE ROLES AND SCRIPTS

Service roles are combinations of social cues that guide and direct behaviour in a given setting.[18] Just as there are roles in dramatic performances, there are roles in service delivery. For example, the role of a hostess in a restaurant is to acknowledge and greet customers, find out how many people are in their group, and then lead them to a table where they will eat. The success of any service performance depends in part on how well the role is performed by the service actor and how well the team of players – the 'role set' of both service employees and customers – act out their roles.[19] Service employees need to perform their roles according to the expectations of the customer; if they do not, the customer may be frustrated and disappointed. If customers are informed and educated about their roles and if they cooperate with the provider in following the script, successful service provision is likely.

One factor that influences the effectiveness of role performance is the service script – the logical sequence of events expected by the customer, involving him or her as either a participant or an observer.[20] Service scripts consist of sequences of actions associated with actors and objects that, through repeated involvement, define what the customer expects.[21] Receiving a dental check-up is a service experience for which a well-defined script exists. For a check-up, the consumer expects the following sequence: enter the reception area, greet a receptionist, sit in a waiting room, follow the dental nurse to a separate room, recline in a chair while teeth are examined by the dentist, then pay for the services. When the service conforms to this script, the customer has a feeling of confirmed expectations and satisfaction. Deviations from the service script lead to confusion and dissatisfaction. Suppose, on moving to a new town, you went to a dentist who had no receptionist and no waiting area, only a doorbell in a cubicle. Suppose, on answering the doorbell, an employee in shorts took you to a large room where all patients were in a dental chairs facing each other. These actions and objects are certainly not in the traditional service script for dentistry and might create considerable uncertainty and doubt in patients.

Some services are more scripted than others. Customers would expect very expensive, customized services such as spa vacations to be less scripted than mass-produced services such as fast food ('Have a nice day!') and airline travel.

THE COMPATIBILITY OF SERVICE CUSTOMERS

We have just discussed the roles of employees and customers receiving service. We now want to focus on the role of *other customers* receiving service at the same time. Consider how central the mere presence of other customers is in churches, restaurants, dances, bars, clubs and spectator sports: if no one else shows up, customers will not get to socialize with others, one of the primary expectations in these types of services. However, if customers become so dense that crowding occurs, customers may also be dissatisfied.[22] The way other customers behave with many services – such as airlines, education, clubs and social organizations – also exerts a major influence on a customer's experience.[23] In general, the presence, behaviour and similarity of other customers receiving services has a strong impact on the satisfaction and dissatisfaction of any given customer.[24]

Customers can be incompatible for many reasons – differences in beliefs, values, experiences, ability to pay, appearance, age and health, to name just a few. The service marketer must anticipate, acknowledge and deal with heterogeneous consumers who have the potential to be incompatible. The service marketer can also bring homogeneous customers together and solidify relationships between them, which increases the cost to the customer of switching service providers.[25] Customer compatibility is a factor that influences customer satisfaction, particularly in high-contact services.

CUSTOMER CO-PRODUCTION

In addition to being audience members, as suggested by the drama metaphor, service users also play a customer co-production role that can have profound influence on the service experience.[26] For example, counselling, personal training or educational services have little value without the full participation of the client, who will most likely have extensive work to do between sessions. In this sense, the client co-produces the service. In business-to-business contexts such as consulting, architecture, accounting and almost any outsourced service, customers also co-produce the service.[27] It has been suggested that customers therefore need to understand their roles and be 'trained' in ways that are similar to the training of service employees, so that they will have the motivation, ability and role clarity to perform.[28]

The idea of customers as 'partners' in the co-creation of products is gaining ground across all industries, not just services.[29] Postmodern consumer behaviour experts propose an even broader interpretation of this idea. They suggest that a fundamental characteristic of the postmodern era is consumers' assertiveness as active participants in creating their world – often evidenced in their demands to adjust, change and use products in customized ways.[30]

SERVICE SPOTLIGHT

In IKEA customers co-produce the service. They identify the items they want, collect them from the warehouse, deliver them to their homes and assemble them. To enable customers to understand their role in these tasks and complete them successfully, IKEA provides a catalogue setting out the product range and instructions as to how to purchase the items. IKEA makes use of comprehensive in-store signage, including arrows on the floor, to direct customers around the store and enable them to find the items they require in the warehouse area. Instructions are also provided on how to assemble items when the customer gets them home. These elements can all be seen as a form of customer training similar to that given to service employees, so that customers will have the motivation, ability and role clarity to co-produce effectively.

EMOTION AND MOOD

Emotion and mood are feeling states that influence people's (and therefore customers') perceptions and evaluations of their experiences. Moods are distinguished from emotions in that *moods* are transient feeling states that occur at specific times and in specific situations, whereas *emotions* are more intense, stable and pervasive.[31]

Because services are experiences, moods and emotions are critical factors that shape the perceived effectiveness of service encounters. If a service customer is in a bad mood when he or she enters a service establishment, service provision will likely be interpreted more negatively than if he or she were in a buoyant, positive mood. Similarly, if a service provider is irritable or sullen, his or her interaction with customers will likely be coloured by that mood. Furthermore, when other customers in a service establishment are cranky or frustrated, whether from problems with the service or from existing emotions unrelated to the service, their mood affects the provision of service for all customers who sense the negative mood. In sum, any service characterized by human interaction is strongly dependent on the moods and emotions of the service provider, the service customer and other customers receiving the service at the same time.

In what specific ways can mood affect the behaviour of service customers? First, positive moods can make customers more obliging and willing to participate in behaviours that help service encounters succeed.[32] Customers in a good emotional state are probably more willing to follow an exercise regimen prescribed by a personal trainer, clear their own dishes at a fast-food restaurant and overlook delays in service. Customers in a negative mood may be less likely to engage in behaviours essential to the effectiveness of the service: abstaining from chocolates when on a diet programme with Weight Watchers, taking frequent aerobic classes from a health club or completing homework assigned in a class.

A second way that moods and emotions influence service customers is to bias the way they judge service encounters and providers. Mood and emotions enhance and amplify experiences, making them either more positive or more negative than they might seem in the absence of these same moods and emotions.[33] After losing a big account, a salesperson catching an airline flight will be more incensed with delays and crowding than he or she might be on a day when business went well. Conversely, the positive mood of a services customer at a dance or restaurant will heighten the experience, leading to positive evaluations of the service establishment. The direction of the bias in evaluation is consistent with the polarity (positive or negative) of the mood or emotion.

Finally, moods and emotions affect the way information about service is absorbed and retrieved in memory. As memories about a service are encoded by a consumer, the feelings associated with the encounter become an inseparable part of the memory. If travellers fall in love during a vacation in Greece, they may hold favourable assessments of the destination due more to their emotional state than to the destination itself. Conversely, if a customer first becomes aware of his or her poor level of fitness when on a guest pass in a health club, the negative feelings may be encoded and retrieved every time he or she thinks of the health club or, for that matter, any health club.

Because emotions and moods play such important roles in influencing customer experiences, 'organizations must manage the emotional component of experiences with the same rigour they bring to the management of product and service functionality'.[34] Organizations may observe customers' emotional responses and attempt to create places, processes and interactions to enhance certain emotions. Some firms believe that consumers' emotional responses may be the best predictors of their ultimate loyalty. Thus, many companies are now beginning to measure emotional responses and connections as well – going beyond traditional measures of satisfaction and behavioural loyalty.

POST-EXPERIENCE EVALUATION

Following the service experience, customers form an evaluation that determines to a large degree whether they will return or continue to patronize the service organization (see Figure 2.2). Historically within the field of marketing, much more attention has been paid to pre-purchase evaluations and consumer choice. Yet, post-purchase and post-experience evaluations are typically most important in predicting subsequent consumer behaviours and repurchase, particularly for services.

Post-experience evaluation is captured by companies in measures of satisfaction, service quality, loyalty and, sometimes, emotional engagement. We devote an entire chapter (Chapter 4) to exploring the specifics of customer satisfaction and service quality. Another chapter (Chapter 7) examines the topic of relationships and loyalty.

WORD-OF-MOUTH COMMUNICATION

Post-experience evaluations will significantly impact what consumers tell others about the service. Because service consumers are strongly influenced by the personal opinions of others, understanding and controlling word-of-mouth communication becomes even more important for service companies. The best way to get positive word of mouth is, of course, to create memorable and positive service experiences. When service is unsatisfactory, it is critical to have an effective service recovery strategy (see Chapter 15) to curb negative word of mouth.

ATTRIBUTION OF DISSATISFACTION

When consumers are disappointed with purchases – because the products did not fulfil the intended needs, did not perform satisfactorily or were not worth the price – their attribution of dissatisfaction may be to a number of different sources, among them the producers, the retailers, or themselves. Because consumers participate to a greater extent in the definition and production of services, they may feel more responsible for their dissatisfaction when they purchase services than when they purchase goods. As an example, consider a consumer purchasing a haircut; receiving the cut that he or she desires depends in part on communicating clear specifications to the stylist. If disappointed, he or she may blame either the stylist (for lack of skill) or him or herself (for choosing the wrong stylist or for not communicating his or her own needs clearly).

The quality of many services depends on the information the customer brings to the service encounter: a pharmacist's accurate diagnosis requires a conscientious case history and a clear articulation of symptoms; a dry cleaner's success in removing a spot depends on the consumer's knowledge of its cause; and a tax adviser's satisfactory performance relies on the receipts saved by the consumer. Failure to obtain satisfaction with any of these services may not be blamed completely on the retailer or producer, because consumers must adequately perform their part in the production process also.

With products, on the other hand, a consumer's main form of participation is the act of purchase. The consumer may attribute failure to receive satisfaction to his or her own decision-making error, but he or she holds the producer responsible for product performance. Goods usually carry warranties or guarantees with purchase, emphasizing that the producer believes that if something goes wrong, it is not the fault of the consumer. With services, consumers attribute some of their dissatisfaction to their own inability to specify or perform their part of the service. They also may complain less frequently about services than about goods because of their belief that they themselves are partly responsible for their dissatisfaction.

POSITIVE OR NEGATIVE BIASES

There is a long history of research in psychology and consumer behaviour that suggests that people remember negative events and occurrences more than positive ones and are more influenced by negative information than by positive information. Research and personal observation suggest that it is easier for consumers to remember the negative service experiences they have than to think of the many routine, or even positive, experiences.

There is also a long stream of research that says that customers will weigh negative information about a product attribute more heavily than positive information in forming their overall brand attitudes. Yet some very interesting and recent research suggests 'positivity bias' for services.[35] The research showed that consumers tend to infer positive qualities for the firm and its employees if they have a good experience with one service employee. When individual service providers are regarded positively, customers' positive perceptions of other service providers in the company are also raised. On the other hand, customers who have a negative experience with one employee are less likely to draw a negative inference about all employees or the firm. That is, customers are more likely to attribute that negative experience to the individual provider, not the entire firm. Although this study is just one piece of research, the results and implications are very intriguing.

BRAND LOYALTY

The degree to which consumers are committed to particular brands of goods or services depends on a number of factors: the cost of changing brands (switching cost), the availability of substitutes, social ties to the company, the perceived risk associated with the purchase, and the satisfaction obtained in the past. Because it may be more costly to change brands of services, because awareness of substitutes is limited and because higher risks may accompany services, consumers are more likely to remain customers of particular companies with services than with goods.

The difficulty of obtaining information about services means that consumers may be unaware of alternatives or substitutes for their brands, or they may be uncertain about the ability of alternatives to increase satisfaction over present brands. Monetary fees may accompany brand switching in many services: dentists sometimes demand new X-rays on the initial visit and health clubs frequently charge 'membership fees' at the outset to obtain long-term commitments from customers.

If consumers perceive greater risks with services, as is hypothesized here, they probably depend on brand names to a greater extent than when they purchase products. Brand loyalty, described as a means of economizing decision effort by substituting habit for repeated, deliberate decision, functions as a device for reducing the risks of consumer decisions.

A final reason that consumers may be more brand loyal with services is the recognition of the need for repeated patronage in order to obtain optimum satisfaction from the seller. Becoming a 'regular customer' allows the seller to gain knowledge of the customer's tastes and preferences, ensures better treatment and encourages more interest in the consumer's satisfaction. Thus a consumer may exhibit brand loyalty to cultivate a satisfying relationship with the seller.

Brand loyalty has two sides. The fact that a service provider's own customers are brand loyal is, of course, desirable. The fact that the customers of the provider's competition are difficult to capture, however, creates special challenges. The marketer may need to direct communications and strategy to the customers of competitors, emphasizing attributes and strengths that his firm possesses and the competitor lacks. Marketers can also facilitate switching from competitors' services by reducing switching costs.

UNDERSTANDING DIFFERENCES AMONG CONSUMERS

To this point in the chapter, we have discussed consumer decision-making and evaluation processes that are applicable across a wide range of consumers and types of services. In the remaining sections, we examine two broad topics that shed light on some of the differences *among* consumers. First, we examine the role of national and ethnic cultures in shaping consumer behaviour. Then we discuss some of the unique differences in consumer decision-making for organizations and households.

GLOBAL DIFFERENCES: THE ROLE OF CULTURE

Culture represents the common values, norms and behaviours of a particular group and is often identified with nations or ethnicity. Culture is learned, shared, multidimensional and transmitted from one generation to the next. Understanding cultural differences is important in services marketing because of its effects on the ways that customers evaluate and use services. Culture also influences how companies and their service employees interact with customers. Culture is important in international services marketing – taking services from one country and offering them in others – but it is also critical within countries. More and more, individual countries are becoming multicultural, and organizations need to understand how this factor affects evaluation, purchase and use of services even within countries.

Research provides considerable evidence that there are differences in how consumers perceive services across cultures. For example, a study showed notable differences in how fast-food and grocery consumers in eight different countries (Australia, China, Germany, India, Morocco, the Netherlands, Sweden and the United States) evaluate these services.[36] Differences in how services are evaluated across cultures can be traced to basic factors that distinguish cultures from each other. In the next sections, we highlight some of the major differences that can influence how people choose, use and evaluate services, including values and attitudes, manners and customers, material culture, and aesthetics. Language, another obvious cultural difference particularly important for services, is discussed in Chapter 16.

Values and Attitudes Differ Across Cultures   Values and attitudes help determine what members of a culture think is right, important and/or desirable. Because behaviours, including consumer behaviours, flow from values and attitudes, services marketers who want their services adopted across cultures must understand these differences.

SERVICE SPOTLIGHT

In 2014, Starbucks withdrew from the Australian market, selling its 24 remaining local stores to 7-Eleven operator Withers Group. Starbucks as a chain was never successful in Australia, owing to the pressure of Australia's thriving independent coffee shop scene. Australians are certainly big purchasers of 'coffee to go' but the coffee shop market is mature and sophisticated. Australians did not need to be introduced to the concept of coffee as many other countries in Asia and Northern Europe did. Early Italian and Greek immigrants introduced Australia to coffee drinking and independent boutique-type coffee shops have served the office-working populations in the large cities for decades. There is a strong sense in Australia of buying local, supporting the community, having relationships with the people you buy from and supporting ethically minded businesses. The Starbucks brand did not take full account of these differences in cultural values and attitudes.

Manners and Customs.   Manners and customs represent a culture's views of appropriate ways of behaving. It is important to monitor differences in manners and customs because they can have a direct effect on the service encounter. For example in fast-food restaurants, Central and Eastern Europeans are perplexed by Western expectations that unhappy workers put on a 'happy face' when dealing with customers. As an example, McDonald's requires Polish employees to smile whenever they interact with customers. Such a requirement strikes many employees as artificial and insincere. The fast-food giant has learned to encourage managers in Poland to probe employee problems and to assign troubled workers to the kitchen rather than to the food counter.[37]

Material Culture.   Material culture consists of the tangible products of culture. What people own and how they use and display material possessions vary around the world. Cars, houses, clothes and furniture are examples of material culture.

The importance of owning your own home varies significantly from country to country, reflecting the different cultural traditions existing within each society. Table 2.2 shows the percentage of residential dwellings that are owner-occupied (with and without a mortgage) in a number of European countries. The difference between Switzerland and Romania is particularly striking. Such differences will impact on

Table 2.2 Housing ownership in European countries

Country	% of population in owner occupied housing with mortgage	% of population in owner occupied housing without mortgage	% of population in owner occupied housing
Romania	1	96	97
Lithuania	7	85	92
Hungary	21	69	90
Croatia	3	87	90
Slovakia	10	80	90
Bulgaria	2	85	87
Norway	65	20	85
Estonia	18	64	82
Latvia	10	72	82
Malta	18	64	82
Poland	10	72	82
Czech Republic	18	62	80
Spain	32	47	79
Slovenia	8	68	76
Greece	15	61	76
Portugal	34	41	75
Finland	42	32	74
Italy	16	58	74
Belgium	43	29	72
Ireland	35	35	70
Sweden	62	8	70
Netherlands	60	8	68
United Kingdom	38	29	67
France	30	34	64
Denmark	52	12	64
Austria	26	32	58
Germany	28	25	53
Switzerland	39	5	44

Source: Eurostat (2014). Distribution of population by tenure status.

property-related services such as decorating, garden maintenance, estate agents, lawyers, architects (for extensions/home improvements) and even do-it-yourself (DIY) retailers.

Aesthetics. Aesthetics refer to cultural ideas about beauty and good taste. These ideas are reflected in music, art, drama and dance as well as the appreciation of colour and form.

Attitudes towards style in clothing, cars, restaurants, retail stores and hotels vary internationally relating to the expectations of local culture. A French café is very different from a Starbucks in terms of atmosphere. Many Scandinavian hotels such as Radisson Blu have very clean lines with utilitarian furniture supported by decor that is striking but simple. The internal design of a French car is generally more 'chic' or quirky than would be the case for a German-built car. These all reflect the aesthetic characteristics of the culture they serve. Care must therefore be taken in designing service environments to ensure that the target market is comfortable with the aesthetic qualities being presented.

GROUP DECISION-MAKING

A group is defined as two or more individuals who have implicitly or explicitly defined relationships to one another such that their behaviour is interdependent.[38] When groups make decisions about services – a household purchasing a family vacation or a kitchen redesign, or an organization purchasing information technology consulting or marketing research services – many of the same issues arise as for individuals. Groups purchasing services encounter greater perceived risk, more reliance on word-of-mouth communication, greater difficulty in comparing alternatives and often a higher level of customer participation than do groups purchasing goods. For example, although many large organizations have very clear evaluation processes for buying goods, their processes and decision rules for purchasing services are often not as well defined. The intangibility and variability of business services make them more risky and often difficult to compare. Thus, organizations often rely on established partnerships, long-term relationships or referrals from others when it comes to major service purchases. Similar issues arise for households who rely heavily on personal referrals in making significant services purchases such as home repair, landscaping and annual vacations. Even smaller household decisions – where to eat dinner or the choice of a dry cleaner – may be influenced by referrals and may involve a great deal of risk, depending on the occasion. A special anniversary or birthday dinner or where to have an heirloom such as Grandmother's 40-year-old wedding dress dry cleaned can be decisions that carry considerable personal risk.

Despite these similarities, some differences in group decision-making should be considered for a fuller understanding of consumer behaviour in services. Among the aspects that are different for group buying are collective decision-making, mixed motives or goals, roles in the purchasing process, and group culture. We will highlight some of these differences for two major groups: households and organizations.

HOUSEHOLDS

When a family makes a service purchase decision, it has a collective style of decision-making that often differs from what any of the individuals would use if making an independent choice. When a family chooses a vacation destination, for example, its style may involve one of the following: (1) one parent makes a unilateral decision that the family will go on vacation to Disneyland Paris; (2) the family discusses possible vacation destinations at the dinner table, taking each person's ideas and suggestions into account, and selects three locations that a parent will investigate further; (3) the parents provide a budget and a list of the destinations that can be visited within that budget, then allow the children to choose among them. Once a destination has been chosen, the mix of motives or goals of the group comes into play. The mother may want to sightsee, the father to rest and the children to visit local theme parks. In this and other group purchasing decisions, the needs and goals of the various members must be balanced so that the service (in this case the vacation) delivers optimal satisfaction for as many members as possible. Group roles are also a key consideration. In a household, one individual often identifies a need and initiates the purchase, someone else may influence which service provider is selected, someone else may pay and someone else may become the ultimate user of the service. For example, the father may decide that the family needs to visit an optician for an eye test, a teenager may recommend an optician that a friend uses, the mother may pay the bills, and all the family members may go to get their eyes tested. Finally, national and ethnic culture affects household purchase and consumption behaviours. For example, ethnic groups vary, with some being very patriarchal, others egalitarian and still others autocratic.

ORGANIZATIONS

Organizational consumers are a special category of group consumers. These days, companies spend millions on information technology services, call centres, travel management, payroll services and outsourced services for human resource management. Making the right decision on service purchases can be absolutely critical for an organization's success. How do companies make these important decisions? How, for example, do certain companies choose to outsource their call-centre operations to a company in India?

For routine and even complex purchases, organizations often rely on a small number of buyers within the company, many of whom specialize in purchasing. These buyers are typically organized either formally or informally into buying centres, which include all people involved in the decision process.[39] Each of these roles may be taken by a different person, or one person may assume all roles in some cases.

* The *initiator* identifies the organization's service needs.
* The *gatekeeper* collects and controls information about the purchase.
* The *decider* determines what service to purchase.
* The *buyer* or purchasing agent physically acquires the service.
* The *user* consumes the service and may or may not have any influence over the purchase decision.

Among the characteristics that distinguish organizational from individual decision-making are economic forces such as current business climate and technology trends; organizational strategies and culture; whether purchasing is a centralized or decentralized function; and the group forces that influence purchasing decisions.[40] Organizational purchases also tend to differ by magnitude and include new task purchases (large purchases that require careful consideration of needs and evaluation of alternative), straight rebuys (simple reorders of past service purchases) and modified rebuys (a mix of new and straight rebuy features).[41]

As companies outsource more services and particularly when these services are outsourced around the globe, purchase decisions become complex and difficult. Often companies must rely on outside consultants such as Accenture or PriceWaterhouseCoopers to help them with these multifaceted and financially risky decisions.

Organizational purchasers also rely on references and the experience of other organizations in making their service purchase decisions. Referrals and testimonials can be very helpful to other organizations considering similar business service purchases. In fact, many business service providers have customer stories, cases and testimonials on their websites to help reduce the risk of these complex decisions.

SUMMARY

The intention of this chapter was to provide understanding about how consumers choose and evaluate services. Services possess high levels of experience and credence properties, which in turn make them challenging to evaluate, particularly prior to purchase. The chapter isolated and discussed three stages of consumer behaviour for services, and it looked at how experience and credence properties result in challenges and opportunities in all three stages. The three stages are consumer choice (including need recognition, information search, evaluation of alternatives and service purchase); consumer experience; and post-experience evaluation. Consumer behaviour theories, current research and insights for managers were highlighted in each of these sections.

Although the three stages are relevant for all types of consumer behaviour in services, important differences exist in behaviour across global cultures and for groups versus individuals. Global differences in consumer behaviour were presented, particularly as they relate to service consumption. The chapter ended with a discussion of the differences in group versus individual consumer decision-making related to households and organizations.

KEY CONCEPTS

EXERCISES

1   Choose a particular end-consumer services industry and one type of service provided in that industry (such as the financial services industry for mortgage loans, the legal services industry for wills or the travel industry for a holiday package). Talk to five customers who have purchased that service and determine to what extent the information in this chapter described their behaviour in terms of consumer choice, consumer experience and post-experience evaluation for that service.

2   Choose a particular business-to-business service industry and one type of service provided in that industry (such as the information services industry for computer maintenance services or the consulting industry for management consulting). Talk to five customers in that industry and determine to what extent the information in this chapter described their behaviour in terms of consumer choice, consumer experience and post-experience evaluation for that service.

3   Visit a service provider of your choice. Experience the service at first hand if possible and observe other customers for a period of time. Describe the consumer (service) experience in detail in terms of what happened throughout the process and how customers, including yourself, felt about it. How could the service experience be improved?

4   Interview three people who come from countries other than your own. Ask them about their consumer behaviour patterns with regard to a variety of services. Note the differences and similarities to your own consumer behaviour. What are possible causes of the differences?

DISCUSSION QUESTIONS

1   Based on the chapter, which aspects of consumer behaviour are similar and which are different for services versus goods?

2   Where does a college or university education fit on the continuum of evaluation for different types of products? Where does computer software fit? Consulting? Retailing? Fast food? What are the implications for consumer behaviour?

3   What are examples (other than those given in the chapter) of services that are high in credence properties? How do high credence properties affect consumer behaviour for these services?

4   Which services do you consider to be unsuited to the introduction of self-service technology? Why?

5   How do you reduce risk when choosing a restaurant in a city you haven't visited before?

6   Why are consumer experiences so important in the evaluation process for services?

7   Using the service drama metaphor, describe the services provided by a health club, a fine restaurant or a cruise liner.

8   What are some differences in service choice, purchase and consumption processes for organizations and households compared with individuals? What are some similarities?

FURTHER READING

Beatson, A., Lee, N. and Coote, L.V. (2007). Self-service technology and the service encounter. *Service Industries Journal*, 27(1), 75–82.

Girard, T. and Dion, P. (2010). Validating the search, experience and credence product classification framework. *Journal of Business Research*, 63(9–10), 1079–87.

Hofstede, G. (2003). *Culture's Consequences: Comparing Values, Behaviours, Institutions and Organisations across Nations*, 2nd edn. London: Sage Publications.

McKoll-Kennedy, J.R. and Fetter, R. (1999). Dimensions of consumer search behaviour in services. *Journal of Services Marketing*, 13(3), 242–63.

Murray, K. and Schlacter, J. (1990). The impact of services versus goods on consumers' assessments of perceived risk and variability. *Journal of the Academy of Marketing Science*, 18(1), 51–65.

Solomon, M., Bamossy, G.J., Askegaard, S. and Hogg, M. (2009). *Consumer Behaviour: A European Perspective*, 4th edn. London: FT Prentice Hall.

Sparks, B. and Browning V. (2011). The Impact of Online Reviews on Hotel Booking Intentions and Perception of Trust. *Tourism Management*, 32(6), 1310–1323.

Tynan, C. and McKechnie, S. (2009). Experience marketing: a review and reassessment. *Journal of Marketing Management*, 25(5/6), 501–17.

Wilson, A., Murphy, H. and Cambra Fierro, J. (2012). Hospitality and Travel: The Nature and Implications of User-Generated Content. *Cornell Hospitality Quarterly*, 53(3), 220–229.

CHAPTER 3

Customer Expectations
of Service

CHAPTER OUTLINE

LEARNING OBJECTIVES

This chapter's objectives are to:

1 Recognize that customers hold different types of expectations for service performance.
2 Discuss the sources of customer expectations of service, including those that are controllable and uncontrollable by marketers.
3 Acknowledge that the types and sources of expectations are similar for end consumers and business customers, for pure service and product-related service, for experienced customers and inexperienced customers.
4 Understand the most important current issues surrounding the management of customer expectations.

OPENING EXAMPLE
The ash cloud - KLM and British Airways response

In 2010 a volcanic eruption in south Iceland grounded thousands of flights and left millions of passengers stranded. During the eruption more than 75 per cent of European airspace was closed for a week, affecting more than 90,000 flights and 10 million passengers. While the circumstances were beyond the control of the airlines, the main expectation of the stranded passengers was that their airlines would keep them updated with information. In tense, time-sensitive circumstances, consumers were increasingly turning to social media for real-time information and advice. In the seven days when most of Europe's largest airlines were grounded, there were more than 55,000 mentions on Twitter of #ashtag, as people tried to source information about flights, accommodation and up-to-date news of their situation.

The rapidly evolving situation meant that the flight information on static websites quickly became obsolete. This led to airlines following customer demand and turning to social media – some for the first time – to update their customers. Although this was a struggle for many, the crisis did highlight two airlines, KLM and British Airways, who excelled at meeting customer expectations by issuing updates via social media channels.

These companies not only provided users with flight status updates, but also engaged in public conversations and looked to make the information to frequently asked questions easily available.

KLM sent out regular Twitter updates filled with advice on re-booking, information about local areas and links to news stories, and dedicated time to replying to many individual customer questions, comments and concerns. KLM also created a bespoke 'Volcanic Eruption' Q&A sidebar on its Facebook page and had official representatives available to respond to questions continuously. Using their social media platforms, KLM was able not only to update a large number of customers and people affected by the ash cloud, but also grow its number of followers on Twitter by more than 4,000 in that one week.

British Airways targeted a different user base by posting a number of videos of its CEO, Willie Walsh, on YouTube. These were done to reassure customers that the airline was doing everything possible to minimize disruption. British Airways also had representatives on all of its official social media channels responding to direct questions in real time.

Not only did these airlines show their competences in managing a crisis, but the organized way in which they provided information and responded to questions has had a very positive effect on their brand perceptions.

The explosion in social media has created a critical tipping point with organizations struggling to cope with the 'noise' and potential damage it can create, but for KLM and British Airways, the ash cloud did them no lasting harm. In effect, it raised their profiles on the various social media platforms, gained them followers and cemented their positions as trusted airlines that address the expectations of their customers.

Social media represents a wealth of opportunity to shape customers relationships with airlines and travel agents, and this is most effectively achieved when firms integrate it with their other service channels. This ensures that dedicated customer service staff can respond to all enquiries in a timely manner, and that consumers get access to the same information no matter which channel they use.

Source: Adapted from post on Mycustomer.com by Dee Roche 3/5/2011.

IMPORTANCE OF CUSTOMER EXPECTATIONS

Customer expectations are beliefs about service delivery that serve as standards, or reference points, against which performance is judged. Because customers compare their perceptions of performance with these reference points when evaluating service quality, thorough knowledge about customer expectations is critical to services marketers. Knowing what the customer expects is the first and possibly most critical step in delivering good-quality service. Being wrong about what customers want can mean losing a customer's business when another company hits the target exactly. Being wrong can also mean expending money, time and other resources on things that do not matter to the customer. Being wrong can even mean not surviving in a fiercely competitive market.

Among the aspects of expectations that need to be explored and understood for successful services marketing are the following: what types of expectation standards do customers hold about services? What factors most influence the formation of these expectations? What role do these factors play in changing expectations? How can a service company meet or exceed customer expectations?

In this chapter we provide a framework for thinking about customer expectations.[1] The chapter is divided into three main sections: (1) the meaning and types of expected service, (2) factors that influence customer expectations of service, and (3) current issues involving customer service expectations.

MEANING AND TYPES OF SERVICE EXPECTATIONS

To say that expectations are reference points against which service delivery is compared is only a beginning. The level of expectation can vary widely depending on the reference point the customer holds. Although almost everyone has an intuitive sense of what expectations are, service marketers need a far more thorough and clear definition of expectations if they are to comprehend, measure and manage them.

Imagine that you are planning to go to a restaurant. Figure 3.1 shows a continuum along which different possible types of service expectations can be arrayed from low to high. On the left of the continuum are different types or levels of expectations, ranging from high (top) to low (bottom). At each point we give a name to the type of expectation, and illustrate what it might mean in terms of a restaurant you are considering. Note how important the expectation you hold will be to your eventual assessment of the restaurant's performance. Suppose you went into the restaurant for which you held the minimum tolerable expectation, paid very little money and were served immediately with good food. Next suppose that you went to the restaurant for which you had the highest (ideal) expectations, paid a lot of money and were served good (but not fantastic) food. Which restaurant experience would you judge to be best? The answer is likely to depend a great deal on the reference point that you brought to the experience.

Because the idea of customer expectations is so critical to evaluation of service, we start this chapter by talking about the levels of expectations.

EXPECTED SERVICE: LEVELS OF EXPECTATIONS

As we show in Figure 3.1, customers hold different types of expectations about service. For purposes of our discussion in the rest of this chapter, we focus on two types. The highest can be termed *desired service*: the level of service the customer hopes to receive – the 'wished for' level of performance. Desired service is a blend of what the customer believes 'can be' and 'should be'. For example, consumers who sign up for a computer dating service expect to find compatible, attractive, interesting people to date and perhaps even someone to marry. The expectation reflects the hopes and wishes of these consumers; without these hopes and wishes and the belief that they may be fulfilled, consumers would probably not purchase the dating service. In a similar way, you may use an online travel-planning and flight-booking site such as Expedia to book a short holiday to Venice at Easter. What are your expectations of the service? In all likelihood you want

Figure 3.1 Possible levels of customer expectations

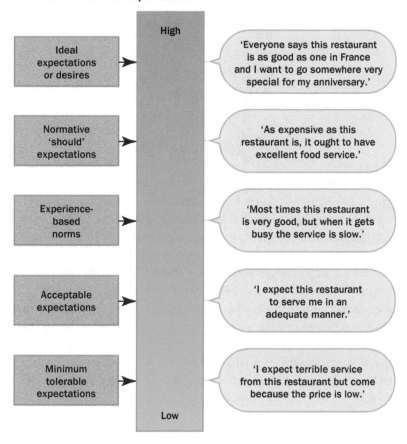

Ideal expectations or desires

'Everyone says this restaurant is as good as one in France and I want to go somewhere very special for my anniversary.'

Normative 'should' expectations

'As expensive as this restaurant is, it ought to have excellent food service.'

Experience-based norms

'Most times this restaurant is very good, but when it gets busy the service is slow.'

Acceptable expectations

'I expect this restaurant to serve me in an adequate manner.'

Minimum tolerable expectations

'I expect terrible service from this restaurant but come because the price is low.'

High

Low

Source: Adapted from R.K. Teas, 'Expectations, performance evaluation and consumers' perceptions of quality', *Journal of Marketing* (October 1993), pp. 18–34.

Expedia to find you a flight exactly when you want to travel and a hotel close to the key sights in Piazza San Marco at a price you can afford – because that is what you hope and wish for.

However, you probably also see that demand at Easter may constrain the availability of airline seats and hotel rooms. And not all airlines or hotels you may be interested in may have a relationship with Expedia. In this situation and in general, customers hope to achieve their service desires but recognize that this is not always possible. We call the threshold level of acceptable service *adequate service* – the level of service the customer will accept.[2] So the customer may put up with a flight at a less than ideal time and stay at a hotel further away from the key Venetian sites if he or she really wants to travel at Easter. Adequate service represents the 'minimum tolerable expectation',[3] the bottom level of performance acceptable to the customer.

Figure 3.2 shows these two expectation standards as the upper and lower boundaries for customer expectations. This figure portrays the idea that customers assess service performance on the basis of two standard boundaries: what they desire and what they deem acceptable.

Among the intriguing questions about service expectations is whether customers hold the same or different expectation levels for service firms in the same industry. For example, are desired service expectations the same for all restaurants? Or just for all fast-food restaurants? Do the levels of adequate service expectations vary across restaurants? Consider the following quotation:

> *Levels of expectation are why two organizations in the same business can offer far different levels of service and still keep customers happy. It is why McDonald's can extend excellent industrialized service with few employees per customer and why an expensive restaurant with many tuxedoed waiters may be unable to do as well from the customer's point of view.*[4]

Figure 3.2   Dual customer expectation levels

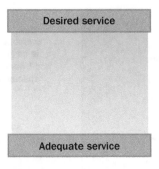

Customers typically hold similar desired expectations across categories of service, but these categories are not as broad as whole industries. Among subcategories of restaurants are expensive restaurants, ethnic restaurants, fast-food restaurants and airport restaurants. A customer's desired service expectation for fast-food restaurants is quick, convenient, tasty food in a clean setting. The desired service expectation for an expensive restaurant, on the other hand, usually involves elegant surroundings, gracious employees, candlelight and fine food. In essence, desired service expectations seem to be the same for service providers within industry categories or subcategories that are viewed as similar by customers.

The adequate service expectation level, on the other hand, may vary for different firms within a category or subcategory. Within fast-food restaurants, a customer may hold a higher expectation for McDonald's than for Burger King, having experienced consistent service at McDonald's over time and somewhat inconsistent service at Burger King. It is possible therefore that a customer can be more disappointed with service from McDonald's than from Burger King, even though the actual level of service at McDonald's may be higher than the level at Burger King.

★ SERVICE SPOTLIGHT

In the past, hotels built their business around employing highly attentive people. In the future, they may replace many of their staff with technology. As a regular guest, on the day of your arrival, when you get within 10 kilometres of the hotel, an alert from your phone ensures that the temperature and humidity levels of your room are automatically adjusted to your liking so they will meet your expectations when you arrive.

Upon arrival, you will be greeted by an automated luggage attendant using auto-tracking technology designed to quickly transfer your bags to your room. Upon entering the hotel lobby, you will be automatically registered without having to check in. Your room number and directions to the room will display on your smartphone. Virtual receptionists will be positioned at key locations in the hotel to help out whenever the need arises. As you approach your room, the door will automatically unlock and you will see your luggage already waiting for you. Upon entering your room, the sound system will automatically be playing music that syncs with your personality at the perfect volume. Temperature and humidity will have been programmed into the room-electrics specifically for you. Window shades will open or close depending on your position in the room, time of day, and intensity of the sunlight. Even when stepping into the shower, the controls will anticipate your desired water temperature, spray selection, and pressure.

Although this may seem far off in the future, Citizen M hotels already provide a smart tablet in each room which commands all essential room functions from lighting to room temperature and air conditioning, TV and entertainment, whilst also serving as a portal for all branded hotel services and as a regular web browsing device. A number of hotels have self-check-in facilities and bedrooms that are unlocked using your smart phone.

Adapted from: **Thomas Frey, www.futuristspeaker.com.**

Figure 3.3   The zone of tolerance

THE ZONE OF TOLERANCE

As we discussed in earlier chapters, services are heterogeneous in that performance may vary across providers, across employees from the same provider, and even with the same service employee. The extent to which customers recognize and are willing to accept this variation is called the zone of tolerance and is shown in Figure 3.3. If service drops below adequate – the minimum level considered acceptable – customers will be frustrated and their satisfaction with the company will be undermined. If service performance is higher than the zone of tolerance at the top end – where performance exceeds desired service – customers will be very pleased and probably quite surprised as well. You might consider the zone of tolerance as the range within which customers do not particularly notice service performance. When it falls outside the range (either very low or very high), the service gets the customer's attention in either a positive or negative way. As an example, consider the service at a checkout queue in a grocery store. Most customers hold a range of acceptable times for this service encounter – probably somewhere between five and ten minutes. If service consumes that period of time, customers probably do not pay much attention to the wait. If a customer enters the line and finds sufficient checkout personnel to serve him or her in the first two or three minutes, he or she may notice the service and judge it as excellent. On the other hand, if a customer has to wait in a queue for 15 minutes, he or she may begin to grumble and look at his or her watch. The longer the wait is below the zone of tolerance, the more frustrated the customer becomes.

Customers' service expectations are characterized by a range of levels (like those shown in Figure 3.2), bounded by desired and adequate service, rather than a single level. This tolerance zone, representing the difference between desired service and the level of service considered adequate, can expand and contract with each customer. An airline customer's zone of tolerance will narrow when he or she is running late and is concerned about making it in time for his or her plane. A minute seems much longer, and the customer's adequate service level increases. On the other hand, a customer who arrives at the airport early may have a larger tolerance zone, making the wait in line far less noticeable than when he or she is pressed for time. This example shows that the marketer must understand not just the size and boundary levels for the zone of tolerance but also when and how the tolerance zone fluctuates with a given customer.

★ SERVICE SPOTLIGHT

When British Airways created an advertising campaign for its business class service on its overnight flights from New York to London, it undertook a significant amount of research to identify what was important to travellers. Certainly schedules, comfortable lounges, connections, in-flight service and price all played a part. However, the research identified that, critically for most passengers, the service experience had to meet their expectations for sleeping. In New York most passengers would get a meal and a couple of drinks prior to boarding the plane. On board, they would get comfortable even before take-off and be ready to push the recline button the minute the seat belt sign went off. Some might graze on a film, book or magazine, allowing the food and drink to settle, but the main objective of every traveller was to get as much sleep before arriving in London in the early morning. It was all about sleep. If they slept, not a lot else mattered and the zone of tolerance for other aspects of the experience was quite wide. If they didn't manage to sleep, everything else mattered a lot and the zone of tolerance for other aspects of the flight tended to be quite narrow. This explains why British Airways along with other airlines has invested so much money on business seats that can recline into flat beds. Their advertising campaign also focused on showing a business traveller getting into a bed in Times Square, New York and waking up fully rested, in the same bed in Piccadilly Circus in London.

Source: **Account Planning Group (UK) Gold Creative Planning Awards.**

DIFFERENT CUSTOMERS POSSESS DIFFERENT ZONES OF TOLERANCE

Another aspect of variability in the range of reasonable services is that different customers possess different tolerance zones. Some customers have narrow zones of tolerance, requiring a tighter range of service from providers, whereas other customers allow a greater range of service. For example, very busy customers would likely always be pressed for time, desire short wait times in general and hold a constrained range for the length of acceptable wait times. When it comes to meeting plumbers or repair personnel at their home for problems with leaking pipes or domestic appliances, customers who work outside the home have a more restricted window of acceptable time duration for that appointment than do customers who work in their homes or do not work at all.

The zone of tolerance of an individual customer increases or decreases depending on a number of factors, including company-controlled factors such as price. When prices increase, customers tend to be less tolerant of poor service. In this case, the zone of tolerance decreases because the adequate service level shifts upward. Later in this chapter we will describe many different factors, some company-controlled and others customer-controlled, that lead to the narrowing or widening of the tolerance zone.

ZONES OF TOLERANCE VARY FOR SERVICE DIMENSIONS

Customers' tolerance zones also vary for different service attributes or dimensions. The more important the factor, the narrower the zone of tolerance is likely to be. In general, customers are likely to be less tolerant about unreliable service (broken promises or service errors) than about other types of service deficiency, which means that they have higher expectations for this factor. In addition to higher expectations for the most important service dimensions and attributes, customers are likely to be less willing to relax these expectations than those for less important factors, making the zone of tolerance for the most important service dimension smaller and the desired and adequate service levels higher.[5] Figure 3.4 portrays the likely difference in tolerance zones for the most important and the least important factors.[6]

The fluctuation in the individual customer's zone of tolerance is more a function of changes in the adequate service level, which moves readily up and down because of situational circumstances, than in the desired service level, which tends to move upward incrementally because of accumulated experiences. Desired service is relatively idiosyncratic and stable compared with adequate service, which moves up and down and in response to competition and other factors. Fluctuation in the zone of tolerance can be likened to an accordion's movement, but with most of the movement coming from one side (the adequate service level) rather than the other (the desired service level).

In summary, we can express the boundaries of customer expectations of service with two different levels of expectations: desired service and adequate service. The desired service level is less subject to change than the adequate service level. A zone of tolerance separates these two levels. This zone of tolerance varies across customers and expands or contracts with the same customer.

Figure 3.4   Zones of tolerance for different service dimensions

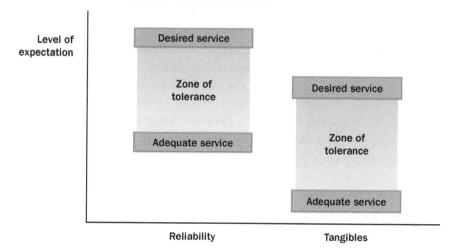

Source: Adapted from L.L. Berry, A. Parasuraman and V.A. Zeithaml, 'Ten lessons for improving service quality', Marketing Science Institute, Report No. 93–104 (May 1993).

FACTORS THAT INFLUENCE CUSTOMER EXPECTATIONS OF SERVICE

Because expectations play such a critical role in customer evaluation of services, marketers need and want to understand the factors that shape them. Marketers would also like to have control over these factors as well, but many of the forces that influence customer expectations are uncontrollable. In this section, we try to separate the many influences on customer expectations.

SOURCES OF DESIRED SERVICE EXPECTATIONS

As shown in Figure 3.5, the two largest influences on desired service level are personal needs and philosophies about service. Personal needs, those states or conditions essential to the physical or psychological well-being of the customer, are pivotal factors that shape what customers desire in service. Personal needs can fall into many categories, including physical, social, psychological and functional. A cinema-goer who regularly goes to see films straight from work, and is therefore thirsty and hungry, hopes and desires that the food and drink counters at the cinema will have short queues and attentive staff, whereas a cinema-goer who regularly has dinner elsewhere has a low or zero level of desired service from the food and drink counters. A customer with high social and dependency needs may have relatively high expectations for a hotel's ancillary services, hoping, for example, that the hotel has a bar with live music and dancing.

Figure 3.5   Factors that influence desired service

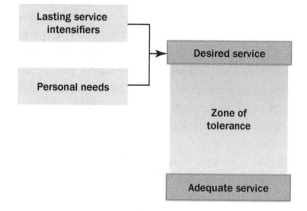

Some customers are more demanding than others, having greater sensitivity to, and higher expectations of, service. Lasting service intensifiers are individual, stable factors that lead the customer to a heightened sensitivity to service. One of the most important of these factors can be called *derived service expectations*, which occur when customer expectations are driven by another person or group of people. A niece from a big family who is planning a ninetieth birthday party for a favourite aunt is representing the entire family in selecting a restaurant for a successful celebration. Her needs are driven in part by the derived expectations from the other family members. A parent choosing a vacation for the family, a spouse selecting a home-cleaning service, an employee choosing an office for the firm – all these customers' individual expectations are intensified because they represent and must answer to other parties who will receive the service. In the context of business-to-business service, customer expectations are driven by the expectations of their own customers. The head of an information technology department in an insurance company, who is the business customer of a large computer company, has expectations based on those of the insurance customers he or she serves: when the computer equipment is down, his or her customers complain. The need to keep the system up and running is not just his or her own expectation but is derived from the pressure of customers.

Business-to-business customers may also derive their expectations from their managers and supervisors. Employees of a marketing research department may speed up project cycles (increase their expectations for speed of delivery) when pressured by their management to deliver the study results. Corporate buyers may increase demands for faster delivery at lower costs when company management is emphasizing cost reduction in the company.

Another lasting service intensifier is *personal service philosophy* – the customer's underlying generic attitude about the meaning of service and the proper conduct of service providers. If you have ever been employed as a member of waiting staff in a restaurant, you are likely to have standards for restaurant service that were shaped by your training and experience in that role. You might, for example, believe that waiters should not keep customers waiting longer than 15 minutes to take their orders. Knowing the way a kitchen operates, you may be less tolerant of lukewarm food or errors in the order than customers who have not held the role of waiter or waitress. In general, customers who are themselves in service businesses or have worked for them in the past seem to have especially strong service philosophies.

To the extent that customers have personal philosophies about service provision, their expectations of service providers will be intensified. Personal service philosophies and derived service expectations elevate the level of desired service.

SOURCES OF ADEQUATE SERVICE EXPECTATIONS

A different set of determinants affects adequate service, the level of service the customer finds acceptable. In general, these influences are short term and tend to fluctuate more than the factors that influence desired service. In this section we explain the five factors shown in Figure 3.6 that influence adequate service: (1) temporary service intensifiers, (2) perceived service alternatives, (3) customer self-perceived service role, (4) situational factors, and (5) predicted service.

The first set of elements, *temporary service intensifiers*, consists of short-term, individual factors that make a customer more aware of the need for service. Personal emergency situations in which service is urgently needed (such as an accident and the need for car insurance or a breakdown in office equipment during a busy period) raise the level of adequate service expectation, particularly the level of responsiveness required and considered acceptable. A mail-order company that depends on freephone numbers for receiving all customer orders will tend to be more demanding of the telephone service during peak periods of the week, month and year. Any system breakdown or lack of clarity on the lines will be tolerated less during these intense periods than at other times.

Problems with the initial service can also lead to heightened expectations. Performing a service right the first time is very important because customers value service reliability above all other dimensions. If the service fails in the recovery phase, putting it right the second time (that is, being reliable in service recovery)

Figure 3.6   Factors that influence adequate service

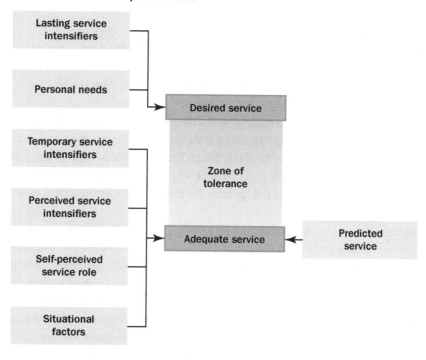

is even more critical than it was the first time. Car repair service provides a case in point. If a problem with your car's brakes sends you to a car repairer, you expect the company to fix the brakes. But if you experience further problems with the brakes after the repair (a not uncommon situation with car repairs), your adequate service level will increase. In these and other situations where temporary service intensifiers are present, the level of adequate service will increase and the zone of tolerance will narrow.

Perceived service alternatives are other providers from whom the customer can obtain service. If customers have multiple service providers to choose from, or if they can provide the service for themselves (such as lawn care or personal grooming), their levels of adequate service are higher than those of customers who believe it is not possible to get better service elsewhere. An airline customer who lives in a provincial town with a small airport, for example, has a reduced set of options in airline travel. This customer will be more tolerant of the service performance of the carriers in the town because few alternatives exist. He or she will accept the scheduling and lower levels of service more readily than will the customer in a big city who has myriad flights and airlines to choose from. The customer's perception that service alternatives exist raises the level of adequate service and narrows the zone of tolerance.

It is important that service marketers fully understand the complete set of options that customers view as perceived alternatives. In the provincial town, small airport example just discussed, the set of alternatives from the customer's point of view is likely to include more than just other airlines: taxi service to a nearby large city, rail service or driving. In general, service marketers must discover the alternatives that the customer views as comparable rather than those in the company's competitive set.

A third factor affecting the level of adequate service is the *customer's self-perceived service role*. We define this as customer perceptions of the degree to which customers exert an influence on the level of service they receive. In other words, customers' expectations are partly shaped by how well they believe they are performing their own roles in service delivery.[7] One role of the customer is to specify the level of service expected. A customer who is very explicit with a waiter about how rare he or she wants his or her steak cooked in a restaurant will probably be more dissatisfied if the meat comes to the table overcooked than a customer who does not articulate the degree of cooking expected. The customer's active participation in the service also affects this factor. A customer who does not get his or her car serviced regularly is likely to be more lenient on the car manufacturer when he or she experiences problems than one who conscientiously follows the manufacturer's service schedule.

A final way the customer defines his or her role is in assuming the responsibility for complaining when service is poor. A dissatisfied customer who complains will be less tolerant than one who does not voice his or her concerns. A car insurance customer acknowledged responsibility in service provision this way: 'You can't blame it all on the insurance broker. You need to be responsible too and let the broker know what exactly you want.'

Customers' zones of tolerance seem to expand when they sense they are not fulfilling their roles. When, on the other hand, customers believe they are doing their part in delivery, their expectations of adequate service are heightened and the zone of tolerance contracts. The comment of a car repair customer illustrates this: 'Service staff don't listen when you tell them what is wrong. I now prepare a written list of problems in advance, take it to the car dealership, and tell them to fix these.' This customer will expect more than one who did not prepare so well.

Levels of adequate service are also influenced by *situational factors*, defined as service performance conditions that customers view as beyond the control of the service provider. For example, where personal emergencies such as serious car accidents would be likely to intensify customer service expectations of insurance companies (because they are temporary service intensifiers), catastrophes that affect a large number of people at one time (floods or storms) may lower service expectations because customers recognize that insurers are inundated with demands for their services. Customers who recognize that situational factors are not the fault of the service company may accept lower levels of adequate service, given the context. In general, situational factors temporarily lower the level of adequate service, widening the zone of tolerance.

The final factor that influences adequate service is *predicted service*, the level of service that customers believe they are likely to get (Figure 3.7). This type of service expectation can be viewed as predictions made by customers about what is likely to happen during an impending transaction or exchange. Predicted service performance implies some objective calculation of the probability of performance or estimate of anticipated service performance level. If customers predict good service, their levels of adequate service are likely to

Figure 3.7   Factors that influence desired and predicted service

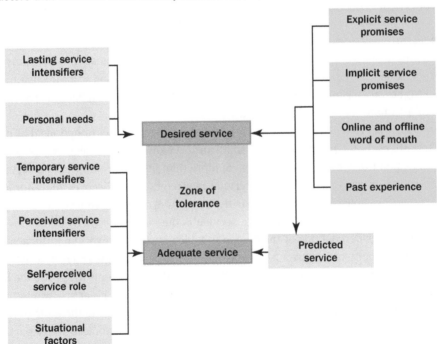

be higher than if they predict poor service. For example, travellers may expect poorer service from some of the no-frills airlines such as Ryanair or easyJet in comparison to some of the full-cost airlines such as British Airways, KLM or Air France). This prediction will mean that higher standards for adequate service will exist in the full-cost airlines. On the other hand, customers of mobile phone companies may know that the companies' call centre operations will provide poor service around Christmas time when myriad people are setting up the mobiles that they have received as gifts. In this case, levels of adequate service decrease and zones of tolerance widen.

Predicted service is typically an estimate or calculation of the service that a customer will receive in an individual transaction rather than in the overall relationship with a service provider. Whereas desired and adequate service expectations are global assessments comprising many individual service transactions, predicted service is almost always an estimate of what will happen in the next service encounter or transaction that the customer experiences. For this reason, predicted service is viewed in this model as an influencer of adequate service.

Because predictions are about individual service encounters, they are likely to be more concrete and specific than the types of expectation levels customers hold for adequate service or desired service. For example, your predicted service expectations about the length of time you will spend in the waiting room the next time you visit your doctor will likely be expressed in terms of the number of minutes or hours you have spent in the waiting room on your last visit.

SERVICE ENCOUNTER EXPECTATIONS VERSUS OVERALL SERVICE EXPECTATIONS

In Chapter 4 we discuss the difference between overall service quality and service encounter quality, viewing the service encounter as a discrete event occurring over a definable period of time (such as a particular hotel stay or a particular check-in experience at the hotel). Customers hold expectations of the quality of each service encounter, just as they hold expectations about the overall service quality of a firm. When the expectations are about individual service encounters, they are likely to be more specific and concrete (such as the number of minutes one must wait for a receptionist) than the expectations about overall service quality (like speedy service).

SOURCES OF BOTH DESIRED AND PREDICTED SERVICE EXPECTATIONS

When consumers are interested in purchasing services, they are likely to seek or take in information from several different sources. For example, they may call a store, ask a friend or deliberately track newspaper advertisements to find the needed service at the lowest price. They may also receive service information by watching television or hearing an unsolicited comment from a colleague about a service that was performed well. In addition to these active and passive types of external search for information, consumers may conduct an internal search by reviewing the information held in their memory about the service. This section discusses one internal and three external factors that influence both desired service and predicted service expectations: (1) explicit service promises, (2) implicit service promises, (3) online and offline word-of-mouth communications and (4) past experience.

Explicit service promises are personal and non-personal statements about the service made by the organization to customers. The statements are personal when they are communicated by salespeople or service or repair personnel; they are non-personal when they come from advertising, brochures and other written publications. Explicit service promises are one of the few influences on expectations that are completely in the control of the service provider.

Promising exactly what will ultimately be delivered would seem a logical and appropriate way to manage customer expectations and ensure that reality fits the promises. However, companies and the personnel who represent them often deliberately over-promise to obtain business or inadvertently over-promise by stating their best estimates about delivery of a service in the future. In addition to over-promising, company representatives simply do not always know the appropriate promises to make because services are often customized and therefore not easily defined and repeated; the representative may not know when or in what final form the service will be delivered.

All types of explicit service promises have a direct effect on desired service expectation. If the sales visit portrays a banking service that is available 24 hours a day, the customer's desires for that service (as well as the service of competitors) will be shaped by this promise.

⭐ SERVICE SPOTLIGHT

The 15-Minute Satisfaction Guarantee offered by Ibis hotels is an example of explicit service promise. This guarantee is a contractual agreement between Ibis and every hotel guest. Ibis invites every guest to immediately report any issue that may arise. If the hotel is responsible and the issue takes more than 15 minutes to resolve, the affected service will be free of charge.

Ibis claims to be able to offer this guarantee by:

- Recruiting and training all team members with the uppermost goal of achieving these quality objectives and encouraging team members to develop their professional skills
- Setting coherent and measureable targets for quality improvement on an annual basis
- Performing rigorous quality assurance tests at every hotel to ensure that these commitments are being met
- Building an organization that constantly challenges decisions at every hierarchy level
- Integrating the company's contractors and suppliers into the quality process
- Conforming with the company's Quality Management System, which is updated regularly.

Source: **www.ibis.com.**

Explicit service promises influence the levels of both desired service and predicted service. They shape what customers desire in general as well as what they predict will happen in the next service encounter from a particular service provider or in a certain service encounter.

Implicit service promises are service-related cues other than explicit promises that lead to inferences about what the service should and will be like. These quality cues are dominated by price and the tangibles associated with the service. In general, the higher the price and the more impressive the tangibles, the more a customer will expect from the service. Consider a customer who shops for insurance, finding two firms charging radically different prices. He or she may infer that the firm with the higher price should and will provide higher-quality service and better coverage. Similarly, a customer who stays at a five-star hotel is likely to desire and predict a higher standard of service than from a hotel with less impressive facilities.

The importance of **online and offline word-of-mouth communication** in shaping expectations of service is well documented.[8] These personal and sometimes non-personal statements made by parties other

than the organization convey to customers what the service will be like and influence both predicted and desired service. Word-of-mouth communication carries particular weight as an information source, because it is perceived as unbiased. Word of mouth tends to be very important in services that are difficult to evaluate before purchase and before direct experience of them. Online reviews such as those on Tripadvisor, friends and family, individuals on social media platforms as well as industry experts are all word-of-mouth sources that can affect the levels of desired and predicted service. Positive comments on social media or posted on a review site about a restaurant may result in customers having overinflated expectations of the service offering they will receive. This could ultimately lead to disappointment when they visit the restaurant. However, if the comments are neutral or negative, the same restaurant experience may result in the customers being reasonably satisfied, as they would not have high expectations for the service.

Past experience, the customer's previous exposure to service that is relevant to the focal service is another force in shaping predictions and desires. The service relevant for prediction can be previous exposure to the focal firm's service. For example, you probably compare each stay in a particular hotel with all previous stays in that hotel. But past experience with the focal hotel is likely to be a very limited view of your past experience. You may also compare each stay with your experiences in other hotels and hotel chains. Customers also compare across industries: hospital patients, for example, compare hospital stays against the standard of hotel visits. In a general sense, past experience may incorporate previous experience with the focal brand, typical performance of a favourite brand, experience with the brand last purchased or the top-selling brand, and the average performance a customer believes represents a group of similar brands.[9]

THE MANAGEMENT OF CUSTOMER EXPECTATIONS

How might a manager of a service organization use the information we have developed in this chapter to create, improve, or market services? First, managers need to know the pertinent expectation sources and their relative importance for a customer population, a customer segment and, perhaps, even a particular customer. They need to know, for instance, the relative weight of word of mouth, explicit service promises and implicit service promises in shaping desired service and predicted service. Some of these sources are more stable and permanent in their influence (such as lasting service intensifiers and personal needs) than the others, which fluctuate considerably over time (like perceived service alternatives and situational factors).

The different sources vary in terms of their credibility as well as their potential to be influenced by the marketer. Table 3.1 shows the breakdown of various factors and how services marketers can influence them. Chapter 16 details these and other strategies that services marketers can use to match delivery to promises and thereby manage expectations.

ISSUES INVOLVING THE MANAGEMENT OF CUSTOMER SERVICE EXPECTATIONS

The following issues represent current topics of particular interest to service marketers about customer expectations. In this section we discuss five of the most frequently asked questions about customer expectations:

1　What does a service marketer do if customer expectations are 'unrealistic'?
2　Should a company try to delight the customer?
3　How does a company exceed customer service expectations?
4　Do customer service expectations continually escalate?
5　How does a service company stay ahead of competition in meeting customer expectations?

WHAT DOES A SERVICES MARKETER DO IF CUSTOMER EXPECTATIONS ARE 'UNREALISTIC'?

One inhibitor to learning about customer expectations is management's and employees' fear of asking. This apprehension often stems from the belief that customer expectations will be extravagant and unrealistic and that, by asking about them, a company will set itself up for even loftier expectation levels (that is, 'unrealistic' levels). Compelling evidence, shown in Table 3.2, suggests that customers' main expectations of service are quite simple and basic: 'Simply put, customers expect service companies to do what they are supposed to do. They expect fundamentals, not fanciness; performance, not empty promises.'[10] Customers want service to be delivered as promised. They want planes to take off on time, hotel rooms to be clean, food to be hot and service providers to show up when scheduled. Unfortunately, many service customers are disappointed and let down by companies' inability to meet these basic service expectations.

Asking customers about their expectations does not so much raise the levels of the expectations themselves but rather heightens the belief that the company will do something with the information that

Table 3.1   How services marketers can influence factors

Factor	Possible influence strategies
Explicit service promises	Make realistic and accurate promises that reflect the service actually delivered rather than an idealized version of the service.
	Ask contact people for feedback on the accuracy of promises made in advertising and personal selling.
	Avoid engaging in price or advertising wars with competitors because they take the focus off customers and escalate promises beyond the level at which they can be met.
	Formalize service promises through a service guarantee that focuses company employees on the promise and that provides feedback on the number of times promises are not fulfilled.
Implicit service promises	Ensure that service tangibles accurately reflect the type and level of service provided. Ensure that price premiums can be justified by higher levels of performance by the company on important customer attributes.
Lasting service intensifiers	Use market research to determine sources of derived service expectations and their requirements. Focus advertising and marketing strategy on ways the service allows the focal customer to satisfy the requirements of the influencing customer.
	Use market research to profile personal service philosophies of customers and use this information in designing and delivering services.
Personal needs	Educate customers on ways the service addresses their needs.
Temporary service intensifiers	Increase service delivery during peak periods or in emergencies.
Perceived service alternatives	Be fully aware of competitive offerings and, where possible and appropriate, match them.
Self-perceived service role	Educate customers to understand their roles and perform them better.
Word-of-mouth communications	Simulate word of mouth in advertising by using testimonials and opinion leaders. Identify influencers and opinion leaders for the service and concentrate marketing efforts on them.
	Use incentives with existing customers to encourage them to say positive things about the service.
Past experience	Use marketing research to profile customers' previous experience with similar services.
Situational factors	Use service guarantees to assure customers about service recovery regardless of the situational factors that occur.
Predicted service	Tell customers when service provision is higher than what can normally be expected so that predictions of future service encounters will not be inflated.

surfaces. Arguably the worst thing a company can do is show a strong interest in understanding what customers expect and then never act on the information. At a minimum, a company should acknowledge to customers that it has received and heard their input and that it will expend effort trying to address their issues. The company may not be able to – and indeed does not always have to – deliver to expressed expectations. An alternative and appropriate response would be to let customers know the reasons that desired service is not being provided at the present time and describe the efforts planned to address them. Another approach could be a campaign to educate customers about ways to use and improve the service they currently receive.

Table 3.2 Service customers want the basics

Type of service	Type of customer	Principal expectations
Car repair	Consumers	Be competent. ('Fix it right the first time.') Explain things. ('Explain why I need the suggested repairs – provide an itemized list.') Be respectful. ('Don't treat me like I am stupid.')
Car insurance	Consumers	Keep me informed. ('I shouldn't have to learn about insurance law changes from the newspaper.') Be on my side. ('I don't want them to treat me like a criminal just because I have a claim.') Play fair. ('Don't drop me when something goes wrong.') Protect me from catastrophe. ('Make sure my family is provided for in the event of a major accident.') Provide prompt service. ('I want fast settlement of claims.')
Hotel	Consumers	Provide a clean room. ('Don't have a deep-pile carpet that can't be completely cleaned ... you can literally see germs down there.') Provide a secure room. ('Good bolts and peephole on door.') Treat me like a guest. ('It is almost like they're looking you over to decide whether they're going to let you have a room.') Keep your promise. ('They said the room would be ready, but it wasn't at the promised time.')
Property and accident insurance	Business customers	Fulfil obligations. ('Pay up.') Learn my business and work with me. ('I expect them to know me and my company.') Protect me from catastrophe. ('They should cover my risk exposure so there is no single big loss.') Provide prompt service. ('Fast claim service.')
Equipment repair	Business customers	Share my sense of urgency. ('Speed of response. One time I had to buy a second piece of equipment because of the huge downtime with the first piece.') Be competent. ('Sometimes you are quoting stuff from their instruction manuals to their own people and they don't even know what it means.') Be prepared. ('Have all the parts ready.')
Vehicle rental/leasing	Business customers	Keep the equipment running. ('Need to have equipment working all of the time – that is the key.') Be flexible. ('The leasing company should have the flexibility to rent us equipment when we need it.') Provide full service. ('Get rid of all the paperwork and headaches.')

Source: Adapted from 'Understanding customer expectations of service' by A. Parasuraman, L.L. Berry and V.A. Zeithaml, *MIT Sloan Management Review* (Spring 1991), pp. 33–46, Copyright © 1991 by Massachusetts Institute of Technology. All rights reserved.

Giving customers progress updates as service is improved to address their needs and desires is sensible because it allows the company to get credit for incremental efforts to improve service.

Some observers recommend deliberately under-promising the service to increase the likelihood of meeting or exceeding customer expectations.[11] While under-promising makes service expectations more realistic, thereby narrowing the gap between expectations and perceptions, it may also reduce the competitive appeal of the offer. Some research has indicated that under-promising may also have the inadvertent effect of lowering customer *perceptions* of service, particularly in situations in which customers have little experience with a service.[12] In these situations customer expectations may be self-fulfilling; that is, if the customer goes into the service experience expecting good service, he or she will focus on the aspects of service provision that are positive, but if he or she expects low service, then that customer may focus on the negative. Thus a salesperson who sells to a customer with a realistic promise may lose the sale to another who inflates the offering. In Chapter 16 we describe various techniques for controlling a firm's promises, but for now consider two options.

First, if the salesperson knows that no competitor can meet an inflated sales promise in an industry, he or she could point that fact out to the customer, thereby refuting the promise made by competitive salespeople.

The second option is for the provider to follow a sale with a 'reality check' about service delivery. Imagine buying a new house from a builder. In order to make the sale, typical sales promises are made about the quality of the home, some less than accurate. Before you are given the keys to the new house, the builder accompanies you on a final check of everything. At the front door the builder points out that each new home has between 3,000 and 5,000 individual elements and that, in his experience, the typical new home has 100 to 150 defects. Armed with this reality check, you would perceive a total of 30–40 defects found in your house as being good. Consider your response in the absence of that reality check.

SHOULD A COMPANY TRY TO DELIGHT THE CUSTOMER?

Some management consultants urge service companies to 'delight' customers to gain a competitive edge. The *delight* that they refer to is a profoundly positive emotional state that results from having one's expectations exceeded to a surprising degree.[13] One author describes the type of service that results in delight as 'positively outrageous service' – that which is unexpected, random, extraordinary and disproportionately positive.[14]

A way that managers can conceive of delight is to consider product and service features in terms of concentric rings.[15] The innermost bull's-eye refers to attributes that are central to the basic function of the product or service, called *musts*. Their provision is not particularly noticeable, but their absence would be. Around the musts is a ring called *satisfiers*: features that have the potential to further satisfaction beyond the basic function of the product. At the next and final outer level are *delights*, or product features that are unexpected and surprisingly enjoyable. These features are things that consumers would not expect to find and they are therefore highly surprised and sometimes excited when they receive them. For example, a student may consider the musts to consist of lecturers, rooms, class outlines and lectures/seminars. Satisfiers might include lecturers who are entertaining or friendly, interesting lectures and good audiovisual aids. A delight might include a free textbook for students signing up for the course.

Delighting customers may seem like a good idea, but this level of service provision comes with extra effort and cost to the firm. Therefore, the benefits of providing delight must be weighed. Among the considerations are the staying power and competitive implications of delight.

Staying power involves the question of how long a company can expect an experience of delight to maintain the consumer's attention. If it is fleeting and the customer forgets it immediately, it may not be worth the cost. Alternatively, if the customer remembers the delight and adjusts his or her level of expectation upward accordingly, it will cost the company more just to satisfy, effectively raising the bar for the future. Recent research indicates that delighting customers does in fact raise expectations and makes it more difficult for a company to satisfy customers in the future.[16]

The competitive implication of delight relates to its impact on expectations of other firms in the same industry. If a competitor in the same industry is unable to copy the delight strategy, it will be disadvantaged by the consumer's increased expectations. If students were offered that free textbook in one of their classes, they might then expect to receive one in each of their classes. Those classes not offering the free textbook might not have high enrolment levels compared with the delighting class. If a competitor can easily copy the delight strategy, however, neither firm benefits (although the consumer does!), and all firms may be hurt because their costs increase and profits erode. The implication is that if companies choose to delight, they should do so in areas that cannot be copied by other firms.

HOW DOES A COMPANY EXCEED CUSTOMER SERVICE EXPECTATIONS?

Many companies today talk about exceeding customer expectations – delighting and surprising them by giving more than they expect. This philosophy raises the question: should a service provider try simply to meet customer expectations or to exceed them?

First, it is essential to recognize that exceeding customer expectations of the basics is virtually impossible. Honouring promises – having the reserved room available, meeting deadlines, showing up for meetings, delivering the core service – is what the company is supposed to do. Companies are *supposed* to be accurate and dependable and provide the service they promised to provide.[17] As you examine the examples of basic expectations of customers in Table 3.2, ask yourself if a provider doing any of these things would delight you. The conclusion you should reach is that it is very difficult to surprise or delight customers consistently by delivering reliable service.

How, then, does a company delight its customers and exceed their expectations? In virtually any service, developing a customer relationship is one approach for exceeding service expectations. Ritz-Carlton Hotels provide highly personalized attention to their customers. In each hotel within the chain, a special database called guest recognition is used to remember over 800,000 guests and generate information for all relevant staff. It stores: likes/dislikes; previous difficulties; family interests; personal interests; preferred credit card; recency/frequency of stays; lifetime usage/amount of purchase. In this way staff are able to understand what is 'new or different' about an individual customer.[18]

Another way to exceed expectations is to deliberately under-promise the service to increase the likelihood of exceeding customer expectations. The strategy is to under-promise and over-deliver. If every service promise is less than what will eventually happen, customers can be delighted frequently. Although this reasoning sounds logical, a firm should weigh two potential problems before using this strategy.

Firstly, customers with whom a company interacts regularly are likely to notice the under-promising and adjust their expectations accordingly, negating the desired benefit of delight. Customers will recognize the pattern of under-promising when time after time a firm promises one delivery time (we cannot get that to you before 5 p.m. tomorrow) yet constantly exceeds it (by delivering at noon).

SERVICE SPOTLIGHT

Many airlines have adopted under-performing strategies with regard to flight duration. easyJet produces a timetable that suggests that flights will be longer than they actually are, allowing them to give the impression that their timekeeping is good as most flights will arrive early or on time. However, with experience, regular customers may come to expect an early arrival and be disappointed when this does not happen.

Secondly, under-promising in a sales situation potentially reduces the competitive appeal of an offering and must be tempered by what the competition is offering. When competitive pressures are high, presenting a cohesive and honest portrayal of the service both explicitly (through advertising and personal selling) and implicitly (such as through the appearance of service facilities and the price of the service) may be wiser. Controlling the firm's promises, making them consistent with the deliverable service, may be a better approach.

A final way to exceed expectations without raising them in the future is to position unusual service as unique rather than standard. Emphasizing that because of special circumstances or a special situation, the service will deviate from the norm. For example, a restaurant may offer customers a free dessert by claiming that the chef is trying out some new recipes/creations.

DO CUSTOMER SERVICE EXPECTATIONS CONTINUALLY ESCALATE?

As we illustrated at the beginning of this chapter, customer service expectations are dynamic. In the credit card industry, as in many competitive service industries, battling companies seek to outdo each other and thereby raise their level of service above that of competing companies. Service expectations – in this case adequate service expectations – rise in step with service delivery or promises. In a highly competitive and rapidly changing industry, expectations can thus rise quickly. For this reason companies need continually to monitor adequate service expectations – the more turbulent the industry, the more frequent the monitoring that is needed.

Desired service expectations, on the other hand, are far more stable. Because they are driven by more enduring factors, such as personal needs and lasting service intensifiers, they tend to be high to begin with and remain high.

HOW DOES A SERVICE COMPANY STAY AHEAD OF COMPETITION IN MEETING CUSTOMER EXPECTATIONS?

All else being equal, a company's goal is to meet customer expectations better than its competitors can. Given the fact that adequate service expectations change rapidly in a turbulent environment, how can a company ensure that it stays ahead of competition?

The adequate service level reflects the minimum performance level expected by customers after they consider a variety of personal and external factors (Figure 3.6), including the availability of service options from other providers. Companies whose service performance falls short of this level are clearly at a competitive disadvantage, with the disadvantage escalating as the gap widens. These companies' customers may well be 'reluctant' customers, ready to take their business elsewhere the moment they perceive an alternative.

If they are to use service quality for competitive advantage, companies must perform above the adequate service level. This level, however, may signal only a temporary advantage. Customers' adequate service levels, which are less stable than desired service levels, will rise rapidly when competitors promise and deliver a higher level of service. If a company's level of service is barely above the adequate service level to begin with, a competitor can quickly erode that advantage. Companies currently performing in the region of competitive advantage must stay alert to the need for service increases to meet or beat competition.

To develop a true customer franchise with customer loyalty, companies must not only consistently exceed the adequate service level but also reach the desired service level. Exceptional service can intensify customers' loyalty to a point at which they are impervious to competitive options.

SUMMARY

Using a conceptual framework of the nature and determinants of customer expectations of service, we showed in this chapter that customers hold different types of service expectations: (1) desired service, which reflects what customers want; (2) adequate service, or what customers are willing to accept; and (3) predicted service, or what customers believe they are likely to get. These different levels of service are reflected within the customer's zone of tolerance which establishes the variability in the service delivery that the customer is willing to accept.

Customer expectations and tolerance levels are influenced by a variety of factors. The types and sources of these are the same for end consumers and business customers, for pure service and product-related service, and for experienced customers and inexperienced customers.

KEY CONCEPTS

EXERCISES

1 Keep a service journal for a day and document your use of services. Record your predicted service before every service encounter. Then, following the encounter, note whether your expectations were met or exceeded. How does your journal log relate to your desire to do business with that service firm again?

2 List five incidents in which a service company has exceeded your expectations. How did you react to the service? Did these incidents change the way you viewed subsequent interactions with the companies? In what way?

3 Map out your expectations for a course delivered by a University or College. Consider whether these expectations are being met.

4 Compare your expectations for a service with friends and with people from different ages and backgrounds. How do they differ?

DISCUSSION QUESTIONS

1 What is the difference between desired service and adequate service? Why would a services marketer need to understand both types of service expectations?

2 Consider a recent service purchase that you have made. Which of the factors influencing expectations were the most important in your decision? Why?

3 Why are desired service expectations more stable than adequate service expectations?

4 How do the technology changes such as the Internet and social media influence customer expectations?

5 Describe several instances in which a service company's explicit service promises were inflated and led you to be disappointed with the service outcome.

6 Do you believe that any of your service expectations are unrealistic? Which ones? Should a service marketer try to address unrealistic customer expectations?

7 Intuitively, it would seem that managers would want their customers to have wide tolerance zones for service. But if customers do have these wide zones of tolerance for service, is it more difficult for firms with superior service to earn customer loyalty? Would superior service firms be better off attempting to narrow customers' tolerance zones to reduce the competitive appeal of mediocre providers?

8 Should service marketers delight their customers?

FURTHER READING

Bebko, C.P. (2000). Service intangibility and its impact on customer expectations of service quality. *Journal of Services Marketing*, 14(1), 9–26.

Licata, J.W., Chakraborty, G. and Krishnan, B.C. (2008). The consumer's expectation formation process over time. *Journal of Services Marketing*, 22(3), 176–87.

Schneider, B. and Bowen, D. E. (2010). *Winning the service game*. Springer US.

Sparks, B. A. and Browning, V. (2011). The impact of online reviews on hotel booking intentions and perception of trust. *Tourism Management*, 32(6), 1310–23.

Wilson, A., Murphy, H. and Fierro, J. C. (2012). Hospitality and travel: the nature and implications of user-generated content. *Cornell hospitality quarterly*, 53(3), 220–28.

Yap, K.B. and Sweeney, J.C. (2007). Zone of tolerance moderates the service quality-outcome relationship. *Journal of Services Marketing*, 21(2), 137–48.

Zhang, J., Beatty, S.E. and Walsh, G. (2008). Review and future directions of cross-cultural consumer services research'. *Journal of Business Research*, 61(3), 211–24.

CHAPTER 4

Customer Perceptions of Service

LEARNING OBJECTIVES

This chapter's objectives are to:

1 Provide a solid basis for understanding what influences customer perceptions of service and the relationships among customer satisfaction, service quality and individual service encounters.

2 Demonstrate the importance of customer satisfaction – what it is, the factors that influence it and the significant outcomes resulting from it.

3 Develop critical knowledge of service quality and its five key dimensions: reliability, responsiveness, empathy, assurance and tangibles.

4 Show that service encounters or the 'moments of truth' are the essential building blocks from which customers form their perceptions.

OPENING EXAMPLE
Changing Perceptions – Virgin Money

As part of its expansion into the UK retail banking sector, Virgin Money are attempting to change customers' perceptions of the service delivered by bank branches through the opening of five Virgin Money Lounges in major cities. These lounges do have areas where customers can do their online banking or receive service relating to their Virgin Money products, but they are about more than money and banking. They are designed to be places where customers can relax and local communities come together.

They provide free hot and cold drinks, fruit and snacks as well as free Wi-Fi and access to free iPads. Television is available all day as well as newspapers and a selection of magazines. Children are welcomed; there is a dedicated children's area in every Lounge, complete with toys, books and games consoles. There are also customer toilets and baby changing facilities. The Glasgow lounge even has a fish tank, a dance floor and a cinema room.

Customers can come in to relax with friends or family-members, use the lounge facility to brush up on a few points before a meeting, or simply unwind with a newspaper. The lounges are furnished with a mix of sofas and writing desks.

Often social and entertainment events are put on in the evenings for customers. In addition, local communities are able to benefit from the proximity of a Lounge by booking it for free to hold a community event or meeting. In 2014, the lounges were used for after-hours community events like exhibitions, talks and book signings.

Brian Brodie, Virgin Money's sales and marketing director said: 'We know our customers expect something different and this is a real key manifestation of that. As we entered the world of banking, we knew the expectations would be high. Virgin is a business built on innovation and excellent customer service. This would also be the first time the Virgin Money brand would be seen on the high street. So we wanted to do something completely different, something traditional banks wouldn't do.'

Source: www.uk.virginmoney.com.

CUSTOMER PERCEPTIONS

How customers perceive services, how they assess whether they have experienced quality service, and whether they are satisfied with their overall experience are the subjects of this chapter. Companies today recognize that they can compete more effectively by distinguishing themselves with respect to service quality and improved customer satisfaction.

SATISFACTION VERSUS SERVICE QUALITY

Practitioners and writers in the popular press tend to use the terms *satisfaction* and *quality* interchangeably, but researchers have attempted to be more precise about the meanings and measurement of the two concepts, resulting in considerable debate.[1] Consensus is that the two concepts are fundamentally different in terms of their underlying causes and outcomes.[2] Although they have certain things in common, satisfaction is generally viewed as a broader concept, whereas service quality focuses specifically on dimensions of service. Based on this view, *perceived service quality* is a component of customer satisfaction. Figure 4.1 graphically illustrates the relationships between the two concepts.

Figure 4.1   The quality–satisfaction link

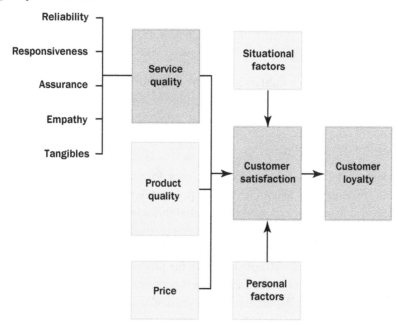

Service quality is a focused evaluation that reflects the customer's perception of reliability, responsiveness, assurance, empathy and tangibles.[3] Satisfaction, on the other hand, is more inclusive: it is influenced by perceptions of service quality, product quality and price as well as situational factors and personal factors. For example, the *service quality* of a health club is judged on attributes such as whether equipment is available and in working order when needed, how responsive the staff are to customer needs, how skilled the trainers are and whether the facility is well maintained. *Customer satisfaction* with the health club is a broader concept that will certainly be influenced by perceptions of service quality but will also include perceptions of product quality (such as quality of products sold in the bar/restaurant), price of membership,[4] personal factors (such as the consumer's emotional state), and even uncontrollable situational factors (such as weather conditions and experiences driving to and from the health club).[5]

TRANSACTION VERSUS CUMULATIVE PERCEPTIONS

In considering perceptions, it is also important to recognize that customers will have perceptions of single, transaction-specific encounters as well as overall perceptions of a company based on all their experiences.[6] For example, a bank customer will have a perception of how he or she was treated in a particular encounter with a bank employee at a branch and will form a perception based on elements of the service experienced during that specific transaction. That perception is at a very micro, transaction-specific level. The same bank customer will also have overall perceptions of the bank based on his or her encounters over a period of time. These experiences might include multiple in-person encounters at the bank branch, online banking experiences and experiences using the bank's ATMs across many different cities. At an even more general level, the customer may have perceptions of banking services or the whole banking industry as a result of all his or her experiences with banks and everything he or she knows about banking.

Research suggests that it is important to understand all these types of perceptions for different reasons and that they reveal complementary rather than competing points of view.[7] Understanding perceptions at the transaction-specific level is critical for diagnosing service issues and making immediate changes. These isolated encounters are also the building blocks for overall, cumulative experience evaluations, as you will learn later in this chapter. On the other hand, cumulative experience evaluations are likely to be better predictors of overall loyalty to a company. That is, customer loyalty most often results from the customer's assessment of all his or her experiences, not just from one single encounter.

CUSTOMER SATISFACTION

'Everyone knows what satisfaction is, until asked to give a definition. Then, it seems, nobody knows'.[8] This quote from Richard L. Oliver, respected expert and long-time writer and researcher on the topic of customer satisfaction, expresses the challenge of defining this most basic of customer concepts.

WHAT IS CUSTOMER SATISFACTION?

Building from previous definitions, Oliver offers his own formal definition (p. 13): 'Satisfaction is the consumer's fulfillment response. It is a judgment that a product or service feature, or the product or service itself, provides a pleasurable level of consumption-related fulfillment.' In less technical terms, we interpret this definition to mean that *satisfaction* is the customer's evaluation of a product or service in terms of whether that product or service has met the customer's needs and expectations. Failure to meet needs and expectations is assumed to result in *dissatisfaction* with the product or service.

In addition to a sense of *fulfilment* in the knowledge that one's needs have been met, satisfaction can also be related to other types of feelings, depending on the particular context or type of service.[9] For example, satisfaction can be viewed as *contentment* – more of a passive response that consumers may associate with services they do not think a lot about or services that they receive routinely over time. Satisfaction may also be associated with feelings of *pleasure* for services that make the consumer feel good or are associated with a sense of happiness. For those services that really surprise the consumer in a positive way, satisfaction may mean *delight*. In some situations, where the removal of a negative leads to satisfaction, the consumer may associate a sense of *relief* with satisfaction. Finally, satisfaction may be associated with feelings of *ambivalence* when there is a mix of positive and negative experiences associated with the product or service.

Although consumer satisfaction tends to be measured at a particular point in time as if it were static, satisfaction is a dynamic, moving target that may evolve over time, influenced by a variety of factors.[10] Particularly when product usage or the service experience takes place over time, satisfaction may be highly variable depending on which point in the usage or experience cycle one is focusing on. Similarly, in the case of very new services or a service not previously experienced, customer expectations may be barely forming at the point of initial purchase; these expectations will solidify as the process unfolds and the consumer begins to form his or her perceptions. Through the service cycle the consumer may have a variety of different experiences – some good, some not good – and each will ultimately impact satisfaction.

WHAT DETERMINES CUSTOMER SATISFACTION?

As shown in Figure 4.1, customer satisfaction is influenced by specific product or service features, perceptions of product and service quality, and price. In addition, personal factors such as the customer's mood or emotional state and situational factors such as the opinions of family members will also influence satisfaction.

PRODUCT AND SERVICE FEATURES

Customer satisfaction with a product or service is influenced significantly by the customer's evaluation of product or service features.[11] For a service such as a resort hotel, important features might include the pool area, access to golf facilities, restaurants, room comfort and privacy, helpfulness and courtesy of staff, room price, and so on. In conducting satisfaction studies, most firms will determine through some means (often focus groups) what the important features and attributes are for their service and then measure perceptions of those features as well as overall service satisfaction. Research has shown that customers of services will make trade-offs among different service features (for example, price level versus quality versus friendliness of personnel versus level of customization), depending on the type of service being evaluated and the criticality of the service.[12]

CONSUMER EMOTIONS

Customers' emotions can also affect their perceptions of satisfaction with products and services.[13] These emotions can be stable, pre-existing emotions – for example, mood state or life satisfaction. Think of times when you are at a very happy stage in your life (such as when you are on holiday), and your good, happy mood and positive frame of mind influence how you feel about the services you experience. Alternatively, when you are in a bad mood, your negative feelings may carry over into how you respond to services, causing you to overreact or respond negatively to any little problem.

Specific emotions may also be induced by the consumption experience itself, influencing a consumer's satisfaction with the service. Research done in a white-water rafting context showed that the guides had a strong effect on their customers' emotional responses to the trip and that those feelings (both positive and negative) were linked to overall trip satisfaction.[14] Positive emotions such as happiness, pleasure, elation and a sense of warm-heartedness enhanced customers' satisfaction with the rafting trip. In turn, negative emotions such as sadness, sorrow, regret and anger led to diminished customer satisfaction. Overall, in the rafting context, positive emotions had a stronger effect than negative ones. In online services, the usability of a website or mobile app may also impact on the emotions of the user, producing feelings of pleasure or frustration which result in satisfaction or dissatisfaction.

SERVICE SPOTLIGHT

Similar effects of emotions on satisfaction were found in a Finnish study that looked at consumers' satisfaction with a government labour bureau service.[15] In that study, negative emotions, including anger, depression, guilt and humiliation, had a strong effect on customers' dissatisfaction ratings.

ATTRIBUTIONS FOR SERVICE SUCCESS OR FAILURE

Attributions – the perceived causes of events – influence perceptions of satisfaction as well.[16] When they have been surprised by an outcome (the service is either much better or much worse than expected), consumers tend to look for the reasons, and their assessments of the reasons can influence their satisfaction. For example, if a customer of a weight-loss organization fails to lose weight as hoped for, he or she will likely search for the causes – was it something he or she did, was the diet plan ineffective or did circumstances simply not allow him or her to follow the diet regime? – before determining his or her level of satisfaction or dissatisfaction with the weight-loss company.[17] For many services, customers take at least partial responsibility for how things turn out. This is often the case in online services where customers may blame their own technical abilities for failing to get a service to work correctly.

Even when customers do not take responsibility for the outcome, customer satisfaction may be influenced by other kinds of attributions. For example, research done in a travel agency context found that customers were less dissatisfied with a pricing error made by the agent if they felt that the reason was outside the agent's control or if they felt that it was a rare mistake, unlikely to occur again.[18]

PERCEPTIONS OF EQUITY AND FAIRNESS

Customer satisfaction is also influenced by perceptions of equity and fairness.[19] Customers ask themselves: have I been treated fairly compared with other customers? Did other customers get better treatment, better prices, or better quality service? Did I pay a fair price for the service? Was I treated well in exchange for what I paid and the effort I expended? Notions of fairness are central to customers' perceptions of satisfaction with products and services, particularly in service recovery situations. As you will learn in Chapter 15, satisfaction with a service provider following a service failure is largely determined by perceptions of fair treatment.

OTHER CONSUMERS, FAMILY MEMBERS AND CO-WORKER

In addition to product and service features and one's own individual feelings and beliefs, consumer satisfaction is often influenced by other people.[20] For example, satisfaction with a family holiday is a dynamic phenomenon, influenced by the reactions and expressions of individual family members over the duration of the holiday. Later, what family members express in terms of satisfaction or dissatisfaction with the holiday will be influenced by stories that are retold among the family and selective memories of the events. Similarly, the satisfaction of people on a white-water rafting adventure is certainly influenced by individual perceptions, but it is also influenced greatly by the experiences, behaviour and views of the other rafters. In a business setting, satisfaction with a new service or technology – for example, a new customer relationship management software service – will be influenced not only by individuals' personal experiences with the software itself, but also by what others say about it in the company, how others use it and feel about it, and how widely it is adopted in the organization.

NATIONAL CUSTOMER SATISFACTION INDICES

Because of the importance of customer satisfaction to firms and overall quality of life, many countries have a national index that measures and tracks customer satisfaction at a macro level.[21] Many public policy-makers believe that these measures could and should be used as tools for evaluating the health of the nation's economy, along with traditional measures of productivity and price. National customer satisfaction indices aim to measure the *quality* of economic output, whereas more traditional economic indicators tend to focus only on *quantity*. The first such index was the Swedish Customer Satisfaction Barometer introduced in 1989.[22] Throughout the 1990s similar indices were introduced in Germany (Deutsche Kundenbarometer, or DK, in 1992), the United States (American Customer Satisfaction Index, ACSI, in 1994), Norway (Norsk Kundebarometer, in 1996) and Switzerland (Swiss Index of Customer Satisfaction, SWICS, in 1998).[23] These indices measure customer satisfaction over a wide range of different industries and organizations, including public sector organizations. They are intended to be complementary to productivity measures, with productivity reflecting the quantity of output and customer satisfaction measuring the customers' view of quality of output. The research is carried out through interviews with hundreds of current customers. Each of the organizations involved receives a satisfaction score computed from its customers' perceptions of quality, value, satisfaction, expectations, complaints and future loyalty.

A multitude of ways to measure customer satisfaction, loyalty, and quality exists, and all are not equally useful. Some are too complex, others are too simple, and yet others measure the wrong things. Some are better for predicting outcomes such as growth and performance, while other types of satisfaction and quality measures are needed for diagnosing underlying problems and making improvements.

One measurement approach, 'Net Promoter', was developed by loyalty expert Frederick Reichheld.[24] This was based on business case studies conducted by his firm. Net Promoter has gained tremendous popularity across industries in a very short time. The research promotes *one* customer loyalty question as the best for most industries in terms of predicting repeat customer purchases, growth, or referrals. The question is: 'How likely is it that you would recommend [company X] to a friend or colleague?'

Customers respond using a standard scale that ranges from 0 (not at all likely) to 10 (extremely likely). Based on their responses, each customer is classified into one of three groups:

Promoters (those giving scores of 9 or 10) are the customers who are loyal and enthusiastic about the organization, will continue buying and referring others and are exceptionally enthusiastic fans.

Passives (those giving scores of 7 or 8) are generally satisfied customers, but lack the enthusiasm of Promoters. They may be vulnerable to competitive offerings and not immune to trying other suppliers.

Detractors (those giving scores of 6 or less) are less happy with the service provider and may communicate negative word of mouth.

Once customers have been classified, an index score is calculated by subtracting the percentage of Detractors from the percentage of Promoters. The score is generally displayed as a whole number by dropping the percent sign for the final number and scores range from anywhere between –100 (all Detractors) to +100 (all Promoters).

Many firms now use Reichheld's Net Promoter metric (the proportional difference between a firm's promoters and detractors, based on the single question '*How likely are you to recommend…*') to predict growth and loyalty. While the measure enjoys tremendous popularity, there is continuing controversy about its superiority as a predictor. Academic researcher Timothy Keiningham and colleagues have concluded that it is no better at predicting growth than other measures such as a Customer Satisfaction Index.[25] However, it can be used over time to track a firm's service delivery performance.

Although tools such as Net Promoter or customer satisfaction indices help firms to determine where they stand with their customers and to monitor trends, these global measures do not provide the detail that companies need to diagnose underlying causes or to make improvements. Additional, deeper, and more detailed assessment (as discussed in this chapter and Chapter 6) can help firms evaluate potential issues and what improvements may be needed.

Improving service and satisfaction most often involves a series of strategic and tactical actions related to employees, service operations and customers. A successful corporate-wide customer satisfaction, loyalty, or service strategy will involve all the functional areas that can influence it.

 SERVICE SPOTLIGHT

Satmetrix, produces Net Promoter Industry Benchmarks for banking, car and home insurance, Internet service, mobile phone carriers, mobile phone handsets, computer hardware, televisions, and utilities. Its benchmark results for 2011 suggest the brands with the highest scores in the UK are First Direct, Saga, Sky, O2, Apple, and Samsung. The results are based on detailed responses from more than 6,800 UK consumers who had purchased products or services from each company within the previous 12 months.

Source: **www.satmetrix.com.**

ENSURING HIGH CUSTOMER SATISFACTION

A recent qualitative study[26] undertaken by *Marketing Magazine* looking at consumers' satisfaction with brands identified the following critical requirements in customer comments:

1. **Be Customer Centric** – '*Fit service around me – knowing what I said, and calling me back when I have got the time. That would show me I'm really valued, rather than just offering me a discount.*'
   Brands need to look at each situation from a customer's point of view and work from the assumption that their customers are reasonable people. Consumers are demanding that brands fit around their hectic schedules, and availability and 24/7 access are becoming more important.

2. **Have Superior Staff** – '*Brand X is just let down by dreadful unknowledgeable weekend staff – they have no idea what they're talking about.*'
   Spending millions on a TV campaign when staff don't know the basics about the product or service doesn't cut it with consumers. Communication skills on the ground are essential: BMW and Virgin

Atlantic are great examples of this – sexy, aspirational brands the personalities of which permeate their staff.

3. **Delight the Customer** – *'When my flowers from Brand X arrived at my wife's doorstep wilted, I phoned the company and they sent me £50 in vouchers. It was really good of them.'*

    A maxim that brands often overlook: over-delivering, whether through excellent customer service or exceeding post-purchase expectations.

4. **Keep your Promises** – *'I was on hold with my insurance company and then an automated message tells me it will call me back in 10 minutes – and you know what, they actually did.'*

    Well-articulated promises that set clear expectations are the key to customer satisfaction.

5. **Sort out Service Recovery** – *'Everyone understands that things go wrong... The art is how you put it right. Having a manager on hand so that you can speak to someone who actually knows what they are talking about really does help.'*

    Inevitably, services or products sometimes fail. Dealing with this promptly and effectively is paramount to maintaining a brand's reputation.

6. **Build a relationship** – *'With Brand X, you can never trace who you've spoken to and which country they're in. There's no relationship at all, it's confusing.'*

    Being put on hold for a lengthy period only to discover that the person you finally get through to knows nothing about your problem and wants to put you through to another department is the bugbear of many a consumer. The 'one-stop-shop' concept – where the left hand of a company knows what the right is doing – is essential.

SERVICE QUALITY

We now turn to service quality, a critical element of customer perceptions. In the case of pure services (e.g. healthcare, financial services, education), service quality will be the dominant element in customers' evaluations. In cases in which customer service or services are offered in combination with a physical product (e.g. IT services, car repairs), service quality may also be very critical in determining customer satisfaction. Figure 4.1 highlighted these relationships. We will focus here on the left-hand side of Figure 4.1, examining the underlying factors that influence perceptions of service quality. First we discuss *what* customers evaluate; then we look specifically at the five dimensions of service that customers rely on in forming their judgements.

OUTCOME, INTERACTION AND PHYSICAL ENVIRONMENT QUALITY

What is it that consumers evaluate when judging service quality? Over the years, services researchers have suggested that consumers judge the quality of services based on their perceptions of the technical outcome provided, the process by which that outcome was delivered, and the quality of the physical surroundings where the service is delivered.[27] For example, in the case of a lawsuit, a client will judge the quality of the technical outcome, or how the court case was resolved, and the quality of the interaction. Interaction quality would include such factors as the lawyer's timeliness in returning telephone calls, his or her empathy for the client, and his or her courtesy and listening skills. Similarly, a restaurant customer will judge the service on his or her perceptions of the meal (technical outcome quality), how the meal was served and how the employees interacted with him or her (interaction quality). The decor and surroundings (physical environment quality) of the restaurant will also impact on the customer's perceptions of overall service quality.

This depiction of service quality as outcome quality, interaction quality and physical environment quality is most recently captured by Michael Brady and Joseph Cronin in their empirical research published in the *Journal of Marketing*.[28] Other researchers have defined similar aspects of service in their examinations of service quality.[29]

SERVICE QUALITY DIMENSIONS

Research suggests that customers do not perceive quality in a unidimensional way but rather judge quality based on multiple factors relevant to the context. The dimensions of service quality have been identified through the pioneering research of Parsu Parasuraman, Valarie Zeithaml and Leonard Berry. Their research identified five specific dimensions of service quality that apply across a variety of service contexts.[30] The five dimensions defined here are shown in Figure 4.1 as drivers of service quality. These five dimensions appear again in Chapter 6, along with the scale developed to measure them, SERVQUAL.

- **Reliability**: ability to perform the promised service dependably and accurately
- **Responsiveness**: willingness to help customers and provide prompt service
- **Assurance**: employees' knowledge and courtesy and their ability to inspire trust and confidence
- **Empathy**: caring, individualized attention given to customers
- **Tangibles**: appearance of physical facilities, equipment, personnel and written materials.

These dimensions represent how consumers organize information about service quality in their minds. On the basis of exploratory and quantitative research, these five dimensions were found relevant for banking, insurance, appliance repair and maintenance, securities brokerage, long-distance telephone service, car repairs and others. The dimensions are also applicable to retail and business services, and logic suggests they would be relevant for internal services as well. At times customers will use all the dimensions to determine service quality perceptions, at other times not. For example, for an ATM, empathy is not likely to be a relevant dimension, while in a telephone encounter to schedule a repair, tangibles will not be relevant. Research suggests that cultural differences may also affect the relative importance placed on the five dimensions in different countries. In the following pages we expand on each of the dimensions and provide illustrations of how customers judge them.

RELIABILITY: DELIVERING ON PROMISES

Of the five dimensions, reliability has been consistently shown to be the most important determinant of perceptions of service quality.[31] Reliability is defined as the ability to perform the promised service dependably and accurately. In its broadest sense, reliability means that the company delivers on its promises – about delivery, service provision, problem resolution and pricing. Customers want to do business with companies that keep their promises, particularly when it comes to service outcomes and core service attributes.

⭐ SERVICE SPOTLIGHT

One company that communicates effectively and delivers on the reliability dimension is Whistl, the express parcel service. The reliability message of Whistl is evident in its aim: 'To satisfy customers every time' – this reflects the company's service positioning. But even when firms do not choose to position themselves explicitly on reliability, as Whistl has, this dimension is extremely important to consumers.

All firms need to be aware of customer expectations of reliability. Firms that do not provide the core service that customers think they are buying fail them in the most direct way.

RESPONSIVENESS: BEING WILLING TO HELP

Responsiveness is the willingness to help customers and to provide prompt service. This dimension emphasizes attentiveness and promptness in dealing with customer requests, questions, complaints and problems. Responsiveness is communicated to customers by the length of time they have to wait for assistance, answers to questions or attention to problems. Responsiveness also captures the notion of flexibility and ability to customize the service to customer needs.

To excel on the dimension of responsiveness, a company must view the process of service delivery and the handling of requests from the customer's point of view rather than from the company's point of view. Standards for speed and promptness that reflect the company's view of internal process requirements may be very different from the customer's requirements for speed and promptness. To truly distinguish themselves on responsiveness, companies need well-staffed customer service departments as well as responsive front-line people in all contact positions. Responsiveness perceptions diminish when customers wait to get through to a company by telephone, are put on hold, are put through to a complex voice mail system, or have trouble accessing the firm's website.

ASSURANCE: INSPIRING TRUST AND CONFIDENCE

Assurance is defined as employees' knowledge and courtesy and the ability of the firm and its employees to inspire trust and confidence. This dimension is likely to be particularly important for services that customers perceive as high risk or for services whose outcomes customers do not feel they can evaluate properly – for example, banking, insurance, medical and legal services.

Trust and confidence may be embodied in the person who links the customer to the company, such as insurance agents, lawyers or advisers. In such service contexts the company seeks to build trust and loyalty between key contact people and individual customers. The 'personal banker' concept captures this idea: customers are assigned to a banker who will get to know them individually and who will coordinate all their banking services.

In certain situations, trust and confidence are embodied in the organization itself. Financial services companies such as AXA Insurance ('Be Life Confident') and ING Direct ('It's Your Money We're Saving') illustrate efforts to create trusting relationships between customers and the company as a whole.

EMPATHY: TREATING CUSTOMERS AS INDIVIDUALS

Empathy is defined as the caring, individualized attention that the firm provides its customers. The essence of empathy is conveying, through personalized or customized service, that customers are unique and special and that their needs are understood. Customers want to feel that they are understood by, and important to, the firms that provide them service. Personnel at small service firms often know customers by name and build relationships that reflect their personal knowledge of customer requirements and preferences. When such a small firm competes with larger firms, the ability to be empathetic may give it a clear advantage.

In business-to-business services, customers want supplier firms to understand their industries and issues. Many small computer consulting firms successfully compete with large vendors by positioning themselves as specialists in particular industries. Even though larger firms have superior resources, the small firms are perceived as more knowledgeable about customers' issues and needs and are able to offer more customized services.

TANGIBLES: REPRESENTING THE SERVICE PHYSICALLY AND VIRTUALLY

Tangibles are defined as the appearance of physical facilities, equipment, personnel, websites, mobile phone apps and communication materials. Tangibles provide physical and virtual representations or images of the service that customers, particularly new customers, will use to evaluate quality. Service industries that emphasize physical tangibles in their strategies include hospitality services in which the customer visits the establishment to receive the service, such as restaurants and hotels, retail stores and entertainment companies. However, there is growing importance of the virtual tangibles through online services and apps in travel, banking and even government services.

Although tangibles are often used by service companies to enhance their image, provide continuity and signal quality to customers, most companies combine tangibles with another dimension to create a service quality strategy for the firm.

SERVICE SPOTLIGHT

Emirates Airline promotes its quality by emphasizing world class service from its staff and by advertising the fact that it flies one of the youngest fleets of aircraft in the world. It highlights that Emirates employees work hard to anticipate a customer's every need and supports this with a range of high-quality tangibles. These include the ICE inflight entertainment system, flat bed seating, the latest cabin design, interesting menus, luxurious lounges and a user-friendly online booking site. This combination is also evident in their promotional messaging: 'Making your Emirates experience world class in every class'.

In contrast, firms that do not pay attention to the tangibles dimension of the service strategy can confuse and even negate an otherwise good strategy.

Table 4.1 provides examples of how customers judge each of the five dimensions of service quality across a variety of service contexts.

DIMENSIONS IN THE NORDIC MODEL OF SERVICE QUALITY

Grönroos's 1984 Nordic model of the service experience categorized the dimensions into those relating to technical quality and those relating to functional quality.[32] Technical quality relates to the outcome of the service process such as the meal in the restaurant or the haircut at the hairdresser's. Functional quality relates to the manner in which the service is delivered in terms of the interactions during the service encounter relating to friendliness, care and attention, etc. The model emphasizes that the interaction between the buyer and the seller in a service setting is as important as the eventual outcome. Staff may need to be trained in technical aspects to ensure the correct outcome and may also require training on softer issues relating to customer care. Rust and Oliver[33] developed these two dimensions further into a three-component model consisting of service product, service delivery and service environment. The service product relates to the service offering and outcome, service delivery relates to the process of consuming the service and the service environment relates to the internal culture and external physical environment associated with the supplier. Other researchers[34] have built on this three-dimensional model to conceptualize expectations. There is overlap across the dimensions used by all of the researchers; the arguments tend to arise around whether each set of dimensions is applicable in all situations. One area that is perceived to be different relates to the delivery of a service over the Internet.

E-SERVICE QUALITY

The growth of e-tailing and e-services has led many companies to wonder how consumers evaluate service quality on the Web and whether the criteria are different from those used to judge the quality of non-Internet services.[35] Some commercial groups, such as the online comparison sites Bizrate and Kelkoo, capture customer perceptions of specific sites. A more systematic study, sponsored by the Marketing Science Institute, has been conducted to understand how consumers judge e-service quality (e-SQ).[36] In that study, e-SQ is defined as the extent to which a website facilitates efficient and effective shopping, purchasing and delivery. Through exploratory focus groups and two phases of empirical data collection and analysis, this research identified seven dimensions that are critical for core service evaluation (four dimensions) and service recovery evaluation (three dimensions).

Social Media and Digital Marketing

Table 4.1   Examples of how customers judge the five dimensions of service quality

	Reliability	Responsiveness	Assurance	Empathy	Tangibles
Car repair (consumer)	Problem fixed the first time and ready when promised	Accessible; no waiting; responds to requests	Knowledgeable mechanics	Acknowledges customer by name; remembers previous problems and preferences	Repair facility; waiting area; uniforms; equipment
Airline (consumer)	Flights to promised destinations depart and arrive on schedule	Prompt and speedy system for ticketing, in-flight baggage handling	Trusted name; good safety record; competent employees	Understands special individual needs; anticipates customer needs	Aircraft; ticketing counters; baggage area; website; mobile apps; uniforms
Dental care (consumer)	Appointments are kept on schedule; diagnoses prove accurate	Accessible; no waiting; willingness to listen	Knowledge; skills; credentials; reputation	Acknowledges patient as a person; remembers previous problems; listens well; has patience	Waiting room; examination room; equipment; written materials
Architecture (business)	Delivers plans when promised and within budget	Returns telephone calls; adapts to changes	Credentials; reputation; name in the community; knowledge and skills	Understands client's industry; acknowledges and adapts to specific client needs; gets to know the client	Office area; reports; plans themselves; billing statements; web site; dress of employees
Information processing (internal)	Provides needed information when requested	Prompt response to requests; not 'bureaucratic'; deals with problems promptly	Knowledgeable staff; well trained; credentials	Knows internal customers as individuals; understands individual and departmental needs	Internal reports; office area; intranet provision; dress of employees
Internet brokerage (consumer and business)	Provides correct information and executes customer requests accurately	Quick website with easy access and no down time	Credible information sources on the site; brand recognition; credentials apparent on site	Responds with human interaction as needed	Appearance of the website and collateral

The four core dimensions that customers use to judge websites at which they experience no questions or problems are:

1 *Efficiency:* the ability of customers to access the website, find their desired product and information associated with it, and check out with minimal effort.

2 *Fulfilment:* the accuracy of service promises, having products in stock, and delivering the products in the promised time.

3 *Reliability:* the technical functioning of the site, particularly the extent to which it is available and functioning properly.

4 *Privacy:* the assurance that shopping behaviour data are not shared and that credit information is secure.

The study also revealed three dimensions that customers use to assess recovery service when they have problems or questions:

1 *Responsiveness:* the ability of e-tailers to provide appropriate information to customers when a problem occurs, to have mechanisms for handling returns, and to provide online guarantees.
2 *Compensation:* the degree to which customers are to receive money back and are reimbursed for shipping and handling costs.
3 *Contact:* the availability of live customer service agents online or by telephone.

In comparing the dimensions of traditional service quality and e-service quality, we can make several observations. First, the traditional dimensions can and should be considered for e-tailing and Internet-based services, as illustrated by the Internet brokerage example in Table 4.1. However, both similar and different dimensions emerge in the research on e-tailing. Reliability and responsiveness are shared dimensions, but new Internet-specific dimensions appear to be critical in that context. Efficiency and fulfilment are core dimensions in e-service quality, and both share some elements of the traditional reliability and responsiveness dimensions. The empathy dimension (that is, the personal, friendly and understanding flavour) of perceived service quality is not required on the Internet except as it makes transactions more efficient in non-routine or problem situations. While not emerging as a dimension of e-service quality, tangibles are clearly relevant given that the entire service is delivered through technology. The tangible, visual elements of the site will be critical to efficiency as well as to overall perceptions of the firm and the brand.

⭐ SERVICE SPOTLIGHT

Organizations like Skyscanner, an international flight booking website that is also available as a mobile app, are dependent on e-service quality.

When a potential traveller opens Skyscanner, the website/app automatically presents the option to fly from the person's location to anywhere. The customer can enter start and end locations for a trip, along with dates, his or her preferred flying class and the number of passengers.

The site's search engine produces a list of the flights that match the criteria. This list can be filtered in a number of ways, including best price, least amount of interim stops, and so on. Clicking a particular flight takes the customer to a page with more detailed information and an option to book.

It can also display a chart of flight prices (including low-cost airlines) around the chosen flight dates. This identifies if cheaper flights can be found by adjusting the departure/return dates or by flying to/from neighbouring airports. Skyscanner also has a 'search everywhere' feature which allows potential travellers to enter their departure airport and identify what flights are available to anywhere in the world on their preferred dates.

The deals come from different flight-booking providers that are not controlled by Skyscanner but the website connects its users directly with them or forwards the booking request straight to a chosen provider's online booking system.

Travellers will only use Skyscanner in preference to other travel sites if it can demonstrate efficiency, fulfilment, reliability and privacy/security.

Source: **www.skyscanner.com.**

SERVICE ENCOUNTERS: THE BUILDING BLOCKS FOR CUSTOMER PERCEPTIONS

We have just finished a discussion of customer perceptions, specifically customer satisfaction and service quality. Here we turn to what have been termed the building blocks for customer perceptions – service encounters, or 'moments of truth'. Service encounters – sometimes called 'real-time marketing' – are where promises are kept or broken and where the proverbial rubber meets the road. It is from these service encounters that customers build their perceptions.

SERVICE ENCOUNTERS OR MOMENTS OF TRUTH

From the customer's point of view, the most vivid impression of service occurs in the **service encounter** or *'moment of truth'*,[37] when the customer interacts with the service firm. For example, among the service encounters that a hotel customer experiences are: checking into the hotel, being taken to a room by a hotel porter, eating a restaurant meal, requesting a wake-up call and checking out. You could think of the linking of these moments of truth as a service encounter cascade (see Figure 4.2). It is in these encounters that customers receive a snapshot of the organization's service quality, and each encounter contributes to the customer's overall satisfaction and willingness to do business with the organization again. From the organization's point of view, each encounter thus presents an opportunity to prove its potential as a quality service provider and to increase customer loyalty.

Figure 4.2   A service encounter cascade for a hotel visit

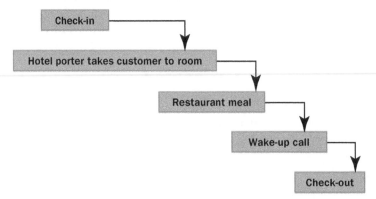

Some services have few service encounters, and others have many. The Disney Corporation estimates that each of its amusement park customers experiences about 74 service encounters and that a negative experience in any one of them can lead to a negative overall evaluation. Mistakes or problems that occur in the early levels of the service cascade may be particularly critical. Marriott Hotels learned this through their extensive customer research to determine what service elements contribute most to customer loyalty. They found that four of the top five factors came into play in the first ten minutes of the guest's stay.[38]

THE IMPORTANCE OF ENCOUNTERS

Although early events in the encounter cascade are likely to be especially important, *any* encounter can potentially be critical in determining customer satisfaction and loyalty. If a customer is interacting with a firm for the first time, that initial encounter will create a first impression of the organization. In these first encounter situations, the customer frequently has no other basis for judging the organization, and the initial telephone contact or face-to-face experience with a representative of the firm can take on excessive importance in the customer's perceptions of quality. A customer calling for a repair service on a household appliance may well hang up and call a different company if he or she is treated rudely by a customer service representative, put on hold for a lengthy period or told that two weeks is the soonest someone can be sent out to make the repair. Even if the technical quality of the firm's repair service is superior, the firm may not get the chance to demonstrate it if the initial telephone encounter drives the customer away.

Even when the customer has had multiple interactions with a firm, each individual encounter is important in creating a composite image of the firm in the customer's memory. Many positive experiences add up to a composite image of high quality, whereas many negative interactions will have the opposite effect. On the other hand, a combination of positive and negative interactions will leave the customer feeling unsure of the firm's quality, doubtful of its consistency in service delivery and vulnerable to the appeals of competitors. For example, a large corporate customer of a commercial catering company that provides food service in all its employee canteens and cafeterias could have a series of positive encounters with the account manager or salesperson who handles the account. These experiences could be followed by positive encounters with the operations staff who actually set up the food service facilities. However, even with these positive encounters, later negative experiences with the staff who serve the food or the accounting department that administers the billing procedures can result in a mixture of overall quality impressions. This variation in experiences could result in the corporate customer wondering about the quality of the organization and unsure of what to expect in the future. Each encounter with different people and departments representing the food service provider adds to or detracts from the potential for a continuing relationship.

Logic suggests that not all encounters are equally important in building relationships. For every organization, certain encounters are probably key to customer satisfaction. For Marriott Hotels, as noted, the early encounters are most important. In a hospital context, a study of patients revealed that encounters with nursing staff were more important in predicting satisfaction than were encounters with catering or administrative staff.[39]

In addition to these key encounters, there are some momentous encounters that, like the proverbial 'one bad apple', simply ruin the rest and drive the customer away no matter how many or what type of encounters have occurred in the past. These momentous encounters can occur in connection with very important events (such as the failure to deliver an essential piece of equipment before a critical deadline). Similarly, momentous positive encounters can sometimes bind a customer to an organization for life.

TYPES OF SERVICE ENCOUNTERS

A service encounter occurs every time a customer interacts with the service organization. There are three general types of service encounters: *remote encounters*, *telephone encounters* and *face-to-face encounters*.[40] A customer may experience any of these types of encounters, or a combination of all three, in his or her relations with a service firm.

First, encounters can occur without any direct human contact (remote encounters), such as when a customer interacts with a bank through the ATM system, with a car park management company through an automated ticketing machine, with a retailer through its Internet website or with a mail-order service through automated touch-tone telephone ordering. Remote encounters also occur when the firm sends its billing statements or communicates other types of information to customers by mail. Although there is no direct human contact in these remote encounters, each represents an opportunity for the firm to reinforce or establish quality perceptions in the customer. In remote encounters the tangible evidence of the service and the quality of the technical processes and systems become the primary bases for judging quality.

More and more services are being delivered through technology, particularly with the advent of Internet applications. Retail purchases, airline ticketing, repair and maintenance troubleshooting, and package and shipment tracking are just a few examples of services available via the Internet. All these manifestations of service encounters can be considered remote encounters.

In many organizations (such as insurance companies, utilities and telecommunications), many encounters between an end customer and the firm still occur over the telephone (*telephone encounters*). Many firms (whether goods manufacturers or service businesses) rely on telephone encounters to some extent for customer service, general inquiry or order-taking functions. The judgement of quality in telephone encounters is different from remote encounters, because there is greater potential variability in the interaction.[41] Tone of voice, employee knowledge and effectiveness/efficiency in handling customer issues become important criteria for judging quality in these encounters.

A third type of encounter is the one that occurs between an employee and a customer in direct contact (*face-to-face encounters*). At Disney theme parks, face-to-face encounters occur between customers and ticket-takers, maintenance personnel, actors in Disney character costumes, ride personnel, food and beverage servers, and others. For a company such as Ericsson, in a business-to-business setting direct encounters occur between the business customer and salespeople, delivery personnel, maintenance representatives and professional consultants. Determining and understanding service quality issues in face-to-face contexts is the most complex of all. Both verbal and non-verbal behaviours are important determinants of quality, as are tangible cues such as employee dress and other symbols of service (equipment, informational brochures, physical setting). In face-to-face encounters, the customer also plays a role in creating quality service for him or herself through his or her own behaviour during the interaction.

SOURCES OF PLEASURE AND DISPLEASURE IN SERVICE ENCOUNTERS

Researchers have extensively analysed service encounters in many contexts to determine the sources of customers' favourable and unfavourable impressions. The research uses the critical incident technique to get customers and employees to provide verbatim stories about satisfying and dissatisfying service encounters they have experienced.[42] With this technique, customers (either internal or external) are told, 'Think of a time when, as a customer, you had a particularly satisfying (or dissatisfying) interaction with _____', and are asked the following questions:

- When did the incident happen?
- What specific circumstances led up to this situation?
- Exactly what did the employee (or firm member) say or do?
- What resulted that made you feel the interaction was satisfying (or dissatisfying)?
- What could or should have been done differently?

Sometimes contact employees are asked to think about incidents from the other side and answer the same questions: '*Put yourself in the shoes of customers of your firm. In other words, try to see your firm through your customers' eyes. Now think of a recent time when a customer of your firm had a particularly satisfying/unsatisfying interaction with you or a fellow employee.*' The stories are then analysed to determine common themes of satisfaction/dissatisfaction underlying the events. On the basis of thousands of service encounter stories, four common themes – service recovery (after failure), adaptability, spontaneity and coping – have been identified as the sources of customer satisfaction/dissatisfaction in memorable service encounters.[43] Each of the themes is discussed here, and sample stories of both satisfying and dissatisfying incidents for each theme are given in Table 4.2. The themes encompass service behaviours in encounters spanning a wide variety of industries.

RECOVERY – EMPLOYEE RESPONSE TO SERVICE DELIVERY SYSTEM FAILURES

The first theme includes all incidents in which there has been a failure of the service delivery system and an employee is required to respond in some way to consumer complaints and disappointments. The failure may be, for example, a hotel room that is not available, a flight that is delayed six hours, an incorrect item sent from a mail-order company or a critical error on an internal document. The content or form of the employee's response is what causes the customer to remember the event either favourably or unfavourably.

ADAPTABILITY – EMPLOYEE RESPONSE TO CUSTOMER NEEDS AND REQUESTS

A second theme underlying satisfaction/dissatisfaction in service encounters is how adaptable the service delivery system is when the customer has special needs or requests that place demands on the process. In these cases, customers judge service encounter quality in terms of the flexibility of the employees and the system. Incidents categorized within this theme all contain an implicit or explicit request for customization of

Table 4.2 Service encounter themes

THEME 1: RECOVERY	
Satisfactory	**Unsatisfactory**
They lost my room reservation but the manager gave me the top suite for the same price.	We had made advance online reservations at the hotel. When we arrived we found we had no room – no explanation, no apologies and no assistance in finding another hotel.
Even though I did not make any complaint about the hour-and-a-half wait, the waitress kept apologizing and said the bill was on the house.	One of my suitcases was damaged and looked like it had been dropped from 30,000 feet. When I tried to make a claim for the damage, the employee insinuated that I was lying and trying to cheat them.

THEME 2: ADAPTABILITY	
Satisfactory	**Unsatisfactory**
I did not have an appointment to see a doctor; however, the practice nurse spoke to the doctor's receptionist and worked me into the schedule. I received treatment after a 10-minute wait. I was very satisfied with the special treatment I received, the short wait and the quality of the service.	My young son, flying alone, was to be assisted by the flight attendant from start to finish. At Heathrow airport she left him alone in the airport with no one to escort him to his connecting flight.
It was snowing outside – my car had broken down. I checked 10 hotels and there were no rooms. Finally, one understood my situation and offered to rent me a bed and set it up in a small banquet room.	Despite our repeated requests, the hotel staff would not deal with the noisy people partying in the corridor at 3 a.m.

THEME 3: SPONTANEITY	
Satisfactory	**Unsatisfactory**
Our children always travel with their teddy bears. When we got back to our room at the hotel we saw that the cleaning person had arranged the bears very comfortably in a chair. The bears were holding hands.	The lady at the front desk acted as if we were bothering her. She was watching television and paying more attention to the television than to the hotel guests.
The medical staff took extra time to explain exactly what I would be aware of and promised to take special care in making sure I did not wake up during the surgical operation.	I needed a few more minutes to choose from the menu. The waitress said, 'If you would read the menu and put down your mobile phone, you would know what you want to order'.

THEME 4: COPING	
Satisfactory	**Unsatisfactory**
A person who became intoxicated on a flight started speaking loudly, annoying the other passengers. The flight attendant asked the passenger if he would be driving when the plane landed and offered him coffee. He accepted the coffee and became quieter and friendlier.	An intoxicated man began pinching the female flight attendants. One attendant told him to stop, but he continued and then hit another passenger. The co-pilot was called and asked the man to sit down and leave the others alone, but the passenger refused. The co-pilot then placed the man's hands in restraints.

the service to meet a need. Much of what customers see as special needs or requests may actually be rather routine from the employee's point of view; what is important is that the customer perceives that something special is being done for him or her based on his or her own individual needs. External customers and internal customers alike are pleased when the service provider makes an effort to accommodate and adjust the system to meet their requirements. On the flip side, they are angered and frustrated by an unwillingness to try to accommodate and by promises that are never followed through. Contact employees also see their abilities to adapt the system as being a prominent source of customer satisfaction, and often they are equally frustrated by constraints that keep them from being flexible.

SPONTANEITY – UNPROMPTED AND UNSOLICITED EMPLOYEE ACTIONS

Even when there is no system failure and no special request or need, customers can still remember service encounters as being very satisfying or very dissatisfying. Employee spontaneity in delivering memorably good or poor service is the third theme. Satisfying incidents in this group represent very pleasant surprises for the customer (special attention, being treated like royalty, receiving something nice but not requested), whereas dissatisfying incidents in this group represent negative and unacceptable employee behaviours (rudeness, stealing, discrimination, ignoring the customer).

COPING – EMPLOYEE RESPONSE TO PROBLEM CUSTOMERS

The incidents categorized in this group came to light when employees were asked to describe service encounter incidents in which customers were either very satisfied or dissatisfied. In addition to describing incidents of the types outlined under the first three themes, employees described many incidents in which customers were the cause of their own dissatisfaction. Such customers were basically uncooperative – that is, unwilling to cooperate with the service provider, other customers, industry regulations and/or laws. In these cases, nothing the employee could do would result in the customer feeling pleased about the encounter. The term *coping* is used to describe these incidents because coping is the behaviour generally required of employees to handle problem customer encounters. Rarely are such encounters satisfying from the customer's point of view.[44] Also of interest is that customers themselves did not relate any 'problem customer' incidents. That is, customers either do not see, or choose not to remember or retell, stories of the times when they themselves were unreasonable to the point of causing their own unsatisfactory service encounter.

Table 4.3 summarizes the specific employee behaviours that cause satisfaction and dissatisfaction in service encounters according to the four themes just presented: recovery, adaptability, spontaneity and coping. The left-hand side of the table suggests what employees do that result in positive encounters, whereas the right-hand side summarizes negative behaviours within each theme.

THE EVIDENCE OF SERVICE

Because services are intangible, customers are searching for evidence of service in every interaction they have with an organization.[45] Figure 4.3 depicts the three major categories of evidence as experienced by the customer: people, process and physical evidence. Together, these categories represent the service and provide the evidence that makes the offering tangible. The new mix elements essentially *are* the evidence of service in each moment of truth.

All these evidence elements, or a subset of them, are present in every service encounter a customer has with a service firm and are critically important in managing service encounter quality and creating customer satisfaction. For example, when a dental patient has an appointment with a local dentist, the first encounter is frequently with a receptionist in a waiting area. The quality of that encounter will be judged by how the appointment registration *process* works (Is there a queue? How long is the wait? Is the registration system computerized and accurate?), the actions and attitude of the *people* (Is the receptionist courteous, helpful, knowledgeable? Does he or she treat the patient as an individual? Does he or she handle enquiries fairly and efficiently?) and the *physical evidence* of the service (Is the waiting area clean and comfortable? Is the signage clear?). The three types of evidence may be differentially important depending on the type of service encounter (remote, telephone, face-to-face). All three types will operate in face-to-face service encounters like the one just described.

Table 4.3 General service behaviours based on service encounter themes – dos and don'ts

Theme	Do	Don't
Recovery	Acknowledge problem Explain causes Apologize Compensate/upgrade Lay out options Take responsibility	Ignore customer Blame customer Leave customer to fend for himself or herself Downgrade Act as if nothing is wrong Blame the problem on someone else
Adaptability	Recognize the seriousness of the need Acknowledge Anticipate Attempt to accommodate Adjust the system Explain rules/policies Take responsibility	Ignore Promise, but fail to follow through Show unwillingness to try Embarrass the customer Laugh at the customer Avoid responsibility Blame the problem on someone else
Spontaneity	Take time Be attentive Anticipate needs Listen Provide information Show empathy	Exhibit impatience Ignore Yell/laugh/swear Steal from customers Discriminate
Coping	Listen Try to accommodate Explain Let go of the customer	Take customer's dissatisfaction personally Let customer's dissatisfaction affect others

Figure 4.3 The evidence of service (from the customer's point of view)

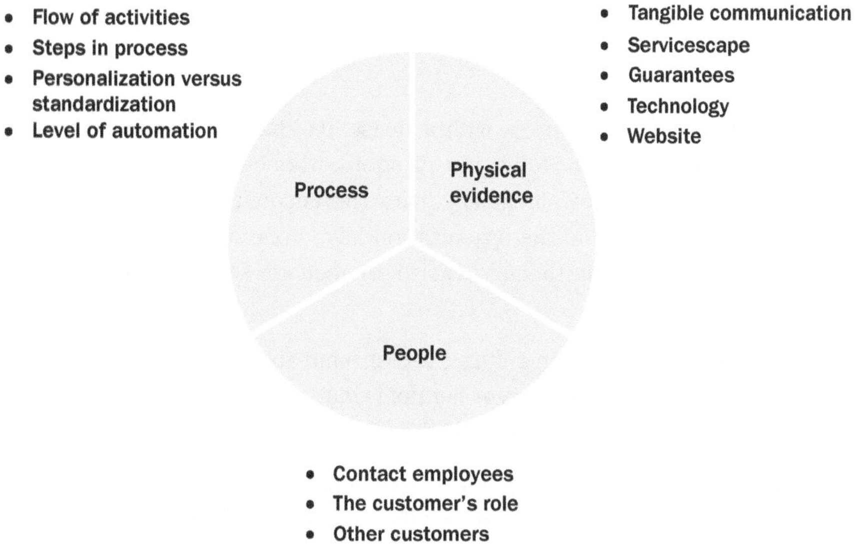

- Flow of activities
- Steps in process
- Personalization versus standardization
- Level of automation

- Tangible communication
- Servicescape
- Guarantees
- Technology
- Website

Process

Physical evidence

People

- Contact employees
- The customer's role
- Other customers

Source: Adapted from 'Managing the evidence of service' by M.J. Bitner from *The Service Quality Handbook*, eds E.E. Scheuing and W.F. Christopher.

SUMMARY

This chapter described customer perceptions of service by first introducing you to two critical concepts: customer satisfaction and service quality. These critical customer perceptions were defined and discussed in terms of the factors that influence each of them. You learned that customer satisfaction is a broad perception influenced by features and attributes of the product as well as by customers' emotional responses, their attributions and their perceptions of fairness. Service quality, the customer's perception of the service component of a product, is also a critical determinant of customer satisfaction. Sometimes, as in the case of a pure service, service quality may be the *most* critical determinant of satisfaction. You learned that perceptions of service quality are based on five dimensions: reliability, assurance, empathy, responsiveness and tangibles.

Another major purpose of this chapter was to introduce the idea of service encounters, or 'moments of truth', as the building blocks for both satisfaction and quality. You learned that every service encounter (whether remote, over the telephone or in person) is an opportunity to build perceptions of quality and satisfaction. The underlying themes of pleasure and displeasure in service encounters were also described. The importance of managing the evidence of service in each and every encounter was discussed.

KEY CONCEPTS

Assurance	78	Remote encounters	83
Critical incident technique (CIT)	84	Responsiveness	77
e-service quality	79	Satisfaction	71
Empathy	78	Service encounter	82
Equity and fairness	73	Service encounter cascade	82
Moment of truth	82	Service quality	71
National customer satisfaction indices	74	Service recovery	84
Nordic model of service quality	79	Tangibles	78
Reliability	77		

EXERCISES

1 Keep a journal of your service encounters with at least five different organizations during the week. For each journal entry, ask yourself the following questions: what circumstances led up to this encounter? What did the employee say or do? How did you evaluate this encounter? What exactly made you evaluate the encounter that way? What should the organization have done differently (if anything)? Categorize your encounters according to the four themes of service encounter satisfaction/dissatisfaction (recovery, adaptability, spontaneity, coping).

2 Interview someone with a non-European cultural background about service quality. Inquire whether the five dimensions of quality are relevant in his or her home culture and which are seen as most important in determining quality of banking services (or some other type of service).

3 Think of an important service experience you have had in the past several weeks. Analyse the encounter according to the evidence of service provided (see Figure 4.3). Which of the three evidence components was (or were) most important for you in evaluating the experience, and why?

4 Interview an employee of a local service business. Ask this person to discuss each of the five dimensions of quality as it relates to his or her company. Which dimensions are most important? Are any dimensions

not relevant in this context? Which dimensions does the company do best? Why? Which dimensions could benefit from improvement? Why?

5 Interview a manager, owner or director of a business. Discuss with this person the strategies he or she uses to ensure customer satisfaction. Does service quality enter into these strategies, and if so, how? Find out how this person's organization measures customer satisfaction and/or service quality.

6 Visit the Amazon website and a traditional bookstore. How would you compare the two experiences? Compare and contrast the factors that most influenced your satisfaction and perceptions of service quality in the two different situations. When would you choose to use one versus the other?

DISCUSSION QUESTIONS

1 What is customer satisfaction, and why is it so important? Discuss how customer satisfaction can be influenced by each of the following: product attributes and features, customer emotions, attributions for success or failure, perceptions of fairness, and family members or other customers.

2 Discuss the differences between perceptions of service quality and customer satisfaction.

3 List and define the five dimensions of service quality. Describe the services provided by a firm you do business with (your bank, your dentist, your favourite restaurant) on each of the dimensions. In your mind, has this organization distinguished itself from its competitors on any particular service quality dimension?

4 Describe a remote encounter, a telephone encounter and a face-to-face encounter that you have had recently. In each case, how did you evaluate the encounter, and what were the most important factors determining your satisfaction/dissatisfaction?

5 Describe an 'encounter cascade' for a commercial flight. In your opinion, what are the most important encounters in this cascade for determining your overall impression of the quality of the airline?

6 Assume that you are a manager of a health club. Discuss general strategies you might use to maximize customers' positive perceptions of your club. How would you know if you were successful?

7 Consider a service and explain how satisfaction with this service could be influenced by the reactions and opinions of other people.

8 Examine the website of a service organization. What aspects of the site do you find satisfying and what aspects do you find dissatisfying? How do these satisfiers and dissatisfiers compare with the service quality dimensions introduced in this chapter?

FURTHER READING

Brady, M. and Cronin, J. (2001). Some new thoughts on conceptualizing perceived service quality: a hierarchical approach. *Journal of Marketing*, 65(3), 34–49.

Carlson, J. and O'Cass, A. (2010). Exploring the relationships between e-service quality, satisfaction, attitudes and behaviours in content-driven e-service websites. *Journal of Services Marketing*, 24(2), 112–27.

Gounaris, S., Dimitriadis, S. and Stathakopoulos, V. (2010). An examination of the effects of service quality and satisfaction on customers' behavioral intentions in e-shopping. *Journal of Services Marketing*, 24(2), 142–56.

Johnson, M.D., Gustafsson, A., Andreassen, T.W., Lervik, L. and Cha, J. (2001). The evolution and future of national customer satisfaction index models. *Journal of Economic Psychology*, 22(2), 217–45.

Keiningham, T.L., Cooil, B., Aksoy, L., Andreassen, T.W. and Weiner, J. (2007). The value of different customer satisfaction and loyalty metrics in predicting customer retention, recommendation and share-of-wallet. *Managing Service Quality*, 17(4), 361–84.

Morgan, N.A. and Rego, L.L. (2006). The value of different customer satisfaction and loyalty metrics in predicting business performance. *Marketing Science*, 25(5), 426–39.

Reichheld, F.F. (2003). The one number you need to grow. *Harvard Business Review*, 81(12), 46–55.

CHAPTER 5

The Gaps Model of Service Quality

CHAPTER OUTLINE

LEARNING OBJECTIVES

This chapter's objectives are to:

1   Introduce a framework, called the gaps model of service quality, which is used to organize the remainder of this textbook.
2   Demonstrate that the gaps model is a useful framework for understanding service quality in an organization.
3   Demonstrate that the most critical service quality gap to close is the customer gap, the difference between customer expectations and perceptions.
4   Show that four gaps that occur in companies, which we call 'provider gaps', are responsible for the customer gap.
5   Identify the factors responsible for each of the four provider gaps.

OPENING EXAMPLE

Amazon – Providing Excellent Service

How can an online company provide excellent service, identify customer expectations and meet them? Amazon is an online retailer that exemplifies the use of the strategies needed to provide consistent, accurate, and even personalized service.

Understanding customer expectations is a strategy that Amazon begins when a customer first starts shopping at its online store. From the very first time customers make choices, the company's computers start to profile them, offering selections based on a database of previous customers who have read similar books or listened to similar music. Initially, some offerings may not seem on target, but the more you shop at Amazon, the more accurately the company identifies your preferences and the more finely tuned suggestions become. In time the company even begins to send emails that are so specific ('We noticed that you purchased the last book by Jonathan Kellerman and we want you to know that he has just published a new one.') that it almost seems like the local librarian is calling to let you know the title you reserved is in. One of the unique features on the company's website is *'Your Amazon'*, a tab on the home page that sends customers to a selection of items that past purchases indicate would be of interest to them.

Customer-defined standards exist for virtually all activities at Amazon, from delivery to communication to service recovery. When you buy a product from Amazon, you select the mode of delivery and the company tells you the expected number of days it will take to receive your merchandise. Standard shipping is three to five days, but one-day shipping is also available. The company has standards for how quickly you are informed when a product is unavailable (immediately), how fast you find out whether an out-of-print book can be located (three weeks), how long you can return items (30 days) and whether you pay return shipping costs (not if it is Amazon's error).

Service performance is where Amazon excels. Orders almost always arrive ahead of the promised date, are accurate and are in excellent condition because of careful shipping practices. The company's copyrighted One-click Ordering allows regular customers to make purchases instantaneously without creating a shopping cart. Customers can track packages and review previous orders at any time. Amazon also makes sure that all its partners, who sell used and new books and other items direct to customers, perform to Amazon's standards. The company verifies performance for each purchase by asking the customer how well the merchant performed, and then posts scores where customers can see them easily.

Managing promises is handled by clear and careful communication on the Amazon website. Virtually every page is easy to understand and navigate. For example, the page dealing with returns eliminates customer misunderstanding by clearly spelling out what can be returned (almost everything) and what cannot (items that are gas powered or have flammable liquids, large televisions, opened CDs). The page describes how to repack items and when refunds are given. The page dealing with a customer's account shows all previous purchases and the exact stage in the shipping process for every item on order.

Amazon's strategies have been well received by its customers and the Amazon brand is known worldwide.

Source: www.Amazon.co.uk.

Effective services marketing similar to that provided by Amazon is a complex undertaking that involves many different strategies, skills and tasks. Executives of service organizations have long been confused about how to approach this complicated topic in an organized manner. This textbook is designed around one approach: viewing services in a structured, integrated way called the *gaps model of service quality*.[1] This model positions the key concepts, strategies and decisions in services marketing and is used to give the rest of this book its structure, with one Part section devoted to each of the gaps described in this chapter.

THE CUSTOMER GAP

The *customer gap* (sometimes known as Gap 5) is the difference between customer expectations and perceptions (see Figure 5.1). Customer expectations are standards or reference points that customers bring to the service experience, whereas customer perceptions are subjective assessments of actual service experiences. Customer expectations often consist of what a customer believes should or will happen. For example, when you visit an expensive restaurant, you expect a high level of service, one that is considerably superior to the level you would expect in a fast-food restaurant. Closing the gap between what customers expect and what they perceive is critical to delivering quality service; it forms the basis for the gaps model.

Figure 5.1   The customer gap

In a perfect world, expectations and perceptions would be identical: customers would perceive that they have received what they thought they would and should. In practice these concepts are often, even usually, separated by some distance. Broadly, it is the goal of services marketing to bridge this distance, and we devote the remainder of this textbook to describing strategies and practices designed to close this customer gap.

THE PROVIDER GAPS

To close the all-important customer gap (*Gap 5*), the gaps model suggests that four other gaps – the *provider gaps* – also need to be closed. These gaps occur within the organization providing the service (hence the term provider gaps) and include:

- *Gap 1:* Not knowing what customers expect
- *Gap 2:* Not selecting the right service quality designs and standards
- *Gap 3:* Not delivering to service designs and standards
- *Gap 4:* Not matching performance to promises.

The rest of this chapter describes the full gaps model. Alternative views of the gaps model can be found in the Further Reading section at the end of this chapter.

PROVIDER GAP 1: NOT KNOWING WHAT CUSTOMERS EXPECT

Provider gap 1 is the difference between customer expectations of service and a company's understanding of those expectations. A primary cause of why many firms fail to meet customers' expectations is that they lack accurate understanding of exactly what those expectations are. Many reasons exist for managers not being aware of what customers expect: they may not interact directly with customers, they may be unwilling to ask about expectations or they may be unprepared to address them. When people with the authority and responsibility for setting priorities do not fully understand customers' service expectations, they may trigger a chain of bad decisions and suboptimal resource allocations which result in perceptions of poor service quality. In this text, we broaden the responsibility for the provider gap 1 from managers alone to any employee in the organization with the authority to change or influence service policies and procedures. In today's changing organizations, the authority to make adjustments in service delivery is often delegated to empowered teams and front-line people. This is particularly true of business-to-business situations, where account teams make their own decisions about how to address their clients' unique expectations.

Figure 5.2 shows the key factors responsible for provider gap 1. An inadequate marketing research orientation is one of the critical factors. When management or empowered employees do not acquire accurate information about customers' expectations, provider gap 1 is large. Formal and informal methods to capture information about customer expectations must be developed through marketing research. Techniques involving a variety of traditional research approaches – among them customer interviews, survey research, complaint systems and customer panels – must be used to stay close to the customer. More innovative techniques, such as structured brainstorming and service quality gap analysis, are often needed.

Another key factor that is related to provider gap 1 is lack of upward communication. Front-line employees often know a great deal about customers; if management is not in contact with front-line employees and does not understand what they know, the gap widens.

Also related to provider gap 1 is a lack of company strategies to retain customers and strengthen relationships with them, an approach called *relationship marketing*. When organizations have strong relationships with existing customers, provider gap 1 is less likely to occur. Relationship marketing is distinct from *transactional marketing*, the term used to describe the more conventional emphasis on acquiring new customers rather than on retaining them. Relationship marketing has always been a practice with large clients of business-to-business firms (such as IBM or Siemens), but firms that sell to end customers often view such situations as sales or transactions rather than as ongoing relationships. When companies focus too much on attracting new customers, they may fail to understand the changing needs and expectations of their current customers. Technology affords companies the ability to acquire and integrate vast quantities of data on customers that can be used to build relationships. Frequent-flyer travel programmes conducted by airlines, car rental companies and hotel chains are among the most familiar programmes of this type.

Figure 5.2   Key factors leading to provider gap 1

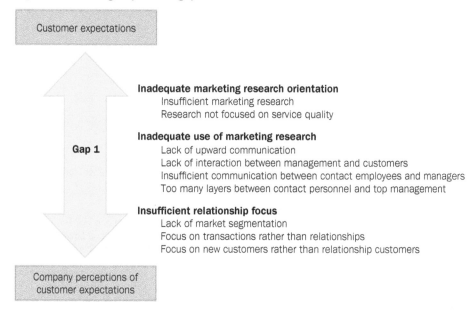

To address the factors in provider gap 1, this text covers topics that include how to understand customers through multiple research strategies (Chapter 6), and how to build strong relationships and understand customer needs over time (Chapter 7). Through these strategies, provider gap 1 can be minimised.

PROVIDER GAP 2: NOT SELECTING THE RIGHT SERVICE QUALITY DESIGNS AND STANDARDS

Accurate perceptions of customers' expectations are necessary, but not sufficient, for delivering superior quality service. Another prerequisite is the presence of service designs and performance standards that reflect those accurate perceptions. A recurring theme in service companies is the difficulty experienced in translating customer expectations into service quality specifications that employees can understand and execute. These problems are reflected in provider gap 2, the difference between company understanding of customer expectations and development of customer-driven service designs and standards. Customer-driven standards differ from the conventional performance standards that companies establish for service in that they are based on pivotal customer requirements that are visible to, and measured by, customers. They are operations standards set to correspond to customer expectations and priorities rather than responses to company concerns such as productivity or efficiency.

Figure 5.3 illustrates a variety of reasons why provider gap 2 exists in service organizations. Those people responsible for setting standards, typically management, sometimes believe that customer expectations are unreasonable or unrealistic. They may also believe that the degree of variability inherent in service defies standardization and that setting standards, therefore, will not achieve the desired goal. Although these assumptions are valid in some situations, they often are mere rationalizations of management's reluctance to tackle head-on the difficult challenges of creating service standards to deliver excellent service.

Because services are intangible, they are difficult to describe and communicate. This difficulty becomes especially evident when new services are being developed. It is critical that all people involved (managers, front-line employees and behind-the-scenes support staff) work with the same concepts of the new service, based on customer needs and expectations. For a service that already exists, any attempt to improve it will also suffer unless everyone has the same vision of the service and associated issues. One of the most important ways to avoid provider gap 2 is clearly to design services without oversimplification, incompleteness,

Figure 5.3   Key factors leading to provider gap 2

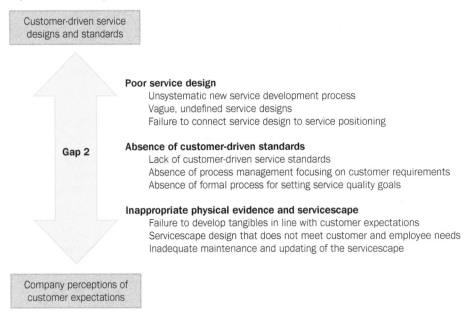

In the figure, between two grey boxes — the top box reading "Customer-driven service designs and standards" and the bottom box reading "Company perceptions of customer expectations" — is labelled **Gap 2** with the following factors:

Poor service design
Unsystematic new service development process
Vague, undefined service designs
Failure to connect service design to service positioning

Absence of customer-driven standards
Lack of customer-driven service standards
Absence of process management focusing on customer requirements
Absence of formal process for setting service quality goals

Inappropriate physical evidence and servicescape
Failure to develop tangibles in line with customer expectations
Servicescape design that does not meet customer and employee needs
Inadequate maintenance and updating of the servicescape

subjectivity and bias. To do so, tools are needed to ensure that new and existing services are developed and improved in as careful a manner as possible. Chapter 8 describes the tools that are most effective in service development and design, including service blueprinting, a unique tool for services.

The quality of service delivered by customer-contact personnel is critically influenced by the standards against which they are evaluated and compensated. Standards signal to contact personnel what the management priorities are and which types of performance really count. When service standards are absent, or when the standards in place do not reflect customers' expectations, the customers' perception of service quality is likely to suffer. When standards do reflect what customers expect, the quality of service they receive is likely to be enhanced. Chapter 9 develops further the topic of customer-defined service standards and shows that, if they are developed appropriately, they can have a powerful positive impact on closing both provider gap 2 and the customer gap.

In Chapter 10 we explore the importance of physical evidence, the variety of roles it plays, and strategies for effectively designing physical evidence and the servicescape to meet customer expectations. By *physical evidence*, we mean everything from business cards to reports, signage, Internet presence, equipment, and facilities used to deliver the service. The *servicescape*, the physical setting where the service is delivered, is a particular focus of Chapter 10. Think of a restaurant, a hotel, a theme park, a health club, a hospital or a university. In these industries, the servicescape – the physical facility – is critical in terms of communicating about the service and making the entire experience pleasurable. In these cases, the servicescape plays a variety of roles, from serving as a visual metaphor for what the company stands for, to actually facilitating the activities of both consumers and employees.

SERVICE SPOTLIGHT

In 2010, the Financial Standards Authority (FSA) undertook a review of the complaint-handling practices of UK banking groups. Their findings indicated that most banks needed to take action to improve the standards of their complaint handling. The FSA stated that it was important to recognize that the degree of change necessary in some banks requires sustained and rigorous effort from senior management to deliver improvement. This includes formally embedding fair complaint handling within the firms' governance structures, so that complaint handling is at the heart of their decision-making and oversight arrangements. This should ensure that senior management are actively involved in improving complaint-handling standards and using the information gathered to identify any underlying issues and make changes to ensure the wider business treats customers fairly.[2]

PROVIDER GAP 3: NOT DELIVERING TO SERVICE DESIGNS AND STANDARDS

Once service designs and standards are put in place, it would seem that the firm is well on its way to delivering high-quality services. This assumption is true, but is still not enough to deliver excellent service. The firm must have systems, processes and people in place to ensure that service delivery actually matches (or exceeds) the designs and standards in place.

Provider gap 3 is the discrepancy between development of customer-driven service standards and actual service performance by company employees. Even when guidelines exist for performing services well and treating customers correctly, high-quality service performance is not a certainty. Standards must be backed by appropriate resources (people, systems and technology) and must be enforced in order to be effective – that is, employees must be measured and compensated on the basis of performance along those standards. Thus, even when standards accurately reflect customers' expectations, if the company fails to provide support for those standards – if it does not facilitate, encourage and require their achievement – standards are of little use. When the level of service delivery falls short of the standards, it falls short of what customers expect as well. Narrowing gap 3 – by ensuring that all the resources needed to achieve the standards are in place – reduces the customer gap.

Research has identified many of the critical inhibitors to closing gap 3 (see Figure 5.4). These factors include employees who do not clearly understand the roles they are to play in the company, employees who experience conflict between customers and company management, poor employee selection, inadequate technology, inappropriate compensation and recognition, and lack of empowerment and teamwork. These factors all relate to the company's human resource function and involve internal practices such as recruitment, training, feedback, job design, building motivation as well as organizational structure. To deliver better service performance, these issues must be addressed across functions, such as involving both marketing and human resources.

Another important variable in provider gap 3 is the customer. Even if contact employees and intermediaries are 100 per cent consistent in their service delivery, the uncontrollable customer variables can have a positive or negative impact on service delivery. If customers do not perform their roles appropriately – if, for example, they fail to provide all the information necessary to the provider or neglect to read and follow instructions – service quality is jeopardized. Customers can also negatively influence the quality of service received by others if they are disruptive or take more than their share of a service provider's time. Understanding customer roles and how customers themselves can influence service delivery and outcomes is critical.

A third difficulty associated with provider gap 3 involves the challenge in delivering service through such intermediaries as retailers, franchisees, agents and brokers. Because quality in service occurs in the human interaction between customers and service providers, control over the service encounter by the company is crucial, yet it rarely is fully possible. Most service (and many manufacturing) companies face an even more formidable task: attaining service excellence and consistency in the presence of intermediaries who represent them and interact with their customers yet are not under their direct control. Franchisers of services depend on their franchisees to execute service delivery as they have specified it. And it is in the execution by the

Figure 5.4   Key factors leading to provider gap 3

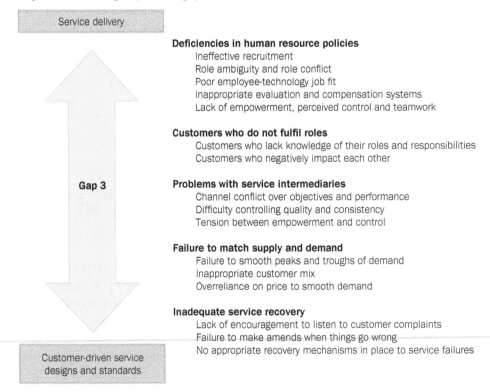

Service delivery

Gap 3

Customer-driven service
designs and standards

Deficiencies in human resource policies
Ineffective recruitment
Role ambiguity and role conflict
Poor employee-technology job fit
Inappropriate evaluation and compensation systems
Lack of empowerment, perceived control and teamwork

Customers who do not fulfil roles
Customers who lack knowledge of their roles and responsibilities
Customers who negatively impact each other

Problems with service intermediaries
Channel conflict over objectives and performance
Difficulty controlling quality and consistency
Tension between empowerment and control

Failure to match supply and demand
Failure to smooth peaks and troughs of demand
Inappropriate customer mix
Overreliance on price to smooth demand

Inadequate service recovery
Lack of encouragement to listen to customer complaints
Failure to make amends when things go wrong
No appropriate recovery mechanisms in place to service failures

franchisee that the customer evaluates the service quality of the company. With franchises and other types of intermediaries, someone other than the producer is responsible for the fulfilment of quality service. For this reason, a firm must develop ways to either control or motivate these intermediaries to meet company standards.

Another issue in provider gap 3 is the need in service firms to synchronize demand and capacity. Because services are perishable and cannot be inventoried, service companies frequently face situations of over-demand or under-demand. Lacking inventories to handle over-demand, companies lose sales when capacity is inadequate to handle customer needs. On the other hand, capacity is frequently underutilized in slow periods. Most companies rely on operations strategies such as cross-training or varying the size of the employee pool to synchronize supply and demand. Marketing strategies for managing demand – such as price changes, advertising, promotion and alternative service offerings – can supplement approaches for managing supply.

The final key factor associated with provider gap 3 is lack of service recovery. Even the best companies, with the best of intentions and clear understanding of their customers' expectations, sometimes fail. It is critical for an organization to understand the importance of service recovery – why people complain, what they expect when they complain, and how to develop effective service recovery strategies for dealing with inevitable service failures. Such strategies might involve a well-defined complaint-handling procedure and an emphasis on empowering employees to react on the spot, in real time, to fix the failure; other times it involves a service guarantee or ways to compensate the customer for the unfulfilled promise.

We discuss strategies to deal with the roles of employees in Chapter 11, customers in Chapter 12, intermediaries in Chapter 13, demand and capacity in Chapter 14 and service recovery in Chapter 15.

PROVIDER GAP 4: NOT MATCHING PERFORMANCE TO PROMISES

Provider gap 4 illustrates the difference between service delivery and the service provider's external communications. Promises made by a service company through its sales force, media advertising and other communications may potentially raise customer expectations, the standards against which customers assess service quality. The discrepancy between actual and promised service therefore has an adverse effect on the customer gap. Broken promises can occur for many reasons: over-promising in advertising or personal selling, inadequate coordination between operations and marketing or differences in policies and procedures across service outlets. Figure 5.5 shows the key factors that lead to provider gap 4.

Figure 5.5   Key factors leading to provider gap 4

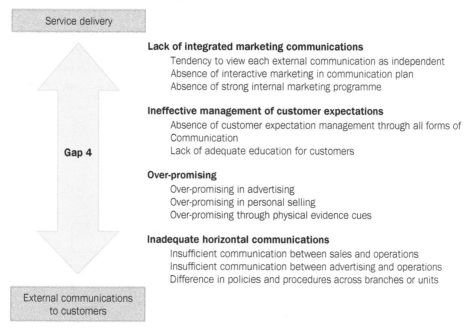

In addition to unduly elevating expectations through exaggerated claims, there are other, less obvious ways in which external communications influence customers' service quality assessments. Service companies frequently fail to capitalize on opportunities to educate customers to use services appropriately. They also neglect to manage customer expectations of what will be delivered in service transactions and relationships.

One of the major difficulties associated with provider gap 4 is that communications to consumers involve issues that cross organizational boundaries. Because service advertising promises what people do, and because what *people* do cannot be controlled like machines that produce physical goods can be controlled, this type of communication involves functions other than the marketing department. This type of marketing is what we call *interactive marketing* – the marketing between contact people and customers – and it must be coordinated with the conventional types of *external marketing* used in product and service firms. When employees who promote the service do not fully understand the reality of service delivery, they are likely to make exaggerated promises or fail to communicate to customers aspects of the service which are intended to serve them well. The result is poor service quality perceptions. Effectively coordinating actual service delivery with external communications, therefore, narrows provider gap 4 and favourably affects the customer gap as well.

Another issue linked with provider gap 4 is pricing of services. In packaged goods (and even in durable goods), customers possess enough price knowledge before purchase to be able to judge whether a price is fair or in line with competition. With services, customers often have no internal reference points for prices before purchase and consumption. Pricing strategies such as discounting, 'everyday prices', and couponing obviously need to be different in service cases in which the customer has no initial sensitivity to prices. Techniques for developing prices for services are more complicated than those for pricing tangible goods.

In summary, external communications – whether from marketing communications or pricing – can create a larger customer gap by raising expectations about service delivery.

In addition to improving service delivery, companies must also manage all communications to customers so that inflated promises do not lead to higher expectations. Chapter 16 discusses integrated services marketing communications, and Chapter 17 covers pricing to accomplish these objectives.

PUTTING IT ALL TOGETHER: CLOSING THE GAPS

The full conceptual model shown in Figure 5.6 conveys a clear message to managers wishing to improve their quality of service: the key to closing the customer gap (gap 5) is to close provider gaps 1 to 4 and keep them closed. To the extent that one or more of provider gaps 1 to 4 exist, customers perceive service quality shortfalls. The gaps model of service quality serves as a framework for service organizations attempting to improve quality service and services marketing.

Figure 5.6   Gaps model of service quality

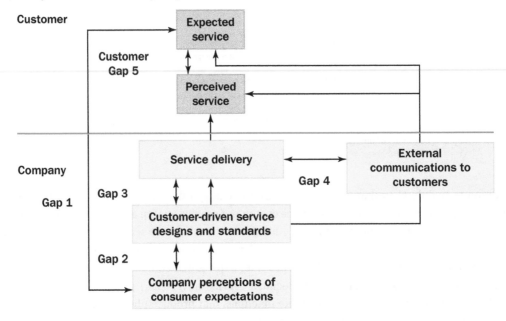

SUMMARY

This chapter presented the integrated gaps model of service quality (shown in Figure 5.6), a framework for understanding and improving service delivery. The remainder of the text is organized around this model of service quality, and focuses on the four provider gaps involved in delivering and marketing a service:

- *Provider gap 1*: Not knowing what customers expect
- *Provider gap 2*: Not selecting the right service quality designs and standards
- *Provider gap 3*: Not delivering to service designs and standards
- *Provider gap 4*: Not matching performance to promises

The gaps model positions the key concepts, strategies and decisions in services marketing in a manner that begins with the customer and builds the organization's tasks around what is needed to close the gap between customer expectations and perceptions. The final chapter in this book, Chapter 18, discusses the financial implications of service quality, reviewing the research and company data that indicate linkages between service quality and financial performance.

EXAMPLE

Using the Gaps Model to Assess an Organization's Service Strategy

The gaps model featured in this chapter is a useful way to audit the service performance and capabilities of an organization. It is the framework that many companies use as an assessment or service audit tool because it is comprehensive and it offers a way for companies to examine all the factors that influence service quality. To use it as an audit tool, a company documents what it knows about each gap and the factors that affect the size of the gap. Although you will learn much more about each of these gaps throughout this book, we provide a basic gaps audit below. In Exercise 1 at the end of the chapter, we propose that you use this audit with a company of your own choosing to determine its service quality gaps.

Service Quality Gaps Model Audit

For each of the following factors in the gaps, indicate the effectiveness of the organization. Use a 1 to 10 scale where 1 is 'poor' and 10 is 'excellent'.

Table 5.1   Customer Gap Audit form

Customer gap 1	Maximum Score	Organization Score 1 = poor 10 = excellent	Organization Score/Maximum Score
1 How well does the company understand customer expectations of service quality?	10		
2 How well does the company understand customer perceptions of service?	10		
Total Score for Customer Gap 1	**20**		
Market research orientation: Is the amount and type of market research adequate to understand customer expectations of service?	10		
Market Research Orientation: Does the company use this information in decisions about service provision?	10		
Upward Communication: Do managers and customers interact enough for management to know what customers expect?	10		
Upward Communication: Do contact people tell management what customers expect?	10		

(Continued)

Customer gap 1	Maximum Score	Organization Score 1 = poor 10 = excellent	Organization Score/Maximum Score
Relationship focus: To what extent does the company understand the expectations of different customer segments?	10		
Relationship focus: To what extent does the company focus on relationships with customers rather than transactions?	10		
Total Score for provider gap 1	**60**		
Provider gap 2	Maximum Score	Organization Score 1 = poor 10 = excellent	Organization Score/Maximum Score
Systematic service design: How effective is the company's service development process?	10		
Systematic service design: How well are new services defined for customers and employees?	10		
Presence of customer-defined standards: How effective are the company's service standards?	10		
Presence of customer-defined standards: Are they defined to correspond to customer expectations?	10		
Presence of customer-defined standards: How effective is the process for setting and tracking service quality goals?	10		
Appropriate physical evidence and servicescape: How appropriate, attractive and effective are the company's physical facilities, equipment and other tangibles?	10		
Total Score for provider gap 2	**60**		
Provider gap 3	Maximum Score	Organization Score 1 = poor 10 = excellent	Organization Score/Maximum Score
Effective human resource policies: How effectively does the company recruit, hire, train, compensate and empower employees?	10		
Effective human resource policies: Is service quality delivery consistent across employees, teams, units and branches?	10		
Effective role fulfilment by customers: Do customers understand their roles and responsibilities?	10		

(Continued)

Provider gap 3	Maximum Score	Organization Score 1 = poor 10 = excellent	Organization Score/Maximum Score
Effective role fulfilment by customers: Does the company manage customers to fulfil their roles, especially customers that are incompatible?	10		
Effective alignment with service intermediaries: How well are service intermediaries aligned with the company?	10		
Effective alignment with service intermediaries: Is there conflict over objectives and performance, costs and rewards?	10		
Effective alignment with service intermediaries: Is service quality delivery consistent across the outlets?	10		
Alignment of supply and demand: How well is the company able to match supply with demand fluctuations?	10		
Service recovery: How effective are the service recovery efforts of the organization?	10		
Service recovery: How well does the organization plan for service failures?	10		
Score for provider gap 3	**100**		

Provider gap 4	Maximum Score	Organization Score 1 = poor 10 = excellent	Organization Score/Maximum Score
Integrated marketing communications: How well do all company communications – including the interactions between company employees and customers – express the same message and level of service quality?	10		
Effective management of customer expectations: How well does the company communicate to customers about what will be provided to them?	10		
Accurate promising in advertising and personal selling: Does the company avoid overpromising and overselling?	10		
Adequate horizontal communications: How well do different parts of the organization communicate with each other so that service quality equals what is promised?	10		
Total Score for provider gap 4	**40**		

The score for each gap should be compared to the maximum score possible. Are particular gaps weaker than others? Which areas in each gap need attention? As you go through the rest of the book, we will provide more detail about how to improve the factors in each of the gaps.

KEY CONCEPTS

Customer gap	93	Provider gaps	94
Gaps model	93		

EXERCISES

1 Choose an organization to interview, and use the integrated gaps model of service quality as a framework. Ask the manager whether the organization suffers from any of the factors listed in the figures in this chapter. Which factor in each of Figures 5.2 through to 5.5 does the manager consider the most troublesome?

2 What does the company do to try to address the problems?

3 Use the Internet to access the website of Ritz-Carlton, IKEA, KLM or any other well-known service organization. Which provider gaps has the company closed? How can you tell?

4 Interview a non-profit or public sector organization in your area (it could be some part of your university or college). Find out if the integrated gaps model of service quality framework makes sense in the context of that organization.

DISCUSSION QUESTIONS

1 Think about a service you receive. Is there a gap between your expectations and your perceptions of that service? What do you expect to receive that you do not?

2 Think about a service that you receive regularly. How would you change it and the way it is provided to make it better for the customer?

3 If you were the manager of a service organization and wanted to apply the gaps model to improve service, which gap would you start with? Why? In what order would you proceed to close the gaps?

4 Can provider gap 4 be closed prior to closing any of the other three provider gaps? How?

5 Which of the four provider gaps do you believe is hardest to close? Why?

FURTHER READING

Bitner, M.J., Zeithaml, V.A. and Gremler, D.D. (2010). Technology's impact on the gaps model of service quality, in Maglio, P.P., Kieliszewski, C.A. and Spoher, J.C. (eds). *Handbook of Service Science*, New York: Springer.

Brady, M. and Cronin, J. (2001). Some new thoughts on conceptualizing perceived service quality: a hierarchical approach. *Journal of Marketing*, 65(3), 34–49.

Ladhari, R. (2009). A review of twenty years of SERVQUAL research. *International Journal of Quality and Service Sciences*, 1(2), 172–98.

Mauri, A. G., Minazzi, R., and Muccio, S. (2013). A review of literature on the gaps model on service quality: a 3-decades period: 1985–2013. *International Business Research*, 6(12), 134–44.

PART 2

Understanding Customer Requirements

THE LISTENING GAP

Not knowing what customers expect is one of the root causes of not delivering to customer expectations. Provider gap 1 is the difference between customer expectations of service and company understanding of those expectations. Note that in its graphic representation we created a link between the customer and the company, showing customer expectations above the line that dissects the model and provider perceptions of customer expectations below that line. This alignment signifies that what customers expect is not always the same as what companies believe they expect.

Part 2 describes two ways to close provider gap 1. In Chapter 6 we detail ways that companies listen to customers through research. Both formal and informal methods of customer research are described, including surveys, critical incident studies and complaint solicitation. Upward communication from front-line employees to managers, another key factor in listening to customers, is also discussed.

Chapter 7 covers company strategies to retain customers and strengthen relationships with them, an approach called relationship marketing. Relationship marketing is distinct from transactional marketing, the more conventional approach that tends to focus on acquiring new customers rather than retaining them. When organizations have strong relationships with existing customers, opportunities for in-depth listening increase over time and provider gap 1 is less likely to occur. A variety of strategies, including the creation of switching barriers and the development of relationship bonds, are suggested as a means of relationship development and, ultimately, the cultivation of customer loyalty.

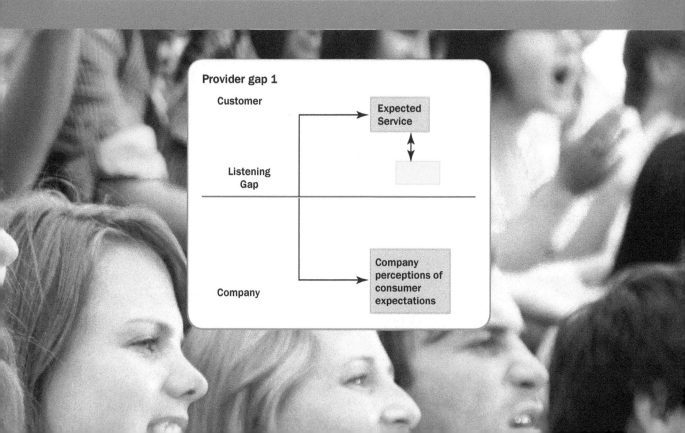

CHAPTER 6

Listening to Customers

CHAPTER OUTLINE

LEARNING OBJECTIVES

This chapter's objectives are to:

1 Understand the role of customer databases and big data.
2 Present the types of, and guidelines for, marketing research in services.
3 Show how marketing research information can and should be used for services.
4 Describe the strategies by which companies can facilitate interaction and communication between management and customers.
5 Present ways that companies can and do facilitate upward communication of customer information from contact people to management.

Airbnb – Understanding Peer-to-Peer Room Rental

Airbnb is part of the broader 'sharing economy', a socio-economic system facilitated by the internet that allows individuals to rent out anything, from spare seats in their cars, to rooms in their homes, tools from their shed or clothes from their wardrobe. The sharing economy is an alternative to the constant accumulation and ownership of things. Since its beginnings, Airbnb has provided peer-to-peer room rental service beds for more than 11 million guests in 192 different countries.

Airbnb was started in 2008 by cash-strapped flatmates Brian Chesky, Nathan Blecharczyk and Joe Gebbia, who had space to share and hosted three travellers looking for a place to stay. Now millions of hosts and travellers choose to create a free Airbnb account so they can list their space and book unique accommodation anywhere in the world. The three founders of Airbnb are each soon to be worth more than $1bn, after the latest round of investment in Airbnb valued the company at $10bn.

The success and rapid growth of Airbnb is due to a consumer thirst for unique travel experiences, which amount to more than just a place to stay. In surveys of guests, one of the reasons why people say they use Airbnb has nothing to do with price or the exact accommodation they choose; it has more to do with the fact that they hate being a tourist and that they want to stay with a local who can give them guidance.

Airbnb allows renters to list their properties free of charge, but takes a percentage of each booking. What motivates renters is the same as the initial impetus behind the company. People start listing their space because they want to make some money. The reason they keep doing it is because they like the experience. It's a mix of financial and personal motivation.

The rapid expansion of Airbnb has been dictated primarily by broad tourism trends. Offices were opened in London, Paris, Berlin and Barcelona because of the sheer numbers of travellers in each market. The service itself provides much of the information that drives the way the business develops, along with in-depth, qualitative discussions with and between users of the service.

When Airbnb started in Europe, they didn't do a large marketing campaign. Instead they bring people together, holding regular meetings with 15–20 new hosts over a bottle of wine to meet them and understand who they are, talk to them and get them to meet each other. They really want to understand the Airbnb community and who the renters are, instead of just looking at the numbers and supply and demand. All Airbnb employees are given a travel coupon every quarter to encourage them to try the product and provide feedback.

Airbnb doesn't employ a team of people to monitor the many user reviews posted on its site, but there are triggers for action, such as a series of low ratings. The focus is on getting users of the service to have a positive experience so that they pass on the message and expand the pool of renters and guests.

Source: Adapted from Impact *magazine, Issue 6, July 2014.*

Despite a genuine interest in meeting customer expectations, many organizations miss the mark by thinking inside out – they believe they know what customers *should* want and deliver that, rather than finding out what they do want. When this happens, organizations provide services that *do not* match customer expectations: important features are left out, and the levels of performance on the features that are provided are inadequate. Because services have few clearly defined and tangible cues, the difficulty of getting at customer needs may be considerably larger than it is in manufacturing firms. A far better approach involves thinking outside in – determining customer expectations and then delivering to them. Thinking outside in uses marketing research and data to fully understand customers and their requirements. Marketing research, the main subject of this chapter, involves far more than conventional surveys. It consists of a portfolio of listening strategies that allow companies to deliver service to meet customer expectations. It also has to be integrated with other information sources such as customer databases.

CUSTOMER DATABASES AND BIG DATA

Over the past 10 years significant improvements in computerization, database management and data capture have meant that many organizations now hold significant amounts of data on their customers. For example, an airline operating a loyalty card scheme will have details on each cardholder, including:

Social Media and Digital Marketing

- Their home address
- The frequency with which they fly
- The days and times they fly
- The value of their annual flights
- The range of destinations they visit
- Their seating and check-in preferences
- Their use of mobile apps for booking and check-in
- The frequency with which they respond to promotional offers
- Their price sensitivity.

In addition, the booking information may indicate whether they always travel alone, travel on business or for pleasure, and use secretaries or travel agents to book their flights.

⭐ SERVICE SPOTLIGHT

Ticketmaster, part of Live Nation Entertainment, provide a service which involves buying tickets for sporting and entertainment events from promoters and selling them on to fans. To the customer, the allure is the convenience of a website or call centre through which they can book, get the tickets delivered and obtain access to the match or gig. Behind the scenes, Ticketmaster is amassing and analysing a huge amount of data about what tickets people buy, who they are, and what interests them.

Ticketmaster is able to work out the patterns of behaviour thanks to the wealth of data it holds on customers. In the UK alone, Ticketmaster has boiled down 46 million separate transactions into some 11 million individual customer records, out of which it is able to figure out whether people who buy one sort of ticket are likely to buy another. In addition to the purchase and user demographic data it gathers, Ticketmaster has a deal covering ten markets with Experian, a global information services company, that allows it to overlay Experian's Mosaic customer segmentation on its own data.

Source: **Adapted from www.research-live.com – January 2014.**

The information available in a database can be categorized into the following groupings:

- information on purchasing behaviour (services purchased, timing and method of purchase, trends);
- information on customer loyalty (relationship length, value, profitability);
- information on customer response (to marketing communications, new products, price changes, etc.).

Where database information has a major strength, it is in the area of tracking customer reactions to different service and promotional offerings. Direct marketing campaigns may be used to obtain a direct one-to-one comparison between two marketing options, e.g. between a service with new features and an unchanged service. By presenting the two different offers to identical samples of the target audience, a measure of the selling power of each can be obtained.

The results of such a test (i.e. how many customers buy each option and what are their specific characteristics) can be stored on the customer database. It can provide an objective and measurable assessment of customers' behaviour in a true-life marketing environment. The data will show what a customer actually does when confronted by an actual proposition that has to be responded to or ignored. It can therefore provide an indication of what is likely to happen when a new offering is provided to the whole market. However, it should be noted that database information is historical and only describes what has happened but not why. Usually, there is no information on why customers' behaviour has changed or why they responded in the way that they have. Further, the data does not depict the whole market, as it only represents current customers and prospects; it provides no information on non-customers or customers' behaviour with other suppliers.

The other major challenge is the size of some of the databases. Organizations such as credit card companies, which experience millions of transactions per week, have very large complex databases of customer behaviour. Such data are often referred to as big data. Big data is an all-encompassing term for any collection of data sets so large and complex that it becomes difficult to process using traditional data processing applications. Data mining software is often used to select, explore and model this big data in order to uncover previously unknown relationships and patterns of behaviour. With complex databases, it can often be difficult for managers to think up all of the possible hypotheses and questions to test with the data when looking for patterns and relationships. Data mining can sometimes overcome this by highlighting and reporting on all possible trends and patterns among the data elements. It uses probabilities and statistics to determine which relationships are least likely to have occurred by chance and can be considered as being significant. Data mining can build models to predict customer behaviour, such as customers' likelihood of renewing fitness centre subscriptions, their likely willingness to use the Internet for booking holidays and the probability of their purchasing software upgrades. The prediction provided by a model is usually called a score. Based on the modelling, a score (typically a numerical value) is assigned to each record in the database and indicates the likelihood that the customer whose record has been scored will exhibit a certain type of behaviour.

SERVICE SPOTLIGHT

In Australia, American Express started using their big data to look for indicators that could predict card loyalty It went on to develop sophisticated predictive models to analyse historical transactions and 115 variables to forecast potential customer churn. The company believes it can now identify 24 per cent of accounts that will close within the next four months.

The availability of both customer databases and marketing research means that many organizations are starting to adopt an integrated approach to collecting, recording, analysing and interpreting information on customers, competitors and markets.[1]

USING MARKETING RESEARCH TO UNDERSTAND CUSTOMER EXPECTATIONS

Although behavioural information may be available from customer databases, finding out through marketing research what customers expect is essential to providing service quality. Marketing research is the key vehicle for understanding customer expectations and perceptions of services. In services, as with any offering, a firm that does no marketing research at all is unlikely to understand its customers. Similarly, a firm that does marketing research, but not on the topic of customer expectations, may fail to uncover what is needed to stay in tune with changing customer requirements. Marketing research must focus on service issues such as what features are most important to customers, what levels of these features customers expect, and what customers think the company can and should do when problems occur in service delivery. Even when a service firm is small and has limited resources to conduct research, avenues are open to explore what customers expect.

In this section we discuss the elements of services marketing research programmes that help companies identify customer expectations and perceptions. In the sections that follow, we will discuss ways in which the tactics of general marketing research may need to be adjusted to maximize its effectiveness in services.

RESEARCH OBJECTIVES FOR SERVICES

The first step in designing services marketing research is without doubt the most critical: defining the problem and research objectives. This is where the services marketer poses the questions to be answered or problems to be solved with research. Does the company want to know what customer requirements are, how customers view the service provided by the company, how they will respond to a new service introduction or what they will want from the company five years from now? Each of these research questions requires a different research strategy. Thus, it is essential to devote time and resources to define the problem thoroughly and accurately. In spite of the importance of this first stage, many marketing research studies are initiated without adequate attention to objectives.

Research objectives translate into action questions. While many different questions are likely to enter into a marketing research programme, the following are the most common research objectives in services:

- To discover customer requirements or expectations for service
- To develop customer-defined standards for service delivery (see Chapter 9)
- To monitor and track service performance
- To assess overall company performance compared with that of competitors
- To assess gaps between customer expectations and perceptions
- To identify dissatisfied customers, so that service recovery can be attempted
- To gauge the effectiveness of changes in service delivery
- To appraise the service performance of individuals and teams for evaluation, recognition and rewards
- To determine customer expectations for a new service
- To monitor changing customer expectations in an industry
- To forecast future expectations of customers.

These research objectives are similar in many ways to the research conducted for physical products: both aim to assess customer requirements, dissatisfaction, and demand. Services research, however, incorporates additional elements that require specific attention.

Services research must continually monitor and track service performance, because performance is subject to human variability and heterogeneity. Conducting performance research at a single point in time, as might be done for a physical product such as a car, would be insufficient in services. A major focus of services research involves capturing human performance – at the level of individual employee, team, branch, organization as a whole and competition. Another focus of services research involves documenting the process by which service is performed. Even when service employees are performing well, a service provider must continue to track performance because the potential for variation in service delivery always exists.

Table 6.1 lists a number of services research objectives. Once objectives such as these have been identified, they will point the way to decisions about the most appropriate type of research, methods of data collection, and ways to use the information. The research approaches in this table are described in later sections of this chapter.

ELEMENTS IN AN EFFECTIVE SERVICES MARKETING RESEARCH PROGRAMME

A good services marketing research programme includes multiple types of information source and research studies. The composite of information and types of research will differ by company because the range of uses for service quality research – from employee performance assessment to advertising campaign development to strategic planning – requires a rich, multifaceted flow of information. If an organization were to engage in virtually all types of service research, the portfolio would look like Table 6.1, but few organizations do all types of research. The particular portfolio for any organization will match organization resources and address the key areas needed to understand the customers of the business. So that it will be easier for you to identify the appropriate type of research for different research objectives, we list the objectives in column 2 of Table 6.1. In the following sections we describe each major type of research and show the way each type addresses the criteria associated with it.

SERVICE SPOTLIGHT

Scandinavian Airlines collect customers' opinions daily through a wide range of channels, including the Internet, letters, paper-based forms and the telephone. In Scandinavia alone, the company has a total of 55 people working on processing around 50,000 spontaneous customer comments a year. The data are presented in a portal environment on the airline's intranet, which means that all employees can access any of the feedback. Customized reports for a large number of department managers are also created, which allows them to see exactly how the areas they are responsible for are experienced and perceived by customers. For example, the data can be interrogated with questions such as 'What can we do to improve the flights between Stockholm and Paris?'

Firms that use complaints as research collect and document them, then use the information to identify dissatisfied customers, correct individual problems where possible and identify common service failure points. Although this research is used for both goods and services, it has a critical real-time purpose in services – to improve failure points and to boost or correct the performance of contact personnel. Research on complaints is one of the easiest types of research for firms to conduct, leading many companies to depend solely on complaints to stay in touch with customers. Unfortunately, there is convincing research evidence that customer complaints alone are a woefully inadequate source of information: only a small percentage of customers with problems actually complain to the company. The rest will stay dissatisfied, telling other people about their dissatisfaction.

To be effective, complaint solicitation requires rigorous recording of numbers and types of complaints through many channels, and then working to eliminate the most frequent problems. Complaint channels include employees at the front line, intermediary organizations like retailers who deliver service, managers, and third parties such as consumer pressure groups who field complaints. Companies must both solve

Table 6.1 Research approaches and primary objectives

Research Approaches	Primary objectives
Complaint solicitation	To identify/attend to dissatisfied customers
	To identify common service failure points
Critical incident studies	To identify 'best practices' at transaction level
	To identify customer requirements as input for quantitative studies
	To identify common service failure points
	To identify systemic strengths and weaknesses in customer-contact services
Researching customer needs	To identify customer requirements as input for quantitative research
Customer satisfaction surveys and SERVQUAL surveys	To monitor and track service performance
	To assess overall company performance compared with that of competition
	To determine links between satisfaction and behavioural intentions
	To assess gaps between customer expectations and perceptions
Database marketing research	To identify the individual requirements of customers using information technology and database information
Exit surveys	To obtain immediate feedback on performance of service transactions
	To measure effectiveness of changes in service delivery
	To assess service performance of individuals and teams
	To use as input for process improvements
	To identify common service failure points
Service expectation meetings and reviews	To create dialogue with important customers
	To identify what individual large customers expect and then to ensure that it is delivered
	To close the loop with important customers
Market-oriented ethnography	To research customers in natural settings
	To study customers while they are in a service encounter
Netnography	To monitor changes in customer expectations over time
	To identify reasons for customer defection
	To research customers in natural settings
	To determine links between satisfaction and behavioural intentions
Mystery shopping	To measure individual employee performance for evaluation, recognition and rewards
	To identify systemic strengths and weaknesses in customer-contact services
Customer panels	To monitor changes in customer expectations over time
	To provide a forum for customers to suggest and evaluate new service ideas
Lost customer follow-up	To identify reasons for customer defection
	To assess gaps between customer expectations and perceptions
Future expectations research	To forecast future expectations of customers
	To develop and test new service ideas

individual customer problems and seek overall patterns to eliminate failure points. More sophisticated forms of complaint resolution define 'complaint' broadly to include all comments – both negative and positive – as well as questions from customers. Firms should build depositories for this information and report results frequently, perhaps weekly or monthly.

COMPLAINT SOLICITATION

Many of you must have complained to employees of service organizations, only to find that nothing happens with your complaint. No one rushes to solve it and the next time you experience the service, the same problem is present. How frustrating! Good service organizations take complaints seriously. Not only do they listen to complaints – they also seek complaints as communications about what can be done to improve their service and the performance of their service employees.

CRITICAL INCIDENT STUDIES

In Chapter 4 we discussed the critical incident technique (CIT), a qualitative interview procedure in which customers are asked to provide verbatim stories about satisfying and dissatisfying service encounters they have experienced. According to a recent summary of the use of the technique in services, CIT has been reported in hotels, restaurants, airlines, amusement parks, car repair, retailing, banking, cable television, public transportation and education.[2] The studies have explored a wide range of service topics: consumer evaluation of services, service failure and recovery, employees, customer participation in service delivery, and service experience.

Critical incident technique has many benefits. First, data are collected from the respondent's perspective and are usually vivid because they are expressed in consumers' own words and reflect the way they think. Second, the method provides concrete information about the way the company and its employees behave and react, thereby making the research easy to translate into action. Third, like most qualitative methods, the research is particularly useful when the topic or service is new and very little other information exists. Finally, the method is well suited for assessing perceptions of customers from different cultures because it allows respondents to share their perceptions rather than answer researcher-defined questions.[3]

> ### ⭐ SERVICE SPOTLIGHT
>
> Asda, the major UK grocery chain which is part of the Walmart group, has trained its staff to undertake qualitative research in two ways: by holding informal group discussions with customers and by accompanying individual shoppers as they proceed around a store. Staff also ask customers about critical incidents they have had when shopping in Asda. The organization perceives this as a very powerful way of getting the service personnel to think about the customer. Usually, staff see the store from an operational perspective, rather than a customer's perspective; accompanying customers on a shopping trip changes that.

RESEARCHING CUSTOMER NEEDS

Researching customer needs involves identifying the benefits and attributes that customers expect in a service. This type of research is very basic and essential because it determines the type of questions that will be asked in surveys and, ultimately, the improvements that will be attempted by the firm. Because these studies are so foundational, qualitative techniques are appropriate to begin them. Quantitative techniques may follow, usually during a pre-test stage of survey development. Unfortunately, many companies do superficial research, often developing surveys on the basis of intuition or company direction rather than through customer probing.

★ SERVICE SPOTLIGHT

Telefónica O_2 used research to create a loyalty programme for its mobile phone customers. The development of the Priority Moments loyalty programme, which the company launched in 2011, began by talking to customers to understand what really mattered to them. This insight informed the structure and content of the programme and continues to do so with ongoing research, social media tracking and behavioural analysis. In order to target and influence customers positively, both qualitative and quantitative research into customer preferences and behaviour were used to identify their favourite brands; moments when they needed a boost (e.g. Monday mornings) and celebratory moments.

The research helped reveal the moments in the customers' relationship with O_2 when their attitude shifted, evidenced in a dip in the net promoter score (NPS), and when the risk of churn increased. It also helped to create customer segmentation based on value. This understanding led to the creation of a tiered reward structure in which each type of reward performs a special function, including to encourage everyday engagement, acquire or reactivate a lapsed user, reward customers based on spend and increase overall satisfaction.

Source: **www.o2priority.co.uk.**

Another approach to researching customer needs that has been effective in services industries is to examine existing research about customer requirements in similar service industries. The five dimensions of quality service are generalizable across industries, and sometimes the way these dimensions are manifest is also remarkably similar. Customers of travel agencies and customers of banks, for example, expect many of the same features when using these two services. Besides expert advice, customers at travel agents expect short queues, brochures, informative websites and a friendly empathetic service – the same features that are desired by bank customers. In these and other industries that share common customer expectations, managers may find it helpful to seek knowledge from existing research in a related service industry.

RELATIONSHIP AND SERVQUAL SURVEYS

One category of surveys could appropriately be named *relationship surveys* because they pose questions about all elements in the customer's relationship with the company (including service, product and price). This comprehensive approach can help a company diagnose its relationship strengths and weaknesses. These surveys typically monitor and track service performance annually with an initial survey providing a baseline. Relationship surveys are also effective in comparing company performance with that of competitors, often focusing on the best competitor's performance as a benchmark. When used for this purpose, the sponsor of the survey is not identified and questions are asked about both the anonymous company and one or more of its competitors.

A sound measure of service quality is necessary for identifying which aspects of service need performance improvement, assessing how much improvement is needed on each aspect, and evaluating the impact of improvement efforts. Unlike goods quality, which can be measured objectively by such indicators as durability and number of defects, service quality is abstract and is best captured by surveys that measure customer evaluations of service. One of the first measures to be developed specifically to measure service quality was the SERVQUAL survey.

The original SERVQUAL scale published in 1988 involved a survey containing 21 service attributes, grouped into the five service quality dimensions (discussed in Chapter 4) of reliability, responsiveness, assurance, empathy and tangibles. The survey sometimes asks customers to provide two different ratings on each attribute – one reflecting the level of service they would expect from excellent companies in a sector and the other reflecting their perception of the service delivered by a specific company within that sector.

The difference between the expectation and perception ratings constitutes a quantified measure of service quality.

Data gathered through a SERVQUAL survey can be used for a variety of purposes:

- To determine the average gap score (between customers' perceptions and expectations) for each service attribute
- To assess a company's service quality along each of the five SERVQUAL dimensions
- To track customers' expectations and perceptions (on individual service attributes and/or on the SERVQUAL dimensions) over time
- To compare a company's SERVQUAL scores against those of competitors
- To identify and examine customer segments that differ significantly in their assessments of a company's service performance
- To assess internal service quality (that is, the quality of service rendered by one department or division to others within the same company).

The SERVQUAL instrument spawned many studies focusing on service quality assessment and is used in many service industries. Despite the fact that SERVQUAL has been productively used in multiple contexts, cultures and countries for measuring service quality, the SERVQUAL instrument has been the centre of criticism from a range of academic researchers. The main criticisms identified by Buttle[4] relate to the instrument's dimensions and shortcomings associated with the disconfirmation paradigm.

There are concerns that the attributes used in the original SERVQUAL instrument are not appropriate for all service offerings and need to be contextualized to reflect different service activities. Therefore, as with any method, care must be taken to ensure that the dimensions that are being measured are appropriate to the situation in which it is to be used. The attributes of the original SERVQUAL instrument do provide a valuable starting point for the development of an appropriate tool; however, it may be necessary to add or delete some of them depending on the context.

DISCONFIRMATION PARADIGM

Grönroos[5] suggested three problems when measuring comparisons between expectations and experiences over a number of attributes:

1   If expectations are measured after the service experience has taken place, which frequently happens for practical reasons, then what is measured is not really expectation but something which has been influenced by the service experience.
2   It may not make sense to measure expectations prior to the service experience either because the expectations that exist before a service is delivered may not be the same as the factors that a person uses when evaluating their experiences. For example, a customer in a restaurant may place no importance on the background music playing before the meal, but the quality or volume of the music heard during the meal may alter a customer's view of the factors to consider in evaluating the quality of the dining experience.
3   A customer's view of their experience in a service encounter is influenced by their prior expectations. Consequently, if expectations are measured and then experiences are measured, then the measures are not independent of each other and the expectations are actually being measured twice.

These issues do not necessarily invalidate the measurement of service quality. However, it has led to researchers looking for alternative ways of measuring service quality. One of the better known alternatives is the SERVPERF instrument, developed by Cronin and Taylor,[6] which measures experiences only and does not ask respondents about their expectations. Experiences are measured over a range of attributes that the researcher has developed to describe the service as conclusively as possible. The resultant instrument may be easier to administer and the data may be easier to analyse. However, SERVPERF has not reached the same level of popularity as exists for SERVQUAL.

EXIT SURVEYS OR POST-TRANSACTION SURVEYS

Whereas the purpose of SERVQUAL surveys is usually to gauge the overall relationship with the customer, the purpose of transaction surveys is to capture information about one or all of the key service encounters with the customer. In this method, customers are asked a short list of questions immediately after a particular transaction (hence the name *exit surveys*) about their satisfaction with the transaction and contact personnel with whom they interacted. Because the surveys are administered continuously to a broad spectrum of customers, they are more effective than complaint solicitation (where the information comes only from dissatisfied customers).

Sport and Leisure Management,[7] which provides leisure management services for the public sector in the UK, needed to refresh its collection of post-transaction customer feedback surveys in order to improve its decision-making. Rather than use paper-based systems, it has installed user-friendly computer terminals in the foyer of leisure centres. These collect customer attitudes about the service experience from users before they leave the premises.

In other companies, transaction surveys are administered by telephone several days after a transaction, such as installation of durable goods or claims adjustment in insurance. Because they are timed to occur close to service transactions, these surveys are useful in identifying sources of dissatisfaction and satisfaction. For example, Kwik Fit, which sells car exhausts and tyres, often calls customers a day after a car has been serviced to ensure that customers are satisfied with the work. A strong benefit of this type of research is that it often appears to customers that the call is following up to ensure that they are satisfied; consequently, the call does double duty as a market research tool and as customer service.

This type of research is simple and fresh and provides management with continuous information about interactions with customers. Further, the research allows management to associate service quality performance with individual contact personnel so that high performance can be rewarded and low performance corrected. It also serves as an incentive for employees to provide better service, because they understand how and when they are being evaluated. One type of post-transaction survey that is becoming more familiar is on websites following online purchases. When a consumer makes a purchase, a message automatically pops up on the site and invites consumers to fill out a survey. Consumers who agree are asked questions about ease of ordering, product selection, website navigation and customer support.

SERVICE EXPECTATION MEETINGS AND REVIEWS

In business-to-business situations when large accounts are involved, a highly effective form of customer research involves eliciting the expectations of the client at a specified time of the year and then following up later (usually after a year) to determine whether the expectations were fulfilled. Even when the company produces a physical product, the meetings deal almost completely with the service expected and provided by an account or sales team assigned to the client. Unlike other forms of research we have discussed, these meetings are not conducted by objective and unbiased researchers but are instead initiated and facilitated by senior members of the account team so that they can listen carefully to the client's expectations. You may be surprised to find that such interaction does not come naturally to sales teams who are used to talking *to* clients rather than listening carefully to their needs. Consequently, teams have to be carefully trained to not defend or explain but rather to comprehend. One company found that the only way it could teach its salespeople not to talk on these interviews was to take a marketing researcher along to gently kick the salesperson under the table whenever he or she strayed from the format!

The format, when appropriate, consists of (1) asking clients what they expect in terms of eight to ten basic requirements determined from focus group research, (2) enquiring what particular aspects of these requirements the account team performed well in the past and what aspects need improvement, and (3) requesting that the client rank the relative importance of the requirements. After getting the input, senior account members go back to their teams and plan their goals for the year around client requirements. The next step is verifying with the client that the account plan will satisfy requirements or, when it will not, managing expectations to let the client know what cannot be accomplished. After executing the plan for the year, the senior account personnel then return to the client, determine whether the plan has been successfully executed and expectations met, then establish a new set of expectations for the coming year.

PROCESS CHECKPOINT EVALUATIONS

With professional services such as consulting, construction and architecture, services are provided over a long period, and there are no obvious ways or times to collect customer information. Waiting until the entire project is complete – which could be years – is undesirable because myriad unresolvable problems could have occurred by then. But discrete service encounters to calibrate customer perceptions are also not usually available. In these situations the smart service provider defines a process for delivering the services and then structures the feedback around the process, checking in at frequent points to ensure that the client's expectations are being met. For example, a management consulting firm might establish the following process for delivering its services to clients: (1) collect information, (2) diagnose problems, (3) recommend alternative solutions, (4) select alternatives, and (5) implement solutions. Next, it could agree with the client up front that it will communicate at major process checkpoints – after diagnosing the problem, before selecting the alternative, and so on – to make certain that the job is progressing as planned.

MARKET-ORIENTED ETHNOGRAPHY

Structured questionnaires make key assumptions about what people are conscious of or can recall about their behaviour and what they are willing to explain to researchers about their opinions. Even focus group interviews depend on norms of participation, or what people are willing to say in front of others and to researchers. To understand fully how customers assess and use services, it may be necessary and effective to use other approaches, such as market-oriented ethnography. This set of approaches allows researchers to observe consumption behaviour in natural settings. The goal is to enter the consumer's world as much as possible – observing how and when a service is used in an actual home environment or consumption environment, such as watching consumers eat in restaurants or attend concerts. Among the techniques used are observation, interviews, documents and examination of material possessions such as artefacts. Observation involves entering the experience as a participant observer and watching what occurs rather than asking questions about it. Such approaches provide valuable insights, especially about lifestyles and usage patterns.[8]

SERVICE SPOTLIGHT

Best Western International used ethnography to better understand its mature market segment. Rather than bringing participants into focus-group facilities and asking them questions, the company paid 25 over-55 couples to videotape themselves on their travels. The firm was able to listen to how couples actually made decisions rather than the way they reported them. The insights they gained from this research were decidedly different from what they would have learned otherwise. Most noteworthy was the finding that seniors who talked hotel receptionists into better deals on rooms did not need the lower price to afford staying at the hotel – they were simply after the thrill of the deal, as illustrated in this description:

The 60-ish woman caught on the grainy videotape is sitting on her hotel bed, addressing her husband after a long day spent on the road. 'Good job!' she exults. 'We beat a great deal out of that receptionist and got a terrific room.'

These customers then spent their discount money on better dinners elsewhere, contributing nothing to Best Western. 'The degree of discount clearly isn't what it used to be in importance – and we got that right out of the research,' claimed the manager of programmes for Best Western.[9] This finding would be highly unlikely using traditional research and asking customers directly, for few customers would admit to being willing to pay a higher price for a service!

NETNOGRAPHY

Netnography, sometimes known as *online ethnography*, is the ethnographic study of online communities. It generally involves a researcher participating fully as a member of the community. Communities which are relevant to the service organization (i.e. world travel) and where there are high levels of interaction and comments are likely to provide the richest sources of information. Customers may speak more freely within their online community than when they are taking part in traditional marketing, as they perhaps feel they are not under as much scrutiny. Balanced against this, however, is the concern that these customers may not be accurately posting their views but may instead be posting comments that enhance their own reputation or reinforce the online persona that they are trying to create. This may lead to new ideas for the design of new services or service components. Data are collected by copying discussions from the forum, or by the researcher taking notes on observations of interactions. There are ethical issues that stem from this type of research, however, particularly around the issue of a researcher taking an active part in the discussions/conversations of a community without the participants being aware of the researcher's identity. In such situations, best practice suggests that the researcher should disclose fully his or her presence, job function, and research intentions to online community members during any research assignment.[10]

MYSTERY SHOPPING

In this form of research, which is unique to services, companies employ outside research organizations to send people into service establishments and experience the service as if they were customers. These 'mystery shoppers' are trained in the criteria important to customers of the establishment. They deliver objective assessments about service performance by completing questionnaires about service standards. Questionnaires contain items that represent important quality or service issues to customers.

In Europe mystery shopping is used quite extensively by organizations in financial services, retailing, motor dealerships, hotels and catering, passenger transportation, public utilities and, even, government departments. Unlike customer satisfaction surveys, the mystery shopping approach is being used to measure the process rather than the outcomes of a service encounter. The emphasis is on the service experience as it unfolds, looking at which activities and procedures do or do not happen rather than gathering opinions about the service experience. Mystery shopping studies are used for three main purposes:

- To act as a diagnostic tool, identifying failings and weak points in an organization's service delivery
- To encourage, develop and motivate service personnel by linking with appraisal, training and reward mechanisms
- To assess the competitiveness of an organization's service provision by benchmarking it against the offerings of others in an industry.

Mystery shopping aims to collect facts rather than perceptions. These facts can relate to basic enquiries, purchases and transactions covering questions such as:

- How many rings did it take before the telephone was answered?
- How long was the queue?
- What form of greeting was used?

They can also relate to more complex encounters, such as in the purchase of a mortgage where the procedures adopted in a two-hour fact-finding meeting can be assessed in terms of service quality and financial compliance.

All the areas on which mystery shoppers need to report are highly structured to minimize the impact of the shoppers' own preferences in terms of areas such as service or cleanliness. Shoppers are often shown videos or photographs of service environments or encounters to illustrate the appropriate rating for a specific type of encounter. Shoppers also receive a detailed briefing on the scenario that they are to enact, focusing on their personal characteristics, the questions they should ask and the behaviours they should adopt. They are then tested on these elements to ensure that the service encounter is realistic and to reduce the risk that service personnel might detect their true purpose as mystery shoppers.

Mystery shopping keeps workers alert because they know they may be evaluated at any time. They know they are being judged on the company's service standards and therefore carry out the standards more consistently than if they were not going to be judged. Mystery shopping can be a very effective way of reinforcing service standards.

SERVICE SPOTLIGHT

London Underground, which operates the underground public transport network in and around London, uses mystery shopping for monitoring and measuring the level and consistency of the Underground's tangible and intangible service performance.

Mystery shoppers travel around the network and follow strictly specified routes, assessing trains and stations on measures such as cleanliness and environment; lighting; maps and information; comfort factors; staff; ticket purchase; safety; and customer mobility and access. The shoppers' routes are organized in such a way that, in each quarter, a number of visits are made to each platform of the 246 London Underground stations. Each shopper is supplied with a questionnaire which includes descriptions of the rating scale to be used for each service measure, together with a short statement explaining what the measure covers. The survey is designed to allow shoppers enough time to complete the train measures between station visits.

When shoppers arrive at the nominated station, they move from the platform, along a route way, through the booking hall and then exit the building. The shoppers then retrace their steps to a designated platform and move on to the next station in the assignment, carrying out a train assessment en route. All of the areas where responses are required are highly structured to minimize the impact of the shoppers' own individual preferences in terms of areas such as service or cleanliness. Shoppers are often shown videos or photographs of service environments or encounters to illustrate the appropriate rating for each type of encounter. London Underground use the mystery shopping scores for setting targets for staff and contractors as well as for developing appropriate action plans to improve performance.[11]

CUSTOMER PANELS

Customer panels are ongoing groups of customers assembled to provide attitudes and perceptions about a service over time. They offer companies regular and timely customer information – virtually a pulse on the market. Firms can use customer panels to represent large segments of end-customers.

Customer panels are used in the entertainment industry to screen movies before they are released to the public. After a rough cut of a film has been created, the movie is viewed by a panel of consumers that matches the demographic target. In the most basic of these panels, consumers participate in post-screening interviews or focus groups in which they report on their responses to the movie. They may be asked questions as general as their reactions to the ending of the movie and as specific as whether they understood different aspects of the plot line. On the basis of these panels' results, movies are revised and edited to ensure that they are communicating the desired message and that they will succeed in the marketplace. In extreme situations, entire movie endings have been changed to be more consistent with customer attitudes. In some of the most sophisticated consumer panel research on movies (also used for television shows and commercials) consumers have digital devices in their seats through which they indicate their responses as they watch films. This instantaneous response allows the producers, directors and editors to make changes at the appropriate places in the film to ensure that the story line, characters and scenery are 'tracking'.

LOST CUSTOMER RESEARCH

This type of research involves deliberately seeking out customers who have dropped the company's service to inquire about their reasons for leaving. Some lost customer research is similar to exit interviews with employees in that it asks open-ended, in-depth questions to expose the reasons for defection and the particular events that led to dissatisfaction. It is also possible to use more standard surveys on lost customers. For example, many utility companies (e.g. Eon), mobile phone operators (e.g. Vodafone) and bank customers (e.g. BNP Paribas) contact former customers, asking them about service performance during different stages of the customer–vendor relationship. The surveys also seek specific reasons for customers' defections and ask customers to describe the problems that triggered the move.

One benefit of this type of research is that it identifies failure points and common problems in the service, and can help establish an early-warning system for future defectors. Another benefit is that the research can be used to calculate the cost of lost customers.

FUTURE EXPECTATIONS RESEARCH

Customer expectations are dynamic and can change very rapidly in markets that are highly competitive and volatile. As competition increases, as tastes change and as consumers become more knowledgeable, companies must continue to update their information and strategies. One such 'industry' is interactive video, representing the merger of computer, telecommunications and cable television. The technologies available in this industry are revolutionary. In dynamic market situations, companies want to understand not just current customer expectations but also future expectations – the service features desired in the future. Future expectations research is new and consists of different types. First, *features research* involves environmental scanning and querying of customers about desirable features of possible services. *Lead user research* brings in customers who are opinion leaders/innovators and asks them what requirements are not being met by existing products or services. Another form of this research is the *synectics approach*, which defines lead users more broadly than in standard lead user research.

The question of customer involvement in expectation studies is often debated. Designers and developers claim that consumers do not know what they might want, especially in industries or services that are new and rapidly changing. Consumers and marketing researchers, on the other hand, counter that services developed independent of customer input are likely to be targeted at needs that do not exist. To study this question, researchers assessed the contributions made by users compared with professional developers for end-user telecom services. Three groups were studied: users alone, developers alone and users with a design expert present to provide information on feasibility. Findings showed that users created more original but less producible ideas. However, inviting users to test and explore possibilities once a prototype has been created can produce positive results.[12]

ANALYSING AND INTERPRETING MARKETING RESEARCH FINDINGS

One of the biggest challenges facing a marketing researcher is converting a complex set of data to a form that can be read and understood quickly by executives, managers and other employees who will make decisions from the research. Many of the people who use marketing research findings have not been trained in statistics and have neither the time nor the expertise to analyse computer printouts and other technical research information. The goal in this stage of the marketing research process is to communicate information clearly to the right people in a timely fashion. Among considerations are the following: who gets this information? Why do they need it? How will they use it? When users feel confident that they understand the data, they are far more likely to apply it appropriately. When managers do not understand how to interpret the data, or when they lack confidence in the research, the investment of time, skill and effort will be lost.

Depicting marketing research findings graphically is a powerful way to communicate research information. Here is a sample of graphic representations of the types of marketing research data we have discussed throughout this chapter.

TRACKING OF PERFORMANCE, GAP SCORES AND COMPETITION

A simple way of tracking performance is shown in Figure 6.1. Both expectations and perceptions are plotted, and the gap between them shows the service quality shortfall. Although any attribute or dimension of service can be tracked in this way, Figure 6.1 shows the scores for service reliability. Competitor service performance is another measurement of service quality that is tracked frequently. It allows managers to have a better grasp of service improvement priorities for their firm by comparing the firm's service strengths and weaknesses against those of key competitors.[13]

Figure 6.1 **Tracking of customer expectations and perceptions of service reliability**

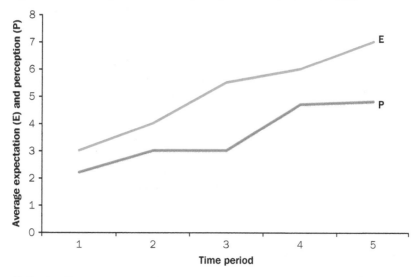

Source: Adapted from E. Sivadas, 'Europeans have a different take on CS [Customer Satisfaction] programs', *Marketing News,* 26 October 1998, p. 39.

ZONES OF TOLERANCE CHARTS

When companies collect data on the dual expectation levels described in Chapter 3 – desired service and adequate service – and performance data, they can convey the information concisely on zones of tolerance charts. Figure 6.2 plots customer service quality perceptions relative to customers' zones of tolerance. Perceptions of company performance are indicated by the circles, and the zones of tolerance boxes are bounded at the top by the desired service score and at the bottom by the adequate service score. When the perception scores are within the boxes or above, the company is delivering service that is above customers' minimum level of expectations. When the perception scores are below the boxes, the company's service performance is lower than the minimum level, and customers are dissatisfied with the company's service.[14]

Figure 6.2   Service quality perceptions relative to zones of tolerance by dimensions

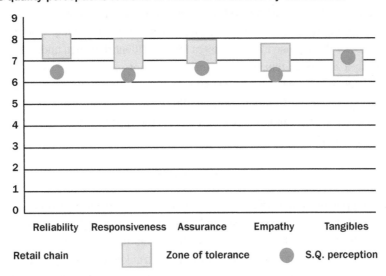

IMPORTANCE/PERFORMANCE MATRICES

One of the most useful forms of analysis in marketing research is the importance/performance matrix. This chart combines information about customer perceptions and importance ratings. An example is shown in Figure 6.3. Attribute importance is represented on the vertical axis from high (top) to low (bottom). Performance is shown on the horizontal axis from low (left) to high (right). There are many variations of these matrices: some companies define the horizontal axis as the gap between expectations and perceptions, or as performance relative to competition. The shading on the chart indicates the area of highest leverage for service quality improvements – where importance is high and performance is low. In this quadrant are the attributes that most need to be improved. In the adjacent upper quadrant are attributes to be maintained, those that a company performs well and that are very important to customers. The lower two quadrants contain attributes that are less important, some of which are performed well and others poorly. Neither of these quadrants merit as much attention in terms of service improvements as the upper quadrants because customers are not as concerned about the attributes that are plotted in them as they are the attributes in the upper quadrants.

Figure 6.3   Importance/performance matrix

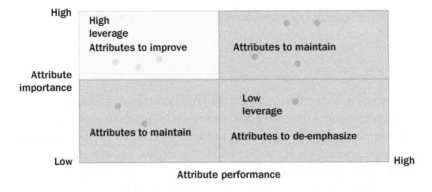

SERVICE SPOTLIGHT

Most visitors to Walt Disney theme parks, whether in France or elsewhere in the world, see magic, but the magic is based on solid research discipline. Disney conducts over 200 different external surveys a year, tracking satisfaction along with demographic profiles of its customers. The company also conducts price sensitivity analysis to determine the tolerance of guests for various levels of pricing. One recent outcome of this price sensitivity analysis was the FastPass, a premium-priced ticket to the park that allows its purchasers to avoid lines and expedite their access to rides and other attractions. The company also has guests evaluate its different attractions, noting the aspects that are pleasing or troublesome, and changing aspects to ensure that the attractions run as smoothly as possible. In addition, the company monitors tens of thousands of letters and comment cards it receives and practises 'management by walking around'. By doing so, Disney gathers critical information that enables the design of a service experience that delights its guests.[15]

USING MARKETING RESEARCH INFORMATION

Conducting research about customer expectations is only the first part of understanding the customer, even if the research is appropriately designed, executed and presented. A service firm must also use the research findings in a meaningful way – to drive change or improvement in the way service is delivered. The misuse (or even non-use) of research data can lead to a large gap in understanding customer expectations. When managers are too busy dealing with the day-to-day challenges of the business to read research reports, companies fail to use the resources available to them. And when customers participate in marketing research studies but never see changes in the way the company does business, they feel frustrated and annoyed with the company. Understanding how to make the best use of research – to apply what has been learned to the business – is a key way to close the gap between customer expectations and management perceptions of customer expectations. Managers must learn to turn research information and insights into action, to recognize that the purpose of research is to drive improvement and customer satisfaction.

The research plan should specify the mechanism by which customer data will be used. The research should be actionable, timely, specific and credible. It can also have a mechanism that allows a company to respond immediately to dissatisfied customers.

ETHICS IN MARKETING RESEARCH

Ethics in the undertaking of research is particularly important in marketing research, as the industry is dependent upon:[16]

- *Goodwill*: the goodwill of the individual respondents is their willingness to volunteer information on their awareness, attitudes and behaviours. Any practice that erodes that goodwill makes future marketing research studies more difficult to undertake.
- *Trust*: marketing decision makers trust researchers to provide accurate information that has been collected in a professional manner. Researchers also trust decision makers to divulge all information that may have an impact on the completion of a marketing research study.
- *Professionalism*: if respondents are to answer questionnaires in a serious and thoughtful manner, they have to feel that the research is going to be used in a professional manner.
- *Confidentiality*: respondents are more willing to express their views and opinions if they know that the information is going to be used in a confidential manner (in other words, taking part in marketing research will not result in the respondent becoming subject to follow-up sales calls).

The behaviour of marketing researchers is therefore controlled by the data protection laws enforced by the government of the country in which the research is being carried out and also by the relevant self-regulatory codes of conduct drawn up by the professional bodies, such as ESOMAR and the Market Research Society, that represent the marketing research industry.

MONITORING USER-GENERATED CONTENT

User-generated content is material such as personal opinions, news, ideas, photos, and video published on the Internet by users of social networks, blogs, online communities and product/service review sites using the applications of Web 2.0. In the past, customers of service organizations may have had to be asked before they gave their views, but now a significant number of customers are willing to express their views in public on a wide variety of sites relating to services, such as www.tripadvisor.com for travel and www.5pm.com for restaurants. All of these interactive sources of feedback, ideas and opinion can provide a service organization with a wealth of information about consumers and their behaviours, actions and attitudes. An organization can tune in to customer conversations to understand the perceptions of their brand and use this to align their business and marketing activity accordingly. Are airline customers talking about punctuality or lost baggage? Are hotel customers talking about location or cleanliness or customer service? Are people talking about a recent advertising campaign and, if so, what are they saying about it? The challenge for the service organization is to search through the Web-based comments, views and opinions and only analyse the material which is relevant and of value. There are many cheap automated Blog search and ranking tools, such as Meltwater Icerocket (http://blogs.icerocket.com) or technorati (www.technorati.com), as well as user-generated media tracking solutions (sometimes known as Listening platforms) developed by providers such as Cision (www.uk.cision.com/uk) and Radian6 (www.radian6.com) which simply identify all information appearing about a brand or company. However, cleaning and relevance checking is needed with user-generated content, as the automated systems struggle with inaccurate spelling, grammar and punctuation. As a result, there are also a number of public relations research agencies, such as TNS Media Intelligence, Millward Brown Precis and Nielsen's BuzzMetrics, which offer services that involve human analysts to examine the information that is collected, verify the material, determine its relevance and assess what it means.

In addition to these hands-off-type monitoring approaches, service organizations may also use their own social networking or websites to create a community that will attract user-generated content.

For example, My Starbucks Idea (www.mystarbucksidea.com) is a site run by Starbucks to generate ideas, opinions and feedback from customers. British Airways post new initiatives nad advertisements on their Facebook site to get customer reactions to them.

UPWARD COMMUNICATION

In some service firms, especially small and localized firms, owners or managers may be in constant contact with customers, thereby gaining first-hand knowledge of customer expectations and perceptions. However, in large service organizations managers do not always get the opportunity to experience at first-hand what their customers want.

The larger a company is, the more difficult it will be for managers to interact directly with the customer, and the less first-hand information they will have about customer expectations. Even when they read and digest research reports, managers can lose touch with the reality of the customer if they never get the opportunity to experience the actual service. A theoretical view of how things are supposed to work cannot provide the richness of the service encounter. To truly understand customer needs, management benefits from hands-on knowledge of what really happens in stores, on customer service telephone lines, in service queues and in face-to-face service encounters.

Table 6.2   Elements in an effective programme of upward communication

Type of interaction or research	Research objective	Qualitative/ quantitative	Cost of information		
			Money	**Time**	**Frequency**
Executive visits to customers	To gain first-hand knowledge about customers	Qualitative	Moderate	Moderate	Continuous
Executive listenings	To gain first-hand knowledge about customers	Qualitative	Low	Low	Continuous
Research on intermediate customers	To gain in-depth information on end customers	Quantitative	Moderate	Moderate	Annual
Employee internal satisfaction surveys	To improve internal service quality	Quantitative	Moderate	Moderate	Annual
Employee visits or listenings	To gain first-hand knowledge about employees	Qualitative	Moderate	Moderate	Continuous
Employee suggestions	To obtain ideas for service improvements	Qualitative	Low	Low	Continuous

OBJECTIVES FOR UPWARD COMMUNICATION

Table 6.2 shows the major research objectives for improving upward communication in an organization. These objectives include gaining first-hand knowledge about customers, improving internal service quality, gaining first-hand knowledge of employees and obtaining ideas for service improvement. These objectives can be met by two types of interactive activities in the organization: one designed to improve the type and effectiveness of communications from customers to management, and the other designed to improve communications between employees and management.

RESEARCH FOR UPWARD COMMUNICATION

EXECUTIVE OR MANAGEMENT LISTENING TO CUSTOMERS

This approach is frequently used in business-to-business services marketing. In some visits, executives of the company make sales or service calls with customer contact personnel (salespeople). In other situations, executives of the selling company arrange meetings with executives at a similar level in client companies. When Lou Gerstner became CEO of IBM in 1993 one of his first actions was to arrange a meeting with 175 of the company's biggest customers for a discussion of how IBM could better meet their needs. The meeting was viewed as a signal that the new IBM would be more responsive and focused on the customer. Alternatively, for a consumer business, senior managers can spend time in their branches or outlets talking to customers in an informal manner.

> ### ⭐ SERVICE SPOTLIGHT
>
> For over 14 years, Asda, the major UK grocery chain which is part of the Walmart Group, has been running a customer listening programme in which managers from head office and from individual stores accompany shoppers around their stores.
>
> 'It is tremendously powerful in getting your managers to think about the customer,' says Asda's head of market research. 'What better way to see the customer's perspective than to accompany them on a shopping trip?' The information collected helps in the redesign of store layouts, signage, shelving displays, lighting, shelf restocking policies and customer service practices.[17]

Given the growth in online communities and blogs where consumers post comments about products, services and organizations, it is important for an organization to monitor such communication. This will give another insight into how customers perceive an organization's offering. Travel sites, in particular, have consumer-generated reviews on hotels, airlines and visitor attractions which may influence the purchasing decisions of other customers. Self-publishing tools and enhanced/user-friendly communication technologies have made consumer-generated content increasingly popular. It is important that managers are aware of the content of such communications. Some organizations may establish their own blogging site, where they treat contributors as VIPs with exclusive previews and consultation on areas such as new products and plans and opportunities to air their views. Software providers such as Microsoft have been doing this for some time but now companies such as BT, Accenture, Thomson Holidays, Benetton and, even, local and national governments are establishing communication channels of this type.

RESEARCH ON INTERMEDIATE CUSTOMERS

Intermediate customers (such as contact employees, dealers, distributors, agents and brokers) are people the company serves and who, in turn, serve the end-customer. Researching the needs and expectations of these customers *in serving the end-customer* can be a useful and efficient way to both improve service to, and obtain information about, end-users. The interaction with intermediate customers provides opportunities for understanding end-customers' expectations and problems. It can also help the company learn about the service expectations of intermediate customers and how to satisfy those, a process critical in their providing quality service to end-customers.

RESEARCH ON INTERNAL CUSTOMERS

Employees who perform services are themselves customers of internal services on which they depend heavily to do their jobs well. There is a strong and direct link between the quality of internal service that employees receive and the quality of service they provide to their own customers. For this reason it is important to conduct employee research that focuses on the service that internal customers give and receive. In many companies this focus requires adapting existing employee opinion research to focus on service satisfaction. Employee research complements customer research when service quality is the issue being investigated. Customer research provides insight into what is occurring, whereas employee research provides insight into why. The two types of research play unique and equally important roles in improving service quality. Companies that focus service quality research exclusively on external customers are missing a rich and vital source of information.[18]

EXECUTIVE OR MANAGEMENT LISTENING APPROACHES TO EMPLOYEES

Employees who actually perform the service have the best possible vantage point for observing the service and identifying impediments to its quality. Customer contact personnel are in regular touch with customers and thereby come to understand a great deal about customer expectations and perceptions.[19] If the information they know can be passed on to top management, top managers' understanding of the customer may improve. In fact, it could be said that in many companies, top management's understanding of the customer depends largely on the extent and types of communication received from customer contact personnel and from non-company contact personnel (such as independent insurance agents and retailers) who represent the company and its services. When these channels of communication are closed, management may not get feedback about problems encountered in service delivery and about how customer expectations are changing.

Upward communication provides information to upper-level managers about activities and levels of performance throughout the organization. Specific types of communication that may be relevant are formal (such as reports of problems and exceptions in service delivery) and informal (like discussions between contact personnel and upper-level managers). Managers who stay close to their contact people benefit not only by keeping their employees happy, but also by learning more about their customers.[20] These companies encourage, appreciate and reward upward communication from contact people. Through this important channel, management learns about customer expectations from employees in regular contact with customers and can thereby reduce the size of gap 1.

EMPLOYEE SUGGESTIONS

Most companies have some form of employee suggestion programme whereby contact personnel can communicate to management their ideas for improving work. Suggestion systems have come a long way from the traditional suggestion box. Effective suggestion systems are those in which employees are empowered to see their suggestions through and are active participants in continuous improvement for their jobs, where supervisors can respond quickly to ideas and implement proposals immediately, and where coaching is provided in ways to handle suggestions.[21] In today's companies, suggestions from employees are facilitated by self-directed work teams that encourage employees to identify problems and then work to develop solutions to those problems.

SUMMARY

This chapter discussed the role of marketing research in understanding customer perceptions and expectations. It defined key forms of services research, including critical incidents studies, mystery shopping, service expectation meetings and reviews, process checkpoint evaluations and database research. Important topics in researching services – including developing research objectives and presenting data – were also described. Finally, upward communication, the ways in which management obtains and uses information from customers and customer contact personnel, was discussed. These topics combine to close gap 1 between customer expectations and company understanding of customer expectations, the first of four provider gaps in the gaps model of service quality.

KEY CONCEPTS

Big Data	111	Panels	121
Complaint solicitation	113	Post-transaction survey	118
Critical incident technique	115	Research objectives	112
Data Mining	111	Research programme	112
Disconfirmation paradigm	117	SERVPERF	117
Ethnography	119	SERVQUAL	116
Lost customer research	122	Upward communication	127
Marketing research	112	User-generated content monitoring	126
Mystery shopping	120	Zones of tolerance charts	123
Netnography	120		

EXERCISES

1 Choose a local services organization to interview about its marketing research. Find out what the firm's objectives are and the types of marketing research it currently uses. Using the information in this chapter, think about the effectiveness of its marketing research. What are its strengths and weaknesses?

2   Choose one of the services you consume. If you were in charge of creating a survey for that service, what questions would you include? Give several examples. What type of survey (relationship versus transaction based) would be most appropriate for this service? What recommendations would you give to management of the company about making such a survey actionable?

3   If you were the marketing director of your college or university, what types of research (see Table 6.1) would be essential for understanding both external and internal customers? If you could choose only three types of research, which ones would you select? Why?

4   Using the SERVQUAL scale presented in this chapter, create a questionnaire for a service firm that you use. Give the questionnaire to ten people, and describe what you learn.

5   To get an idea of the power of the critical incidents technique, try it yourself with reference to restaurant service. Think of a time when, as a customer, you had a particularly satisfying interaction with a restaurant. Follow the instructions below (they are identical to the instructions in an actual study) and observe the insights you obtain about your requirements in restaurant service:

   a   When did the incident happen?

   b   What specific circumstances led up to this situation?

   c   Exactly what did the employee (or firm) say or do?

   d   What resulted that made you feel the interaction was satisfying?

   e   What could or should have been done differently?

DISCUSSION QUESTIONS

1   Give five reasons why research objectives must be established before marketing research is conducted.

2   Why are both qualitative and quantitative research methods needed in a services marketing research programme?

3   Why does the frequency of research differ across the research methods shown in Table 6.1?

4   Compare and contrast the types of research that help a company identify common failure points. Which of the types do you think produces better information? Why?

5   Why would a company undertake a mystery shopping study when it could simply ask customers if they are satisfied?

6   What reasons can you give for companies' lack of use of research information? How might you motivate managers to use the information to a greater extent? How might you motivate front-line workers to use the information?

7   Given a specific marketing research budget, what would be your recommendations for the percentage to be spent on customer research versus upward communication? How would you justify it?

8   What kinds of information could be gleaned from research on intermediate customers? What would intermediate customers know that service providers might not?

9   For what types of products and services would monitoring user-generated content be preferable to traditional research?

10 What challenges exist when measuring comparisons between expectations and experiences?

FURTHER READING

Buttle, F. (1996). SERVQUAL: review, critique, research agenda. *European Journal of Marketing*, 30(1), 8–32.

Cooke, M. and Buckley, N. (2008). Web 2.0, Social Networks and the Future of Market Research. *International Journal of Market Research*, 50(2), 267–92.

Cronin, J. and Taylor S.A. (1992). Measuring service quality: a re-examination and extension. *Journal of Marketing*, 56(3), 55–68.

Cronin, J. and Taylor, S.A. (1994). SERVPERF versus SERVQUAL: reconciling performance-based and perceptions-minus-expectations measurement of service quality. *Journal of Marketing*, 58(1), 125–31.

Kozinets, R.V. (2009). *Netnography: Doing Ethnographic Research Online*. London: Sage.

Ladhari, R. (2009). A review of twenty years of SERVQUAL research. *International Journal of Quality and Service Sciences*, 1(2), 172–98.

Ladhari, R. (2010). Developing E-service quality scales: a literature review. *Journal of Retailing and Consumer Services*, 17(6), 464–77.

McAfee, A., Brynjolfsson, E., Davenport, T. H., Patil, D. J., and Barton, D. (2012). Big Data: The management revolution. *Harvard Business Revue*, 90(10), 61–67.

Parasuraman, A., Berry, L.L. and Zeithanl, V.A. (1991). Refinement and reassessment of the SERVQUAL scale. *Journal of Retailing*, 67(4), 420–50.

Poynter, R. (2010). *The Handbook of Online and Social Media Research: Tools and Techniques for Market Researchers*. London: Wiley.

Wilson, A. (2011). *Marketing Research: An Integrated Approach*, 3rd edn. London: FT Prentice Hall.

Wilson, A.M. (1998). The use of mystery shopping in the measurement of service delivery. *The Service Industries Journal*, 18(3), 148–63.

CHAPTER 7

Building Customer Relationships

CHAPTER OUTLINE

LEARNING OBJECTIVES

This chapter's objectives are to:

1 Explain relationship marketing, its goals, and the benefits of long-term relationships for firms and customers.
2 Explain why and how to estimate customer relationship value.
3 Introduce the concept of customer profitability segments as a strategy for focusing relationship marketing efforts.
4 Present relationship development strategies – including quality core service, switching barriers and relationship bonds.
5 Identify challenges in relationship development, including the somewhat controversial idea that 'the customer is not always right'.

OPENING EXAMPLE
Boots – Focusing on the Customer

Boots The Chemists is one of the best-known and trusted brands in the UK and is the leading health and beauty retailer in the UK, Norway, Republic of Ireland, Netherlands, Lithuania and Thailand. The company, founded in 1849, spans three centuries of successful operations. Currently it offers its products through 3,150 retail stores in 11 countries as well as an online store at www.boots.com. On its website, the Boots Company states that it is a leading international pharmacy-led health and beauty group delivering a range of products to customers.

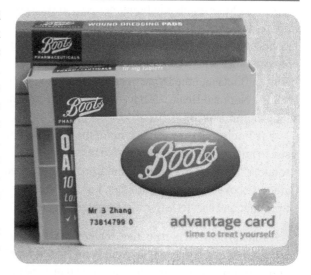

A foundation for Boots's success in recent years is its increased focus on the customer and a desire to develop customer relationships through a number of retention and loyalty strategies. At the heart of the company's loyalty strategy is its Advantage Card, started in 1997. By 31 March 2014, the number of active Boots Advantage Card members (defined as members who have used their card at least once in the last 12 months) totalled 17.8 million, reflecting the programme's well-established position as one of the largest and most valued loyalty schemes in the UK. Around 90 per cent of active members are women, representing nearly 60 per cent of the adult female population in the UK.

The aims of the Advantage card are to:

- Provide unique insights into how Boots customers shop
- Enable targeted marketing and one-to-one communication
- Drive sales through rewarding loyalty.

Members collect four points for every £1 spent in store or online. In addition, Boots periodically runs promotions offering additional points (such as 10 points per £1 or triple points). Boots Advantage Card members receive offers by mail or via email, including special promotions and invitations to special customer evenings for Christmas shopping in larger Boots stores near where they live or work. The first digital Boots Health & Beauty magazine was launched in February 2014.

The points obtained by members can be redeemed for selected products, aimed to treat customers to something special rather than simply offering discounts off purchases. In fact, the card is positioned in a way that emphasizes treating oneself rather than being about discounts. Customers can use their points to treat themselves to a simple lunch or to a full day of pampering at a spa.

Boots Advantage Card members aged over 60 can also join the 'More Treats for Over 60s' scheme, which enables them to collect 10 points per £1 spent on Boots branded products like No7 skincare, plus other benefits. The Boots Parenting Club, which as of 31 March 2014 had almost 1 million active members, is designed to support parents from the early stages of pregnancy to their baby's second birthday.

The Advantage Card uses smart chip technology, enabling customers to to spend their points in any Boots store, and enabling Boots itself to identify unique customers when they use their card at the point of purchase. In 2014, the company launched a dedicated app for use on Android and iOS devices which works with the Advantage Card, so that customers can get continuous access to their vouchers, as opposed to receiving paper vouchers quarterly through the post. The app also features a barcode scanner customers can use to get additional information on a product, including customer ratings and reviews.

Cardholders enjoy additional benefits and discounts using approximately 1,400 interactive kiosks in over 440 stores. The card can be used for purchases at the online store. The Boots website also provides access to 'Treat Street', an online shopping service through which Advantage Card holders collect points when they shop online with around 60 other well-known retailers. A joint initiative between Boots and the Department of Health makes it possible for Advantage Card holders to register with the National Health Service Organ Donor programme and to carry an Advantage Card featuring that programme's logo.

For Boots, the card is much more than a reward programme. Data generated through the card are used to understand customers and to anticipate and identify individual needs in health and beauty care products. Through the programme Boots has learned that the more broadly customers buy, in more categories over time, the more they increase visits to Boots stores. The result has been customization of product and service offerings targeted at specific customer profiles.

From a financial perspective, the company has seen increasing average transaction values among higher-spending customers as well as increased loyalty and spending from people who were already good and profitable customers. Around 60 per cent of Boots retail sales are to Boots Advantage Card members. On average they spend over 60 per cent more per transaction than non-members.

However, building customer relationships is not solely dependent on loyalty cards. It is also about customer service. Each week Boots analyses over 20,000 responses to in-store customer questionnaires to better understand customers' evolving needs. Boots customer satisfaction scores have been improving year on year as a result of an ongoing focus on key areas such as 'value for money', 'quick and easy to pay', 'staff availability and approachableness' and 'time taken to get my prescription'. Boots attributes their success to their passionate focus on customer service and care, with the customer relationship being very much at the heart of their business strategy.

Source: www.boots.com.

Boots provides a strong example of a company that has focused on keeping its customers and building long-term relationships with them. Unlike Boots, however, many companies do not have an accurate understanding of their customers because they fail to focus on customer relationships. They tend to fixate on acquiring new customers rather than viewing existing customers as assets that they need to nurture and retain. By concentrating on customer acquisition, firms can easily fall into the traps of short-term promotions, price discounts or catchy advertisements that bring customers in but are not enough to bring them back. By adopting a relationship philosophy, on the other hand, companies develop in-depth understanding of their customers and are better able to meet their changing needs and expectations.

Marketing strategies for understanding customers over time and building long-term relationships are the subjects of this chapter.

RELATIONSHIP MARKETING

There has been a shift from a transactions to a relationship focus in marketing. Customers become partners and the firm must make long-term commitments to maintaining those relationships with quality, service, and innovation.[1]

Relationship marketing essentially represents a paradigm shift within marketing – away from an acquisitions/transaction focus toward a retention/relationship focus.[2] Relationship marketing (or relationship management) is a philosophy of doing business, a strategic orientation, that focuses on *keeping and improving* relationships with current customers rather than on acquiring new customers. This philosophy assumes that many consumers and business customers prefer to have an ongoing relationship with one organization than to switch continually among providers in their search for value. Building on this assumption, and the fact that it is usually much cheaper to keep a current customer than to attract a new one, successful marketers work on effective strategies for retaining customers. Our opening example showed how Boots has built its business around a relationship philosophy.

It has been suggested that firms frequently focus on attracting customers (the 'first act') but then pay little attention to what they should do to keep them (the 'second act').[3] Ideas expressed in an interview with James L. Schorr, then executive vice president of marketing at Holiday Inns, illustrate this point.[4] Schorr stated that he was famous at Holiday Inns for what is called the 'bucket theory of marketing'. By this he meant that marketing can be thought of as a big bucket: it is what the sales, advertising and promotion programmes do that pours business into the top of the bucket. As long as these programmes are effective, the bucket stays full. However, 'There's only one problem,' he said, 'there's a hole in the bucket.' When the business is running well and the hotel is delivering on its promises, the hole is small and few customers are leaving. When the operation is weak and customers are not satisfied with what they get, however, they start falling out through the holes in the bucket faster than they can replaced by new customers.

The bucket theory (see Figure 7.1) illustrates why a relationship approach that focuses on plugging the holes in the bucket makes so much sense. Historically, marketers have been more concerned with acquisition of customers, so a shift to a relationship approach often represents changes in mindset, organizational culture and employee reward systems. For example, the sales incentive systems in many organizations are set up to reward bringing in new customers. Often, there are fewer (or no) rewards for retaining current accounts. Thus, even when people see the logic of customer retention, the existing organizational systems may not support its implementation.

Figure 7.1   There is a hole in the bucket: why relationship development makes sense

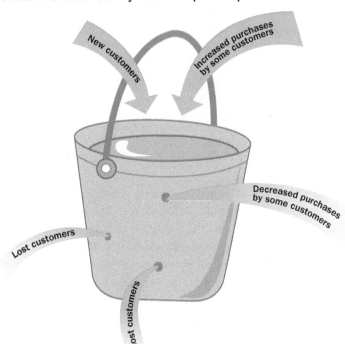

THE EVOLUTION OF CUSTOMER RELATIONSHIPS

Firms' relationships with their customers, like other social relationships, tend to evolve over time. Scholars have suggested that marketing exchange relationships between providers and customers often have the potential to evolve from strangers to acquaintances to friends to partners.[5]

CUSTOMERS AS STRANGERS

Strangers are those customers who are not aware of, or those who have not yet had any transactions (interactions) with, a firm. At the industry level, strangers may be thought of as customers who have not yet entered the market; at the firm level, they may include customers of competitors. Clearly the firm has no relationship with them at this point. Consequently, the firm's primary goal with these strangers (potential customers) is to initiate communication with them in order to *attract* and *acquire* their business. Thus, the primary marketing efforts directed towards such customers deal with familiarizing them with the firm's offerings and, subsequently, encouraging them to give the firm a try.

CUSTOMERS AS ACQUAINTANCES

Once customer awareness and trial are achieved, familiarity is established and the customer and the firm become acquaintances, creating the basis for an exchange relationship. A primary goal for the firm at this stage of the relationship is *satisfying* the customer. In the acquaintance stage, firms are generally concerned about providing a value proposition to customers that is comparable with that of competitors. For a customer, an acquaintanceship is effective as long as the customer is relatively satisfied and what is being received in the exchange is perceived as fair value. With repeat interactions, the customer becomes more familiar with the firm's product offerings. These encounters can help reduce uncertainty about the benefits expected in the exchange and, therefore, increase the attractiveness of the company relative to the competition. Repeat interactions improve the firm's knowledge of the customer, helping to facilitate marketing, sales and service efforts. Thus, an acquaintance relationship facilitates transactions primarily through the reduction of the customer's perceived risk and the provider's costs.

In acquaintance relationships, firms generally focus on providing value comparable to the competition, often through the repetitive provision of standardized offerings. As a result, the potential to develop a sustainable competitive advantage through relationship activities is limited. However, firms that already have acquaintance relationships with their customers can create value for them by learning from all their transactions. For example, Amazon has created value for its acquaintances through a highly developed order-processing system. By processing and organizing historical transaction data from a customer and comparing it with data from other customers demonstrating similar purchase behaviours, the system is able to identify additional products of potential interest to the acquaintance customer and to generate cross-selling opportunities.

CUSTOMERS AS FRIENDS

As a customer continues to make purchases from a firm and to receive value in the exchange relationship, the firm begins to acquire specific knowledge of that customer's needs, allowing it to create an offering that directly addresses the customer's situation. The provision of a unique offering (a differential value) transforms the exchange relationship from acquaintance to friendship. This transition requires the development of trust, particularly in service exchange relationships.[6] As discussed in Chapter 2, customers may not be able to assess a service outcome prior to purchase and consumption, and in the case of services high in credence qualities, customers may not be able to discern service performance even after experiencing it. Therefore, customers must trust the provider to deliver what is promised. As customers become friends, they not only become familiar with the company but they also come to trust that it provides superior value.

A primary goal for firms at the friendship stage of the relationship is customer *retention*. Given their likelihood of past satisfying experiences and repeated purchases, these customers ('friends') are more likely to appreciate the firm's product offerings and are, perhaps, more open to other related services. A firm's potential to develop sustainable competitive advantage through friends should be higher than for acquaintances because the offering is more unique (and more difficult for competition to imitate) and the customer comes to trust that uniqueness.[7]

CUSTOMERS AS PARTNERS

As a customer continues to interact with a firm, the level of trust often deepens and the customer may receive more customized product offerings and interactions. The trust developed in the friendship stage is a necessary but not sufficient condition for a customer–firm partnership to develop.[8] That is, the creation of trust leads to (ideally) the creation of commitment – and that is the condition necessary for customers to extend the time perspective of a relationship.[9] The deepening of trust and the establishment of commitment reduce the customer's need to solve problems in the traditional sense of 'finding a better alternative'. Thus, in order to move the relationship into a partner relationship, a firm must use customer knowledge and information systems to deliver highly personalized and customized offerings.

The key to success in the partnership stage is the firm's ability to organize and use information about individual customers more effectively than competitors. Customers benefit from, and therefore desire to commit to, relationships with firms whose knowledge of their needs translates into the delivery of highly personalized and customized offerings.[10] Over time, the customer–firm relationship may evolve through continuous adaptation and commitment, and the parties may become increasingly interdependent. At this point the relationship has advanced from having the purpose of merely meeting the customer's needs to a situation in which both parties sense a deep appreciation of each other. However, in order to continue to receive such benefits, customers generally must be willing to pay a price premium or to commit themselves to the firm for an extended period of time.

SERVICE SPOTLIGHT

The American Express Centurion Card is an example of an exclusive and expensive partnership, Nicknamed the 'Black Card' because of its distinctive colour obtained from the anodized titanium used to make it, The Amex Centurion is unlike most credit cards, for which anyone can apply. To get a Centurion card, you must be invited. Centurion cardholders earn Membership Rewards points, and enjoy exclusive benefits, including concierge-style perks like guaranteed tables at three-star restaurants, priority bookings at luxury hotels, invitations to private cultural events, personal shoppers at major retailers, access to private jets and the unique status of having a metal card.

The concierge service is able to arrange just about any service or perk for Amex Centurion cardholders. The Amex Centurion, available for personal or business accounts, is a charge card with no interest rate, no pre-set spending limit, and no foreign transaction fees. It requires a one-time initiation fee of around 4,000 euros and a 2,000 euro annual fee. In order to maintain Centurion membership, a cardholder is expected to make and pay off around 200,000 euros-worth of purchases a year.

At the partnership stage the firm is concerned with *enhancing* the relationship. Customers are more likely to stay in the relationship if they feel that the company understands their changing needs and is willing to invest in the relationship by constantly improving and evolving its product and service mix. By enhancing these relationships, the firm expects that customers will be less likely to be lured away by competitors and more likely to buy additional products and services from the company over time. These loyal customers not only provide a solid base for the organization, they may represent growth potential. For example, a bank current account customer becomes a better customer when he or she sets up a savings account, takes out a loan and/or uses the financial advisory services of the bank; likewise, a corporate account becomes a better customer when it chooses to do 75 per cent of its business with a particular supplier rather than splitting the business equally among three suppliers. In recent years, in fact, many companies have aspired to be the 'exclusive supplier' of a particular product or service for their customers. Over time these enhanced relationships can increase market share and profits for the organization.

However, it is important to note that not all customers may be interested in forming relationships with their suppliers or service providers. Depending on the product or service, the level of interest from some customers may vary from a situation where some only want to transact the business, and others want the service provider to have ongoing knowledge of their changing requirements. Grönroos divided customer expectations into three types:[11]

1 *Transactional expectations* – where the customer is looking for solutions to their needs at an acceptable price, and they do not appreciate contacts from the supplier or service provider in between purchases.
2 *Active relational expectations* – where the customer is looking for opportunities to interact with the supplier or service provider in order to get additional value. A lack of contact leaves them disappointed because the value inherent in the relationship is missing.
3 *Passive relational expectations* – where customers are looking for the knowledge that they could contact the service provider if they wanted to. In this sense, they are also seeking contact, but they seldom respond to invitations to interact.

It is important for a service provider to be aware of the relationship expectations of their customers if the most appropriate relationship management strategy is to be adopted.

THE GOAL OF RELATIONSHIP MARKETING

The discussion of the evolution of customer relationships demonstrates how a firm's relationship with its customers might be enhanced as customers move further along this relationship continuum. As the relationship value of a customer increases, the provider is more likely to pursue a closer relationship. Thus, the primary goal of relationship marketing is *to build and maintain a base of committed customers who are profitable for the organization.* From a customer's problem-solving perspective, the formation of satisfaction, trust and commitment corresponds to the customer's willingness to engage in an exchange relationship as an acquaintance, friend and partner, respectively. From a firm's resource-allocation perspective, the delivery of differential, and perhaps customized, value corresponds to the extent of its ability and/or desire to create an acquaintance, friend or partner relationship with the customer. As customers make the transition from satisfaction-based acquaintanceships to trust-based friendships to commitment-based partnerships, increases are required in both the value received and the level of cooperation.

BENEFITS FOR CUSTOMERS AND FIRMS

Both parties in the customer–firm relationship can benefit from customer retention. That is, it is not only in the best interest of the organization to build and maintain a loyal customer base, but customers themselves also benefit from long-term associations.

BENEFITS FOR CUSTOMERS

Assuming they have a choice, customers will remain loyal to a firm when they receive greater value relative to what they expect from competing firms. *Value* represents a trade-off for the consumer between the 'give' and the 'get' components. Consumers are more likely to stay in a relationship when the gets (quality, satisfaction, specific benefits) exceed the gives (monetary and non-monetary costs). When firms can consistently deliver value from the customer's point of view, clearly the customer benefits and has an incentive to stay in the relationship.

Beyond the specific inherent benefits of receiving service value, customers also benefit in other ways from long-term associations with firms. Sometimes these relationship benefits keep customers loyal to a firm more than the attributes of the core service. Research has uncovered specific types of relational benefits that customers experience in long-term service relationships, including confidence benefits, social benefits and special treatment benefits.[12]

CONFIDENCE BENEFITS

Confidence benefits comprise feelings of trust or confidence in the provider, along with a sense of reduced anxiety and comfort in knowing what to expect. Across all the services studied in the research just cited, confidence benefits were the most important to customers.

Human nature is such that most consumers would prefer not to change service providers, particularly when they are considerably invested in the relationship. The costs of switching are frequently high in terms of the monetary costs of transferring business and the associated psychological and time-related costs. Most consumers (whether individuals or businesses) face many competing demands on their time and money, and are continually searching for ways to balance and simplify decision-making to improve the quality of their lives. When they can maintain a relationship with a service provider, it frees up time for other concerns and priorities.

SOCIAL BENEFITS

Over time, customers develop a sense of familiarity and, even, a social relationship with their service providers. These ties make it less likely that they will switch, even if they learn about a competitor that might have better quality or a lower price. This customer's description of her hair stylist illustrates the concept of social benefits: 'I like him … He's really funny and always has lots of good jokes. He's kind of like a friend now… It's more fun to deal with somebody that you're used to. You enjoy doing business with them.'

In some long-term customer–firm relationships, a service provider may actually become part of the consumer's social support system.[13] Hairdressers, as in the example just cited, often serve as personal confidants. Less common examples include proprietors of local retail stores who become central figures in local communities; the health club or restaurant manager who knows his or her customers personally; the pharmacist who knows an entire family and its special needs; or the tour guide who befriends passengers on a long coach tour.[14]

These types of personal relationships can develop for business-to-business customers as well as for end consumers of services. The social support benefits resulting from these relationships are important to the consumer's quality of life (personal and/or work life) above and beyond the technical benefits of the service provided. Many times the close personal and professional relationships that develop between service providers and clients are the basis for the customer's loyalty. The flip side of this customer benefit is the risk to the firm of losing customers when a valued employee leaves and takes customers with him or her.[15]

SPECIAL TREATMENT BENEFITS

Special treatment includes getting the benefit of the doubt, being given a special deal or price, or getting preferential treatment, as exemplified by the following quote from the research:

> *You should get the benefit of the doubt in many situations. For example, I always pay my VISA bill on time, before a service charge is assessed. One time my payment didn't quite arrive on time. When I called them, by looking at my past history, they realized that I always make an early payment. Therefore, they waived the service charge.*

Interestingly, the research showed that special treatment benefits, while important, were deemed less important than the other types of benefits received in service relationships. Although special treatment benefits can clearly be critical for customer loyalty in some industries (think of frequent-flyer benefits in the airline industry), they seem to be less important to customers overall.

BENEFITS FOR FIRMS

The benefits to organizations of maintaining and developing a loyal customer base are numerous. In addition to the economic benefits that a firm receives from cultivating close relationships with its customers, a variety of customer behaviour benefits and human resource management benefits are also often received.

ECONOMIC BENEFITS

One of the most commonly cited economic benefits of customer retention is increased purchases over time, as illustrated in Figure 7.2. The figure summarizes results of studies showing that across industries customers generally spent more each year with a particular relationship partner than they did in the preceding period.[16] As customers get to know a firm and are satisfied with the quality of its services relative to that of its competitors, they tend to give more of their business to the firm.

Another economic benefit is lower costs. Some estimates suggest that repeat purchases by established customers require as much as 90 per cent less marketing expenditure.[17] Many start-up costs are associated with attracting new customers, including advertising and other promotion costs, the operating costs of setting up new accounts and time costs of getting to know the customers. Sometimes these initial costs can outweigh the revenue expected from the new customers in the short term, so it is to the firm's advantage to cultivate long-term relationships. Even ongoing relationship maintenance costs are likely to drop over time. For example, early in a relationship a customer is likely to have questions and encounter problems as he or she learns to use the service; an experienced customer will likely have fewer problems and questions, and the firm will incur fewer costs in serving the latter. In Chapter 18 we provide more specifics on the financial impact of customer retention.

CUSTOMER BEHAVIOUR BENEFITS

The contribution that loyal customers make to a service business can go well beyond their direct financial impact on the firm.[18] The first, and maybe the most easily recognized, customer behaviour benefit that a firm receives from long-term customers is the free advertising provided through word-of-mouth communication. When a complex product is difficult to evaluate and – as is the case with many services – when risk is involved in the decision to buy it, consumers often look to others for advice on which providers to consider. Satisfied, loyal customers are likely to provide strong word-of-mouth endorsements. Such endorsements may also take the form of online reviews or blogs. This form of communication can be more effective than any paid advertising that the firm might use, and it has the added benefit of reducing the costs of attracting new customers. Indeed, loyal customers often talk a great deal about a company and may be responsible for generating much new business over the years.

Figure 7.2   **Profit (in euros) generated by a customer over time**

	Year				
	1	2	3	4	5
Credit card	23	32	33	37	41
Industrial laundry	108	125	144	167	192
Industrial distribution	34	74	91	108	126
Car servicing	19	26	53	66	66

In addition to word-of-mouth communication, a second consumer behaviour benefit is one that is sometimes labelled customer voluntary performance.[19] In a restaurant, such behaviour might include customers clearing their own tables, reporting messy washrooms to an employee or picking up litter in the car park. Such behaviours support the firm's ability to deliver quality services. Although customer voluntary performance could be engaged in by anyone, those customers who have a long-term relationship with the firm are perhaps more likely to do so because they may want to see the provider do well. Third, for some services loyal customers may provide social benefits to other customers in the form of friendships or encouragement. At a health club, for example, a new member is likely to think more highly of the club when fellow members provide encouragement and guidance during fitness sessions and classes. Finally, loyal customers may serve as mentors and, because of their experience with the provider, help other customers understand the explicitly or implicitly stated rules of conduct.[20]

HUMAN RESOURCE MANAGEMENT BENEFITS

Loyal customers may also provide a firm with human resource management benefits. First, loyal customers may, because of their experience with and knowledge of the provider, be able to contribute to the co-production of the service by assisting in service delivery; often the more experienced customers can make the service employees' job easier. For example, a regular patient of a medical clinic is likely to know how the system works; she would know to bring her medication with her on a visit, and to schedule an annual mammogram without waiting for her doctor to prompt her. A second benefit relates to one of the benefits for customers that we have already discussed. We noted that loyal customers receive social benefits as a result of being in a relationship with a firm; employees who regularly interact with the same customers may also receive similar social benefits.[21] A third benefit of customer retention is employee retention. It is easier for a firm to retain employees when it has a stable base of satisfied customers. People like to work for companies whose customers are happy and loyal. Their jobs are more satisfying, and they are able to spend more of their time fostering relationships than scrambling for new customers. In turn, customers are more satisfied and become even better customers – a positive upward spiral. When employees stay with the firm longer, service quality improves and costs of turnover are reduced, adding further to profits.

RELATIONSHIP VALUE OF CUSTOMERS

Relationship value of a customer is a concept or calculation that looks at customers from the point of view of their lifetime revenue and/or profitability contributions to a company. This type of calculation is obviously needed when companies start thinking of building long-term relationships with their customers. Just what is the potential financial value of those long-term relationships? And what are the financial implications of *losing* a customer? Here we will first summarize the factors that influence a customer's relationship value, and then show some ways it can be estimated. In Chapter 18 we provide more detail on lifetime value financial calculations.

FACTORS THAT INFLUENCE RELATIONSHIP VALUE

The lifetime or relationship value of a customer is influenced by the length of an average 'lifetime', the average revenues generated per relevant time period over that lifetime, sales of additional products and services over time, referrals generated by the customer over time, and costs associated with serving the customer. *Lifetime value* sometimes refers to lifetime revenue stream only, but when costs are considered, lifetime value truly means 'lifetime profitability'.

ESTIMATING CUSTOMER LIFETIME VALUE

If companies knew how much it really costs to lose a customer, they would be able accurately to evaluate investments designed to retain customers. One way of documenting the value of loyal customers is to estimate the increased value or profits that accrue for each additional customer who remains loyal to the company rather than defecting to the competition. This is what Bain & Co. has done for a number of industries, as shown in Figure 7.3.[22] The figure shows the percentage of increase in total firm profits when the retention or loyalty rate rises by 5 percentage points. The increases are dramatic, ranging from 35 to 95 per cent. These increases were calculated by comparing the net present values of the profit streams for the average customer life at current retention rates with the net present values of the profit streams for the average customer life at 5 per cent higher retention rates.

Figure 7.3   Profit impact of 5 per cent increase in retention rate

Advertising agency	96%
Bank branch deposits	85%
Publishing	85%
Car/home insurance	84%
Car service	81%
Credit cards	75%
Industrial distribution	45%
Software	35%

Source: Adapted from F.F. Reichheld, 'Loyalty and the renaissance of marketing', *Marketing Management*, vol. 2, no. 4 (1994), p. 15.

With sophisticated accounting systems to document actual costs and revenue streams over time, a firm can be quite precise in documenting the value and costs of retaining customers. These systems attempt to estimate the value of *all* the benefits and costs associated with a loyal customer, not just the long-term revenue stream. The value of word-of-mouth advertising, employee retention and declining account maintenance costs can also enter into the calculation.[23]

LINKING CUSTOMER RELATIONSHIP VALUE TO FIRM VALUE

The emphasis on estimating the relationship value of customers has increased substantially in the past decade. Part of this emphasis has resulted from an increased appreciation of the economic benefits that firms accrue with the retention of loyal customers. Interestingly, recent research suggests that customer retention has a large impact on firm value and that relationship value calculations can also provide a useful proxy for assessing the value of a firm.[24] That is, a firm's market value can be roughly determined by carefully calculating customer lifetime value. The approach is straightforward: estimate the relationship value of a customer, forecast the future growth of the number of customers and use these figures to determine the value of a company's current and future base. To the extent that the customer base forms a large part of a company's overall value, such a calculation can provide an estimate of a firm's value – a particularly useful figure for young, high-growth firms for which traditional financial methods (e.g. discounted cash flow) do not work well.

CUSTOMER PROFITABILITY SEGMENTS

Companies may want to treat all customers with excellent service, but they generally find that customers differ in their relationship value and that it may be neither practical nor profitable to meet (and certainly not to exceed) *all* customers' expectations.[25]

Traditional segmentation approaches using demographics or lifestyles are showing their limitations as individual behaviour becomes more hybridized, as in the case of an individual being ready to spend large amounts on certain services whilst at the same time being very frugal on other services. An example of this would be spending thousands of euros in a destination at a luxury hotel or spa but flying easyJet to travel to the destination and eating Subway sandwiches at the hotel. For the marketer, it may be that they are addressing one consumer, but two segments, exhibiting opposite characteristics. The individual may be price-conscious and frugal in the morning but indulgent and free-spending in the afternoon. Understanding and tracking behaviour becomes very important, as is the need to look after loyal and valuable customers.

SERVICE SPOTLIGHT

Virgin Airlines' Flying Club rewards customers according to their value to the airline. It inducts members at the Club Red tier, then moves them up through Club Silver and Club Gold. Club Red members earn frequent flyer miles and get discounts on rental cars and hotels. Club Silver members earn 50 per cent more points on flights, expedited check-in, and priority stand-by seating. Club Gold members get double miles, priority boarding, and access to exclusive clubhouses where they can grab a drink or get a massage before their flight. It is important to offer a benefit scheme; Club Red tier benefits aim to hook the customer into coming back. Once they do, they realize that making it to the next tier, 'silver' or 'gold' isn't unattainable, and they may keep flying with Virgin.

As the Boots example at the start of this chapter illustrates, companies do try to identify segments – or, more appropriately, tiers of customers – that differ in current and/or future profitability to a firm. This approach goes beyond usage or volume segmentation because it tracks costs and revenues for segments of customers, thereby capturing their financial worth to companies. The hotel guest who eats and drinks on the premises is more valuable than the guest who rents a room but goes outside the hotel to eat and drink. After identifying profitability bands, the firm offers services and service levels in line with the identified segments. Building a high-loyalty customer base of the right customers increases profits.

PROFITABILITY TIERS – THE CUSTOMER PYRAMID

Virtually all firms are aware at some level that their customers differ in profitability, and in particular, that a minority of their customers account for the highest proportion of sales or profit. This finding has often been called the '80/20 rule' – 20 per cent of customers produce 80 per cent of sales or profit.

In this version of tiering, 20 per cent of the customers constitute the top tier, those who can be identified as the most profitable in the company. The rest are indistinguishable from each other but differ from the top tier in profitability. Most companies realize that there are differences among customers within this tier but do not possess the data or capabilities to analyse the distinctions. The 80/20 two-tier scheme assumes that consumers within the two tiers are similar, just as conventional market segmentation schemes typically assume that consumers within segments are similar.

However, it is likely that more than two tiers exist, and provided a company has sufficient data to segment customer tiers more precisely, they can be analysed. Different systems and labels can be helpful. One useful four-tier system, shown in Figure 7.4, includes the following:

1 The *platinum tier* describes the company's most profitable customers, typically those who are heavy users of the product, are not overly price sensitive, are willing to invest in and try new offerings, and are committed customers of the firm.

2 The *gold tier* differs from the platinum tier in that profitability levels are not as high, perhaps because the customers want price discounts that limit margins or they are not as loyal. They may be heavy users who minimize risk by working with multiple vendors rather than just the focal company.

3 The *iron tier* contains essential customers who provide the volume needed to utilize the firm's capacity, but their spending levels, loyalty and profitability are not substantial enough for special treatment.

4 The *lead tier* consists of customers who are costing the company money. They demand more attention than they are due given their spending and profitability, and are sometimes problem customers – complaining about the firm to others and tying up the firm's resources.

Figure 7.4 The customer pyramid

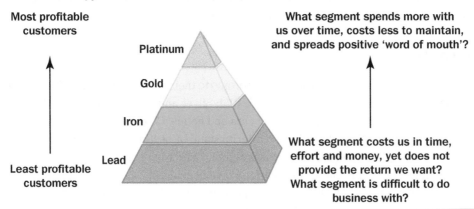

Note that this classification is superficially reminiscent of, but very different from, traditional usage segmentation performed by airlines such as British Airways. Two differences are obvious. First, in the customer pyramid profitability rather than usage defines all levels. Second, the lower levels actually articulate classes of customers who require a different sort of attention. The firm must work either to change the customers' behaviour – to make them more profitable through increases in revenue – or to change the firm's cost structure to make them more profitable through decreases in costs.

Once a system has been established for categorizing customers, the multiple levels can be identified, motivated, served and expected to deliver differential levels of profit. Companies improve their opportunities for profit when they increase shares of purchases by customers who either have the greatest need for the services or show the greatest loyalty to a single provider. By strengthening relationships with the loyal customers, increasing sales with existing customers and increasing the profitability on each sale opportunity, companies increase the potential of each customer.

THE CUSTOMER'S VIEW OF PROFITABILITY TIERS

Whereas profitability tiers make sense from the company's point of view, customers are not always understanding, nor do they appreciate being categorized into a less desirable segment.[26] For example, at some companies the top clients have their own individual account representative whom they can contact personally. The next tier of clients may be handled by representatives who each have 100 clients. Meanwhile, most clients are served by a call centre, an automated voice response system or referral to a website. Customers are aware of this unequal treatment, and many resist and resent it. It makes perfect sense from a business perspective, but customers are often disappointed in the level of service they receive and give firms poor marks for quality as a result.

Therefore, it is increasingly important that firms communicate with customers so they understand what level of service they can expect and what they would need to do or pay to receive faster or more personalized service. The most significant issues result when customers do not understand this and believe they have been singled out for poor service, or feel that the system is unfair. Although many customers refuse to pay for quality service, they react negatively if they believe it has been taken away from them unfairly.

The ability to segment customers narrowly, based on profitability implications, also raises questions of privacy for customers. In order to know who is profitable and who is not, companies must collect large amounts of individualized behavioural and personal data on consumers. Many consumers today resent what they perceive as an intrusion into their lives in this way, especially when it results in differential treatment that they perceive is unfair.

MAKING BUSINESS DECISIONS USING PROFITABILITY TIERS

Prudent business managers are well aware that past customer purchasing behaviour, although useful in making predictions, can be misleading.[27] What a customer spends today, or has spent in the past, may not necessarily reflect what he or she will do (or be worth) in the future. Banks serving students know this well – a typical student generally has minimal financial services needs (i.e. a current account) and tends not to have a high level of deposits. However, within a few years that student may embark on a professional career, start a family and/or purchase a house, and thus require several financial services and become a potentially very profitable customer. Generally, a firm would like to keep its consistent big spenders and lose the erratic small spenders. But all too often a firm also has two other groups they must consider: erratic big spenders and consistent small spenders. So, in some situations where consistent cash flow is a concern, it may be helpful to a firm to have a portfolio of customers that includes steady customers, even if they have a history of being less profitable. Some service providers have actually been quite successful in targeting customers who were previously considered to be unworthy of another firm's marketing efforts.[28] Firms, therefore, need to be cautious in blindly applying customer value calculations without thinking carefully about the implications.

SERVICE SPOTLIGHT

Endsleigh Insurance have targeted customers who were previously considered to be unworthy of other insurance companies. They have become very successful in selling insurance to students and young people, a group that most of the competition did not feel had a sufficient relationship value. Their sales message to students emphasizes the following attributes (in their own words):

Recognized – We are the only insurance provider endorsed by the National Union of Students.

Trusted – We insure more student rooms in the UK than anyone else.

Proven track record – Endsleigh have been the market leaders in student insurance for over four decades.

For students – We operate a network of campus branches throughout the UK.

In tune with student lifestyles – You do not need locks on your door and we even cover you if there is no sign of break-in. Your parents' home insurance may not cover this and over a third of our claims are paid on this basis.

Not just a student insurer – We not only cover more students than anyone else but we have special policies for when you graduate.

Source: **www.endsleigh.co.uk.**

RELATIONSHIP DEVELOPMENT STRATEGIES

To this point in the chapter we have focused on the rationale for relationship marketing, the benefits (to both firms and customers) of the development of strong exchange relationships, and an understanding of the relationship value of a customer. In this section we examine a variety of factors that influence the development of strong customer relationships, including the customer's overall evaluation of a firm's offering, bonds created with customers by the firm, and barriers that the customer faces in leaving a relationship. These factors, illustrated in Figure 7.5, provide the rationale for specific strategies that firms often use to keep their current customers.

Figure 7.5   Relationship development model

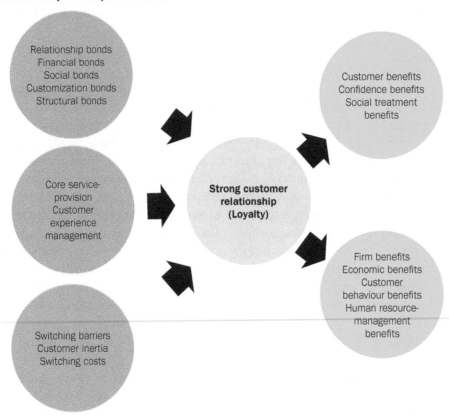

Source: Adapted from D.D. Gremler and S.W. Brown, 'Service loyalty: antecedents, components, and outcomes', in *1998 AMA Winter Educators' Conference: Marketing Theory and Applications*, vol. 9, D. Grewal and C. Pechmann, eds. Chicago, IL: American Marketing Association, pp. 165–6.

CORE SERVICE PROVISION

CUSTOMER EXPERIENCE MANAGEMENT

Clearly, a firm needs to begin the relationship development process by providing a good core service delivery that, at a minimum, meets customer expectations; it does no good to design relationship strategies for inferior services. Managing the customer experience during the service encounter, including the interactions with the organization, its facilities and interactions with the service firm's representatives and other customers is therefore critically important. A company needs to know what is important to customers at each stage of the process and at each 'touchpoint' they experience.[29] This involves identifying the key criteria and putting in place measurement tools to assess whether these criteria are being delivered. There is a need to look at the organization from the viewpoint of the customer, and not at the customer from the viewpoint of the organization. To be effective customer experience management needs to involve the whole organization and not be seen as the responsibility of a customer service department. It is only effective when it is seen as a priority of senior management and when an organization's work processes, systems and structure change to best serve the customer. In seeking consistency of service across all touchpoints, it is necessary to understand the journey that the customer goes through when doing business with the organization and determine where things go very well and where goodwill is destroyed. Developing this understanding makes it possible to create a better customer journey and, as a result, an improved customer experience. Implementing customer experience management is an ongoing and continuous process of listening to customers with the voice of the customer being captured at every opportunity through surveys, focus groups and user panels. This insight is then used to continually enhance the delivery of the service in every 'touchpoint'. Retention strategies will have little long-term success unless the firm has a solid base of service quality and customer experience management on which to build. The firm does not necessarily have to be the very best among its competitors or be world-class in terms of quality and customer satisfaction. It must be competitive, however, and frequently better than that. All the retention strategies that we describe in this section are built on the assumption of competitive quality and value being offered. The earlier example of Boots provides convincing support for the argument that excellence in the core service or product offered is essential to a successful relationship approach. Boots has benefited tremendously from its loyal customer base; it offers excellent quality and uses relationship strategies to enhance its success.

SWITCHING BARRIERS

When considering a switch in service providers, a customer may face a number of barriers that make it difficult to leave one service provider and begin a relationship with another. Literature suggests that switching barriers influence consumers' decisions to exit from relationships with firms and, therefore, facilitate customer retention.[30]

CUSTOMER INERTIA

One reason that customers commit to developing relationships with firms is that a certain amount of effort may be required to change firms. Sometimes consumers simplistically state that 'it's just not worth it' to switch providers. Inertia may even explain why some dissatisfied customers stay with a provider. In discussing why people remain in relationships (in general) that they no longer find satisfying, scholars suggest that people may stay because breaking the relationship would require them to restructure their life – to develop new habits of living, to refashion old friendships and to find new ones.[31] In other words, people do not like to change their behaviour.

To retain customers, firms might consider increasing the perceived effort required on the part of the customer to switch service providers. If a customer believes that a great deal of effort is needed to change companies, he or she is more likely to stay put. For example, car repair facilities might keep a complete and detailed maintenance history of a customer's vehicle. These records remove from the customer the burden of having to remember all the services performed on the vehicle and would force the customer to expend considerable effort in providing a complete maintenance history if the vehicle is taken to a new mechanic. Conversely, if a firm is looking to attract a competitor's customers, it might automate the process for switching providers as much as possible in order to reduce the effort required to switch. Utility companies supplying electricity and gas generally make switching providers as simple as saying 'yes' on the Internet or to a company representative – thereby removing any action required of the customer.

SWITCHING COSTS

In many instances, customers develop loyalty to an organization in part because of costs involved in changing to and purchasing from a different firm. These monetary and non-monetary costs, both real and perceived, are termed *switching costs*. Switching costs include investments of time, money or effort – such as set-up costs, search costs, learning costs and contractual costs – that make it challenging for the customer to move to another provider.[32] To illustrate: a patient may *incur set-up costs* such as paying for new X-rays when switching dentists or paying for a property survey when changing mortgage/housing loan provider. Because services often have characteristics that make them difficult to evaluate – including intangibility, non-standardization, inseparability of production and consumption, as well as high experience and credence qualities – high *search costs* may be required to obtain suitable information about alternative services. *Learning costs* are those costs associated with learning the idiosyncrasies of how to use a product or service; in many situations a customer who wishes to switch firms may need to accumulate new user skills or customer know-how. *Contractual costs* arise when the customer is required to pay a penalty to switch providers (e.g. penalty charges for customer-initiated switching of mortgage companies or mobile phone services), making it financially difficult, if not impossible, for the customer to initiate an early termination of the relationship.

In order to retain customers, firms might consider increasing their switching costs to make it difficult for customers to exit the relationship (or at least create the perception of difficulty). Indeed, many firms explicitly specify such costs in the contracts that they require their customers to sign (e.g. mobile phone services, health clubs). In order to attract new customers, a service provider might consider implementing strategies designed to *lower* the switching costs of customers not currently using the provider. To reduce the set-up costs involved when switching, providers could complete the paperwork required from the customer. Banks, for example, could offer to do all the paperwork to set up a current account, including direct debits and standing orders.

RELATIONSHIP BONDS

Switching barriers tend to serve as constraints that keep customers in relationships with firms because they 'have to'.[33] However, firms can engage in activities that encourage customers to remain in the relationship bond because they 'want to'. Leonard Berry and A. Parasuraman have developed a framework for understanding the types of retention strategies that focus on developing bonds with customers.[34] The framework suggests that relationship marketing can occur at different levels and that each successive level of strategy results in ties that bind the customer a little closer to the firm. At each successive level, the potential for sustained competitive advantage is also increased. Building on the levels of the retention strategy idea, Figure 7.6 illustrates four types of retention strategies, which are discussed in the following sections. Recall, however, that the most successful retention strategies will be built on foundations of core service excellence.

Figure 7.6   Levels of relationship strategies

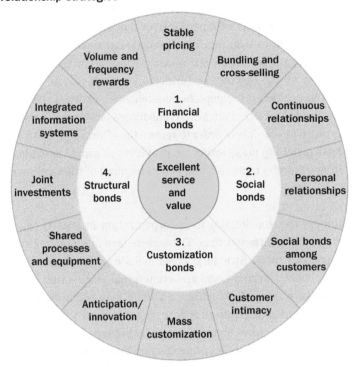

LEVEL 1 – FINANCIAL BONDS

At level 1 the customer is tied to the firm primarily through financial incentives – lower prices for greater volume purchases or lower prices for customers who have been with the firm a long time. Examples of level 1 relationship marketing are not hard to find. Think about the airline industry and related travel service industries like hotels and car rental companies. Frequent-flyer programmes provide financial incentives and rewards for travellers who bring more of their business to a particular airline. Hotels and car rental companies do the same. Mobile phone companies have engaged in a similar battle, trying to provide volume discounts and other price incentives to retain market share and build a loyal customer base. One reason these financial incentive programmes proliferate is that they are not difficult to initiate and frequently result in at least short-term profit gains. Unfortunately, financial incentives do not generally provide long-term advantages to a firm because, unless combined with another relationship approach, they do not differentiate the firm from its competitors in the long run. Many travellers belong to several frequent-flyer programmes and do not hesitate to trade off among them. Although price and other financial incentives are important to customers, they are generally not difficult for competitors to imitate because the primary customized element of the marketing mix is price.

Other types of retention strategies that depend primarily on financial rewards are focused on bundling and cross-selling of services. Frequent-flyer programmes again provide a common example. Many airlines link their reward programmes with hotel chains, car rental and, in some cases, credit card usage. By linking airline mileage points earned to usage of other firms' services, customers can enjoy even greater financial benefits in exchange for their loyalty.

In other cases, firms aim to retain their customers by simply offering their most loyal customers the assurance of stable prices, or at least lower price increases than those paid by new customers. In this way firms reward their loyal customers by sharing with them some of the cost savings and increased revenue that the firm receives through serving them over time.

Although widely and increasingly used as retention tactics, loyalty programmes based on financial rewards merit caution.[35] These programmes are often easily imitated. Thus, any increased usage or loyalty from customers may be short-lived. Second, these strategies are not likely to be successful unless they are structured so that they truly lead to repeat or increased usage rather than serving as a means to attract new customers and potentially causing endless switching among competitors.

⭐ SERVICE SPOTLIGHT

Mastercard decided that it needed to deepen the brand's relationship with customers and position itself as more than just a payment-card company. Rival American Express has long offered its cardholders financial bonds in the form of exclusive deals. In 2011 Mastercard started rolling out a series of city-wide rewards programmes across Europe, claiming to offer exclusive 'experiences'. The first of these was 'Priceless London' which centred on a series of partnerships with attractions, hotels and restaurants, including the Victoria and Albert Museum, the Southbank arts centre and the Society of London Theatres. Cardholders gain access to exclusive exhibitions and performances. All Mastercard users are eligible for the deals, although a few premium offers are restricted to premium card-holders. All promotional activity and email updates for this activity are concentrated in the London area. This 'Priceless Cities' strategy has now being rolled out to 11 other major cities throughout the world. The overall aim is to build loyalty to the Mastercard brand.

LEVEL 2 – SOCIAL BONDS

Level 2 strategies bind customers to the firm through more than financial incentives. Although price is still assumed to be important, level 2 retention marketers build long-term relationships through social and interpersonal as well as financial bonds. Customers are viewed as 'clients', not nameless faces, and become individuals whose needs and wants the firm seeks to understand.

Social, interpersonal bonds are common among professional service providers (lawyers, accountants, architects) and their clients as well as among personal care providers (hairdressers, counsellors, healthcare providers) and their clients. A dentist who takes a few minutes to review his or her patient's file before an appointment jogs his or her memory on personal facts about the patient (occupation, family details, interests, dental health history). By bringing these personal details into the conversation, the dentist reveals a genuine interest in the patient as an individual and builds social bonds. Interpersonal bonds are also common in business-to-business relationships in which customers develop relationships with salespeople and/or relationship managers working with their firms.

Sometimes relationships are formed with the organization because of the social bonds that develop *among customers* rather than between customers and the provider of the service. Such bonds are often formed in health clubs, country clubs, educational settings and other service environments where customers interact with each other. Over time the social relationships they have with other customers are important factors that prevent them from switching to another organization. One company that has built a significant strategy around customer-to-customer bonds is Harley Davidson, with its local Harley Owners Groups (HOGs). Throughout Europe (in Belgium, Germany, Spain, France, Italy, Luxembourg, Netherlands, Austria, Switzerland and the UK) HOGs are involved in local rallies, tours and parties as well as in national HOG events organized by the company. Through the HOGs, Harley customers come to know each other and develop a sense of community around their common interest – motorcycle riding.

Social bonds alone may not tie the customer permanently to the firm, but they are much more difficult for competitors to imitate than are price incentives. In the absence of strong reasons to shift to another provider, interpersonal bonds can encourage customers to stay in a relationship.[36] In combination with financial incentives, social bonding strategies may be very effective.

⭐ SERVICE SPOTLIGHT

Social bonds can also be created through social media by setting up a Facebook page and getting customers to visit the site and interact with it. For example, Subway, the sandwich retailer, has more than 27 million likes for its Facebook pages. There is interaction on the site relating to menu items, competitions, individual stores and special offers. However, interaction only occurs if staff are dedicated to updating the site and posting interesting material.

LEVEL 3 – CUSTOMIZATION BONDS

Level 3 strategies involve more than social ties and financial incentives, although there are common elements of level 1 and 2 strategies encompassed within a customization strategy and vice versa. For example, Royal Bank of Scotland branch managers are relied on not just to form strong personal commitments to customers, but also to feed information back into the bank to help customize services to fit developing customer needs.

Two commonly used terms fit within the customization bonds approach: *mass customization* and *customer intimacy*. Both these strategies suggest that customer loyalty can be encouraged through intimate knowledge of individual customers and through the development of one-to-one solutions that fit the individual customer's needs.

Mass customization has been defined as 'the use of flexible processes and organizational structures to produce varied and often individually customized products and services at the price of standardized, mass-produced alternatives'.[37] Mass customization does not mean providing customers with endless solutions or choices that only make them work harder for what they want; rather, it means providing them through little effort on their part with tailored services to fit their individual needs.

SERVICE SPOTLIGHT

An organization such as Dell Computers provides mass customization. On their website, Dell offers customers the facility to configure their computer to their own needs. Customers can personalize everything including hardware components, design and colour options, electronics, accessories and even services and support.

LEVEL 4 – STRUCTURAL BONDS

Level 4 strategies are the most difficult to imitate; they involve structural as well as financial, social and customization bonds between the customer and the firm. Structural bonds are created by providing services to the client that are frequently designed right into the service delivery system for that client. Often, structural bonds are created by providing customized services to the client that are technology based and make the customer more productive.

 SERVICE SPOTLIGHT

An example of structural bonds can be seen in a business-to-business context with Gist, who manage the UK supply chain and logistics of food products for M&S (Marks and Spencer), duty-free products for British Airways and beer for Carlsberg. By working closely with its retail and service customers, it has developed ways to improve supply ordering, delivery and billing that have greatly enhanced its value as a supplier. For example, Gist can manage physical stock replenishment in such a way that products are delivered to stores (or aeroplanes!) in shop-floor condition. In other words, they manage the whole process of packaging, sorting, tagging and hanging items for a retailer in addition to dealing with returned goods, invoicing, etc. There is, therefore, a strong structural bond between the retailer and a company; for example, M&S have been using this same supplier for over 38 years.

But there is also a potential downside to this arrangement from the customer's perspective. Customers may fear that tying themselves too closely to one provider may not allow them to take advantage of potential price savings from other providers in the future.

RELATIONSHIP CHALLENGES

Given the many benefits of long-term customer relationships, it would seem that a company would not want to refuse or terminate a relationship with any customer. Yet, situations arise in which either the firm, the customer or both want to end (or have to end) their relationship. This final section of the chapter discusses situations in which the firm might actually consider ending the relationship and how that might occur.

THE CUSTOMER IS *NOT* ALWAYS RIGHT

The assumption that all customers are good customers is very compatible with the belief that 'the customer is always right', an almost sacrosanct tenet of business. Yet any service worker can tell you that this statement is *not* always true, and in some cases it may be preferable for the firm and the customer to not continue their relationship. The following discussion presents a view of customer relationships that suggests that all relationships may not be beneficial and that every customer is not right all the time.

THE WRONG SEGMENT

A company cannot target its services to all customers; some segments will be more appropriate than others. It would not be beneficial to either the company or the customer for a company to establish a relationship with a customer whose needs the company cannot meet. For example, a business school offering a daytime MBA programme would not encourage full-time working people to apply to its programme, nor would a law firm specializing in government issues establish a relationship with individuals seeking advice on trusts and estates. These examples seem obvious. Yet firms frequently do give in to the temptation to make a sale by agreeing to serve a customer who would be better served by someone else.

Similarly, it would not be wise to forge relationships simultaneously with incompatible market segments. In many service businesses (such as restaurants, hotels, tour package operators, entertainment and education), customers experience the service together and can influence each other's perceptions about value received. Thus, to maximize service to core segments, an organization may choose to turn away marginally profitable segments that would be incompatible. For example, a conference hotel may find that mixing senior managers in the hotel for a serious training programme with students in the hotel for an end-of-year student ball may not be wise. If the senior management group is a key long-term customer, the hotel may choose to pass up hosting the student ball in the interest of retaining the corporate business.

NOT PROFITABLE IN THE LONG TERM

In the absence of ethical or legal mandates, organizations will prefer *not* to have long-term relationships with unprofitable customers. Some segments of customers will not be profitable for the company even if their needs can be met by the services offered. Some examples of this situation are when there are not enough customers in the segment to make it profitable to develop a marketing approach, when the segment cannot afford to pay the cost of the service, or when the projected revenue flows from the segment would not cover the costs incurred to originate and maintain the business. For example, in the banking industry it has been estimated that 40 to 70 per cent of customers served in a typical bank are not profitable in the sense that the costs of serving these customers exceed the revenues generated.[38]

At the individual customer level, it may not be profitable for a firm to engage in a relationship with a particular customer who has bad credit or who is a poor risk for some other reason. Retailers, banks and credit card companies routinely refuse to do business with individuals whose credit histories are unreliable. Although the short-term sale may be beneficial, the long-term risk of non-payment makes the relationship unwise from the company's point of view. Similarly, some car rental companies check into the driving records of customers and reject bad-risk drivers.[39] This practice, while controversial, is logical from the car rental companies' point of view because they can cut back on insurance costs and accident claims (thus reducing rental costs for good drivers) by not doing business with accident-prone drivers.

Beyond the monetary costs associated with serving the wrong customers, there can be substantial time investments in some customers that, if actually computed, would make them unprofitable for the organization. Everyone has had the experience of waiting in a bank, a retail store or, even, in an education setting while a particularly demanding customer seems to use more than his share of the service provider's time. The monetary value of the time spent with a specific customer is typically not computed or calculated into the price of the service.

In a business-to-business relationship, the variability in time commitment to customers is even more apparent. Some customers may use considerable resources of the supplier organization through inordinate numbers of telephone calls, excessive requests for information and other time-consuming activities. In the legal profession, clients are billed for every hour of the firm's time that they use in this way because time is essentially the only resource the firm has. Yet, in other service businesses, all clients essentially pay the same regardless of the time demands they place on the organization.

DIFFICULT CUSTOMERS

Managers have repeated the phrase 'the customer is always right' so often that you would expect it to be accepted by every employee in every service organization. So why is it not? Perhaps because it simply is not true. The customer is not always right. No matter how frequently it is said, repeating that mantra does not make it become reality, and service employees know it.

In many situations, firms have service encounters that fail because of *dysfunctional customers*. Dysfunctional customer behaviour refers to actions by customers who intentionally, or perhaps unintentionally, act in a manner that in some way disrupts otherwise functional service encounters.[40] Such customers have been described as 'customers from hell' or 'problem customers'. During a recent hotel stay, one of us was awakened at 4.00 a.m. by drunken customers who were arguing with each other in a room above; management eventually called the police and asked them to escort the customers off the property. An Enterprise Rent-A-Car customer demanded that she not be charged for any of the two weeks that she had a car because, near the end of the rental period, she found a small stain in the back seat.[41] These customers often have the objective of gaining faster, superior or perhaps free service, but their behaviour is considered dysfunctional from the perspective of the service provider and perhaps fellow customers.

Dysfunctional customer behaviour can affect employees, other customers and the organization. Research suggests that exposure to dysfunctional customer behaviour can have psychological, emotional, behavioural and physical effects on employees.[42] For example, customer-contact employees who are exposed to rude, threatening, obstructive, aggressive or disruptive behaviour by customers often have their mood or temper negatively affected as well as their motivation and morale. Such customers are difficult to work with and often create stress for employees. The dysfunctional behaviour of some customers can also have an impact on other customers: it can spoil the service experience for other customers, and it may become contagious for other customers witnessing it, particularly if it includes vociferous or illegitimate complaining. Finally, dysfunctional customer behaviour can create both direct costs and indirect costs for the organization. Direct costs can include the expense of restoring damaged property, increased insurance premiums, property loss by theft, costs incurred in compensating customers affected by the dysfunctional behaviour of others, and the costs incurred through illegitimate claims by dysfunctional customers. Indirect costs might include increased workloads for staff required to deal with dysfunctional behaviour as well as increased costs for attracting and retaining appropriate personnel and, perhaps, for absenteeism payments.

Although often these difficult customers will be accommodated and employees can be trained to recognize and deal with them appropriately, at times the best choice may be to not maintain the relationship at all – especially at the business-to-business level, where long-term costs to the firm can be substantial.

SOME CUSTOMERS MAY NOT WANT RELATIONSHIPS

Some customers may simply not want a relationship. This may be due to them seeing relationship marketing activities as being:[43]

- *Irritating* – If customers feel they are being forced into a relationship that isn't genuine and a service company's employees are only acting as if they want to be friendly and caring, then the customer may become irritated. The waiter who is over friendly and continually checks on the customer's perceptions of the meal may become annoying particularly if the guest thinks the waiter is only seeking a bigger tip.
- *Intrusive* – Organizations that overuse their databases to communicate with the customer can be seen as being intrusive and taking advantage of the information held about the customers. Customers may feel exploited in such a one-sided relationship and may raise questions about privacy issues, etc. The mobile phone companies that continuously text their customers about offers may lead to customers moving supplier.
- *Time-consuming* – To establish a relationship with an organization by taking out a store card for example, a customer may have to expend a large amount of time and effort completing paperwork or registering

personal details online. Some customers may consider this as being too much effort for the limited rewards they will get.

- *Unattractive* – Some customers will not value the benefits offered. The rewards for loyalty may seem trivial to a customer if they are difficult to redeem or if so many points or tokens need collecting before anything of any value can be claimed.

Service organizations need to take account of these points and segment their customers as to the relationships and rewards that different customers require. Understanding who wants to remain anonymous and who wants to be recognized as a loyal customer is important. Not all customers want to have a relationship with all their service providers; they may be happy to provide detailed information about their likes and dislikes to hotels and airlines, but be unwilling to do so with their bank and grocery store. Similarly, there will be differences in customer perceptions about being tied into long-term relationships and loyalty programmes. It is therefore unlikely that one relationship solution will be appropriate for all of a service organization's customers. Service organizations need to develop a sensitivity to ways of satisfying each customer in a manner that is relevant and attractive to that particular customer.

SERVICE SPOTLIGHT

It is quite common for European marketing research agencies to choose not to work for certain clients. Difficult clients can paralyse a marketing research agency in a variety of ways. Some ask for complex research projects to be undertaken on limited budgets. Others require so much up-front work and the development of creative research ideas during the bidding process that the companies who aren't selected in the end essentially do much of the preliminary research design work for free. Other clients are stingy; require many meetings before settling on an agency; or insist on a lot of direct, frequently disruptive, involvement in the design of questionnaires or the operations of a group discussion. As a result, agencies have become more wary of chasing every client that comes along.

ENDING BUSINESS RELATIONSHIPS

For the effective management of service relationships, managers should not only know how to establish a relationship but also how to end one. As suggested earlier in this chapter, firms may identify some customers who are not in their targeted segment, who are not profitable in the long run, may be difficult to work with or are dysfunctional. A company may *not* want to continue in a relationship with every customer. However, gracefully exiting a relationship may not be easy. Customers may end up feeling disappointed, confused or hurt if a firm attempts to terminate the relationship.

RELATIONSHIP ENDINGS

Relationships end in different ways – depending on the type of relationship in place.[44] In some situations, a relationship is established for a certain purpose and/or time period and then dissolves when it has served its purpose or the time frame has elapsed. For example, a house-painting service may be engaged with the customer for four days while painting the house exterior, but both parties understand that the end of the relationship is predetermined – the end occurs when the house has been painted and the customer has paid for the service. Sometimes a relationship has a natural ending. Piano lessons for children, for example, often cease as the child gets older and develops interests in other musical areas (such as singing or playing the clarinet); in such situations, the need for the relationship has diminished or become obsolete. In other situations an event may occur that forces the relationship to end; a provider who relocates to the other side of town may force some customers to select a different company. Or a relationship ending may occur because the customer is not fulfilling his or her obligations. For example, a bank may choose to end the relationship with a customer who regularly has insufficient funds in their account. Whatever the reason for ending the relationship, firms should clearly communicate their reasons for wanting (or needing) to terminate it so that customers understand what is occurring and why.

SHOULD FIRMS FIRE THEIR CUSTOMERS?

A logical conclusion to be drawn from the discussion of the challenges firms face in customer relationships is that perhaps firms should seek to get rid of those customers who are not right for them. More and more companies are making these types of decisions based on the belief that troublesome customers are usually less profitable and less loyal, and that attempting to retain their business may be counterproductive.[45] Another reason for 'firing' a customer is the negative effect that these customers can have on employee quality of life and morale. Troublesome airline passengers who are disruptive on a flight may find that the airline refuses to carry them on any future flight.

Although it may sound like a good idea, firing customers is not that simple and needs to be done in a way that avoids negative publicity or negative word of mouth. Sometimes raising prices or charging for services that previously had been given away for free can move unprofitable customers out of the company. Helping a client find a new supplier who can better meet its needs is another way to gracefully exit a non-productive relationship. If the customer has become too demanding, the relationship may be salvaged by negotiating expectations or finding more efficient ways to serve the client. If not, both parties may find an agreeable way to end the relationship.

RELATIONSHIPS FROM THE SERVICE DOMINANT LOGIC PERSPECTIVE

In goods dominated logic, value is intrinsic to goods; it is created by the organization and distributed to those who consume it. In service dominant logic, the organization cannot create value on its own but can only offer value propositions through the use of its resources and then collaboratively create value with the customer. In commercial services, the organization provides inputs for the customer's value-creating activities and the customer does the same for the organization. The customer provides a supply of money but may also:

- help in promoting the service brand;
- offer new ideas and feedback for the service;
- or contribute to the atmosphere for other customers (e.g. in a nightclub or football stadium).

The value created may develop over time: the restaurant meal may spark interest in a new cuisine, leading to the customer attending cooking classes and making menu suggestions when they next visit the restaurant, and finally resulting in their tweeting favourably about the restaurant. This co-creational nature of value is relational in the sense that the extended activities of both parties (as well as those of other parties: the cooking school) interactively and interdependently combine, over time, to create value.[46] It is through these joint, collaborative and reciprocal roles in value co-creation that service dominant logic conceptualizes relationships. Organizations may be seeking to obtain the direct goal of repeat or long-term business from a customer, but there may be value from other types of relationship that do not result in repeat business. The service dominant logic concept of relationship is of the importance of a service oriented and customer oriented view that results in a much broader value creation perspective.

This broader view does not only reflect the type of value obtained but also the range of actors involved in the co-creation of value. Customers and organizations operate in markets that are often complex with networks of suppliers, intermediaries, advisers, friends and families. If a restaurant patron only visits a restaurant once, they may influence other restaurant patrons sitting at adjoining tables and their experience may be communicated to friends or reported on review sites. The value created for the customer on that single visit is impacted upon by the supplier of the meal ingredients to the restaurant, the staff recruitment agency, the interior designer, the credit card processing company and many others. Therefore relationships are not limited to a dyad between the restaurant and the customer but are instead nested within dynamic networks of relationships which achieve mutual benefit for all parties through service provision. As such, the relationship with the one-time customer or occasional purchaser is often as important as the relationships with long-term providers and long-term customers.

SUMMARY

In this chapter we focused on the rationale for, benefits of, and strategies for developing long-term relationships with customers. It should be obvious by now that organizations that focus only on acquiring new customers may well fail to understand their current customers; thus, while a company may be bringing customers in through the front door, equal or greater numbers may be exiting. Estimates of lifetime relationship value accentuate the importance of retaining current customers.

The particular strategy that an organization uses to retain its current customers can and should be customized to fit the industry, the culture and the customer needs of the organization. However, in general, customer relationships are driven by a variety of factors that influence the development of strong customer relationships, including (1) the customer's overall evaluation of the quality of a firm's core service offering, (2) the switching barriers that the customer faces in leaving a relationship, and (3) the relationship bonds developed with that customer by the firm. By developing strong relationships with customers and by focusing on factors that influence customer relationships, the organization will accurately understand customer expectations over time and consequently will narrow service quality gap 1.

Although long-term customer relationships are critical and can be very profitable, firms should not attempt to build relationships with just any customer. In other words, 'the customer is not always right'. Indeed, in some situations it may be best for firms to discontinue relationships with some customers – for the sake of the customer, the firm, or both.

The chapter concluded with a discussion of relationships from a service dominant logic viewpoint and consideration of a much broader value creation perspective.

KEY CONCEPTS

Customer pyramid	144	Relationship endings	154
Customer experience management	146	Relationship marketing	135
Lifetime value	141	Retention strategies	146
Profitability tiers	144	Switching barriers	147
Relationship bonds	148	Touchpoints	146

EXERCISES

1 Interview the manager of a local service organization. Discuss the target market(s) for the service. Estimate the lifetime value of a customer in one or more of the target segments. To do this estimate, you will need to get as much information from the manager as you can. If the manager cannot answer your questions, make some assumptions.

2   In small groups in class, debate the question, 'Is the customer always right?' In other words, are there times when a customer may be the wrong customer for the organization?

3   Design a customer appreciation programme for the organization with whom you currently work. Why would you have such a programme, and to whom would it be directed?

4   Choose a specific company context (your class project company, the company you work for or a company in an industry you are familiar with). Calculate the lifetime value of a customer for this company. You will need to make assumptions to do this calculation, so state them clearly. Using ideas and concepts from this chapter, describe a relationship marketing strategy to increase the number of lifetime customers for this firm.

DISCUSSION QUESTIONS

1   Discuss how relationship marketing or retention marketing is different from the traditional emphasis in marketing.

2   Describe how a firm's relationships with customers may evolve over time. For each level of relationship discussed in the chapter, identify a firm with which you have that level of relationship and discuss how its marketing efforts differ from other firms.

3   Think about a service organization that retains you as a loyal customer. Why are you loyal to this provider? What are the benefits to you of staying loyal and not switching to another provider? What would it take for you to switch?

4   With regard to the same service organization, what are the benefits to the organization of keeping you as a customer? Calculate your 'lifetime value' to the organization.

5   Describe the logic behind 'customer profitability segmentation' from the company's point of view. Also discuss what customers may think of the practice.

6   Describe the various switching barriers discussed in the text. What switching barriers might you face in switching banks, mobile phone service providers, or universities?

7   Describe the four levels of retention strategies, and give examples of each type. Again, think of a service organization to which you are loyal. Can you describe the reason(s) you are loyal in terms of the different levels? In other words, what ties you to the organization?

8   Have you ever worked as a front-line service employee? Can you remember having to deal with difficult or 'problem' customers? Discuss how you handled such situations. As a manager of front-line employees, how would you help your employees deal with difficult customers?

9   Which types of service organization would you want to have a relationship with and what types would you not want to have a relationship? Explain your selections.

10 How can an organization's Facebook site help to build relationships? Will this only work for certain types of services?

FURTHER READING

Baron, S., Conway, T. and Warnaby G. (2010). *Relationship Marketing: A Consumer Experience Approach*. London: Sage Publications.

Fournier, S. and Lee, L. (2009). Getting brand communities right. *Harvard Business Review*, April, 105–11.

Godson, M. (2009). *Relationship Marketing.* Oxford: Oxford University Press.

Grayson, K. and Ambler, T. (1999). The dark side of long-term relationships in marketing services. *Journal of Marketing Research*, 36 (February), 132–41.

Gummesson, E. (2008). *Total Relationship Marketing.* Oxford: Butterworth-Heinemann.

Johnston, R. and Kong, X. (2011). The customer experience: A road-map for improvement. *Managing Service Quality*, 21(1), 5–24.

Kavall, S.G., Tzokas, N.X. and Saren, M.J. (1999). Relationship marketing as an ethical approach: philosophical and managerial considerations. *Management Decision*, 37(7), 573–81.

Lacey, R. and Sneath, J.Z. (2006). Customer loyalty programs: are they fair to consumers? *Journal of Consumer Marketing*, 23(7), 458–64.

MacGillavry, K. and Wilson, A. (2014). *Delivering loyalty via customer experience management at DHL freight.* Global Business and Organizational Excellence, 33(6), 6–20.

Vargo, S. (2009). Toward a transcending conceptualization of relationship: a service-dominant logic perspective. *Journal of Business & Industrial Marketing*, 24(5/6), 373–79.

PART 3
Aligning Service Design and Standards

Meeting customer expectations of service requires not only understanding what the expectations are, it also requires taking action on that knowledge. Action takes several forms: designing services based on customer requirements, setting service standards to ensure that employees perform as customers expect, and providing physical evidence that creates the appropriate cues and ambience for service. When action does not take place, there is a gap – service design and standards gap – as shown in the accompanying figure. In this section you will learn to identify the causes of gap 2 as well as effective strategies for closing this gap.

Chapter 8 describes the tools that are most effective in service development and design, especially a tool called *service blueprinting*. Chapter 9 helps you differentiate between company-defined standards and customer–provider gap 2-defined standards, and to recognize how they can be developed. Chapter 10 explores the strategic importance of physical evidence, the variety of roles it plays, and strategies for effectively designing physical evidence and the servicescape to meet customer expectations.

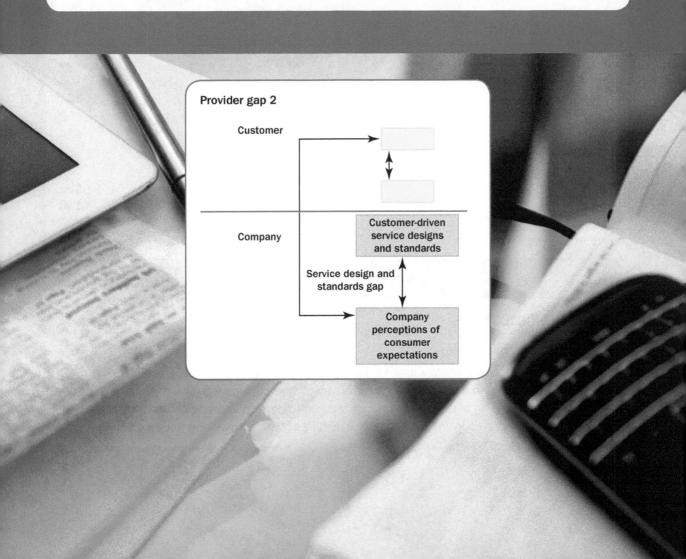

Provider gap 2

Customer

Company

Customer-driven service designs and standards

Service design and standards gap

Company perceptions of consumer expectations

CHAPTER 8

Service Innovation and Design

CHAPTER OUTLINE

LEARNING OBJECTIVES

This chapter's objectives are to:

1 Describe the challenges inherent in service innovation and design.
2 Present the stages and unique elements of the service innovation and development process.
3 Demonstrate the value of service blueprinting and how to develop and read service blueprints.
4 Present lessons learned in choosing and implementing high-performance service innovations.

OPENING EXAMPLE

My Starbucks Idea – Crowdsourcing Innovation

Starbucks initiated its crowdsourcing Web-based platform, 'mystarbucksidea.com' in March 2008. It is a website which encourages customers to submit ideas for better products, improving the customer experience, and defining new community involvement. Customers can submit, view and discuss submitted ideas along with employees from various Starbucks departments known as 'Idea Partners'. In addition, the company regularly polls its customers for their favourite products and has a leader-board to track which customers are the most active in submitting ideas and comments, and poll participation. In its first year the site generated over 70,000 ideas directly from consumers, and by 2014 the site had received 190,000 submitted ideas, with more than 300 of these having been implemented by Starbucks.

There is no financial compensation or reward for ideas submitted or implemented; rather, users are driven by the intrinsic value of contributing to the brand's success. Through the site, Starbucks gets a direct line into those interactions, allowing the company to see what ideas are really taking off and what concerns they should be addressing to help improve their customers' experiences. Some of the ideas implemented thus far include splash sticks to keep drinks from spilling, mobile payment transactions, digital rewards for the use of personal Starbucks Cards, free in-store Wi-Fi, smaller-sized treats such as cake pops, and new flavours such as the Hazelnut Macchiato and Pumpkin Spice Latte.

The success of the site relates to the two-way interaction between the customer and Starbucks. The Starbucks 'Idea Partners' regularly respond to the customer posts and take part in discussions on the topics proposed. Therefore, even though the number of ideas that are actually implemented is relatively small, the company gets the additional benefit of customer loyalty as the customer feels that Starbucks as an organization is listening to them. Also as the Starbucks platform is open to the public, so anyone can view the ideas, which increases loyalty and participation among a wider audience.

In addition to customers, baristas in the coffee shops and in the head office are posting as well, letting the company know about small yet important things they want to see changed. This enhances innovation and builds loyalty and support among the employee team.

Source: www.mystarbucksidea.com.

So what causes new products and services such as those offered by Starbucks to fail or succeed? If you decide to start your own business, what can you do to protect yourself as much as possible from failure?

An analysis of more than 60 studies on new product and service success showed that the dominant and most reliable predictors of success for new introductions relate to ***product/service characteristics*** (product meeting customer needs, product advantage over competing products, technological sophistication); ***strategy characteristics*** (dedicated human resources to support the initiative, dedicated research and development (R&D) focused on the new product initiative); **process characteristics** (marketing, pre-development, technological and launch proficiencies); and **marketplace characteristics** (market potential).[1]

Frequently a good service idea fails because of development, design and specification flaws, topics that are emphasized in this chapter. As more firms across industries move into services as a growth strategy, the challenges and opportunities of developing and delivering service offerings become a reality.

CHALLENGES OF SERVICE INNOVATION POLICY

Because services are largely intangible and process oriented (such as a visit to the dentist, a golf lesson or a Champions League football game), they are difficult to describe and communicate. When services are delivered over a long period – a week's vacation, a six-month consulting engagement, 10 weeks on a Weight Watchers programme – their complexity increases, and they become even more difficult to define and describe. Further, because services are delivered by employees to customers, they are variable. Rarely are two services alike or experienced in the same way. These characteristics of services, which we explored in Chapter 1, are the heart of the challenge involved in designing services. Global companies and governments around the world are awakening to these challenges and the recognition that, despite the dominance of services in the world's economies, there is relatively little formal focus on service research and innovation.[2] The Organisation for Economic Co-operation and Development (OECD) produced a report in 2005 entitled 'Promoting Innovation in Services' in which they stated:

> *Boosting innovation in services is central to improving performance of the service sector ... the sector has traditionally been seen as less innovative than manufacturing and as playing only a supportive role in the innovation system. As the importance of service innovation becomes more and more apparent, significant initiatives are beginning to emerge in countries around the world.*[3]

Since then there have been many different Government initiatives for services innovation across Europe; examples include:[4]

Finland – developed the 'Innovation Strategy 200' of Tekes – the Finnish Funding Agency for Technology and Innovation – which made explicit reference to societal priorities like health and well-being, clean energy, scarce resources and 'the knowledge society for all'. Services innovation is expected to make a major contribution to achieving these objectives. Between 2006 and 2010, Tekes ran the SERVE programme which sought to facilitate service business development in targeted industries, encouraging research, development and innovation activity in these industries and promoting service-related academic research. The total budget was around €100 million.

Germany – the German R&D programme on 'Innovation with Services' was launched in 2006 by the Federal Ministry of Education and Research providing funding in pre-defined thematic fields. The project funding objectives were drawn up in cooperation with representatives of research, industry and social partners integrating the recommendations issued by the 'Partners for Innovation Initiative'. The objectives are threefold: to improve the German service sector's market position by systematically developing new services and ensuring the quality of existing services, to establish the conditions necessary for attractive jobs at various levels and to realign services research on the basis of economic, social and technological development.

Spain – the 'Strategic Action for Tourism' within the framework of the National Research and Development and Innovation Plan (2008–2011) established lines of research and support for science and technology, and fostered innovation in the tourism sector, particularly in the Balearic and Canary Islands). Another example from Spain is 'INGENIO 2010', a programme which put in place initiatives to develop a knowledge economy through investments in services aimed at modernizing the public and private sectors.

Denmark – an innovation strategy for service enterprises was launched in 2008 to help improve the service sector's framework conditions for research and innovation. It set out four strategic targets for the development of service enterprises, specifically focusing on cooperation with knowledge institutions, the proportion of graduates in service enterprises, the interaction of service enterprises with foreign players and increased participation of operational service enterprises in innovation, research and development projects. A number of activities were proposed to achieve these targets, such as new innovation networks for services, the launch of 'Knowledge Pilots' in service enterprises, a better use of the Business PhD scheme in service enterprises, the launch of a user analysis of service enterprises' needs, the facilitation of commercialization of research by new, knowledge-based service enterprises and the enlargement of the 'proof of concept' approach for services. The overall budget for this strategy was approximately €67 million.

Netherlands – focused on three innovation programmes starting in 2009 targeted at creative and financial sectors, retirement management (pensions) and logistics and supply chains.

In addition to specific support mechanisms, many European countries are applying the concept of geographical service clusters, providing eco-systems for services innovation in a region. These clusters involve providing the correct infrastructure and conditions to attract certain types of businesses to coalesce in an area. The most common services in these clusters are in: information and communication technology; education and research; creative industries; financial services; health and well-being; tourism; transport and logistics. Service-related cluster initiatives can be found in Austria, Belgium, Bulgaria, Cyprus, Estonia, Finland, France, Iceland, Ireland, Italy, Luxembourg, Malta, the Netherlands, Norway, Portugal, Spain, Sweden, Switzerland, and the UK. For example in France, the Finance Innovation Competitiveness Cluster brings together in one location major financial firms in banking, insurance and asset management, regulators, business schools, universities and academics, as well as public institutions. This cluster aims to become a 'global competitiveness cluster' meaning that it has a mission to compete on the world stage.

DESCRIBING SERVICE INNOVATIONS

Because services cannot be touched, examined or easily tried out, people have historically resorted to words in their efforts to describe them. Yet, there are a number of risks inherent in attempting to describe services with words alone. The first is *oversimplification*. To say that 'portfolio management' means 'buying and selling stocks' is like describing the space shuttle as 'something that flies'. Some people will picture a bird, some a helicopter, and some an angel.'[5] Words are simply inadequate to describe a complex service system such as financial portfolio management. In our modern-day global economy, service systems have significantly increased in complexity, often involving networks of service firms and customers, and evolution of offerings over time. Within these complex systems, the risks of oversimplification are even more apparent.

The second risk of using words alone is *incompleteness*. In describing services, people (employees, managers, customers) tend to omit details or elements of the service with which they are not familiar. A person might do a fairly credible job of describing how a discount stockbroker service takes orders from customers. But would that person be able to describe fully how the monthly statements are created, how the interactive computer system works, and how these two elements of the service are integrated into the order-taking process?

The third risk is *subjectivity*. Any one person describing a service in words will be biased by personal experiences and degree of exposure to the service. There is a natural (and mistaken) tendency to assume that because all people have gone to a fast-food restaurant, they all understand what that service is. Persons working in different functional areas of the same service organization (a marketing person, an operations person, a finance person) are likely to describe the service very differently as well, biased by their own functional background.

A final risk of describing services using words alone is *biased interpretation*. No two people will define 'responsive', 'quick' or 'flexible' in exactly the same way. For example, a supervisor or manager may suggest to a front-line service employee that he or she should try to be more flexible or responsive in providing service to the customer. Unless the term 'flexibility' is further defined, the employee is likely to interpret the word differently from the manager.

All these risks become very apparent in the innovation and service development process, when organizations attempt to design complex services never before experienced by customers or when they attempt to change existing services. In the sections that follow, we present approaches for new service development and design to address these unique challenges.

NEW SERVICE DEVELOPMENT PROCESSES

Research suggests that products that are designed and introduced via the steps in a structured planning framework have a greater likelihood of ultimate success than those not developed within a framework. Despite the proven value of a structured and analytic approach to innovation, often new services are introduced on the basis of managers' and employees' subjective opinions about what the services should be and whether they will succeed, rather than on objective designs incorporating data about customer perceptions, market needs, and feasibility. A new service design process may be imprecise in defining the nature of the service concept because the people involved believe either that service processes cannot be defined precisely or that 'everyone knows what we mean'. None of these rationalizations for imprecision or lack of planning are justifiable, as we illustrate in this chapter's model for new service innovation and development.[6]

Because services are produced and consumed and co-created in real time, often involving interaction between employees and customers, it is also critical that innovation and the new-service development process involve both employees and customers. Employees frequently *are* the service, or at least they perform or deliver the service, and thus their involvement in choosing which new services to develop and how they should be designed and implemented can be very beneficial. Contact employees are psychologically and physically close to customers and can be very helpful in identifying customer needs for new services. Involving employees in the design and development process also increases the likelihood of new service success because employees can identify the organizational issues that need to be addressed to support the delivery of the service to customers.[7]

Because customers often actively participate in service delivery, they too should be involved in the new service development process. Beyond just providing input on their own needs, customers can help design the service concept and the delivery process, particularly in situations in which the customer personally carries out part of the service process. Examples include:

1 IKEA: Well known for involving its customers in the design of its stores to ensure that the layout will work for the shoppers and not just for the staff or the architects who design the stores.
2 Banco Santander: A significant amount of market research was undertaken by the UK arm of Banco Santander in determining the future of its retail banking branches. As a result, new designs have been developed, some of which incorporate Costa Coffee outlets.

SERVICE SPOTLIGHT

Ford Motor Company manufactures or distributes automobiles across six continents. With about 224,000 employees worldwide, the company's core and affiliated automotive brands include Ford, Lincoln, Mercury, Volvo and Mazda.

Ford conducts market research online and in person, refining and creating new data-gathering processes that influence product and service development. Surveys are undertaken with Ford customers online, over the telephone and through the post to examine customer satisfaction with existing vehicles and services, identifying any improvements required.

In addition to these traditional marketing research approaches, Ford searches for information appearing in customer reviews, chat rooms and blogs about vehicles and dealership services. Ford also has its own Facebook site, where reactions to new ideas can be monitored. This is supported by a variety of Twitter accounts, each one serving a specific purpose as a two-way communication channel with different market segments.

By taking a disciplined and integrated approach to gathering consumer feedback from a wide variety of sources, Ford is gaining a better understanding of consumer expectations for modern vehicles and service support.

TYPES OF NEW SERVICES

As we describe the service innovation and development process, remember that not all new services are 'new' to the same degree. New service options can run the gamut from major innovations to minor style changes:

- *Major or radical innovations* are new services for markets as yet undefined. Past examples include the first broadcast television services and the creation of eBay Internet-based auction sites. Many innovations now and in the future will evolve from information, computer and Internet-based technologies. Often these major innovations create brand-new markets.
- *Start-up businesses* consist of new services for a market that is already served by existing products that meet the same generic needs. Service examples include the creation of Amazon to provide an alternative to bookstores, online banking for financial transactions and door-to-door airport shuttle services that compete with traditional taxi and limousine services.
- *New services for the currently served market* represent attempts to offer existing customers of the organization a service not previously available from the company (although it may be available from other companies). Examples include Tesco offering insurance services, a health club offering nutrition classes and airlines offering telephone and Internet service during flights.
- *Service line extensions* represent augmentations of the existing service line, such as a restaurant adding new menu items, an airline offering new routes, a law firm offering additional legal services and a university adding new courses or degrees.
- *Service improvements* represent perhaps the most common type of service innovation. Changes in features of services that are already offered might involve faster execution of an existing service process, extended hours of service, or augmentations such as added amenities in a hotel room (e.g. the addition of wireless Internet connections).
- *Style changes* represent the most modest service innovations, although they are often highly visible and can have significant effects on customer perceptions, emotions and attitudes. Changing the colour scheme of a restaurant, revising the logo for an organization, redesigning a website or painting aircraft a different colour all represent style changes. These innovations do not fundamentally change the service, only its appearance, similar to how packaging changes are used for consumer products.

These types of service innovations are tied to the offerings themselves, suggesting that innovation occurs when a service offering is altered or expanded in some way – either radically on one extreme or stylistically at the other extreme. It is also possible that service innovations may come about when the customer's usage or co-creation role is redefined. For example, assuming the customer plays the role of user, buyer, or payer in a service context, new services can result when the previous role is redefined.[8]

Many radical innovations effectively redefine the customer's role in these ways. For example, Netflix totally redefined customers' role for movie rentals. While customers used to visit their local Blockbuster store to rent one or more movies for a predetermined period of time and pay for them on a per movie basis, Netflix allows customers to stream movies directly to their Internet-enabled devices. Thus, while movie watching in the home has not changed, the entire service process for renting, receiving, paying for and returning movies is radically different.

STAGES IN SERVICE INNOVATION AND DEVELOPMENT

In this section we focus on the actual steps to be followed in service innovation and development. The steps can be applied to any type of new service. Much of what is presented in this section has direct parallels in the new product development process for manufactured goods. Because of the inherent characteristics of services, however, the development process for new services requires adaptations.[9] Figure 8.1 shows the basic principles and steps in new service development. Although these steps may be similar to those for manufactured goods, their implementation is different for services. The challenges typically lie in defining the concept in the early stages of the development process and again at the prototype development stage. Other challenges come about in the design and implementation of the new service because it can involve coordinating human resources, technology, internal processes, and facilities within already existing

Figure 8.1   Service innovation and development process

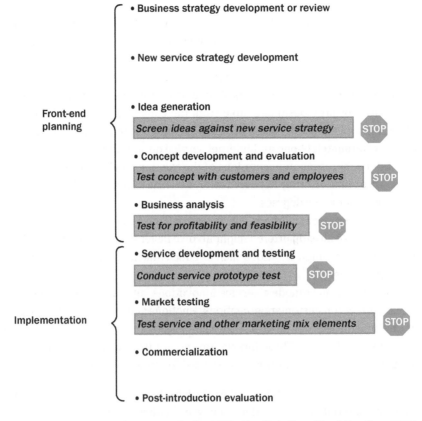

Sources: Booz-Allen & Hamilton, *New Product Management for the 1980s* (New York: Booz-Allen & Hamilton, 1982); M.J. Bowers (1985) 'An exploration into new service development: organization, process, and structure', doctoral dissertation, Texas: A&M University; A. Khurana and S.R. Rosenthal (1997) 'Integrating the fuzzy front end of new product development', *Sloan Management Review* (Winter 1997), pp. 103–20; and R.G. Cooper (2001) *Winning at New Products*, 3rd edn, Cambridge, MA: Perseus Publishing.

systems. Partly because of these challenges, service firms are generally less likely to carry out a structured development process for new innovations than are their manufacturing and consumer-goods counterparts.[10]

An underlying assumption of new product development process models is that new product ideas can be dropped at any stage of the process if they do not satisfy the criteria for success at that particular stage.[11] Figure 8.1 shows the checkpoints (represented by stop signs) that separate critical stages of the development process. The checkpoints specify requirements that a new service must meet before it can proceed to the next stage of development. Despite what Figure 8.1 suggests, however, new service or product development is rarely a completely linear process. Many companies are finding that to speed up new service innovation, some steps can be worked on simultaneously, and in some instances a step may even be skipped, particularly for simple products and services. The overlapping of steps and simultaneous development of various pieces of the new service/product development process has been referred to as 'flexible product development'. This type of flexible, speedy process is particularly important in technology industries, in which products and services evolve extremely quickly. In these environments, computer technology lets companies monitor customer opinions and needs during development and change the final offering right up until it is launched. Often, the next version of the service is in planning stages at the same time that the current version is being launched.[12] Even if the stages are handled simultaneously, the important checkpoints noted in Figure 8.1 must be assessed to maximize chances of success.

The process shown in Figure 8.1 is divided into two sections: front-end planning and implementation. The front end determines what service concepts will be developed, whereas the back end executes or implements the service concept. When asked where the greatest weaknesses in product and service innovation occur, managers typically report problems with the 'fuzzy front end'.[13] The front end is called 'fuzzy' because of its relative abstractness, which is even more apparent with intangible and variable services than with manufactured products.

FRONT-END PLANNING

BUSINESS STRATEGY DEVELOPMENT OR REVIEW

It is assumed that an organization will have an overall strategic orientation, vision and mission. Clearly a first step in new service development is to review that mission and vision. The new service strategy and specific new service ideas must fit within the larger strategic mission and vision of the organization.

⭐ **SERVICE SPOTLIGHT**

The Virgin Group sets its mission to be the consumer champion through delivering to its brand values, which are: value for money; good quality; brilliant customer service; innovative; competitively challenging; and fun. This mission has led to the development of a host of new services, such as holidays, mobile phones, financial services, cosmetics, health clubs and Internet access.

In addition to its strategic mission, the company's underlying orientation toward growth will affect how it defines its new services strategy. Becoming aware of the organization's overall strategic orientation is fundamental to plotting a direction for growth. Noted strategy researchers suggest four primary strategic orientations that are taken by companies:[14] (1) *prospectors* seek to be innovative, searching out new opportunities and taking on risks; (2) *defenders* are experts in their own areas and tend not to seek new opportunities outside their domain of expertise; (3) *analysers* maintain stability in certain areas of operation but are open to experimenting and seeking out opportunities on the margin; (4) *reactors* seldom make adjustments unless forced to do so by environmental pressures. Another noted management strategist suggests that firms can be distinguished by whether they primarily pursue a cost-leadership strategy, a differentiation strategy or a focused strategy.[15] An organization's strategic orientation will affect how it views growth through new service development.

NEW-SERVICE STRATEGY DEVELOPMENT

Research suggests that without a clear new product or service strategy, a well-planned portfolio of new products and services, and an organizational structure that facilitates product development via ongoing communications and cross-functional sharing of responsibilities, front-end decisions become ineffective.[16] Thus, a product portfolio strategy and a defined organizational structure for new product or service development are critical – and are the foundations – for success.

The types of new services that will be appropriate will depend on the organization's goals, vision, capabilities and growth plans. By defining a new service strategy (possibly in terms of markets, types of services, time horizon for development, profit criteria or other relevant factors), the organization will be in a better position to begin generating specific ideas. For example, it may focus its growth on new services at a particular level of the described continuum from major innovations to style changes. Or the organization may define its new service strategy even more specifically in terms of particular markets or market segments or in terms of specific profit-generation goals.

One way to begin formulating a new service strategy is to use the framework shown in Figure 8.2 for identifying growth opportunities. The framework allows an organization to identify possible directions for growth and can be helpful as a catalyst for creative ideas. The framework may also later serve as an initial idea screen if, for example, the organization chooses to focus its growth efforts on one or two of the four cells in the matrix. The matrix suggests that companies can develop a growth strategy around current customers or for new customers, and can focus on current offerings or new service offerings.

Figure 8.2 New service strategy matrix for identifying growth opportunities

Offerings	Markets	
	Current customers	**New customers**
Existing services	Share building	Market development
New services	Service development	Diversification

Sources: Adapted from H.I. Ansoff (1965) *Corporate Strategy*, New York: McGraw-Hill.

IDEA GENERATION

The next step in the process is the generation of new ideas that can be passed through the new service strategy screen described in the preceding step. Many methods and avenues are available for services idea generation. Formal brainstorming, solicitation of ideas from employees and customers, lead user research and learning about competitors' offerings are some of the most common approaches. Some companies are even collaborating with outsiders (e.g. competitors, vendors, alliance partners) or developing licensing agreements and joint ventures in an effort to exploit all possible sources of new ideas.[17] Observing customers and how they use the firm's products and services can also generate creative ideas for new innovations. Sometimes referred to as *empathic design*, observation is particularly effective in situations in which customers may not be able to recognize or verbalize their needs.[18] In service businesses, contact personnel, who actually deliver the services and interact directly with consumers, can be particularly good sources of ideas for complementary services and ways to improve current offerings.

Social media and networks can also be a good source of new ideas. Crowdsourcing seeks out feedback and ideas from the people who know the services best: the customers. The Starbucks example at the start of this chapter is an example of crowdsourcing of ideas. Lego is another well-known brand that encourages customers to redesign its product offerings. The idea has been popularized by various authors including James Surowiecki's book, 'The Wisdom of Crowds'.[19] And it has been transformed by the power and popularity of the Internet which allows major international brands to easily engage a crowd of customers. Marriott Hotels has evolved their crowdsourcing of ideas through their TravelBrilliantly.com website by asking guests to help the hotel chain shape innovative ideas and concepts that are closer to being rolled out. The website has been soliciting theme-travel ideas for design, culinary, wellness and technology since it launched in June 2013. Visitors to the site can also watch videos of innovations that Marriott Hotels is working on for the future of travel. They also run an annual challenge to select best public-generated creative ideas. In 2013 an idea for a healthy and nutritious vending machine was selected by the panel of judges from more than 700 submissions. As a result, the winning entrant travelled to the London Marriott Hotel Grosvenor Square to work with Marriott Hotels' experts and local innovative partners to further develop her winning idea. Once fully developed, the vending machine will be introduced at a Marriott Hotels' property later this year.

Other organizations have found that internal networks of employees, across functions and disciplines, can be great sources of innovative ideas; thus, organizational practices that encourage networking and make collaboration easy are also ways to encourage new ideas.[20] Whether the source of a new idea is inside or outside the organization, some established mechanism should exist for ensuring an ongoing stream of new service possibilities. This mechanism might include a formal service innovation, service R&D department or function with responsibility for generating new ideas; suggestion boxes for employees and customers; new-service development teams that meet regularly; surveys and focus groups with customers and employees; or formal competitive analysis to identify new services.

SERVICE CONCEPT DEVELOPMENT AND EVALUATION

Once an idea surfaces that is regarded as a good fit with both the business and the new service strategies, it is ready for initial development. In the case of a tangible product, this next step in service concept development and evaluation would mean formulating the basic product definition and then presenting consumers with descriptions and drawings to get their reactions.

The inherent characteristics of services, particularly intangibility and simultaneous production and consumption, place complex demands on this phase of the process. Drawing pictures and describing an intangible service in concrete terms is difficult. It is, therefore, important that agreement be reached at this stage on exactly what the concept is and what customer need it fills. The service concept is made up of the core benefit provided to the customer, supported by a variety of tangible and intangible elements that assist in the delivery of that benefit. The core benefit of a passenger flight is getting a customer to a particular destination, but the service concept also involves: booking and check-in procedures; the frequency of in-flight service; the design of the aeroplane; the configuration of the seating; food and drink, etc. The service concept for no-frills airlines is very different from that of the traditional carriers even though the core benefit is the same. It may be necessary to involve multiple parties in sharpening the definition of the service concept. For example, Lynn Shostack relates that the design and development of a new discount share-dealing service was initially described by the bank as a way 'to buy and sell stocks for customers at low prices'.[21] Through the initial concept development phase it became clear that not everyone in the organization had the same idea about how this description would translate into an actual service and that there was a variety of ways the concept could be developed. Only through multiple iterations of the service – and the raising of hundreds of issues, large and small – was an agreement finally reached on the discounted share-dealing concept.

After clear definition of the concept, it is important to produce a description of the service that represents its specific features and characteristics, and then to determine initial customer and employee responses to the concept. The service design document would describe the problem addressed by the service, discuss the reasons for offering the new service, itemize the service process and its benefits and provide a rationale for purchasing the service.[22] The roles of customers and employees in the delivery process would also be described. The new service concept would then be evaluated by asking employees and customers whether they understand the idea of the proposed service, whether they are favourable to the concept and whether they feel it satisfies an unmet need.

BUSINESS ANALYSIS

Assuming that, at the concept development stage, the service idea is favourably evaluated by customers and employees, the next step is to estimate its economic feasibility and potential profit implications. Demand analysis, revenue projections, cost analyses and operational feasibility studies are assessed at this stage. Because the development of service concepts is so closely tied to the operational system of the organization, this stage will involve preliminary assumptions about the costs of staff recruitment and training, delivery system enhancements, facility changes and any other projected operations costs. The organization will pass the results of the business analysis through its profitability and feasibility screen to determine whether the new service idea meets the minimum requirements.

IMPLEMENTATION

Once the new service concept has passed all the front-end planning hurdles, it is ready for the implementation stages of the process.

SERVICE DEVELOPMENT AND TESTING

In the development of new tangible products, the development and testing stage involves construction of product prototypes and testing for consumer acceptance. Again, because services are intangible and simultaneously produced, consumed and frequently co-created, this step presents unique challenges. To address these challenges, this stage of service development should involve all who have a stake in the new service: customers and contact employees as well as functional representatives from marketing, operations and human resources. During this phase, the concept is refined to the point at which a detailed service blueprint representing the implementation plan for the service can be produced. The blueprint is likely to evolve over a series of iterations on the basis of input from all the involved parties.

A final step is for each area involved in rendering the service to translate the final blueprint into specific implementation plans for its part of the service delivery process. Because service development, design and delivery are so intricately intertwined, all parties involved in any aspect of the new service must work together at this stage to delineate the details of the new service. If not, seemingly minor operational details can be overlooked and cause an otherwise good new service idea to fail.

⭐ SERVICE SPOTLIGHT

Beneath the headquarters of Marriott Hotels in Bethesda, Maryland, USA, lies the 'The Underground' — a 10,000 square foot innovation lab designed to promote collaboration. Its floor-to-ceiling white space is like a blank canvas which visitors can mark and manipulate. The facility is built as an ever-changing lab where it is possible to experience innovative ideas, explore concepts, and receive instant feedback from guests. Because the parts of the Innovation Lab are mobile, the Marriott design team can take every detail into consideration, from the positioning of the bed in the room to the layout of the bathroom. Visitors to the space, which opened in 2013, will become an integral part of the design and testing process for guestrooms, hotel lobbies, meetings spaces, and even food & beverage concepts.

MARKET TESTING

At the market testing stage of the development process, a tangible product might be test marketed in a limited number of trading areas to determine marketplace acceptance of the product as well as other marketing mix variables such as promotion, pricing and distribution systems. Because new service offerings are often intertwined with the delivery system for existing services, it is difficult to test new services in isolation. Also, in some cases, such as a one-site retailer, it may not be possible to introduce the service to an isolated market area because the organization has only one point of delivery. There are alternative ways of testing the response to marketing mix variables, however. The new service might be offered to employees of the organization and their families for a time to assess their responses to variations in the marketing mix. Alternatively, the organization might decide to test variations in pricing and promotion in less realistic contexts by presenting customers with hypothetical mixes and getting responses on whether they would try the service under varying circumstances. This approach certainly has limitations compared with an actual market test, but it is better than not assessing market response at all.

It is also extremely important at this stage in the development process to do a pilot run of the service to be sure that the operational details are functioning smoothly. Frequently this step is overlooked, and the actual market introduction may be the first test of whether the service system functions as planned. By this point, mistakes in design are harder to correct. As one noted service expert says, 'There is simply no substitute for a proper rehearsal' when introducing a new service.[23] In the case of the discount share-dealing service described earlier, the bank ran a pilot test by offering employees a special price for one month. The offer was marketed internally, allowing the bank to observe the service process in action before it was actually introduced to the external market.

COMMERCIALIZATION

During the commercialization stage, the service goes live and is introduced to the marketplace. This stage has two primary objectives. The first is to build and maintain acceptance of the new service among large numbers of service delivery personnel who will be responsible day to day for service quality. This task is made easier if acceptance has been built in by involving key groups in the design and development process all along. However, it will still be a challenge to maintain enthusiasm and communicate the new service throughout the system; excellent internal marketing will help.

The second objective is to monitor all aspects of the service during introduction and through the complete service cycle. If the customer needs six months to experience the entire service, then careful monitoring must be maintained through at least six months. Every detail of the service should be assessed – telephone calls, face-to-face transactions, billing, complaints and delivery problems. Operating efficiency and costs should also be tracked.

POST-INTRODUCTION EVALUATION

At this point, the information gathered during commercialization of the service can be reviewed and changes made to the delivery process, staffing or marketing mix variables on the basis of actual market response to the offering.

SERVICE SPOTLIGHT

An example of post-introduction evaluation is when Expedia.com, the travel website, realized that despite pre-launch testing, restrictions on Expedia bargain fares were confusing to customers. A 'hot fix' team was called in to remedy the problem.[24] Within a day, the project team redesigned the presentation of information so that the fare restrictions would be clear to customers.

No service will ever stay the same. Whether deliberate or unplanned, changes will always occur. Therefore, formalizing the review process to make those changes that enhance service quality from the customer's point of view is critical.

SERVICE BLUEPRINTING

A stumbling block in service innovation and development is the difficulty of describing and depicting the service at the concept development, service development and market test stages. One of the keys to matching service specifications to customer expectations is the ability to describe critical service process characteristics objectively and to depict them so that employees, customers and managers alike know what the service is, can see their role in its delivery and understand all the steps and flows involved in the service process. In this section we look in depth at service blueprinting, a useful tool for designing and specifying intangible service processes.[25]

WHAT IS A SERVICE BLUEPRINT?

The manufacturing and construction industries have a long tradition of engineering and design. Can you imagine a house being built without detailed plans? Can you imagine a car, a computer or, even, a simple product like a child's toy or a shampoo being produced without concrete and detailed plans, written specifications and engineering drawings? Yet services commonly lack concrete specifications. A service, even a complex one, might be introduced without any formal, objective depiction of the process.

A service blueprint is a picture, or a map, that accurately portrays the service system so that the different people involved in providing it can understand and deal with it objectively, regardless of their roles or their individual points of view. Blueprints are particularly useful at the design stage of service development. A service blueprint visually displays the service by simultaneously depicting the process of service delivery, the points of customer contact, the roles of customers and employees, and the visible elements of the service (see Figure 8.3). It provides a way to break down a service into its logical components and to depict the steps or tasks in the process, the means by which the tasks are executed and the evidence of service as the customer experiences it.

Figure 8.3   Service blueprinting

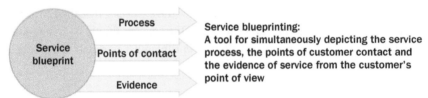

Service blueprinting:
A tool for simultaneously depicting the service process, the points of customer contact and the evidence of service from the customer's point of view

Blueprinting has its origins in a variety of fields and techniques, including logistics, industrial engineering, decision theory and computer systems analysis – all of which deal with the definition and explanation of processes.[26] Because services are 'experiences' rather than objects, blueprinting is a particularly useful tool for describing them.

BLUEPRINT COMPONENTS

The key components of service blueprints are shown in Figure 8.4.[27] They are customer actions, 'onstage' contact employee actions, 'backstage' contact employee actions, and support processes. The conventions for drawing service blueprints are not rigidly defined, and thus the particular symbols used, the number of horizontal lines in the blueprint, and the particular labels for each part of the blueprint may vary somewhat depending on what you read and the complexity of the service being described. These variations are not a problem as long as you keep in mind the purpose of the blueprint and view it as a useful tool rather than as a set of rigid rules for designing services.

The *customer actions* area encompasses the steps, choices, activities and interactions that the customer performs in the process of purchasing, consuming and evaluating the service. The total customer experience

Figure 8.4   Service blueprint components

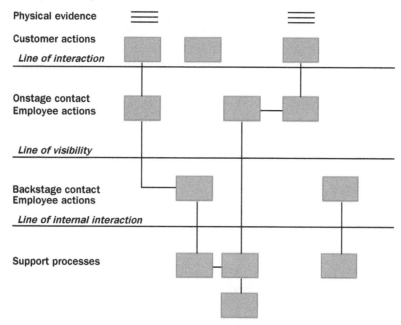

is apparent in this area of the blueprint. In a legal services example, the customer actions might include a decision to contact a lawyer, telephone calls to the lawyer, face-to-face meetings, receipt of documents and receipt of a bill.

In parallel to the customer actions are two areas of contact employee actions. The steps and activities that the contact employee performs that are visible to the customer are the *onstage contact employee actions*. In the legal services setting, the actions of the lawyer (the contact employee) that are visible to the client are, for example, the initial interview, intermediate meetings and final delivery of legal documents. Those contact employee actions that occur behind the scenes to support the onstage activities are the *backstage contact employee actions*. In the example, anything the lawyer does behind the scenes to prepare for the meetings or to prepare the final documents will appear in this section of the blueprint, together with telephone call contacts the customer has with the lawyer or other front-line staff in the firm. All *non-visible* contact employee actions are shown in this area of the blueprint.

The *support processes* section of the blueprint covers the internal services, steps and interactions that take place to support the contact employees in delivering the service. Again, in our legal example, any service support activities such as legal research by staff, preparation of documents and secretarial support to set up meetings will be shown in the support processes area of the blueprint.

At the very top of the blueprint you see the *physical evidence* of the service. Typically, above each point of contact the actual physical evidence of the service is listed. In the legal example, the physical evidence of the face-to-face meeting with the lawyer would be such items as office decor, written documents, lawyer's clothing, and so on.

The four key action areas are separated by three horizontal lines. First is the *line of interaction*, representing direct interactions between the customer and the organization. Whenever a vertical line crosses the horizontal line of interaction, a direct contact between the customer and the organization, or a service encounter, has occurred. The next horizontal line is the critically important *line of visibility*. This line separates all service activities that are visible to the customer from those that are not visible. In reading blueprints it is immediately obvious whether the consumer is provided with much visible evidence of the service simply by analysing how much of the service occurs above the line of visibility versus the activities carried out below the line. This line also separates what the contact employees do onstage from what they do backstage. For example, in a medical examination situation, the doctor would perform the actual examination and answer the patient's questions above the line of visibility, or onstage, whereas he or she might read the patient's chart in advance and dictate notes following the examination below the line of visibility, or backstage. The third line is the *line of internal interaction*, which separates contact employee activities from those of other service support activities and people. Vertical lines cutting across the line of internal interaction represent internal service encounters.

One of the most significant differences between service blueprints and other process flow diagrams is the inclusion of customers and their views of the service process. In fact, in designing effective service blueprints it is recommended that the diagramming start with the customer's view of the process and work back into the delivery system. The boxes shown within each action area depict steps performed or experienced by the actors at that level.

SERVICE BLUEPRINT EXAMPLES

Figure 8.5 shows a service blueprint for an overnight hotel stay. This blueprint is deliberately kept very simple, showing only the most basic steps in the services. Complex diagrams could be developed for each step, and the internal processes could be much more fully developed. In addition to the four action areas separated by the three horizontal lines, these blueprints also show the physical evidence of the service from the customer's point of view at each step of the process.

In the case of the overnight hotel stay depicted in Figure 8.5, the guest first checks in, then goes to the hotel room where a variety of steps take place (receiving bags, sleeping, showering, eating breakfast, and so on) and, finally, checks out. Imagine how much more complex this process could be, and how many more interactions might occur, if the service blueprint depicted a week-long vacation at the hotel, or even a three-day business conference. The service blueprint makes clear also (by reading across the line of interaction) those employees with whom the guest interacts and thus those employees who provide evidence of the service to the customer. Several interactions occur with a variety of hotel employees, including the bellperson, the front desk clerk, the food service order-taker and the food delivery person. Each step in the customer action area is also associated with various forms of physical evidence, from the hotel parking area and hotel exterior and interior to the forms used at guest registration, the lobby, the room and the food. The hotel facility itself is critical in communicating the image of the hotel company, in providing satisfaction for the guest through the manner in which the hotel room is designed and maintained, and in facilitating the actions and interactions of both the guest and the employees of the hotel. In the hotel case, the process is relatively complex (although again somewhat standardized), the people providing the service are a variety of front-line employees, and the physical evidence includes everything from the guest registration form to the design of the lobby and room to the uniforms worn by front-line employees.

Any of the steps in the blueprint could be exploded into a detailed blueprint if needed for a particular purpose. For example, if the hotel learned that the 'room service' step was taking too long and causing unacceptable delays, that step could be blueprinted in much greater detail to isolate the problems.

BLUEPRINTS FOR TECHNOLOGY-DELIVERED SELF-SERVICE

Up to this point our discussion of service blueprints has only related to services that are delivered in person, services in which employees interact directly with customers at some point in the process. But what about technology-delivered services like self-service websites (Expedia's travel information site, Dell's customer self-service site) and interactive kiosks (ATMs, airline self-check-in machines)? Can service blueprinting be used effectively to design these types of services? Certainly it can, but the lines of demarcation change, and some blueprint labels may need to be adapted (see Figure 8.6)

As Figure 8.6 shows, if no employees are involved in the service (except when there is a problem or the service does not function as planned), the contact person areas of the blueprint are not needed. Instead, the area above the line of visibility can be used to illustrate the interface between the customer and the computer

Figure 8.5   Blueprint for overnight hotel stay service

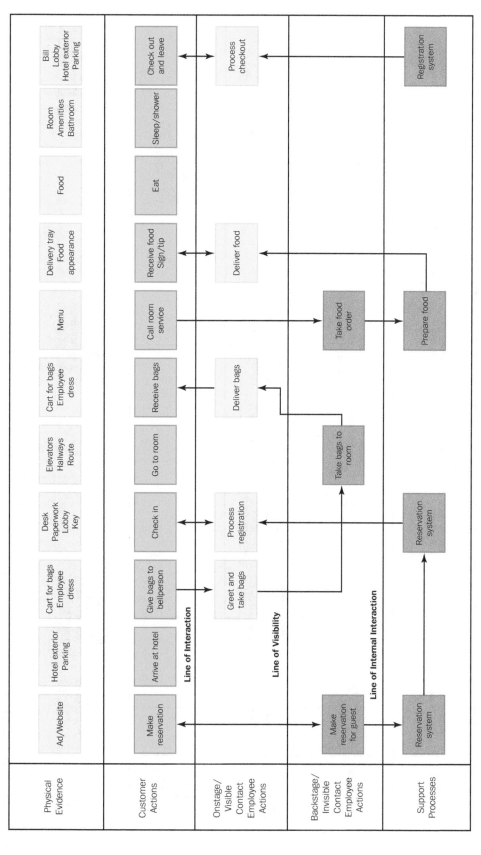

Source: Bitner, M.J., Ostrom, A.L. and Morgan F.C. (2007) 'Service Blueprinting: A Practical Approach for Service Innovation', Centre for Services Leadership Working Paper, Arizona State University.

Figure 8.6 **Blueprint for an automated DVD rental kiosk**

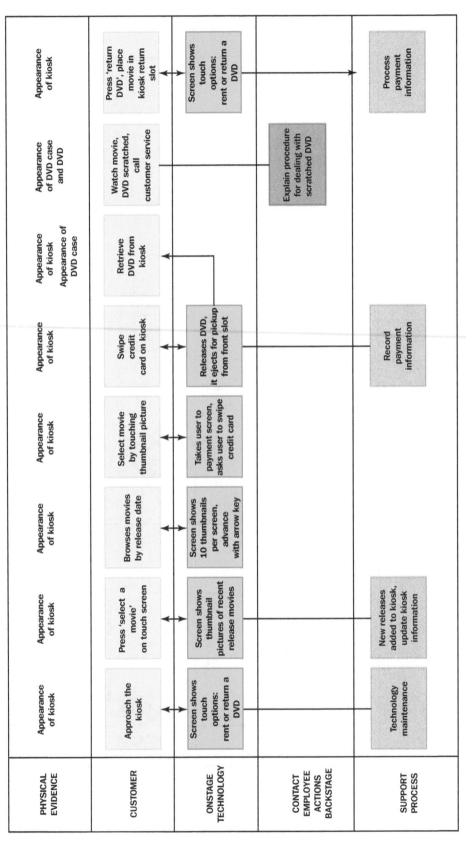

PHYSICAL EVIDENCE	Appearance of kiosk	Appearance of kiosk	Appearance of kiosk	Appearance of kiosk	Appearance of kiosk	Appearance of kiosk Appearance of DVD case	Appearance of DVD case and DVD	Appearance of kiosk
CUSTOMER	Approach the kiosk	Browses movies by release date	Select movie by touching thumbnail picture	Swipe credit card on kiosk		Retrieve DVD from kiosk	Watch movie, DVD scratched, call customer service	Press 'return DVD', place movie in kiosk return slot
ONSTAGE TECHNOLOGY	Screen shows touch options: rent or return a DVD	Screen shows thumbnail pictures of recent release movies	Screen shows 10 thumbnails per screen, advance with arrow key	Takes user to payment screen, asks user to swipe credit card	Releases DVD, it ejects for pickup from front slot			Screen shows touch options: rent or return a DVD
CONTACT EMPLOYEE ACTIONS BACKSTAGE							Explain procedure for dealing with scratched DVD	
SUPPORT PROCESS	Technology maintenance	New releases added to kiosk, update kiosk information			Record payment information			Process payment information

Adapted from source: Bitner, M.J., Ostrom, A.L. and Morgan F.C. (2007) 'Service Blueprinting: A Practical Approach for Service Innovation', Centre for Services Leadership Working Paper, Arizona State University.

website or the physical interaction with the kiosk. This area can be relabelled onstage/visible technology. The backstage contact person actions area would be irrelevant in this case.

If the service involves a combination of human and technology interfaces, as with airline computerized check-in, the onstage area can be cut into two distinct spaces divided by an additional horizontal line. In the airline computerized check-in example, the human contact with the airline employee who takes the bags and checks identification would be shown in one area and the technology interactions with the check-in computer kiosk would be shown in the second area, both above the line of visibility.

READING AND USING SERVICE BLUEPRINTS

A service blueprint can be read in a variety of ways, depending on the purpose. If the purpose is to understand the customer's view of the process or the customer experience, the blueprint can be read from left to right, tracking the events in the customer action area. Questions that might be asked include: how is the service initiated by the customer? What choices does the customer make? Is the customer highly involved in creating the service or are few actions required of the customer? What is the physical evidence of the service from the customer's point of view? Is the evidence consistent with the organization's strategy and positioning?

If the purpose is to understand contact employees' roles, the blueprint can also be read horizontally, but this time focusing on the activities directly above and below the line of visibility. Questions that might be asked include: how rational, efficient and effective is the process? Who interacts with customers, when and how often? Is one person responsible for the customer, or is the customer passed off from one contact employee to another?

If the purpose is to understand the integration of the various elements of the service process, or to identify where particular employees fit into the bigger picture, the blueprint can be analysed vertically. In this analysis, it becomes clear what tasks and which employees are essential in the delivery of service to the customer. The linkages from internal actions deep within the organization to front-line effects on the customer can also be seen in the blueprint. Questions that might be asked include: what actions are being performed backstage to support critical customer interaction points? What are the associated support actions? How are handoffs from one employee to another taking place?

If the purpose is service redesign, the blueprint can be looked at as a whole to assess the complexity of the process, how it might be changed, and how changes from the customer's point of view would impact the contact employee and other internal processes, and vice versa. Blueprints can also be used to assess the overall efficiency and productivity of the service system and to evaluate how potential changes will impact the system.[28] The blueprint can also be analysed to determine likely failure points or bottlenecks in the process. When such points are discovered, a firm can introduce measures to track failures, or that part of the blueprint can be exploded so that the firm can focus in much greater detail on that piece of the system.

Blueprinting applications in a variety of contexts have demonstrated benefits and uses including:[29]

- Providing a platform for innovation
- Recognizing roles and interdependencies among functions, people and organizations
- Facilitating both strategic and tactical innovations
- Transferring and storing innovation and service knowledge
- Designing moments of truth from the customer's point of view
- Suggesting critical points for measurement and feedback in the service process
- Clarifying competitive positioning
- Understanding the ideal customer experience.

Clearly, one of the greatest benefits of blueprinting is education.[30] When people begin to develop a blueprint, what is actually known about the service quickly becomes apparent. Sometimes the shared knowledge is minimal. Biases and prejudices are made explicit, and agreements and compromises must be reached. The process itself promotes cross-functional integration and understanding. In the attempt to visualize the entire service system, people are forced to consider the service in new and more comprehensive ways.

BUILDING A BLUEPRINT

Recall that many of the benefits and purposes of building a blueprint evolve from the process of doing it. Thus the final product is not necessarily the only goal. Through the process of developing the blueprint, many intermediate goals can be achieved: clarification of the concept, development of a shared service vision, recognition of complexities and intricacies of the service that are not initially apparent, and delineation of roles and responsibilities, to name a few. The development of the blueprint needs to involve a variety of functional representatives as well as information from customers. Drawing or building a blueprint is not a task that should be assigned to one person or one functional area. Figure 8.7 identifies the basic steps in building a blueprint.

Figure 8.7   Building a service blueprint

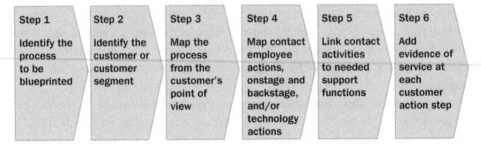

EXAMPLE

FREQUENTLY ASKED QUESTIONS ABOUT SERVICE BLUEPRINTING

The following provides answers to frequently asked questions about service blueprints.

WHAT PROCESS SHOULD BE BLUEPRINTED?

What process to map depends on the team or organization's objectives. If these are not clearly defined, then identifying the process can present a challenge. Questions to ask: why are we blueprinting the service? What is our objective? Where does the service process begin and end? Are we focusing on the entire service, a component of the service, or a period of time?

CAN MULTIPLE MARKET SEGMENTS BE INCLUDED ON ONE BLUEPRINT?

Generally, the answer to this question is no. Assuming that market segments require different service processes or attributes, the blueprint for one segment may look very different from the blueprint for another. Only at a very high level (sometimes called a *concept blueprint*) might it be relevant to map multiple segments simultaneously.

WHO SHOULD 'DRAW' THE BLUEPRINT?

A blueprint is a team effort. It should not be assigned as an individual task, certainly not in the development stages. All relevant parties should be involved or represented in the development effort. The task might include employees across multiple functions in the organization (marketing, operations, human resources, facilities design) as well as customers in some cases.

SHOULD THE ACTUAL OR DESIRED SERVICE PROCESS BE BLUEPRINTED?

If a new service is being designed, then clearly it is important to start with the desired service process. However, in cases of service improvement or service redesign, it is very important to map (at least at a conceptual level) the actual service process first. Once the group knows how the service is actually functioning, then the blueprint can be modified or used as a basis for changes and improvements.

SHOULD EXCEPTIONS OR RECOVERY PROCESSES BE INCORPORATED WITHIN THE BLUEPRINT?

It may be possible to map relatively simple, commonly occurring recovery processes onto a blueprint, assuming there are not a lot of these. However, this process can quickly become complex and cause the blueprint to be confusing or unreadable. Often a better strategy is to indicate common fail points on the blueprint and, if needed, develop sub-blueprints for the service recovery processes.

WHAT IS THE APPROPRIATE LEVEL OF DETAIL?

The answer to this question depends again on the objective or purpose for doing the blueprint in the first place. If it is to be used primarily to communicate the general nature of the service, then a concept blueprint with few details is best. If it is being used to focus on diagnosing and improving the service process, then more detail is needed. Because some people are more detail oriented than others, this particular question will always arise and needs to be resolved in any team blueprinting effort.

WHAT SYMBOLS SHOULD BE USED?

At this point in time, there is not a lexicon of blueprinting symbols that is commonly used or accepted across companies. What is most important is that the symbols be defined, be kept relatively simple, and be used consistently by the team and across the organization if blueprints are being shared internally.

SHOULD TIME OR FINANCIAL COSTS BE INCLUDED ON THE BLUEPRINT?

Blueprints are very versatile. If reducing the time taken for various parts of the service process is an objective of the blueprinting effort, then time can definitely be included. The same is true for financial costs or anything else that is relevant as an objective. However, it is not advisable to put such information on the blueprint unless it is of central concern.

STEP 1: IDENTIFY THE SERVICE PROCESS TO BE BLUEPRINTED

Blueprints can be developed at a variety of levels, and there needs to be agreement on the starting point. For example, in an express mail delivery blueprint, specific blueprints could be developed for two-day express mail, large accounts, Internet-facilitated services and/or high street drop-off centres. Each of these blueprints would share some features but would also include unique features. Or if the 'sort packages' and 'loading' elements of the process were found to be problem areas or bottlenecks that were slowing service to customers, a detailed blueprint of the sub-processes at work in those two steps could be developed. A firm can identify the process to be mapped once it has determined the underlying purpose for building the blueprint.

STEP 2: IDENTIFY THE CUSTOMER OR CUSTOMER SEGMENT EXPERIENCING THE SERVICE

A common rationale for market segmentation is that each segment's needs are different and therefore will require variations in the service or product features. Thus, blueprints are most useful when developed for a particular customer or customer segment, assuming that the service process varies across segments. At a very abstract or conceptual level it may be possible to combine customer segments on one blueprint. However, once almost any level of detail is reached, separate blueprints should be developed to avoid confusion and maximize their usefulness.

STEP 3: MAP THE SERVICE PROCESS FROM THE CUSTOMER'S POINT OF VIEW

Step 3 involves charting the choices and actions that the customer performs or experiences in purchasing, consuming and evaluating the service. Identifying the service from the customer's point of view first will help avoid focusing on processes and steps that have no customer impact.

This step forces agreement on who the customer is (sometimes no small task) and may involve considerable research to determine exactly how the customer experiences the service.

Sometimes the beginning and ending of the service from the customer's point of view may not be obvious. For example, research in a haircutting context revealed that customers viewed the process as beginning with the telephone call to the salon and making the appointment, whereas the hairstylists did not typically view the making of appointments as part of the service process.[31] Similarly, in a mammogram screening service, patients viewed driving to the clinic, parking and locating the screening office as part of the service experience. If the blueprint is being developed for an existing service, it may be helpful at this point in the process to videotape or photograph the service process from the customer's point of view. Managers, and others who are not on the front line, often do not actually know what the customers are experiencing and may be quite surprised when they view the actual service experience.

STEP 4: MAP CONTACT EMPLOYEE ACTIONS, BOTH ONSTAGE AND BACKSTAGE, AND/OR TECHNOLOGY ACTIONS

First the lines of interaction and visibility are drawn, and then the process from the customer-contact person's point of view is mapped, distinguishing visible or onstage activities from invisible backstage activities. For existing services this step involves questioning front-line operations employees to learn what they do and which activities are performed in full view of the customer versus which activities are carried out behind the scenes.

For technology-delivered services or those that combine technology and human delivery, the required actions of the technology interface will be mapped above the line of visibility as well. If no employees are involved in the service, the area can be relabelled 'onstage technology actions'. An additional horizontal line can separate 'onstage contact employee actions' from 'onstage technology actions' if both human and technology interactions are involved. Using the additional line will facilitate reading and interpretation of the service blueprint.

STEP 5: LINK CONTACT ACTIVITIES TO NEEDED SUPPORT FUNCTIONS

The line of internal interaction can then be drawn and linkages from contact activities to internal support functions can be identified. In this process, the direct and indirect impact of internal actions on customers becomes apparent. Internal service processes take on added importance when viewed in connection with their link to the customer. Alternatively, certain steps in the process may be viewed as unnecessary if there is no clear link to the customer's experience or to an essential internal support service.

STEP 6: ADD EVIDENCE OF SERVICE AT EACH CUSTOMER ACTION STEP

Finally, the evidence of service can be added to the blueprint to illustrate what the customer sees and receives as tangible evidence of the service at each step in the customer experience. A photographic blueprint, including photos, slides or video of the process, can be very useful at this stage to aid in analysing the impact of tangible evidence and its consistency with the overall strategy and service positioning.

HIGH-PERFORMANCE SERVICE INNOVATIONS

Up to this point in the chapter we have discussed approaches and tools for developing and designing new services. A dilemma in most companies is that there are too many new ideas from which to choose. New technologies, changing customer needs, deregulation, competitors' actions – all these areas result in myriad potential new offerings to consider. The question is which to pursue. How can a company decide which new offerings will likely be major successes, and which may be less successful or even fail? How can they decide which are worthy of investment and which are not?

In this section we summarize some of what has been learned about successful new services in terms of measures of success, key success drivers and the importance of integrating new services.

⭐ SERVICE SPOTLIGHT

Firms in many industries are discovering the value of strategically focusing on service innovations to provide value for their customers as well as profits and growth for the firm. Using this strategic approach, services are developed to enhance relationships with customers by providing them total packages of offerings, sometimes referred to as 'solutions'. By adding services to their traditional offerings, firms can differentiate themselves from their competitors and frequently make higher profit margins on the new services compared with traditional manufactured offerings. Here we highlight three firms from very diverse industries and their growth-through-services strategies.

ROLLS-ROYCE

Many of the Rolls-Royce engines on commercial aeroplanes are owned by Rolls-Royce rather than the airline or the plane manufacturer. The company's CorporateCare is a flexible and comprehensive cost-per-flight-hour leasing service, designed to deliver engines with an engine maintenance programme. Engine management plans are developed that combine engine condition monitoring, customer specific operational information and fleet-wide experience to produce tailored repair and engine overhaul schedules. The CorporateCare programme covers lease engine costs and also covers the cost of repairing or replacing parts. There is minimal interruption to flying for scheduled engine maintenance as Rolls-Royce guarantees access to spare engines. Rolls-Royce also uses computer and satellite technology to track in-flight engine performance from its information centre in Derby in the UK. The company can direct replacement parts and repair teams to the airport locations where they are needed. As Rolls-Royce takes responsibility for the performance of the aircraft engines, the airlines can concentrate more of their efforts on delivering their core services of flying and looking after passengers. CorporateCare also allows Rolls-Royce to build close relationships with airlines as well as a continuous income stream and higher margins.

ERICSSON

Headquartered in Sweden, Ericsson is a leading global provider of telecommunications equipment and related services and solutions. Since the mid-1990s it has pursued a growth strategy focused on customers and services that enhance and add value to its sophisticated technology products. Among its services, the company lists an array of 'solutions' for end users, business operations, and network infrastructure. For example, since the 1980s Ericsson has worked in a partnership with the New Zealand police force to support its telecommunication needs through products and services.

In 2007 Ericsson signed a 21-year exclusive agreement to supply and support a flexible and scalable point-to-point microwave radio network system. The goal for the system is to provide community safety through a customized and secure telecommunications network for the country. As Ericsson continues to move away from its traditional base in manufacturing, the company has reoriented its entire organization toward providing integrated solutions for customers such as the one being developed for the New Zealand police force.

PHILIPS ELECTRONICS

Companies such as Philips Electronics, the European electronics giant, are faced with the realities of price competition from cheaper products produced primarily in Asia. The results for many companies are declining sales and growing losses from their products. Part of the solution for these companies is a venture into services.

For Philips this has meant branching out into healthcare by marrying its expertise in consumer marketing and the knowledge in its professional medical division with an unmet demand for personal healthcare monitoring. The Philips Lifeline service is a medical-alert system that allows elderly patients immediate connection to a call centre, where Personal Response Associates, with access to their health profiles, can help them. The immediate access is gained by pushing a button on an electronic bracelet that the patient wears.

Other services which Philips has in the works include one that allows doctors to monitor patients' vital signs from their homes via the Internet, and an intelligent pill box that can detect when a person has not taken his or her medication. A box with excess pills would automatically alert the system and an operator would call the patient to remind them.

For each of these companies, the move to services represented a significant strategic choice that initially took them into uncharted waters. For Ericsson it meant moving away from a manufacturing and technology mindset to one that focuses on customers and solutions. For Philips the move was even more dramatic as it began to understand a whole new industry in healthcare delivery. Yet the potential rewards are great and customer demands for services and solutions are real. These rewards and demands are what compel more and more firms to pursue the strategic service path.

Sources: **http://www.rolls-royce.com/civil/services/corporatecare/; A. Davies, T. Brady, and M. Hobday (2006) 'Charting a Path toward Integrated Solutions',** *Sloan Management Review,* **47 (Spring 2006), pp. 39–48; M. Sawhney, S. Balasubramanian, and V. V. Krishnan (2004) 'Creating Growth with Services',** *Sloan Management Review* **45 (Winter 2004), pp. 34–43; www.ericsson.com; www.medical.philips.com; and L. Abboud (2007) 'Electronics Giant Seeks a Cure in Health Care,'** *The Wall Street Journal,* **11 July 2007, p. Al.**

CHOOSE THE RIGHT PROJECTS

Success with new services is going to be determined by two things: choosing the right projects and doing the projects right.[32] Researchers confirm that following the new service development process discussed earlier in this chapter and illustrated in Figure 8.2 will help with both these goals.[33] Service blueprinting, also presented in this chapter, will help as well, primarily with the second goal of getting the projects rights.

Another concept, *portfolio management for new products*, is very useful in helping companies choose the right projects in the first place.[34] Using this approach, companies manage their product portfolio like they manage their financial portfolio. The approach helps companies prioritize projects, choose which ones to accelerate, and determine the best balance between risk versus return, maintenance versus growth and short-term versus long-term projects. Methods for portfolio management include financial models, scoring models and checklists, mapping approaches, and behavioural approaches.[35]

INTEGRATE NEW SERVICES

Because of the nature of services – they are processes, typically delivered at least in part by people, consumed and produced simultaneously – any new service introduction will affect the existing systems and services.

Unlike when a manufacturer adds a new product to its production facility, new service introductions are frequently visible to customers and may even require their participation. Explicit recognition of these potential impacts, and planning for the integration of people, processes and physical evidence, will facilitate success.[36] This recognition will help in both (1) deciding which projects to pursue – sometimes the disruptive effect on existing systems is too great to warrant the investment – and (2) knowing how to proceed with implementation – what elements of existing processes, people and physical facilities will need to be adjusted, added or changed.

CONSIDER MULTIPLE MEASURES OF SUCCESS

In predicting the success of a new service, multiple performance measures may be considered.[37] First, and most commonly used, is near-term *financial performance* including revenue growth, profitability, market share and return on investment (ROI). In other cases, *relationship enhancement* may be a more appropriate measure of success. This measurement might include (1) the new service's effect on customer loyalty, (2) image enhancement and (3) the effect on the success of other products and services. Or success may be measured in terms of *market development* – the degree to which the new service opens up new markets or new customer segments. Successful projects will lead to increases in one, or perhaps more than one, of these measures.

MAINTAIN SOME FLEXIBILITY

New service success depends on market-driven, customer-focused new product processes; emphasis on planning for and executing the launch; integration of services within existing processes (including staff training); and strong marketing communications, both external and internal. Yet, firms must be cautioned about being too rigid in their service innovation approach. Steps in the development process should be allowed some flexibility, and there will no doubt be overlapping processes. Initial service development, for example, can be occurring simultaneously with additional gathering of customer information. Because services, particularly business-to-business services, are often very complex, some creativity and 'out of order' decisions will be needed. There must be some elements of improvisation, anarchy, and internal competition in the development of new services. 'Consequently, the innovation and adoption of new services must be both a planned process and a happening!'[38]

SUMMARY

Service providers must effectively match customer expectations to new service innovations and actual service process designs. However, because of the very nature of services – their intangibility and variability and co-creation elements – the design and development of service offerings are complex and challenging. Many services are only vaguely defined before their introduction to the marketplace. This chapter has outlined some of the challenges involved in innovating and designing services and some strategies for effectively overcoming the challenges.

Through adaptations of the new product development process that is commonplace in goods production and manufacturing companies, service providers can begin to not only make their offerings more explicit but also avoid failures. The new service development process presented in the chapter includes nine stages, beginning with the development of a business and new service strategy and ending with post-introduction evaluation of the new service. Between these initial and ending stages are a number of steps and checkpoints designed to maximize the likelihood of new service success. Carrying out the stages requires the inclusion of customers, contact employees, business partners and anyone else who will affect or be affected by the new service. Because successful new service introduction is often highly dependent on service employees (often they are the service), integration of employees at each stage is critical.

Service blueprinting is a particularly useful tool in the new service development process. A blueprint can make a complex and intangible service concrete through its visual depiction of all the steps, actors, processes and physical evidence of the service. The key feature of service blueprints is their focus on the customer – the customer's experience is documented first and is kept fully in view as the other features of the blueprint are developed.

The final section of the chapter summarized some of the key factors driving successful new service innovations, including the need for portfolio planning and integration of new services with existing processes and systems. The need to consider multiple measures of success was highlighted as well as the importance of maintaining flexibility in the innovation and new service development process.

KEY CONCEPTS

Business analysis	173	New service development	167
Crowdsourcing	171	Service blueprint	173
Idea generation	171	Service concept development and evaluation	172
Market testing	173		

EXERCISES

1 Think of a new service you would like to develop if you were an entrepreneur. How would you go about it? Describe what you would do and where you would get your information.

2 Find a new and interesting service in your local area, or a service offered on your campus. Document the service process via a service blueprint. To do this exercise, you will probably need to interview one of the service employees. After you have documented the existing service, use blueprinting concepts to redesign the service or change it in some way.

3 Choose a service you are familiar with and document the customer action steps through a photographic blueprint. What is the 'evidence of service' from your point of view as a customer?

4 Develop a service blueprint for a technology-delivered service (such as an Internet-based travel service). Compare and contrast this blueprint to one for the same service delivered via more traditional channels (such as a personal travel agent).

5 Compare two services on the Internet. Discuss the design of each in terms of whether it meets your expectations. How could the design or the service process be changed? Which one is most effective, and why?

DISCUSSION QUESTIONS

1 Why is it challenging to design and develop services?

2 Why is service innovation so critical for firms and countries?

3 Identify where ideas for service innovation might come from.

4 What are the risks of attempting to describe services in words alone?

5 Compare and contrast the blueprints in Figures 8.5 and 8.6.

6 How might a service blueprint be used for marketing, human resource and operations decisions? Focus on the blueprint example in Figure 8.5 as a context for your answer.

7 Assume that you are a multi-product service company that wants to grow through adding new services. Describe a logical process you might use to introduce a new service to the marketplace. What steps in the process might be most difficult and why? How might you incorporate service blueprinting into the process?

8 Discuss Figure 8.2 in terms of the four types of opportunities for growth represented there. Choose a company or service, and explain how it could grow by developing new services in each of the four cells.

9 What role can social media play in innovation?

FURTHER READING

Akao, Y. (2004). *Quality Function Deployment*. Shelton: CTL Productivity Press.

Berry, L.L. and Kampo, S.K. (2000). Teaching an old service new tricks: the promise of service redesign. *Journal of Service Research*, 2(3), 265–75.

Cohen, L. (1995). *Quality Function Deployment: How to Make QFD Work for You*. New York: Addison-Wesley Prentice Hall.

Den Hertog, P., van der Aa, W. and de Jong, M.W. (2010). Capabilities for managing service innovation: towards a conceptual framework. *Journal of Service Management*, 21(4), pp. 490–514.

Edvardsson, B., Enquist, B. and Johnston, R. (2005). Cocreating customer value through hyperreality in the prepurchase service experience. *Journal of Service Research*, 8(2), 149–61.

Edvardsson, B., Gustafsson, A. and Kristensson, P. (2006). *Involving Customers in New Service Development*. Imperial College Press.

Hatch, M.J. and Schultz, M. (2010). Toward a theory of brand co-creation with implications for brand governance. *Journal of Brand Management*, 17(8), 590–604.

Matthing, J. Sandén, B. and Edvardsson, B. (2004). New service development: learning from and with customers. *International Journal of Service Industry Management*, 15(5), 479–498.

Poetz, M. K. and Schreier, M. (2012). The value of crowdsourcing: can users really compete with professionals in generating new product ideas? *Journal of Product Innovation Management*, 29(2), 245–256.

Ramaswamy, V. and Gouillart, F. (2010). Building the co-creative enterprise. *Harvard Business Review*, October, 100–09.

Shostack, G.L. (1984). Designing services that deliver. *Harvard Business Review* (January/February), 133–39.

'*Succeeding through Service Innovation: a service perspective for education, research, business and government*', a white paper published by the University of Cambridge Institute for Manufacturing and IBM, October 2007.

CHAPTER 9

Customer-Defined Service Standards

CHAPTER OUTLINE

LEARNING OBJECTIVES

This chapter's objectives are to:

1 Distinguish between company-defined and customer-defined service standards.
2 Differentiate among one-time service fixes and 'hard' and 'soft' customer-defined standards.
3 Explain the critical role of the service encounter sequence in developing customer-defined standards.
4 Illustrate how to translate customer expectations into behaviours and actions that are definable, repeatable and actionable.
5 Explain the process of developing customer-defined service standards.
6 Emphasize the importance of service performance indexes in implementing strategy for service delivery.

OPENING EXAMPLE

DHL Freight – Understanding Service Standards from a Customer Perspective

DHL Freight is a leading provider of international road transportation solutions in Europe and beyond. The road freight market is highly fragmented, with many providers offering seemingly similar services. Unlike many consumer businesses, the level of emotional engagement between the customer and the provider is low and the relationship is often reduced to a negotiation around operational service quality (e.g., on-time delivery) and price. This results in price competition and yield erosion for the road freight provider. Customers tend to switch provider easily and do not demonstrate any

loyalty behaviour. It is therefore important for DHL Freight to deliver the highest standard of service that meets the needs of customers.

In order to determine if shippers are truly driven by price alone, DHL Freight undertook a survey with 700 road freight customers in 5 countries (France, Germany, the Netherlands, Poland, and Sweden) and asked them to identify the most important attributes of a road freight provider as well as what they would most like their current provider to improve. The research demonstrated that shippers care about more than just operational quality; they are also concerned with the quality of the service support and the ease of doing business with the road freight provider.

DHL Freight found that there was a big difference between the operating standards used by the company to measure performance and the factors used by customers to rate the quality of the service. Like most companies, DHL Freight uses functional scorecards to measure how well their functions perform in terms of aspects such as deliveries made, invoice claims, invoice correctness and number of complaints, but the performance of DHL Freight on these measures did not correlate with customer survey results relating to satisfaction, loyalty or likelihood of recommending the road freight provider to others.

From a customer's perspective, operational quality and price were considered very important, as was expected, but they are not the only or most important aspects. The survey identified that ease of contact with the freight provider, acting quickly and having knowledgeable staff are equally important, or even more so. DHL Freight has therefore introduced standards and customer satisfaction and net promoter score measures to address these softer attributes.

Clearly the relationship between a company and its customers in road freight is more complex than is widely assumed.

Source: Adapted from MacGillavry, K and Wilson, A. (2014) Delivering Loyalty via Customer Experience Management at DHL Freight, Global Business and Organizational Excellence, Vol. 33(6), 6–20.

As we saw in Chapters 6 and 7, understanding customer requirements is the first step in delivering high service quality. Once managers of service businesses accurately understand what customers expect, they face a second critical challenge: using this knowledge to set service quality standards and goals for the organization. Service companies often experience difficulty in setting standards to match or exceed customer expectations – partly because doing so requires that the marketing and operations departments within a company work together. In most service companies, integrating the work of the marketing function and the operations function (appropriately called *functional integration*) is not a typical approach; more frequently these two functions operate separately – setting and achieving their own internal goals – rather than pursuing a joint goal of developing the operations standards that best meet customer expectations.

Creating service standards that address customer expectations is not a common practice in service firms. Doing so often requires altering the very process by which work is accomplished, which is ingrained in tradition in most companies. Often change requires new equipment or technology. Change also necessitates aligning executives from different parts of the firm to understand collectively the comprehensive view of service quality from the customer's perspective. And almost always, change requires a willingness to be open to different ways of structuring, calibrating and monitoring the way service is provided.

FACTORS NECESSARY FOR APPROPRIATE SERVICE STANDARDS

The translation of customer expectations into specific service quality standards depends on the degree to which tasks and behaviours to be performed can be standardized or routinized. Some executives and managers believe that services cannot be standardized – that customization is essential for providing high-quality service. Managers also may feel that standardizing tasks is inconsistent with employee empowerment – that employees will feel controlled by the company if tasks are standardized. Further, they feel that services are too intangible to be measured. This view leads to vague and loose standard setting with little or no measurement or feedback.

In reality, many service tasks are routine (such as those needed for opening bank accounts or servicing domestic gas central heating boilers) and, for these, specific rules and standards can be fairly easily established and effectively executed. Employees may welcome knowing how to perform actions most efficiently: it frees them to use their ingenuity in the more personal and individual aspects of their jobs.

STANDARDIZATION OF SERVICE BEHAVIOURS AND ACTIONS

Standardization of service can take three forms: (1) substitution of technology for personal contact and human effort, (2) improvement in work methods, and (3) combinations of these two methods.[1] Examples of technology substitution include automatic teller machines, automatic car washes and airport X-ray machines. Improvements in work methods are illustrated by restaurant salad bars and routinized tax and accounting services developed by firms such as Pizza Hut and Sage (Accounting Software).

Technology and work improvement methods facilitate the standardization of service necessary to provide consistent delivery to customers. By breaking tasks down and providing them efficiently, technology also allows the firm to calibrate service standards such as the length of time a transaction takes, the accuracy with which operations are performed and the number of problems that occur. In developing work improvements, the firm comes to understand completely the process by which the service is delivered. With this understanding, the firm more easily establishes appropriate service standards.

Standardization, whether accomplished by technology or by improvements in work processes, reduces gap 2. Standardization does not mean that service is performed in a rigid, mechanical way. Customer-defined standardization ensures that the most critical elements of a service are performed as expected by customers, not that every action in a service is executed in a uniform manner. In fact, using customer-defined standardization can allow for, and be compatible with, employee empowerment. One example of this compatibility involves the time limits many companies establish for customer service calls. If their customers' highest priorities involve feeling good about the call or resolving problems, then setting a limit for calls would be decidedly company-defined and not in customers' best interests.

> ⭐ **SERVICE SPOTLIGHT**
>
> Some companies use customer priorities rather than company priorities to determine service standards. Barclaycard, the personal and business credit card provider, have no set standard for the amount of time an employee should spend on the telephone with a customer. Instead, they have defined standards that focus on making the customer satisfied and comfortable, letting telephone representatives use their own judgement about the duration of calls. They recognize that standardization of service is not appropriate in some situations.

WHEN IS THE STRATEGY OF CUSTOMIZATION BETTER THAN STANDARDIZATION?

This chapter focuses on the benefits of customer-defined standards in the context of situations – hotels, retail stores, service outlets – in which it is important to provide the same service to all or most customers. In these situations, standards establish strong guidelines for technology and employees in order to ensure consistency and reliability. In other services, providing standardization is neither appropriate nor possible, and customization – providing unique types and levels of service to customers – is a deliberate strategy.

In most 'expert' services – such as accounting, consulting, engineering and dentistry, for example – professionals provide customized and individualized services; standardization of the tasks is perceived as being impersonal, inadequate and not in the customer's best interests. Because patient and client needs differ, these professionals offer very customized services that address individual requirements. They must adapt their offerings to the particular needs of each customer because each situation is different. Even within a given medical specialty, few patients have the same illness with precisely the same symptoms and the same medical history. Therefore, standardizing the amount of time a doctor spends with a patient is rarely possible, one of the reasons why patients usually must wait before receiving medical services even though they have advance appointments. Because professionals such as accountants and lawyers cannot usually standardize what they provide, they often charge by the hour rather than by the job, which allows them to be compensated for the customized periods of time they spend with clients. It is important to recognize, however, that even in highly customized services, some aspects of service provision can be routinized. Physiotherapists and dentists, for example, can and do standardize recurring and non-technical aspects such as checking patients in, weighing patients, taking routine measurements, billing patients and collecting payment. In delegating these routine tasks to assistants, the professional staff can spend more of their time on the expert service of diagnosis or patient care.

Another situation in which customization is the chosen strategy is in business-to-business contexts, particularly with key accounts. When accounts are large and critical to a provider, most aspects of service provision are customized. At a very basic level, this customization takes the form of service contracts such as those described for ISS (See Service Spotlight on page 192) in which the client and the provider agree on issues such as cleaning standards, speed of response, etc. At a higher level, customization involves creative problem-solving and innovative ideas (as in consulting services).

Finally, many consumer services are designed to be (or appear) very customized. These services include spa and upmarket hotel visits, exotic vacations such as safaris, and even haircuts from expensive salons. In these situations, the steps taken to ensure the successful delivery of service are often standardized behind the scenes but appear to the customer to be very individualized. Even Disney theme parks use this approach, employing hundreds of standards to ensure the delivery of 'magic' to each individual customer.

FORMAL SERVICE TARGETS AND GOALS

Companies that have been successful in delivering consistently high service quality are noted for establishing formal standards to guide employees in providing service. These companies have an accurate sense of how well they are performing service that is critical to their customers – how long it takes to conduct transactions, how frequently service fails, how quickly they settle customer complaints – and strive to improve by defining goals that lead them to meet or exceed customer expectations.

One type of formal goal-setting that is relevant in service businesses involves specific targets for individual behaviours or actions. As an example, consider the behaviour 'calls the customer back quickly', an action that signals responsiveness in contact employees. If the service goal for employee behaviour is stated in such a general term as 'call the customer back quickly', the standard provides little direction for service employees. Different employees will interpret this vague objective in their own ways, leading to inconsistent service: some may call the customer back in ten minutes whereas others may wait two to four days. And the firm itself will not be able to determine when or if individual employees meet the goal because its expression is not measurable – one could justify virtually any amount of time as 'quickly'. On the other hand, if the individual employee's service goal is to call each customer back within four hours, employees have a specific, unambiguous guideline about how quickly they should execute the action (four hours). Whether the goal is met is also unequivocal: if the call occurs within four hours the company meets the goal; otherwise it does not.

Another type of formal goal setting involves the overall department or company target, most frequently expressed as a percentage, across all executions of the behaviour or action. For example, a department might set as its overall goal 'to call the customer back within four hours 97 per cent of the time' and collect data over a month's or years' time to evaluate the extent to which it meets the target.

Service firms that produce consistently excellent service – firms such as Disneyland Paris, DHL and British Airways – have very specific, quantified, measurable service goals. Disneyland calibrates employee performance on myriad behaviours and actions that contribute to guest perceptions of high service quality. Whether they are set and monitored using audits (such as timed actions) or customer perceptions (such as opinions about courtesy), service standards provide a means for formal goal setting.

⭐ SERVICE SPOTLIGHT

Integrated Service Solutions (ISS), headquartered in Copenhagen, Denmark, is one of the world's largest facility service providers, with market presence in Europe, Asia, South America and Australia. ISS employs more than 520,000 people serving 200,000 public and private-sector customers in over 60 countries. It offers services such as catering, office support, security, cleaning, property services and facility management. ISS's service offering has been developed to meet customer needs. ISS has to meet standards of service set by its customers. For example, in Singapore, where the company cleans the Raffles Link shopping area, the standards for cleanliness may be among the most challenging in the world. ISS Singapore uses the most modern and environmentally friendly cleaning equipment, chemicals and methods to serve their demanding customers in Singapore.

'First of all, managing demanding customer expectations means understanding the customer's requirements and needs. When I come here early in the morning, I have to ensure that all areas are attended to and cleaned before my client arrives. The result at the end of the day matters a lot to me,' explains Project Manager Jason Foo of ISS Singapore.

Jason heads the 60 employees in the shopping and office area connected to the Raffles Link Station. They have more than 300,000 square metres to clean.

'When I first worked with this client, he used a white handkerchief to check the cleanliness of surfaces. As time has passed, he found less and less dirt on his handkerchief. In the past year, we managed to gain his trust and confidence, and he no longer uses his handkerchief when inspecting our work,' explains Jason. However, every day ISS uses its own inspectors to continue to check whether the customer's standards are being met.

Source: **Adapted from www.issworld.com.**

CUSTOMER- NOT COMPANY-DEFINED STANDARDS

Virtually all companies possess service standards and measures that are *company defined* – they are established to reach internal company goals for productivity, efficiency, cost or technical quality. A current company-defined standard that does not meet customer expectations is the common practice of voice-activated telephone support systems that do not allow consumers to speak to humans. Because these systems save companies money (and actually provide faster service to some customers), many organizations have switched from the labour-intensive practice of having customer representatives to using these systems.

To close gap 2, standards set by companies must be based on customer requirements and expectations (identified using some of the methods outlined in Chapter 6) rather than just on internal company goals. In this chapter we make the case that company-defined standards are not typically successful in driving behaviours that close provider gap 2. Instead, a company must set *customer-defined standards:* operational standards based on pivotal customer requirements that are visible to and measured by customers. These standards are deliberately chosen to match customer expectations and to be calibrated the way the customer views and expresses them. Because these goals are essential to the provision of excellent service, the rest of this chapter focuses on customer-defined standards.

Knowing customer requirements, priorities and expectation levels can be both effective and efficient. Anchoring service standards on customers can save money by identifying what the customer values, thus eliminating activities and features that the customer either does not notice or will not pay for. Through precise measurement of expectations, the company often discovers that it has been over-delivering to many customer needs.

A bank might add several extra tellers and reduce the average peak waiting time in queues from seven minutes to five minutes. If customers expect, however, to wait up to eight minutes during peak time, the investment in extra tellers may not be effective. An opportunity thus exists to capture the value of this information through reduced teller costs and higher profits.[2]

Although customer-defined standards need not conflict with productivity and efficiency, they are not developed for these reasons. Rather, they are anchored in and steered by customer perceptual measures of service quality or satisfaction. The service standards that evolve from a customer perspective are likely to be different from company-defined service standards.

Virtually all organizations have lists of actions that they measure regularly, most of which fall into the category of company-defined standards. Often these standards deal with activities or actions that reflect the history of the business rather than the reality of today's competitive marketplace or the needs of current customers.

SERVICE SPOTLIGHT

Scottish and Southern Energy, a supplier of gas and electricity to domestic consumers, follows the Energy Supplier Guaranteed Standards set by the UK energy regulator (Ofgem). These standards are aimed at meeting customer expectations and requirements, including:

- **Keeping Appointments** – Scottish and Southern Energy (SSE) issues guarantees about punctuality when it sets appointments with customers in relation to their gas or electricity supply. Customers can select either a morning or afternoon slot, Monday through Friday and can also specify a two-hour window. If SSE can't keep this appointment, or fails to give advance notice, customers receive £20 (gas) or £22 (electricity) off their bill.
- **Electricity bill queries** – SSE promises to reply in writing within five working days with an explanation about customer billing inquiries; for example, if customers think that they are due

a refund, have noticed a billing error, or are in disagreement with SSE about changes to their mode of payment. If not, the company pays the customer £22.

- **Meter disputes** – When customers believe that their meter is faulty and SSE are unable to resolve the query over the telephone, the company sends a written explanation within five working days or offers an appointment to visit within seven working days. If the company fails to do so, it promises to send the customers a £22 (electricity) or £20 (gas) payment.
- SSE also ensures that their customers are compensated quickly, and promises payment within 10 working days, or the customer receives a further £20 (gas) or £22 (electricity).

TYPES OF CUSTOMER-DEFINED SERVICE STANDARDS

The type of standards that close provider gap 2 are *customer-defined standards:* operational goals and measures based on pivotal customer requirements that are visible to and measured by customers rather than on company concerns such as productivity or efficiency. Take a typical operations standard such as inventory control. Most firms control inventory from the company's point of view.

However, supermarkets such as Tesco and Sainsbury's capture every single service measurement related to inventory control *from the customer's point of view.* The companies begin with the question, 'What does the customer see?' and answer, 'The average number of stockouts per week'. These supermarkets then design a customer-focused measurement system based on measures such as the number of empty shelves, the number of unfulfilled product requests and complaints as well as transaction-based data linked to the use of customer loyalty cards at the tills. These and other customer-defined standards allow for the translation of customer requirements into goals and guidelines for employee performance. Two major types of customer-defined service standards can be distinguished: 'hard' and 'soft'. These standards are discussed in the following two sections.

HARD CUSTOMER-DEFINED STANDARDS

As we stressed in Chapter 3, customer expectations of reliability – fulfilment of service promises – are high. Recent studies across numerous industries have found that the most frequent customer complaints are associated with poor product performance (29 per cent of all complaints) and service mistakes or problems (24 per cent of all complaints).[3]

To address the need for reliability, companies can institute a 'do it right the first time' and an 'honour your promises' value system by establishing reliability standards. An example of a generic reliability standard that would be relevant to virtually any service company is 'right first time', which means that the service performed is done correctly the first time according to the customer's assessment. If the service involves delivery of products, 'right first time' to the customer might mean that the shipment is accurate – that it contains all that the customer ordered and nothing that the customer did not order. If the service involves installation of equipment, 'right the first time' would likely mean that the equipment was installed correctly and could be used immediately by the customer. Another example of a reliability standard is 'right on time', which means that the service is performed at the scheduled time. The company representative arrives when promised or the delivery is made at the time the customer expects it. In more complex services, such as disaster recovery or systems integration in computer service, 'right on time' would likely mean that the service was completed by the promised date.

Reliability is often the single most important concern of service customers. In online retailing, on time and accurate fulfilment of orders is one of the most important aspects of reliability. One of the best examples of hard customer-defined service standards in the Internet context is the set of summary metrics that Dell Computer uses for fulfilment.[4] They include:

- *Ship to target* (STT) – the percentage of orders delivered on time with complete accuracy
- *Initial field incident rate* (IFIR) – the frequency of customer problems
- *On time first time fix* (OTFTF) – the percentage of problems fixed on the first visit by a service representative arriving at the time promised.

Dell tracks its performance to these standards and rewards employees on the basis of their 'met promises' or reliability, which is often higher than 98 per cent.

Hard service standards for responsiveness are set to ensure the speed or promptness with which companies deliver products (within two working days), handle complaints (by sundown each day), answer questions (within two hours), answer the telephone and arrive for repair calls (within 30 minutes of the estimated time). In addition to standard-setting that specifies levels of response, companies must have well-staffed customer service departments. Responsiveness perceptions diminish when customers wait to get through to the company by telephone, are put on hold, or are dumped into a telephone mail system.

Table 9.1   Examples of hard standards include:

Company	Customer priorities	Customer-defined standards
DHL	On-time delivery	Number of packages right day late Number of packages wrong day late Number of missed pickups
Dell Computer	On-time delivery Computer works properly	Ship to target Initial field incident rate Missing, wrong, and damaged rate

SOFT CUSTOMER-DEFINED STANDARDS

Not all customer priorities can be counted, timed or observed through audits. As Albert Einstein once said, 'Not everything that counts can be counted, and not everything that can be counted counts'. For example, 'understanding and knowing the customer' is not a customer priority that can be adequately captured by a standard that counts, times or observes employees. In contrast to hard measures, soft measures are those that must be documented using perceptual data. We call the second category of customer-defined standards soft standards and measures because they are opinion-based measures and cannot be directly observed. They must be collected by talking to customers, employees or others. Soft customer-defined service standards provide direction, guidance and feedback to employees in ways to achieve customer satisfaction and can be quantified by measuring customer perceptions and beliefs. Soft standards are especially important for person-to-person interactions such as the selling process and the delivery process for professional services.

ONE-TIME FIXES

When customer research is undertaken to find out what aspects of service need to be changed, requirements can sometimes be met using one-time fixes. One-time fixes are *technology, policy or procedure changes that, when instituted, address customer requirements*. We further define one-time fixes as those company standards that can be met by an outlet (a franchisee, for example) making a one-time change that does not involve employees and therefore does not require motivation and monitoring to ensure compliance. We include one-time fixes in our discussion of standards because organizations with multiple outlets often must clearly define these standards to ensure consistency.

Table 9.2 Examples of soft customer-defined standards include:

Company	Customer priorities	Customer-defined standards
Ritz-Carlton*	Being treated with respect	'Gold Standards' Uniforms are to be immaculate Wear proper and safe footwear Wear name tag Adhere to grooming standards Notify supervisor immediately of hazards Use proper telephone etiquette Ask the caller, 'May I place you on hold?' Do not screen calls Eliminate call transfers when possible
American Express	Resolution of problems	Resolve problem at first contact (no transfers, other calls or multiple contacts); communicate and give adequate instructions; take all the time necessary
	Treatment	Listen; do everything possible to help; be appropriately reassuring (open and honest)
	Courtesy of representative	Put card member at ease; be patient in explaining billing process; display sincere interest in helping card member; listen attentively; address card member by name; thank card member at end of call

*Source: 'The Ritz-Carlton Basics', flyer distributed by the Ritz-Carlton to all employees and www. Americanexpress.com.

Examples of successful one-time fixes include Europcar and other car rental companies' express check-in, Tesco's self-scanning tills or KLM's online check-in facility. In each of these examples, customers expressed a desire to be served in ways different from the past. All had clearly indicated their frustration at waiting in long lines. Whereas most companies in these industries decided for various reasons not to address these customer requirements, Europcar, Tesco and KLM each responded with one-time fixes that virtually revolutionized the service quality delivered by their companies. One-time fixes are often accomplished by technology. Technology can simplify and improve customer service, particularly when it frees company personnel by handling routine, repetitious tasks and transactions. Customer service employees can then spend more time on the personal and possibly more essential portions of the job. Some technology, in particular computer databases that contain information on individual needs and interests of customers, allows the company to standardize the essential elements of service delivery.

One-time fixes also deal with the aspects of service relating to rules and policies, operating hours, product quality and price. An example of a one-time fix involving a policy change is that of allowing front-line employees to refund money to dissatisfied customers. An example of operating-hour changes is extending the operating hours of call centres to include Sundays.

DEVELOPMENT OF CUSTOMER-DEFINED SERVICE STANDARDS
BASING STANDARDS ON THE SERVICE ENCOUNTER SEQUENCE

A customer's overall service quality evaluation is the accumulation of evaluations of multiple service experiences. Service encounters are the component pieces needed to establish service standards in a company. In establishing standards we are concerned with service encounter quality, because we want to understand for each service encounter the specific requirements and priorities of the customer. When we know these priorities, we can focus on them as the aspects of service encounters for which standards should be established. Therefore, one of the first steps in establishing customer-defined standards is to delineate the service encounter sequence. Identifying the sequence can be done by listing the sequential steps and activities that the customer experiences in receiving the service. Alternatively, service blueprints (see Chapter 8) can be used to identify the sequence by noting all the customers' activities across the top of the blueprint. Vertical lines from customer activities into the lower levels of the blueprint signal the points at which service encounters take place. Standards that meet customer expectations can then be established.

Because many services have multiple encounters, companies and researchers have examined whether some encounters (for example, the first or the last) are more important than others. The Marriott Corporation identified the encounters that occur in the first ten minutes of a hotel stay as the most critical, leading the hospitality company to focus on hotel front-desk experiences (such as express check-in) when making improvements. Although service practice and management literature have emphasized strong starts, recent research indicates that strong finishes in the final event of the encounter have a greater impact on overall satisfaction. Further, the research shows that consistent performance throughout the encounter – widely believed to produce the most favourable evaluations – is not as effective as a pattern of improving performance that culminates in a strong finish.[5] An implication of this research for hotels is that managers should focus on the 'back end' of the hotel experience – checkout, parking, concierge services – to leave a strong final impression.

EXPRESSING CUSTOMER REQUIREMENTS AS SPECIFIC BEHAVIOURS AND ACTIONS

Setting a standard in broad conceptual terms, such as 'improve skills in the company', is ineffective because the standard is difficult to interpret, measure and achieve. When a company collects data, it often captures customer requirements in very abstract terms. In general, contact or field people often find that data are not diagnostic – they are too broad and general. Research neither tells them specifically what is wrong and right in their customer relationships nor helps them understand what activities can be eliminated so that the most important actions can be accomplished. In most cases, field people need help translating the data into specific actions to deliver better customer service.

Effective service standards are defined in very specific ways that enable employees to understand what they are being asked to deliver. At best, these standards are set and measured in terms of specific responses of human behaviours and actions.

Figure 9.1 shows different levels of abstraction/concreteness for standards in a service firm, arrayed from top (most abstract) to bottom (most concrete and specific). At the very abstract level are customer requirements that are too general to be useful to employees: customers want satisfaction, value and relationships. One level under these very general requirements are abstract dimensions of service quality already discussed in this text: reliability, responsiveness, empathy, assurance and tangibles. One level further down are attributes more specific in describing requirements. If we dig still deeper beneath the attribute level, we get to specific behaviours and actions that are at the right level of specificity for setting standards.

Figure 9.1   What customers expect: getting to actionable steps

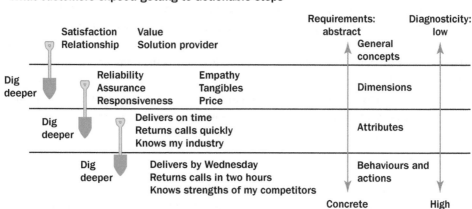

A real-world example of the difference in requirements across these levels will illustrate their practical significance. In a traditional measurement system for a major company's training division, only one aspect of the instructor was included in its class evaluation: ability of instructor. During qualitative research relating to the attributes that satisfy students, three somewhat more specific requirements were elicited: (1) instructor's style, (2) instructor's expertise and (3) instructor's management of class. Although the articulation of the three attributes was more helpful to instructors than the broad 'ability of instructor', management found that the attributes were still too broad to help instructors wanting to improve their course delivery. When the company invested in a customer-defined standards project, the resulting measurement system was far more useful in diagnosing student requirements because the research focused on *specific behaviours and actions* of instructors that met student requirements. Instead of a single broad requirement or three general attributes, the requirements of students were articulated in 14 specific behaviours and actions that related to the instructor and 11 specific behaviours and actions that related to the course content. These behaviours and actions were clearly more diagnostic for communicating what was good and bad in the courses. An additional benefit of this approach was that feedback on behaviours and actions was less personal than feedback on traits or personal characteristics. It was also easier for employees of the company to make changes that related to behaviours rather than to personality traits.

MEASURING BEHAVIOURS AND ACTIONS

Hard measurements for measuring behaviours and actions consist of counts or audits or timed actions that provide feedback about the operational performance of a service standard. What distinguishes these data from soft measurements is that they can be captured continuously and operationally without asking the customer's opinion about them.

⭐ SERVICE SPOTLIGHT

Here are some of the actual hard measurements used by Federal Express in its international operations:

- *Missing proofs of delivery:* the number of invoices that do not include proof-of-delivery paperwork
- *Overgoods:* lost and found packages that lack, or have lost, identifying labels for the sender and the addressee, and are sent to the Overgoods Department
- *Wrong day late deliveries:* number of packages delivered after the commitment date
- *Traces:* the number of 'proof of performance' requests from customers that cannot be answered through data contained in the computer system.[6]

In these and other hard measurements, the actual gauge involves a count of the number and type of actions or behaviours that are correct or incorrect. Somewhere in the operation system these actions and behaviours are tabulated, frequently through information technology. Other gauges of hard measures include service guarantee lapses (the number of times a service guarantee is invoked because the service did not meet the promise), amounts of time (as in the number of hours or days to respond to a question or complaint or of minutes spent in a queue) and frequencies associated with relevant standards (such as the number of visits made to customers).

The appropriate hard measure to deliver to customer requirements is not always intuitive or obvious, and the potential for counting or tracking an irrelevant aspect of operations is high. For this reason it is desirable to link the measure of operational performance with soft measures (relationship surveys or follow-up satisfaction surveys) to be sure that they are strongly correlated.

SOFT MEASUREMENTS

Two types of perceptual measurement that were described in Chapter 6 can document customers' opinions about whether performance met the standards established: satisfaction surveys and relationship surveys.

Relationship and SERVQUAL surveys cover all aspects of the customer's relationship with the company, are typically expressed in attributes, and are usually completed once a year. Follow-up satisfaction surveys are associated with specific service encounters, are short (approximately six or seven questions) and are administered as close in time to a specific service encounter as possible. Such surveys can be administered in various ways: company-initiated telephone calls following the interactions, postcards to be mailed, letters requesting feedback, customer-initiated calls to a freephone number or online electronic surveys. For requirements that are longer term and at a higher level of abstraction (such as at the attribute level), annual relationship surveys can document customer perceptions on a periodic basis. Follow-up satisfaction surveys are administered continuously, whenever a customer experiences a service encounter of the type being considered, and they provide data on a continuous basis. The company must decide on a survey strategy combining relationship surveys and follow-up satisfaction surveys to provide soft measurement feedback.

SERVICE SPOTLIGHT

As one of the world's leading operators of luxury hotels and resorts, Four Seasons manages 63 properties in 29 countries, and successfully accomplishes this goal by balancing universal services standards with standards that vary by country.[7] The company owes much of its success to its seven 'service culture standards' expected of *all* staff *all* over the world at *all* times. The seven standards, which form the word SERVICE, are:

1 Smile: employees will actively greet guests, smile and speak clearly in a friendly manner
2 Eye: employees will make eye contact, even in passing, with an acknowledgement
3 Recognition: all staff will create a sense of recognition by using the guest's name, when known, in a natural and discreet manner
4 Voice: staff will speak to guests in an attentive, natural and courteous manner, avoiding pretension and in a clear voice
5 Informed: all guest contact staff will be well informed about their hotel, their product, will take ownership of simple requests, and will not refer guests elsewhere
6 Clean: staff will always appear clean, crisp, well-groomed and well fitted
7 Everyone: everyone, everywhere, all the time, shows their care for our guests.

In addition to these culture standards that are expected of all staff all over the world, the hotel has 270 core standards that apply to different aspects of service provision (examples include 'the staff will be aware of arriving vehicles and will move toward them, opening doors within 30 seconds' and 'unanswered guest room phones will be picked up within 5 rings, or 20 seconds'). Exceptions to these 270 standards are allowed if they make local or cultural sense. For example, in the United States, coffee pots are left on tables at breakfast; in many parts of Europe, including France, customers perceive this practice as a lack of service, and servers personally refill coffee cups as needed. Standards for uniforms and decor differ across cultures, but minimum expectations must be met everywhere.

ADAPTING STANDARDS GLOBALLY OR LOCALLY

How do companies adjust for cultural or local differences in service standards if they recognize that these geographic differences are related to varying customer expectations? Companies with worldwide brands have much to lose if their service standards vary too much across countries, and therefore they must find ways to achieve universally high quality while still allowing for local differences.

DEVELOPING CUSTOMER-DEFINED STANDARDS

Figure 9.2 shows the general process for setting customer-defined service standards.

STEP 1: IDENTIFY EXISTING OR DESIRED SERVICE ENCOUNTER SEQUENCE

The first step involves delineating the customer journey through the service encounter sequence. In many cases a service blueprint may be used to identify the service encounter sequence and the various customer touchpoints. Ideally, the company would be open to discovering customers' desired customer journey, exploring the ways customers want to do business with the firm.

Figure 9.2   Process for setting customer-defined standards

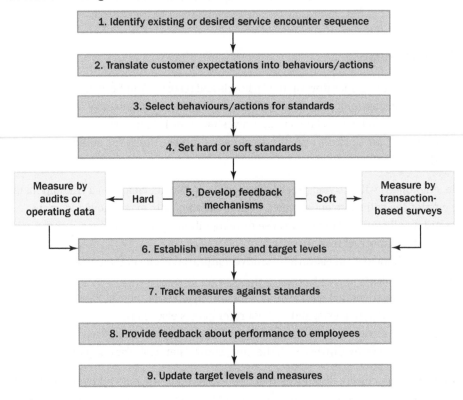

STEP 2: TRANSLATE CUSTOMER EXPECTATIONS INTO BEHAVIOURS AND ACTIONS FOR EACH SERVICE ENCOUNTER

The input to step 2 is existing research on customer expectations. In this step, abstract customer requirements and expectations must be translated into concrete, specific behaviours and actions associated with each service encounter. Abstract requirements (like reliability) can call for a different behaviour or action in each service encounter, and these differences must be probed. Eliciting these behaviours and actions is likely to require additional qualitative research because in most service companies, marketing information has not been collected for this purpose.

Information on behaviours and actions must be gathered and interpreted by an objective source such as a research firm or an internal department with no stake in the ultimate decisions. If the information is filtered through company managers or front-line people with an internal bias, the outcome would be company-defined rather than customer-defined standards.

Research techniques discussed in Chapter 6 that are relevant for eliciting behaviours and actions include in-depth interviewing of customers and focus group interviews.

STEP 3: SELECT BEHAVIOURS AND ACTIONS FOR STANDARDS

This stage involves prioritizing the behaviours and actions, of which there will be many, into those for which customer-defined standards will be established. The following are the most important criteria for creation of the standards.

1 *The standards are based on behaviours and actions that are very important to customers.* Customers have many requirements for the products and services that companies provide. Customer-defined standards need to focus on what is *very important* to customers. Unless very important behaviours/actions are chosen, a company could show improvement in delivering to standards with no impact on overall customer satisfaction or business goals.

2 *The standards cover performance that needs to be improved or maintained.* Customer-defined standards should be established for behaviour that needs to be improved or maintained. The company gets the highest leverage or biggest impact from focusing on behaviours and actions that need to be improved. Figure 9.3 shows an importance/performance matrix for a computer manufacturer. It combines the importance and performance criteria and indicates them by the shading in the cell in the matrix where behaviours and actions should be selected to meet those criteria.

3 *The standards cover behaviours and actions employees can improve.* Employees perform consistently according to standards only if they understand, accept and have control over the behaviours and actions specified in the standards. Holding contact people to standards that they cannot control (such as product quality or time lag in introduction of new products) does not result in improvement. For this reason, service standards should cover controllable aspects of employees' jobs.

4 *The standards are accepted by employees.* Employees will perform to standards consistently only if they understand and accept the standards. Imposing standards on unwilling employees often leads to resistance, resentment, absenteeism, even turnover. Many companies establish standards for the amount of time it should take (rather than for the time it does take) for each service job and gradually cut back on the time to reduce labour costs. This practice inevitably leads to increasing tensions among employees. In these situations, managers, financial personnel and union representatives can work together to determine new standards for the tasks.

5 *The standards are predictive rather than reactive.* Customer-defined standards should not be established on the basis of complaints or other forms of reactive feedback. Reactive feedback deals with past concerns of customers rather than with current and future customer expectations. Rather than waiting for dissatisfied customers to complain, the company should actively seek both positive and negative perceptions of customers in advance of complaints.

6 *The standards are challenging but realistic.* A large number of studies on goal-setting show that highest performance levels are obtained when standards are challenging but realistic. If standards are not challenging, employees get little reinforcement for mastering them. On the other hand, unrealistically high standards leave an employee feeling dissatisfied with performance and frustrated by not being able to attain the goal.

Table 9.3 shows an example of the set of behaviours and actions selected by a company for its complaint-handling service encounter. Some of these are different across the two segments of customers for which standards were set (small and large customers). Three other behaviours were chosen for standards across all customers.

⭐ SERVICE SPOTLIGHT

It isn't only commercial bodies that develop service standards. Public bodies such as government departments and local government set standards for delivery. The following service standards are used by Derby City Council, a local government organization based in England.

We will:

- treat you politely and with respect
- listen to you and take your views, wishes and needs seriously
- make sure that our employees are trained to give you the help and advice that you need
- use plain language and not use jargon
- provide information in other languages and arrange for a British Sign Language (BSL) interpreter where needed
- not discriminate against you.

When answering the telephone and minicom, we will:

- aim to answer your call within six rings
- greet you politely and clearly
- tell you who you are speaking to and the name of the service or place you are calling
- put calls through to the right place first time
- take a message or give you the correct number to phone if we cannot transfer your call
- return your messages within one working day.

When dealing with your letters and faxes, we will:

- provide an acknowledgement where requested
- give you details of who is dealing with your enquiry
- respond to your enquiry within five working days.

When dealing with your emails, text or other electronic communications, we will:

- provide an acknowledgement
- give you details of who is dealing with your enquiry
- respond to your enquiry within five working days.

When you visit Council buildings, we will:

- create an accessible environment that is welcoming, safe and friendly
- provide clear signs in reception areas
- provide self service facilities where appropriate
- make sure you are greeted within three minutes of arriving.

When we meet you face-to-face, we will:

- be on time
- wear name badges or carry official identification
- arrange a time and place for you to discuss issues in private
- where appropriate, make other arrangements to see you if you cannot visit us
- provide a follow up card with contact details, where appropriate.

Dealing with complaints, comments and compliments, we will:

- provide you with information about how to report a complaint, comment or compliment
- record complaints, comments and compliments and use them to review and improve our services
- respond to all complaints within 10 working days

- treat complaints confidentially, while making sure we are fair to everyone concerned
- inform you how you can take your complaint further if you are not satisfied with our response
- apologise when we are at fault and do our very best to put things right.

  We will keep customers informed and involved by:

- producing information about the Council and our services that is accurate, useful and up to date
- providing information in other languages and making this accessible if you are a disabled person
- publishing regularly how well we are meeting our Customer Service Standards
- reviewing the Customer Standards every year
- using your feedback to help us make decisions.

Source: **Derby City Council, UK - www.derby.gov.uk.**

Figure 9.3   Importance/performance matrix: delivery, installing, performing

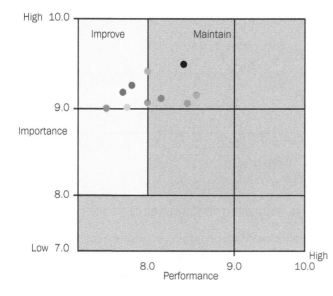

- Delivers on promises specified in proposal contract (9.49,8.51)
- Does whatever it takes to correct problems (9.26, 7.98)
- Gets project within budget, on time (9.31, 7.87)
- Gets price we originally agreed upon (9.21, 8.64)
- Complete projects correctly on time (9.29, 7.98)
- Gets back to me when promised (9.04, 7.63)
- Tells me cost aheed of time (9.08, 8.45)
- Provides equipment that operates as vendor said it would (9.24, 8.14)
- Takes responsibility for their mistakes (9.18, 8.01)
- Delivers or installs on promised date (9.02, 7.84)

Table 9.3   Customer-defined standards for complaint handling by segment

Large customers	All complaint-handling personnel trained to
Are assigned an individual to call with complaints Have a four-hour standard for resolving problems	Paraphrase problems Ask customers what solution they prefer
Small customers	
Can call service centre or individual Have an eight-hour standard for resolving problems	Verify that problem has been fixed

STEP 4: DECIDE WHETHER HARD OR SOFT STANDARDS ARE APPROPRIATE

The next step involves deciding whether hard or soft standards should be used to capture the behaviour and action. One of the biggest mistakes companies make in this step is to choose a hard standard hastily. Companies are accustomed to operational measures and have a bias towards them. However, unless the hard standard adequately captures the expected behaviour and action, it is not customer defined. The best way to decide whether a hard standard is appropriate is first to establish a soft standard by means of follow-up satisfaction surveys and then determine over time which operational aspect most correlates to this soft measure. Figure 9.4 shows the linkage between speed of complaint handling (a hard measure) and satisfaction (a soft measure), and illustrates that satisfaction strongly depends on the number of hours it takes to resolve a complaint.

Figure 9.4   Linkage between soft and hard measures for speed of complaint handling

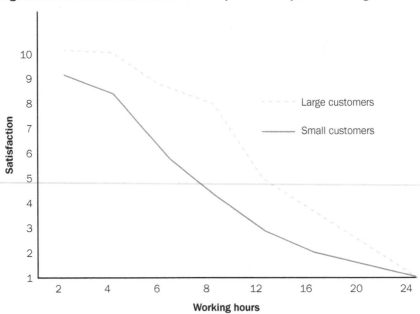

STEP 5: DEVELOP FEEDBACK MECHANISMS FOR MEASUREMENT TO STANDARDS

Once companies have determined whether hard or soft standards are appropriate and which specific standards best capture customer requirements, they must develop feedback mechanisms that adequately capture those standards. Hard standards typically involve mechanical counts or technology-enabled measurement of time or errors. Soft standards require perceptual measurements through the use of follow-up satisfaction surveys or employee monitoring. Employee monitoring is illustrated by the practice of supervisors listening in on employee calls. You may have experienced this practice when you called customer service numbers for many organizations and noticed that the voice prompts tell you that calls may be monitored for quality purposes. The purpose of this monitoring is to provide feedback on employee performance to the standards set by the organization to meet customer needs. One critical aspect of developing feedback mechanisms is ensuring that performance captures the process from the customer's view rather than the company's perspective. A supervisor monitoring an employee's handling of a customer service call, for example, should focus less on how quickly the employee gets the customer off the telephone and more on how adequately he or she handles the customer's request.

STEP 6: ESTABLISH MEASURES AND TARGET LEVELS

The next step requires that companies establish target levels for the standards. Without this step the company lacks a way to quantify whether the standards have been met. Figure 9.4 provided a good example of the approach used to set standards for timeliness in a service company. Each time a complaint was made to the company, and each time a complaint was resolved, employees logged in the times. They also asked each customer his or her satisfaction with the performance in resolving the complaint. The company was then able to plot the information from each complaint on the chart to determine how well the company was performing as well as where the company wished to be in the future. The vertical axis in Figure 9.4 shows the satisfaction levels of customers, and the horizontal axis shows the number of hours it took the company to resolve customer problems. This technique is one of several for determining the target level.

Another technique is a simple perception–action correlation study. When the service consists of repetitive processes, companies can relate levels of customer satisfaction with actual performance of a behaviour or task. Consider, for example, a study to determine the standard for customers' wait time in a queue. The information needed includes customer perceptions of their queuing up (soft perceptual measure) and the amount of time they actually stand in the queue (hard operations measure). The joint collection of these data over many transactions provides evidence of the sensitivity of customers to different wait times.

An airline conducted precisely this study by having airline staff intercept customers as they approached the check-in counter. As each customer entered the line, the attendant stamped the entry time on a ticket and handed the customer the stamped ticket. As the customer exited the queue at the end of the transaction, airline staff restamped the ticket with the exit time and asked the customer three or four questions about their perceptions of queuing up and their satisfaction with the transaction. Aggregating the individual customer data provided a graph that allowed the company to evaluate the impact on perceptions of various levels of line waits.

STEP 7: TRACK MEASURES AGAINST STANDARDS

Successful service businesses such as the Royal Bank of Scotland, London Undergound and Ritz-Carlton have careful and comprehensive fact-based systems about their operations.

The Royal Bank of Scotland uses customer satisfaction, actual performance and operational measures as the drivers of service performance measurement. Qualitative research involving trade-off analysis was used to identify customers' perceptions of the key service attributes from a bank. These attributes were then established as service standards which were measured through an index which was constructed from scores relating to:

- Customer satisfaction questionnaire (70 per cent)
- Mystery shopping activity (20 per cent)
- An inventory of tangibles relating to physical aspects of each branch (10 per cent).

Table 9.4   The attributes that were measured by each method.

Attributes	Satisfaction questionnaire	Mystery shopping	Inventory
Courtesy	X	X	
Telephone handling	X	X	
Queuing	X	X	
Product/service knowledge	X	X	
Problem-solving	X		
Efficiency	X		
Appearance	X	X	
Loyalty	X		
Tangibles			X

London Underground measures service quality through customer satisfaction surveys, mystery shopping activities and the monitoring of complaints. However, the quality of service is also measured through operational information relating to areas such as:

- Percentage of trains cancelled
- Percentage of ticket offices open
- Percentage of ticket machines in operation
- Average journey times
- Headway: the average time between each train arriving at a platform.

These combine with the other service quality measures to provide guidance for management priorities and investment decisions.

Ritz-Carlton has created a service quality indicator (SQI). The Ritz's SQI spells out the 12 most serious defects that can occur in the operation of a hotel and weights them by their seriousness. The defects and points associated with them include:

1 Missing guest preferences (10 points)
2 Unresolved difficulties (50 points)
3 Inadequate guest-room housekeeping (1 point)
4 Abandoned reservation calls (5 points)
5 Guest-room changes (5 points)
6 Inoperable guest-room equipment (5 points)
7 Unready guest-room (10 points)
8 Inappropriate hotel appearance (5 points)
9 Meeting event difficulties (5 points)
10 Inadequate food/beverage (1 point)
11 Missing/damaged guest property/accidents (50 points)
12 Invoice adjustment (3 points).

The hotel calculates the SQI by multiplying the total number of occurrences by their points, totals the points and divides by the number of working days to get an average daily point value. This value is communicated every day to employees.[8]

STEP 8: PROVIDE FEEDBACK ABOUT PERFORMANCE TO EMPLOYEES

Data and facts need to be analysed and distributed to support evaluation and decision-making at multiple levels within the company. The data also must be deployed quickly enough that the people who need it to make decisions about service or processes can do so. Responsibility for meeting service requirements must also be communicated throughout the organization. All parts of the organization must be measuring their services to internal customers and, ultimately, measuring how that performance relates to external customer requirements.[9]

STEP 9: PERIODICALLY UPDATE TARGET LEVELS AND MEASURES

The final step involves revising the target levels, measures and, even, customer requirements regularly enough to keep up with customer expectations.

DEVELOPING SERVICE PERFORMANCE INDICES

One outcome from following the process for developing customer-defined standards is a service performance index. *Service performance indices* are comprehensive composites of the most critical performance standards. Development of an index begins by identifying the set of customer-defined standards that the company will use to drive behaviour. Not all service performance indices contain customer-defined standards, but the best are based on them. Most companies build these indices by (1) understanding the most important requirements of the customer, (2) linking these requirements to tangible and measurable aspects of service provision, and (3) using the feedback from these indices to identify and improve service problems. The most progressive companies also use the feedback for reward and recognition systems within the company.

Among the issues that companies must tackle when developing service performance indices are (1) the number of components to be contained, (2) what overall or summary measures will be included, (3) whether the index should be weighted or unweighted (to put greater emphasis on the performance of the attributes considered most important to customers), and (4) whether all parts of the business (departments, sectors or business units) will be held to the same performance measures. One of the most important goals of an index is to simply and clearly communicate business performance in operational and perceptual terms. Companies must develop the same rigour in these measurement areas that they have in financial performance.

SUMMARY

This chapter discussed the discrepancy between company perceptions of customer expectations and the standards they set to deliver to these expectations. Among the major causes for provider gap 2 are inadequate standardization of service behaviours and actions, absence of formal processes for setting service quality goals, and lack of customer-defined standards. These problems were discussed and detailed, along with strategies to close the gap.

Customer-defined standards are at the heart of delivery of service that customers expect: they are the link between customers' expressed expectations and company actions to deliver to those expectations. Creating these service standards is not always done by service organizations. Doing so requires that companies' marketing and operations departments work together by using the marketing research as input for operations design. Unless the operations standards are defined by customer priorities, they are not likely to have an impact on customer perceptions of service.

KEY CONCEPTS

Customization v. standardization	191	One-time fixes	195
Goal-setting	192	Service performance indices	205
Hard customer-defined service standards	195	Service standards	189
Measuring behaviours and actions	198	Soft customer-defined service standards	194

EXERCISES

1 Select a local service firm. Visit the firm and ascertain the service measurements that the company tracks. What hard measures does it monitor? What soft measures? On the basis of what you find, develop a service performance index.

2 Choose one of the peripheral services (such as computer, library, placement) provided by your university or college. What hard standards would be useful to track to meet student expectations? What soft standards? What one-time fixes would improve service?

3 Think about a specific service that you have delivered or received. Using Figure 9.1, write in the customer requirements at each of the levels. How far down in the chart can you describe requirements? Is that far enough? What would you need to do to find out more?

4 Look at three websites from which you can order products (such as amazon.co.uk or tesco.com). What are the companies' delivery promises? What types of standards might they set for these promises? Are these customer- or company-defined standards?

DISCUSSION QUESTIONS

1 How does the service measurement that we describe in this chapter differ from the service measurement in Chapter 6? Which of the two types do you think is most important? Why?

2 In what types of service industries are standards most difficult to develop? Why? Recommend three standards that might be developed in one of the firms from the industries you specify. How would employees react to these standards? How could you gain buy-in for them?

3 Given the need for customer-defined service standards, do firms need company-defined standards at all? Could all standards in a company be customer defined? Why or why not? What functional departments in a firm would object to having all standards customer defined?

4 What is the difference between hard and soft standards? Which do you think would be more readily accepted by employees? By management? Why?

5 Consider the university or college you currently attend. What are examples of hard standards, soft standards and one-time fixes that would address student requirements? Does the university or college currently use these standards for delivery of service to students? Why or why not? Do you think your reasons would apply to private sector companies as well? To public or non-profit companies?

6 Think about a service that you currently use, and then map out the service encounter sequence for that service. What is your most important requirement in each interaction? Document these requirements and make certain that they are expressed at the concrete level of behaviours and actions.

7 From a customer perspective, what standards would you expect the following customer service personnel to meet;
   a) a hotel receptionist?
   b) a lawyer?
   c) a hospital cleaner?

8 Should standards vary by segment?

FURTHER READING

Boksberger, P. E. and Melsen, L. (2011). Perceived value: a critical examination of definitions, concepts and measures for the service industry. *Journal of Services Marketing*, 25(3), 229–40.

Caemmerer, B. and Wilson A. (2010). Customer Feedback Mechanisms and Organisational Learning in Service Operations. *International Journal of Operations and Production Management*, 30(3), 288–311.

Kontoghiorges, C. (2003). Examining the association between quality and productivity performance in a service organisation. *The Quality Management Journal*, 10(1), 32–42.

Parasuraman, A. (2002). Service quality and productivity: a synergistic perspective. *Managing Service Quality*, 12(1), 6–9.

Taticchi, P., Tonelli, F. and Cagnazzo, L. (2010). Performance measurement and management: a literature review and a research agenda. *Measuring Business Excellence*, 14(1), 4–18.

Wilson, A. (2000). The use of performance information in the management of service delivery. *Marketing Intelligence and Planning'*, 18(3), 127–34.

CHAPTER 10

The Physical and Virtual Servicescape

LEARNING OBJECTIVES

This chapter's objectives are to:

1 Explain the profound impact of physical evidence, particularly the servicescape, on customer perceptions and experiences.
2 Illustrate differences in types of physical and virtual servicescapes, the roles played by the servicescape, and the implications for strategy.
3 Explain *why* the servicescape affects customer and employee behaviour, using a framework based in marketing, organizational behaviour and environmental psychology.
4 Present elements of an effective physical evidence strategy.

OPENING EXAMPLE

Redesigning Fast Food

Fast-food giant McDonald's has continued to invest considerably in its restaurants and supply chain throughout the UK. In 2013, the business invested £95 million in new outlets, refurbishments and equipment. Over the last 5 years the total value of the investment in new restaurants and in refurbishment of older ones in the UK has been £428 million.

A spokeswoman for the company says the aim of the project was to bring its restaurants 'into the 21st century' and create a 'more welcoming environment' for customers. The programme has contributed to significant growth for the company, with sales rising by about 6 per cent since its inception.

Refit projects are slow and, therefore, do not necessarily offer an immediate return on investment. However, the eventual benefits can be significant. Big brands may never be able to roll out a refit in all stores at once. However, the brand message being conveyed by the refit can be input into other stores, through staff training and imagery, to make it seem as though the brand is evolving as a whole.

Refurbishments can be used to demonstrate that a brand genuinely wants to change. However, service managers must be wary of believing that a programme of refurbishment will solve all their problems. McDonald's says its new-look restaurants are part of a culmination of the changes it has made as a brand over the past few years. 'It is just one part of the changes in our restaurants,' says the spokeswoman. 'There is also a focus on improving customer service, installing new technology and equipment.'

The redesigned restaurants feature McDonald's signature style with a bright, modern interior and exterior design, often including an Express Lane Walk Thru making it even easier and quicker to be served. The new-look restaurants aim to offer more seating options, free WiFi, and power supplies in the dining area. In addition, the restaurant makeovers include the introduction of a range of energy-efficient measures, including water-saving urinals, low-energy hand dryers, LED spotlights and energy-saving external signage. For the employees, there are also improved kitchen facilities and a 'crew room' with seating, a television and a computer. Staff can use the area to study for nationally recognized qualifications in maths or English through a specially designed website.

Ensuring that a series of store overhauls extends beyond merely the physical changes to its overall look is vital, according to Elliot Wilson, managing director of branding agency Elmwood. 'It must also involve staff training and experimentation. Concept stores should push the boundaries of what a brand can achieve,' he says. There should be a surprise element to such activity, the creation of something unexpected and special. You need to give people a reason to keep visiting an outlet. New looks might be impressive when they are first rolled out, but interiors can soon become tired in appearance. Refurbishments offer a good starting point for drawing people in, but to maintain the momentum, companies must maximize the broader potential of the in-store experience.

Source: Adapted from: Golding, A. (2009) 'Behind the Façade', Marketing, *2 December, p.16. and McDonald's (2013)* Serving the UK: McDonald's at 40.

In this chapter we explore the importance of physical evidence for communicating service quality attributes, setting customer expectations, and creating the service experience. In Chapter 1, when we introduced the expanded marketing mix for services, we defined physical evidence as *the environment in which the service is delivered and in which the firm and the customer interact, and any tangible commodities that facilitate performance or communication of the service.* The first part of this definition encompasses the actual physical or virtual facility in which the service is performed, delivered and consumed; throughout this chapter this facility is referred to as the *servicescape*.[1]

Physical evidence is particularly important for communicating about credence services (such as hairstyling), but it is also important for services such as hotels, hospitals and theme parks that are dominated by experience attributes. Think of how effectively Disney uses the physical evidence of its service to excite its customers. The brightly coloured displays, the music, the fantastic rides and the costumed characters all reinforce the feelings of fun and excitement that Disney seeks to generate in its customers. Think also of how effective Disney is in portraying consistent physical evidence that is compatible with its goals. The physical evidence and servicescape, or the 'stage' in Disney's terms, is always stimulating to the extreme, is always clean, is always in top repair and never fails to deliver what it has promised to consumers, and more. In this chapter we present many examples of how physical evidence communicates with customers and how it can play a role in creating the service experience, in satisfying customers, and in enhancing customers' perceptions of quality.

PHYSICAL EVIDENCE

WHAT IS PHYSICAL EVIDENCE?

Customers often rely on tangible cues, or physical evidence, to evaluate the service before its purchase and to assess their satisfaction with the service during and after consumption. Effective design of physical, tangible evidence is important for closing provider gap 2.

General elements of physical evidence are shown in Table 10.1. They include all aspects of the organization's physical facility (the servicescape) as well as other forms of tangible communication. Elements of the servicescape that affect customers include both exterior attributes (such as signage, parking, and the landscape) and interior attributes (such as design, layout, equipment and decor). Note that web pages and virtual servicescapes conveyed over the Internet are more recent forms of physical evidence that companies can use to communicate about the service experience, making services more tangible for customers both before and after purchase. For example, travellers can now preview destinations, tour natural environments and 'experience' entertainment venues online before booking their trips or even deciding where to travel. Virtual tours and 360-degree views of hotels and their rooms allow potential guests to view the facilities in and out before booking.

⭐ SERVICE SPOTLIGHT

Sofitel, the upmarket hotel chain owned by the French company Accor, allows potential guests to undertake a virtual visit to each of their hotels on the company website (www.sofitel.com) using 360-degree views of their public areas and bedrooms. Users can examine panoramic images by clicking on the left-hand button of their mouse. They can also zoom in by pushing their mouse cursor towards the centre of the screen.

 Digital and internet technology clearly provides tremendous opportunities for firms to communicate about their services. Tangible images on the Web create expectations for customers that set standards for service delivery, and it is critical that the actual services live up to these

Table 10.1   Elements of physical evidence

Servicescape	Other tangibles
Facility exterior	Business cards
Exterior design	Stationery
Signage	Billing statements
Parking	Reports
Landscape	Employee dress
Surrounding environment	Uniforms
Facility interior	Brochures
Interior design	
Equipment	
Signage	
Layout	
Air quality/temperature	
Lighting	
Floor coverings	
Aromas/scents	
Virtual environment	
Web page design	
Web-cams	
Photographs	
360 degree views	
Online chat facilities	

expectations. Images and virtual service tours presented on the Internet also need to support the positioning of the service brand and be consistent with other marketing messages.

Physical evidence examples from different service contexts are given in Table 10.2. It is apparent that some services (like hospitals, resorts and child care) rely heavily on physical evidence to communicate and create customer experiences. Others (like insurance, express mail) provide limited physical evidence for customers. All the elements of evidence listed for each service communicate something about the service to consumers, facilitate performance of the service and/or add to the customer's total experience. Although we focus in this chapter primarily on the servicescape and its effects, keep in mind that what is said applies to the other forms of evidence as well.

HOW DOES PHYSICAL EVIDENCE AFFECT THE CUSTOMER EXPERIENCE?

Physical evidence, particularly the servicescape, can have a profound effect on the customer experience. This is true whether the experience is mundane (e.g. a bus or train ride), personally meaningful (e.g. a wedding or a birthday celebration), or spectacular (e.g. a weeklong travel adventure). In all cases, the physical evidence of the service will influence the flow of the experience, the meaning customers attach to it, their satisfaction and their emotional connections with the organization delivering the experience.

Table 10.2   Examples of physical evidence from the customer's point of view

| Service | Physical evidence | |
	Servicescape	Other tangibles
Insurance	Website	Policy itself Billing statements Periodic updates Company brochure Letters/cards Claims forms
Hotel	Building exterior Parking Reception area Lift/corridors Bedroom Bathroom Restaurant layout Bar Leisure facilities Website	Uniforms Reports/stationery Billing statements
Airline	Airline check-in area Airline gate area Aeroplane exterior Aeroplane interior (decor, seats, air quality) Self-service check-in terminals Website	Tickets Food Uniforms
Express mail	Drop-off service points Website	Packaging Vehicles Uniforms Computers
Sporting event	Parking Stadium exterior Ticketing area Entrance Seating Toilets Catering outlets Playing field Website	Signs Tickets Programmes Employee uniforms

As marketers and corporate strategists begin to pay more attention to experiences, they have recognized the impact of physical space and tangibles in creating those experiences. Lewis Carbone, a leading consultant on experience management, has developed an entire lexicon and management process around the basic idea of 'experience engineering' through 'clue management'.[2] *Clue management* refers to the process of clearly identifying and managing *all* the various clues that customers use to form their impressions and feelings about the company. Included in this set of clues are what Carbone refers to as *mechanics clues*, or the physical and tangible clues that we focus on in this chapter. Other writers and consultants who focus on managing customer experiences also zero in on the importance of tangible evidence and physical facilities in shaping those experiences.[3] Throughout this chapter are numerous examples of how physical evidence communicates with customers and shapes their experiences.

 SERVICE SPOTLIGHT

Italian bank ChiantiBanca has opened a string of new branches that are designed to look more like traditional local eateries than financial institutions. Italian design studio DINN! and branding agency Crea International devised the Restaurant Experience Banking concept to integrate ChiantiBanca's customer services with a relaxing and familiar local environment to enhance the social and economic potential of the branches.

Traditional cash desks are nowhere to be seen; they are replaced by clusters of tables surrounded by bar stools, chairs and cushioned seating cubes. Brochures displayed on the tables are arranged to look like restaurant menus. Digital technologies include video teller machines (VTMs), which replace the standard ATMs, and a touch-screen wall displaying information and advertisements. This showcase, called 'Bacheca del Chianti', communicates the values and identity of the bank through information and graphical tools that mirror the physical design of the branch office. Informal spaces at the front of the banks function as welcome zones, complete with play areas for young children. Each branch shares a similar colour and materials palette, including timber, Corten steel and earthy shades of brown and green. The first two branches are located in Florence's Piazza Duomo and in the town of Poggibonsi. Others have opened across Tuscany.

Source: **www.chiantibanca.it**

TYPES OF SERVICESCAPES

In this chapter we explain the roles played by the servicescape and how it affects employees and customers, and their interactions. The chapter relies heavily on ideas and concepts from environmental psychology, a field that encompasses the study of human beings and their relationships with built (human-made), natural and social environments.[4] The physical setting may be more or less important in achieving the organization's marketing and other goals depending on certain factors. Table 10.3 is a framework for categorizing service organizations on two dimensions that capture some of the key differences that will impact the management of the servicescape. Organizations that share a cell in the matrix will face similar issues and decisions regarding their physical spaces.

SERVICESCAPE USAGE

First, organizations differ in terms of *whom* the servicescape will actually affect. That is, who actually comes into the service facility and thus is potentially influenced by its design – customers, employees, or both groups? The first column of Table 10.3 suggests three types of service organizations that differ on this dimension.

At one extreme is the *self-service* environment, in which the customer performs most of the activities and few if any employees are involved. Examples of self-service environments include ATMs, cinemas, self-service entertainment such as golf courses and theme parks, and online services. In these primarily self-service environments the organization can plan the servicescape to focus exclusively on marketing goals such as attracting the right market segment, making the facility pleasing and easy to use, and creating the desired service experience.

Table 10.3   Typology of service organizations based on variations in form and use of the servicescape

Complexity of the servicescape		
Servicescape usage	Elaborate	Lean
Self-service (customer involvement and limited interaction with employees)	Golf course eBay Amazon	ATM Car wash Mobile Banking App
Interpersonal services (customer and employee interaction and involvement)	Restaurant Hospital Airline School	Car repair Hair salon
Remote service (employee involvement with limited interaction with customers and limited customer involvement)	Mobile Network Provision House Insurance Electricity Supply	Warehousing Provision of traffic information

Source: Adapted from M.J. Bitner (1992) 'Servicescapes: the impact of physical surroundings on customers and employees', *Journal of Marketing* 56 (April 1992), pp. 57–71.

At the other extreme of the use dimension is the *remote service*, which has little or no customer involvement with the servicescape. Telecommunications, online services, utilities, financial consultants and mail-order services are examples of services that can be provided without the customer ever seeing the service facility. In fact, the facility may be in a different region or a different country. In remote services, the facility can be set up to keep employees motivated and to facilitate productivity, teamwork, operational efficiency or whatever organizational behaviour goal is desired without any consideration of customers because they will never need to see the servicescape.

Interpersonal services are placed between these two extremes and represent situations in which both the customer and the employee are present and active in the servicescape. Examples abound, such as hotels, restaurants, hospitals, educational settings and banks. In these situations, the servicescape must be planned to attract, satisfy and facilitate the activities of both customers and employees simultaneously. Special attention must also be given to how the servicescape affects the nature and quality of the social interactions between and among customers and employees. A cruise ship provides a good example of a setting in which the servicescape must support customers and the employees who work there, and facilitate interactions between the two groups.

SERVICESCAPE COMPLEXITY

The horizontal dimension of Table 10.3 suggests another factor that will influence servicescape management. Some service environments are very simple, with few elements, few spaces and few pieces of equipment. Such environments are termed *lean*. Shopping-centre information kiosks and ATMs would be considered lean environments because both provide service from one simple structure. For lean servicescapes, design decisions are relatively straightforward, especially in self-service or remote service situations in which there is no interaction among employees and customers.

Other servicescapes are very complicated, with many elements and many forms. They are termed *elaborate* environments. An example is a hotel with its many floors and rooms, sophisticated equipment and complex variability in functions performed within the physical facility. In such an elaborate environment, the full range of marketing and organizational objectives theoretically can be approached through careful management of the servicescape. For example, a guest's hotel room can be designed to enhance comfort and satisfaction while simultaneously facilitating low-energy usage and costs. Firms such as hotels that are positioned in the elaborate interpersonal service cell face the most complex servicescape decisions.

STRATEGIC ROLES OF THE SERVICESCAPE

Within the cells of the typology, the servicescape can play many strategic roles simultaneously. An examination of the variety of roles and how they interact makes clear how strategically important it is to provide appropriate physical evidence of the service. In fact, the servicescape is frequently one of the most important elements used in positioning a service organization.

PACKAGE

Similar to a tangible product's package, the servicescape and other elements of physical evidence essentially 'wrap' the service and convey to consumers an external image of what is 'inside'. Product packages are designed to portray a particular image as well as to evoke a particular sensory or emotional reaction. The physical setting of a service does the same thing through the interaction of many complex stimuli. The servicescape is the outward appearance of the organization, and thus can be critical in forming initial impressions or setting up customer expectations – it is a visual metaphor for the intangible service. This packaging role is particularly important in creating expectations for new customers and for newly established service organizations that are trying to build a particular image. The physical surroundings offer an organization the opportunity to convey an image in a way not unlike the way an individual chooses to 'dress for success'. The packaging role extends to the appearance of contact personnel through their uniforms or dress and other elements of their outward appearance.[5]

SERVICE SPOTLIGHT

Eurostar, the operators of the trains running between the UK and France has ditched the contemporary styling of their customer areas for a retro look evocative of the 'golden age of travel'. The makeover aims to create a 'less pedestrian travel experience'.

The new London Ticket Hall combines Art Nouveau and Victorian Gothic. In the Eurostar terminal at St Pancras station, furniture and fittings for both the standard and business class ticket offices have been styled to incorporate materials and shapes common in the late 19th and early 20th century. Christopher Jenner, Eurostar's creative director stated, 'A good travel brand is judged by how it responds to its clients' needs. We've designed a space which is functional, yet embodies the narrative of connection and journey within its DNA.'

A Venetian plaster wall in the business class office is interrupted with curvy panels of walnut edged in brass. The same combination of wood and metal is used for the cabinetry, and bespoke blown-glass lampshades are suspended over the ticket desk made of formed Corian edged with wood. A 30-metre-long hand-drawn illustration of the journey from London to Paris is recreated on photo-etched stainless steel to cover the main walls of the standard class office. Curved desks are formed out of Corian, edged in steel and English oak. Limestone has been used to create new flooring for both spaces, which will retain their glazed frontages.

Art Nouveau and Victorian Gothic were radical movements which shared common values. These values – fluidity, organic, enriched and symbolic – were key inspiration points in the development of Eurostar's new design.[6]

Interestingly, the same care and resource expenditures given to package design in product marketing are often not provided for services, even though the service package serves a variety of important roles. There are many exceptions to this generality, however. Smart companies like H&M, KLM and Novotel spend a lot of time and money relating their servicescape design to their brand, providing their customers with strong visual metaphors and 'service packaging' that conveys the brand positioning.

FACILITATOR

The servicescape can also serve as a facilitator in aiding the performance of persons in the environment. How the setting is designed can enhance or inhibit the efficient flow of activities in the service setting, making it easier or harder for customers and employees to accomplish their goals. A well-designed, functional facility can make the service a pleasure to experience from the customer's point of view and a pleasure to perform from the employee's. On the other hand, poor and inefficient design may frustrate both customers and employees. For example, an international air traveller who finds him or herself in a poorly designed airport with few signs, poor ventilation and few places to sit or eat will find the experience quite dissatisfying, and employees who work there will probably be unmotivated as well. The same international traveller will appreciate seats on the aeroplane that are conducive to work and sleep. The seating itself, part of the physical surroundings of the service, has been improved over the years better to facilitate travellers' needs to sleep. In fact, the competition for better seat design continues as a major point of contention among the international airline carriers, and the results have translated into greater customer satisfaction for business travellers.[7] British Airways has even seen its market share increase on some routes as a direct result of its award-winning Club-World seat.[8] Citizen M boutique hotels located in the Netherlands and the UK provide all guests with a Phillips moodpad which is described as a technological personal assistant. It wakes you up, opens the blinds, turns on the lights, controls the television and adapts the room to your chosen theme in terms of colour, digital art and music.[9] Amazon's website is designed in such a way as to enable the user to quickly find products to purchase using a very clear search facility and simple shopping cart controls to speedily process payment. All these examples emphasize the facilitator role of the servicescape.

SOCIALIZER

The design of the servicescape serves as a socializer of both employees and customers in the sense that it helps convey expected roles, behaviours and relationships. For example, a new employee in a professional services firm would come to understand his or her position in the hierarchy partly through noting the office he or she has been allocated, the quality of the office furnishings and his or her location relative to others in the organization.

The design of the facility can also suggest to customers what their role is relative to employees, what parts of the servicescape they are welcome in and which are for employees only, how they should behave while in the environment and what types of interactions are encouraged. For example, consider a Club Med vacation environment that is set up to facilitate customer–customer interactions as well as guest interactions with Club Med staff. The organization also recognizes the need for privacy, providing areas that encourage solitary activities. To illustrate further, in many Starbucks locations, the company has shifted to more of a traditional coffeehouse environment in which customers spend social time rather than coming in for a quick cup of coffee on the run. To encourage this type of socializing, these Starbucks locations have comfortable lounge chairs and tables set up to encourage customers to interact and to stay longer.

DIFFERENTIATOR

The design of the physical facility can differentiate a firm from its competitors and signal the market segment that the service is intended for. Given its power as a differentiator, changes in the physical environment can be used to reposition a firm and/or to attract new market segments. In shopping malls the signage, the colours used in decor and displays, and the type of music wafting from a store signal the intended market segment.

SERVICE SPOTLIGHT

Omega Bank, a private bank with branches across Greece, has designed its branch interiors to communicate a feeling of 'understated quality', avoiding ostentation and short-lived trendiness. Instead of using Greek marble and granite flooring, they imported honed green slate from the Lake District in the UK which better matched the 'understated quality' image. The teller desks were designed in etched glass and steel, with maple timber slab ends. Aesthetically, they are meant to be very open and welcoming in appearance, accentuated by 'floating' all the surface planes on stainless steel spacers, so that none of the major elements actually touch each other.

The same design system is incorporated into graphic and print items such as banking and ATM cards, promotional leaflets and private banking communication and print items.[10]

The design of a physical setting can also differentiate one area of a service organization from another. For example, in the hotel industry, one large hotel may have several levels of dining possibilities, each signalled by differences in design. Price differentiation is also often partly achieved through variations in physical setting. Bigger rooms with more physical amenities cost more, just as larger seats with more leg room (generally in first class) are more expensive on an airline.

FRAMEWORK FOR UNDERSTANDING SERVICESCAPE EFFECTS ON BEHAVIOUR

Although it is useful from a strategic point of view to think about the multiple roles of the servicescape and how they interact, making actual decisions about servicescape design requires an understanding of why the effects occur and how to manage them. The next sections of this chapter present a framework or model of environment and behaviour relationships in service settings.

THE UNDERLYING FRAMEWORK – THE PHYSICAL SERVICESCAPE

The framework for understanding servicescape effects on behaviour follows from basic *stimulus–organism–response theory*. In the framework the multidimensional environment is the *stimulus*, consumers and employees are the *organisms* that respond to the stimuli, and behaviours directed at the environment are the *responses*. The assumptions are that dimensions of the servicescape will impact customers and employees and that they will behave in certain ways depending on their internal reactions to the servicescape.

A specific example will help illustrate the theory in action. Assume there is a fresh coffee outlet close to the lecture theatres on a university campus. This coffee outlet has large comfortable sofas, and an aroma of fresh coffee wafts from it. The design and the aroma are two elements of the servicescape that will impact customers in some way. Now assume you are a tired student, just out of class, strolling across campus. The comfortable sofas attract your attention and, simultaneously, you smell the coffee. The furniture and the delicious smell cause you to feel happy, relaxed and thirsty at the same time. You are attracted to the coffee outlet and decide to buy a coffee and cookie because you have another class to attend before lunch. The movement toward the outlet and the purchase of a coffee are behaviours directed at the servicescape. Depending on how much time you have, you may even choose to relax in a sofa and read a newspaper with your coffee, other forms of behaviour directed at the servicescape.

The framework shown in Figure 10.1 is detailed in the next sections. It represents a comprehensive stimulus–organism–response model that recognizes complex dimensions of the environment, impacts on multiple parties (customers, employees and their interactions), multiple types of internal responses (cognitive, emotional and physiological) and a variety of individual and social behaviours that can result.

Figure 10.1   A framework for understanding environment–user relationships in service organizations

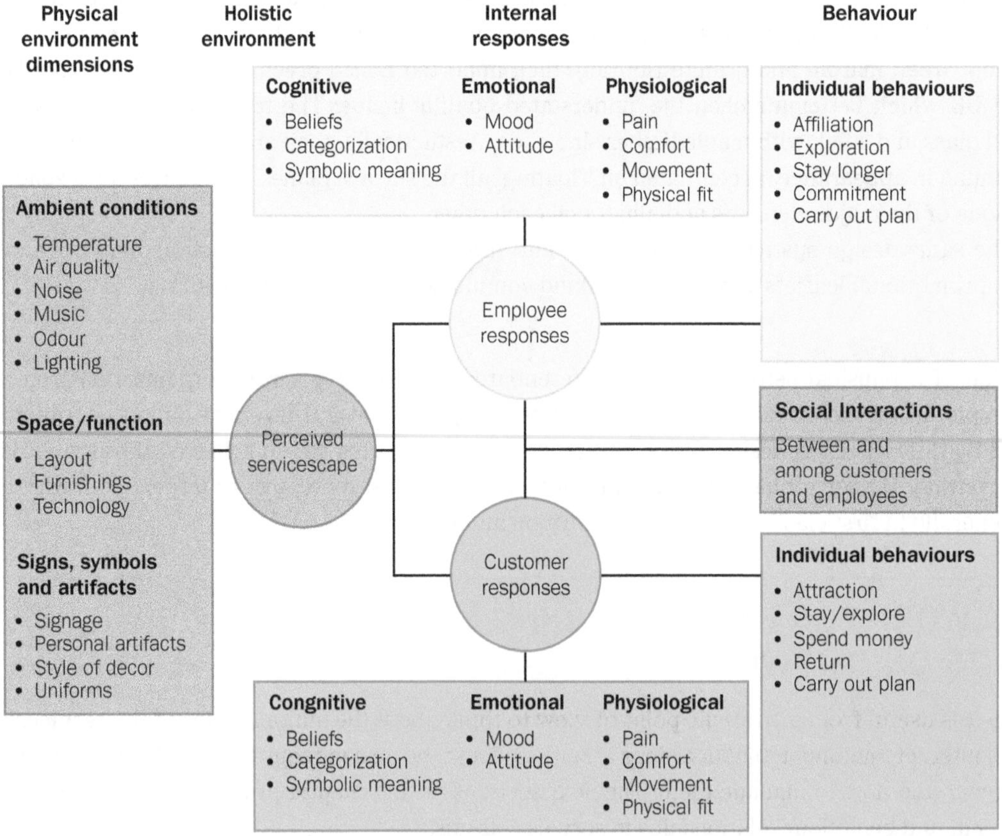

Physical environment dimensions	Holistic environment	Internal responses	Behaviour

Ambient conditions
- Temperature
- Air quality
- Noise
- Music
- Odour
- Lighting

Space/function
- Layout
- Furnishings
- Technology

Signs, symbols and artifacts
- Signage
- Personal artifacts
- Style of decor
- Uniforms

Cognitive
- Beliefs
- Categorization
- Symbolic meaning

Emotional
- Mood
- Attitude

Physiological
- Pain
- Comfort
- Movement
- Physical fit

Individual behaviours
- Affiliation
- Exploration
- Stay longer
- Commitment
- Carry out plan

Employee responses

Perceived servicescape

Social Interactions
Between and among customers and employees

Customer responses

Individual behaviours
- Attraction
- Stay/explore
- Spend money
- Return
- Carry out plan

Congnitive
- Beliefs
- Categorization
- Symbolic meaning

Emotional
- Mood
- Attitude

Physiological
- Pain
- Comfort
- Movement
- Physical fit

Source: Adapted from M.J. Bitner (1992) 'Servicescapes: the impact of physical surroundings on customers and employees', *Journal of Marketing* 56 (April 1992), pp. 57–71.

Our discussion of the framework begins on the right side of the model with *behaviours*. Next we explain and develop the *internal responses* portion of the model. Finally we turn to the dimensions of the *environment* and the holistic perception of the environment.

BEHAVIOURS IN THE SERVICESCAPE

That human behaviour is influenced by the physical setting in which it occurs is essentially a truism. Interestingly, however, until the 1960s psychologists largely ignored the effects of physical setting in their attempts to predict and explain behaviour. Since that time a large and steadily growing body of literature within the field of environmental psychology has addressed the relationships between human beings and their built environments. Recent marketing focus on the customer experience has also drawn attention to the effects of physical spaces and design on customer behaviour.[11]

INDIVIDUAL BEHAVIOURS

Environmental psychologists suggest that individuals react to places with two general, and opposite, forms of behaviour: approach and avoidance. Approach behaviours include all positive behaviours that might be directed at a particular place, such as desire to stay, explore, work and affiliate.[12] Avoidance behaviours reflect the opposite – a desire not to stay, to explore, to work or to affiliate. In a study of consumers in retail environments, researchers found that approach behaviours (including shopping enjoyment, returning, attraction and friendliness towards others, spending money, time spent browsing, and exploration of the store) were influenced by perceptions of the environment.[13] At one 7-Eleven store, the owners played 'easy-listening music' to drive away the youthful market segment that was detracting from the store's image. And our coffee outlet example is reminiscent of bakeries in supermarkets that attract patrons through the power of smell.

In addition to attracting or deterring entry, the servicescape can actually influence the degree of success that consumers and employees experience in executing their plans once inside. Each individual comes to a particular service organization with a goal or purpose that may be aided or hindered by the setting. Sports fans are aided in their enjoyment of the game by adequate and easy-access parking, clear signage directing them to their seats, efficient food service and clean washrooms. The ability of employees to do their jobs effectively is also influenced by the servicescape. Adequate space, proper equipment, and comfortable temperature and air quality all contribute to an employee's comfort and job satisfaction, causing him or her to be more productive, stay longer and affiliate positively with co-workers.

SOCIAL INTERACTIONS

In addition to its effects on their individual behaviours, the servicescape influences the nature and quality of customer and employee interactions, most directly in interpersonal services. It has been stated that 'all social interaction is affected by the physical container in which it occurs'.[14] The 'physical container' can affect the nature of social interaction in terms of the duration of interaction and the actual progression of events. In many service situations, a firm may want to ensure a particular progression of events (a 'standard script') and limit the duration of the service. Environmental variables such as physical proximity, seating arrangements, size and flexibility can define the possibilities and limits of social episodes such as those occurring between customers and employees, or customers and other customers. The design of the servicescape can help define the social rules, conventions and expectations in force in a given setting, thus serving to define the nature of social interaction.[15] The close physical proximity of passengers on the sunbathing deck on a cruise ship will in and of itself prescribe certain patterns of behaviour. This vacation is not designed for a social recluse! Some researchers have implied that recurring social behaviour patterns are associated with particular physical settings and that when people encounter typical settings, their social behaviours can be predicted.[16]

Examples of how environments shape social interactions – and how these interactions in turn influence the environment – are abundant.[17] Even casual observation of the retail phenomenon 'Nike Town' shows how this form of 'entertainment retail' shapes the behaviours of consumers but at the same time allows them to interpret and create their own realities and experiences.[18] In a mountain biking trip, the 'wilderness servicescape' profoundly influences the behaviours, interactions and total experiences of cyclists consumers and their guides. In this case the natural, and for the most part uncontrollable, environment is the setting for the service.[19]

SERVICE SPOTLIGHT

'Nike Town', a retail concept that exists in London and fifteen other locations around the world, is built as a theatre where our consumers are the audience participating in the production. Nike Town gives us the opportunity to explore and experiment with innovative ways to connect with our consumers.'

Source: **Nike press release.**

Nike Towns epitomize the role of servicescape design in building the brand, providing customers with a way to interact with the brand, and making Nike come alive. Nike Town represents the height of retail theatre.

So what is so special about Nike Town? What sets it apart from other retail environments? First, it is a showcase for the full range of Nike products. A common reaction of consumers is that they had no idea Nike made and carried all of the products displayed. In addition, every designed element of the servicescape encourages impulsive behaviour, inviting instant gratification. But the prices are very high – higher than prices on the same items in other stores. This is by design. Here the servicescape and the experience of Nike Town are meant to build the brand – not necessarily to sell the products, and especially not to compete with other Nike stores and dealers.

The Nike Town store in London is a concept 'town'. Buildings, each housing a specific sport, surround a central square, the store's focal point. In its centre sits the core – a three-storey high, 360-degree projector screen – which springs to life every 20 minutes as window blinds snap shut and customers are surrounded by Nike sports images. Nike Town is more than just a shop; each week there are special events: athletes come in for interviews, and they even organize a running club. With 70,000 square feet of shopping space Nike Town manages to fit everything in, and more besides. The store boasts the largest women's sports clothing and footwear area in Europe.[20]

INTERNAL RESPONSES TO THE SERVICESCAPE

Employees and customers respond to dimensions of their physical surroundings cognitively, emotionally and physiologically, and those responses are what influence their behaviours in the environment (as shown in the middle portion of Figure 10.1). In other words, the perceived servicescape does not directly *cause* people to behave in certain ways. Although the internal responses are discussed independently here, they are clearly interdependent: a person's beliefs about a place, a cognitive response, may well influence the person's emotional response, and vice versa. For example, patients who come into a dentist's waiting room that is designed to calm and sooth their anxieties (emotional responses) may believe as a result that the dentist is caring and competent (cognitive responses).

ENVIRONMENT AND COGNITION

The perceived servicescape can have an effect on people's beliefs about a place and their beliefs about the people and products found in that place. In a sense the servicescape can be viewed as a form of non-verbal communication, imparting meaning through what is called 'object language'.[21] For example, particular environmental cues such as the type of office furniture and decor and the clothing worn by a lawyer may influence a potential client's beliefs about whether the lawyer is successful, expensive and trustworthy. In a consumer study, variations in descriptions of store atmospheres were found to alter beliefs about a product (perfume) sold in the store.[22] Another study showed that a travel agent's office decor affected customer attributions and beliefs about the travel agent's behaviour.[23] Travel agents whose facilities were more organized and professional were viewed more positively than were those whose facilities were disorganized and unprofessional.

In other cases, perceptions of the servicescape may simply help people distinguish a firm by influencing how it is categorized. The overall perception of the servicescape enables the consumer or employee to categorize the firm mentally. Research shows that in the restaurant industry a particular configuration of environmental cues such as hard furnishings suggests 'fast food', whereas another configuration (soft furnishings) suggests 'elegant sit-down restaurant'.[24] In such situations, environmental cues serve as a shortcut device that enables customers to categorize and distinguish among types of restaurants.

ENVIRONMENT AND EMOTION

In addition to influencing beliefs, the perceived servicescape can directly elicit emotional responses that, in turn, influence behaviours. Just being in a particular place can make a person feel happy, light-hearted and relaxed, whereas being in another place may make that person feel sad, depressed and gloomy. The colours, decor, music and other elements of the atmosphere can have an unexplainable and sometimes subconscious effect on the moods of people in the place. For some people, certain environmental stimuli (noises, smells) common in a dental office can bring on immediate feelings of fear and anxiety. In very different contexts, the marble interior and grandeur of a government building or palace may call up feelings of pride and respect; lively music and bright decor in a local night spot may cause people to feel excited and happy. In all these examples, the response from the consumer probably does not involve thinking but, rather, is just an unexplained feeling. Consumers' responses to Nike Town (on page 222) are in large part emotional.

SERVICE SPOTLIGHT

Another example of emotional connection through architectural design and the servicescape has been designed by London architect Farshid Moussavi, who created the first physical retail space for Victoria Beckham's fashion label in London's West End.

The ground floor space features concrete floors and a ceiling covered with mirrored stainless steel, and is fitted with bespoke pieces of furniture. A four-metre-wide flight of polished concrete stairs located at the back leads up to a flat white wall at the rear of the top floor that is used to project images of Beckham's collections. A similar flight leads down to the basement level.

Diagonal sections of the floor and ceiling have been cut away with the intention of creating a visual connection between all three levels of the 560-square-metre space. These triangular holes accommodate the staircases, while clear glass balustrades maintain a sense of openness. Lengths of blonde-gold coloured chain are used to display clothes throughout the store. These are suspended from recessed tracks in the ceiling and can be moved to make way for installations and other displays. Further hanging space is proved by zig-zagging strips of metal in the same colour, suspended on wires.

Shelving has been designed to be 'wafer thin'and can retract into the walls. American walnut wood and bottle-green coloured glass have been used to create the fitting rooms and cash desk. The same wood is used to create bespoke modular benches that rest on the tips of triangular shaped bottoms. Stainless steel has been used to wrap display counters, with built-in glass display cases, as well as columns and the ceiling of the lower-ground floor.

Source: **www.dezeen.com/2014/10/01/farshid-moussavi-victoria-beckham-36-dover-street-london-shop-interior/.**

Environmental psychologists have researched people's emotional responses to physical settings.[25] They have concluded that any environment, whether natural or engineered, will elicit emotions that can be captured by two basic dimensions: (1) pleasure/displeasure and (2) degree of arousal (amount of stimulation or excitement). Servicescapes that are both pleasant and arousing would be termed *exciting*, whereas those that are pleasant and non-arousing, or sleepy, would be termed *relaxing*. Unpleasant servicescapes that are arousing would be called *distressing*, whereas unpleasant, sleepy servicescapes would be *gloomy*. These basic emotional responses to environments can be used to begin predicting the expected behaviours of consumers and employees who find themselves in a particular type of place. Certain organizations may try to stimulate strong emotional responses; for examples of this, look at the European hotel websites **www. propeller-island.de** and **www.roughluxe.co.uk**.

ENVIRONMENT AND PHYSIOLOGY

The perceived servicescape may also affect people in purely physiological ways. Noise that is too loud may cause physical discomfort, the temperature of a room may cause people to shiver or perspire, the air quality may make it difficult to breathe, and the glare of lighting may decrease ability to see and may induce physical discomfort. All these physical responses may, in turn, directly influence whether people stay in and enjoy a particular environment. It is well known that the comfort of seating in a restaurant influences how long people stay. The hard seats in fast-food restaurants cause most people to leave within a predictable period of time, whereas the soft, cosy chairs of Starbucks coffee shops have the opposite effect, encouraging people to stay. Similarly, environmental design and related physiological responses affect whether employees can perform their job functions well.

A vast amount of research in engineering and design has addressed human physiological responses to ambient conditions as well as physiological responses to equipment design.[26] Such research fits under the rubric of *human factors design or ergonomics*. Human factors research systematically applies relevant information about human capabilities and limitations to the design of items and procedures that people use. For example, First Group, one of the largest bus operators in the UK, has introduced new low-floor buses to offer easier access for parents with pushchairs, wheelchairs and the elderly.

VARIATIONS IN INDIVIDUAL RESPONSES

In general, people respond to the environment in the ways just described – cognitively, emotionally, physiologically – and their responses influence how they behave in the environment. However, the response will not be the same for every individual, every time. Personality differences as well as temporary conditions such as moods or the purpose for being there can cause variations in how people respond to the servicescape.[27]

One personality trait that has been shown to affect how people respond to environments is *arousal-seeking*. Arousal-seekers enjoy and look for high levels of stimulation, whereas arousal-avoiders prefer lower levels of stimulation. Thus an arousal-avoider in a loud, bright disco with flashing lights might feel strong dislike for the environment, whereas an arousal-seeker would be very happy. In a related vein, it has been suggested that some people are better *screeners* of environmental stimuli than others.[28] Screeners of stimuli would be able to experience a high level of stimulation but not be affected by it. Non-screeners would be highly affected and might exhibit extreme responses even to low levels of stimulation.

The particular purpose for being in a servicescape can also affect a person's response to it. A passenger on an aeroplane for a one-hour flight will likely be less affected by the atmosphere on the plane than will the traveller who is embarking on a 14-hour long-haul flight. Similarly, a day-surgery hospital patient will likely be less sensitive and demanding of the hospital environment than would a patient who is spending two weeks in the hospital. And a person who is staying at a hotel for a business meeting will respond differently to the environment than will a couple on their honeymoon.

Temporary mood states can also cause people to respond differently to environmental stimuli. A person who is feeling frustrated and fatigued after a long day at work is likely to be affected differently by a highly arousing restaurant than the person would be after a relaxing three-day weekend.

ENVIRONMENTAL DIMENSIONS OF THE PHYSICAL SERVICESCAPE

The preceding sections have described customer and employee behaviours in the servicescape and the three primary responses – cognitive, emotional and physiological – that lead to those behaviours. In this section we turn to the complex mix of environmental features that influence these responses and behaviours (the left-hand portion of Figure 10.1). Specifically, environmental dimensions of the physical surroundings can include all the objective physical factors that can be controlled by the firm to enhance (or constrain) employee and customer actions. There is an endless list of possibilities: lighting, colour, signage, textures, quality of materials, style of furnishings, layout, wall decor, temperature, and so on. In Figure 10.1, and in the discussion that follows here, the hundreds of potential elements have been categorized into three composite dimensions: ***ambient conditions***; **spatial layout and functionality**; and ***signs***, ***symbols and artefacts***.

Although we discuss the three dimensions separately, environmental psychology explains that people respond to their environments holistically. That is, although individuals perceive discrete stimuli (for example, they can perceive noise level, colour and decor as distinct elements), it is the total configuration of stimuli that determines their reactions to a place. Hence, though the dimensions of the environment are defined independently in the following sections, it is important to recognize that they are perceived by employees and customers as a holistic pattern of interdependent stimuli. The holistic response is shown in Figure 10.1 as the 'perceived servicescape'.

AMBIENT CONDITIONS

Ambient conditions include background characteristics of the environment such as temperature, lighting, noise, music, scent and colour. All these factors can profoundly affect how people feel, think, and respond to a particular service establishment. For example, a number of studies have documented the effects of music on consumers' perceptions of products, their perceptions of how long they have waited for service, and the amount of money they spend.[29] When there is music, shoppers tend to perceive that they spend less time shopping or in queues than when there is no music. Slower music tempos at lower volumes tend to make people shop more leisurely and, in some cases, they spend more. Shoppers also spend more time when the music 'fits' the product or matches their musical tastes. Other studies have similarly shown the effects of scent on consumer responses.[30] Scent in bakeries, coffee shops and cheese shops, for example, can be used to draw people in, and pleasant scents can increase lingering time. The presence of a scent can reduce perceptions of time spent and improve store evaluations. There is a distinct scent in the cabins of Singapore Airlines. They have used the same cologne since the airline was founded. The cologne, Stefan Floridian Waters originates and is available to buy in Singapore perfumeries. It is blended into the hot towels and is infused into the entire fleet. The perfume is described as exotic and feminine. Combined with the sound, touch, sight and taste sensations of Singapore Airlines, the scent aims to make the airline stand out in the increasingly competitive airline industry. Singapore Airlines markets itself as an experience, not just a means of travel.[31]

The effects of ambient conditions are especially noticeable when they are extreme. For example, people attending a music concert in a hall which is hot and stuffy because the air conditioning has failed will be uncomfortable, and their discomfort will be reflected in how they feel about the concert. If the temperature and air quality were within a comfort tolerance zone, these ambient factors would probably go unnoticed. Ambient conditions also have a greater effect when the customer or employee spends considerable time in the servicescape. The impact of temperature, music, odours and colours builds over time. Another instance in which ambient conditions will be particularly influential is when they conflict with what the customer or employee expects. As a general rule, ambient conditions affect the five senses. Sometimes such dimensions may be totally imperceptible (gases, chemicals, equipment noise) yet have profound effects, particularly on employees who spend long hours in the environment.

⭐ **SERVICE SPOTLIGHT**

Abercrombie & Fitch is well known for the musky scent of its stores. This unmistakable scent is that of Abercrombie's signature cologne, Fierce, which generates more than $80 million annually, according to CEO Mike Jeffries. Employees regularly spray it into the air at Abercrombie stores to keep the scent fresh.

Source: **www.abercrombie.co.uk.**

SPATIAL LAYOUT AND FUNCTIONALITY

Because service environments generally exist to fulfil specific purposes or needs of customers, spatial layout and functionality of the physical surroundings are particularly important. *Spatial layout* refers to the ways in which machinery, equipment and furnishings are arranged, the size and shape of those items, and the spatial relationships among them. *Functionality* refers to the ability of the same items to facilitate the accomplishment of customer and employee goals. The spatial layout and functionality of the environment are particularly important for customers in self-service environments, where they must perform the service on their own and cannot rely on employees to assist them. Thus, the functionality of an ATM machine and of self-serve restaurants, service stations and Internet shopping are critical to success and customer satisfaction.

The importance of facility layout is particularly apparent in retail, hospitality and leisure settings, where research shows it can influence customer satisfaction, store performance and consumer search behaviour.[32]

SIGNS, SYMBOLS AND ARTEFACTS

Many items in the physical environment serve as explicit or implicit signals that communicate about the place to its users. Signs displayed on the exterior and interior of a structure are examples of explicit communicators. They can be used as labels (name of company, name of department, and so on), for directional purposes (entrances, exits) and to communicate rules of behaviour (no smoking, children must be accompanied by an adult). Adequate signs have even been shown to reduce perceived crowding and stress.

Other environmental symbols and artefacts may communicate less directly than signs, giving implicit cues to users about the meaning of the place and norms and expectations for behaviour in the place. Quality construction materials, artwork, certificates and photographs, floor coverings, and personal objects displayed in the environment can all communicate symbolic meaning and create an overall aesthetic impression. Restaurant managers, for example, know that white tablecloths and subdued lighting symbolically convey full service and relatively high prices, whereas counter service, plastic furnishings and bright lighting symbolize the opposite. In office environments, certain cues such as desk size and placement symbolize status and may be used to reinforce professional image.[33]

Signs, symbols and artefacts are particularly important in forming first impressions and for communicating service concepts. When customers are unfamiliar with a particular service establishment, they look for environmental cues to help them categorize the place and form their expectations. A study of dentists' offices found that consumers use the environment, in particular its style of decoration and level of quality, as a clue to the competence and manner of the service provider.[34]

THE UNDERLYING FRAMEWORK – THE VIRTUAL SERVICESCAPE

Although the framework in Figure 10.1 was originally developed for physical servicescapes, a large part of it (excluding the employee responses) could also be seen to be relevant to virtual servicescapes such as online services and websites. A number of the environmental dimensions would be different, but the perceived servicescape would create similar customer responses and behaviours. In the Web environment, ambient conditions may include music/sound effects, colour schemes and font sizes. Spatial layout and functionality, procedures for signing in or progressing through the website, search facilities relate to ease of navigation. Signs, symbols and artifacts will include photographs, auto-play videos, pop-up advertisements and the general style of the website. All of these impact on the cognition, emotion and physiology of users, resulting in their behaviours on the site. They may be attracted by the environmental dimensions of a particular site, which may result in them spending more time and money with that service provider. Alternatively they may become annoyed or frustrated with a site and go to an alternative service provider.

Social Media and Digital Marketing

GUIDELINES FOR PHYSICAL EVIDENCE STRATEGY

To this point in the chapter we have presented ideas, frameworks and psychological models for understanding the effects of physical evidence, and most specifically the effects of the physical facility or servicescape. In this section we suggest some general guidelines for an effective physical evidence strategy.[35]

RECOGNIZE THE STRATEGIC IMPACT OF PHYSICAL EVIDENCE

Physical evidence can play a prominent role in determining service quality expectations and perceptions. For some organizations, just acknowledging the impact of physical evidence is a major first step. Once they have taken it, they can take advantage of the potential of physical evidence and plan strategically.

For an evidence strategy to be effective, it must be linked clearly to the organization's overall goals and vision. Thus planners must know what those goals are and then determine how the physical evidence strategy can support them. At a minimum, the basic service concept must be defined, the target markets (both internal and external) identified and the firm's broad vision of its future known. Because many evidence decisions are relatively permanent and costly (particularly servicescape decisions), they must be planned and executed deliberately.

BLUEPRINT THE PHYSICAL EVIDENCE OF SERVICE

The next step is to map the service. Everyone should be able to see the service process and the existing elements of physical evidence. An effective way to depict service evidence is through the service blueprint. (Service blueprinting was presented in detail in Chapter 8.) Although service blueprints clearly have multiple purposes, they can be particularly useful in visually capturing physical evidence opportunities. People, process and physical evidence can all be seen in the blueprint. Firms can read the actions involved in service delivery, the complexity of the process, the points of human interaction that provide evidence opportunities and the tangible representations present at each step. To make the blueprint even more useful, photographs or videotape of the process can be added to develop a photographic blueprint that provides a vivid picture of physical evidence from the customer's point of view.

CLARIFY STRATEGIC ROLES OF THE SERVICESCAPE

Early in this chapter we discussed the varying roles played by the servicescape and how firms could locate themselves in the typology shown in Table 10.3 to begin to identify their roles. For example, a child-care company would locate itself in the 'elaborate, interpersonal' cell of the matrix, and quickly see that its servicescape decisions would be relatively complex and that its servicescape strategy (1) would have to consider the needs of both the children and the service providers, and (2) could impact on marketing, organizational behaviour and consumer satisfaction goals.

Sometimes the servicescape may have no role in service delivery or marketing from the customer's point of view, such as in telecommunications services or utilities. Clarifying the roles played by the servicescape in a particular situation will aid in identifying opportunities and deciding who needs to be consulted in making facility design decisions. Clarifying the strategic role of the servicescape also forces recognition of the importance of the servicescape in creating customer experiences.

ASSESS AND IDENTIFY PHYSICAL EVIDENCE OPPORTUNITIES

Once the current forms of evidence and the roles of the servicescape are understood, possible changes and improvements can be identified. One question to ask is: are there missed opportunities to provide service evidence? The service blueprint of an insurance or utility service may show that little if any evidence of service is ever provided to the customer. A strategy might then be developed to provide more physical or virtual evidence of service to show customers exactly what they are paying for.

Or it may be discovered that the evidence provided is sending messages that do not enhance the firm's image or goals or that do not match customer expectations. For example, a restaurant might find that its high-price menu cues are not consistent with its design which suggests 'family dining' to its intended market segment. Either the pricing or the facility design would need to be changed, depending on the restaurant's overall strategy.

Another set of questions addresses whether the current physical evidence of service suits the needs and preferences of the target market. To begin answering such questions, the framework for understanding environment–user relationships (Figure 10.1) and the research approaches suggested in this chapter could be employed. Finally, does the evidence strategy take into account the (sometimes incompatible) needs of both customers and employees? This last question is particularly relevant in making decisions regarding the servicescape.

SERVICE SPOTLIGHT

McDonald's strategy is to have its restaurants worldwide reflect the cultures and communities in which they are found – to mirror the communities they serve. At the same time that it allows this creative energy to flourish in design and marketing strategies, McDonald's is extremely tight on its operating procedures and menu standards.

Although the Golden Arches are always present, a brief tour around the globe shows the wide variation in McDonald's face to the community:

- Bologna, Italy: in Bologna, known as the 'City of Arches' for hundreds of years, McDonald's has taken on the weathered, crafted look of the neighbouring historic arches. Even the floor in the restaurant was done by hand, using old-world techniques. The restaurant used local architects and artists to bring the local architectural feel to the Golden Arches.
- Paris, France: near the Sorbonne university in Paris, the local McDonald's reflects its studious neighbour. The servicescape there has the look of a leather-bound library with books, statues and heavy wood furniture.
- Salen, Sweden: within the Lindvallen Resort, MacDonald's operates the world's first 'ski-thru' restaurant, named McSki, located on the slopes, next to the main ski lift. The building, built in a typical mountain style with wood panels and natural stone from the surroundings, is different from any other McDonald's restaurant. Skiers can simply glide to the counter without taking off their skis, or they can be seated indoors or out.[36]

BE PREPARED TO UPDATE AND MODERNIZE THE EVIDENCE

Some aspects of the evidence, particularly the servicescape, require frequent or at least periodic updating and modernizing. Even if the vision, goals and objectives of the company do not change, time itself takes a toll on physical and virtual evidence, necessitating change and modernization. Clearly, an element of fashion is involved, and over time different colours, designs and styles may come to communicate different messages. Organizations obviously understand this concept when it comes to advertising strategy, but sometimes they overlook other elements of physical evidence.

WORK CROSS-FUNCTIONALLY

In presenting itself to the consumer, a service brand is concerned with communicating a desired image, with sending consistent and compatible messages through all forms of evidence, and with providing the type of service evidence the target customers want and can understand. Frequently, however, physical evidence decisions are made over time and by various functions within the organization. For example, decisions regarding employee uniforms may be made by the human resources area, servicescape design decisions may be made by the facilities management group, process design decisions are most frequently made by operations managers, webpages are designed by the IT department and advertising and pricing decisions may be made by the marketing department. Thus, it is not surprising that the physical evidence of service may at times be less than consistent. Service blueprinting can be a valuable tool for communicating within the firm, identifying existing service evidence and providing a springboard for changing or providing new forms of physical evidence.

A multifunction team approach to physical evidence strategy is often necessary, particularly for making decisions about the servicescape. It has been said that 'Facility planning and management . . . is a problem-solving activity that lies on the boundaries between architecture, interior space planning and product design, organizational [and consumer] behaviour, planning and environmental psychology'.[37]

SUMMARY

In this chapter we explored the roles of physical evidence in forming customer and employee perceptions and shaping customer experiences. Because services are intangible and because they are often produced and consumed at the same time, they can be difficult to comprehend or evaluate before their purchase. The physical evidence of the service thus serves as a primary cue for setting customer expectations before purchase. These tangible cues, particularly the servicescape, also influence customers' responses as they experience the service. Because customers and employees often interact in the servicescape, the physical surroundings also influence employees and the nature of employee–customer interactions.

The chapter focused primarily on the physical and virtual servicescapes – the physical surroundings or the physical facility where the service is produced, delivered and consumed. We presented a typology of servicescapes that illustrated their range of complexity and usage. By locating itself in the appropriate cell of the typology, an organization can quickly see who needs to be consulted regarding servicescape decisions, what objectives might be achieved through careful design of the facility, and how complex the decisions are likely to be. General strategic roles of the servicescape were also described. The servicescape can serve as a package (a 'visual metaphor' for the service itself), a facilitator in aiding the accomplishment of customer and employee goals, a socializer in prescribing behaviours in the environment and a differentiator to distinguish the organization from its competitors.

With this grounding in the importance of physical evidence, in particular the servicescape, we presented a general framework for understanding physical and virtual servicescape effects on employee and customer behaviours. The servicescape can affect the approach and avoidance behaviours of individual customers and employees as well as their social interactions. These behavioural responses come about because the physical environment influences (1) people's beliefs or cognitions about the service organization, (2) their feelings or emotions in response to the place, and (3) their actual physiological reactions while in the physical facility. The chapter also pointed out that individuals may respond differently to the servicescape depending on their personality traits, the mood they are in or the goals they are trying to accomplish.

Three categories of environmental dimensions capture the complex nature of the servicescape: ambient conditions; spatial layout and functionality; and signs, symbols and artefacts. These dimensions affect people's beliefs, emotions and physical responses, causing them to behave in certain ways while in the servicescape.

Given the importance of physical evidence and its potentially powerful influence on both customers and employees, it is important for firms to think strategically about the management of the tangible evidence of service. The impact of physical evidence and design decisions needs to be researched and planned as part of the marketing strategy. The chapter concluded with specific guidelines for physical evidence strategy. If physical evidence is researched, planned and implemented effectively, key problems leading to service quality shortcomings can be avoided. Through careful thinking about physical evidence decisions, an organization can avoid miscommunicating to customers via incompatible or inconsistent evidence or over-promising and raising customer expectations unrealistically. Beyond its role in helping avoid these negative outcomes, an effective physical evidence strategy can play a critically important role in communicating to customers and in guiding them in understanding the firm's offerings and setting up accurate expectations. During the service experience, the physical and virtual servicescape can play a major role in creating memorable outcomes and emotional connections with customers.

KEY CONCEPTS

Clue management	214	Servicescape	212
Environmental psychology	215	Socializer	218
Environmental dimensions	224	Stimulus–organism–response theory	219
Package v. facilitator v. differentiator	218	Virtual servicescapes	212

EXERCISES

1 Choose two very different firms (different market segments or service levels) in the same industry. Observe both establishments. Describe the service 'package' in both cases. How does the package help distinguish the two firms? Do you believe that the package sets accurate expectations for what the firm delivers? Is either firm over-promising through the manner in which its servicescape (or other types of physical evidence) communicates with customers?

2 Think of a particular service organization (it can be a class project company, the company you work for or some other organization) for which you believe physical evidence is particularly important in communicating with and satisfying customers. Prepare the text of a presentation you would give to the manager of that organization to convince him or her of the importance of physical evidence in the organization's marketing strategy.

3 Choose a service organization and collect all forms of physical evidence that the organization uses to communicate with its customers. If customers see the firm's facility, also take a photograph of the servicescape. Analyse the evidence in terms of compatibility, consistency and whether it over-promises or under-promises what the firm can deliver.

4 Visit the websites of several service providers. Does the physical evidence of the website portray an image consistent with other forms of evidence provided by the organizations?

5 Visit a hotel review site such as tripadvisor.com and examine what proportion of reviews mention elements of the physical environment. What aspects of the environment do reviewers specifically focus on?

DISCUSSION QUESTIONS

1 What is physical evidence, and why have we devoted an entire chapter to it in a marketing text?

2 Describe and give an example of how servicescapes play each of the following strategic roles: package, facilitator, socializer and differentiator.

3 Imagine that you own an independent copying and printing shop. In which cell would you locate your business in the typology of servicescapes shown in Table 10.3? What are the implications for designing your physical facility?

4 How can an effective physical evidence strategy help close provider gap 2? Explain.

5 Why are both customers and employees included in the framework for understanding servicescape effects on behaviour (Figure 10.1)? What types of behaviours are influenced by the servicescape according to the framework? Think of examples.

6 Using your own experiences, give examples of times when you have been affected cognitively, emotionally and physiologically by elements of the servicescape (in any service context).

7 Why is everyone not affected in exactly the same way by the servicescape?

8 Describe the physical environment of your favourite restaurant in terms of the three categories of servicescape dimensions: ambient conditions; spatial layout and functionality; and signs, symbols and artefacts.

9 Imagine that you are serving as a consultant to a local health club. How would you advise the health club to begin the process of developing an effective physical evidence strategy?

10 How can virtual servicescapes on the Internet be used by companies? Do they have any weaknesses?

FURTHER READING

Harris, L.C. and Ezeh, C. (2008). Servicescape and loyalty intentions: an empirical investigation. *European Journal of Marketing*, 42(3/4), 390–422.

Harris, L.C. and Goode, M.M.H. (2010). Online servicescapes, trust and purchase intentions. *Journal of Services Marketing*, 24(3) 230–43.

Heinonen, K. (2006). Temporal and spatial e-service value. *International Journal of Service Industry Management*, 17(4), 380–400.

Hoffman, K.D. and Turley, L.W. (2002). Atmospherics, service encounters and consumer decision-making: an integrative perspective. *Journal of Marketing Theory and Practice*, 10(3), 33–47.

Hulten, B., Broweus, N. and van Dijk, M. (2009). *Sensory Marketing*. UK: Palgrave Macmillan.

Lee, S. and Jeong, M. (2012). Effects of e-servicescape on consumers' flow experiences. *Journal of Hospitality and Tourism Technology*, 3(1), 47–59.

Mari, M. and Poggesi, S. (2013). Servicescape cues and customer behavior: a systematic literature review and research agenda. *The Service Industries Journal*, 33(2), 171–99.

Mattila, A.S. and Wirtz, J. (2001). Congruency of scent and music as a driver of in-store evaluations and behavior. *Journal of Retailing*, 77(2), 273–89.

Oakes, S. (2000). The influence of the musicscape within service environments. *Journal of Services Marketing*, 14(7), 539–56.

Rosenbaum, M.S. and Massiah, C. (2011). An expanded servicescape perspective. *Journal of Service Management*, 22(4), 471–90

Zomerdijk, L.G. and Voss, C.A. (2010). Service design for experience-centric services. *Journal of Service Research*, 13(1), 67–82.

PART 4
Delivering and Performing Service

In the gaps model of service quality, provider gap 3 (the service performance gap) is the discrepancy between customer-driven service standards and actual service delivery (see the accompanying figure). Even when guidelines exist for performing service well and treating customers correctly, high-quality service performance is not a certainty. Part 4 deals with all the ways in which companies ensure services are performed according to customer-defined designs and standards.

In Chapter 11, we focus on the key roles that employees play in service delivery and strategies that ensure they are effective in their roles.

In Chapter 12 we discuss the variability in service performance caused by customers. If customers do not perform appropriately – if they do not follow instructions or if they disturb other customers receiving service at the same time – service quality is jeopardized.

Chapter 13 describes service delivery through electronic channels and intermediaries such as retailers, franchisees, agents and brokers. Firms must develop ways to either control or motivate these intermediaries to meet company goals and deliver consistent quality service.

Chapter 14 emphasizes the need to synchronize demand and capacity in service organizations in order to deliver consistent, high-quality service.

Chapter 15 describes service recovery management, which involves understanding why customers complain, what they expect when they complain, and how to deal with service failures.

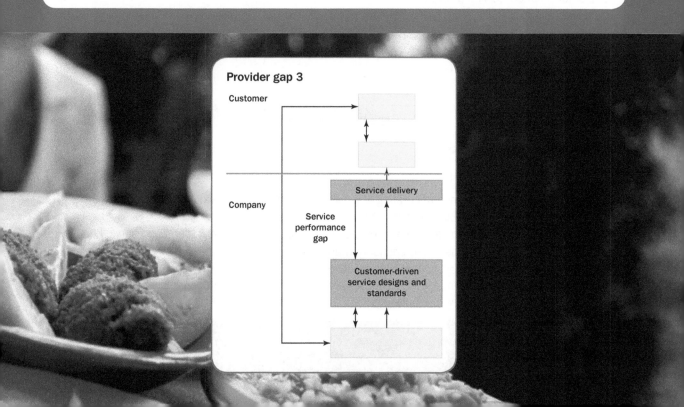

CHAPTER 11

Employees' Roles in Service Delivery

CHAPTER OUTLINE

LEARNING OBJECTIVES

This chapter's objectives are to:

1 Demonstrate the importance of creating a service culture in which providing excellent service to both internal and external customers is a way of life.

2 Illustrate the pivotal role of service employees in creating customer satisfaction and service quality.

3 Identify the challenges inherent in boundary-spanning roles.

4 Provide examples of strategies for creating customer-oriented service delivery through hiring the right people, developing employees to deliver service quality, providing needed support systems and retaining the best service employees.

OPENING EXAMPLE
The Critical Role of the Employees

The reviews below illustrate the important roles played by service employees in creating satisfied customers and in building customer relationships. The front-line service providers in each example are enormously important to the success of the organizations they represent. They are responsible for understanding customer needs and for interpreting customer requirements in real time. They represent the organization's brand in the eye of the customer.

- We arrived at the hotel early to leave our bags with the concierge and we stood at the desk for twenty minutes and were finally greeted with a grunt; this seemed to set the tone for the majority of the staff for the rest of our stay, not once were we made to feel welcome. On leaving the hotel I eventually spoke to the Duty Manager, the look on his face gave the expression 'not again', and after he listened to me he just rolled his eyes and said it was just as well we were leaving.

- The staff here are FANTASTIC – I could not fault them in any way, The reception staff made me feel welcome whilst checking in; the light-haired lady that checked us out this morning was extremely friendly and helpful. She also looked after our bags while we did one more trip around the city. She is a credit to your hotel, she did not make us feel as if we were rushed out and she asked us questions regarding our stay and what we had planned for the day. She seemed genuinely interested and cared if our stay was comfortable.

- I arrived at this hotel to be greeted by a grumpy receptionist who didn't even acknowledge me when she walked past. She was messing about with a till drawer and continued to not even make eye contact with me. Once she finally came over and spoke to me it took ages to check in. She didn't explain any of the hotel's facilities or anything, and I even had to ask where the lift was!

- Every single member of staff went out of their way to be friendly, polite and helpful. What more can you want from a hotel? It was a great experience and I congratulate the hotel on their training and their attitude towards doing business!

In this chapter we focus on service employees and human resource practices that facilitate delivery of quality services. The assumption is that even when customer expectations are well understood (gap 1) and services have been designed and specified to conform to those expectations (gap 2), there may still be discontinuities in service quality when the service is not delivered as specified. These discontinuities are labelled gap 3 – the service performance gap – in the service quality framework. Because employees frequently deliver or perform the service, human resource issues are a major cause of this gap. By focusing on the critical role of service employees, and by developing strategies that will lead to effective customer-oriented service, organizations can begin to close the service performance gap.

The failure to deliver services as designed and specified can result from a number of employee and human performance factors: ineffective recruitment of service-oriented employees; role ambiguity and role conflict among contact employees; poor employee–technology–job fit; inappropriate evaluation and compensation systems; and lack of empowerment, perceived control and teamwork.

SERVICE CULTURE

Before addressing the role of the employee in service delivery, we should look at the bigger picture. The behaviour of employees in an organization will be heavily influenced by its organization, or the pervasive norms and values that shape individual and group behaviour. *Corporate culture* has been defined as 'the pattern of shared values and beliefs that give the members of an organization meaning and provide them with the rules for behaviour in the organization'.[1] *Culture* has been defined more informally as 'the way we do things around here'.

To understand at a personal level what corporate culture is, think of different places you have worked or organizations you have been a member of, such as sports clubs, schools or associations. Your behaviour and the behaviours of others were no doubt influenced by the underlying values, norms and culture of the organization. Even when you attend an interview for a new job, you can begin to get a sense of the culture through talking to a number of employees and observing their behaviour. Once you are in the job, your formal training and informal observation of behaviour will work together to give you a better picture of the organization's culture.

Experts have suggested that a customer-oriented, service-oriented organization will have at its heart a *service culture*, defined as 'a culture where an appreciation for good service exists, and where giving good service to internal as well as ultimate, external customers is considered a natural way of life and one of the most important norms by everyone'.[2] This very rich definition has many implications for employee behaviours. First, a service culture exists if there is an 'appreciation for good service'. This phrase does not mean that the company has an advertising campaign that stresses the importance of service, but 'in that underneath sort of way' people know that good service is appreciated and valued. A second important point in this definition is that good service is given to internal as well as external customers.[3] It is not enough to promise excellent service to final customers; all people within the organization deserve the same kind of service. Finally, in a service culture good service is 'a way of life' and it comes naturally because it is an important norm of the organization.

Service culture has been linked to competitive advantage in companies.[4] Why is it so important? No realistic amount of supervision would allow a firm to exercise sufficient control over *all* employee behaviour. In many service settings, employees interact with customers with no management present. In such instances, the firm must rely on its service culture to influence employee thoughts, feelings and behaviours.

EXHIBITING SERVICE LEADERSHIP

A strong service culture begins with leaders in the organization who demonstrate a passion for service excellence. Leonard Berry suggests that leaders of successful service firms tend to have similar core values, such as integrity, joy and respect, and they 'infuse those values into the fabric of the organization'.[5] Service leadership does not consist of bestowing a set of commands from a thick rulebook but, rather, the regular and consistent demonstration of one's values. Employees are more likely to embrace a service culture when they see management living out these values. Espoused values – what managers *say* the values are – tend to have less impact on employees than enacted values – what employees believe the values to be because of what they observe management actually *doing*.[6] That is, culture is what employees perceive that management *really* believes, and employees gain an understanding of what is important in the organization through the daily experiences they have with those people in key roles throughout the organization.

The Virgin Group, driven by Sir Richard Branson, has the following brand values: quality; innovation; value for money; fun; and sense of challenge. These values reflect those of Sir Richard himself: for example the sense of challenge is evident in his world-record-breaking attempts at crossing the Atlantic and Pacific in fast boats and hot-air balloons. In terms of innovation, he is involved in organizing the first passenger flights into space, and in terms of fun he is regularly involved in the activities of the Comic Relief charity and has undertaken stunts involving him dressing up as an air hostess, shaving off his beard, etc. He has also positioned himself as a campaigner against big business, placing an emphasis on quality and value for money for the customer. He has a well-stated philosophy of putting staff at the heart of his organizations' brand positioning. He has asserted that you have to have employees on board as the best representation of the brand, and success in business will follow from that.

DEVELOPING A SERVICE CULTURE

A service culture cannot be developed overnight, and there is no magic, easy way to sustain a service culture. The human resource and internal marketing practices discussed later in this chapter can help develop a service culture over time. If, however, an organization has a culture that is rooted in product- or operations-oriented government regulation or traditions, no single strategy will change it overnight. Hundreds of little (but significant) factors, not just one or two big factors, are required to build and sustain a service culture.[7] Successful companies such as Hilton Hotels and IBM Global Services have all found that it takes years of consistent, concerted effort to build a service culture and to shift the organization from its old patterns to new ways of doing business. Even for companies that started out with a strong service and customer focus, such as Eurostar, Disney and Ritz-Carlton, sustaining their established service cultures still takes constant attention to hundreds of details.

TRANSPORTING A SERVICE CULTURE

Transporting a service culture through international business expansion is also very challenging. Attempting to 'export' a corporate culture to another country creates additional issues. For instance, will the organization's service culture clash with a different national culture? If there is a clash, is it over *what* the actual values are or over *how* they are to be enacted? If the issue is over what the values are, and they are core values critical to the firm's competitive advantage, then perhaps the company cannot be successful in that setting. Although tremendous opportunities exist in the global marketplace, the many legal, cultural and language barriers become particularly evident for services that depend on human interaction.

What sets Prêt-à-Manger(Pret) apart, is a commitment to fresh, healthy food (every shop has its own kitchen and there is no sell-by date on anything), and an obsession with speedy service. But there's something else too: they call it the 'Pret Buzz', which every customer should feel within seconds of entering, and which is principally to do with the people who work there.

Pret claim to 'only employ people who are friendly and lively … people who are good-humoured by nature.' To support this philosophy, every Team Member is issued with a little book of 'Pret Behaviours' that are applicable to any job in the company. In terms of dress-code, the requirements include 'smart' blue jeans, black polishable shoes, no visible piercings or offensive tattoos and hair kept tidy.

Everyone applying for a job is assessed against three core Pret behaviours of passion, clear speaking and team working, and, if accepted, is sent to a shop for a trial day. At the end of that day, the rest of the staff in the branch vote on whether to keep the new recruit; if they vote yes, the applicant becomes the latest member of the team, but if they vote no, the applicant gets a day's wages and a polite 'thanks, but no thanks'.

Fresh recruits begin a 10-day training in hygiene, safety and the Pret way, at the end of which, provided they pass various tests, they graduate as Team Members. They then go on a further 10-week training in every aspect of what goes on in the kitchen and at the front of the store, which leads to graduation as a Team Member Star. Thereafter, a Star can become a Hot Chef, a Barista (coffee expert) or Team Member Trainer; then Team Leader, Assistant Manager and General Manager.[8]

The McDonald's way – The fast-food giant has been very successful in its international expansion. In some ways it has remained very 'American' in everything it does – people around the world want an American experience when they go to McDonald's. However, the company is sensitive to cultural differences as well. This subtle blending of the 'McDonald's way' with adaptations to cultural nuances has resulted in great success. One way McDonald's has found to maintain its standards is through its Hamburger University (HU), which is required training for *all* McDonald's employees worldwide before they can become managers. Each year approximately 3,000 employees from nearly 100 countries enroll and attend the Advanced Operations Course at HU, located in Oak Brook, Illinois. The curriculum is 80 per cent devoted to communications and human relations skills.

Because of the international scope of McDonald's, translators and electronic equipment enable professors to teach and communicate in 22 languages at one time. The result is that all managers in all countries have the same 'ketchup in their veins', and the restaurant's basic human resources and operating philosophies remain fairly stable from operation to operation. Certain adaptations in decor, menu and other areas of cultural differences are then allowed (see Chapter 10 for some specific examples).

THE CRITICAL IMPORTANCE OF SERVICE EMPLOYEES

A popular quotation about service organizations goes like this: 'In a service organization, if you're not serving the customer, you'd better be serving someone who is.'[9] People – front-line employees and those supporting them from behind the scenes – are critical to the success of any service organization. The importance of people in the marketing of services is captured in the people element of the services marketing mix, which we described in Chapter 1 as *all the human actors who play a part in service delivery and thus influence the buyer's perceptions; namely, the firm's personnel, the customer, and other customers in the service environment.*

The key focus in this chapter is on customer-contact service employees because:

- They *are* the service.
- They *are* the organization in the customer's eyes.
- They *are* the brand.
- They *are* marketers.

In many cases, the contact employee is the *service* – there is nothing else. For example, in most personal and professional services (like haircutting, personal trainers, child care, cleaning/maintenance, limousine services, counselling and legal services) the contact employee provides the entire service single-handedly. The offering *is* the employee. Thus, investing in the employee as a means to improve the service parallels a direct investment in the improvement of a manufactured product.

Even if the contact employee does not perform the service entirely, he or she may still *personify the brand in the customer's eyes*. All the employees of a law firm or a health clinic – from the professionals who provide the service to the receptionists and office staff – represent the firm's brand to the client, and everything these individuals do or say can influence perceptions of the organization. Even off-duty employees, such as flight attendants or restaurant employees on a break, reflect on the organizations they represent. If they are unprofessional or make rude remarks about or to customers, customers' perceptions of the organization will suffer even though the employee is not on duty.

Disneyland Paris insists that its employees maintain 'onstage' attitudes and behaviours whenever they are in front of the public and that they relax these behaviours only when they are out of the customers' sight or 'backstage' in their off-duty times.

Service employees are the brand. A Barclays Bank financial adviser, an IKEA sales assistant, a KLM flight attendant – in each case, the primary image that a customer has of the firm is formed by his or her interactions with the employees of that firm. A customer sees Barclays Bank as a good provider of financial services if the employees he or she interacts with are knowledgeable, understanding and concerned about the customer's financial situation and goals. Similarly, a customer sees IKEA as a professional and empathetic company because of interactions he or she has with its sales assistants.

⭐ SERVICE SPOTLIGHT

In the UK, Starbucks has overhauled its recruitment and training by giving its employees the chance to get National Vocational Qualifications (NVQs) supported by the national Employment Service, management training and funding opportunities for community projects that contribute to the personal development of their staff. By providing staff better opportunities, the theory is that Starbucks will have a better trained, more knowledgeable workforce with lower levels of staff turnover, which, in turn, will give the coffee chain more motivated and engaged brand advocates. Brian Waring, Starbucks VP of marketing, stated: 'We've upweighted our commitment in the training and development of our people because as brand ambassadors our partners must truly embrace the values of our company. We know that the longer we keep and develop our baristas, and the more they embrace our values the better our coffee and our service'.[10]

Because contact employees represent the organization and can directly influence customer satisfaction, they *perform the role of marketers*. They physically embody the product and are walking billboards, from a promotional standpoint. Some service employees may also perform more traditional selling roles. For example, bank tellers are often responsible for cross-selling bank products, a departure from the traditional teller role limited to the operations function. Whether acknowledged or not, whether actively selling or not, service employees perform marketing functions. They can perform these functions well, to the organization's advantage, or poorly, to the organization's detriment. In this chapter we examine frameworks, tools and strategies for ensuring that service employees perform their marketing functions well.

EMPLOYEE SATISFACTION, CUSTOMER SATISFACTION AND PROFITS

Satisfied employees make for satisfied customers (and satisfied customers can, in turn, reinforce employees' sense of satisfaction in their jobs). Some researchers have even gone so far as to suggest that unless service employees are happy in their jobs, customer satisfaction will be difficult to achieve.[11]

Through their research with customers and employees in 28 different bank branches, Benjamin Schneider and David Bowen have shown that both a *climate for service* and *a climate for employee well-being* are highly correlated with overall customer perceptions of service quality.[12] That is, both service climate and human resource management experiences that *employees* have within their organizations are reflected in how *customers* experience the service. Other research suggests that employees who feel they are treated fairly by their organizations will treat customers better, resulting in greater customer satisfaction.[13]

The underlying logic connecting employee satisfaction and loyalty to customer satisfaction and loyalty, and ultimately profits, is illustrated by the service profit chain shown in Figure 11.1.[14] In earlier chapters we focused on customer satisfaction and retention; here we focus on employee satisfaction and employee retention. The service profit chain suggests that there are critical linkages among internal service quality; employee satisfaction/productivity; the value of services provided to the customer; and, ultimately, customer satisfaction, retention and profits.

Figure 11.1 The service profit chain

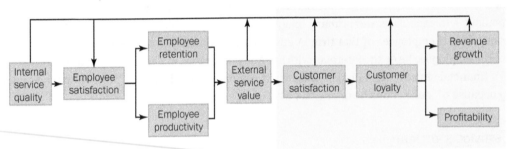

Source: Adapted and reprinted by permission of *Harvard Business Review*, an excerpt from J.L. Heskett, T.O. Jones, G.W. Loveman, W.E. Sasser Jr and L.A. Schlesinger, 'Putting the service-profit chain to work', *Harvard Business Review* (March–April 1994). Copyright © 1994 by The Harvard Business School Publishing Corporation; all rights reserved.

Service profit chain researchers are careful to point out that the model does not suggest causality. That is, employee satisfaction does not *cause* customer satisfaction; rather the two are interrelated and feed off each other. The model does imply that companies that exhibit high levels of success on the elements of the model will be more successful and profitable than those that do not. This finding is borne out in other research, which reports that companies that manage people right will outperform by 30 to 40 per cent companies that do not.[15]

THE EFFECT OF EMPLOYEE BEHAVIOURS ON SERVICE QUALITY DIMENSIONS

Customers' perceptions of service quality will be impacted by the customer-oriented behaviours of employees.[16] In fact, all five dimensions of service quality (reliability, responsiveness, assurance, empathy and tangibles) can be influenced directly by service employees.

Delivering the service as promised – *reliability* – is often totally within the control of front-line employees. Even in the case of automated services (such as ATMs, automated ticketing machines or self-serve service stations), behind-the-scenes employees are critical for making sure all the systems are working properly. When services fail or errors are made, employees are essential for setting things right and using their judgement to determine the best course of action for service recovery.

Front-line employees directly influence customer perceptions of *responsiveness* through their personal willingness to help and their promptness in serving customers. Consider the range of responses you receive from different retail staff when you need help finding a particular item of clothing. One employee may ignore your presence, whereas another offers to help you search and calls other stores to locate the item. One may help you immediately and efficiently, whereas another may move slowly in accommodating even the simplest request.

The *assurance* dimension of service quality is highly dependent on employees' ability to communicate their credibility and to inspire trust and confidence. The reputation of the organization will help, but in the end, individual employees with whom the customer interacts confirm and build trust in the organization or detract from its reputation and ultimately destroy trust. For start-up or relatively unknown organizations, credibility, trust and confidence will be tied totally to employee actions.

It is difficult to imagine how an organization would deliver 'caring, individualized attention' to customers independent of its employees. *Empathy* implies that employees will pay attention, listen, adapt and be flexible in delivering what individual customers need.[17] For example, research documents that when employees are customer oriented, have good rapport with customers and exhibit perceptive and attentive listening skills, customers will evaluate the service more highly and be more likely to return.[18] Employee appearance and dress are important aspects of the *tangibles* dimension of quality, along with many other factors that are independent of service employees (the service facility, decor, brochures, signage, and so on).

SERVICE SPOTLIGHT

In order to demonstrate responsiveness and assurance, airlines such as British Airways, KLM, Iberia and Air France have provided Apple iPads to their cabin crews. These provide cabin crew with a library of information on the popular computer tablet. Safety manuals, customer service updates and timetables are all at the cabin crew's fingertips, allowing them to answer any questions from passengers. The device also helps staff identify where each customer is seated, who they are travelling with and their Loyalty Programme status, as well as any meal requirements. Overall, the iPads give staff the opportunity to offer a more personalized service and the ability to log incidents that happen both on the ground and in the air. These can then be synced with a main database once the devices are brought back to an airport.

BOUNDARY-SPANNING ROLES

Our focus in this chapter is on front-line service employees who interact directly with customers, although much of what is described and recommended can be applied to internal service employees as well. The front-line service employees are referred to as *boundary spanners* because they operate at the organization's boundary. Boundary spanners provide a link between the external customer and environment and the internal operations of the organization. They serve a critical function in understanding, filtering and interpreting information and resources to and from the organization and its external constituencies.

Who are these boundary spanners? What types of people and positions comprise critical boundary-spanning roles? Their skills and experience cover the full spectrum of jobs and careers. In industries such as fast food, hotels, telecommunication and retail, the boundary spanners are the least skilled, lowest-paid employees in the organization. They are order-takers, front-desk employees, telephone operators, store clerks, truck drivers and delivery people. In other industries, boundary spanners are well-paid, highly educated professionals – for example, doctors, lawyers, accountants, consultants, architects and teachers.

No matter what the level of skill or pay, boundary-spanning positions are often high-stress jobs. In addition to mental and physical skills, these positions require extraordinary levels of emotional labour, frequently demand an ability to handle interpersonal and inter-organizational conflict, and call on the employee to make real-time trade-offs between quality and productivity on the job. These stresses and trade-offs can result in failure to deliver services as specified, which widens the service performance gap.

EMOTIONAL LABOUR

The term *emotional labour* was coined by Arlie Hochschild to refer to the labour that goes beyond the physical or mental skills needed to deliver quality service.[19] In general, boundary-spanning service employees are expected to align their displayed emotions with organizationally desired emotions via their use of emotional labour.[20] Such labour includes delivering smiles, making eye contact, showing sincere interest and engaging in friendly conversation with people who are essentially strangers and who may or may not ever be seen again. Friendliness, courtesy, empathy and responsiveness directed towards customers all require huge amounts of emotional labour from the front-line employees who shoulder this responsibility for the organization. Emotional labour draws on people's feelings (often requiring them to suppress their true feelings) to be effective in their jobs. A front-line service employee who is having a bad day or is not feeling just right is still expected to put on the face of the organization when dealing with customers. One of the clearest examples of emotional labour is the story (probably apocryphal) of the flight attendant who was approached by a businessman who said, 'Let's have a smile.' 'Okay,' she replied, 'I'll tell you what, first you smile and then I'll smile, okay?' He smiled. 'Good,' she said. 'Now hold that for 15 hours,' and walked away.[21]

Many of the strategies we will discuss later in this chapter can help organizations and employees deal with the realities of emotional labour on the job. For the organization, such strategies include carefully selecting people who can handle emotional stress, training them in the required skills (like listening and problem-solving) and teaching or giving them coping abilities and strategies (via job rotation, scheduled breaks, teamwork or other techniques).[22]

STRATEGIES FOR MANAGING EMOTIONAL LABOUR

Customer-contact employees in service positions are often required to display (or, conversely, to hide) a variety of emotions. In many situations, such employees are increasingly being required to invest personal identity and expression into their work. The following description suggests how the experience of the service employee, even in the most routine of occupations, is markedly different from that of the traditional manufacturing worker:

> *The assembly-line worker could openly hate his job, despise his supervisor, and even dislike his coworkers, and while this might be an unpleasant state of affairs, if he [completes] his assigned tasks efficiently, his attitude [is] his own problem. For the service worker, inhabiting the job means, at the very least, pretending to like it, and, at most, actually bringing his whole self into the job, liking it, and genuinely caring about the people with whom he interacts.[23]*

Emotional labour occurs more often when the job requires frequent and long durations of voice contact or face-to-face contact with customers. Employees in these roles often need emotional management to deal with such situations. The following activities help to foster an environment that helps employees deal with the realities of emotional labour on the job:

1 Screen for emotional labour activities
2 Teach emotional management skills and appropriate behaviours
3 Carefully fashion the physical work environment
4 Allow employees to air their views
5 Put management on the front line
6 Give employees a break
7 Hand off demanding customers to managers.

SCREEN FOR EMOTIONAL LABOUR ABILITIES

Many firms look to hire employees who are well suited to meet the emotional labour requirements of the job. Retailers such as Marks and Spencer or Asda (Wal-Mart) put prospective employees through simulated customer contact exercises to see the kind of friendliness and warmth they naturally communicate. Such practices help in identifying employees whose values, background and personalities match the job's emotional labour requirements.

TEACH EMOTIONAL MANAGEMENT SKILLS AND APPROPRIATE BEHAVIOURS

Most customer-contact employees are taught that they need to be courteous to customers. However, customers have no obligation to return empathy or courtesy. In situations in which customers exercise the privilege of 'the customer is always right', employees face real challenges in suppressing their true feelings. Seldom do firms provide much training to assist employees in facing these challenges. Arlie Hochschild identifies two forms of emotional labour: *surface acting*, in which employees pretend to feel emotions that are not really present and, in doing so, deliberately and consciously create an outward appearance in order to deceive others; and *deep acting*, in which employees attempt to experience the real feelings they must express to the customer, including the active invocation of 'thoughts, images, and memories to induce the associated emotion'.[24] Hair salon stylists and airline flight attendants are often encouraged to engage in deep acting strategies such as imagining that the client is a friend or that the passenger is a frightened little child flying for the first time. Often, in order to persuade clients to buy hair products or colour their hair, stylists have to moderate their language or behaviour; they may use deep acting to justify these behaviours to themselves. Companies may also train employees in how to avoid absorbing a customer's bad mood, perhaps by having employees spend hours role-playing to suppress their natural reaction to retaliate with their own negative emotions.

CAREFULLY FASHION THE PHYSICAL WORK ENVIRONMENT

As we discussed in Chapter 10, the environment in which the service is delivered can have an impact on employee behaviours and emotions. Many of the better call centres working for insurance companies or banks attempt to reduce staff stress and boredom through bright airy decoration with windows that allow employees to see the weather, trees, grass, people and cars driving by.

ALLOW EMPLOYEES TO AIR THEIR VIEWS

Employees who must exert emotional labour often need to have an outlet to 'let off steam'. Allowing employees to air their views lets them get rid of their frustrations. If such venting is done in a group setting, it can provide emotional support and encouragement, as well as allowing employees to see that others are experiencing the same problems and that they are not alone. If part of the work day (or week) is explicitly set aside to allow employees to share their frustrations, it delivers a message to employees that the company is aware of, and acknowledges, the emotional contribution that they have made. Ritz-Carlton, Wal-Mart and other companies regularly set aside time for such venting. In addition to the cathartic benefit this experience can provide, other employees may reveal coping strategies that they have found useful.

PUT MANAGEMENT ON THE FRONT LINE

Customer-contact employees often feel that management does not truly understand or appreciate the emotional labour they must expend. Managers should regularly be required to interact with customers. Scottish and Southern Energy has its management team work alongside its customer service representatives in fielding customers' telephone calls. In addition to understanding what the issues are, managers are truly able to empathize with employees. Managers who do so not only have an appreciation for the emotional labour requirements of their employees, but they are also in a better position to serve as role models and mentors in using emotional management skills.

GIVE EMPLOYEES A BREAK

In situations in which an employee has just handled a particularly tough customer, especially if the employee has frequent and long durations of voice or face-to-face contact with customers, a particularly helpful strategy is to allow the employee a short break to regroup. Retailers rotate employees into different positions throughout the day so that they do not spend the entire time working on checkouts. Customer contact employees can be re-energized and refreshed after spending a little time away from the situation, even if they take only a few minutes to finish paperwork or complete some other job responsibility.

HAND OFF DEMANDING CUSTOMERS TO MANAGERS

Some customers may be too much for an employee to handle. In such situations, to alleviate pressure on the customer-contact employee, firms may shift responsibility for the interaction to managers. Norwich Union Insurance call-centre operators are trained to pass difficult customers on to supervisors or managers.

SOURCES OF CONFLICT

Front-line employees often face interpersonal and inter-organizational conflicts on the job. Many, such as waiters, bus drivers and hotel receptionists may perceive themselves performing roles that give them a status below that of the customer. This is often described as a *subordinate service role*.[25] They may feel that the customer has more control over their role than they do. As a result some employees may develop their own approach to get even and overcome the perceived inequality between customers and themselves. For instance, the hotel receptionist who speaks French when dealing with English guests, despite being able to speak excellent English, is shifting the balance of power to give herself greater control over the situation.

The frustration and confusion of front-line employees can, if left unattended, lead to stress, job dissatisfaction, a diminished ability to serve customers and burnout.[26] Managers need to understand the perceived roles and challenges faced by their front-line employees and in particular the conflicts that they have to deal with, including person/role conflicts, organization/client conflicts and inter-client conflicts, as discussed in the next three points.[27]

PERSON/ROLE CONFLICTS

In some situations boundary spanners feel conflicts between what they are asked to do and their own personalities, orientations or values. Service workers may feel role conflict when they are required to subordinate their feelings or beliefs, as when they are asked to live by the motto 'The customer is always right – even when he [or she] is wrong'. Sometimes there is a conflict between role requirements and the self-image or self-esteem of the employee.

Person/role conflict also arises when employees are required to wear specific clothing or change some aspect of their appearance to conform to the job requirements. A young lawyer, just out of school, may feel an internal conflict with his new role when his employer requires him to cut his long hair and trade his casual clothes for a suit.

ORGANIZATION/CLIENT CONFLICT

A more common type of conflict for front-line service employees is the conflict between their two bosses, the organization and the individual customer. Service employees are typically rewarded for following certain standards, rules and procedures. Ideally these rules and standards are customer based, as described in Chapter 10. When they are not, or when a customer makes excessive demands, the employee has to choose whether to follow the rules or satisfy the demands. The conflict is greatest when the employee believes the organization is wrong in its policies and must decide whether to accommodate the client and risk losing his or her job, or to follow the policies. The employee may attempt to apply the agreed policies, but given the potential stressful situation with the customer, they can frequently side with the customer against the organization or show signs of frustration and irritation. Such conflicts are especially severe when service employees depend directly on the customer for income. For example, employees who depend on tips or commissions are likely to face greater levels of organization/client conflict because they have even greater incentives to identify with the customer.

INTER-CLIENT CONFLICT

Sometimes conflict occurs for boundary spanners when incompatible expectations and requirements arise from two or more customers. This situation occurs most often when the service provider is serving customers in turn (a bank teller, a supermarket checkout operator, a doctor) or is serving many customers simultaneously (a teacher, an entertainer).

When serving customers in turn, the provider may satisfy one customer by spending additional time, customizing the service, and being very flexible in meeting the customer's needs. Meanwhile, waiting customers are becoming dissatisfied because their needs are not being met in a timely way. Beyond the timing issue, different clients may prefer different modes of service delivery. Having to serve one client who prefers personal recognition and a degree of familiarity in the presence of another client who is all business and would prefer little interpersonal interaction can also create conflict for the employee.

When serving many customers at the same time, employees often find it difficult or impossible simultaneously to serve the full range of needs of a group of heterogeneous customers. This type of conflict is readily apparent in any classroom in which the teacher must meet a multitude of expectations and different preferences for formats and style.

QUALITY/PRODUCTIVITY TRADE-OFFS

Front-line service workers are asked to be both effective and efficient: they are expected to deliver satisfying service to customers and at the same time to be cost-effective and productive in what they do. A dentist, for example, is expected to deliver caring, quality, individualized service to his or her patients, but at the same time to serve a certain number of patients within a specified time frame. A checkout operator at a grocery store is expected to know his or her customers and to be polite and courteous, yet also to process the groceries accurately and move people through the line quickly. An architectural draftsperson is expected to create quality drawings, yet to produce a required quantity of drawings in a given period of time. These essential trade-offs between quality and quantity, and between maximum effectiveness and efficiency, place real-time demands and pressures on service employees.

Research suggests that these trade-offs are more difficult for service businesses than for manufacturing and packaged goods businesses, and that pursuing goals of customer satisfaction and productivity simultaneously is particularly challenging in situations in which service employees are required to customize service offerings to meet customer needs.[28]

Jagdip Singh, a noted services researcher, has studied productivity and quality as two types of performance inherent in front-line service jobs.[29] He explains the difficult trade-offs that employees face and has developed ways to measure these two types of performance together with a theoretical model to predict the causes and consequences of these trade-offs. He finds that quality of job performance is particularly susceptible to burnout and job stress. He also finds that internal support from understanding managers and control over the job tasks can help employees in making quality and productivity trade-offs, avoiding burnout and maintaining their performance. Technology is being used to an ever-greater degree to balance the quality/quantity trade-off to increase productivity of service workers and at the same time free them to provide higher-quality service for the customer. Through software applications, calls coming into call centres are identified (by telephone number and market segment) and routed to the right customer service personnel even before the calls are answered. Employees get the calls that they are trained for and best able to handle. The software also allows the employee to view the entire account history of the caller, and this information is available on the employee's computer screen simultaneously with the incoming call. Employees have at their fingertips information on the wide variety of services on offer and other options available to customers. The person who answers the call is empowered to make decisions, answer questions and encourage sales in ways that were totally impractical prior to this technology.

Although front-office customer relationship management (CRM) systems hold great promise and have provided tremendous bottom-line benefits for companies already, they come with their own, often significant, challenges. They can require major monetary and human investments. They often mandate integration of incompatible information systems, significant internal training costs and incentives to be sure they are used effectively. Frequently they fail, at least on the initial try, for a variety of reasons. Some companies do not anticipate the amount of work involved, and many do not realize how resistant their employees will be to making the necessary changes. Even a corporate giant such as Microsoft faced significant challenges when it attempted to integrate all of its 36 distinct customer information applications worldwide. Microsoft underestimated the internal demands of such a large deployment and cut back on end-user training at the wrong time. It learned that training (of employees and, sometimes, customers) is critical to the success of the technology. Despite some difficulties, however, the system soon began to pay for itself, allowing Microsoft service staff and salespeople to make decisions better and in a more timely fashion, satisfying customers and building the business.

STRATEGIES FOR DELIVERING SERVICE QUALITY THROUGH PEOPLE

A complex combination of strategies is needed to ensure that service employees are willing and able to deliver quality services and that they stay motivated to perform in customer-oriented, service-minded ways. These strategies for enabling service promises are often referred to as *internal marketing*, as shown in the service triangle (Figure 1.4) in Chapter 1.[30] Even during slow economic times, the importance of attracting, developing and retaining good people in knowledge- and service-based industries cannot be over-emphasized, as *Fast Company magazine* suggested: 'When it comes to building great companies, the most urgent business challenge is finding and keeping great people. Sure a Web strategy is important, and the stock market is scary, but still the best companies know that people are the foundation of greatness.'[31]

By approaching human resource decisions and strategies from the point of view that the primary goal is to motivate and enable employees to deliver successfully customer-oriented promises, an organization will move towards delivering service quality through its people. The strategies presented here are organized around four basic themes. To build a customer-oriented, service-minded workforce, an organization must (1) hire the right people, (2) develop people to deliver service quality, (3) provide the needed support systems, and (4) retain the best people. Within each of these basic strategies are a number of specific sub-strategies for accomplishing the goal, as shown in Figure 11.2.

HIRE THE RIGHT PEOPLE

To deliver service quality effectively, considerable attention should be focused on recruiting and hiring service employees. Such attention is contrary to traditional practices in many service industries, where service personnel are the lowest on the corporate ladder and work for a minimum wage. At the other end of the spectrum, in the professional services, the most important recruiting criteria are typically technical training, certifications and expertise. However, many organizations are now looking above and beyond the technical qualifications of applicants to assess their customer and service orientation as well. Figure 11.2 shows three ways to go about hiring the right people.

COMPETE FOR THE BEST PEOPLE

To get the best people, an organization needs to identify them and compete with other organizations to hire them. L. Berry and A. Parasuraman refer to this approach as 'competing for talent market share'.[32] They suggest that firms act as marketers in their pursuit of the best employees, just as they use their marketing expertise to compete for customers. Firms that think of recruiting as a marketing activity will address issues of market (employee) segmentation, product (job) design and promotion of job availability in ways that attract potential long-term employees.

Figure 11.2   Human resource strategies for delivering service quality through people

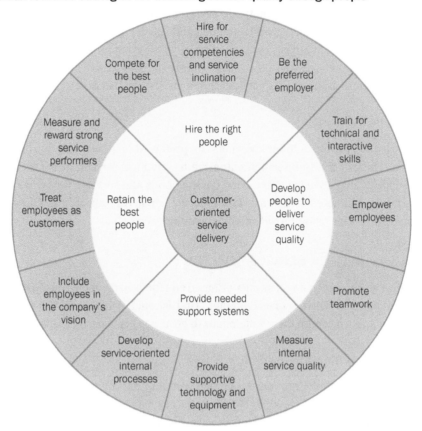

HIRE FOR SERVICE COMPETENCIES AND SERVICE INCLINATION

Once potential employees have been identified, organizations need to be conscientious in interviewing and screening them to truly select the best people from the pool of candidates. Service employees need two complementary capacities: *service competencies* and *service inclination*.[33]

Service competencies are the skills and knowledge necessary to do the job. In many cases, employees validate competencies by achieving particular degrees and certifications, such as attaining a degree and passing the relevant professional qualifications. These are required of doctors, airline pilots, university professors, teachers and many other job seekers before they are ever interviewed for service jobs in their fields. In other cases, service competencies may not be degree related but may instead relate to basic intelligence or physical requirements. A checkout assistant, for example, must possess basic mathematical skills and the potential to operate a cash register.

Given the multidimensional nature of service quality, service employees should be screened for more than their service competencies. They must also be screened for *service inclination* – their interest in doing service-related work – which is reflected in their attitudes towards service and orientation toward serving customers and others on the job. Self-selection suggests that most service jobs will draw applicants with some level of service inclination and that most employees in service organizations are inclined towards service. However, some employees clearly have a greater service inclination than others. Research has shown that service effectiveness is correlated with service-oriented personality characteristics such as helpfulness, thoughtfulness and sociability.[34] An ideal selection process for service employees assesses both service competencies and service inclination, resulting in employee hires who are high on both dimensions.[35]

In many cases a component of the selection process will include a form of work simulation that allows employees to demonstrate how they would actually perform on the job. A simulation may take the form of role-playing or a series of exercises that parallel the demands of the actual job. In addition to being a good way to assess potential employee abilities, simulations can give the potential recruit a better view of what the job is actually like. Those candidates who do not like what they experience can withdraw their application before being hired and then finding out that the job is not what they had expected.

BE THE PREFERRED EMPLOYER

One way to attract the best people is to be known as the preferred employer in a particular industry or in a particular location. This is achieved through extensive training, career and advancement opportunities, excellent internal support, attractive incentives, and quality goods and services that employees are proud to be associated with. Organizations such as Marks and Spencer, British Airways, Hilton, Ritz-Carlton, Mercedes and Accenture would all be seen as preferred employers in their sector.

DEVELOP PEOPLE TO DELIVER SERVICE QUALITY

To grow and maintain a workforce that is customer oriented and focused on delivering quality, an organization must develop its employees to deliver service quality. That is, once it has hired the right individuals, the organization must train and work with these employees to ensure service performance.

TRAIN FOR TECHNICAL AND INTERACTIVE SKILLS

To provide quality service, employees need ongoing training in the necessary technical skills and knowledge and in process or interactive skills.[36] Examples of technical skills and knowledge are working with accounting systems in hotels, cash machine procedures in a retail store, underwriting procedures in an insurance company and any operational rules the company has for running its business. Most service organizations are quite conscious of, and relatively effective at, training employees in technical skills. These skills may be taught through formal education, as is the case at McDonald's Hamburger University, which trains McDonald's managers from all over the world. Additionally, technical skills are often taught through on-the-job training, as when education students work with experienced teachers in internship programmes or when telephone service trainees listen in on the conversations of experienced employees. Companies are increasing their use of information technology to train employees in the technical skills and knowledge needed on the job.

★ **SERVICE SPOTLIGHT**

CitizenM, the Dutch boutique hotel chain, attempts to be the preferred employer by emphasizing the following benefits in their human resource strategy:

- **Training programme**: Our first gift to you is a special training programme in the language and lifestyle of citizenM. We inspire, empower and coach you as a professional in:
  - citizenM hospitality
  - citizenM knowledge and know-how
  - citizenM (food) retail
  - citizenM Barista and professional cocktail shaker.
- **Personal development plan**: Our second gift to you is a personal development plan. Whether you like to learn more about hospitality, personal presentation or sushi, you can pick your flavour from our à la carte system.

- **Pays & perks**: We love to reward our ambassadors for good performance, excellent guest service and overall team success. The basic salary is set to meet market conditions and a performance-based reward. We also love to give you and your family the opportunity of a good night sleep in one of our hotels at a very special rate.
- **Food**: We offer free delicious and healthy food and beverages.
- **Multi-tasking job**: Working for citizenM is never dull or standard. Every employee has a mobile job being responsible for a variety of tasks. But we have one thing in common; We are all ambassadors to our guests.
- **Outfit**: We want you to be mobile. So no dull, impractical uniforms but a stylish, easy and fitting citizenM outfit.
- **Community**: As a citizen you are automatically part of the citizenM community. Here you can chat with your colleagues and keep yourself up-to-date about what's new on citizenM.

Source: **www.citizenm.com.**

Service employees also need training in interactive skills that allow them to provide courteous, caring, responsive and empathetic service. Successful companies invest heavily in training and make sure that the training fits their business goals and strategies.

SERVICE SPOTLIGHT

In the Accor hotel group which encompasses hotel brands such as Ibis, Novotel, Mercure and Sofitel, learning and development is provided by the organization's Académie Accor. This is a training resource supported by a global network of 17 campuses that offer training in every aspect of hospitality-related expertise and jobs. Courses may be attended by any employee of an Accor-brand hotel, regardless of job, family circumstance, educational background, position or seniority. The Académie Accor's primary mission is to train employees so that every hotel guest enjoys impeccable quality of service. It can train employees on-site as well as through e-learning modules, virtual classrooms and other computer-mediated activities.[37]

EMPOWER EMPLOYEES

Many organizations have discovered that to be truly responsive to customer needs, front-line providers need to be empowered to accommodate customer requests and to recover on the spot when things go wrong. *Empowerment* means giving employees the desire, skills, tools and authority to serve the customer. Although the key to empowerment is giving employees authority to make decisions on the customer's behalf, authority alone is not enough. Employees need the knowledge and tools to be able to make these decisions, and they need incentives that encourage them to make the right decisions. Organizations do not succeed in empowering their employees if they simply tell them, 'You now have the authority to do whatever it takes to satisfy the customer'. First, employees often do not believe this statement, particularly if the organization has functioned hierarchically or bureaucratically in the past. Second, employees often do not know what it means to 'do whatever it takes' if they have not received training, guidelines and the tools needed to make such decisions.

Research suggests positive benefits to empowering front-line service workers. Some of these benefits include reduction in job-related stress, improved job satisfaction, greater adaptability and better outcomes for customers.[38] But such success does not come easily. In fact, some experts have concluded that few organizations have truly taken advantage of, or properly implemented, successful empowerment strategies.[39]

Nor is empowerment the answer for all organizations. David Bowen and Edward Lawler, experts on this subject, suggest that organizations well suited to empowerment strategies are ones in which (1) the business strategy is one of differentiation and customization, (2) customers are long-term relationship customers, (3) technology is non-routine or complex, (4) the business environment is unpredictable, and (5) managers and employees have high growth and social needs and strong interpersonal skills.[40] They also enumerate the costs and benefits of empowerment[41] as follows:

BENEFITS

- *Quicker online responses to customer needs during service delivery.* Employees who are allowed to make decisions on behalf of the customer can make decisions more quickly, bypassing what in the past might have meant a long chain of command, or at least a discussion with an immediate supervisor.

(Social Media and Digital Marketing)

- *Quicker online responses to dissatisfied customers during service recovery.* When failures occur in the delivery system, customers hope for an immediate recovery effort on the part of the organization. Empowered employees can recover on the spot, and a dissatisfied customer can potentially be turned into a satisfied, even loyal, one.
- *Employees feel better about their jobs and themselves.* Giving employees control and authority to make decisions makes them feel responsible and gives them ownership for the customer's satisfaction. Decades of job design research suggest that when employees have a sense of control and of doing meaningful work, they are more satisfied. The result is lower turnover and less absenteeism.
- *Employees will interact with customers with more warmth and enthusiasm.* Employees feel better about themselves and their work, and these attitudes will spill over into their feelings about customers and will be reflected in their interactions.
- *Empowered employees are a great source of service ideas.* When employees are empowered, they feel responsible for the service outcome and they will be excellent sources of ideas about new services or how to improve current offerings.
- *Great word-of-mouth advertising from customers.* Empowered employees do special and unique things that customers will remember and tell their friends, family and associates about.

COSTS

- *A potentially greater investment in selection and training.* To find employees who will work well in an empowered environment requires creative, potentially more costly selection procedures. Training will also be more expensive in general because employees need more knowledge about the company, its products and how to work in flexible ways with customers.
- *Higher labour costs.* The organization may not be able to use as many part-time or seasonal employees, and it may need to pay more for asking employees to assume responsibility.
- *Potentially slower or inconsistent service delivery.* If empowered employees spend more time with all, or even some, customers, then service overall may take longer and may annoy customers who are waiting. Empowerment also means that customers will get what they need or request. When decisions regarding customer satisfaction are left to the discretion of employees, there may be inconsistency in the level of service delivered.
- *May violate customers' perceptions of fair play.* Customers may perceive that sticking to procedures with every customer is fair. Thus, if they see that customers are receiving different levels of service or that employees are cutting special deals with some customers, they may believe that the organization is not fair.
- *Employees may 'give away the store' or make bad decisions.* Many people fear that empowered employees will make costly decisions that the organization cannot afford. Although this situation can happen, good training and appropriate guidelines will help.

PROMOTE TEAMWORK

The nature of many service jobs suggests that customer satisfaction will be enhanced when employees work as teams. Because service jobs are frequently frustrating, demanding and challenging, a teamwork environment will help alleviate some of the stresses and strains. Employees who feel supported and feel that they have a team backing them up will be better able to maintain their enthusiasm and provide quality service.[42] 'An interactive community of co-workers who help each other, commiserate and achieve together is a powerful antidote to service burnout',[43] and, we would add, an important ingredient for service quality. By promoting teamwork, an organization can enhance the employees' *abilities* to deliver excellent service while the camaraderie and support enhance their *inclination* to be excellent service providers.

One way of promoting teamwork is to encourage the attitude that 'everyone has a customer'. That is, even when employees are not directly responsible for or in direct interaction with the final customer, they need to know whom they serve directly and how the role they play in the total service picture is essential to the final delivery of quality service. If each employee can see how he or she is somehow integral in delivering quality to the final customer and if each employee knows who to support to make service quality a reality, teamwork will be enhanced. Service blueprints (described in Chapter 8) can serve as useful tools to illustrate for employees their integral roles in delivering service quality to the ultimate customer.

Team goals and rewards also promote teamwork. When a firm rewards teams of individuals rather than basing all rewards on individual achievements and performance, team effort and team spirit are encouraged.

PROVIDE NEEDED SUPPORT SYSTEMS

To be efficient and effective in their jobs, service workers require internal support systems that are aligned with their need to be customer focused. This point cannot be over-emphasized. In fact, without customer-focused internal support and customer-oriented systems, it is nearly impossible for employees to deliver quality service no matter how much they want to. For example, a bank teller who is rewarded for customer satisfaction as well as for accuracy in bank transactions needs easy access to up-to-date customer records, a well-staffed branch (so that he or she is not constantly facing a long line of impatient customers), and supportive customer-oriented supervisors and back-office staff. In examining customer service outcomes in Australian call centres, researchers found that internal support from supervisors, teammates and other departments as well as evaluations of technology used on the job were all strongly related to employee satisfaction and ability to serve customers.[44] The following sections suggest strategies for ensuring customer-oriented internal support.

MEASURE INTERNAL SERVICE QUALITY

One way to encourage supportive internal service relationships is to measure and reward internal service. By first acknowledging that everyone in the organization has a customer and then measuring customer perceptions of internal service quality, an organization can begin to develop an internal quality culture. Internal customer service audits can be used to implement a culture of internal service quality. Through the audit, internal organizations identify their customers, determine their needs, measure how well they are doing and make improvements. The process parallels market research practices used for external customers.

One risk of measuring and focusing on internal service quality and internal customers is that people can sometimes get so involved in meeting the needs of internal customers that they forget they are in business to serve the ultimate, external customers.[45] In measuring internal service quality, therefore, it is important to constantly draw the linkages between what is being delivered internally and how it supports the delivery of the final service to customers. Service blueprinting, introduced in Chapter 8, can help to illustrate these critical linkages.

PROVIDE SUPPORTIVE TECHNOLOGY AND EQUIPMENT

When employees do not have the right equipment or their equipment fails them, they can be easily frustrated in their desire to deliver quality service. To do their jobs effectively and efficiently, service employees need the right equipment and technology. Having the right technology and equipment can extend into strategies regarding workplace and workstation design.

DEVELOP SERVICE-ORIENTED INTERNAL PROCESSES

To best support service personnel in their delivery of quality service on the front line, an organization's internal processes should be designed with customer value and customer satisfaction in mind. In other words, internal procedures must support quality service performance. In many companies internal processes are driven by bureaucratic rules, tradition, cost efficiencies or the needs of internal employees. Providing service- and customer-oriented internal processes can therefore imply a need for total redesign of systems. This kind of wholesale redesign of systems and processes has become known as 'process re-engineering'. Although developing service-oriented internal processes through re-engineering sounds sensible, it is probably one of the most difficult strategies to implement, especially in organizations that are steeped in tradition. Refocusing internal processes and introducing large amounts of new, supportive technology were among the changes made by British Telecom in its transition from a traditional, operations-driven company to a customer-focused one.

RETAIN THE BEST PEOPLE

An organization that hires the right people, trains and develops them to deliver service quality, and provides the needed support must also work to retain them. Employee turnover, especially when the best service employees are leaving, can be very detrimental to customer satisfaction, employee morale and overall service quality. And, just as they do with customers, some firms spend a lot of time attracting employees but then tend to take them for granted (or even worse), causing these good employees to search for alternative jobs. Although all the strategies depicted in Figure 11.2 will support the retention of the best employees, here we focus on some strategies that are particularly aimed at this goal.

INCLUDE EMPLOYEES IN THE COMPANY'S VISION

For employees to remain motivated and interested in sticking with the organization and supporting its goals, they need to share an understanding of the organization's vision. People who deliver service day after day need to understand how their work fits into the big picture of the organization and its goals.

EXAMPLE
Steps Involved in Conducting an Internal Customer Service Audit[46]

1 *Define your customer.*
   a List all the people or departments in the organization who need help from you or your department in any way. This list may include specific departments, particular staff people, the CEO, certain executives or the board of directors.
   b Prioritize the names on the list, placing the people or departments that rely on you the most at the top.
2 *Identify your contribution.*
   a For each of these customers, specify the primary need you think they have to which you can contribute. Talk to your internal customers about what problems they are trying to solve and think about how you can help.

3 *Define service quality.*

   a What are the critical moments of truth that really define the department–internal customer interface from your customer's point of view? Blueprint the process and list the moments of truth.

   b For each major internal customer, design a customer report card (based on customer input) and a set of evaluation criteria for your department's service package, as seen through the eyes of that customer. The criteria might include such dimensions as timeliness, reliability and cost.

4 *Validate your criteria.*

   a Talk to your customers. Allow them to revise, as necessary, how you saw their needs and the criteria they used in assessing your performance. This dialogue itself can go a long way toward building internal service teamwork.

5 *Measure service quality.*

   a Evaluate your service (using internal measures and/or customer surveys) against the quality criteria you established in talking to your customers. See how you score. Identify opportunities for improvement. Set up a process and timetable for following through.

6 *Develop a mission statement based on what you contribute.*

   a Consider drafting a brief, meaningful service mission statement for your operation. Be certain to frame it in terms of the value you *contribute*, not what you *do*. For example, the mission of the HR department should not be 'to deliver training' (the action); it would be 'to create competent people' (the contribution).

SERVICE SPOTLIGHT

Insurance provider Allianz, which sells its products through insurance brokers, ran an internal campaign to engage and motivate its staff. They wanted a programme to attract and retain the best employees within the company. The campaign involved a roadshow of around 11 top athletes from the 2012 London Olympics visiting each of the company's 22 UK offices. Sporting events were held for employees who were able to question athletes about competing in Olympic events. The campaign focused on the theme of 'performance' to inspire staff and encourage their collaboration to succeed.

Employees will be motivated to some extent by their pay and other benefits, but the best ones will be attracted away to other opportunities if they are not committed to the vision of the organization. Employees cannot be committed to the vision if that vision is kept secret from them. What this vision-sharing strategy means in practice is that the vision is communicated frequently to employees and that it is communicated by top managers, often by the CEO.[47]

Respected CEOs such as Richard Branson of the Virgin Group and Ingvar Kamprad of IKEA are known for communicating their vision clearly and often to employees. When the company's vision and direction are clear and motivating, employees are more likely to stay on through the inevitable rough spots on the way to accomplishing the company's goals.

TREAT EMPLOYEES AS CUSTOMERS

If employees feel valued and their needs are taken care of, they are more likely to stay with the organization. Many companies have adopted the idea that employees are also customers of the organization and that basic marketing strategies can be directed at them.[48] The products that the organization has to offer its employees are jobs (with assorted benefits) and quality of work life. To determine whether the job and work-life needs of employees are being met, organizations conduct periodic internal marketing research to assess employee satisfaction and needs.

In addition to basic internal research, organizations can apply other marketing strategies to their management of employees. For example, segmentation of the employee population is apparent in many of the flexible benefit plans and career path choices now available to employees. Organizations that are set up to meet the needs of specific segments and to adjust as people proceed through their lives will benefit from increased employee loyalty. Advertising and other forms of communication directed at employees can also increase their sense of value and enhance their commitment to the organization.[49]

MEASURE AND REWARD STRONG SERVICE PERFORMERS

If a company wants the strongest service performers to stay with the organization, it must reward and promote them. This strategy may seem obvious, but often the reward systems in organizations are not set up to reward service excellence. Reward systems may value productivity, sales or some other dimension that can potentially work *against* good service. Even those service workers who are intrinsically motivated to deliver high service quality will become discouraged at some point and start looking elsewhere if their efforts are not recognized and rewarded.

Reward systems need to be linked to the organization's vision and to outcomes that are truly important. For instance, if customer satisfaction and retention are viewed as critical outcomes, service behaviours that increase those outcomes need to be recognized and rewarded. In the Royal Bank of Scotland and National Westminster Bank, employees in branches do not receive their sales bonuses unless their branch has achieved the required customer service scores.

Companies with a goal of customer satisfaction in every service encounter often need to adjust the criteria by which employee performance is judged. Mystery shopping scores may be used in determining rewards for staff in organizations such as Burger King.

⭐ SERVICE SPOTLIGHT

Carphone Warehouse (incorporating the Phone House brand) is Europe's biggest independent mobile phone retailer with over 2,440 branches in eight different countries. The company pays employees for giving good customer service rather than for individual sales. Carphone Warehouse moved away from a commission reward mechanism for employees based on sales to one that is more team and customer service based. Sales staff (by now they are called 'customer consultants') receive a basic salary and a share of a percentage of store profits that goes into a bonus pool. Staff can double the amount in the pool by meeting customer service targets, or halve it if they do not deliver these scores. This approach is aimed at driving a team effort rather than a competitive employee culture. It also offers an opportunity to move from a short-term sales focus on one-off sales to the development of long-term relationships with customers.

Aligning reward systems with customer outcomes can be challenging. Reward systems are usually well entrenched, and employees have learned over time how they need to perform within the old structures. Change is difficult both for the managers who may have created, and may still believe in, the old systems and for employees who are not sure what they need to do to succeed under the new rules. In many organizations, however, reward and incentive systems are still not matched with customer satisfaction and loyalty goals.[50]

In developing new systems and structures to recognize customer focus and customer satisfaction, organizations have turned to a variety of rewards. Traditional approaches such as higher pay, promotions and one-off monetary awards or prizes can be linked to service performance.

Other types of rewards include special organizational and team celebrations for achieving improved customer satisfaction or for attaining customer retention goals. In most service organizations it is not only the major accomplishments but the daily perseverance and attention to detail that move the organization forward, so recognition of the 'small wins' is also important.

In many situations, a customer's relationship is with a specific employee and may be stronger with the *employee* than with the firm. If this employee leaves the firm and is no longer available to the customer, the firm's relationship with the customer may be jeopardized.[51] Clearly, a firm should make great efforts to retain such employees; however, in spite of its best efforts, some good employees are going to leave. If the firm is not successful at retaining a key customer-contact employee, what can it do to reduce the impact on the customer? Employees could be rotated occasionally in order to ensure that the customer has exposure to, and is comfortable with, more than one employee. Firms might also form teams of employees who are responsible for interacting with each customer. In both cases, the idea is that the customer would have multiple contacts with several employees in the organization, thus reducing the firm's vulnerability to losing the customer should any one employee leave. Emphasis should also be placed on creating a positive firm image in the minds of its customers and in so doing convey that *all* its employees are capable.[52]

CUSTOMER-ORIENTED SERVICE DELIVERY

As the examples presented in this chapter illustrate, specific approaches for hiring and energizing front-line workers take on a different look and feel across companies, based on the organization's values, culture, history and vision.[53] For example, 'developing people to deliver service quality' is accomplished quite differently at TGIF restaurants than at Disney. At Disney the orientation and training process is highly structured, scripted and standardized. At TGIF restaurants, the emphasis is more on developing needed skills and then empowering employees to be spontaneous and non-scripted in their approach to customers. Although the style and culture of the two organizations are different, both pay special attention to all four basic themes shown in Figure 11.2. Both have made significant investments in their people, recognizing the critical roles they play.

Throughout this book we have advocated a strong customer focus. Firms that have a strong service culture clearly put an emphasis on the customer and the customer's experience. To do so, firms must also create an environment that staunchly supports the customer-contact employee because, in the organization, this person is frequently the most responsible for ensuring that the customer's experience is delivered as designed. Historically, many firms have viewed senior management as the most important people in the firm and, indeed, organizational charts reflect this view in their structure. This approach places management at the top of the structure and (implicitly) the customer at the bottom, with customer-contact employees just above them. If the organization's most important people are customers, they should be at the top of the chart, followed by those with whom they have contact. Such a view, illustrated in Figure 11.3, is more consistent with a customer-oriented focus. In effect, the role of top-level management changes from that of commanding employees to that of facilitating and supporting those employees in the organization who are closest to the customer.

The human resource strategies that we have offered in this chapter are suggested as a means to support the customer contact employee. Indeed, a truly customer-oriented management team might actually 'flip' the services marketing triangle (discussed in Chapter 1), with customers and employees equally placed at the top – as illustrated in Figure 11.4. A statement by Michel Bon, CEO of France Telecom, succinctly summarizes the philosophy behind this approach:

> *If you sincerely believe that 'the customer is king', the second most important person in this kingdom must be the one who has a direct interaction on a daily basis with the one who is king.*[54]

Figure 11.3   Customer-focused organizational chart

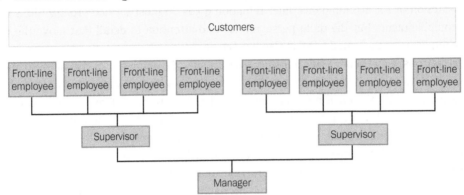

By flipping the services marketing triangle in Figure 11.4, the two groups that are the most important people to the organization, customers and those who interact with customers, are placed in a position of prominence.

Figure 11.4   Inverted services marketing triangle

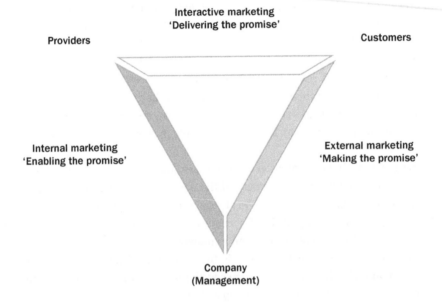

SUMMARY

Because many services are delivered by people in real time, closing the service performance gap is heavily dependent on human resource strategies. The successful execution of such strategies begins with the development and nurturing of a true service culture throughout the organization.

Often service employees *are* the service, and in all cases they represent the organization in the customers' eyes. They affect service quality perceptions to a large degree through their influence on the five dimensions of service quality: reliability, responsiveness, empathy, assurance and tangibles. It is essential to match what the customer wants and needs with service employees' abilities to deliver.

In this chapter we focused on service employees to provide you with an understanding of the critical nature of their roles and an appreciation of the inherent stresses and conflicts they face. You learned that front-line service jobs demand significant investments of emotional labour and that employees confront a variety of on-the-job conflicts. Sometimes service employees are personally uncomfortable with the roles they are asked to play; other times the requirements of the organization may conflict with client expectations and employees must resolve the dilemma on the spot. Sometimes there are conflicting needs among customers who are being served in turn (such as in a bank teller line) or among customers being served simultaneously (as in a college classroom). At other times a front-line employee may be faced with a decision about whether to satisfy a customer or meet productivity targets (such as a dentist who is required to see a certain number of patients in a defined period of time).

Grounded in this understanding of the importance of service employees and the nature of their roles in the organization, you learned strategies for integrating appropriate human resource practices into service firms. The strategies are aimed at allowing employees to effectively satisfy customers as well as be efficient and productive in their jobs. The strategies were organized around four major human resource goals in service organizations: to hire the right people, to develop people to deliver service quality, to provide needed support systems, and to retain the best people. A company that works toward implementing these strategies is well on its way to delivering service quality through its people, thereby diminishing gap 3 – the service performance gap.

KEY CONCEPTS

EXERCISES

1 Visit the websites of companies with known world-class service cultures (such as Ritz-Carlton, FedEx or SAS airlines). How does the information conveyed on their websites reinforce these companies' service culture?

2 Review the section of the chapter on boundary-spanning roles. Interview at least two front-line service personnel regarding the stresses they experience in their jobs. How do the examples they provide relate to the sources of conflict and trade-offs described in the text?

3 Assume that you are the manager of a team of front-line customer-service employees in a credit card company. Assume that these employees work over the telephone and that they deal primarily with customer requests, questions and complaints. In this specific context,

(a) Define what is meant by *boundary-spanning roles*, and discuss the basic purposes or functions performed by participants in these roles.

(b) Discuss two of the potential conflicts that your employees may face on the basis of their roles as boundary spanners.

(c) Discuss how you, as their supervisor, might deal with these conflicts based on what you have learned.

4 Choose one or more of the human resource strategy themes (hire the right people, develop people to deliver service quality, provide needed support systems, retain the best people). Interview a manager in a service organization of your choice regarding his or her current practices within the theme you have chosen. Describe the current practices and recommend any appropriate changes for improving them.

DISCUSSION QUESTIONS

1 Define *service culture*. Why is service culture so important? Can a manufacturing firm have a service culture? Why or why not?

2 Why are service employees critical to the success of any service organization? Why do we include an entire chapter on service employees in a marketing course?

3 What is *emotional labour*? How can it be differentiated from physical or mental labour?

4 Reflect on your own role as a front-line service provider, whether in a current job or in any full- or part-time service job you have had in the past. Did you experience the kinds of conflicts described in the boundary-spanning roles section of the chapter? Be prepared with some concrete examples for class discussion.

5 Select a service provider (your dentist, doctor, lawyer, hair stylist) with whom you are familiar, and discuss ways this person could positively influence the five dimensions of service quality in the context of delivering his or her services. Do the same for yourself (if you are currently a service provider).

6 Describe the four basic human resource strategy themes and why each plays an important role in building a customer-oriented organization.

7 What is the difference between technical and interactive service skills? Provide examples (preferably from your own work context or from another context with which you are familiar). Why do service employees need training in both?

8 Is empowerment always the best approach for effective service delivery? Why is employee empowerment so controversial?

9 Visit the jobs page of the citizenM website at www.citizenM.com, and describe the types of people, i.e. personality, clothing tastes, etc., they are trying to recruit.

10 What reasons would you give to explain the high turnover of staff in fast-food restaurants?

FURTHER READING

Bernoff, J. and Schadler, T. (2010). Empowered. *Harvard Business Review*, July/August, 5–101.

Chebat, J.C. and Kollias P. (2000). The impact of empowerment on customer contact employees' roles in service organizations, *Journal of Service Research*, 3(1), 66–81.

Edvardsson, B. and Enqvist, B. (2002). The IKEA saga: how service culture drives service strategy. *The Service Industries Journal*, 22(4), 153–86.

Evanschitzky, H., Wangenheim, F. V., and Wünderlich, N. V. (2012). Perils of managing the service profit chain: The role of time lags and feedback loops. *Journal of Retailing*, 88(3), 356–66.

Gruman, J. A. and Saks, A. M. (2011). Performance management and employee engagement. *Human Resource Management Review*, 21(2), 123–36.

Hesket, J.L., Jones, T.O., Loveman, G.W., Earl Sasser Jr, W. and Schlesinger L.L. (2008). Putting the service-profit chain to work. *Harvard Business Review*, July/August, 118–29.

Lashley, C. (2012). *Empowerment: HR strategies for service excellence*. Routledge.

Mosley, W.M. (2007). Customer experience, organizational culture and the employer brand. *Brand Management*, 15(2), 123–34.

Schneider, B. and Bowen, D. (2010). Winning the service game: revisiting the rules by which people co-create value. *Handbook of Service Science*, Part 1, 31–59.

Wilson, A.M. (2001). Understanding organisational culture and the implications for corporate marketing. *European Journal of Marketing*, 35(3/4), 353–67.

CHAPTER 12

Customers' Roles in Service Delivery

CHAPTER OUTLINE

LEARNING OBJECTIVES

This chapter's objectives are to:

1. Illustrate the importance of customers in successful service delivery and co-creation of service experiences.
2. Discuss the variety of roles that service customers play: productive resources for the organization; contributors to quality and satisfaction; competitors.
3. Explain strategies for involving service customers effectively to increase both quality and productivity.

OPENING EXAMPLE

IKEA – Customers Create Value for Themselves

IKEA of Sweden has managed to transform itself from a small mail-order furniture company in the 1950s into the world's largest retailer of home furnishings with over 315 stores in 27 countries. In 2014, 716 million store visits and 1.5 billion Web visits generated more than 29,300 million euros in revenues. The company sells simple Scandinavian design furnishings, charging 25 to 50 per cent less than its competitors.

A key to IKEA's success is the company's relationship with its customers. IKEA has drawn the customer into its production system: 'If customers agree to take on certain key tasks traditionally done by manufacturers and retailers – the assembly of products and their delivery to customers' homes – then IKEA promises to deliver well-designed products at substantially lower prices.' In effect, IKEA's customers become essential contributors to value – they create value for themselves through participating in the manufacturing, design and delivery processes.

IKEA has made being part of the value creation process an easy, fun and pleasant experience for customers. The stores are set up with 'inspirational displays', including realistic room settings and real-life homes that allow customers to get comfortable with the furnishings, try them out and visualize the possibilities in their own homes. To make shopping easy, free pushchairs and supervised child care are provided as well as wheelchairs for those who need them.

When customers enter the store they are given catalogues, tape measures, pens and notepaper to use as they shop, allowing them to perform functions commonly done by sales and service staff. After payment, customers take their purchases to their cars on trolleys; if necessary they can rent or buy a roof rack to carry larger purchases. Thus, customers also provide furniture loading and delivery services for themselves. At home, IKEA customers then take on the role of manufacturer in assembling the new furnishings following simple visual instructions.

IKEA prints 217 million catalogues in more than 30 different languages, making its products and instructions for their use accessible worldwide. In addition to tailoring its catalogues, another key to IKEA's successful global expansion has been the company's policy of allowing each store to tailor its mix according to local market needs and budgets. For example, in its China stores, layouts reflect the design of many Chinese apartments. Because many of the apartments have balconies, the stores have a selection of balcony furnishings and displays. And because Chinese kitchens are generally small, fewer kitchen items and furnishings are shown. Even IKEA's famous 'do it yourself' (DIY) assembly concept has also been adapted to some extent in China. Because fewer people have cars and therefore use public transport, IKEA has a more extensive delivery service in China than in most countries. And because labour is cheaper in China, many customers choose to have their furniture assembled for them rather than doing it themselves. Although IKEA has not abandoned its DIY strategy, it has been somewhat more flexible in China to suit customer realities in that country.

IKEA's success is attributable in part to recognizing that customers can be part of the business system, performing roles they have never performed before. The company's flexible implementation of this idea through clearly defining customers' new roles and making it fun to perform these roles is the genius of its strategy. Through the process, customers co-create their own experiences and contribute to their own satisfaction.[1]

In this chapter we examine the unique roles played by customers in service delivery situations. Service customers are often present in the 'factory' (the place the service is produced and/or consumed), interacting with employees and with other customers. For example, in a classroom or training situation, students (the customers) are sitting in the factory interacting with the instructor and other students as they consume and co-create the educational services. Because they are present during service production, customers can contribute to, or detract from, the successful delivery of the service and to their own satisfaction. In a manufacturing context, rarely does the production facility contend with customer presence on the factory floor, nor does it rely on the customer's immediate real-time input to manufacture the product. As our opening vignette illustrates, service customers can actually produce the service themselves and to some extent are responsible for their own satisfaction. Buying IKEA furniture, customers co-create value for themselves and in the process also reduce the prices they pay.

Because customers are participants in service production and delivery, they can potentially contribute to the widening of gap 3, the service performance gap: that is, customers themselves can influence whether the delivered service meets customer-defined specifications. Sometimes customers contribute to gap 3 because they lack understanding of their roles and exactly what they should do in a given situation, particularly if the customer is confronting a service concept for the first time. Customers visiting IKEA for the first time need detailed, but simple, instructions to help them understand how to use the service effectively and get the greatest value.

At other times customers may understand their roles but be unwilling or unable to perform for some reason. In a health club context, members may understand that to get into good physical shape they must follow the workout guidelines set up by the trainers. If work schedules or illness keep members from living up to their part of the guidelines, the service will not be successful because of customer inaction. In a different service situation, customers may choose not to perform the roles defined for them because they are not rewarded in any way for contributing their effort. When service customers are enticed through price reductions, greater convenience or some other tangible benefit, they are more likely to perform their roles willingly, as in the case of our opening vignette about IKEA.

Finally, the service performance gap may be widened not through actions or inactions on the part of the customer, but because of what *other* customers do. Other customers who are in the service outlet, either receiving the service simultaneously (passengers on an aeroplane flight) or waiting their turn to receive the service sequentially (bank customers waiting in a queue, Disneyland customers waiting to go on one of the rides), can influence whether the service is effectively and efficiently delivered.

This chapter focuses on the roles of customers in service delivery and co-creation of service experiences as well as strategies to effectively manage them.

THE IMPORTANCE OF CUSTOMERS IN SERVICE CO-CREATION AND DELIVERY

Customer participation at some level is inevitable in service delivery and co-creation. Services are actions or performances, typically produced and consumed simultaneously. In many situations employees, customers and, even, others in the service environment interact to produce the ultimate service outcome. Because they participate, customers are indispensable to the production process of service organizations, and they can actually control or contribute to their own satisfaction.[2] This view of participatory customers is consistent with the service-dominant logic of marketing that promotes the idea customers are always co-creators of value.[3]

The importance of customers in successful service delivery is obvious if service performances are looked at as a form of drama. The drama metaphor for services (discussed in Chapter 2) suggests the reciprocal, interactive roles of employees (actors) and customers (audience) in creating the service experience. The service actors and audience are surrounded by the service setting or the servicescape (discussed in

Chapter 10). The drama metaphor argues that the development and maintenance of an interaction (a service experience) relies on the audience's input as well as the actors' presentation. Through this 'services as drama' metaphor, service performances or service delivery situations are viewed as tenuous, fragile processes that can be influenced by behaviours of customers as well as by employees.[4] Service performance results from actions and interactions among individuals in both groups.

Consider the services provided by a cruise ship company. The actors (ship's personnel) provide the service through interactions with their audience (the passengers) and among each other. The audience also produces elements of the service through interactions with the actors and other audience members. Both actors and audience are surrounded by an elaborate setting (the cruise ship itself) that provides a context to facilitate the service performance. The drama metaphor provides a compelling frame of reference for recognizing the interdependent roles of actors and audience in service delivery.[5]

Recognition of the role of customers is also reflected in the definition of the *people* element of the services marketing mix given in Chapter 1: *all human actors who play a part in service delivery and thus influence the buyer's perceptions; namely, the firm's personnel, the customer, and other customers in the service environment.* Chapter 11 thoroughly examined the role of the firm's employees in delivering service quality. In this chapter we focus on the customer receiving the service and on fellow customers in the service environment.

CUSTOMER RECEIVING THE SERVICE

Because the customer receiving the service participates in the delivery process, he or she can contribute to narrowing or widening gap 3 through behaviours that are appropriate or inappropriate, effective or ineffective, productive or unproductive. Even in a relatively simple service such as retail, customers' actions and preparation can have an effect on service delivery. Customers who are unprepared in terms of what they want to buy can soak up the customer service representative's time as they seek advice. Similarly, shoppers who are not prepared with their credit card numbers can put the call centre representative on hold while they search for their cards or retrieve them from another room or their cars. Meanwhile, other customers and calls are left unattended, causing longer wait times and potential dissatisfaction.

The level of customer participation – low, medium or high – varies across services, as shown in Table 12.1. In some cases, all that is required is the customer's physical presence *(low level of participation)*, with the employees of the firm doing all the service production work, as in the example of an orchestral concert. Concert-goers must be present to receive the entertainment service, but little else is required once they are seated. In other situations, consumer inputs are required to aid the service organization in creating the service *(moderate level of participation)*. Inputs can include *information, effort* or *physical possessions*. All three of these are required for an accountant to effectively prepare a client's tax return: information in the form of tax history, marital status and number of dependents; effort in putting the information together in a useful fashion; and physical possessions such as receipts and past tax returns. In some situations, customers are truly co-creators of the service *(high level of participation)*. For these services, customers have important participation roles that will affect the nature of the service outcome. In a complex or long-term business-to-business consulting engagement, the client can be involved in activities such as identification of issues, shared problem-solving, ongoing communication, provision of equipment and work space, and implementation of solutions.

FELLOW CUSTOMERS

In many service contexts customers receive the service simultaneously with other customers or must wait their turn while other customers are being served. In both cases 'fellow customers' are present in the service environment and can affect the nature of the service outcome or process. Fellow customers can either *enhance* or *detract* from customer satisfaction and perceptions of quality.[6] Some of the ways fellow customers can negatively affect the service experience are by exhibiting disruptive behaviours, causing delays, excessively

Table 12.1   Levels of customer participation across different services

Low: consumer presence required during service delivery	Moderate: consumer inputs required for service creation	High: customer co-creates the service
Products are standardized	Client inputs (information, materials) to customize a standard service	Active client participation guides the customized service
Service is delivered regardless of any individual purchase	Delivery of service only occurs when customer purchases	Service cannot be created apart from the customer's purchase and active participation
Payment may be the only required customer input	Customer inputs are necessary for an adequate outcome, but the service firm provides the service	Customer inputs are mandatory and co-create the outcome
Airline travel	Haircut	Marriage counselling
Hotel stay	Tax advice	Personal training
Fast-food restaurant	Full-service restaurant	Weight reduction programme

crowding and manifesting incompatible needs. In restaurants, hotels, aeroplanes and other environments in which customers are in very close proximity to each other as they receive the service, crying babies, loud patrons and unruly groups can be disruptive and detract from the experiences of their fellow customers.

The customer is disappointed through no direct fault of the provider. In other cases, overly demanding customers (even customers with legitimate problems) can cause a delay for others while their needs are met. This occurrence is common in banks, post offices and customer service counters in retail stores. Excessive crowding or overuse of a service can also affect the nature of the customer's experience. For example, the quality of mobile phone networks and the ability to make a call can suffer on special holidays such as Christmas and New Year's Eve when large numbers of customers all try to use the service at the same time.

Finally, customers who are being served simultaneously but who have incompatible needs can negatively affect each other. This situation can occur in restaurants, university lecture theatres, hospitals and any service establishment in which multiple segments are served simultaneously. In a study of critical service encounters occurring in tourist attractions, researchers found that customers negatively affected each other when they failed to follow either explicit or implicit 'rules of conduct'. Customers reported such negative behaviours as shoving, smoking, drinking alcohol, being verbally abusive or pushing into the line. Other times, dissatisfaction resulted when other customers were impersonal, rude, unfriendly or even spiteful.[7]

We can offer just as many examples of other customers enhancing satisfaction and quality for their fellow customers as detracting from them. Sometimes the mere presence of other customers enhances the experience – for example, at sporting events, in cinemas and in other entertainment venues. The presence of other patrons is essential for true enjoyment of these experiences. In other situations, fellow customers provide a positive social dimension to the service experience. At health clubs, churches and resorts such as Club Med, other customers provide opportunities to socialize and build friendships.

In some situations, customers may actually help each other achieve service goals and outcomes. The success of the Weight Watchers organization, for example, depends significantly on the camaraderie and support that group members provide each other. The study of tourist attractions mentioned earlier found that customers increased the satisfaction of others by having friendly conversations while waiting in line, by taking photographs, by assisting with children and by returning dropped or lost items.[8] An ethnographic study that observed hundreds of hours of customer interactions among travellers on the UK rail system found that customers often helped each other by (1) providing important service-related information (e.g. schedules, interesting features en route) that can reduce trip-related anxiety; (2) engaging in enjoyable conversation, thus making the trip more pleasant; and (3) serving as someone to complain to when mishaps and service failures occurred.[9]

The influence of fellow customers in helping others is even more apparent in some online service environments such as Amazon, travel review sites and eBay. Customers will provide reviews of their experiences with the service or book or trader in order to assist others with purchasing decisions. They may also provide advice on how to use the service effectively. Computer and software suppliers often have online user groups who share ideas and solutions to issues and problems with fellow users.

Social Media and Digital Marketing

⭐ SERVICE SPOTLIGHT

TomTom, the makers of satellite navigation systems for cars, have an online community of users who talk about the products and services as well as provide technical help and support to other users. It has over 50,000 registered users and operates in English, German and French. Members earn badges by sharing their 'tips & tricks', and by helping other community members. The community through their forum can provide answers to problems from a user's perspective and the company receives feedback on issues with their products and services. Since the community was established in 2011, TomTom have found that enquiries to their call centres have reduced by over 15 per cent (resulting in cost savings). Also, positive word of mouth through the community (such as the following example) may have more impact and be more trusted than corporate promotional material.

Amidst all of this negative sentiment, I'd just like to add some encouragement. HD Traffic and IQ Routes save me between twenty and forty minutes in traffic almost every single day. I have not been able to find a better, or even remotely similar, solution at any price, to my daily traffic challenges. So thank you for what has already been achieved, even if we still always crave ever more!

CUSTOMERS' ROLES

The following subsections examine in more detail three major roles played by customers in service delivery: customers as productive resources; customers as contributors to quality and satisfaction; and customers as competitors.

CUSTOMERS AS PRODUCTIVE RESOURCES

Service customers have been referred to as 'partial employees' of the organization – human resources who contribute to the organization's productive capacity.[10] Some management experts have suggested that the organization's boundaries be expanded to consider the customer as part of the service system. In other words, if customers contribute effort, time or other resources to the service production process, they should be considered as part of the organization. (Later in this chapter we devote a section to defining customers' jobs and strategies for managing them effectively.)

Customer inputs can affect the organization's productivity through both the quality of what they contribute and the resulting quality and quantity of output generated. In a business-to-business services context, the contributions of the client can enhance the overall productivity of the firm in both quality and quantity of service.[11] easyJet depends on customers to perform critical service roles for themselves, thus increasing the overall productivity of the airline. Passengers are asked to carry their own bags when transferring to other flights, print their own boarding passes and, in certain airports, print their own bag tags.

Customer participation in service production raises a number of issues for organizations. Because customers can influence both the quality and quantity of production, some experts believe the delivery system should be isolated as much as possible from customer inputs in order to reduce the uncertainty they can bring into the production process. This view sees customers as a major source of uncertainty – in the timing of their demands and the uncontrollability of their attitudes and actions. The logical conclusion is that any service activities that do not require customer contact or involvement should be performed away from customers: the less direct contact there is between the customer and the service production system, the greater the potential for the system to operate at peak efficiency.[12]

Other experts believe that services can be delivered most efficiently if customers are truly viewed as partial employees and their co-production roles are designed to maximize their contributions to the service creation process. The logic behind this view is that organizational productivity can be increased if customers learn to perform service-related activities they currently are not doing or are educated to perform more effectively the tasks they are already doing.[13]

For example, when self-service service stations first came into being, customers were asked to fill their own tanks. With customers performing this task, fewer employees were needed and the overall productivity of service stations improved. Now many service stations offer customers the option of paying for their fuel at the pump by popping their credit cards into a slot on the pump and leaving the station without dealing directly with a cashier. Similarly, the introduction of many automated airline services such as self-service baggage drop-off and self-ticketing are intended to speed up the process for customers while freeing employees for other tasks.[14] Organizational productivity is increased by using customers as a resource to perform tasks previously completed by employees. In both business-to-business and business-to-consumer contexts, organizations are turning to automated and online customer service. One prominent goal with online customer service is to increase organizational productivity by using the customer as a partial employee, performing his or her own service.

SERVICE SPOTLIGHT

At Schiphol airport in Amsterdam, KLM use a self-service baggage drop, where customers feed the luggage they wish to check into a machine. The technology automatically checks whether a bag is acceptable by determining its weight, dimensions, volume, shape, conveyability and label bar code. The bag is photographed, further processed in a controlled way and tracked from moment of entry and dispatched to the airport's baggage handling area. The self-service baggage drop is located next to a pay terminal which offers the airline the option to recover costs of overweight or bag handling.

Although organizations derive obvious productivity benefits by involving customers as co-producers, customers do not always like or accept their new roles, especially when they perceive the purpose to be bottom-line cost savings for the company. If customers see no clear benefit to being involved in co-production (e.g. lower prices, quicker access, better quality outcome), then they are likely to resent and resist their co-production roles.

CUSTOMERS AS CONTRIBUTORS TO SERVICE QUALITY AND SATISFACTION

Another role customers can play in services co-creation and delivery is that of contributor to their own satisfaction and the ultimate quality of the services they receive. Customers may care little that they have increased the productivity of the organization through their participation, but they likely care a great deal about whether their needs are fulfilled. Effective customer participation can increase the likelihood that needs are met and that the benefits the customer seeks are actually attained. Think about services such as health care, education, personal fitness and weight loss, in which the service outcome is highly dependent on customer participation. In these services, unless the customers perform their roles effectively, the desired service outcomes are not possible.

Research has shown that in education, active participation by students – as opposed to passive listening – increases learning (the desired service outcome) significantly.[15] The same is true in health care; patient compliance, in terms of taking prescribed medications or changing diet or other habits, can be critical to whether patients regain their health (the desired service outcome).[16] Other research in financial and medical service settings has shown that effective coproduction by customers leads to greater loyalty toward the service provider.[17] In all of these examples, the customers contribute directly to the quality of the outcome and to their own satisfaction with the service. In a business-to-business context, couriers and parcel carriers have found that in many situations customers cause their own *dissatisfaction* with the service by failing to pack shipments appropriately, resulting in breakage or delays while items are repacked. Thus, ineffective coproduction can result in negative outcomes and dissatisfaction.

Research suggests that customers who believe they have done their part to be effective in service interactions are more satisfied with the service. In a study of the banking industry, bank customers were asked to rate themselves (on a scale from 'strongly agree' to 'strongly disagree') on questions related to their contributions to service delivery, as follows:

- *What they did – outcome quality of customer inputs*
  I clearly explained what I wanted the bank employee to do.
  I gave the bank employee proper information.
  I tried to cooperate with the bank employee.
  I understand the procedures associated with this service.
- *How they did it – interaction quality of customer inputs*
  I was friendly to the bank employee.
  I have a good relationship with the bank employee.
  I was courteous to the bank employee.
  Receiving this service was a pleasant experience.

Results of the study indicated that the customers' perceptions of both what they did and how they did it were significantly related to customers' satisfaction with the service they received from the bank.[18] That is to say, those customers who responded more positively to the questions listed above were also more satisfied with the bank. Research in another context showed that customers' perceptions of service quality increased with greater levels of participation. Specifically, customers (in this case members of a YMCA) who participated more in the club gave the club higher ratings on aspects of service quality than did those who participated less.[19]

Customers contribute to quality service delivery when they ask questions, take responsibility for their own satisfaction, and complain when there is a service failure. The following four scenarios illustrate the wide variations in customer participation that can result in equally wide variations in service quality and customer satisfaction.

SCENARIO 1
A Major International Hotel

Guest A called the desk right after check-in to report that his television was not working and that the light over the bed was burnt out; both problems were fixed immediately. The hotel staff exchanged his television for one that worked and fixed the light bulb. Later they brought him a plate of fruit to make up for the inconvenience. Guest B did not communicate to management until check-out time that his television did not work and he could not read in his bed. His complaints were overheard by guests checking in, who wondered whether they had chosen the right place to stay.

SCENARIO 2

Office of a Tax Adviser

Client A has organized into categories the information necessary to do her taxes and has provided all documents requested by the accountant. Client B has a box full of papers and receipts, many of which are not relevant to her taxes but which she brought along 'just in case'.

SCENARIO 3

An Airline Flight from London to New York

Passenger A arrives for the flight with an MP3 player and reading material and wearing warm clothes; passenger A also called ahead to order a special meal. Passenger B, who arrives empty-handed, becomes annoyed when the crew runs out of blankets, complains about the magazine selection and the meal, and starts fidgeting after the movie.

SCENARIO 4

Architectural Consultation for Renovating an Office Building

Client A has invited the architects to meet with its design committee made up of managers, staff and customers in order to lay the groundwork for a major redesign job that will affect everyone who works in the building as well as customers. The committee has already formulated initial ideas and surveyed staff and customers for input. Client B has invited architects in following a decision the week previously to redesign the building; the design committee is two managers who are preoccupied with other, more immediate tasks and have little idea what they need or what customers and staff would prefer in terms of a redesign of the office space.

Customers who take responsibility and providers who encourage their customers to become their partners in identifying and satisfying their own needs will together produce higher levels of service quality. In addition to contributing to their own satisfaction by improving the quality of service delivered to them, some customers simply enjoy participating in service delivery. These customers find the act of participating to be intrinsically attractive.[20] They enjoy using the Internet to attain airline tickets, or doing all their banking via ATMs and the Internet, or refuelling their own car. Often customers who like self-service in one setting are predisposed to serving themselves in other settings as well.

★ SERVICE SPOTLIGHT

Waitrose supermarkets in the UK have installed 'Quick Check' in many of their stores. This is a self-scan system which involves customers taking a handset round the store and scanning items as they put them into their bags within their shopping trolley. Customers see a running total of their spending on the device's screen. They then pay on exiting the store without having to remove their items from the trolley. As part of the process, service personnel will occasionally rescan the items, just to make sure that everything scanned correctly and that there is no attempt at theft. The benefit to the customer is that they can bypass the usual queues at check out and there is no need for emptying a trolley and repacking.

Interestingly, because service customers must participate in service delivery, they frequently blame themselves (at least partially) when things go wrong. Why did it take so long to reach an accurate diagnosis of my health problem? Why can't I operate this self-scanning handset correctly? Why was the room we reserved for our meeting unavailable when we arrived? If customers believe they are partially (or totally) to blame for the failure, they may be less dissatisfied with the service provider than when they believe the provider is responsible.[21] A recent series of studies suggests the existence of this 'self-serving bias'. That is, when services go better than expected, customers who have participated tend to take credit for the outcome and are less satisfied with the firm than are those customers who have not participated. However, when the outcome is worse than expected, customers who have chosen to participate in service production are less dissatisfied with the service than are those who choose not to participate – presumably because the participating customers have taken on some of the blame themselves.[22]

CUSTOMERS AS COMPETITORS

A final role played by service customers is that of potential competitor. If self-service customers can be viewed as resources of the firm, or as 'partial employees', they could in some cases partially perform the service or perform the entire service for themselves and not need the provider at all. Thus, in a sense customers are competitors of the companies that supply the service. Whether to produce a service for themselves (*internal exchange*) – for example, child care, home maintenance, car repair – or have someone else provide the service for them (*external exchange*) is a common dilemma for consumers.[23]

Similar internal versus external exchange decisions are made by organizations. Firms frequently choose to outsource service activities such as payroll, data processing, call centres, accounting, or maintenance and facilities management. They find that it is advantageous to focus on their core businesses and leave these essential support services to others with greater expertise. Alternatively, a firm may decide to stop purchasing services externally and bring the service production process in-house.

Whether a household or a firm chooses to produce a particular service itself or contract externally for the service depends on a variety of factors. A proposed model of internal/external exchange suggests that such decisions depend on the following:[24]

- *Expertise capacity:* the likelihood of producing the service internally is increased if the household or firm possesses the specific skills and knowledge needed to produce it. Having the expertise will not necessarily result in internal service production, however, because other factors (available resources and time) will also influence the decision. (For firms, making the decision to outsource is often based on recognizing that although they may have the expertise, someone else can do it better.)
- *Resource capacity:* to decide to produce a service internally, the household or firm must have the needed resources including people, space, money, equipment and materials. If the resources are not available internally, external exchange is more likely.
- *Time capacity:* time is a critical factor in internal/external exchange decisions. Households and firms with adequate time capacity are more likely to produce services internally than are groups with time constraints.
- *Economic rewards:* the economic advantages or disadvantages of a particular exchange decision will be influential in choosing between internal and external options. The actual monetary costs of the two options will sway the decision.
- *Psychic rewards:* these are rewards of a non-economic nature which have a potentially strong influence on exchange decisions. Psychic rewards include the degree of satisfaction, enjoyment, gratification or happiness that is associated with the external or internal exchange.
- *Trust:* in this context *trust* means the degree of confidence or certainty the household or firm has in the various exchange options. The decision will depend to some extent on the level of self-trust in producing the service versus trust of others.

- *Control:* the household or firm's desire for control over the process and outcome of the exchange will also influence the internal/external choice. Entities that desire and can implement a high degree of control over the task are more likely to engage in internal exchange.

> **⭐ SERVICE SPOTLIGHT**
>
> The travel agency outlets of Tui, a multinational travel and tourism company, have suffered from customers acting as competitors, resulting from people booking their travel and holidays directly through the Internet. Younger, independent travellers, who are used to the Web and getting instant information, see little benefit of having to wait on somebody else booking their trip for them. This is particularly the case for short-haul destinations or destinations where they have been before.

The important thing to remember from this section is that in many service scenarios customers can, and often do, choose to fully or partially produce the service themselves. Thus, in addition to recognizing that customers can be productive resources and co-creators of quality and value, organizations also need to recognize the customer's role as a potential competitor.

SELF-SERVICE TECHNOLOGIES – THE ULTIMATE IN CUSTOMER PARTICIPATION

Self-service technologies (SSTs) are services produced entirely by the customer without any direct involvement or interaction with the firm's employees. SSTs represent the ultimate form of customer participation along a continuum from services that are produced entirely by the firm to those that are produced entirely by the customer. This continuum is depicted in Figure 12.1, using the example of a service station to illustrate the various ways the same service could be delivered along all points on the continuum. At the far right end of the continuum, the service station attendant does everything from refuelling the car to taking payment. On the other end of the spectrum, the customer does everything; in between are various

Figure 12.1   Services production continuum

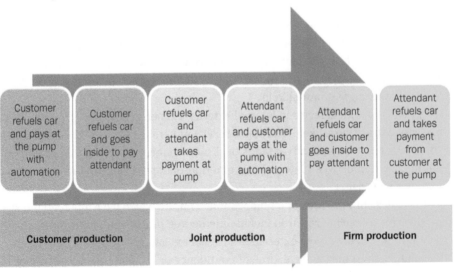

Source: Adapted from M.L. Meuter and M.J. Bitner, 'Self-service technologies: extending service frameworks and identifying issues for research', in *Marketing Theory and Applications*, eds D. Grewal and C. Pechmann (American Marketing Association Winter Educators' Conference, 1998), pp. 12–19.

forms and levels of customer participation. Many service delivery options, across industries, could be laid out on this type of continuum from total customer production through total firm production.

A PROLIFERATION OF NEW SSTs

Advances in technology, particularly the Internet, have allowed the introduction of a wide range of self-service technologies that occupy the far left end of the customer participation continuum in Figure 12.1. These technologies have proliferated as companies see the potential cost savings and efficiencies that can be achieved, potential sales growth, increased customer satisfaction and competitive advantage. A partial list of some of the self-service technologies available to consumers includes:

- ATMs
- Self-service petrol pumps
- Airline check-in
- Self-service airline bag drop
- Hotel check-in and check-out
- Automated car rental
- Automated filing of legal claims
- Online tax returns
- Automated betting machines
- Electronic blood pressure machines
- Various vending services
- Tax preparation software

- Self-scanning at retail stores
- Internet banking
- Vehicle registration online
- Online auctions
- Home and car buying online
- Automated investment transactions
- Insurance online
- Package tracking
- Internet shopping
- Internet information search
- Interactive voice response telephone systems
- Distance education.

The rapid proliferation of new SSTs is occurring for several reasons.[25] Many times firms are tempted by the cost savings that they anticipate by shifting customers to technology-based, automated systems and away from expensive personal service. If cost saving is the only reason for introducing an SST and if customers see no apparent benefits, the SST is likely to fail. Customers quickly see through this strategy and are not likely to adopt the SST if they have alternative options for service. Other times, firms introduce new SSTs based on customer demand. More and more, customers are expecting to find access to information, services and delivery options online or through applications on their smartphones. When they do not find what they want from a particular firm in a mobile application or online, they are likely to choose a competitor. Thus, customer demand in some industries is forcing firms to develop and offer their services via technology. In particular, there has been an explosion in mobile phone apps to assist customers in booking accommodation, track flights, undertake banking or investment transactions and provide a wide variety of information services. Using such technology can also open up new geographic, socio-economic and lifestyle markets for organizations that were not available to them through traditional channels.

⭐ SERVICE SPOTLIGHT

The Hilton chain of hotels is replacing room keys with a mobile phone app. The app allows guests to check in before they arrive, even enabling them to choose which room they would like on which floor. No longer needing to queue at reception, guests can proceed straight to their room and scan their smart phone on the sensor on the door.

CUSTOMER USAGE OF SSTs

Some of the SSTs listed above – ATMs, self-service fuel pumps, mobile apps, Internet information search – have been very successful, embraced by customers for the benefits they provide in terms of convenience, accessibility and ease of use.[26] Benefits to firms, including cost savings and revenue growth, can also result for those SSTs that succeed. Others (automated hotel check-in/check-out, using ATMs to pay money into an account and grocery self-scanning) have been more slowly embraced by customers.

Failure results when customers see no personal benefit in the new technology or when they do not have the ability to use it or know what they are supposed to do. Often, adopting a new SST requires customers to change significantly their traditional behaviours, and many are reluctant to make those changes. Research looking at customer adoption of SSTs found that 'customer readiness' was a major factor in determining whether customers would even try a new self-service option.[27] Customer readiness results from a combination of personal motivation (What is in it for me?), ability (Do I have the ability to use this SST?) and role clarity (Do I understand what I am supposed to do?). Other times customers see no value in using the technology when compared to the alternative interpersonal mode of delivery; or the SSTs may be so poorly designed that customers may prefer not to use them.[28]

There is also a condition called self-service anxiety which can be defined as the fear and apprehension of using technology to execute a service along with the perceived social pressures of performing the service. Users of self-service technology may not only feel anxiety from the technical aspects of using the technology, but also the social aspects of performing the service in the presence of others. People may become more stressed about using self-service technology where there is a queue of people watching and waiting for them to complete their transaction.

A major problem with SSTs is that so few of them incorporate service recovery systems. In many instances, when the process fails, there is no simple way to recover on the spot. If your ATM rejects or keeps your bank card, you have to phone or visit the branch to resolve your problem. A self-service checkout in a supermarket will cease to operate if its sensor tells it that the customer hasn't put the purchased item in the bagging area. The customer then has to wait for a member of staff to reset the equipment. These failures will add to the length of the transaction and the likely dissatisfaction of the customer. It is therefore critical that organizations provide back-up systems and support for their SSTs. That may be a freephone number on the ATM machine or an employee available to support customers on self-service checkouts.

SUCCESS WITH SSTs

Technologies have been successful because they offer clear benefits (such as faster service or discounts) to customers, the benefits are well understood and appreciated compared with the alternative delivery modes, and the technology is user-friendly and reliable. In addition, customers understand their roles and have the capability to use the technology.

From a strategic perspective, research suggests that as firms move into SSTs as a mode of delivery, these questions are important to ask:[29]

- What is our strategy? What do we hope to achieve through the SST (cost savings, revenue growth, competitive advantage)?
- What are the benefits to customers of producing the service on their own through the SST? Do they know and understand these benefits?
- How can customers be motivated to try the SST? Do they understand their role? Do they have the capability to perform this role?
- How 'technology ready' are our customers?[30] Are some segments of customers more ready to use the technology than others?
- How can customers be involved in the design of the service technology system and processes so that they will be more likely to adopt and use the SST?
- What forms of customer education will be needed to encourage adoption? Will other incentives be needed?
- How will inevitable SST failures be handled to regain customer confidence?

STRATEGIES FOR ENHANCING CUSTOMER PARTICIPATION

The level and the nature of customer participation in the service process are strategic decisions that can impact an organization's productivity, its positioning relative to competitors, its service quality and its customers' satisfaction. In the following sections we will examine the strategies captured in Figure 12.2 for effectively involving customers in the service delivery process. The overall goals of a customer participation strategy will typically be to increase organizational productivity and customer satisfaction while simultaneously decreasing uncertainty due to unpredictable customer actions.

Figure 12.2   Strategies for enhancing customer participation

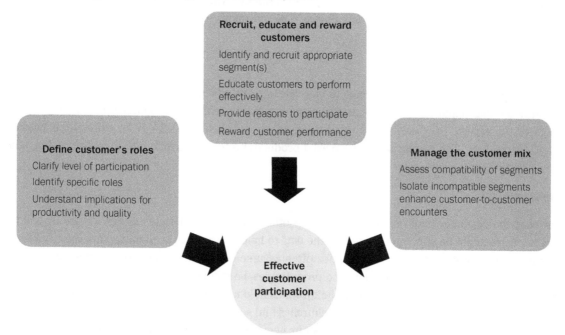

Source: Adapted from M.L. Meuter and M.J. Bitner, 'Self-service technologies: extending service frameworks and identifying issues for research', in *Marketing Theory and Applications*, eds D. Grewal and C. Pechmann (American Marketing Association Winter Educators' Conference, 1998), pp. 12–19.

DEFINE CUSTOMERS' JOBS

In developing strategies for addressing customer involvement in service delivery, the organization first determines what type of participation it wants from customers, thus beginning to define the customer's 'job'. Identifying the current level of customer participation can serve as a starting point. Customers' roles may be partially predetermined by the nature of the service, as suggested in Table 12.1. The service may require only the customer's presence (a concert, airline travel) or it may require moderate levels of input from the customer in the form of effort or information (a haircut, tax preparation) or it may require the customer to actually co-create the service outcome (fitness training, consulting, self-service offerings).

The organization may decide that it is satisfied with the existing level of participation it requires from customers but wants to make the participation more effective. For example, IKEA has positioned itself as a company whose customers are highly involved in the purchase, transportation and construction of their products. It may see no added benefit in getting customers to use self-scanning equipment at the checkout or buy their restaurant products from vending machines.

Alternatively, the organization may choose to increase the level of customer participation, which may reposition the service in the customers' eyes. Experts have suggested that higher levels of customer participation are strategically advisable when service production and delivery are inseparable, marketing benefits (cross-selling, building loyalty) can be enhanced by on-site contact with the customer, and customers can supplement for the labour and information provided by employees.[31]

Finally, the organization may decide it wants to reduce customer participation owing to all the uncertainties it causes. In such situations the strategy may be to isolate all but the essential tasks, keeping customers away from the service facility and employees as much as possible.[32] Mail order is an extreme example of this form of service. Customers are in contact with the organization via telephone or the Internet, never see the organization's facility and have limited employee interactions. The customer's role is thus extremely limited and can interfere very little with the service delivery process.

Once the desired level of participation is clear, the organization can define more specifically what the customer's 'job' entails.[33] The customer's 'job description' will vary with the type of service and the organization's desired position within its industry. The job might entail helping oneself, helping others or promoting the company.

HELPING ONESELF

In many cases the organization may decide to increase the level of customer involvement in service delivery through active participation. In such situations the customer becomes a productive resource, performing aspects of the service previously performed by employees or others. IKEA is an example of customers 'helping themselves'. The result may be increased productivity for the firm and/or increased value, quality and satisfaction for the customer.

HELPING OTHERS

Sometimes the customer may be called on to help others who are experiencing the service. A child at a day-care centre might be appointed 'buddy of the day' to help a new child acclimatize into the environment. Long-time residents of retirement communities often assume comparable roles to welcome new residents. Many universities have established mentoring programmes, particularly for students from minority groups, in which experienced students with similar backgrounds help newcomers adjust and learn the system. Many membership organizations (like health clubs, churches and social organizations) also rely heavily, although often informally, on current members to help orientate new members and make them feel welcome. In engaging in these types of roles, customers are again performing productive functions for the organization, increasing customer satisfaction and retention. Acting as a mentor or facilitator can have very positive effects on the person performing the role and is likely to increase his or her loyalty as well.

PROMOTING THE COMPANY

In some cases the customer's job may include a sales or promotional element. As you know from previous chapters, service customers rely heavily on word-of-mouth endorsements in deciding which providers to try. They are more comfortable getting a recommendation from someone who has actually experienced the service than from advertising alone. A positive recommendation from a friend, relative, colleague or an acquaintance can pave the way for a positive service experience. Many service organizations have been very imaginative in getting their current customers to work as promoters or salespeople:

- A bowling alley holds a prize draw for its regular patrons. The person whose name is drawn is given a party at the bowling alley to which he or she can invite friends for free bowling. This effectively creates a 'word-of-mouth champion' who brings new people into the establishment.
- To increase membership, an insurance company published a member referral coupon in its newsletter. Those who referred new members were then given a monetary reward.
- A credit card that gives customers frequent-flyer points every time they use their credit card offers 10,000 free miles to those who solicit a new credit card customer.

INDIVIDUAL DIFFERENCES: NOT EVERYONE WANTS TO PARTICIPATE

In defining customers' jobs it is important to remember that not everyone will want to participate.[34] Some customer segments enjoy self-service, whereas others prefer to have the service performed entirely for them. Companies that provide education and training services to organizations know that some customers want to be involved in designing the training and perhaps in delivering it to their employees. Other companies want to hand over the entire training design and delivery to the consulting organization, staying at arm's length with little of their own time and energy invested in the service. In health care, it is clear that some patients want lots of information and want to be involved in their own diagnosis and treatment decisions. Others simply want the doctor to tell them what to do. Despite all the customer service and purchase options now available via the Internet, many customers still prefer human, high-contact service delivery rather than self-service. Research has shown, for example, that customers with a high 'need for human interaction' are less likely to try new self-service options offered via the Internet and automated telephone systems.[35] Because of these differences in preferences, most companies find they need to provide service delivery choices for different market segments.

Often an organization can customize its services to fit the needs of these different segments – those who want to participate and those who prefer little involvement. Banks typically customize their services by offering both automated self-service options and high-touch, human delivery options. At other times, organizations such as IKEA can effectively position themselves to specifically serve segments of customers who want a high level of participation.

★ **SERVICE SPOTLIGHT**

The UK shopworkers' union USDAW claimed that self-service tills in supermarkets posed a risk to staff who find themselves on the receiving end of frustrated customers' anger at announcements of 'unexpected items in the baggage area', rejection of banknotes and the need for a shopworker to verify the age of anyone buying alcohol. 'In our latest survey, self-service checkouts were cited for the first time as a cause of abuse of staff by customers,' said John Hannett, USDAW's general secretary.

Source: The *Independent*, 22/8/10.

RECRUIT, EDUCATE AND REWARD CUSTOMERS

Once the customer's role is clearly defined, the organization can think in terms of facilitating that role. In a sense, the customer becomes a 'partial employee' of the organization at some level, and strategies for managing customer behaviour in service production and delivery can mimic to some degree the efforts aimed at service employees discussed in Chapter 11. As with employees, customer participation in service production and delivery will be facilitated when (1) customers understand their roles and how they are expected to perform, (2) customers are able to perform as expected, and (3) customers receive valued rewards for performing as expected.[36] Through these means, the organization will also reduce the inherent uncertainty associated with the unpredictable quality and timing of customer participation.

RECRUIT THE RIGHT CUSTOMERS

Before the company begins the process of educating and socializing customers for their roles, it must attract the right customers to fill those roles. The expected roles and responsibilities of customers should be clearly communicated in advertising, personal selling and other company messages. By previewing their roles and what is required of them in the service process, customers can self-select into (or out of) the relationship. Self-selection should result in enhanced perceptions of service quality from the customer's point of view and reduced uncertainty for the organization.

To illustrate, a child-care centre that requires parent participation on the site at least one-half day per week needs to communicate that expectation before it enrols any child in its programme. For some families, this level of participation will not be possible or desirable, thus precluding them from enrolling in the centre. The expected level of participation needs to be communicated clearly in order to attract customers who are ready and willing to perform their roles. In a sense this situation is similar to a manufacturing firm exercising control over the quality of inputs into the production process.[37]

EDUCATE AND TRAIN CUSTOMERS TO PERFORM EFFECTIVELY

Customers need to be educated, or in essence 'socialized', so that they can perform their roles effectively. Through the socialization process, service customers gain an appreciation of specific organizational values, develop the abilities necessary to function within a specific context, understand what is expected of them and acquire the skills and knowledge to interact with employees and other customers.[38] Customer-education programmes can take the form of formal orientation programmes, written literature provided to customers, directional cues and signage in the service environment, and information obtained from employees and other customers.

Many services offer 'customer orientation' programmes to assist customers in understanding their roles and what to expect from the process before experiencing it. For example, health clubs provide guidance on the layout of the club, details on fitness classes and training on how the different fitness machines operate.

Customer education can also be partially accomplished through written literature and customer 'handbooks'. Many hospitals have developed patient handbooks, very similar in appearance to employee handbooks, to describe what the patient should do in preparation for arrival at the hospital, what will happen when he or she arrives, and policies regarding visiting hours. The handbook may even describe the roles and responsibilities of family members.

Although formal training and written information are usually provided in advance of the service experience, other strategies can continue customer socialization during the experience itself. On site, customers require two kinds of orientation: *place orientation* (Where am I? How do I get from here to there?) and *function orientation* (How does this organization work? What am I supposed to do?).[39] Signage, the layout of the service facility and other orientation aids can help customers answer these questions, allowing them to perform their roles more effectively. Orientation aids can also take the form of rules that define customer behaviour for safety (airlines, health clubs), appropriate dress (restaurants, entertainment venues) and noise levels (hotels, classrooms, theatres). Customers may also be socialized to their expected roles through information provided by employees and by observing other customers.

REWARD CUSTOMERS FOR THEIR CONTRIBUTIONS

Customers are more likely to perform their roles effectively, or to participate actively, if they are rewarded for doing so. Rewards are likely to come in the form of increased control over the delivery process, time savings, monetary savings and psychological or physical benefits. For instance, some accountants have their clients complete extensive forms before meeting. If the forms are completed, the accountants will have less work to do and the clients will be rewarded with fewer billable hours. Those clients who choose not to perform the requested role will pay a higher price for the service. Automated teller machine customers who perform banking services for themselves are also rewarded through greater access to the bank, in terms of both locations and times. In some situations ATM customers are also rewarded because they avoid fees that are assessed for interpersonal transactions with tellers. In healthcare contexts, patients who perform their roles effectively are likely to be rewarded with better health or quicker recovery. For a long time airlines have offered price discounts for passengers who ordered tickets online, providing a monetary incentive for customer participation.

Customers may not realize the benefits or rewards of effective participation unless the organization makes the benefits apparent to them. In other words, the organization needs to clarify the performance-contingent benefits that can accrue to customers just as it defines these types of benefits to employees. The organization also should recognize that not all customers are motivated by the same types of rewards. Some may value the increased access and time savings they can gain by performing their service roles effectively. Others may value the monetary savings. Still others may be looking for greater personal control over the service outcome.

AVOID NEGATIVE OUTCOMES OF INAPPROPRIATE CUSTOMER PARTICIPATION

If customers are not effectively socialized, the organization runs the risk that inappropriate customer behaviours will result in negative outcomes for customers, employees, and the organization itself:[40]

1   Customers who do not understand the service system or the process of delivery may slow down the service process and negatively affect their own as well as other customers' outcomes. In a rental car context, customers who do not understand the reservation process, the information needed from them, insurance coverage issues and the pick-up and drop-off procedures can slow the flow for employees and other customers, lowering both productivity and quality of service.

2   If customers do not perform their roles effectively, it may not be possible for employees to provide the levels of technical and process quality promised by the organization. For example, in a management consulting practice, clients who do not provide the information and cooperation needed by the consultants will likely receive inferior service in terms of both the usefulness of the management report and the timeliness of the delivery.

3   If customers are frustrated because of their own inadequacies and incompetencies, employees are likely to suffer emotionally and be less able to deliver quality service. For example, if customers routinely enter the service delivery process with little knowledge of how the system works and their role in it, they are likely to take out their frustrations on front-line employees. This negative impact on individual employees can take its toll on the organization in the form of turnover and decreased motivation to serve.

MANAGE THE CUSTOMER MIX

Because customers frequently interact with each other in the process of service delivery and consumption, another important strategic objective is to effectively manage the mix of customers who simultaneously experience the service. If a restaurant chooses to serve two segments during the dinner hour that are incompatible with each other – for example, students who want to party and business people who want quiet to discuss work – it may find that the two groups do not merge well. Of course, it is possible to manage these segments so that they do not interact with each other by seating them in separate sections or by attracting the two segments at different times of day. Major tourism attractions around the world face the challenge of accommodating visitors who differ in the languages they speak, the foods they want to eat, their values and their perceptions of appropriate behaviours. Sometimes these visitors can clash when they do not understand and appreciate each other.

The process of managing multiple and sometimes conflicting segments is known as *compatibility management*, broadly defined as 'a process of first attracting homogeneous consumers to the service environment, then actively managing both the physical environment and customer-to-customer encounters in such a way as to enhance satisfying encounters and minimize dissatisfying encounters'.[41] Compatibility management will be critically important for some businesses (such as health clubs, public transportation and hospitals) and less important for others. Table 12.2 lists seven interrelated characteristics of service businesses that will increase the importance of compatibility management.

Table 12.2   Characteristics of service that increase the importance of compatible segments

Customers are in close physical proximity to each other	Customers will more often notice each other and be influenced by each other's behaviour when they are in close physical proximity	Aeroplane flights Entertainment events Sports events
Verbal interaction takes place among customers	Conversation (or lack thereof) can be a component of both satisfying and dissatisfying encounters with fellow patrons	Full-service restaurants Cocktail lounges Educational settings
Customers are engaged in numerous and varied activities	When a service facility supports varied activities all going on at the same time, the activities themselves may not be compatible	Libraries Health clubs Resort hotels
The service environment attracts a heterogeneous customer mix	Many service environments, particularly those open to the public, will attract a variety of customer segments	Public parks Public transportation Shopping centres
The core service is compatibility	The core service is to arrange and nurture compatible relationships between customers	Speed-dating events Weight-loss group programmes Mental health support groups
Customers must occasionally wait for the service	Waiting in line for service can be monotonous or anxiety producing. The boredom or stress can be magnified or lessened by other customers, depending on their compatibility	Dentists Tourist attractions Restaurants
Customers are expected to share time, space or service utensils with each other	The need to share space, time and other service factors is common in many services but may become a problem if segments are not comfortable with sharing with each other or if the need to share is intensified because of capacity constraints	Golf courses Hospitals Retirement communities Aeroplanes

Source: Adapted from C.I. Martin and C.A. Pranter, 'Compatibility management: customer-to-customer relationships in service environments', *Journal of Services Marketing* 3, no. 3 (Summer 1989), pp. 5–15.

To manage multiple (and sometimes conflicting) segments, organizations rely on a variety of strategies. Attracting homogeneous groups of customers through careful positioning and segmentation strategies is one approach.

Other strategies for enhancing customer compatibility include customer 'codes of conduct' such as the regulation of smoking behaviour and dress codes. Clearly such codes of conduct may vary from one service establishment to another. Finally, training employees to observe customer-to-customer interactions and to be sensitive to potential conflicts is another strategy for increasing compatibility among segments. Employees can also be trained to recognize opportunities to foster positive encounters among customers in certain types of service environments.

SUMMARY

This chapter focused on the role of customers in service creation and delivery. The customer receiving the service and the fellow customers in the service environment can all potentially cause a widening of gap 3 if they fail to perform their roles effectively. A number of reasons why customers may widen the service delivery gap were suggested: customers lack understanding of their roles; customers are unwilling or unable to perform their roles; customers are not rewarded for good performance; other customers interfere; or market segments are incompatible.

Managing customers in the process of service delivery is a critical challenge for service firms. Whereas manufacturers are not concerned with customer participation in the manufacturing process, service managers constantly face this issue because their customers are often present and active partners in service production. As participants in service creation, production and delivery, customers can perform three primary roles, discussed and illustrated in the chapter: *productive resources* for the organization, *contributors* to service quality and satisfaction and *competitors* in performing the service for themselves.

Through understanding the importance of customers in service delivery and identifying the roles played by the customer in a particular context, managers can develop strategies to enhance customer participation. Strategies discussed in the text include defining the customers' roles and jobs, recruiting customers who match the customer profile in terms of desired level of participation, educating customers so they can perform their roles effectively, rewarding customers for their contributions, and managing the customer mix to enhance the experiences of all segments. By implementing these strategies, organizations should see a reduction in gap 3 due to effective, efficient customer contributions to service delivery.

KEY CONCEPTS

Customer 'codes of conduct'	278	Self-service anxiety	272
Customer participation	262	Self-service technologies	270
Customers as competitors	265	Services as drama	263
Manage the mix of customers	277		

EXERCISES

1 Visit a service establishment where customers can influence each other (such as a theme park, entertainment establishment, resort, shopping mall, restaurant, airline, school or hospital). Observe or interview customers and record cases of positive and negative customer influence. Discuss how you would manage the situation to increase overall customer satisfaction.

2 Interview someone regarding his or her decision to outsource a service – for example, legal services, payroll, or maintenance in a company; or cleaning, child care or pet care in a household. Use the criteria for internal versus external exchange described in the text to analyse the decision to outsource.

3 Think of a service in which a high level of customer participation is necessary for the service to be successful (health club, weight loss, educational setting, healthcare, golf lessons, or the like). Interview a service provider in such an organization to find out what strategies the provider uses to encourage effective customer participation.

4 Visit a service setting in which multiple types of customer segments use the service at the same time (such as a theatre, golf course, resort or theme park). Make your own observations or interview the

manager about the organization's strategies to manage these segments effectively. Would you do anything differently if you were in charge?

DISCUSSION QUESTIONS

1   Using your own personal examples, discuss the general importance of customers in the successful creation and delivery of service experiences.

2   Why might customer actions and attitudes cause the service performance gap to occur? Use your own examples to illustrate your understanding.

3   Using Table 12.1, think of specific services you have experienced that fall within each of the three levels of customer participation: low, medium and high. Describe specifically what you did as a customer in each case. How did your involvement vary across the three types of service situations?

4   Describe a time when your satisfaction in a particular situation was *increased* because of something another customer did. Could (or does) the organization do anything to ensure that this experience happens routinely? What does it do? Should it try to make this situation a routine occurrence?

5   Describe a time when your satisfaction in a particular situation was *decreased* because of something another customer did. Could the organization have done anything to manage this situation more effectively? If so, what?

6   Discuss the customer's role as a *productive resource* for the firm. Describe a time when you played this role. What did you do and how did you feel? Did the firm help you perform your role effectively? How?

7   Discuss the customer's role as a *contributor to service quality and satisfaction*. Describe a time when you played this role. What did you do and how did you feel? Did the firm help you perform your role effectively? How?

8   Discuss the customer's role as a potential *competitor*. Describe a time when you chose to provide a service for yourself rather than pay someone to provide the service for you. Why did you decide to perform the service yourself? What could have changed your mind, causing you to contract with someone else to provide the service?

9   Identify the main frustrations of using self-service technologies. How can these frustrations be reduced?

10 Choose a service that customers co-produce and outline the specific tasks that customers need to undertake to satisfactorily produce the service.

FURTHER READING

Åkesson, M., Edvardsson, B. and Tronvoll, B. (2014). Customer experience from a self-service system perspective. *Journal of Service Management*, 25(5), 677–698.

Cunningham, L. F., Young, C. E. and Gerlach, J. (2009). A comparison of consumer views of traditional services and self-service technologies. *Journal of Services Marketing*, 23(1), 11–23.

Giebelhausen, M., Robinson, S. G., Sirianni, N. J. and Brady, M. K. (2014). Touch versus tech: When technology functions as a barrier or a benefit to service encounters. *Journal of Marketing*, 78(4), 113–24.

Grissemann, U. S. and Stokburger-Sauer, N. E. (2012). Customer co-creation of travel services: The role of company support and customer satisfaction with the co-creation performance. *Tourism Management*, 33(6), 1483–92.

Johnson, D.S., Bardhi, F. and Dunn, D.T. (2008). Understanding how technology paradoxes affect customer satisfaction with self-service technology: the role of performance ambiguity and trust in technology. *Psychology and Marketing*, 25(5), 416–43.

Shamdasani, P., Mukherjee, A. and Malhotra, N. (2008). Antecedents and consequences of service quality in consumer evaluation of self-service Internet technologies. *Service Industries Journal*, 28(1), 117–38.

CHAPTER 13

Delivering Service Through Electronic Channels and Intermediaries

CHAPTER OUTLINE

LEARNING OBJECTIVES

This chapter's objectives are to:

1 Identify the primary channels through which services are delivered to end customers.
2 Examine the manner in which services can be delivered through technology and electronic channels.
3 Provide examples of each of the key service intermediaries.
4 View delivery of service from two perspectives – the service provider and the service deliverer.
5 Discuss the benefits and challenges of each method of service delivery.
6 Outline the strategies that are used to manage service delivery through intermediaries.

OPENING EXAMPLE

Shakespeare Goes Online

Shakespeare's Globe theatre is a replica of the original Globe Theatre, an Elizabethan playhouse on the south bank of the River Thames in London, built in 1599 and destroyed by fire in 1613. It was where many of William Shakespeare's plays were originally performed. The modern reconstruction, opened in 1997 under the name 'Shakespeare's Globe Theatre', is an academic approximation based on available evidence of the 1599 and 1614 buildings.

Shakespeare's Globe Theatre has staged plays every summer since 1997 and attempts to duplicate the experience that audiences would have had in Elizabethan times. The auditorium is open to the sky and productions use no stage lights, microphones, speakers or amplification; all music is performed live. There is no seating at the foot of the stage and the crowding audience stands very close to the actors, adding to the feeling of a shared experience and of a community event.

To widen the audience for the performances, the theatre sought to add delivery channels. Initially, this took the form of plays being filmed and released to cinemas through Shakespeare Globe on Screen productions. This allowed theatre enthusiasts to see the plays in local cinemas in the UK, mainland Europe, USA, Canada, Australia and New Zealand. Although this was partially successful, it was clear that audiences wanted greater flexibility as to where and when they could watch a production. To address this, another delivery channel was developed, the Globe Player. This video-on-demand service allows the user to download and watch HD films of productions anywhere and anytime. Subscribers can opt between renting (around €5.50) or buying (around €11) the films. Shakespeare's Globe is also releasing an app for use on mobile phones and tablets, enabling users to browse videos as well as gain access to any films they have purchased previously.

These new electronic channels have extended the customer base for the Shakespeare's Globe Theatre from people visiting or living in London to anybody with a computer, tablet or smartphone anywhere in the world. In the first 6 months following launch, Globe Player had 100,500 users from 174 countries with 35 per cent of users accessing on mobile or tablet.

Source: www.globeplayer.tv.

DELIVERING SERVICE THROUGH ELECTRONIC CHANNELS

The Internet has 'transformed every aspect of our lives – including how we socialize, manage our money, purchase goods and services, and gather information.'[1] Electronic channels have vastly expanded the opportunities for goods and services marketers to distribute their offerings. They differ from the other types of channel that we discuss in this chapter as they do not require direct human interaction. What they do require is some predesigned service (such as information, education or entertainment) and an electronic vehicle to deliver it. You are probably all familiar with telephone and

Social Media and Digital Marketing

Table 13.1   Benefits and challenges in electronic distribution of services

Benefits	Challenges
Consistent delivery for standardized services	Price competition
Low cost	Inability to customize because of standardized nature of the service
Customer convenience	Lack of consistency due to customer involvement
Wide distribution	Changes in consumer behaviour
Customer choice and ability to customize	Security concerns
Quick customer feedback	Competition from widening geographies

television channels, the Internet and mobile apps. The consumer and business services that are made possible through these channels include movies on demand, interactive news and music, banking and financial services, multimedia libraries and databases, distance learning, desktop videoconferencing, remote health services and interactive network-based games.

The more a service relies on technology and/or equipment for service production and the less it relies on face-to-face contact with service providers, the less the service is characterized by inseparability and non-standardization. As you will see in the following section, using electronic channels overcomes some of the problems associated with service inseparability and allows a form of standardization not previously possible in most services. Table 13.1 summarizes the benefits and challenges of electronic distribution.

BENEFITS OF ELECTRONIC CHANNELS

CONSISTENT DELIVERY FOR STANDARDIZED SERVICES

Electronic channels such as the Internet do not alter the service, as channels with human interaction tend to do. Unlike delivery from a personal provider, electronic delivery does not interpret the service and execute it according to that interpretation. Its delivery is likely to be the same in all transmissions. The process of booking a flight on the easyJet website or mobile phone app is the same for every customer, no matter where they are or who they are.

LOW COST

Electronic media offer more efficient means of delivery than interpersonal distribution. Critics could rightly claim that personal sales interaction is more powerful and effective, but with interactive services, companies such as Amazon are able to gain some of the credibility benefits of personal interaction (such as being able to answer individual questions or tailor the service, book recommendations and website for individuals).

CUSTOMER CONVENIENCE

With electronic channels, customers are able to access a firm's services when and where they want. 'Retailers still tell customers, "You have to come to us. But online consumers are saying, No way – *you* have to come to *us*. My place, my time is the new mantra of consumers everywhere".[2] Just as catalogue shopping freed working women from the perceived drudgeries of having to go to the shops, e-commerce is changing the way people shop. Many companies with call centres and telephone ordering still limit their hours of availability, a real mistake if they are going to match the customer convenience of being able to order online 24 hours a day, seven days a week. For the marketer, electronic channels allow access to a large group of customers who would otherwise be unavailable to them because of busy schedules that do not allow them to shop in other ways.

> ## ★ SERVICE SPOTLIGHT
>
> Just Eat, a company founded in Denmark, offers convenience to consumers by providing an online hub for takeaway food ordering. The company claims to operate the largest site of its kind, with listings for more than 40,000 restaurants in 13 countries stretching from Ireland to India.
>
> Just Eat forms partnerships with bricks-and-mortar takeout food outlets to give them a reliable Web interface, search engine and ordering service. Consumers get a single convenient site to access all takeaways in their local area; restaurants get increased customer traffic; and Just Eat acts as the broker and makes a margin on each sale.
>
> That model was perfected over five years working in and around Copenhagen, but Just Eat is now headquartered in London, with operations throughout Europe and beyond.

WIDE DISTRIBUTION

Electronic channels do more than allow the service provider to interact with a large number of geographically dispersed consumers. They also allow the service provider to interact (often simultaneously) with a large number of intermediaries. The costs and effort to inform, promote and motivate consumers to buy through offline channels are higher than the costs to accomplish the same activities with electronic channels. A service that places an advertisement on the right-hand side of a Google search results page only pays Google when a potential customer clicks on the advertisement and visits the organization's Web page. It can be far more difficult and expensive to make potential customers aware of the physical location of a service outlet and motivate them to get in their car and travel to it.

CUSTOMER CHOICE AND ABILITY TO CUSTOMIZE

Consider the options available in movies and videos to customers who use video-on-demand services. Just as Dell Computer allows customers to configure entire products to their own particular needs and desires, the Internet allows many companies to design services from the beginning. Individuals who want to renovate their kitchen may now go to many Internet sites, specify their requirements and order what they wish. Whether the supplier is a large retailer such as B&Q (www.diy.com) or a small start-up company, customers get exactly what they want.

QUICK CUSTOMER FEEDBACK

Rapid customer feedback is without doubt one of the major strengths of e-commerce. Companies can find out immediately what customers think of services and can gain far higher participation from customers in surveys. With quick customer feedback, changes can be made rapidly to service assortments, problems can be addressed immediately and the learning cycles of companies can speed up dramatically. Online customers may not be aware that they are giving feedback, but companies can monitor which Web pages they access, the length of time that they spend on each page and whether they make a purchase (or at what stage they leave the website).

CHALLENGES IN DISTRIBUTING SERVICES THROUGH ELECTRONIC CHANNELS

PRICE COMPETITION

One of the traditional differences between goods and services has been the difficulty of directly comparing features and prices of services with each other. Whereas goods can typically be compared in retail settings, few retail settings exist that offer services from multiple sources. The Internet has changed all that. Services such as trivago.com and Kelkoo.com make it simple for customers to compare prices for a wide variety of services.

★ SERVICE SPOTLIGHT

Online travel has been one of the biggest success stories in electronic channels. The Internet has proved an extremely effective channel for travel for three key reasons:

1 Prices are more competitive online, and the technology can conjure up literally thousands of providers in an instant.
2 Online travel companies do not have to pay commission to intermediaries such as travel agents and can therefore offer cheaper prices.
3 Travel sites that focus narrowly on a specific clientele draw significant advertising revenue because advertisers know that all users are potential buyers of their travel-related services and products.

One of the most successful online travel sites is Expedia. Like other online sites, it sells airline tickets, hotel rooms and car rentals directly to consumers, bypassing travel agents. The site also offers *Expedia Hotel View*, which combines customer reviews and hotel pricing information augmented by imagery from Google Street View to people a virtual tour of the area surrounding their selected accommodation so they can book with confidence.

INABILITY TO CUSTOMIZE DUE TO THE STANDARDIZED NATURE OF ELECTRONIC SERVICES

Some of you may be on a distance learning course using video or online support materials. If you consider what you miss in learning this way compared with learning directly from a lecturer, you will understand this challenge. You may not be able to interact directly with the lecturer, ask questions, raise points for clarification or experience the connection that you receive in person. In online classes – as in videoconferences that are springing up in many businesses – the quality of the service can also be impeded by the way the audience reacts (or does not react) in those situations. People talk among themselves, leave, laugh and criticize, among other behaviours.

LACK OF CONSISTENCY BECAUSE OF CUSTOMER INVOLVEMENT

Although electronic channels are very effective in minimizing the inconsistency from employees or providers of service, customer variability still presents a problem. Many times, customers use the technology themselves to produce the service but often this can lead to errors or frustration unless the technology is highly user friendly. Manoeuvring online can sometimes be overwhelming, broadband speeds can vary enormously and not all websites are easy to use. Furthermore, many customers may not have computers and, even if they do, may be reluctant to use this medium.

CHANGES IN CONSUMER BEHAVIOUR

A consumer purchasing a service through electronic channels engages in very different behaviour to a consumer entering a retail store and talking to a salesperson. Considerable changes – in the willingness to search for information, in the willingness to perform some aspects of the services themselves, in the acceptance of different levels of service – are necessary when customers use electronic channels. Behaviour change is difficult, even for a consumer wanting to make a change; therefore, marketers wishing to motivate consumers to alter long-established patterns will be challenged.

SECURITY CONCERNS

One issue confronting marketers using electronic channels is concern about the security of information, particularly health and financial information. Many customers are still hesitant about giving credit card numbers on the Internet. These problems can undermine consumers' trust in the Internet as a safe place to do business. Companies doing business through the Internet must continually devise ways to protect their systems from penetration, vandalism, eavesdropping and identity theft.[3] With penetration, intruders steal passwords and exploit unprotected modems and connections, actually taking over the sites. With vandalism, hackers crash corporate and other computers. To combat these problems, firewalls and other software scan for unusual activity. With eavesdropping, hackers snoop on information as it passes through multiple computers to the Internet. The typical solution is encryption software that scrambles electronic mail and other data to make it unintelligible to eavesdroppers. Finally, with identity theft, criminals steal consumers' identities in order to buy goods and services. A form of encryption technology is often used to deal with this problem, and special service companies confirm signature holders.[4]

COMPETITION FROM WIDENING GEOGRAPHIES

Historically, many services were somewhat protected from competition because customers had limited choice among the providers they could physically drive to. Banks, for example, supplied all local customers with current accounts, savings accounts and mortgages. In fact, it used to be said that because services could not be transported they were limited in their scope. Not any longer – and not with electronic channels. Through the Internet, many services, including financial services, can be purchased from service providers far from the local area.

DELIVERING SERVICE THROUGH MOBILE CHANNELS

SMARTPHONE APPLICATIONS

The growth in smartphones and tablet computers has provided an important platform for delivering services. Software developed specifically for these platforms is called mobile application software (app). The original apps were developed to provide information retrieval, access to emails, personal calendars, personal contacts and weather information. However, they now provide information and reservation systems for hotels and airlines; communication channels; retailing channels (e.g. Amazon app); services for monitoring health and fitness (e.g. Fitnet); entertainment and games; banking and financial services; map and navigation services (e.g. Google Maps, MapQuest); education; transport information (e.g. Uber taxis) and many others. These all allow people to access information and services whilst they are on the move; no longer do they need to be in the service provider's premises or even in their own homes or offices. As there are no manuals or service personnel on hand when the user accesses an app, it needs to be easy to use and function in the way it is meant to. If someone is trying to check in for a flight using their mobile between meetings or when they are in transit, simplicity and functionality are critical. The app also needs to seamlessly link with other delivery channels. A bank customer that transfers money between his bank accounts on his mobile phone wants to see that same transaction recorded on the Web, at the ATM machine and on the screen of the bank employee in the local branch or in the call centre.

Smartphones also allow the service provider to provide location-based services based on the GPS information provided by the phone. The app can highlight the location of local services and car parking spaces, as well as promotional offers relevant to the individual user and details on stock levels in specific retail outlets.

The growth in location-based services and apps is likely to expand significantly as the number of smartphones continues to grow.

⭐ **SERVICE SPOTLIGHT**

House of Fraser, a department store group with locations across the UK, has introduced beacon-powered mannequins in clothing departments to capitalize on mobile technologies and engage with customers. Beacon mannequins throughout the store send alerts about items of clothing on display or where they can be found in the store to customers who come within 50 feet of the source. The technology is enabled by a smartphone app that customers download.. House of Fraser hopes that customers will use the app to share products with friends via social media, or link directly to the House of Fraser's online store where they can later purchase the items.

OTHER FORMS OF SERVICE DISTRIBUTION

Except for situations where electronic channels can distribute services, providers and consumers come into direct contact in service provision. Because of the inseparability of production and consumption in service, providers must either be present themselves when customers receive service or find ways to involve others in distribution. Involving others can be problematic because quality in service occurs in the service encounter between company and customer. Unless the service distributor is willing and able to perform in the service encounter as the service principal would, the value of the offering decreases and the reputation of the original service may be damaged. Chapter 11 pointed out the challenges of controlling encounters within service organizations themselves, but most service (and many manufacturing) companies face an even more formidable task: attaining service excellence and consistency when intermediaries represent them to customers. As we have indicated throughout this textbook, services are generally intangible and experiential in nature. Thus, service distribution does not typically involve moving items through a chain of firms that begins with a manufacturer and ends with a consumer, as is the case for goods distribution. In fact, many services are delivered directly from the service producer to the consumer. That is, in contrast to channels for goods, channels for services are often direct – with the creator of the service (i.e. the service principal) selling directly to and interacting directly with the customer. Examples include air travel (easyJet), opticians (Vision Express) and consulting services (Accenture). Because services cannot be owned, there are no titles or rights to most services that can be passed along a delivery channel. Because services are intangible and perishable, inventories cannot exist, making warehousing a dispensable function. In general, because services cannot be produced, warehoused and then retailed, as goods can, many channels available to goods producers are not feasible for service firms. Thus, many of the primary functions that distribution channels serve – inventorying, securing and taking title to goods – have no meaning in services, allowing the service principal to deliver the service directly to the customer.

DELIVERY OF SERVICE THROUGH INTERMEDIARIES

Two distinct service marketers are involved in delivering service through intermediaries: the service principal, or originator, and the service deliverer, or intermediary. The service principal is the entity that creates the service concept (whose counterpart is the manufacturer of physical goods), and the service deliverer is the entity that interacts with the customer in the actual execution of the service (whose counterpart is the distributor or wholesaler of physical goods).

Even though many of the functions that intermediaries provide for goods manufacturers are not relevant for service firms, intermediaries often deliver services and perform several important functions for service principals. First, they may co-produce the service, fulfilling service principals' promises to customers. Franchise services such as haircutting, key-making and dry-cleaning are produced by the intermediary (the franchisee) using a process developed by the service principal. Service intermediaries also make services locally available, providing time and place convenience for the customer. Because they represent multiple service principals, such intermediaries as travel and insurance agents provide a retailing function for customers, gathering together in one place a variety of choices. And in many financial or professional services, intermediaries function as the glue between the brand or company name and the customer by building the trusting relationship required in these complex and expert offerings.

The primary types of intermediaries used in service delivery are franchisees, agents and brokers. *Franchisees* are service outlets licensed by a principal to deliver a unique service concept it has created or popularized. Examples include fast-food chains (McDonald's, Burger King), business services (Mailboxes etc.) and hotels (Holiday Inn). Agents and brokers are representatives who distribute and sell the services of one or more service suppliers. Examples include insurance (AA Insurance Services), financial services (through any one of the many independent financial advisers) and travel services (American Express).

We do not include retailers in our short list of service intermediaries because most retailers – from department stores to discount stores – are channels for delivering physical goods rather than services. Retailers that sell only services (cinemas, restaurants) or retail services that support physical products (car dealers, service stations) can also be described as dealers or franchises. For our purposes in this chapter, such retailers are grouped into the franchise category because they possess the same characteristics, strengths and weaknesses as franchises.

Goods retailers, by the way, are service organizations themselves; they are intermediaries for goods and perhaps services. Manufacturing companies depend on retailers to represent, explain, promote and insure their products – all of which are pre-sale services. Manufacturers also need retailers to return, exchange, support and service products – all of which are post-sale services. These roles are increasingly critical as products become more complex, technical and expensive. For example, camera and computer firms rely on retailers carrying their products to understand and communicate highly technical information so that customers choose products that fit their needs. A retailer that leads the customer to the wrong product choice or that inadequately instructs the customer on how to use the product creates service problems that strongly influence the manufacturer's reputation.

Service principals depend on their intermediaries to deliver service to their specifications. Service intermediaries determine how the customer evaluates the quality of the company. When a McDonald's franchisee undercooks McNuggets, the customer's perception of the company – and of other McDonald's franchisees – is tarnished. When one Holiday Inn franchisee has hygiene issues, it reflects on all other Holiday Inns and on the Holiday Inn brand itself. Unless service providers ensure that the intermediary's goals, incentives and motives are consistent with their own, they lose control over the service encounters between the customer and the intermediary. When someone other than the service principal is critical to the fulfilment of quality service, a firm must develop ways to either control or motivate these intermediaries to meet company goals and standards. In the sections that follow, we discuss both direct delivery of service by the service principal and indirect delivery of the service through intermediaries.

DIRECT OR COMPANY-OWNED CHANNELS

Although we call this chapter 'Delivering service through technology and intermediaries', it is important to acknowledge that many services are distributed directly from provider to customer. Some of these are local services – doctors, dry-cleaners and hairstylists – whose area of distribution is limited. Others are national chains with multiple outlets but are considered direct channels because the provider owns all the outlets. HSBC bank,[5] is an example of a service provider with all company-owned outlets enabling service delivery to be controlled and managed in a consistent manner thereby maintaining the bank's image.

Perhaps the major benefit of distributing through company-owned channels is that the company has complete *control* over the outlets. One of the most critical implications of this type of control is that the owner can maintain consistency in service provision. Standards can be established and will be carried out as planned because the company itself monitors and rewards proper execution of the service. Control over hiring, firing and motivating employees is also a benefit of company-owned channels. Using company-owned channels also allows the company to expand or contract sites without being bound by contractual agreements with other entities.

A final benefit of company-owned channels is that the company owns the customer relationship. In service industries in which skilled or professional workers have individual relationships with customers, a major concern is whether the loyalty the customer feels is for the company or for the individual service employee. It is well known, for example, that most people are loyal to individual hairstylists and will follow them from one place of business to another. Therefore, one of the important issues in service delivery is who owns the customer relationship – the store or the employee. With company-owned channels, the company owns both the store and the employee, and therefore has complete control over the customer relationship.

However, several disadvantages exist with company-owned channels. First, and probably the largest impediment to most service chains, the company must bear all the financial risk. When expanding, the firm must find all the capital, sometimes using it for geographical expansion rather than for other uses (such as advertising, service quality or new service development) that would be more profitable. Second, large companies are rarely experts in local markets – they know their businesses but not all markets. When adjustments are needed in business formats for different markets, they may be unaware of what these adjustments should be. This disadvantage is especially evident when companies expand into other cultures and other countries. Partnering or joint venturing is almost always preferred to company-owned channels in these situations.

When two or more service companies want to offer a service and neither have the full financial capability or expertise, they often undertake service partnerships. These partnerships operate very much like company-owned channels except that they involve multiple owners. The benefit is that risk and effort are shared, but the disadvantage is that control and returns are also distributed among the partners. Several areas in which partnerships are common are telecommunications, high-technology services, Internet-based services and entrepreneurial services. Service partnerships also proliferate when companies expand beyond their country boundaries – typically one partner provides the business format and the other provides knowledge of the local market.

FRANCHISING

Franchising is the most common type of distribution in services. In the UK the franchise industry is worth around 19 billion euros and employs more than 561,000 people with more than 930 franchisors licensing their brand names, business processes or formats, unique products, services or reputations in return for fees and royalties.[6] Franchising works well with services that can be standardized and duplicated through the delivery process, service policies, warranties, guarantees, promotion and branding. Body Shop[7], Domino's Pizza[8], Prontaprint[9], Toni & Guy[10] and Vision Express[11] are examples of companies that are ideal for franchise operations. At its best, franchising is a relationship or partnership in which the service provider – the franchisor – develops and optimizes a service format that it licenses for delivery by other parties – the franchisees.

⭐ SERVICE SPOTLIGHT

Subway, the franchised sandwich chain, was first opened in 1965 in Bridgeport, Connecticut, USA and was called Pete's Super Submarines. The first franchised Subway unit opened in 1974 and its popularity soon spread and there are now more than 43,000 Subway franchises in 110 countries worldwide. All Subway sandwiches are made on freshly baked bread and are prepared by 'sandwich artists' in front of the customer to a standardized Subway format. Franchisees receive national and local support, national and regional advertising, a two-week training programme, ongoing training for staff, store development assistance, design support; lease negotiations and construction guidance. In return, Subway charges franchisees an initial fee of around 11,000 euros and then takes 12.5 per cent of a store's gross weekly income.

Table 13.2   **Benefits and challenges in franchising**

Benefits	Challenges
For franchisors	
Leveraged business format for greater expansion and revenues	Difficulty in maintaining and motivating franchisees
Consistency in outlets	Highly publicized disputes and conflict
Knowledge of local markets	Inconsistent quality
Shared financial risk and more working capital	Control of customer relationship by intermediary
For franchisees	
An established business format	Encroachment of other outlets into franchisee territory
National or regional brand marketing	Disappointing profits and revenues
Minimized risk of starting a business	Lack of perceived control over operations
	High fees

There are benefits and disadvantages for both the franchisor and the franchisee in this relationship (see Table 13.2).

THE FRANCHISOR'S PERSPECTIVE

A franchisor typically begins by developing a business concept that is unique in some way. Perhaps it is a fast-food concept (such as McDonald's) with unique cooking or delivery processes. Perhaps it is a hairstylist (such as Toni & Guy) with established formats for marketing to customers, pricing and hiring employees. Or maybe it is a retail store (such as Krispy Kreme) with unique store environments, employee training, purchasing and computer systems. A franchisor typically expands business through this method because it expects the following benefits:

- *Leveraged business format for greater expansion and revenues.* Most franchisors want wider distribution – and increased revenues, market share, brand name recognition and economies of scale – for their concepts and practices than they can support in company outlets.
- *Consistency in outlets.* When franchisors have strong contracts and unique formats, they can require that service be delivered according to their specifications.
- *Knowledge of local markets.* National chains are unlikely to understand local markets as well as the business people who live in the geographic areas. With franchising, the company obtains a connection to the local market.
- *Shared financial risk and more working capital.* Franchisees must contribute their own capital for equipment and personnel, thereby bearing part of the risk of doing business.

Franchising is not without its challenges, however. Most franchisors encounter the following disadvantages:

- *Difficulty in maintaining and motivating franchisees.* Motivating independent operators to price, promote, deliver and hire according to standards the principal establishes is a difficult job, particularly when business is down.
- *Highly publicized disputes between franchisees and franchisors.* Franchisees are organizing and hiring lobbyists and lawyers to gain more economic clout. Many countries are looking at implementing legislation to boost franchisee rights.

- *Inconsistent quality.* Although some franchisees deliver the service in the manner in which the franchisor intended, other franchisees do not perform the service as well as desired. This inconsistency can undermine the company's image, reputation and brand name.
- *Customer relationships controlled by the franchisee rather than the franchisor.* The closer a company is to the customer, the better able it is to listen to that customer's concerns and ideas. When franchisees are involved, a relationship forms between the customer and the franchisee rather than between the customer and the franchisor. All customer information, including demographics, purchase history and preferences, is in the hands of the intermediary rather than the principal. This can be overcome by having a loyalty card scheme that links the customer and their transactions to the customer relationship management system of the franchisor.

THE FRANCHISEE'S PERSPECTIVE

From the perspective of the franchisee, one of the main benefits of franchising is obtaining an established business format on which to base a business, something one expert has defined as an 'entrepreneur in a prepackaged box, a super-efficient distributor of services and goods through a decentralized web'.[12] A second benefit is receiving national or regional brand marketing. Franchisees obtain advertising and other marketing expertise as well as an established reputation. Finally, franchising minimizes the risks of starting a business.

Disadvantages for franchisees also exist. One of the most problematic is *encroachment* – the opening of new units near existing ones without compensation to the existing franchisee. When encroachment occurs, potential revenues are diminished and competition is increased. Another frequent disadvantage involves disappointment over profits and revenues which is exacerbated by having to pay fees to the franchisor (averaging around 7–8 per cent in the UK).[13] Other disadvantages include lack of perceived control over operations and high fees. Many of these problems are due to over-promising by the franchisor, but others are caused by unrealistic expectations about what will be achieved in a franchise agreement.

AGENTS AND BROKERS

An *agent* is an intermediary who acts on behalf of a service principal (such as an estate agent) or a customer and is authorized to make agreements between the principal and the customer. Some agents, called *selling agents*, work with the principal and have contractual authority to sell a principal's output (such as travel, insurance or financial services), usually because the principal lacks the resources or desire to do so. Other agents, called *purchasing agents*, often have long-term relationships with buyers and help them in evaluating and making purchases. Such agents are frequently hired by companies and individuals to find art, antiques and rare jewellery. A *broker* is an intermediary who brings buyers and sellers together while assisting in negotiation. Brokers are paid by the party who hired them, rarely become involved in financing or assuming risk and are not long-term representatives of buyers or sellers. The most familiar examples are insurance brokers.

Agents and brokers do not take title to services but instead deliver the rights to them. They have legal authority to market services as well as to perform other marketing functions on behalf of producers. The benefits and challenges in using agents and brokers are summarized in Table 13.3.

BENEFITS OF AGENTS AND BROKERS

The travel industry provides an example of both agents and brokers. Three main categories of travel intermediaries exist: tour packagers, retail travel agents and speciality channellers (including incentive travel

Table 13.3   Benefits and challenges in distributing services through agents and brokers

Benefits	Challenges
Reduced selling and distribution costs	Loss of control over pricing
Intermediary's possession of special skills and knowledge	Representation of multiple service principals
Wide representation	
Knowledge of local markets	
Customer choice	

firms, meeting and convention planners, hotel representatives and corporate travel offices). You are likely to be most familiar with traditional retail travel agents. Industry convention terms the travel companies as brokers and the individuals who work for them as travel agents or sales associates. This traditional industry is changing rapidly because of electronic channels, with online travel agents (OTAs) such as Expedia and Booking.com. These OTAs can operate using two different models:[14]

- **Agent model**: the website has direct access to the hotel's inventory of rooms and sells them, gaining a commission. The hotel collects the payment from the guest before forwarding the commission on to the OTA.
- **Merchant model**: hotels sell their rooms at discounted rates to the OTAs, which in turn mark them up, at contract-specified margins and sell to the public. The OTA collects the payment from the guest and then remits the discounted price to the hotel.

The OTAs have a significant advantage over the individual hotels as they offer a choice of hotels to travellers as well as bundled services (flight, hotel, car hire and excursions). The agreements that OTAs set up with the hotels, often limit the extent to which the hotel can charge a different price from the one being offered by the OTA. Many hotels agree to this in order to have a presence in the OTAs search engine and in front of the many users of such OTA sites.

Agents and brokers, whether online or offline, offer significant benefits and challenges to the service principal. The following illustrate some of these in the travel industry.

REDUCED SELLING AND DISTRIBUTION COSTS

Traditionally (before the Internet), if an airline or resort hotel needed to contact every potential traveller to promote its offerings, costs would be exorbitant. Because most travel services are transactional rather than long term, travellers would need to expend tremendous effort to find services that meet their needs. Online travel agents and brokers accomplish the intermediary role by assembling information from travel suppliers and offering it to travellers.

POSSESSION OF SPECIAL SKILLS AND KNOWLEDGE

Agents and brokers have special knowledge and skills in their areas. For example, retail travel agents know the industry well and know how to access the information they do not possess, often through reference materials and online services. Tour packagers have a more specialized role – they assemble, promote and price bundles of travel services from travel suppliers, then offer these bundles either to travellers themselves or to retail travel agents. Speciality channellers have even more specialized roles. Some work in corporate travel offices to lend their skills to an entire corporation; others are business meeting and convention planners who act almost as tour packagers for whole companies or associations; and some are incentive travel firms that focus on travel recognition programmes in corporations or associations.

WIDE REPRESENTATION

Because agents and brokers are paid by commission rather than by salary, there is little risk or disadvantage to the service principal in extending the service offerings to a wide geography. Thus companies have representatives in many places, far more than if fixed costs such as buildings, equipment and salaries were required.

KNOWLEDGE OF LOCAL MARKETS

Another key benefit of agents and brokers is that they become experts in the local markets they serve. They know or learn the unique needs of different markets, including international markets. They understand what their clients' preferences are and how to adapt the principal's services to match the needs of clients. This benefit is particularly needed and appreciated when clients are dispersed internationally. Knowing the culture and taboos of a country is critical for successful selling. Most companies find that obtaining local representation by experts with this knowledge is necessary.

CUSTOMER CHOICE

Travel and insurance agents provide a retailing service for customers – they represent the services of multiple suppliers. If a traveller needed to visit six or eight different websites or agencies, each of which carried the services of a single supplier, imagine the effort a customer would need to make to plan a trip! Similarly, independent insurance agents have the right to sell a wide variety of insurance, which allows them to offer customers a choice. These types of agents are also able to compare prices across suppliers and get the best prices for their clients. Insurance comparison websites are good examples of this.

CHALLENGES OF DELIVERING SERVICE THROUGH AGENTS AND BROKERS

LOSS OF CONTROL OVER PRICING

As representatives of service principals and experts on customer markets, agents and brokers are typically empowered to negotiate price, configure services and otherwise alter the marketing of a principal's service. This issue could be particularly important – and possibly detrimental – when a service provider depends on a particular (high) price to convey a level of service quality. If the price can be changed, it might drop to a level that undermines the quality image. In addition, the agent often has the flexibility to give different prices to different customers. As long as the customers are geographically dispersed, this variation will not create a problem for the service principal; however, if buyers compare prices and realize they are being given different prices, they may perceive the service principal as unfair or unethical.

REPRESENTATION OF MULTIPLE SERVICE PRINCIPALS

When independent agents represent multiple suppliers, they offer customer choice. From service principal's point of view, however, customer choice means that the agent represents – and in many cases advocates – a competitive service offering. This is the same challenge a manufacturer confronts when distributing products in a retail store. Only in rare cases are its products the only ones in a given category on the retail floor. In a service context, consider the use of independent insurance agents. These agents carry a range of insurance products from different companies, serving as a surrogate service retail store for customers. When they find a customer who needs insurance, they sell from their portfolio the offerings that best match the customer's requirements.

COMMON ISSUES INVOLVING INTERMEDIARIES

Key problems with intermediaries include conflict over objectives and performance, difficulty controlling quality and consistency across outlets, tension between empowerment and control, and channel ambiguity.

CHANNEL CONFLICT OVER OBJECTIVES AND PERFORMANCE

The parties involved in delivering services do not always agree about how the channel should operate. Channel conflict can occur between the service provider and the service intermediary, among intermediaries in a given area, and between different types of channels used by a service provider (such as when a service principal has its own outlets as well as franchised outlets). The conflict most often centres on the parties having different goals, competing roles and rights, and conflicting views of the way the channel is performing. Sometimes the conflict occurs because the service principal and its intermediaries are too dependent on each other.

DIFFICULTY CONTROLLING QUALITY AND CONSISTENCY ACROSS OUTLETS

One of the biggest difficulties for both principals and their intermediaries involves the inconsistency and lack of uniform quality that result when multiple outlets deliver services. When poor performance occurs, even at a single outlet, the service principal suffers because the entire brand and reputation are jeopardized, and other intermediaries endure negative attributions to their outlets. The problem is particularly acute in highly specialized services such as management consulting or architecture, in which execution of the complex offering may be difficult to deliver to the standards of the principal.

TENSION BETWEEN EMPOWERMENT AND CONTROL

McDonald's and other successful service businesses were founded on the principle of performance consistency. Both they and their intermediaries have attained profits and longevity because the company controls virtually every aspect of their intermediaries' businesses. McDonald's, for example, is famous for its demanding and rigid service standards (such as 'turn, never flip, hamburgers on the grill'), carefully specified supplies, and performance monitoring. The strategy makes sense: unless an intermediary delivers service exactly the same way the successful company outlets provide it, the service may not be as desirable to customers. From the principal's point of view, its name and reputation are on the line in each outlet, making careful control a necessity.

Control, however, can have negative ramifications within intermediaries. Many service franchisees, for example, are entrepreneurial by nature and select service franchising because they can own and operate their own businesses. If they are to deliver according to consistent standards, their independent ideas must be integrated into and often subsumed by the practices and policies of the service principal. In these situations they often feel like automatons with less freedom than they have anticipated as owners of their own businesses.

CHANNEL AMBIGUITY

When control is not the chosen strategy, doubt exists about the roles of the company and the intermediary. Who will undertake market research to identify customer requirements, the company or an intermediary? Who owns the results and in what way are they to be used? Who determines the standards for service delivery, the franchisor or the franchisee? Who should train a dealer's customer service representatives, the company or the dealer? In these and other situations, the roles of the principal and its intermediaries are unclear, leading to confusion and conflict.

STRATEGIES FOR EFFECTIVE SERVICE DELIVERY THROUGH INTERMEDIARIES

Service principals, of course, want to manage their service intermediaries to improve service performance, solidify their images and increase profits and revenues. The principal has a variety of choices, which range from strict contractual and measurement control to partnering with intermediaries in a joint effort to improve service to the customer. One of the biggest issues a principal faces is whether to view intermediaries as extensions of its company, as customers or as partners. We discuss three categories of intermediary management strategies: control, empowerment and partnering strategies.

CONTROL STRATEGIES

In the control strategies category, the service principal believes that intermediaries will perform best when it creates standards both for revenues and service performance, measures results and compensates or rewards on the basis of performance level. To use these strategies the principal must be the most powerful participant in the channel, possessing unique services with strong consumer demand or loyalty, or other forms of economic power.

MEASUREMENT

Some franchisors maintain control of the service quality delivered by their franchisees by ongoing measurement programmes that feed data back to the principal. Virtually all car dealers' sales and service performance is monitored regularly by the manufacturer, which creates the measurement programme, administers it and maintains control of the information. The company surveys customers at key points in the service encounter sequence: after sale, 30 days out, 90 days out and after a year. The manufacturer designs the survey instruments (some of them with the assistance of dealer councils) and obtains the customer feedback directly. On the basis of this information, the manufacturer rewards and recognizes both individuals and dealerships that perform well and can potentially punish those that perform poorly. The obvious advantage to this approach is that the manufacturer retains control; however, the trust and goodwill between manufacturers and dealers can easily be eroded if dealers feel that the measurement is used to control and punish.

REVIEW

Some franchisors control through terminations, non-renewals, quotas and restrictive supplier sources. Expansion and encroachment are two of the tactics being used today. Another means by which franchisors exert control over franchisees is through quotas and sales goals, typically by offering price breaks after a certain volume is attained.

EMPOWERMENT STRATEGIES

Empowerment strategies – in which the service principal allows greater flexibility to intermediaries based on the belief that their talents are best revealed in participation rather than acquiescence – are useful when the service principal is new or lacks sufficient power to govern the channel using control strategies. In empowerment strategies, the principal provides information, research or processes to help intermediaries perform well in service.

HELP THE INTERMEDIARY DEVELOP CUSTOMER-ORIENTED SERVICE PROCESSES

Individual intermediaries rarely have the funds to sponsor their own customer research studies or training programmes. One way for a company to improve intermediary performance is to conduct research or standard-setting studies relating to service performance, then provide the results as a service to intermediaries. Service originators can invest in training or other forms of development to improve the skills and knowledge of intermediaries and their employees.

⭐ SERVICE SPOTLIGHT

After the Ford Motor Company conducted customer research and identified six sales standards and six service standards that address the most important customer expectations, it found that dealers and service centres did not know how to apply these standards to implement, measure and improve service. For example, one sales standard specified that customers be approached within the first minute they enter the dealership and be offered help when and if they need it. Although dealers could see that this standard was desirable, they did not immediately know how to make it happen. Ford stepped in and provided the research and process support to help the dealers. As another form of support, the company created national advertising featuring dealers discussing the quality care standards.

PROVIDE NEEDED SUPPORT SYSTEMS

In airlines and hotels as well as other travel and ticketing services, the service principal's reservation system is an important support system. Holiday Inn has a franchise service delivery system that adds value to the Holiday Inn franchise and differentiates it from competitors.

CHANGE TO A COOPERATIVE MANAGEMENT STRUCTURE

Companies such as TGI Fridays[15] use the technique of empowerment to manage and motivate franchisees. They develop worker teams in their outlets to hire, discipline and handle financial tasks such as deposits and audits.

PARTNERING STRATEGIES

The group of strategies with the highest potential for effectiveness involves partnering with intermediaries to learn together about end customers, set specifications, improve delivery and communicate honestly. This approach capitalizes on the skills and strengths of both principal and intermediary, and engenders a sense of trust that improves the relationship.

ALIGNMENT OF GOALS

One of the most successful approaches to partnering involves aligning company and intermediary goals early in the process. Both the service principal and the intermediary have individual goals that they strive to achieve. If channel members can see that they benefit the ultimate consumer of services and in the process optimize their own revenues and profit, they begin the relationship with a target in mind.

CONSULTATION AND COOPERATION

A strategy of consultation and cooperation is not as dramatic as setting joint goals, but it does result in intermediaries participating in decisions. In this approach, which could involve virtually any issue, from compensation to service quality to the service environment, the principal makes a point of consulting intermediaries and asking for their opinions and views before establishing policy. For example, when a franchisor finds that the outlets need greater support in promotion, the company can began to make customer mailings for franchisees. This approach makes the franchisees feel that they have some control over the way they do business and also generates a steady stream of improvement ideas.

SUMMARY

This chapter discussed the benefits and challenges of delivering service through intermediaries. Service intermediaries perform many important functions for the service principal – co-producing the service, making services locally available and functioning as the link between the principal and the customer. The focus in service distribution is on identifying ways to bring the customer and principal or its representatives together.

In contrast to channels for products, channels for services are almost always direct, if not to the customer then to the intermediary that sells to the customer. Many of the primary functions that distribution channels serve – stock-holding, securing and taking title to goods – are irrelevant because of services' intangibility. Because services cannot be owned, most have no titles or rights that can be passed along a delivery channel. Because services are intangible and perishable, stock-holding cannot exist, making warehousing dispensable. In general, because services cannot be produced, warehoused, and then retailed as goods can, many channels available to goods producers are not feasible for service firms.

Four forms of distribution in service were described in the chapter: electronic channels, franchisees, agents/brokers and direct. The benefits and challenges of each type of intermediary were discussed, and examples of firms successful in delivering services through each type were detailed. Discussion centred on strategies that could be used by service principals to improve management of intermediaries.

KEY CONCEPTS

Agents and brokers	289	Franchising	290
Channel ambiguity	295	Location-based services	287
Channel conflict	295	Mobile apps	284
Control, empowerment and partnering		Service deliverer	288
strategies	296	Service principal	288
Electronic channels	283		

EXERCISES

1   On the Internet, locate three services that you believe are interesting. What are the benefits of buying these services on the Internet versus elsewhere?

2   Develop a brief franchising plan for a service concept or idea that you believe could be successful.

3   Visit a franchisee and discuss the pros and cons of the arrangement from his or her perspective. How closely does this list of benefits and challenges fit the one provided in this chapter? What would you add to the list to reflect the experience of the franchisee you interviewed?

4   Select a service industry with which you are familiar. How do service principals in that industry distribute their services? Develop possible approaches to manage intermediaries using the three categories of strategies in the last section of this chapter. Which approach do you believe would be most effective? Why? Which approaches are currently used by service principals in the industry?

DISCUSSION QUESTIONS

1   In what specific ways does the distribution of services differ from the distribution of goods?

2   Identify other service firms that are company owned and see whether the services they provide are more consistent than ones provided by franchisees.

3 Why are franchises so common in the fast-food sector?

4 List five services that could be distributed on the Internet that are not mentioned in this chapter. Why are these particular services appropriate for electronic distribution? Choose two that you particularly advocate. How would you address the challenges to electronic media discussed in this chapter?

5 List services that are sold through selling agents. Why is the use of agents the chosen method of distribution for these services? Could any be distributed in the other ways described in this chapter?

6 Look at the website www.just-eat.com. Why do you think this service has been successful?

7 What are the main differences between agents and brokers?

8 What types of services are bought through purchasing agents? What qualifies a purchasing agent to represent a buyer in these transactions? Why don't buyers themselves engage in the purchase, rather than hiring someone to do so?

9 Which of the reasons for channel conflict described in this chapter is the most problematic? Why? What can be done to address the problem you selected? Base your answer on the strategies discussed at the end of the chapter, selecting then ranking them from most to least effective.

10 Which of the three categories of strategies for effective service delivery through intermediaries do you believe is most successful? Why? Why are the other two categories less successful?

FURTHER READING

Cassab, H. and Maclachlan, D.L. (2009). A consumer-based view of multi-channel service. *Journal of Service Management*, 20(1), 52–75.

Combs, J. G., Ketchen, D. J., Shook, C. L. and Short, J. C. (2011). Antecedents and consequences of franchising: Past accomplishments and future challenges. *Journal of Management*, 37(1), 99–126.

Guillet, B. D., & Law, R. (2013). An examination of the relationship between online travel agents and hotels: a case study of choice hotels international and Expedia. com. *Cornell Hospitality Quarterly*, 54(1), 95–107.

Heinonen, K. (2006). Temporal and spatial e-service value. *International Journal of Service Industry Management*, 17(4), 380–400.

Herington, C. and Weaven, S. (2009). E-retailing by banks: e-service quality and its importance to customer satisfaction. *European Journal of Marketing*, 43(9/10), 1220–31.

Kim, E., Lin, J. S. and Sung, Y. (2013). To app or not to app: Engaging consumers via branded mobile apps. *Journal of Interactive Advertising*, 13(1), 53–65.

Mendelsohn, M. (2004). *The Guide to Franchising*, 7th edn. London: Cengage Learning EMEA.

Rowley, J. (2006). An analysis of the e-service literature: towards a research agenda. *Internet Research*, 16(3), 339–58.

CHAPTER 14

Managing Demand and Capacity

LEARNING OBJECTIVES

This chapter's objectives are to:

1. Explain the underlying issue for capacity-constrained services: lack of inventory capability.
2. Present the implications of time, labour, equipment and facilities constraints combined with variations in demand patterns.
3. Lay out strategies for matching supply and demand through (a) shifting demand to match capacity, or (b) adjusting capacity to meet demand.
4. Demonstrate the benefits and risks of revenue management strategies in forging a balance among capacity utilization, pricing, market segmentation and financial return.
5. Provide strategies for managing waiting lines for times when capacity and demand cannot be aligned.

OPENING EXAMPLE

Hilton Worldwide RMCC – Revenue Management Consolidated Centre

Revenue management is a sophisticated approach to managing supply and demand under varying degrees of constraint. The objective is to maximize the revenue (or contribution) that can be obtained from available capacity at any given point in time. It is, therefore, highly appropriate for services such as airlines, hotels and car rental.

The right revenue management decisions make an immediate and quantifiable impact on an individual hotel's profitability. Yet finding and keeping a revenue manager with

the skills and experience to fit a hotel's profile is both difficult and costly.

To address this challenge, Hilton Worldwide established a Revenue Management Consolidated Centre (RMCC) in 2004, to 'help hotels achieve superior market share and profitability'. The RMCC operates from four locations around the world, providing Hilton Worldwide hotels with world-class revenue management talent, powerful market intelligence, cutting-edge tools and business processes. The centre manages over 45,000 rooms in 195 hotels across 35 countries taking in city centre, convention, airport and resort hotels. Its success is dependant on finding, developing and motivating the best revenue management professionals, and then fitting their experience to the needs and profile of each individual hotel.

The RMCC provides service and cost modes tailored to each hotel, reflecting business complexity, size and market environment. The consolidated approach means Hilton Worldwide maximize cost and scale efficiencies, rapidly sharing best practice, market and trend intelligence to optimize the hotel's market share and deliver market-beating RevPAR (revenue per available room) results. The centre recruits team members from top schools' graduates and experienced professionals, who bring with them a wealth of knowledge from various markets and economies. Before starting on the job, each recruit participates in a dedicated 8-week training programme on the tools and business processes which are the foundation of RMCC's commercial focus.

Source: Darcy VanWyck Senior Director RMCC Europe, Hilton WorldWide 2015.

For Hilton and other hotels, managing demand and utilizing the hotel's fixed capacity of rooms, restaurants and meeting facilities can be a seasonal, weekly and, even, daily challenge. Although the hotel industry epitomizes the challenges of demand and capacity management, many service providers face similar problems. For example, tax advisers and air-conditioning maintenance services face seasonal demand fluctuations, whereas services such as commuter trains and restaurants face weekly and, even, hourly variations in customer demand. For some businesses, demand is predictable, as for a tax adviser. For others, such as management or technology consultants, demand may be less predictable, fluctuating based on customer needs and business cycles. Sometimes firms experience too much demand for the existing capacity and sometimes capacity sits idle.

Overuse or underuse of a service can directly contribute to gap 3: failure to deliver what was designed and specified. For example, when demand for services exceeds maximum capacity, the quality of service may drop because staff and facilities are over-taxed. Also, some customers may be turned away, not receiving the service at all. During periods of slow demand it may be necessary to reduce prices or cut service amenities, changing the make-up of the clientele and the nature of the service, and thus running the risk of not delivering what customers expect. For example, older travellers or business groups who are in a hotel on a weekend may resent the invasion of families and children because it changes the nature of the service they expected. At the pool, for example, collisions can occur between adults trying to swim laps and children playing water games.

In this chapter we focus on the challenges of matching supply and demand in capacity-constrained services. The service performance gap can occur when organizations fail to smooth the peaks and valleys of demand, overuse their capacities, attract an inappropriate customer mix in their efforts to build demand or rely too much on price in smoothing demand. The chapter gives you an understanding of these issues and strategies for addressing them. The effective use of capacity is frequently a key success factor for service organizations.

THE UNDERLYING ISSUE: LACK OF INVENTORY CAPABILITY

The fundamental issue underlying supply and demand management in services is the lack of inventory capability. Unlike manufacturing firms, service firms cannot build up inventories during periods of slow demand to use later when demand increases. This lack of inventory capability is due to the perishability of services and their simultaneous production and consumption. An airline seat that is not sold on a given flight cannot be resold the following day. The productive capacity of that seat has perished. Similarly, an hour of a lawyer's billable time cannot be saved from one day to the next. Services also cannot be transported from one place to another or transferred from person to person. Thus Hilton's hotel services in Mallorca cannot be moved to an alternative location in off-peak months – say, to a skiing area where conditions are ideal for tourists and demand for hotel rooms is high.

The lack of inventory capability combined with fluctuating demand leads to a variety of potential outcomes, as illustrated in Figure 14.1.[1] The horizontal lines in Figure 14.1 indicate service capacity, and the curved line indicates customer demand for the service. In many services, capacity is fixed; thus capacity can be designated by a flat horizontal line over a certain time period. Demand for service frequently fluctuates, however, as indicated by the curved line. The topmost horizontal line in Figure 14.1 represents maximum capacity. For example, it could represent all 160 rooms in a hotel or it could represent the approximately 70,000 seats in a large football stadium. The rooms and the seats remain constant, but demand for them fluctuates. The band between the second and third horizontal lines represents optimum capacity – the best use of the capacity from the perspective of both customers and the company (the difference between optimal and maximum capacity utilization is discussed later in the chapter). The areas in the middle of Figure 14.1 are labelled to represent four basic scenarios that can result from different combinations of capacity and demand:

1   *Excess demand.* The level of demand exceeds maximum capacity. In this situation some customers will be turned away, resulting in lost business opportunities. For the customers who do receive the service, its quality may not match what was promised because of crowding or overtaxing of staff and facilities.

2   *Demand exceeds optimum capacity.* No one is being turned away, but the quality of service may still suffer because of overuse, crowding or staff being pushed beyond their abilities to deliver consistent quality.

3   *Demand and supply are balanced at the level of optimum capacity.* Staff and facilities are occupied at an ideal level. No one is overworked, facilities can be maintained and customers are receiving quality service without undesirable delays.

4 *Excess capacity*. Demand is below optimum capacity. Productive resources in the form of labour, equipment and facilities are underutilized, resulting in lost productivity and lower profits. Customers may receive excellent quality on an individual level because they have the full use of the facilities, no waiting and complete attention from the staff. If, however, service quality depends on the presence of other customers, customers may be disappointed or may worry that they have chosen an inferior service provider.

Not all firms will be challenged equally in terms of managing supply and demand. The seriousness of the problem will depend on the extent of demand fluctuations over time and the extent to which supply is constrained. Some types of organizations will experience wide fluctuations in demand (telecommunications, hospitals, transportation, restaurants), whereas others will have narrower fluctuations (insurance, laundry, banking). For some, peak demand can usually be met even when demand fluctuates (electricity or gas supply), but for others peak demand may frequently exceed capacity (hospital emergency rooms, restaurants, hotels). Those firms that have difficulty in matching supply with fluctuations in demand, will find the issues and strategies in this chapter particularly important to their success.

To identify effective strategies for managing supply and demand fluctuations, an organization needs a clear understanding of the constraints on its capacity and the underlying demand patterns.

CAPACITY CONSTRAINTS

For many firms, service capacity is fixed. Depending on the type of service, critical fixed capacity factors can be time, labour, equipment, facilities or (in many cases) a combination of these.

TIME, LABOUR, EQUIPMENT, FACILITIES

For some service businesses, the primary constraint on service production is *time*. For example, a lawyer, a consultant, a hairdresser, a plumber and a personal counsellor all primarily sell their time. In such contexts, if the service worker is not available or if his or her time is not used productively, profits are lost. If there is excess demand, time cannot be created to satisfy it. From the point of view of the individual service provider, time is the constraint.

From the point of view of a firm that employs a large number of service providers, *labour* or staffing levels can be the primary capacity constraint. A law firm, a university department, a consulting firm, a tax accounting firm and a repair and maintenance contractor may all face the reality that at certain times demand for their organizations' services cannot be met because staff are already operating at peak capacity. However, it does not always make sense (nor may it be possible in a competitive labour market) to hire additional service providers if low demand is a reality a large percentage of the time.

In other cases, *equipment* may be the critical constraint. For road transport or airfreight delivery services, the lorries or aeroplanes needed to service demand may be the capacity limitation. During the Christmas holidays, DHL, TNT and other delivery service providers face this issue. Health clubs also deal with this limitation, particularly at certain times of the day (before work, during lunch hours, after work) and in certain months of the year. For network service providers, bandwidth, servers and switches represent their perishable capacity.

Finally, many firms face restrictions brought about by their limited *facilities*. Hotels have only a finite number of rooms to sell, airlines are limited by the number of seats on the aircraft, universities are constrained by the number of rooms and the number of seats in each lecture theatre, and restaurant capacity is restricted to the number of tables and seats available.

⭐ **SERVICE SPOTLIGHT**

Yodel, the UK's biggest delivery company after Royal Mail, handles 155 million packages every year. In the lead-up to Christmas 2014, the delivery company admitted that it would stop collecting parcels from retailers as it was unable to deliver them to customers in time for Christmas. Yodel, which works for 85 per cent of the UK's retailers, including Amazon, Argos, Boots and Tesco Direct, and delivers to every postcode in the country, blamed poor forecasting by retailers for its difficulties. Special Black Friday, Cyber Monday and other retail promotions resulted in unexpectedly high parcel volumes across the carrier industry. Yodel had been expecting to handle 15 per cent more parcels than during the Christmas 2013 season but, despite investing in another 13 handling sites, sourcing an extra 200 vehicles to ship goods from client warehouses to its own sorting centres and extending working hours, it was unable to meet the increased demand.[2]

Understanding the primary capacity constraint, or the combination of factors that restricts capacity, is a first step in designing strategies to deal with supply and demand issues.

OPTIMAL VERSUS MAXIMUM USE OF CAPACITY

To fully understand capacity issues, it is important to know the difference between optimum and maximum use of capacity. As suggested in Figure 14.1, optimum and maximum capacity may not be the same. Using capacity at an optimum level means that resources are fully employed but not overused and that customers are receiving quality service in a timely manner. Maximum capacity, on the other hand, represents the absolute limit of service availability. In the case of a football game, optimum and maximum capacity may be the same. The entertainment value of the game is enhanced for customers when every seat is filled, and obviously the profitability for the team is greatest under these circumstances. On the other hand, in a university classroom it is usually not desirable for students or teaching staff to have every seat filled. In this case, optimal use of capacity is less than the maximum. In some cases, maximum use of capacity may result in excessive waiting by customers, as in a popular restaurant. From the perspective of customer satisfaction, optimum use of the restaurant's capacity will again be less than maximum use.

Figure 14.1   **Variations in demand relative to capacity**

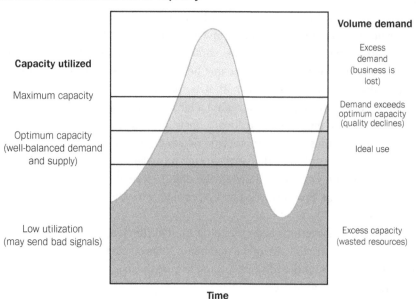

Adapted from source: Lovelock, Wintz, Jochen, *Services Marketing*, 7th edition, © 2011, ch. 9, p.230 and Palmer, *Services Marketing*, 7th edition, © 2014, ch.12, p.392. Reprinted by permission of The McGraw-Hill Companies.

Table 14.1   Constraints on capacity

Nature of the constraint	Type of service*
Time	Legal
	Consulting
	Accounting
	Medical
Labour	Law firm
	Accounting firm
	Consulting firm
	Health clinic
Equipment	Delivery services
	Telecommunications
	Network services
	Utilities
	Health club
Facilities	Hotels
	Restaurants
	Hospitals
	Airlines
	Schools
	Theatres
	Churches

* The examples illustrate the most common capacity constraint for each type of service. In reality, any of the service organizations listed can be operating under multiple constraints. For example, a law firm may be operating under constrained labour capacity (too few lawyers) and facilities constraints (not enough office space) at the same time.

In the case of equipment or facilities constraints, the maximum capacity at any given time is obvious. There are only a certain number of weight machines in the health club, a certain number of seats in the aeroplane and a limited amount of space in a cargo carrier. In the case of a bottling plant, when maximum capacity on the assembly line is exceeded, bottles begin to break and the system shuts down. Thus it is relatively easy to observe the effects of exceeding maximum equipment capacity.

When the limitation is people's time or labour, maximum capacity is harder to specify because people are in a sense more flexible than facilities and equipment. When an individual service provider's maximum capacity has been exceeded, the result is likely to cause decreased service quality, customer dissatisfaction, and employee burnout and turnover, but these outcomes may not be immediately observable even to the employee him or herself. It is often easy for a consulting firm to take on one more assignment, taxing its employees beyond their maximum capacity, or for a dental clinic to schedule a few more appointments in a day, stretching its staff and dentists beyond their maximum capacity. Given the potential costs in terms of reduced quality and customer and employee dissatisfaction, it is critical for the firm to understand optimum and maximum human capacity limits.

DEMAND PATTERNS

To manage fluctuating demand in a service business, it is necessary to have a clear understanding of demand patterns, why they vary, and the market segments that comprise demand at different points in time.[3] A number of questions need to be answered regarding the predictability and underlying causes of demand.

THE RECORDING OF DEMAND PATTERNS

To begin to understand demand patterns, the organization needs to record the level of demand over relevant time periods. Organizations that have good computerized customer information systems can record this information very accurately. Others may need to record demand patterns more informally. Daily, weekly and monthly demand levels should be followed, and if seasonality is a suspected problem, graphs should be drawn for data from at least the past year. In some services, such as restaurants or health care, hourly fluctuations within a day may also be relevant. Sometimes demand patterns are intuitively obvious; in other cases patterns may not reveal themselves until the data are collected.

PREDICTABLE CYCLES

In looking at the graphic representation of demand levels, predictable cycles may be detected, including daily (variations occur by hours), weekly (variations occur by day), monthly (variations occur by day or week) and/or yearly (variations occur according to months or seasons). In some cases, predictable patterns may occur at all periods. For example, in the restaurant industry, especially in seasonal tourist locations, demand can vary predictably by month, by week, by day and by hour.

If a predictable cycle is detected, what are its underlying causes? Tax advisers can predict demand based on when taxes are due. Services catering to children and families respond to variations in school hours and vacations. Retail and telecommunications services have peak periods at certain holidays and times of the week and day. When predictable patterns exist, generally one or more causes can be identified.

RANDOM DEMAND FLUCTUATIONS

Sometimes the patterns of demand appear to be random – there is no apparent predictable cycle. Yet even in this case, causes can often be identified. For example, day-to-day changes in the weather may affect use of recreational, shopping or entertainment facilities. Good weather can increase the use of outdoor activities such as amusement parks and bicycle rental but it has the opposite effect on cinemas and art galleries. Although the weather cannot be predicted far in advance, it may be possible to anticipate demand a day or two ahead. Health-related events also cannot be predicted. Accidents, heart attacks and births all increase demand for hospital services, but the level of demand cannot generally be determined in advance. Natural disasters such as floods, fires and storms can dramatically increase the need for such services as insurance, telecommunications, builders and health care.

DEMAND PATTERNS BY MARKET SEGMENT

An organization that has detailed records on customer transactions may be able to disaggregate demand by market segment, revealing patterns within patterns. Or the analysis may reveal that demand from one segment is predictable, whereas demand from another segment is relatively random. For example, for a bank, the visits from its business customers may occur daily at a predictable time, whereas personal account holders may visit the bank at seemingly random intervals. Health clinics often notice that walk-in or 'same-day requests to see a doctor' patients tend to concentrate their arrivals on Monday, with fewer needing immediate attention on other days of the week. Knowing that this pattern exists, some clinics schedule more future appointments (which they can control) for later days of the week, leaving more of Monday available for same-day appointments and walk-ins.

STRATEGIES FOR MATCHING CAPACITY AND DEMAND

When an organization has a clear grasp of its capacity constraints and an understanding of demand patterns, it is in a good position to develop strategies for matching capacity and demand. There are two general approaches for accomplishing this match. The first is to smooth the demand fluctuations themselves by shifting demand to match existing supply. This approach implies that the peaks and valleys of the demand curve (Figure 14.1) will be flattened to match as closely as possible the horizontal optimum capacity line. The second general strategy is to adjust capacity to match fluctuations in demand. This implies moving the horizontal capacity lines shown in Figure 14.1 to match the ups and downs of the demand curve. Each of these two basic strategies is described next with specific examples.

SHIFTING DEMAND TO MATCH CAPACITY

With this strategy an organization seeks to shift customers away from periods in which demand exceeds capacity, perhaps by convincing them to use the service during periods of slow demand. This change may be possible for some customers but not for others. For example, many business travellers are not able to shift their needs for airline, car rental and hotel services; leisure travellers, on the other hand, can often shift the timing of their trips. Customers who cannot shift and cannot be accommodated will represent lost business for the firm.

During periods of slow demand, the organization seeks to attract more and/or different customers to utilize its productive capacity. A variety of approaches, detailed in the following sections, can be used to shift or increase demand to match capacity. Frequently, a firm uses a combination of approaches. Ideas for how to shift demand during both slow and peak periods are shown in Figure 14.2.

REDUCE DEMAND DURING PEAK TIMES

One strategic approach to matching capacity and demand for a service provider focuses on reducing demand during times when customer demand is at its peak for the service.

COMMUNICATE WITH CUSTOMERS

Another approach for shifting demand is to communicate with customers, letting them know the times of peak demand so they can choose to use the service at alternative times and avoid crowding or delays. For example, signs in banks and post offices that let customers know their busiest hours and busiest days of the week

Figure 14.2 Strategies for shifting demand to match capacity

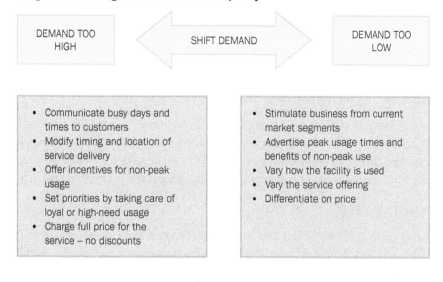

can serve as a warning, allowing customers to shift their demand to another time if possible. Forewarning customers about busy times and possible waits can have added benefits. Many customer service telephone lines provide a similar warning by informing waiting customers of approximately how long it will be until they are served. Those who do not want to wait may choose to call back later when the queues are less busy or to visit the company's website for faster service.

MODIFY TIMING AND LOCATION OF SERVICE DELIVERY

Some firms adjust their hours and days of service delivery to more directly reflect customer demand. Historically, UK banks were open only during 'bankers' hours' from 10 a.m. to 3 p.m. every weekday. Obviously these hours did not match the times when most people preferred to do their personal banking. Now UK banks open earlier, stay open until 5 p.m. many days, and are open on Saturdays, better reflecting customer demand patterns. Online banking has also shifted demand from branches to 'anytime, anywhere' websites. Theatres accommodate customer schedules by offering matinees on weekends and holidays when people are free during the day for entertainment. Cinemas are sometimes rented during weekdays by business groups – an example of varying the service offering during a period of low demand.

OFFER INCENTIVES FOR NON-PEAK USAGE

In an attempt to shift demand away from peak times, some firms will offer incentives to encourage customers to shift their use of the service to other times. Fitness centres often offer different membership rates to customers who limit their usage to off-peak times.

SET PRIORITIES

When demand for the service is high and there is limited capacity, service providers can prioritise who is served by taking care of loyal or high-need customers first. Theatres often offer tickets to their regular patrons in their theatre club before tickets are offered through the box-office to other customers.

CHARGE FULL PRICE

Organizations generally charge full price for service during those periods of time when they know their services are historically in high demand; no discounts are allowed during such times. One of the busiest periods of the year for airlines are those days just before and just after the Christmas period; for this reason, most airlines give priority for seating to those paying full fares and prohibit the redeeming of frequent flyer miles for bookings. Because demand is so high, customers looking for discounted or free tickets find that the days around this holiday have been 'blacked out' and they must purchase tickets at regular fares if they wish to travel.

INCREASE DEMAND TO MATCH CAPACITY

Other approaches that service providers may consider in matching capacity and demand focus on increasing demand for service during times when the service is at less than full capacity.

STIMULATE BUSINESS FROM CURRENT MARKET SEGMENTS

Advertising and other forms of promotion can emphasize different service benefits to customers during peak and slow periods. Advertising and sales messages can remind customers about times when demand is low. For example, car tyre replacement centres such as Kwik Fit increase their service advertising during periods when demand is slow by sending out reminders and offering discounts for replacing more than one tyre.

VARY HOW THE FACILITY IS USED

One approach is to change how the service facility is used, depending on the season of the year, day of the week, or time of day. Novotel, the hotel chain, has bedrooms, restaurants and meeting facilities all available to guests 365 days and nights of the year. Yet natural demand for them varies tremendously. Because Novotel hotels cater to business travellers and business meetings, demand has a weekly cycle in addition to any seasonal fluctuations. Business travellers do not stay over weekends. Thus, demand for rooms from the hotel's primary market segment drops on Friday and Saturday nights.

To smooth the peaks and valleys of demand for its facilities, Novotel has employed a number of strategies. Group business (primarily business conferences) is pursued throughout the year to fill the lower-demand periods. A variety of special events, weddings and getaway packages are offered year round to increase weekend demand for rooms. Most city centre hotels have tried to cater to families and children on the weekends. For many working parents, weekend getaways are a primary form of relaxation and vacation. The city centre hotels cater to these couples and families by offering discounted room rates, child-oriented activities and amenities, and an environment in which families feel comfortable. At weekends, children stay free. On arrival, each child receives a gift featuring 'Dolfi', the hotel's dolphin mascot. The hotels also do special weekend promotions with local theme parks and visitor attractions.

VARY THE SERVICE OFFERING

A similar approach entails changing the nature of the service offering. For example, a ski resort that offers facilities and accommodation for skiers in the winter offer may adapt their services to attract executive development and training programmes during the summer when snow skiing is not possible. Airlines even change the configuration of their plane seating to match the demand from different market segments. Some planes may have no first-class section. On routes with a large demand for first-class seating, a significant proportion of seats may be placed in first class. The Pizza Express restaurant chain which is primarily a sit-in restaurant offers take away services in certain branches as a way to increase demand for its service.

In these examples, the service offering and associated benefits are changed to smooth customer demand for the organization's resources. Care should be exercised in implementing strategies to change the service offering, because such changes may easily imply and require alterations in other marketing mix variables – such as promotion, pricing and staffing – to match the new offering. Unless these additional mix variables are altered effectively to support the offering, the strategy may not work. Even when done well, the downside of such changes can result in confusion in the organization's image from the customers' perspective, or a loss of strategic focus for the organization and its employees.

DIFFERENTIATE ON PRICE

A common response during slow demand is to discount the price of the service. This strategy relies on basic economics of supply and demand. To be effective, however, a price differentiation strategy depends on solid understanding of customer price sensitivity and demand curves. For example, business travellers are far less price sensitive than are families travelling for pleasure. For Novotel hotels, lowering prices during the slow summer months is not likely to increase dramatically bookings from business travellers. However, lower summer prices attract considerable numbers of families and local guests who want an opportunity to experience a good quality hotel but are not able to afford the rooms during peak season.

The maximum capacity of any hotel, airline, restaurant or other service establishment could be reached if the price were low enough. But the goal is always to ensure the highest level of capacity utilization without sacrificing profits (see Hilton example at the start of this chapter). We explore this complex relationship among price, market segments, capacity utilization and profitability later in the chapter in the section on revenue management.

Heavy use of price differentiation to smooth demand can be a risky strategy. Overreliance on price can result in price wars in an industry in which eventually all competitors suffer. Price wars are well known in the airline industry, and total industry profits often suffer as a result of airlines simultaneously trying to attract customers through price discounting. Another risk of relying on price is that customers grow accustomed to the lower price and expect to get the same deal the next time they use the service. If communications with customers are unclear, customers may not understand the reasons for the discounts and will expect to pay the same during peak demand periods. Overuse or exclusive use of price as a strategy for smoothing demand is also risky because of the potential impact on the organization's image, the potential for attracting undesired market segments, and the possibility that higher-paying customers will feel they have been treated unfairly.

ADJUSTING CAPACITY TO MEET DEMAND

A second strategic approach to matching supply and demand focuses on adjusting capacity. The fundamental idea here is to adjust, stretch and align capacity to match customer demand (rather than working on shifting demand to match capacity, as just described). During periods of peak demand the organization seeks to stretch or expand its capacity as much as possible. During periods of slow demand it tries to shrink capacity so as not to waste resources. General strategies for adjusting the four primary service resources (time, people, equipment and facilities) are discussed throughout the rest of this section. In Figure 14.3, we summarize specific ideas for adjusting capacity during periods of peak and slow demand. Often, a number of different strategies are used simultaneously.

STRETCH EXISTING CAPACITY

The existing capacity can often be expanded temporarily to match demand. In such cases no new resources are added; rather the people, facilities and equipment are asked to work harder and longer to meet demand:

- *Stretch time temporarily.* It may be possible to extend the hours of service temporarily to accommodate demand. A health clinic might stay open longer during flu epidemics, retailers are open longer hours during the Christmas shopping season, and accountants have extended appointment hours (evenings and Saturdays) before tax deadlines.
- *Stretch labour temporarily.* In many service organizations, employees are asked to work longer and harder during periods of peak demand. For example, consulting organizations face extensive peaks and troughs with respect to demand for their services. During peak demand, associates are asked to take on additional projects and work longer hours, and front-line service personnel in banks, tourist attractions, restaurants and telecommunications companies are asked to serve more customers per hour during busy times than during 'normal' hours or days.

Figure 14.3   Strategies for adjusting capacity to match demand

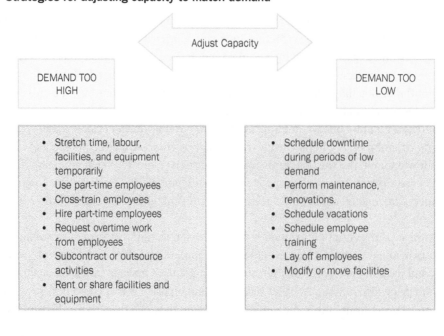

- *Stretch facilities temporarily.* Theatres, restaurants, meeting facilities and classrooms can sometimes be expanded temporarily by the addition of tables, chairs or other equipment needed by customers. Or, as in the case of a commuter train, a carriage that holds a fixed number of people seated comfortably can 'expand' by accommodating standing passengers.
- *Stretch equipment temporarily.* Computers, power lines and maintenance equipment can often be stretched beyond what would be considered the maximum capacity for short periods to accommodate peak demand.

In using these types of 'stretch' strategies, the organization needs to recognize the wear and tear on resources and the potential for inferior quality of service that may go with the use. These strategies should thus be used for relatively short periods in order to allow for later maintenance of the facilities and equipment, and refreshment of the people who are asked to exceed their usual capacity. Sometimes it is difficult to know in advance, particularly in the case of human resources, when capacity has been stretched too far.

SERVICE SPOTLIGHT

Swedish Railways, along with railways in countries such as Finland, France, Germany, the Netherlands, and Spain have expanded their capacity by using bi-level trains. Such trains with double-decker carriages, can resolve capacity problems on a rail line via rolling stock improvements, rather than via the other options of longer trains (requiring longer platforms at stations), more trains per hour (which signalling systems may not allow) or adding extra tracks besides the existing line (which is very expensive). The double-decker design solution usually involves lowering the bottom floor to below the top level of the wheels, closer to the rails, and then adding an upper floor. Such a design fits under bridges and through tunnels whilst carrying more passengers on the same length of track.

ALIGN CAPACITY WITH DEMAND FLUCTUATIONS

This basic strategy is sometimes known as a 'chase demand' strategy. By adjusting service resources creatively, organizations can in effect chase the demand curves to match capacity with customer demand patterns. Time, labour, facilities and equipment are again the focus, this time with an eye towards adjusting the basic mix and use of these resources. Specific actions might include the following:[4]

- *Use part-time employees.* In this situation the organization's labour resource is being aligned with demand. Retailers hire part-time employees during the holiday rush, tax accountants engage temporary help during the tax return season, tourist resorts bring in extra workers during peak season. Restaurants often ask employees to work split shifts (work the lunch shift, leave for a few hours, and come back for the dinner rush) during peak mealtime hours.
- *Outsource.* Firms that find they have a temporary peak in demand for a service that they cannot perform themselves may choose to outsource the entire service. For example, in recent years, many firms have found they do not have the capacity to fulfil their own needs for technology support, Web design and software-related services. Rather than try to hire and train additional employees, these companies look to firms that specialize in outsourcing these types of functions as a temporary (or sometimes long-term) solution.
- *Rent or share facilities or equipment.* For some organizations it is best to rent additional equipment or facilities during periods of peak demand. For example, express mail delivery services such as DHL rent or lease trucks during the peak holiday delivery season. It would not make sense to buy trucks that would sit idle during the rest of the year. Sometimes organizations with complementary demand patterns can share facilities. An example is a church that shares its facilities with a pre-school during the week. The school needs the facilities Monday to Friday during the day; the church needs the facilities evenings and

at the weekend. There are whole businesses that have been created to satisfy other businesses' fluctuating demand. For example, a firm may offer temporary office suites and clerical support to individuals who do not need such facilities and support on a continuous basis.

- *Schedule downtime during periods of low demand.* If people, equipment and facilities are being used at maximum capacity during peak periods, then it is imperative to schedule repair, maintenance and renovations during off-peak periods. This schedule ensures that the resources are in top condition when they are most needed. Vacations and training are also scheduled during slow demand periods.

- *Cross-train employees.* If employees are cross-trained, they can shift among tasks, filling in where they are most needed. Cross-training increases the efficiency of the whole system and avoids underutilizing employees in some areas while others are being overworked. Many airlines, such as easyJet, cross-train their employees to move from ticketing to working on boarding gates to assisting with baggage if needed. In some fast-food restaurants employees specialize in one task (like making French fries) during busy hours, and the team of specialists may number ten people. During slow hours the team may shrink to three, with each person performing a variety of functions. Grocery stores also use this strategy, with most employees able to move as needed from operating checkouts to stocking shelves to bagging groceries.

- *Modify or move facilities and equipment.* Sometimes it is possible to adjust, move or creatively modify existing capacity to meet demand fluctuations. Hotels utilize this strategy by reconfiguring rooms – two rooms with a locking door in-between can be rented to two different parties in high demand times or turned into a suite during slow demand. The airline industry offers dramatic examples of this strategy. Using an approach known as 'demand-driven dispatch', airlines have begun to experiment with methods that assign aeroplanes to flight schedules on the basis of fluctuating market needs.[5] The method depends on accurate knowledge of demand and the ability to quickly move aeroplanes with different seating capacities to flights that match their capacity. The Boeing 777 aircraft is so flexible that it can be reconfigured within hours to vary the number of seats allocated to one, two or three classes.[6] The aircraft can thus be quickly modified to match demand from different market segments, essentially moulding capacity to fit demand. Another strategy may involve moving the service to a new location to meet customer demand or even bringing the service to customers. Mobile training facilities, libraries and blood donation facilities are examples of services that physically follow customers.

★ SERVICE SPOTLIGHT

Jet2.com, a no frills passenger airline specializing in chartered flights, uses Boeing 737-300 QC aircraft. This model is equipped with a 'Quick Change' (QC) system designed to alter the aircraft from a 148-passenger carrier to a 16-tonne payload freighter in 30 minutes. As a result, Jet2 can continue flying for a different purpose in the evenings. After holidaymakers have been flown back to Edinburgh Airport, a large cargo door, just to the left of the standard passenger door, opens up and the seats are slid out of the fuselage. The aircraft, now transformed into a freighter, is then loaded with Royal Mail containers of letters and packages. These are then transported overnight to and from London Stansted Airport before the plane is reconfigured for passengers and takes off from Edinburgh with another group of holidaymakers in the morning.

COMBINING DEMAND AND CAPACITY STRATEGIES

Many firms use multiple strategies, combining marketing-driven demand management approaches with operations-driven capacity management strategies. Figuring out which is the best set of strategies for maximizing capacity utilization, customer satisfaction and profitability can be challenging, particularly when the service offering is a constellation of offerings within one service setting – for example, theme parks with rides, restaurants, shopping; hotel vacation villages with hotels, shopping, spas, pools, restaurants; or ski resorts with ski slopes, spas, restaurants and entertainment. Firms face complex problems in trying to balance demand across all the different offerings with an eye to quality and profitability.

REVENUE MANAGEMENT

Revenue management (also referred to as *yield management*) is a term that has become attached to a variety of methods, some very sophisticated, matching demand and supply in capacity-constrained services. Using revenue management models, organizations find the best balance at a particular point in time among the prices charged, the segments sold to and the capacity used. The goal of revenue management is to produce the best possible financial return from a limited available capacity. Specifically, revenue management has been defined as 'the process of allocating the right type of capacity to the right kind of customer at the right time at the right price so as to maximize revenue or yield'.[7]

It involves a range of activities including pricing, segmentation, capacity allocation and demand modelling.

Although the implementation of revenue management can involve complex mathematical models and computer programs, the underlying effectiveness measure is the ratio of actual revenue to potential revenue for a particular measurement period:

$$\text{Yield} = \frac{\text{Actual revenue}}{\text{Potential revenue}}$$

where:

$$\text{Actual revenue} = \text{Actual capacity used} \times \text{Average actual price}$$
$$\text{Potential revenue} = \text{Total capacity} \times \text{Maximum price}$$

The equations indicate that yield is a function of price and capacity used. Recall that capacity constraints can be in the form of time, labour, equipment or facilities. Yield is essentially a measure of the extent to which an organization's resources (or capacities) are achieving their full revenue-generating potential. Assuming that total capacity and maximum price cannot be changed, yield approaches as actual capacity utilization increases or when a higher actual price can be charged for a given capacity used. For example, in an airline context, a manager could focus on increasing revenue by finding ways to bring in more passengers to fill the capacity, or by finding higher-paying passengers to fill a more limited capacity. In reality, expert revenue managers work on capacity and pricing issues simultaneously to maximize revenue across different customer segments. The following shows simple yield calculations and the inherent trade-offs for two types of services: hotel and legal.

EXAMPLE

Simple Yield Calculations: Examples from Hotel and Legal Services

You can do basic yield calculations for any capacity-constrained service assuming you know the actual capacity, average price charged for different market segments, and maximum price that could be charged. Ideally, yield will approach the number 1, or 100 per cent, where:

Yield = Actual revenue/Potential revenue

We describe yield calculations for two simple examples – a 200-room hotel and a lawyer with a 40-hour work week – under different assumed pricing and usage situations. Although companies use much more complex mathematical models to determine yield, the underlying ideas are the same. The goal is to maximize the revenue-generating capability of the organization's capacity.

200-room hotel with maximum room rate of €100 per room per night

$$\text{Potential revenue} = 100 \text{ euros} \times 200 \text{ rooms} = 20{,}000 \text{ euros per night}$$

1 Assume: the hotel rents all its rooms at a discounted rate of 50 euros per night.

$$\text{Yield} = 50 \text{ euros} \times 200 \text{ rooms}/20{,}000 \text{ euros} = 50\%$$

At this rate, the hotel is maximizing capacity utilization, but not getting a very good price.

2 Assume: the hotel charges its full rate, but can only rent 40 per cent of its rooms at that price, due to price sensitivity.

$$\text{Yield} = 100 \text{ euros} \times 80 \text{ rooms}/20{,}000 \text{ euros} = 40\%$$

In this situation the hotel has maximized the per-room price, but the yield is even lower than in the first situation because so few rooms were rented at that relatively high rate.

3 Assume: the hotel charges its full rate of 100 euros for 40 per cent of its rooms and then gives a discount of 50 euros for the remaining 120 rooms.

$$\text{Yield} = [(100 \text{ euros} \times 80) + (50 \text{ euros} \times 120)]$$
$$20{,}000 \text{ euros} = 14{,}000 \text{ euros}/20{,}000 \text{ euros} = 70\%$$

Clearly, the final alternative, which takes into account price sensitivity and charges different prices for different rooms or market segments, will result in the highest yield.

40 hours of a lawyer's time across a typical work week at €200 per hour maximum (private client rate)

$$\text{Potential revenue} = 40 \text{ hours} \times 200 \text{ euros per hour} = 8{,}000 \text{ euros per week}$$

1 Assume: the lawyer is able to bill out 30 per cent of her billable time at 200 euros per hour.

$$\text{Yield} = 200 \text{ euros} \times 12 \text{ hours}/8{,}000 \text{ euros} = 30\%$$

In this case the lawyer has maximized her hourly rate, but has only enough work to occupy 12 billable hours.

2 Assume: the lawyer decides to charge 100 euros for non-profit or government clients and is able to bill out all 40 hours at this rate for these types of clients.

$$\text{Yield} = 100 \text{ euros} \times 40 \text{ hours}/8{,}000 \text{ euros} = 50\%$$

In this case, although she has worked a full week, yield is still not very good given the relatively low rate per hour.

3 Assume: the lawyer uses a combined strategy in which she works 12 hours for private clients and fills the rest of her time with non-profit clients at 100 euros per hour.

$$\text{Yield} = [(200 \text{ euros} \times 12) + (100 \text{ euros} \times 28)]/8{,}000 \text{ euros}$$
$$= 5{,}200 \text{ euros}/8{,}000 \text{ euros} = 65\%$$

Again, catering to two different market segments with different price sensitivities is the best overall strategy in terms of maximizing revenue-generating capacity of the lawyer's time.

IMPLEMENTING A REVENUE MANAGEMENT SYSTEM

To implement a revenue management system, an organization needs detailed data on past demand patterns by market segment as well as methods of projecting current market demand. The data can be combined through mathematical programming models, threshold analysis or use of expert systems to project the best allocation of limited capacity at a particular point in time.[8] Allocations of capacity for specific market segments can then be communicated to sales representatives or reservations staff as targets for selling rooms, seats, time or other limited resources. Sometimes the allocations, once determined, remain fixed. At other times allocations change weekly, or even daily or hourly, in response to new information.

☆ SERVICE SPOTLIGHT

AIR BERLIN

Air Berlin, Germany's second largest airline, provides relatively low-cost services from more than 20 German airports to popular European holiday destinations as well as to major cities in Europe. The airline uses revenue management in an effort to maximize passenger revenue. Its revenue management process begins six to nine months prior to a flight's scheduled departure date. Air Berlin often sells initial blocks of seats at what it terms 'headline prices' to price-sensitive customers and to tour operators; any seats not initially sold are then managed through Air Berlin's revenue management technology. Its revenue management system requires massive amounts of data that take into account the season when the flight takes place, general popularity of the route, local holiday schedules and upcoming events, and the exact time of departure. Similar to other airlines, Air Berlin adjusts its fares frequently, sometimes several times daily as the flights' departure date nears, to reflect customer demand and the time remaining until the departure date. However, because Air Berlin's focus is on relatively short routes, it offers only a single class of service on all of its flights, and each flight is available on a one-way ticket basis. This practice means that each flight is subject to its own price management, enabling Air Berlin to charge passengers different fares on outbound and return flights. By developing profiles for each flight, Air Berlin's revenue management technology helps it to maximize passenger revenue by flight and by regions while maintaining high passenger loads.[9]

MARRIOTT HOTELS

The hotel industry has also embraced the concept of revenue management, and Marriott Hotels has been a leader. The systems at Marriott, for example, maximize profits for a hotel across full weeks rather than by day. In the hotels that target business travellers, Marriott has peak days during the middle of the week. Rather than simply sell the hotel out on those nights on a first-come, first-served basis with no discounts, the revenue management system (which is reviewed and revised daily) now projects guest demand both by price and length of stay, providing discounts in some cases to guests who will stay longer, even on a peak demand night. One early test of the system was at the Munich Marriott during Oktoberfest. Typically no discounts would be offered during this peak period. However, the revenue management system recommended that the hotel offer some rooms at a discount, but only for those guests who stayed an extended period before or after the peak days. Although the average daily rate was down 11.7 per cent for the period, occupancy was up over 20 per cent, and overall revenues were up 12.3 per cent. Using revenue management practices, Marriott Hotels estimates an additional 300 million euros per year in revenue.[10]

Research indicates that traditional revenue management approaches are most profitable when

1 They have relatively fixed capacity
2 They have perishable inventory

3 They have different market segments or customers, who arrive or make their reservations at different times

4 They have low marginal sales costs and high marginal capacity change costs

5 The product is sold in advance

6 There is fluctuating demand.

7 Customers who arrive or reserve early are more price sensitive than those who arrive or reserve late.[11]

When these conditions are present, revenue management approaches can generally be employed to identify the best mix of service offerings to produce and sell in the period, and at what prices, to generate the highest expected revenue. These criteria exactly fit the situation for airlines, car rental agencies and many hotels – industries that have effectively and extensively used revenue management techniques to allocate capacity. In other services (entertainment, sports, fashion), those customers willing to pay the higher prices are the ones who buy early rather than late. People who really want to see a particular performance reserve their seats at the earliest possible moment. Discounting for early purchases would reduce profits. In these situations, the price generally starts out high and is reduced later to fill capacity if needed.

Interestingly, some airlines now use both these strategies effectively. They start with discounted seats for customers who are willing to buy early, usually leisure and discretionary travellers. They charge a higher fare for those who want a seat at the last minute, typically the less price-sensitive business travellers whose destinations and schedules are inflexible. However, in some cases a bargain fare can be found at the last minute as well, commonly via Internet sales, to fill seats that would otherwise go unoccupied. Online auctions and services offered by companies like Internet-based Lastminute.com serve a purpose in filling capacity at the last minute, often charging much lower fares.

CHALLENGES AND RISKS IN USING REVENUE MANAGEMENT

Revenue management programmes can significantly improve revenues. However, although revenue management may appear to be an ideal solution to the problem of matching supply and demand, it is not without risks. By becoming focused on maximizing financial returns through differential capacity allocation and pricing, an organization may encounter these problems:[12]

- *Loss of competitive focus.* Revenue management may cause a firm to over-focus on profit maximization and inadvertently neglect aspects of the service that provide long-term competitive success.
- *Customer alienation.* If customers learn that they are paying a higher price for service than someone else, they may perceive the pricing as unfair, particularly if they do not understand the reasons. However, a study done in the restaurant industry found that when customers were informed of different prices being charged by time of day, week or table location, they generally felt the practice was fair, particularly if the price difference was framed as a discount for less desirable times rather than a premium for peak times or table locations.[13] Customer education is thus essential in an effective revenue management programme.
- *Overbooking.* Customers can be further alienated if they fall victim (and are not compensated adequately) to overbooking practices often necessary to make revenue management systems work effectively. Research suggests that customers who experience negative consequences of revenue management (i.e. denied service or downgrades), particularly high-value customers, subsequently reduce their number of transactions with the firm.[14]
- *Employee morale problems.* Revenue management systems take much guesswork and judgement in setting prices away from sales and reservations people. Although some employees may appreciate the guidance, others may resent the rules and restrictions on their own discretion.
- *Incompatible incentive and reward systems.* Employees may resent revenue management systems that do not match incentive structures. For example, many managers are rewarded on the basis of either capacity utilization or average rate charged, whereas revenue management balances the two factors.

- *Lack of employee training.* Extensive training is required to make a revenue management system work. Employees need to understand its purpose, how it works, how they should make decisions, and how the system will affect their jobs.
- *Inappropriate organization of the revenue management function.* To be most effective with revenue management, an organization must have centralized reservations. Although airlines and some large hotel chains and shipping companies do have such centralization, smaller organizations may have decentralized reservations systems and thus find it difficult to operate a revenue management system effectively.

MEASURING THE EFFECTIVENESS OF REVENUE MANAGEMENT ACTIVITIES

Within each service sector, measures will be used to ascertain how well capacity has been utilized and revenue has been maximized. In the hotel industry the main measures that are used include:

Occupancy rate – the percentage share of all rooms that are occupied for a given time. To allow for rooms being renovated or used for accommodating staff, the figure is usually calculated using the total number of rooms available to guests rather than all rooms in the hotel. Some hotels also produce a percentage of beds occupied which may be different from room occupancy figures as rooms may be configured differently with one, two, three or even more beds.

Average Daily Rate (ADR) – also known as the average room rate (ARR) represents the average rental rate per occupied in a given period of time. It is calculated by dividing the total room revenue for a period of time by the number of rooms sold.

RevPOR (Revenue per Occupied Room) – is the total revenue (including rooms, food and beverage, etc.) divided by the number of occupied rooms. This differs from ADR since it includes ancillary spending done by guests when staying in a room.

RevPAR (Revenue per Available Room) – currently this is the most common measure used by hotels as it is simple to understand and takes account of occupancy levels and room rates. It is often used as a proxy for a hotel's profitability. It can be calculated in two ways, by either: a) dividing the rooms revenue by the number of rooms available, or b) multiplying the occupancy percentage by the average daily room rate (ADR).

Total RevPAR (Total Revenue per Available Room) – this is a measure which is growing in importance and is particularly useful in resorts or hotels where a larger component of the revenue is additional to room revenue and is calculated in a similar manner to RevPAR, by either: a) dividing the total revenue for a hotel by the number of rooms available, or b) multiplying the occupancy percentage by the revenue per available room (RevPOR).

GOPPAR (Gross Operating Profit per Available Room) – this is another measure which is growing in popularity and involves taking the total revenue of a hotel less costs and expenses and dividing it by the number of rooms available. This gives an impression of operating efficiency on a per room basis and can demonstrate whether costs are controlled properly.

All of these measures are of most use in benchmarking one hotel against others within a branded chain or against other competing hotels in a city or region. In order to enable such benchmarking to be undertaken, a number of consultancies collect data from hotels via voluntary surveys and provide blinded reports back to the participants.

Similar measures exist for other service organizations: for example, in the airline industry, revenue per available seat mile (RASM) is used (calculated by dividing operating income by available seat miles) and in freight transport there is revenue per tonne mile (RTM).

QUEUING STRATEGIES: WHEN DEMAND AND CAPACITY CANNOT BE MATCHED

Sometimes it is not possible to manage capacity to match demand, or vice versa. It may be too costly – for example, most health clinics would not find it economically feasible to add additional facilities or doctors to handle peaks in demand during periods of flu epidemics; patients usually simply have to wait to be seen. Or demand may be very unpredictable and the service capacity very inflexible (it cannot be easily stretched to match unpredictable peaks in demand). Sometimes waits may occur when demand backs up because of the variability in length of time for service. For example, even though patients are scheduled by appointments in a doctor's surgery, frequently there is a wait because some patients take longer to serve than the time allotted to them.

For most service organizations, waiting customers are a fact of life at some point. Waiting can occur on the telephone (customers put on hold when they call in to ask for information, order something or make a complaint) and in person (customers queuing at the bank, post office, Disneyland or a doctor's surgery). Waiting can occur even with service transactions through the mail – delays in mail-order delivery or backlogs of correspondence on a manager's desk.

In today's fast-paced society, waiting is not something most people tolerate well. As people work longer hours, as individuals have less leisure, and as families have fewer hours together, the pressure on people's time is greater than ever. In this environment, customers are looking for efficient, quick service with no wait. Organizations that make customers wait take the chance that they will lose business or at the very least that customers will be dissatisfied.[15] Research suggests that waiting time satisfaction is nearly as important as service delivery satisfaction with respect to customer loyalty.[16] To deal effectively with the inevitability of waits, organizations can utilize a variety of queuing strategies, for general strategies are described next.

EMPLOY OPERATIONAL LOGIC

If customer waits are common, a first step is to analyse the operational processes to remove any inefficiencies. It may be possible to redesign the system to move customers along more quickly.

⭐ **SERVICE SPOTLIGHT**

Modifications in the operational system were part of the solution employed by Tesco in its efforts to reduce customer waiting and improve service. The retailer introduced self-service checkouts, hired 'peak-time' checkout operators, expanded its hours in some stores to 24-hour operations, and provided customers with alternative delivery channels (Tesco.com). Collectively these efforts reduced customer wait time, increased productivity and improved customer satisfaction.

When queues are inevitable, the organization faces the operational decision of what kind of queuing system to use, or how to configure the queues. Queue configuration refers to the number of queues, their locations, their spatial requirement and their effect on customer behaviour.[17] Several possibilities exist, as shown in Figure 14.4. In the multiple-queue alternative, the customer arrives at the service facility and must decide which queue to join and whether to switch later if the wait appears to be shorter in another line. In the single-queue alternative, fairness of waiting time is ensured in that the first-come, first-served rule applies to everyone; the system can also reduce the average time customers spend waiting overall. However, customers may leave if they perceive that the line is too long or if they have no opportunity to select a particular service provider. The last option shown in Figure 14.4 is the take-a-number option in which arriving customers take a number

Figure 14.4   Waiting-line configurations

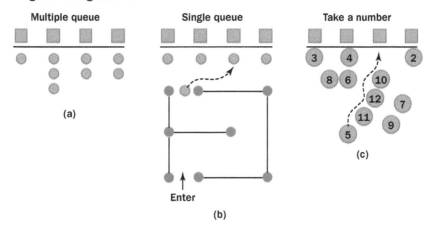

(a)

(b)

(c)

Enter

Multiple queue

Single queue

Take a number

Source: J.A. Fitzsimmons and M.J. Fitzsimmons, *Service Management: Operations, Strategy, Information Technology*, 8/e, ch. 12, p. 345. © 2014 by The McGraw-Hill Companies, Inc. Reprinted by permission of The McGraw-Hill Companies.

to indicate line position. Advantages are similar to the single-queue alternative with the additional benefit that customers are able to mill about, browse and talk to each other. The disadvantage is that customers must be on the alert to hear their numbers when they are called. Recent research suggests that length of the queue and perceived cost of waiting are not the only influences on customers' likelihood of staying in line. In a series of experiments and field tests, researchers showed that the larger the number of customers queuing *behind* a consumer, the more likely that consumer is to stay in the queue and wait for the service.[18]

ESTABLISH A RESERVATION PROCESS

When waiting cannot be avoided, a reservation system can help to spread demand. Restaurants, transportation companies, theatres, doctors and many other service providers use reservation systems to alleviate long waits. The idea behind a reservation system is to guarantee that the service will be available when the customer arrives.

SERVICE SPOTLIGHT

Even at Disneyland Paris a FASTPASS service is used to reserve times for visitors and cut the waiting time on the most popular attractions. As a result visitors spend less time waiting in line and more time enjoying the park. Here is how it works. The visitor inserts their park entrance ticket into the FASTPASS machine at an attraction and they receive a designated ride time. Then they are free to go enjoy the rest of the park until their allotted time when they come back to the Disney's FASTPASS entrance and hop on board with no further wait.

Beyond simply reducing waiting time, a reservation system has the added benefit of potentially shifting demand to less desirable time periods. A challenge inherent in reservation systems, however, is what to do about 'no shows'. Inevitably there will be customers who reserve a time but do not show up. Some organizations deal with this problem by overbooking their service capacity on the basis of past records of no-show percentages. If the predictions are accurate, overbooking is a good solution. When predictions are inaccurate, however, customers may still have to wait and sometimes may not be served at all, as when airlines overbook the number of seats available on a flight. Victims of overbooking may be compensated for their inconvenience in such cases. To minimize the no-show problem, some organizations (such as hotels, airlines, conferences/training programmes and theatres) charge customers who fail to show up or cancel their reservations within a certain time frame.

DIFFERENTIATE WAITING CUSTOMERS

Not all customers necessarily need to wait the same length of time for service. On the basis of need or customer priority, some organizations differentiate among customers, allowing some to experience shorter waits for service than others. Known as 'queue discipline', such differentiation reflects management policies regarding whom to select next for service.[19] The most popular discipline is first-come, first-served. However, other rules may apply. Differentiation can be based on factors such as:[20]

- *Importance of the customer.* Frequent customers or customers who spend large amounts with the organization can be given priority in service by providing them with a special waiting area or segregated lines.
- *Urgency of the job.* Those customers with the most urgent need may be served first. This strategy is used in emergency health care. It is also used by maintenance services such as central-heating or air-conditioning repair that give priority to customers whose system is not functioning over those who call for routine maintenance.
- *Duration of the service transaction.* In many situations, shorter service jobs get priority through 'express lanes'. At other times, when a service provider sees that a transaction is going to require extra time, the customer is referred to a designated provider who deals only with these special-needs customers.
- *Payment of a premium price.* Customers who pay extra (first class on an airline, for example) are often given priority via separate check-in lines or express systems.

MAKE WAITING PLEASURABLE OR AT LEAST TOLERABLE

Even when they have to wait, customers can be more or less satisfied depending on how the wait is handled by the organization. Of course, the actual length of the wait will affect how customers feel about their service experience, but it is not just the actual time spent waiting that has an impact on customer satisfaction – it is how customers feel about the wait and their perceptions during it. The type of wait (for example, a standard queue versus a wait due to a delay of service) can also influence how customers will react.[21] In a classic article entitled 'The psychology of waiting lines', David Maister proposes several principles about the psychology of queuing, each of which has implications for how organizations can make waiting more pleasurable or at least tolerable.[22]

UNOCCUPIED TIME FEELS LONGER THAN OCCUPIED TIME

When customers are unoccupied they will likely be bored and will notice the passage of time more than when they have something to do. Providing something for waiting customers to do, particularly if the activity offers a benefit in and of itself or is related in some way to the service, can improve the customer's experience and may benefit the organization as well.[23] Examples include giving customers menus to look at while waiting in a restaurant, providing interesting information to read in a dentist's office or playing entertaining music over the telephone while customers are on hold. At Disney customers waiting to get on a ride wind their way through a themed environment such as space tunnels or pirates' caves that become part of the total service adventure.[24]

PRE-PROCESS WAITS FEEL LONGER THAN IN-PROCESS WAITS

If wait time is occupied with activities that relate to the upcoming service, customers may perceive that the service has started and they are no longer actually waiting. This in-process activity will make the length of the wait seem shorter and will also benefit the service provider by making the customer better prepared when the service actually does begin. Filling out medical information while waiting to see the doctor, reading a menu while waiting to be seated in a restaurant, and watching a videotape of the upcoming service event are all activities that can both educate the customer and reduce perceptions of waiting.

Research in a restaurant context found that customers reacted less negatively to in-process waits than to either pre-process or post-process waits.[25] Other researchers have found the same for waits due to routine slowness of the process. However, if the wait is due to a service failure, then the in-process wait is viewed more negatively than the pre-process wait.[26] Thus, how customers perceive pre-process, in-process and post-process waits may depend to some extent on the cause of the wait.

ANXIETY MAKES WAITS SEEM LONGER

When customers fear that they have been forgotten or do not know how long they will have to wait, they become anxious, and this anxiety can increase the negative impact of waiting. Anxiety also results when customers are forced to choose in a multiple-line situation and they discover they have chosen the 'wrong line'. To combat waiting-line anxiety, organizations can provide information on the length of the wait. At its theme parks, Disney uses signs at intervals along the line that let customers know how long the wait will be from that point on. Using a single line also alleviates customer anxiety over having chosen the wrong line. Explanations and reassurances that no one has forgotten them help alleviate customer anxiety by taking away their cause for worry.

UNCERTAIN WAITS ARE LONGER THAN KNOWN, FINITE WAITS

Anxiety is intensified when customers do not know how long they will have to wait. Healthcare providers combat this problem by letting customers know when they check in how far behind the doctor is that day. Some patients resolve this uncertainty themselves by calling ahead to ask. Maister provides an interesting example of the role of uncertainty, which he terms the 'appointment syndrome'. Customers who arrive early for an appointment will wait patiently until the scheduled time, even if they arrive very early. However, once the expected appointment time has passed, customers grow increasingly anxious. Before the appointment time the wait time is known; after that, the length of the wait is not known.

Research in an airline context has suggested that as uncertainty about the wait increases, customers become angrier, and their anger in turn results in greater dissatisfaction.[27] Research also shows that giving customers information on the length of the anticipated wait or their relative position in the queue can result in more positive feelings and acceptance of the wait and, ultimately, more positive evaluation of the service.[28]

UNEXPLAINED WAITS ARE LONGER THAN EXPLAINED WAITS

When people understand the causes for waiting, they frequently have greater patience and are less anxious, particularly when the wait is justifiable. An explanation can reduce customer uncertainty and may help customers estimate how long they will be delayed. Customers who do not know the reason for a wait begin to feel powerless and irritated.

UNFAIR WAITS ARE LONGER THAN EQUITABLE WAITS

When customers perceive that they are waiting while others who arrived after them have already been served, the apparent inequity will make the wait seem even longer. This situation can easily occur when there is no apparent order in the waiting area and many customers are trying to be served. Queuing systems that work on a first-come, first-served rule are best at combating perceived unfairness. However, other approaches may be required to determine who will be served next. For example, in an emergency medical care situation, the most seriously ill or injured patients would be seen first. When customers understand the priorities and the rules are clearly communicated and enforced, fairness of waiting time should not be an issue. To understand more about perceptions of fairness, see the 'Fair treatment' section in Chapter 15.

THE MORE VALUABLE THE SERVICE, THE LONGER THE CUSTOMER WILL WAIT

Customers who have substantial purchases or who are waiting for a high-value service will be more tolerant of long wait times and may even expect to wait longer. For example, in a supermarket, customers who have a full cart of groceries will generally wait longer than customers who have only a few items and expect to be checked through quickly. Similarly, diners expect to wait longer for service in an expensive restaurant than they do when eating at a 'greasy spoon'.

SOLO WAITS FEEL LONGER THAN GROUP WAITS

People will wait longer when they are in a group than when they are alone because of the distractions provided by other members of the group. People also feel comfort in waiting with a group rather than alone.[29] In some group waiting situations, such as at Disneyland or when patrons are waiting in long lines to purchase concert tickets, customers who are strangers may begin to talk to each other and the waiting experience can actually become fun and a part of the total service experience.

SUMMARY

Because service organizations lack the ability to inventory their products, the effective use of capacity can be critical to success. Idle capacity in the form of unused time, labour, facilities or equipment represents a direct drain on bottom-line profitability. When the capacity represents a major investment (for example, aircraft, expensive medical imaging equipment, lawyers and doctors), the losses associated with underuse of capacity are even more accentuated. Overused capacity is also a problem. People, facilities and equipment can become worn out over time when used beyond optimum capacity constraints. People can quit, facilities become run down and equipment can break. From the customer's perspective, service quality also deteriorates. Organizations focused on delivering quality service, therefore, have a natural drive to balance capacity utilization and demand at an optimum level in order to meet customer expectations.

This chapter has provided you with an understanding of the underlying issues of managing supply and demand in capacity-constrained services by exploring the lack of inventory capability, the nature of service constraints (time, labour, equipment, facilities), the differences in optimal versus maximum use of capacity, and the causes of fluctuating demand.

Based on a grounding in the fundamental issues, the chapter presented a variety of strategies for matching supply and demand. The basic strategies fall under two headings: *demand strategies* (shifting demand to match capacity) and *capacity strategies* (adjusting capacity to meet demand). Demand strategies seek to flatten the peaks and valleys of demand to match the flat capacity constraint, whereas supply strategies seek to align, flex or stretch capacity to match the peaks and valleys of demand. Organizations frequently employ several strategies simultaneously to solve the complex problem of balancing supply and demand.

Revenue management (also known as *yield management*) was presented as a sophisticated form of supply and demand management that balances capacity utilization, pricing, market segmentation and financial return. Long practised by the passenger airline industry, this strategy is growing in use by hotel, shipping, car rental and other capacity-constrained industries in which bookings are made in advance. Essentially, revenue management allows organizations to decide on a monthly, weekly, daily or hourly basis to whom they want to sell their service capacity and at what price.

The last section of the chapter discussed situations in which it is not possible to align supply and demand. In these unresolved capacity utilization situations, the inevitable result is customer wait. Strategies were described for effectively managing waiting lines, such as employing operational logic, establishing a reservation process, differentiating waiting customers and making waiting fun or at least tolerable.

KEY CONCEPTS

EXERCISES

1 Choose a local service organization that is challenged by fixed capacity and fluctuating demand. Interview the marketing manager (or another knowledgeable person) to learn (a) in what ways capacity is constrained, (b) the basic patterns of demand, and (c) strategies the organization has used to align supply and demand. Write up the answers to these questions, and make your own recommendations regarding other strategies the organization might use.

2 Assume you manage a winter ski resort. (a) Explain the underlying pattern of demand fluctuation that is likely to occur at your resort and the management challenges it would present. Is the pattern of demand predictable or random? (b) Explain and give examples of how you might use both demand-oriented and supply-oriented strategies to smooth the peaks and troughs of demand.

3 Choose a local organization in which people have to queue for service. Design a queuing strategy for the organization.

4 Visit the website of Royal Bank of Scotland (www.rbs.co.uk), a leader in online banking. What online services does the bank currently offer? How do these online services help Royal Bank of Scotland manage the peaks and troughs of customer demand? How do its strategies to use more ATMs and other alternative delivery strategies complement the online strategies?

DISCUSSION QUESTIONS

1 Discuss the four scenarios (excess demand, demand exceeds optimum capacity, demand and supply are balanced, excess capacity) illustrated in Figure 14.1 and presented in the text in the context of a football team selling seats for its games. What are the challenges for management under each scenario?

2 Discuss the four common types of constraints (time, labour, equipment, facilities) facing service businesses and give an example of each (real or hypothetical).

3 How does optimal capacity utilization differ from maximum capacity utilization? Give an example of a situation in which the two might be the same and one in which they are different.

4 Choose a local restaurant or some other type of service with fluctuating demand. What is the likely underlying pattern of demand? What causes the pattern? Is it predictable or random?

5 Describe the two basic strategies for matching supply and demand, and give at least two specific examples of each.

6 What is revenue management? Discuss the risks in adopting a revenue management strategy.

7 How might revenue management apply in the management of the following: a major theatre? A consulting firm? A commuter train?

8 What are the advantages and disadvantages of outsourcing?

9 Identify examples of pre-process waits and in-process waits. What can be done to reduce these waiting times?

10 Describe the four basic queuing strategies, and give an example of each one, preferably based on your own experiences as a consumer.

FURTHER READING

Adenso-Diaz, B., Gonzalez-Torre, P. and Garcia, V. (2002). A capacity management model in service industries. *International Journal of Service Industry Management*, 13(3/4), 286–302.

Borges, A., Herter, M. M. and Chebat, J. C. (2015). 'It was not that long!': The effects of the in-store TV screen content and consumers emotions on consumer waiting perception. *Journal of Retailing and Consumer Services*, 22, 96–106.

Hayes, D.K. and Miller, A. (2010). *Revenue Management for the Hospitality Industry.* John Wiley & Sons.

Jack, E.P. and Powers, T.L. (2009). A review and synthesis of demand management, capacity management and performance in health care services. *International Journal of Management Reviews*, 11(2), 149–74.

Klassen, K.J. and Rohleder, T.R. (2002). Demand and capacity management decisions in services: how they impact on one another. *International Journal of Operations and Production Management*, 22(5), 527–48.

Maister, D. H. (1984). *The psychology of waiting lines.* Harvard Business School.

Mauri, A.G. (2012). *Hotel Revenue Management: Principles and Practices.* Milan, Italy, Pearson.

Noone, B.M. and Mattila, A.S. (2009) Hotel revenue management and the Internet: the effect of price presentation strategy on customers' willingness to book. *International Journal of Hospitality Management*, 28(2), 272–79.

CHAPTER 15

Service Recovery

LEARNING OBJECTIVES

This chapter's objectives are to:

1 Illustrate the importance of recovery from service failures in keeping customers and building loyalty.
2 Discuss the nature of consumer complaints and why people do and do not complain.
3 Provide evidence of what customers expect and the kind of responses they want when they do complain.
4 Present strategies for effective service recovery, together with examples of what does and does not work.
5 Discuss service guarantees – what they are, the benefits of guarantees and when to use them – as a particular type of service recovery strategy.

OPENING EXAMPLE

Revenge on YouTube – United Airlines Breaks Guitars

Although the following service recovery failure occurred in the USA, its notoriety has spread throughout Europe and around the globe, all thanks to the power of a YouTube video.

Dave Carroll is a musician who performed in a pop-folk music band, Sons of Maxwell. The band went on tour in the USA and Canada, performing in small venues and music festivals. On 31 March 2008 the band members were flying from their hometown of Halifax, Canada to Omaha, Nebraska. During a connection in Chicago, passengers including Carroll noticed some very rough handling of luggage by United Airlines baggage handlers, including Dave's $3,500 Taylor guitar. When Carroll complained to the cabin crew, he was told that he should speak to the lead agent at the gate. Carroll did so, but was told that he should lodge his complaint with the ground staff at his destination airport in Omaha. However, on arriving at Omaha airport, he could find no ground staff as it was after midnight.

On returning to the airport in Omaha for his return flight, he spoke with a United agent who advised him that he would need to lodge a claim at his originating airport in Halifax. Once back in Halifax, he was told he would have to phone a call centre based in India. After several calls he was told to take his guitar 1,200 miles to Chicago Airport for inspection. When he stated he couldn't travel that far, he was told to contact United Airlines central baggage centre in New York which rerouted his call back to a call centre in India. Eventually, after a number of other steps and a seven-month wait, Dave received an e-mail from United Airlines, apologizing for the damage to his guitar, but rejecting his claim for $1,200 damage because the claim had not been officially submitted within 24 hours of the flight (a requirement of the United Airlines claim policy). In response to further complaints from Carroll, he was told that his case had been closed and United Airlines would be making no further communication on the matter.

As a result, Carrol decided to write songs and produce a video about United Airline breaking guitars and posting it on YouTube. He produced the video on a budget of $150 and posted it on YouTube on Monday 6 July 2009 at 10 p.m, using Twitter and other social media channels to publicize the video. The story was picked up by consumer websites, newspapers and television channels. In less than 24 hours the video had received 24,000 views and 461 comments, most of them maligning United Airlines. By the end of July 2009, the number of views was up to 4.6 million. The song on the video became a Top 20 iTunes download in Canada and the number one country music download in the United Kingdom. At the time of writing this book, the video is still on YouTube and has received over 15 million views.

United monitored the large amount of traffic about the video and tried to enter the conversation very early on by tweeting using the airline's Twitter account that 'this has struck a chord with us' and they were trying to contact Carroll by phone to put things right. They offered Carroll compensation (which he refused – so they donated $3,000 to a music school) and asked if they could use the video for training purposes in trying to change the United culture.

Worldwide, the video has had a major impact on the image and reputation of United Airlines. The power of online social media demonstrates the impact of negative word of mouth and the need for immediate and effective handling of customers' dissatisfaction and complaints as and when they happen.

Sources: C. Ayers (2009) 'Revenge is best served cold on YouTube', The Times, 22 July; M. Tran (2009) 'Singer gets his revenge on United Airlines and soars to fame', Guardian, 23 July; J. Deighton and L. Kornfield (2010) 'United breaks guitars'. Harvard Business Review Case Study, 6 January.

In all service contexts – whether customer service, consumer services or business-to-business services – service failure is inevitable. Failure is inevitable even for the best of firms with the best of intentions, even for those with world-class service systems.

To fully understand and retain their customers, firms must know what customers expect when service failures occur, and must implement effective strategies for service recovery. Our chapter-opening vignette illustrates what can happen, particularly since the advent of social media channels and customer review sites, when companies do not address service failures effectively.

THE IMPACT OF SERVICE FAILURE AND RECOVERY

A *service failure* is generally described as service performance that falls below a customer's expectations in such a way that leads to customer dissatisfaction. *Service recovery* refers to the actions taken by an organization in response to a service failure. Failures occur for all kinds of reasons – the service may be unavailable when promised, it may be delivered late or too slowly, the outcome may be incorrect or poorly executed or employees may be rude or uncaring.[1] These types of failures bring about negative feelings and responses from customers. Research suggests that only a portion (45 per cent) of customers who experience a problem with service delivery actually complain to the employees serving them, and a very small number (1 to 5 per cent) complain to someone at the company headquarters.[2] This phenomenon, commonly referred to as the 'tip of the iceberg', suggests that every complaint that management receives at company headquarters represents 20 to 100 other customers who experienced the problem but did not complain. Service failures left unfixed can result in customers leaving, telling other customers about their negative experiences, leaving negative reviews online, and, even, challenging the organization through consumer rights organizations or legal channels.

SERVICE RECOVERY EFFECTS

Research has shown that resolving customer problems effectively has a strong impact on customer satisfaction, loyalty, word-of-mouth communication and bottom-line performance.[3] That is to say, customers who experience service failures but who are ultimately satisfied thanks to recovery efforts by the firm will be more loyal than those whose problems are not resolved. That loyalty translates into profitability, as you learned in Chapter 7. Data from TARP Worldwide verify this relationship, as shown in Figure 15.1.[4] Among customers of service businesses who complain and have their problems satisfactorily resolved, 43 per cent indicate they would definitely purchase again from the same provider – illustrating the power of good service recovery. However, this study and other research have found that customers who are dissatisfied with the recovery process after making a complaint are less likely to repurchase than are those who do not complain – suggesting the power of poor service recovery.[5]

Figure 15.1 **Unhappy customers' repurchase intentions**

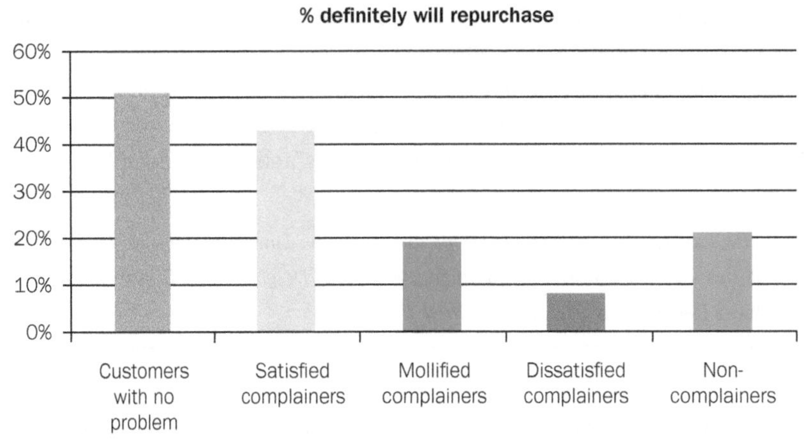

% definitely will repurchase

Source: TARP Worldwide Inc Service Industry Data 2007.

An effective service recovery strategy has multiple potential impacts. It can increase customer satisfaction and loyalty and generate positive word-of-mouth communication. A well-designed, well-documented service recovery strategy also provides information that can be used to improve service as part of a continuous improvement effort. By making adjustments to service processes, systems and outcomes based on previous service recovery experiences, companies increase the likelihood of 'doing it right the first time'. In turn, this reduces costs of failures and increases initial customer satisfaction.

Unfortunately, many firms do not employ effective recovery strategies. Studies suggest as much as 60 per cent of customers who experienced a serious problem received no response from the firm.[6] There are tremendous downsides to having no service recovery or ineffective service recovery strategies. Poor recovery following a bad service experience can lead to customers who are so dissatisfied that they become 'terrorists', actively pursuing opportunities to openly criticize the company using online review sites and online social media such as Facebook. When customers experience a service failure, they talk about it to others no matter what the outcome. Research has found that customers who are satisfied with a firm's recovery efforts talk to an average of eight people, whereas those customers who were dissatisfied with the response talk to an average of 18.5 people.[7] With the ability to share such stories on social media and the Internet, the potential reach of such dissatisfied customers is even greater. Further, repeated service failures without an effective recovery strategy in place can aggrieve even the best employees. The reduction in employee morale and even the loss of employees can be huge but are often the overlooked costs of not having an effective service recovery strategy.

THE SERVICE RECOVERY PARADOX

Occasionally some businesses have customers who are initially dissatisfied with a service experience and go on to experience a high level of excellent service recovery, seemingly leading them to be even more satisfied and more likely to repurchase than if no problem had occurred at all; that is, they appear to be more satisfied after they experience a service failure than they otherwise would have been![8] To illustrate: consider a hotel customer who arrives to check in and finds that no room is available. In an effort to recover, the hotel front-desk person immediately upgrades this guest to a better room at the original price. The customer, thrilled with this compensation, reports that he or she is extremely satisfied with this experience, is even more impressed with the hotel than before, and vows to be loyal into the future. Although such extreme instances are relatively rare, this idea – that an initially disappointed customer who has experienced good service recovery might be even more satisfied and loyal as a result – has been labelled the *service recovery paradox*.

So, should a firm 'screw up' just a little so that it can 'fix the problem' superbly? If doing so would actually lead to more satisfied customers, is this strategy worth pursuing? The logical, but not very rational, conclusion is that companies should *plan to disappoint customers* so they can recover well and (hopefully!) gain even greater loyalty from them. What are the problems with such an approach?

- As we indicated earlier in this chapter, the vast majority of customers do not complain when they experience a problem. The possibility of a recovery exists only in situations in which the firm is aware of a problem and is able to recover well; if customers do not make the firm aware of the failure – and most do not – dissatisfaction is most likely to be the result.
- It is expensive to fix mistakes; re-creating or reworking a service may be quite costly to a firm.
- It would appear somewhat ludicrous to encourage service failures – after all, reliability ('doing it right the first time') is the most critical determinant of service quality across industries.
- Research suggests that even if a customer's satisfaction with the firm increases as a result of the great service recovery, repurchase intentions and image perceptions of the firm do not increase – that is, customers do not necessarily think more highly of the firm in the long run.[9]
- Although the recovery paradox suggests that a customer *may* end up more satisfied after experiencing excellent recovery, there is certainly *no* guarantee that the customer actually *will* end up more satisfied.

The recovery paradox is highly dependent on the context and situation; although one customer may find it easy to forgive a restaurant who provides him with a gift certificate for a later date to make up for having lost his or her dinner reservation, another customer who had planned to propose marriage to his or her date over dinner may not be all that happy with the same recovery scenario.

The intrigue stimulated by the recovery paradox has led to empirical research specifically on this issue. Although anecdotal evidence provides limited support for the recovery paradox, research seems to indicate that this phenomenon is not pervasive. In one study researchers found that only the very highest levels of customers' service recovery ratings resulted in increased satisfaction and loyalty.[10] This research suggests that customers weigh their most recent experiences heavily in their determination of whether to buy again. If the most recent experience is negative, overall feelings about the company will decrease and repurchase intentions will also diminish significantly. Unless the recovery effort is absolutely superlative, it cannot overcome the negative impression of the initial experience enough to build repurchase intentions beyond the point at which they would be if the service had been provided correctly in the first place. Other studies suggest the conditions under which a service recovery paradox is most likely to occur is when the failure is not considered by the customer to be severe, the customer has not experienced prior failures with the firm, the cause of the failure is viewed as transient by the customer, or the customer perceives that the company had little control over the cause of the failure.[11] Apparently conditions must be just right in order for the recovery paradox to be present.

Given the mixed opinions on the extent to which the recovery paradox exists, 'doing it right the first time' is still the best and safest strategy in the long run. However, when a failure does occur, then every effort at a superior recovery should be made to mitigate its negative effects. If the failure can be fully overcome, if the failure is less critical or if the recovery effort is clearly superlative, it may be possible to observe evidence of the recovery paradox.

HOW CUSTOMERS RESPOND TO SERVICE FAILURES

Customers who experience service failures can respond in a variety of ways, as illustrated in Figure 15.2.[12] It is assumed that following a failure, dissatisfaction at some level will occur for the customer. In fact, research suggests that a variety of negative emotions can occur following a service failure, including such feelings as anger, discontent, disappointment, self-pity and anxiety.[13] These initial negative responses will affect how customers evaluate the service recovery effort and presumably their ultimate decision to return to the provider or not.[14]

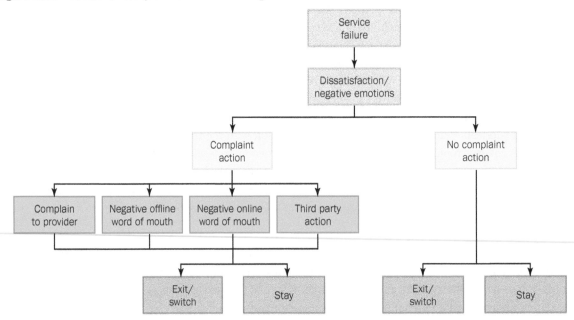

Figure 15.2 **Customer complaint actions following service failure**

Many customers are very passive about their dissatisfaction, simply saying or doing nothing. Whether they take action or not, at some point the customers will decide whether to stay with that provider or switch to a competitor. As we have already pointed out, customers who do not complain are least likely to return. For companies, customer passivity in the face of dissatisfaction is a threat to future success.

WHY PEOPLE DO (AND DO NOT) COMPLAIN

Some customers are more likely to complain than others for a variety of reasons. These consumers believe that positive consequences may occur and that there are social benefits of complaining, and their personal norms support their complaining behaviour. They believe they should and will be provided compensation for the service failure in some form. They believe that fair treatment and good service are their due, and that in cases of service failure someone should make good. In some cases they feel a social obligation to complain – to help others avoid similar situations or to punish the service provider. A very small number of consumers have 'complaining' personalities – they just like to complain or cause trouble.

Consumers who are unlikely to take any action hold the opposite beliefs. They often see complaining as a waste of their time and effort. They do not believe anything positive will occur for them, or others, as a result of their actions. Sometimes they do not know how to complain – they do not understand the process or may not realize that avenues are open to them to voice their complaints. In some cases non-complainers may engage in 'emotion-focused coping' to deal with their negative experiences. This type of coping involves self-blame, denial and, possibly, seeking social support.[15] They may feel that the failure was somehow their fault and that they do not deserve redress.

Personal relevance of the failure can also influence whether people complain.[16] If the service failure is really important, if the failure has critical consequences for the consumer, or if the consumer has much ego involvement in the service experience, then he or she is more likely to complain. Consumers are more likely to complain about services that are expensive, high risk and ego-involving (like vacation packages, airline travel and medical services) than they are about less expensive, frequently purchased services (fast-food drive-through service, a taxi ride, a call to a customer service helpline). These latter services are simply not important enough to warrant the time to complain. Unfortunately, even though the experience may not be important to the consumer at that moment, a dissatisfying encounter can still drive him or her to a competitor next time the service is needed.

Finally people are more likely to complain when there are remote channels set up by service providers to make it easy for customers to provide feedback.[17] Organizations that have twitter feeds, facebook pages, online customer forums and online customer satisfaction surveys are more likely to find dissatisfied customers voicing their complaints.

TYPES OF CUSTOMER COMPLAINT ACTIONS

When customers initiate responses following service failure, these customer complaint actions can be of various types. A dissatisfied customer can choose to complain on the spot to the service provider, giving the company the opportunity to respond immediately. This reaction is often the Social Media and Digital Marketing

best-case scenario for the company, because it has a second chance at that moment to satisfy the customer, keep his or her business in the future and, potentially, avoid any negative word of mouth. Customers who do not complain immediately may choose to complain later to the provider by telephone, in writing or via the corporate website or the company's Facebook and Twitter accounts. Again, the company has a chance to recover. Researchers refer to these proactive types of complaining behaviour as *voice* responses or *seeking redress*.

Some customers choose not to complain directly to the provider but rather spread negative word of mouth about the company to friends, relatives and co-workers. This negative word-of-mouth communication can be extremely detrimental because it can reinforce the customer's feelings of negativism and spread that negative impression to others. Further, the company has no chance to recover unless the negative word of mouth is accompanied by a complaint directly to the company. In recent years, customers have taken to complaining via the Internet. A variety of websites, including Web-based consumer opinion platforms such as Tripadvisor or flyertalk.com have been created to facilitate customer feedback and, in doing so, have provided customers with the opportunity of spreading negative word-of-mouth communication to a much broader audience. Some customers become so dissatisfied with a product or service failure that they construct websites or Facebook sites targeting the firm's current and prospective customers. On these sites[18] angry customers convey their grievances against the firm in ways designed to convince other consumers of the firm's incompetence.[19]

Finally, customers may choose to complain to third parties such as the Consumers Association, to trading standards departments of local or national government, to a licensing authority, to a professional association or to radio or television programmes that focus on consumer issues. No matter the action (or inaction), ultimately the customers determine whether to patronize the service provider again or to switch to another provider.

TYPES OF COMPLAINERS

Research suggests that people can be grouped into categories based on how they respond to failures. Four categories of response types were identified in a study that focused on grocery stores, car repair services, medical care, and banking and financial services:[20] *passives*, *voicers*, *irates* and *activists*. Although the proportion of the types of complainers is likely to vary across industries and contexts, it is likely that these four types of complainers will be relatively consistent and that each type can be found in all companies and industries.

PASSIVES

This group of customers is least likely to take any action. They are unlikely to say anything to the provider, less likely than others to spread negative word of mouth and unlikely to complain to a third party. They often doubt the effectiveness of complaining, thinking that the consequences will not merit the time and effort they will expend. They feel uncomfortable complaining in public. Sometimes their personal values or norms argue against complaining. These folks tend to feel less alienated from the marketplace than irates and activists.

VOICERS

These customers actively complain to the service provider, but they are less likely to spread negative word of mouth, to switch patronage or to go to third parties with their complaints. *These customers should be viewed as the service provider's best friends!* They actively complain and thus give the company a second chance. As with the passives, these customers are less alienated from the marketplace than those in the other two groups. They tend to believe complaining has social benefits and therefore do not hesitate to voice their opinions. They believe that the consequences of complaining to the provider can be very positive, and they believe less in other types of complaining such as spreading word of mouth or talking to third parties. Their personal norms are consistent with complaining.

IRATES

These consumers are more likely than are others to engage in negative word-of-mouth communication with friends and relatives and to switch providers. They are about average in their propensity to complain to the provider. They are unlikely to complain to third parties. These folk tend to feel somewhat alienated from the marketplace. As their label suggests, they are angrier with the provider, although they do believe that complaining to the provider can have social benefits. They are less likely to give the service provider a second chance and instead will switch to a competitor, spreading the word to friends and relatives along the way.

ACTIVISTS

These consumers are characterized by above average propensity to complain on all dimensions: they will complain to the provider, they will tell others and they are more likely than any other group to complain to third parties. Complaining fits with their personal norms. As with the irates, these consumers are more alienated from the marketplace than the other groups. They have a very optimistic sense of the potential positive consequences of all types of complaining.

⭐ SERVICE SPOTLIGHT

This is an example of a typical complaint from an irate customer appearing on the flightsfromhell.com website.

'I had booked my honeymoon travel tickets from Mumbai to Nice and back to Mumbai via London with *** Airlines. Let me start by saying that this has been the worst flight I have taken in my life. My honeymoon started as a flop because of *** Airlines. The staff were rude and arrogant.

I thought I had booked comfort class as my agent said that he booked me in it. While checking in I didn't realize that they had given me an economy seat. After the flight took off I realized that I am in economy. We thought there was a mistake at the check-in counter and we would get some clarity at Istanbul Airport. At the airport the guys at the counter were too busy chatting with each other to answer us properly. Their response: "What do you want us to do now? Your ticket was not premium economy." I asked him if my ticket was comfort class or not as my agent had charged me for comfort class. His response: "Why are you asking me, talk to your agent and ask him." He then turned his back and resumed his chat.

On the flight from Mumbai to Istanbul, the steward and stewardess were high-handed and were not willing to hear us out if we had any queries or wanted to make a request. We had ordered a vegetarian meal which we did not get. We had an option of chicken or fish. When we told them that we had requested vegetarian, their only response was, and I quote, "It's not mentioned in our system; there is nothing we can do about it."

Also while booking the tickets at London Gatwick, I informed the counter staff person who was punching in my details that I was unhappy with the service we got while coming from Mumbai. Her response to that was, "Why are you telling me; send a mail if you want."

Let's just say that this has been the worst experience of my life, and definitely I'm going to make it a point to try to reach each and every media source to share my experience about this ridiculous airline, and make it a point that at least my friends and family won't have to go through the experience I had to go through. Cursing myself for selecting *** Airlines for my honeymoon. Rest assured that I will not be flying with *** Airlines again.' [21]

CUSTOMERS' RECOVERY EXPECTATIONS

When they take the time and effort to complain, customers generally have high recovery expectations. They expect the firm to be accountable. They expect to be helped quickly. They expect to be compensated for their grief and for the hassle of being inconvenienced. And they expect to be treated nicely in the process.

UNDERSTANDING AND ACCOUNTABILITY

In many service failure situations, customers are not looking for extreme actions from the firm; however, they are looking to understand what happened and for firms to be accountable for their actions (or inactions).[22] One study identified the eight most common 'remedies' that customers seek when they experience a serious problem;[23] three of these remedies were to have the product repaired or service fixed, be reimbursed for the hassle of having experienced a problem, and receive a product or service free of charge in the future. Interestingly, however, the other five remedies – including an apology from the firm, an explanation by the firm as to what happened, an assurance that the problem would not be repeated, a thank you for the customer's business and an opportunity for the customer to vent his or her frustrations to the firm – cost the firm very little to provide.

These five non-monetary remedies consist primarily of affording employees the opportunity to communicate with customers. Understanding and accountability are very important to many customers after a service failure, for if they perceive an injustice has occurred, someone is to blame. Customers expect an apology when things go wrong, and a company that provides an apology demonstrates courtesy and respect; customers also want to know what the company is going to do to ensure that the problem does not reoccur.[24]

As the percentages in Table 15.1 suggest, customer discontent can be moderated if firms simply communicate well with customers. Customers clearly value such communication, because these non-monetary remedies are positively related to satisfaction with the complaint process, continued loyalty, and positive word-of-mouth communication.[25]

FAIR TREATMENT

Customers also want justice and fairness in handling their complaints. Service recovery experts Steve Brown and Steve Tax have documented three specific types of justice that customers are looking for following their complaints: *outcome justice, procedural justice* and *interactional justice*.[26] Outcome justice concerns the results that customers receive from their complaints; procedural justice refers to the policies, rules

Table 15.1   Customer dissatisfaction from firm responses to service failures

Firm Response	Percentage of Customers Dissatisfied with Action Taken
Do nothing	79%
Explain what happened	20%
Provide customer an opportunity to vent frustrations	17%
Apologies to customer	10%
Thank customer for business	10%
Assure customer problem will not recur	6%

Source: 2007 National Consumer Rage Study conducted by Customer Care Alliance.

and timeliness of the complaint process; and interactional justice focuses on the interpersonal treatment received during the complaint process.[27] Table 15.2 shows examples of each type of justice taken from Brown and Tax's study of consumers who reported on their experiences with complaint resolution.

Table 15.2   Fairness themes in service recovery

	Fair	Unfair
Outcome justice: the results that customers receive from complaints	*'The waitress agreed that there was a problem. She took the sandwiches back to the kitchen and had them replaced. We were also given a free drink.'* *'They were very thorough with my complaint. One week later I received a coupon for a free oil change and an apology from the shop owner.'*	*'Their refusal to refund our money or make up for the inconvenience and cold food was inexcusable.'* *'If I wanted a refund, I had to go back to the store the next day. It's a 20-minute drive; the refund was barely worth the trouble.'*
Procedural justice: the policies, rules and timeliness of the complaint process	*'The hotel manager said that it didn't matter to her who was at fault, she would take responsibility for the problem immediately.'* *'The sales manager called me back one week after my complaint to check if the problem was taken care of to my satisfaction.'*	*'They should have assisted me with the problem instead of giving me a phone number to call. No one returned my calls, and I never had a chance to speak to a real person.'* *'I had to tell my problem to too many people. I had to become irate in order to talk with the manager, who was apparently the only one who could provide a solution.'*
Interactional justice: the interpersonal treatment received during the complaint process	*'The loan officer was very courteous, knowledgeable and considerate – he kept me informed about the progress of the complaint.'* *'The teller explained that they had a power outage that morning so things were delayed. He went through a lot of files [effort] so that I would not have to come back the next day.'*	*'The person who handled my complaint about the faulty air-conditioner repair wasn't going to do anything about it and didn't seem to care.'* *'The receptionist was very rude; she made it seem like the doctor's time was important but mine was not.'*

Source: Adapted from 'Recovering and learning from service failure', by S.S. Tax and S.W. Brown, MIT *Sloan Management Review* (Fall 1998), p. 79. Copyright © 1998 by Massachusetts Institute of Technology. All rights reserved.

OUTCOME JUSTICE

Customers expect outcomes, or compensation, to match the level of their dissatisfaction. This compensation can take the form of actual monetary compensation, an apology, future services for free, reduced charges, repairs and/or replacements. Customers expect equity in the exchange – that is, they want to feel that the company has 'paid' for its mistakes in a manner at least equal to what the customer has suffered. The company's 'punishment should fit the crime'. Customers expect equality – that is, they want to be compensated no more or less than other customers who have experienced the same type of service failure. They also appreciate it when a company gives them choices in terms of compensation. For example, a hotel guest could be offered the choice of a refund or a free upgrade to a better room in compensation for a room not being available on arrival. Outcome justice is especially important in settings in which customers have particularly negative emotional responses to the service failure; in such situations recovery efforts should focus on improving the outcome from the customer's point of view.[28]

However, it should also be noted that customers can feel uncomfortable if they are overly compensated.

★ SERVICE SPOTLIGHT

Early in its experience with service guarantees, Domino's Pizza offered not to charge for the pizza if the driver arrived after the 30-minute guaranteed delivery time. Many customers were not comfortable asking for this level of compensation, especially if the driver was only a few minutes late. In this case 'the punishment was greater than the crime'. For a while Domino's changed the compensation to a more reasonable reduced price for late deliveries. Later the time guarantee was dropped altogether because of problems it caused with employees who were driving too fast in order to make their deliveries.

PROCEDURAL JUSTICE

In addition to fair compensation, customers expect fairness in terms of policies, rules and timeliness of the complaint process. They want easy access to the complaint process, and they want things handled quickly, preferably by the first person they contact. They appreciate companies that can be adaptable in their procedures so that the recovery effort can match their individual circumstances. In some cases, particularly in business-to-business services, companies actually ask the customer, 'What can we do to compensate you for our failure?' Many times what the customer asks for is actually less than the company might have expected.

Fair procedures are characterized by clarity, speed and absence of difficulties. Unfair procedures are those that customers perceive as slow, prolonged and inconvenient. Customers also feel it is unfair if they have to prove their case – when the assumption seems to be they are wrong or lying until they can prove otherwise.

INTERACTIONAL JUSTICE

Above and beyond their expectations of fair compensation and difficulty-free, quick procedures, customers expect to be treated politely, with care and honesty. This form of fairness can dominate the other forms if customers feel the company and its employees have uncaring attitudes and have done little to try to resolve the problem. This type of behaviour on the part of employees may seem strange – why would they treat customers rudely or in an uncaring manner under these circumstances? Often it is due to lack of training and empowerment – a frustrated front-line employee who has no authority to compensate the customer may easily respond in an aloof or uncaring manner, especially if the customer is angry and/or rude.

CULTURAL DIFFERENCES IN CUSTOMERS' RECOVERY EXPECTATIONS

Service firms operating internationally, as well as those operating in multi-ethnic countries within Europe, need to be sensitive to the cultural diversity and subsequently differing expectations of service and of service recovery.

DIFFERING ATTRIBUTION EXPECTATIONS

When service failures occur, customers spontaneously make assumptions about, or attribute blame for, the unexpected event. Researchers[29] have explored service recovery across cultures and found in Western countries, when the failure is caused by some external factor beyond the control of the service firm, customers will often attribute the problem to the context or situation surrounding the service failure – particularly if an explanation is offered by the firm as to what happened. Such action can diminish the blame customers attribute to the firm and its staff, thus avoiding any lowering of their perceptions of overall perceived quality.

For customers from East Asian cultures, on the other hand, a causal explanation has relatively little impact on where the blame for the failure is attributed. These customers prefer other remedies, such as a speedy resolution to the problem and a genuine apology from a manager (rather than a front-line employee) to regain 'face' in the eyes of their family and friends. East Asian customers also have a lower tolerance towards uncertain and ambiguous situations. Thus, when a failure is being remedied, these customers would prefer having a sense of control, which the firm can provide by keeping them informed of exactly what is being done to rectify the situation.

DIFFERING VIEWS OF OUTCOME JUSTICE

Western customers are more interested in, and expect to receive, tangible compensation (i.e. a discount) when a service failure occurs than are Asian customers. Offering compensation is particularly effective in restoring a sense of fairness among American customers; apparently American consumers are particularly concerned with outcome justice. Indeed, American customers are generally more assertive and more used to 'asking for reparation' than consumers from other cultures. Previous research on service recovery in Western contexts consistently shows that compensation has a positive effect on post-recovery satisfaction and loyalty. East Asian customers, who typically tend to be high on uncertainty avoidance, prefer other types of remedies when service failure occurs. In Asian cultures there is a tendency to focus on avoidance of losses rather than on individual gains. East Asian customers emphasize the need to fit in with others and to avoid conflict and confrontation.

DIFFERING VIEWS OF INTERACTIONAL JUSTICE

The research also suggests that, in Western cultures, offering an explanation for service failure might shift the customer's focus away from thinking that the service provider is incompetent, uncaring, or lazy. Such an explanation tends to cause Western customers to pay more attention to the situation as a cause of the failure. East Asian customers, meanwhile, are more likely to be aware of situational constraints, seek to maintain social harmony, and avoid causing a loss of face. For them, interactional fairness appears to be particularly salient. Thus, providing an explanation and treating the offended East Asian customers in a courteous, formal, and empathetic manner is more important than the compensation offered.

PROCEDURAL JUSTICE

For service firms operating in Western countries, hassle-free and fast recovery procedures that lead to compensation for any losses or inconveniences triggered by a service failure are preferred by customers. In East Asian cultures, a genuine apology from a manager (rather than a customer-contact employee) is particularly desirable; such a procedure allows customers to regain 'face' in the eyes of their family and friends. East Asian customers would also prefer to have a sense of control, so having management constantly inform them of what is being done to rectify the situation is also appealing to them.

In service recovery, as in any service situation, companies need to be sensitive to the fact that culture and other factors play a role. Customers in all cultures expect strong service recovery but preferences for the type of recovery or which fairness dimension to emphasize may vary.

SWITCHING VERSUS LOYALTY FOLLOWING SERVICE RECOVERY

Ultimately, how a service failure is handled, and the customer's reaction to the recovery effort, can influence future decisions to remain loyal to the service provider or to switch to another provider. Whether customers switch to a new provider following service failure will depend in addition on a number of other factors. The magnitude and criticality of the failure will clearly be a factor in future repurchase decisions. The more serious the failure, the more likely the customer is to switch, regardless of the recovery effort.[30]

The nature of the customer's relationship with the firm may also influence whether the customer stays or switches providers. Research suggests that customers who have 'true relationships' with their service providers are more forgiving of poorly handled service failures and are less likely to switch than are those who have a 'pseudo-relationship' or a 'first-time encounter' type of relationship.[31] A true relationship is one in which the customer has had repeated contact over time with the same service provider. A first-time encounter relationship is one in which the customer has had only one contact, on a transaction basis, with the provider. A pseudo-relationship is one in which the customer has interacted many times with the same company, but with different service providers each time.

Other research reveals that the individual customer's attitude towards switching will strongly influence whether he or she ultimately stays with the provider and that this attitude toward switching will be even more influential than basic satisfaction with the service.[32] This research suggests that certain customers will have a greater propensity to switch service providers no matter how their service failure situations are handled. Research in an online service context, for example, shows that demographic factors such as age and income, as well as individual factors such as risk aversion, will influence whether a customer continues to use an online service or switches to another provider.[33] The profile of an 'online service switcher' emerged in the research as a person who was influenced to subscribe to the service through positive word-of-mouth communication; who used the service less; who was less satisfied and less involved with the service; who had a lower income and education level; and who also had a lower propensity for taking risks.

Finally, the decision to switch to a different service provider may not occur immediately following service failure or poor service recovery, but may follow an accumulation of events. That is, service switching can be viewed as a process resulting from a series of decisions and critical service encounters over time rather than one specific moment in time when a decision is made.[34] This process orientation suggests that companies could potentially track customer interactions and predict the likelihood of defection based on a series of events, intervening earlier in the process to head off the customer's decision to switch.

Although customers may decide to switch service providers for a variety of reasons, service failure and poor service recovery are often a cause of such behaviour. A study of approximately 500 service-switching incidents identified eight broad themes underlying the decision to defect.[35] These themes are shown in Figure 15.3.

In about 200 of the incidents, a single theme was identified as the cause for switching service providers, and the two largest categories were related to service failure. Core service failure was the cause of switching for 25 per cent of the respondents, and service encounter failure was the reason for switching services for an additional 20 per cent of the sample. In incidents that listed two themes, 29 per cent listed core service failure and 18 per cent service encounter failure as contributing to their desire to switch providers; poor response to failure was mentioned by an additional 11 per cent of the respondents as the cause for switching. As these findings suggest, service failure can cause customers to switch companies. To minimize the impact of

Figure 15.3 Causes behind service switching

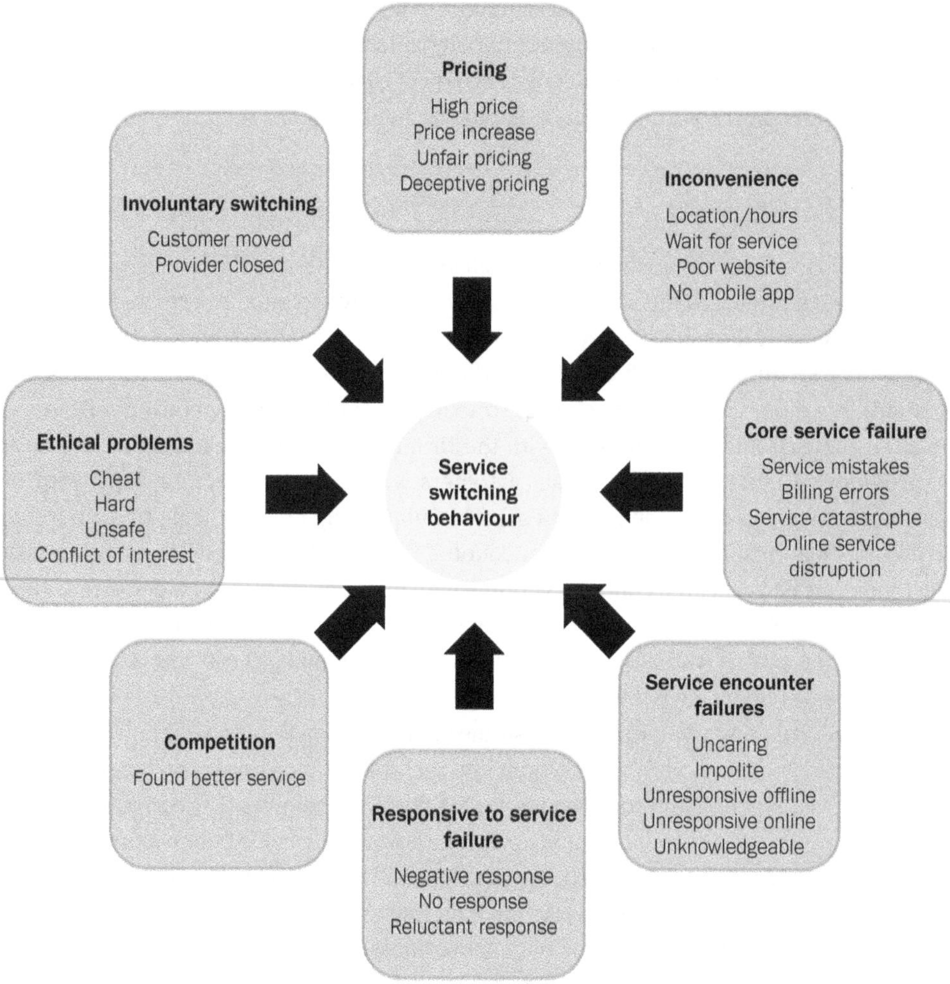

Pricing
High price
Price increase
Unfair pricing
Deceptive pricing

Involuntary switching
Customer moved
Provider closed

Inconvenience
Location/hours
Wait for service
Poor website
No mobile app

Ethical problems
Cheat
Hard
Unsafe
Conflict of interest

Service switching behaviour

Core service failure
Service mistakes
Billing errors
Service catastrophe
Online service distruption

Competition
Found better service

Responsive to service failure
Negative response
No response
Reluctant response

Service encounter failures
Uncaring
Impolite
Unresponsive offline
Unresponsive online
Unknowledgeable

Source: Adapted from S. Keaveney, 'Customer switching behaviour in service industries: an exploratory study', *Journal of Marketing* 59 (April 1995), pp. 71–82.

service failure, excellent service recovery is needed. In the next section we discuss several service recovery strategies that attempt to keep dissatisfied customers from defecting.

SERVICE RECOVERY STRATEGIES

Many companies have learned the importance of providing excellent recovery for disappointed customers. In this section we examine their strategies and share examples of benchmark companies and what they are doing. It will become clear that excellent service recovery is really a combination of a variety of strategies that need to work together, as illustrated in Figure 15.4. We discuss each of the strategies shown in the figure, starting with the basic 'do it right the first time'.

MAKE THE SERVICE FAIL-SAFE – DO IT RIGHT THE FIRST TIME!

The first rule of service quality is to do it right the first time. In this way recovery is unnecessary, customers get what they expect and the costs of redoing the service and compensating for errors can be avoided. As you have already learned, reliability, or doing it right the first time, is the most important dimension of service quality across industry contexts.[36]

Figure 15.4   Service recovery strategies

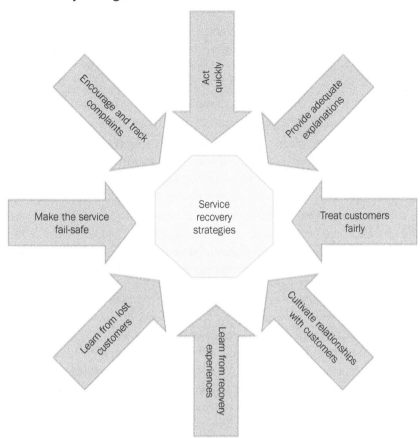

What specific strategies do firms employ to achieve reliability? Total quality management or TQM, practices aimed at 'zero defects' are commonly used. However, given the inherent differences between services and manufactured products, these tools typically require considerable adaptation to work well in service contexts. Firms that blindly adopt TQM practices without considering services implications often fail in their efforts.

It is frequently suggested that services adopt the TQM notion of *poka yoke* to improve service reliability.[37] *Poka yoke* is a Japanese term that means 'fail safing' or 'mistake proofing'. These are automatic warnings or controls in place to ensure that mistakes are not made; essentially they are quality-control mechanisms, typically used on assembly lines. They can be devised in service settings to 'mistake-proof' the service, to ensure that essential procedures are followed and that service steps are carried out in the proper order and in a timely manner. In a hospital, setting numerous poka-yokes ensures that procedures are followed to avoid potentially life-threatening mistakes. For example, trays for surgical instruments have indentations for specific instruments, and each instrument is nested in its appropriate spot. In this way surgeons and their staff know that all instruments are in their places prior to operating.[38]

Similarly, poka-yokes can be devised to ensure that the tangibles associated with the service are clean and well maintained, and that documents are accurate and up-to-date. Poka-yokes can also be implemented for employee behaviours (checklists, role-playing and practice, reminder signs) and even for ensuring that customers perform effectively. Many of the strategies we discuss in Parts 3 and 4 of this text ('Aligning service design and standards' and 'Delivering and performing service') are aimed at ensuring service reliability and can be viewed as applications of the basic fail-safe notion of *poka yoke*.

Even more fundamentally, it is for a firm to create a culture of zero defections to ensure it is doing it right the first time.[39] Within a zero defections culture everyone understands the importance of reliability. Employees and managers aim to satisfy every customer and look for ways to improve service. Employees in a zero defections culture fully understand and appreciate the 'relationship value of a customer' concept that was presented in Chapter 7. Thus they are motivated to provide quality *service every time* and to *every customer*.

ENCOURAGE AND TRACK COMPLAINTS

Even in a zero defections organization that aims for 100 per cent service quality, failures occur. A critical component of a service recovery strategy is thus to encourage and track complaints. Service failures can occur in a variety of ways and at numerous times throughout the service delivery process. However, in many cases it is difficult, if not impossible, for the firm to know that a service failure has occurred unless the customer informs the firm accordingly. Unfortunately, a relatively low percentage of customers (5–10 per cent) will actually complain to the firm. Thus, a major challenge facing management is how to get customers to complain when they experience a service failure and/or they are not satisfied with service delivery. So what can a firm do to elicit complaints? Here are some issues to consider:[40]

- *Develop the mind-set that complaints are good.* Too often the complaining customer is seen by employees in the organization as the *enemy* – someone to be conquered and subdued. The more prudent approach is to develop the mind-set that the complaining customer is the firm's *friend*. Complaints provide valuable feedback to the firm, giving it the opportunity not only to address the service failure for the complaining customer, but also to identify problems that other (less vocal) customers may also be experiencing. It has been suggested that complainers should be treated with the dignity and respect given to the best analysts and consultants. One company puts all customers who have complained on a VIP list. Accepting complaints is truly reflective of firms who are close to their customers.
- *Make complaining easy.* If the firm truly wants to hear from customers who experience poor service, it needs to make it easy for them to share their experiences with the firm. Sometimes customers have no idea whom to speak to if they have a complaint, what the process is or what will be involved. Complaining should be easy – the last thing customers want when they are dissatisfied is to face a complex, difficult-to-access process for complaining. Customers should know where to go and/or who to talk to when they encounter problems, and they should be made to feel confident that something positive will result from their efforts. Technological advances have made it possible to provide customers with multiple avenues to complain, including freephone customer call centres, company email addresses, twitter feeds and website feedback forms. The firm should regularly communicate to customers that complaining is easy and that it welcomes and appreciates such feedback.

SERVICE SPOTLIGHT

KLM uses social media to make obtaining feedback easy. The company aims to respond to each Twitter tweet or Facebook post within one hour and resolve all issues within 24 hours. KLM receives around 35,000 questions every week on social media. 75 per cent of these are posted on Facebook, with the other 25 per cent coming predominantly via Twitter.

KLM has 130 employees fully focused on social customer care. The average response time is 23 minutes. It is a 24/7 service available in 10 languages.

Flight attendants carry an iPad on board to field any social enquiries from passengers on their flight. The customer care team can ask the cabin crew to take the enquiries offline, solve any problems and report back.

An example of such social customer care is when a customer complained about being given a cold meal on a flight. On the return flight, the cabin crew made sure this passenger was among the first to get their meal and received an apology for what happened on the outbound journey.[41]

- *Be an active listener.* Employees should be encouraged and trained to listen actively to customers, particularly to see if they can pick up on any cues to suggest less than ideal service. A restaurant customer might respond 'fine' to the waiter's question, 'How is your meal?' However, the customer's body language and tone of voice, or the amount of food not eaten, might indicate that all is not fine. Some customers may not be assertive in voicing their displeasure, but they may drop clues to suggest that something is amiss. Employees as well as managers should be consistently listening not only to the customer's actual words but also to what he or she may really be trying or wanting to communicate.
- *Ask customers about specific service issues.* A very simple, informal way to find out about any service failure is simply to ask. Managers at one hotel with a high percentage of business travellers make it a point to be at the front desk between 7.45 a.m. and 8.45 a.m. every day, because approximately 80 per cent of their business travellers check out at that time. During the checkout process, managers avoid questions that can be answered with a simple 'yes', 'OK', or 'fine' (e.g. 'Was the room to your satisfaction?') and instead ask questions that force customers to provide specific feedback (e.g. 'How could we have improved the technology in your room?' or 'What needs to be done to improve our gym?'). Asking customers very specific questions that cannot be answered with a simple 'yes' or 'no' may provide customers with an easy way to point out expectations that were not fulfilled.
- *Conduct short surveys.* A follow-up telephone call to a customer still in the midst of the service experience can help to identify problems in real time and thus enable real-time recovery.

SERVICE SPOTLIGHT

An example of using follow-up telephone calls is the Enterprise Rent-A-Car Company. It regularly calls customers the day after they have picked up a rental car to ask the customer if everything is OK with the vehicle. Customers who report problems, such as a broken window or a car that smells of smoke, are brought a replacement vehicle that day without any additional questions.

As we have just seen, firms can utilize a number of ways to encourage and track complaints. Customer research can be designed specifically for this purpose through satisfaction surveys, critical incidents studies and lost customer research, as discussed in Chapter 6. Nowadays, freephone call centres, email, Facebook pages and the use of pagers are commonplace to facilitate, encourage and track complaints. Software applications in a number of companies also allow complaints to be analysed, sorted, responded to, and tracked automatically.[42]

In some cases technology can anticipate trouble and complaints before they happen, allowing service employees to diagnose problems before the customer recognizes they exist. At companies such as Ericsson and Siemens, information systems are being implemented to anticipate equipment failures and to send out an electronic alert to the local field technician with the nature of the problem as well as which parts and tools will be needed to make the repair – a repair the customer does not yet know is needed.

ACT QUICKLY

Complaining customers want quick responses.[43] Thus, if the company welcomes, even encourages, complaints, it must be prepared to act on them quickly. Unfortunately, many companies require customers to contact multiple employees before getting a problem resolved. Research suggests that, if a problem can be handled by the first contact, customers are satisfied with the firm's response 46 per cent of the time; however, once three or more contacts are needed, the percentage of customers who are satisfied with the response drops to 21 per cent.[44] An unsolved problem can quickly escalate. Take, for example, a true story of a company director who sent an email to his bank to register a complaint while he was attempting a transaction through its Internet banking service. The email was never answered. The customer then sent an email directly to the chairman of the bank. That email was never answered either. Ultimately the customer withdrew his approximately 75,000 euro account, dissatisfied that his complaint was not handled in a timely manner. In this case the technology was not effectively linked to other systems, nor, ultimately, to employees. Internet access encouraged the complaint, but the response never occurred. The lesson here? A quick response to a service failure can go a long way in appeasing a dissatisfied customer. The ability to provide an immediate response requires not only systems and procedures that allow quick action, but empowered employees also.

Employees must be trained and empowered to solve problems as they occur. Empowerment of employees, a practice discussed in more detail in Chapter 11, can often allow for quick responses and help placate dissatisfied customers.

Service employees have a specific and real need for recovery training. Because customers demand that service recovery take place on the spot and quickly, front-line employees need the skills, authority and incentives to engage in effective recovery. Effective recovery skills include hearing the customer's problems, taking initiative, identifying solutions, improvising and perhaps bending the rules from time to time.

Not only do employees need the authority to act (usually within defined limits), but they also should not be punished for taking action. In fact, incentives should exist that encourage employees to exercise their recovery authority. At the Ritz-Carlton employees are authorized to spend up to 1,500 euros on behalf of the customer to solve a problem. This amount of money is rarely needed, but knowing that they have the clearance to use it encourages employees to be responsive without fear of retribution.

Sometimes employees can even anticipate problems before they arise and surprise customers with a solution. For example, the cabin crew on a flight severely delayed due to weather conditions anticipated that passengers would be hungry, particularly young children. Once in flight, they announced to the harried travellers, 'Thank you for your extreme patience in waiting with us. Now that we're on our way, we'd like to offer you complimentary beverages and dinner. Because we have a number of very hungry children on board, we'd like to serve them first, if that's OK with all of you'. The passengers nodded and applauded their efforts, knowing that hungry, crying children could make the situation even worse. The cabin crew had anticipated a problem and solved it before it escalated.

Another way that problems or complaints can be handled quickly is by building systems that allow customers to actually solve their own service needs and fix their own problems. Typically this approach is done through technology. Customers directly interface with the company's technology to perform their own customer service, which provides them with instant answers. DHL uses this strategy for its package tracking services, for example.

SERVICE SPOTLIGHT

Cisco Systems – Customers Recover for Themselves[45]

Cisco provides the equipment and produces networking devices that keep businesses running. If the network is not working, the business is not working. Failures in this environment become extremely costly very quickly. Customers want to know that their problems can be solved immediately, and they want a sense of control over the solution.

To address this issue, Cisco Systems turned to the Internet. It built a world-class model of online customer service. Essentially, Cisco has put customers in charge of their own service through the

Internet. In many cases customers are now able to completely solve their own service problems, with no intervention of Cisco personnel. Access to information is immediate, and solutions can be highly customized for the individual customer. The system includes the following types of service:

- *Support Community* – a searchable database for answers to networking questions. If the question is too complex, the customer can escalate the request to a highly trained service representative. However, most questions can be answered without human intervention. Plus, the questions asked are used to further enhance and develop the information system to answer similar questions in the future.
- *Troubleshooting engine* – an expert system that takes the user through the problem identification and resolution process. Here customers actually solve problems and are instructed on how to fix their systems. This system saves time for customers and gives them a much greater sense of control, particularly in critical situations when every minute of downtime is extremely costly.
- *Bug tool-kit* – collection of interactive tools for identifying, tracking and resolving software bugs.
- *Software centre* – a comprehensive vending machine for Cisco software. This system provides one-stop shopping for Cisco software and helps customers upgrade in a timely manner and be sure that they have the latest release of a particular software.
- *Service order agent* – a parts information, ordering and tracking system that allows customers to conduct transactions online. This system provides fast service for orders and saves on administrative costs for both Cisco and its customers.
- *Service contract centre* – a system that allows customers to view the contents and/or status of their contracts with Cisco.

Currently 80 per cent of customer problems are handled via the Internet through information provided by Cisco and self-help tools that allow customers to diagnose and solve their own problems.

PROVIDE ADEQUATE EXPLANATIONS

In many service failures, customers look to try to understand why the failure occurred. Explanations can help to defuse negative reactions and convey respect for the customer.[46] Research suggests that when the firm's ability to provide an adequate outcome is not successful, further dissatisfaction can be reduced if an adequate explanation is provided to the customer.[47] In order for an explanation to be perceived as adequate, it must possess two primary characteristics. First, the content of the explanation must be appropriate; relevant facts and pertinent information are important in helping the customer understand what occurred. Second, the style of the delivery of the explanation, or how the explanation is delivered, can also reduce customer dissatisfaction. Style includes the personal characteristics of the explanation givers, including their credibility and sincerity. Explanations perceived by customers as honest, sincere and not manipulative are generally the most effective.

TREAT CUSTOMERS FAIRLY

In responding quickly, it is also critical to treat each customer fairly. Customers expect to be treated fairly in terms of the outcome they receive, the process by which the service recovery takes place, and the interpersonal treatment received from employees attempting to address the service failure. Acknowledging a problem has occurred, apologizing for the inconvenience, and putting effort into resolving the issue are generally perceived by customers as fair treatment. In the section titled 'Customers' recovery expectations', we discussed examples, strategies and results of research that focused on fairness in service recovery. Here we remind you that fair treatment is an essential component of an effective service recovery strategy.

CULTIVATE RELATIONSHIPS WITH CUSTOMERS

In Chapter 7, we discussed the importance of developing long-term relationships with customers. One additional benefit of relationship marketing is that, if the firm fails in service delivery, those customers who have a strong relationship with the firm are often more forgiving of service failures and more open to the firm's service recovery efforts. Research suggests that strong customer–firm relationships can help shield the firm from the negative effects of failures on customer satisfaction.[48] To illustrate: one study demonstrated that the presence of rapport between customers and employees provided several service recovery benefits, including increased post-failure satisfaction, increased loyalty intentions and decreased negative word-of-mouth communication.[49] Another study found that customers who expect the relationship to continue also tend to have lower service recovery expectations and may demand less immediate compensation for a failure, because they consider the balance of equity across a longer time horizon.[50] Thus, cultivation of strong customer relationships can provide an important buffer to service firms when failures occur.

LEARN FROM RECOVERY EXPERIENCES

Problem-resolution situations are more than just opportunities to fix flawed services and strengthen ties with customers. 'They are also a valuable – but frequently ignored or underutilized – source of diagnostic, prescriptive information for improving customer service.'[51] By tracking service recovery efforts and solutions, managers can often learn about systematic problems in the delivery system that need fixing. By conducting root-cause analysis, firms can identify the sources of the problems and modify processes, sometimes eliminating almost completely the need for recovery.

★ SERVICE SPOTLIGHT

At Ritz-Carlton Hotels all employees carry service recovery forms called 'instant action forms' with them at all times so that they can immediately record service failures and suggest actions to address them. Each individual employee 'owns' any complaint that he or she receives and is responsible for seeing that service recovery occurs. For example, if a maintenance employee hears a complaint from a customer while in the middle of fixing a light in the hotel corridor, he or she owns that complaint and must be sure that it is handled appropriately by the hotel before returning to the task at hand.

In turn, the employees report to management the sources of service failure and the remedies. This information is then entered into the customer database and analysed for patterns and systemic service issues that need to be fixed. If common themes are observed across a number of failure situations, changes are made to service processes or attributes. In addition, the information is entered into the customer's personal data file so when that customer stays at a Ritz-Carlton again (no matter at which hotel), employees are made aware of the prior experience, ensuring that it does not happen again for that particular customer.

LEARN FROM LOST CUSTOMERS

Another key component of an effective service recovery strategy is to learn from the customers who defect or decide to leave. Formal market research to discover the reasons customers have left can assist in preventing service failures in the future. This type of research is difficult, even painful for companies, however. No one really likes to examine their failures. Yet such examination is essential for preventing the same mistakes and losing more customers in the future.[52]

As presented in Chapter 6, lost customer research typically involves in-depth probing of customers to determine their true reasons for leaving. This information is most effectively obtained by in-depth interviews administered by skilled interviewers who truly understand the business. It may be best to have this type of research done by senior people in the company, particularly in business-to-business contexts in which customers are large and the impact of even one lost customer is great. This type of in-depth analysis often requires a series of 'why' questions or 'tell me more about that' prompts to get at the actual reason for the customer's defection.[53]

In conducting this kind of research, a firm must focus on important or profitable customers who have left – not just everyone who has dropped the company. An insurance company in Australia once began research to learn about their lost customers, only to find that the customers they were losing tended to be their least profitable customers anyway. They quickly determined that in-depth research on how to keep these unprofitable customers would not be a good investment!

ACT QUICKLY BEFORE BEING FORCED TO DO SO THROUGH LEGISLATION

If an industry or large organization is not seen to be responding to the complaints of customers, national or European governmental bodies may step in and impose regulations and legislation to ensure the protection of the consumer. Many utilities such as water, gas, electricity, telephone and broadcasting are controlled by bodies who regulate prices and issue guidelines for service delivery. Another example is the airline industry, where the European Union introduced legislation to protect air passenger rights with regard to flight cancellations and delays. Air passengers are entitled to the following compensation in the case of arrivals delayed by over three hours:

€250 (≈ £197) for flights of up to 1,500 km
€400 (≈ £315) for flights between 1,500 km and 3,500 km
€400 (≈ £315) for all intra-community flights of more than 1,500 km
€600 (≈ £473) for flights over 3,500 km

Airlines have to pay compensation on this scale for flights that are delayed by more than three hours. Passengers are also compensated for late cancellation of their flight and should receive assistance in the event of long delays. There is therefore an incentive to address problems before the cost of addressing the issue increases as a result of having to comply with externally imposed regulations.

SERVICE GUARANTEES

A guarantee is a particular type of recovery tool. In a business context, a guarantee is a pledge or assurance that a product offered by a firm will perform as promised and, if not, then some form of reparation will be undertaken by the firm. Although guarantees are relatively common for manufactured products, they have only recently been used for services. Traditionally, many people believed that services simply could not be guaranteed given their intangible and variable nature. What would be guaranteed? With a product, the customer is guaranteed that it will perform as promised and, if not, that it can be returned. With services, it is generally not possible to take returns or to 'undo' what has been performed. Scepticism about service guarantees is being dispelled, however, as more and more companies find they can guarantee their services and that there are tremendous benefits for doing so.

Companies are finding that effective service guarantees can complement the company's service recovery strategy – serving as one tool to help accomplish the service recovery strategies.

BENEFITS OF SERVICE GUARANTEES

'Service organizations, in particular, are beginning to recognize that guarantees can serve not only as a marketing tool but as a means for defining, cultivating, and maintaining quality throughout an organization.'[54] The benefits to the company of an effective service guarantee are numerous:[55]

- *A good guarantee forces the company to focus on its customers*. To develop a meaningful guarantee, the company must know what is important to its customers – what they expect and value. In many cases 'satisfaction' is guaranteed, but in order for the guarantee to work effectively, the company must clearly understand what satisfaction means for its customers (what they value and expect).
- *An effective guarantee sets clear standards for the organization*. It prompts the company to define clearly what it expects of its employees and to communicate that expectation to them. The guarantee gives employees service-oriented goals that can quickly align employee behaviours around customer strategies.

⭐ SERVICE SPOTLIGHT

Lands' End, the clothing retailer, publicizes its customer service guarantee on its website, stating:

> *In complete contrast to today's throwaway culture, quality counts for everything at Lands' End. We take great pride in the design and manufacture of our products to ensure their longevity and, ultimately, your satisfaction. So that you can be assured of our commitment to this, everything we sell is Quality. Guaranteed. No ifs, no buts, no problem.*

Simply put, if you're not 100 per cent happy with a purchase, you can return it at any time for an exchange or refund.[56]

This lets employees know exactly what they should do if a customer complains. It is also clear to employees that making it right for the customer is an important company goal.

- *A good guarantee generates immediate and relevant feedback from customers*. It provides an incentive for customers to complain, thereby providing more representative feedback to the company than simply relying on the relatively few customers who typically voice their concerns. The guarantee communicates to customers that they have the right to complain.
- *When the guarantee is invoked there is an instant opportunity to recover*, thus satisfying the customer and helping customer retention.
- *Information generated through the guarantee can be tracked and integrated into continuous improvement efforts*. A feedback link between customers and service operations decisions can be strengthened through the guarantee.
- *Studies of the impact of service guarantees suggest that employee morale and loyalty can be enhanced as a result*. A guarantee generates pride among employees. Through feedback from the guarantee, improvements can be made in the service that benefit customers and, indirectly, employees.
- *For customers, the guarantee reduces their sense of risk* and builds confidence in the organization. Because services are intangible and often highly personal or ego-involving, customers seek information and cues that will help reduce their sense of uncertainty. Guarantees have been shown to reduce risk and increase positive evaluation of the service prior to purchase.[57]

The bottom line for the company is that an effective guarantee can affect profitability through building customer awareness and loyalty, through positive word of mouth, and through reduction in costs as service improvements are made and service recovery expenses are reduced. Indirectly, the guarantee can reduce costs of employee turnover through creating a more positive service culture.

TYPES OF SERVICE GUARANTEES

SATISFACTION VERSUS SERVICE ATTRIBUTE GUARANTEES

Service guarantees can be *unconditional satisfaction guarantees* or *service attribute guarantees*. Radisson hotels operate the 100 per cent guest satisfaction guarantee. That is, if a customer complains, they will respond speedily. If the guest remains disappointed, any staff member can evoke the 100 per cent Guest Satisfaction Guarantee, and that guest will not have to pay for their room or the service in question.

Radisson's guarantee is an unconditional satisfaction guarantee. Travelodge and Hotel ibis offer similar types of guarantee.

SERVICE SPOTLIGHT

Hotel ibis, the budget hotel chain owned by Accor, have a commitment through all of their activities:

To make our customers' sleep happy.

Hotel ibis demonstrate their confidence in delivering on this commitment by operating the '*15-Minute Promise*'. If a customer doesn't get what they expected, the hotel has 15 minutes to set it right or the specific service will be provided free of charge to the guest.

In other cases, firms offer guarantees for particular aspects of the service that are important to customers. Tesco has developed a 'One in Front' policy, which ensures that each customer should have no more than one person ahead of him or her in the checkout queue. If they do, another checkout will be opened. Pizza Hut guarantees delivery to the table in 20 minutes or the pizza is free. In both cases, the companies have guaranteed elements of the service that they know are important to customers.

EXTERNAL VERSUS INTERNAL GUARANTEES

Interestingly, guarantees do not have to be just for external customers. Some companies are finding that internal service guarantees – one part of the organization guaranteeing its services to others – are effective ways of aligning internal service operations. For example, the housekeeping supplies department at Embassy Suites guarantees the housekeeping staff, its internal customer, that they can get supplies on the day they requested them. If not, the supply department pays approximately 4 euros to the housekeeper. At one direct-mail firm, the sales force guarantees to give the production department all the specifications needed to provide service to the external customer, or the offending salesperson will take the production department to lunch, will sing a song at their next department meeting, or will personally input all the specifications into the computer.[58]

CHARACTERISTICS OF EFFECTIVE GUARANTEES

No matter the type of guarantee, certain characteristics make some guarantees more effective than others. These characteristics are as follows: [59]

- *Unconditional.* The guarantee should be unconditional – no strings attached. Some guarantees can appear as if they were written by the legal department (they often are), with all kinds of restrictions, proof required and limitations. Such guarantees are generally not effective.
- *Meaningful.* Guaranteeing what is obvious or expected is not meaningful to customers. For example, a water delivery company offered a guarantee to deliver water on the day promised, or a free container of water would be provided next time. In that industry, delivery on the day scheduled was an expectation nearly always met by every competitor – thus the guarantee was not meaningful to the customer. It was a bit like guaranteeing four wheels on a car! The payout should also be meaningful. Customers expect to be reimbursed in a manner that fully compensates them for their dissatisfaction, their time and for the inconvenience involved.
- *Easy to understand.* The guarantee should communicate clearly to both customers and employees. Sometimes the wording of a guarantee is confusing, the language is verbose, or the guarantee contains

so many restrictions and conditions that neither customers nor employees are certain what is being guaranteed.

- *Easy to invoke.* The guarantee should be easy to invoke. Requiring customers to write a letter and/or provide documented proof of service failure are common pitfalls that make invoking the guarantee time-consuming and not worth it to the customer, particularly if the monetary value of the service is relatively low.

WHEN TO USE (OR NOT USE) A GUARANTEE

Service guarantees are not appropriate for every company and certainly not in every service situation. A guarantee is probably *not* the right strategy when:

- *Existing service quality in the company is poor.* Before instituting a guarantee, the company should fix any significant quality problems. Although a guarantee will certainly draw attention to these failures and the poor quality of the service, the costs of implementing it could easily outweigh any benefits. These costs include actual monetary payouts to customers for poor service as well as the costs associated with customer goodwill.

- *A guarantee does not fit the company's image.* If the company already has a reputation for very high quality, and in fact implicitly guarantees its service, then a formal guarantee is most likely unnecessary. For example, if Ritz-Carlton Hotels were to offer an explicit guarantee, it could potentially confuse customers who already expect the highest quality, implicitly guaranteed, from this high-end hotel chain. Research suggests that the benefits of offering a guarantee for a high-end hotel like the Ritz-Carlton may be significantly less than the benefits that a hotel of lesser standing would enjoy, and in fact the benefits might not be justified by the costs.[60]

- *Service quality is truly uncontrollable.* Uncontrollable service quality is often an excuse for not employing a guarantee, but firms encounter few situations in which service quality is truly uncontrollable. Here are a couple of examples to illustrate such situations. If success depends in large part on the participants' own effort, it would not be good practice for a training organization to guarantee that all participants will pass a particular examination on completion of the training course. The company could, however, guarantee satisfaction with the training or particular aspects of the training process. Similarly, a ferry company operating in the Western Isles of Scotland in the winter would probably not guarantee on-time departure because of the unpredictability and uncontrollability of the weather.

- *Potential exists for customer abuse of the guarantee.* Fear of opportunistic customer behaviour, including customer cheating or fraudulent invocation of service guarantees, is a common reason that firms hesitate to offer guarantees.[61] For example, at one large pizza chain students occasionally 'cheated' the company by invoking the service guarantee without cause in order to receive free food.[62] In those situations in which abuse of the service guarantee can easily occur, firms should carefully consider the consequences of offering a guarantee. A recent study found that guarantees are more likely to be abused when offered in situations in which a large percentage of customers are not regular (repeat) customers.[63] In general, customer abuse of service guarantees is fairly minimal and not at all widespread.[64]

- *Costs of the guarantee outweigh the benefits.* As it would with any quality investment, the company will want to carefully calculate expected costs (payouts for failures and costs of making improvements) against anticipated benefits (customer loyalty, quality improvements, attraction of new customers, word-of-mouth advertising).

- *Customers perceive little risk in the service.* Guarantees are usually most effective when customers are uncertain about the company and/or the quality of its services. The guarantee can allay uncertainties and help reduce risk.[65] If customers perceive little risk, if the service is relatively inexpensive with lots of potential alternative providers, and if quality is relatively invariable, then a guarantee will likely produce little effectiveness for the company, other than perhaps delivering some promotional value.

• *Customers perceive little variability in service quality among competitors.* Some industries exhibit extreme variability in quality among competitors. In these cases a guarantee may be quite effective, particularly for the first company to offer one. Guarantees may also be effective in industries in which quality is perceived to be low overall across competitors. The first firm with a guarantee can often distinguish itself from competitors. A study of guarantees offered by several service firms in Singapore found that those companies which were unique in their industry in offering a guarantee attributed more of their success to having one than did companies in industries in which guarantees were more common.[66]

SUMMARY

This chapter focused on the importance of an effective service recovery strategy for retaining customers and increasing positive word-of-mouth communication. Another major benefit of an effective service recovery strategy is that the information it provides can be useful for service improvement. The potential downsides of poor service recovery are tremendous – negative word of mouth, lost customers and declining business when quality issues are not addressed.

You learned how customers respond to service failures and why some complain while others do not. You learned that customers who complain expect to be treated fairly – not just in terms of the actual outcome or compensation they receive, but also in terms of the procedures that are used and how they are treated interpersonally. We pointed out that there is tremendous room for improvement in service recovery effectiveness across firms and industries.

The second half of the chapter focused on specific strategies that firms use for service recovery: (1) making the service fail-safe, or doing it right the first time, (2) encouraging and tracking complaints, (3) acting quickly, (4) providing adequate explanations, (5) treating customers fairly, (6) cultivating relationships with customers, (7) learning from recovery experiences, (8) learning from lost customers. To these, we added enacting recovery mechanisms before regulation imposes them.

The chapter ended with a discussion of service guarantees as a tool many firms use to build a foundation for service recovery. You learned the benefits of service guarantees, the elements of a good guarantee, and the pros and cons of using guarantees under various circumstances.

KEY CONCEPTS

EXERCISES

1 Write a letter of complaint (or voice your complaint in person) to a service organization from which you have experienced less than desirable service. What do you expect the organization to do to recover? (Later, report to the class the results of your complaint, whether you were satisfied with the recovery, what could/should have been done differently and whether you will continue using the service.)

2 Interview five people about their service recovery experiences as customers. What happened and what did they expect the firm to do? Were they treated fairly based on the definition of recovery fairness presented in this chapter? Will they give the company their custom in the future?

3 Interview a manager about the service recovery strategies used in his or her firm. Use the strategies shown in Figure 15.4 to frame your questions.

4 Reread the example relating to Cisco Systems on page 342. Visit Cisco System's website (www.cisco.com). Review what the company is currently doing to help its customers solve their own problems. Compare Cisco's initiatives with the self-service efforts of another service provider of your choice.

5 Choose a service you are familiar with. Explain what it offers and develop a good service guarantee for it. Discuss why your guarantee is a good one, and list the benefits to the company of implementing it.

DISCUSSION QUESTIONS

1 Why is it important for a service firm to have a strong recovery strategy? Think of a time when you received less than desirable service from a particular service organization. Was any effort made to recover? What should/could have been done differently? Do you still buy services from the organization? Why or why not? Did you tell others about your experience?

2 Discuss the benefits to a company of having an effective service recovery strategy. Describe an instance in which you experienced (or delivered as an employee) an effective service recovery. In what ways did the company benefit in this particular situation?

3 For a particular service, identify examples of unfairness in outcomes, procedures and interactions.

4 Explain the recovery paradox, and discuss its implications for a service firm manager.

5 Discuss the types of actions that customers can take in response to a service failure. Of the four types of complainer described in this chapter, which one are you? Why? As a manager, would you want to encourage your customers to be voicers? If so, how?

6 Explain the logic behind these two quotes: 'a complaint is a gift' and 'the customer who complains is your friend'.

7 Choose a firm you are familiar with. Describe how you would design an ideal service recovery strategy for that organization.

8 What are the benefits to the company of an effective service guarantee? Should every service organization have one?

9 Research and describe three service guarantees that are currently offered by companies or organizations (other than the ones already described in this chapter). Are your examples good guarantees or poor guarantees based on the criteria presented in this chapter?

10 What is the value of undertaking research with lost customers? Suggest ways in which this research could be done.

FURTHER READING

Andreassen, T.W. and Streukens, S. (2013). Online complaining. *Managing Service Quality: An International Journal*, 23(1) pp. 4–24.

De Matos, C.A., Henrique, J.L. and C.A.V. Rossi, C.A.V. (2007). Service recovery paradox: a meta-analysis. *Journal of Service Research* 10 (August), 60–77.

De Matos, C.A., Von der Heyde Fernandes, D., Leis, R.P., and Trez, G. (2011). A cross cultural investigation of customer reactions to service failure and recovery. *Journal of International Consumer Marketing* 23(3/4), 211–28.

De Ruyter, K. and Wetzels, M. (2000). Customer equity considerations in service recovery: a cross-industry perspective. *International Journal of Service Industry Management*, 11(1), 91–108.

Edvardsson, B., Tronvoll, B. and Höykinpuro, R. (2011). Complex service recovery processes: how to avoid triple deviation. *Managing Service Quality: An International Journal*, 21(4), 331–49.

Michel, S. and Meuter, M.L. (2008). The service recovery paradox: true but overrated? *International Journal of Service Industry Management*, 19(4), 441–57.

Schoefer, K. and Ennew, C. (2005). The impact of perceived justice on consumers' responses to service complaint experiences. *Journal of Services Marketing*, 19(5), 261–70.

Tax, S.S., Brown, S.W. and Chandrashekaran, M. (1998). Customer evaluations of service complaint experiences: implications for relationship marketing. *Journal of Marketing*, 62 (April), 60–76.

PART 5
Managing Service Promises

CHAPTER 16   Managing External and Internal Communications

CHAPTER 17   Pricing of Services

The fourth provider gap illustrates the difference between service delivery and the service provider's external communications. Promises made by a service company through its media advertising, online activity and other communications may potentially raise customer expectations that serve as the standard against which customers assess service quality. Broken promises can occur for many reasons: ineffective marketing communications, over-promising in advertising or personal selling, inadequate coordination between operations and marketing, and differences in policies and procedures across service outlets.

In service companies, a fit between communications about service and actual service delivery is necessary, as shown in the figure below. Chapter 16 is devoted to the topic of managing external and internal communications – careful integration and organization of all of a service organization's external and internal communications channels. The chapter describes why this communication is necessary and how companies can do it well.

Chapter 17 deals with another issue related to managing promises, the pricing of services. In packaged goods (and even in durable goods), many customers possess enough price knowledge before purchase to be able to judge whether a price is fair or in line with competition. With services, customers often have no internal reference point for prices before purchase and consumption.

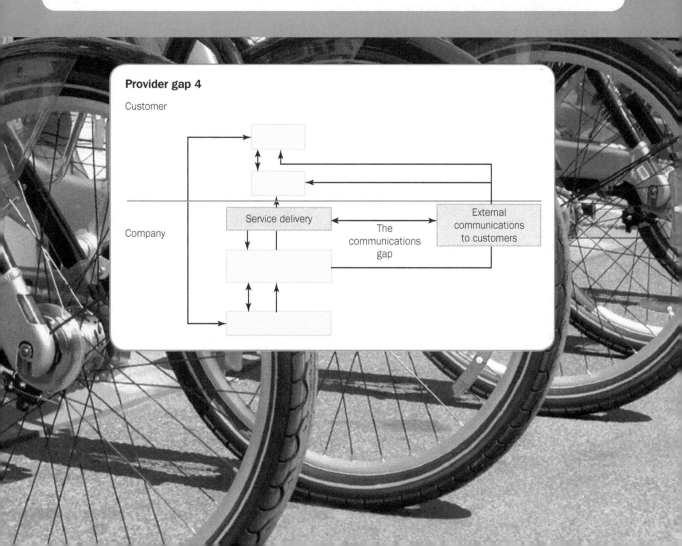

Provider gap 4

Customer

Company

Service delivery

The communications gap

External communications to customers

CHAPTER 16

Managing External and Internal Communications

LEARNING OBJECTIVES

This chapter's objectives are to:

1 Discuss the key reasons for service communication challenges.
2 Introduce the concept of integrated service marketing communications.
3 Present four ways to integrate online and offline marketing communications in service organizations.
4 Present specific strategies for managing promises, managing customer expectations, educating customers and managing internal communications.

OPENING EXAMPLE

Santander's Cycle Partnership

Santander UK has been awarded the title sponsorship of London's self-service bike sharing scheme for a seven year period (2015–2022). The 11,500 bikes, 748 docking stations, and 32 service vehicles used in the scheme have been branded with the Santander Cycles name and red colour, down to the staff uniforms and membership keys. Users log more than 10 million journeys across London on the bicycles each year. The £43.75 m deal is the largest public-sector sponsorship in the world.

The sponsorship is supported with the launch of a branded mobile phone app that enables Santander Cycles users to unlock a bike remotely and share journey information. Santander staff, known as 'cycle champions', are on call in the bank's London branches to offer advice to those using the bikes for the first time. Cyclists who have a current account with Santander also receive cashback on every journey.

The sponsorship aims to bring Santander's brand values to life. It is designed to encourage interactions between people and to embody the bank's motto 'simple, personal and fair': *simple* through events and cycle champions, *personal* through the app, and *fair* through the cashback scheme. In addition to the London scheme, Santander UK is also sponsoring a number of cycling events throughout the UK.

In 2015, television advertisements for a Santander credit card featured McLaren Honda driver Jenson Button riding a Santander Cycle to promote the new cashback offer on the card. Major public relations activity was undertaken at the launch of the new sponsorship ensuring significant coverage over all media types.

Social media (Facebook and Twitter) are integrated in the PR for the sponsorship. On April 1st 2015, the bank even tweeted its own April Fools' joke with photographs of the first Santander Cycle-through bank. Within 2 months of launch, the Santander Cycles twitter feed had over 36,000 followers and around 4,000 tweets.

However, if Santander UK truly want to demonstrate commitment to their brand positioning (and for any integrated marketing communication campaign to work), it is important that the service activities of the organization also match the service promise that it is trying to communicate.[1]

The message at the end of this Santander example is clear: a major cause of poorly perceived service is the difference between what a firm promises about a service and what it actually delivers. Customer expectations are shaped by both uncontrollable and company-controlled factors. Word-of-mouth communication, social media, publicity, customer generated media, customer experiences with other service providers and customer needs are key factors that influence customer expectations; they are rarely controllable by the firm. Controllable factors such as company advertising, corporate websites, mobile apps, personal selling and promises made by service personnel also influence customer expectations. In this chapter we discuss both types of communication, but focus more heavily on the controllable factors as the ones that can be more directly influenced by the company. Accurate, coordinated and appropriate company communication – advertising, websites, social media, personal selling and other communication channels that do not over-promise or misrepresent – is essential to delivering services that customers perceive as high in quality.

Because company communications about services promise what people will do and because people's behaviour cannot be standardized like physical goods produced by machines, the potential for a mismatch between what is communicated and perceptions of actual service delivery (provider gap 4, the communications gap) is high. By coordinating communication within and outside the organization, companies can minimize the size of this gap.

THE NEED FOR COORDINATION IN ONLINE AND OFFLINE MARKETING COMMUNICATION CHANNELS

Marketing communication is more complex today than it used to be. In the past customers received marketing information about goods and services from a limited number of sources, usually mass-communication ones such as television and newspapers. With a limited number of sources, marketers could easily convey a uniform brand image and coordinate promises. By contrast, today's consumers of both goods and services receive communications from a far richer variety of advertising vehicles – websites, direct mail, and interactive communication tools such as virtual communities (Facebook, Linkedin, Twitter, YouTube, Foursquare, etc.), blogs, mobile phone apps, viral marketing and gaming.

In addition, consumers of services also receive additional communication from servicescapes, customer service departments and everyday service encounters with employees. These service interactions add to the variety, volume and complexity of information that a customer receives. While a company cannot control outside sources, ensuring that messages from all company sources provide a consistent message about the service brand is a major challenge for marketers of services.

Any company that disseminates information through multiple channels needs to be certain that customers receive unified messages and promises. These channels include not only marketing communication messages that flow directly from the company but also personal messages that employees send to customers. Figure 16.1 shows an enhanced version of the services marketing triangle that we presented in Chapter 1, emphasizing that the customer of services is the target of two types of communication. First, external marketing communication includes traditional channels such as advertising, corporate websites, sales promotion and public relations. Second, interactive marketing communication involves the messages

Figure 16.1 Communications and the services marketing triangle

Source: Adapted from P. Kotler, *Marketing Management: Analysis, Planning, Implementation, and Control*, 9th edn, © 1997.

that employees give to customers through such channels as personal selling, customer service interactions, service encounter interactions and servicescapes (discussed in Chapter 10). A service company must ensure that these interactive messages remain consistent, both among themselves and with those sent through external communications. To do so, the third side of the triangle, internal marketing communications, must be managed so that information from the company to employees is accurate, complete and consistent with what customers are hearing or seeing.

The need for integrated marketing campaigns is evident in both business-to-business situations and business-to-consumer instances. In business-to-business situations, the problem often comes about because multiple parts of a service organization deal with a client and do not communicate well internally. For example, consider a large client of a major accountancy firm which provides it with audit services, taxation advice and management consultancy services. If the client organization deals with someone different for each service, the accountancy firm needs to – but may not – coordinate internally to ensure that they are sending the customer consistent messages. Not only that, but each internal division may have its own promotional campaign with different promises and messages. Think of an example from your own experience that may illustrate what happens when services marketing communications are not integrated. Have you ever seen an advertisement for a service, such as a special sandwich offer from a fast-food chain, then gone to your local outlet and found it is not available there? Did the employee behind the counter provide a reason for the sandwich offer not being available? Did he or she even realize that it was advertised for sale in all locations? This may be due to corporate advertising being changed frequently and quickly to meet competitive offerings, but the branch training in the new offerings is failing to keep pace with the changes in advertising. As a result, customers come in expecting new offerings to be available, and employees are embarrassed because they have not been informed.

This example demonstrates one of the main reasons that integrated marketing communications have not been the norm in many companies. All too often, various parts of the company are responsible for different aspects of communication. The sales department develops and executes sales communication. The marketing department prepares and disseminates advertising. A public relations firm is responsible for publicity. Functional specialists handle sales promotions, direct marketing, company websites and social media. The human resources department trains front-line employees for service interactions, and still another area is responsible for the customer service department. Rarely is one person responsible for the overall communications strategy in a company, and all too often people responsible for the different communication components do not coordinate their efforts.

Today, however, more companies are adopting the concept of ***integrated marketing communications*** (IMC), where the company carefully integrates and organizes all of its external communications channels. As a marketing executive explained it,

> *Integrated marketing communications build a strong brand identity in the marketplace by tying together and reinforcing all your images and messages. IMC means that all your corporate messages, positioning and images, and identity are coordinated across all venues. It means that your PR materials say the same things as your direct mail campaign, and your advertising has the same 'look and feel' as your website.[2]*

In this chapter we propose that a more complex type of integrated marketing communication is needed for services than for goods. External communications channels must be coordinated, as with physical goods, but both external communications and internal communication channels must be integrated to create consistent service promises. To do that, internal marketing communications channels must be managed so that employees and the company are in agreement about what is communicated to the customer. We call this more complicated version of IMC *integrated services marketing communications* (ISMC). ISMC requires that everyone involved with communication clearly understand both the company's marketing strategy and its promises to consumers.

KEY SERVICE COMMUNICATION CHALLENGES

Discrepancies between what is communicated about a service and what a customer receives – or perceives that they receive – can powerfully affect consumer evaluations of service quality. The factors that contribute to these communication challenges include (1) service intangibility (2) management of service promises, (3) management of customer expectations, (4) customer education, and (5) internal marketing communications. In this chapter, we first describe the challenges stemming from these factors and then detail strategies that firms have found useful in dealing with them.

SERVICE INTANGIBILITY

Because services are performances rather than objects, their essence and benefits are difficult to communicate to customers. Intangibility makes marketing communication for services more challenging for both marketers and consumers. The intangible nature of services creates problems for consumers both before and after purchase. Before buying services, consumers have difficulty understanding what they will be buying and evoking names and types of services to consider? During purchase, consumers often cannot clearly see the differences among services. After purchase, consumers have trouble evaluating their service experiences.

The difficulties associated with intangibility can be divided into five properties, each of which has implications for services marketing communication. Intangibility involves incorporeal existence, abstractness, generality, non-searchability, and mental impalpability.[3]

- *Incorporeal existence.* The service product does not occupy physical space. Although the delivery mechanism may use facilities that occupy space (such as a dry-cleaning shop), the service itself (dry cleaning) does not. The implication is that showing the service is difficult, if not impossible.
- *Abstractness.* Service benefits such as financial security, fun, or health do not correspond directly with objects, making them difficult to visualize and understand. When businesses need consulting, for example, they often do not know where to begin because the concept is so vague that they do not understand the specific goals processes, or cannot articulate what deliverables they are seeking.
- *Generality* refers to a class of things, persons, events, or properties, whereas *specificity* refers to particular objects, people, or events. Many service and service promises are described in generalities (wonderful experience, superior education, completely satisfied customers), making them difficult to differentiate from those of competitors.
- *Non-searchability.* Because service is a performance, it often cannot be previewed or inspected in advance of purchase. If we are interested in finding a doctor, a heating repair firm, a personal trainer, or virtually any service, we cannot search the options as easily as we can search the shelves in a grocery store. Considerably more effort must be expended, and what we find may not be useful. For example, if a customer needs a plumber, the information contained in a source such as the telephone directory does not adequately discriminate among the choices. As we discussed in Chapter 2, non-searchability is particularly true of services that are classified as either experience or credence services.
- *Mental impalpability.* Services are often complex, multidimensional, and difficult to grasp mentally. When customers have not had prior exposure, familiarity, or knowledge services are difficult to interpret. You may have experienced this when buying car insurance for the first time.

These five aspects of service intangibility make customers feel more uncertain about their purchases, and evidence indicates that the greater the risk that customers perceive in purchasing services, the more actively they will seek and rely on online or offline word-of-mouth communications to guide their choices.[4] Word of mouth can be a very convincing source of information about services for consumers, but it is not under the control of the service provider.

> **★ SERVICE SPOTLIGHT**
>
> Thorpe Park, a theme park in England, has seats on five big roller coasters to sell. Although the park can put out advertisements showing people enjoying its attractions, they don't really get across the emotional thrill of the rides. Thorpe Park has honed on a social media strategy to leverage user-generated content, such as the photos that visitors take and post on Instagram to tell of their personal experience in the park. The best pictures are recognized for awards each week. Campaigns such as 'Happy Height Day', which the park runs in association with Mumsnet, a social media channel for parents, celebrate when children reach 1.4 metres, which is the minimum height for the big rides. Another social media presence creates excitement: the five vlogger videos (videos made by a video blogger) posted on YouTube relating to the Halloween 'Fright Nights'. All of these are aimed at communicating the excitement and emotions associated with the big thrill rides.

MANAGEMENT OF SERVICE PROMISES

A serious problem occurs when companies fail to manage service marketing communications – the vows made by salespeople, advertising and service personnel – and service falls short of what is promised. This sometimes occurs because the part of the company making the promise lacks the information necessary to make accurate statements. For example, salespeople often sell services, particularly new business services such as software, before they are actually available and without having an exact date of when they will be ready for market. Demand and supply variations make service provision possible at some times, improbable at others and, generally, difficult to predict. The traditional functional structure of many companies, with their marketing and sales, operations, production human resources, and finance departments (often called silos), also makes communication about promises and delivery difficult internally.

MANAGEMENT OF CUSTOMER EXPECTATIONS

Appropriate and accurate communication about services is the responsibility of both marketing and operations. Marketing must accurately (if compellingly) reflect what happens in actual service encounters; operations must deliver what is promised in communications. For example, when a management consulting firm introduces a new offering, the marketing and sales departments must make the offering appealing enough to be viewed as superior to competing services. In promoting and differentiating the service, however, the company cannot afford to raise expectations above the level at which its consultants can consistently perform. If advertising, websites, personal selling or any other external communication sets up unrealistic expectations, customers will be disappointed by the actual encounters.

Because of increasing deregulation and intensifying competition in the services sector, many service firms feel pressure to acquire new business and to meet or beat competition. To accomplish these ends, service firms often over-promise in selling, advertising and other company communications. In the airline industry, advertising is a constant battlefield of competing offers and price reductions to gain the patronage of customers. The greater the extent to which a service firm feels pressured to generate new customers, and perceives that the industry norm is to over-promise ('everyone else in our industry over-promises'), the greater is the firm's propensity to over-promise.

If advertising shows a smiling young worker at the counter in a Carrefour commercial, the customer expects that, at least most of the time, there will be a smiling young worker in the local Carrefour. If a brochure claims that a customer's wake-up call will always be on time at an ibis Hotel, the customer expects no mistakes. Raising expectations to unrealistic levels may lead to more initial business but invariably fosters customer disappointment and discourages repeat business.

Many product and service companies also find themselves in the position of having to actively manage customer expectations downward – to tell customers that service previously provided will be discontinued or available only at a higher price. Airlines change flight schedules and charge for food. Credit card companies adjust their interest rates and change their value-added services. Hotels close their leisure facilities for refurbishment. In these situations – perhaps more than any others – the need to manage customer expectations is critical.

CUSTOMER EDUCATION

Service companies must educate their customers. If customers are unclear about how the service will be provided, what their role in delivery involves, and how to evaluate services they have never used before, they will be disappointed. When this happens, customers will hold the service company responsible, not themselves. Errors or problems in service – even when they are 'caused' by the customer – still lead customers to defect. For this reason the firm must assume responsibility for educating customers.

For services high in credence properties – expert services that are difficult for customers to evaluate even after they have received the services – many customers do not know the criteria by which they should judge the service. For high-involvement services, such as long-term dental treatment or purchase of a first home, customers are also unlikely to comprehend and anticipate the service process. First-time home buyers rarely understand the complex set of services (surveys, conveyancing, insurance) and processes (securing a mortgage, offers and counteroffers) that will be involved in their purchases. Professionals and other providers of high-involvement services often forget that customers are novices who must be educated about each step in the process. They assume that giving an overview at the start of the service, or providing a manual or a set of instructions, will equip the customer. Unfortunately these steps are rarely sufficient, and customers defect because they can neither understand the process nor appreciate the value received from the service.

A final condition under which customer education can be beneficial involves services in which demand and supply are not synchronized, as discussed in Chapter 14. If the customer is not informed about peaks and troughs in demand, service overloads and failures, not to mention underutilized capacity, defections are likely to result.

INTERNAL MARKETING COMMUNICATIONS

Multiple functions in the organization, such as marketing and operations, must be coordinated to achieve the goal of service provision. Because service advertising and personal selling promise what *people* do, frequent and effective communication across functions – horizontal communication – is critical. If internal communication is poor, perceived service quality is at risk. If company advertising and other promises are developed without input from operations, contact personnel may not be able to deliver service that matches the image portrayed in marketing efforts.

Not all service organizations advertise, but all need coordination or integration across departments or functions to deliver quality service. All need internal communication between the sales force and service providers. Horizontal communication also must occur between the human resource and marketing departments. To deliver excellent customer service, firms must be certain to inform and motivate employees to deliver what their customers expect. If marketing and sales personnel who understand customer expectations do not communicate this information to contact employees, the lack of knowledge for these employees will affect the quality of service that they deliver.

A final form of internal coordination central to providing service excellence is consistency in policies and procedures across departments and branches. If a service organization operates many outlets under the same name, whether franchised or company owned, customers expect similar performance across those outlets. If managers of individual branches or outlets have significant autonomy in procedures and policies, customers may not receive the same level of service quality across the branches.

FIVE CATEGORIES OF STRATEGIES TO MATCH SERVICE PROMISES WITH DELIVERY

Figure 16.2 shows the major approaches to overcome the service communication challenges that we just described. The goal is to deliver service that is greater than, or equal to, promises made. To do so, all three sides of the marketing service triangle must be addressed.

Figure 16.2   Five major approaches to overcome service communication challenges

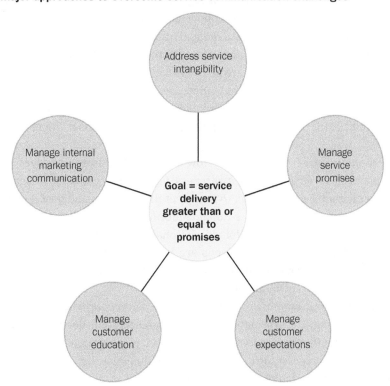

ADDRESS SERVICE INTANGIBILITY

Approaches to address service intangibility include advertising and other communication strategies that clearly communicate service attributes and benefits to consumers, and strategies designed to encourage word-of-mouth and social media communication.

If service companies recognize the challenges they face due to intangibility, they can use selected strategies to compensate. In one way or another, each of the individual strategies we discuss here focuses on ways to make the message dramatic and memorable.

- *Use narratives to demonstrate the service experience.* Many services are experiential, and a uniquely effective approach to communicating them involves story-based appeals. Research has concluded that consumers with relatively low familiarity with a service category prefer appeals based on stories to appeals based on lists of service attributes. Furthermore, the relative advantage of the story is intensified when the novice consumer is in a happy mood rather than a sad one.[5] For example, young consumers needing their first home mortgage will react more positively to an advertisement that shows a couple in their situation finding a house they love and then a banker quickly finding them a mortgage than to an advertisement about interest rates.

- *Present vivid information.* Effective service marketing communication creates a strong or clear impression on the senses and produces a distinct mental picture. One way to use vivid information is to evoke strong emotion, such as in British Airways' classic 'To Fly. To Serve' advertising campaign. Vividness can also be achieved by concrete language and dramatization.

- *Use interactive imagery.* One type of vividness involves what is called *interactive imagery.*[6] Imagery (defined as a mental event that involves the visualization of a concept or relationship) can enhance recall of names and facts about service. Interactive imagery integrates two or more items in some mutual action, resulting in improved recall. Some service companies effectively integrate their logos or symbols with an expression of what they do, such as Orange where the colour of the logo and the brand name help to maintain high awareness of the mobile phone company. The Legal & General Insurance company use a multi-coloured umbrella in their logo to demonstrate that they provide protection. The logo of the international fast-food restaurant chain Nando's is a Portuguese cockerel, hinting at the origins of their cuisine and the fact that their meat dishes are all made with chicken.

- *Focus on the tangibles.*[7] Another way that advertisers can increase the effectiveness of services communications is to feature the tangibles associated with the service, such as showing a bank's marble columns or gold credit card. Showing the tangibles provides clues about the nature and quality of the service.

- *Use brand icons to make the service tangible.* How does an advertiser of services improve competitive differentiation and achieve strong brand awareness in a highly competitive market? Some service organizations use a character or brand icon to represent the company and generate brand visibility. One of the most enduring service brand icons is Ronald McDonald, the red-and-yellow clown that represents McDonald's and its children's charity, the Ronald McDonald House. McDonald's competitor, KFC, has its own mascot, Colonel Sanders. Advertising icons are even more critical in industries in which service is complex and difficult to understand. In the UK, talking dogs, horses and even meerkats are used by different insurance providers to generate brand visibility.

- *Use association, physical representation, documentation and visualization.* Berry and Clark propose four strategies of tangibilization: association, physical representation, documentation and visualization.[8] *Association* means linking the service to a tangible person, place or object, such as linking Virgin with Richard Branson. *Physical representation* means showing tangibles that are directly or indirectly part of the service, such as employees, buildings or equipment. *Documentation* means featuring objective data and factual information. *Visualization* is a vivid mental picture of a service's benefits or qualities, such as showing people on vacation having fun.

- *Feature service employees in communication.* Customer contact personnel are an important second audience for services advertising.[9] Featuring actual employees doing their jobs or explaining their services in communications is effective for both the primary audience (customers) and the secondary audience (employees) because it communicates to employees that they are important. Furthermore, when employees who perform a service well are featured in advertising, they become standards for other employees' behaviours. B&Q, the international DIY chain, has its own employees appearing in its advertisements.

- *Feature satisfied customers in the communication.* One way to generate positive word of mouth is to feature satisfied customers in the communications. Testimonials featuring actual service customers simulate personal communications between people and are thereby a credible way to communicate the benefits of service.

- *Encourage word-of-mouth communication.* Because services are usually high in experience and credence properties, people frequently turn to others for information rather than to traditional marketing channels. Services advertising and other external messages can generate word-of-mouth communication that extends the investment in paid communication and improves the credibility of the messages. Communications that generate talk because they are humorous, compelling or unique can be particularly effective. The Santander Cycle-through branch mentioned in the case study at the start of this chapter is a good example of this.

- *Leverage social media.* Online Social Media on sites such as Facebook, Linkedin and Twitter are becoming very important avenues for consumers exchanging information about service providers and their personal experiences when interacting with them. Service organizations run the risk of their information and marketing function being performed by peer groups with user-generated content who ask/offer advice to customers, bypassing the company and the opportunity to either improve their services or recover from service failures. This may impact further on brand value as users revert to user-generated sources on social media and networks to ensure credibility, trustworthiness and expertise. It is clear that service companies that have a significant volume of customers actively engaged in user-generated content increasingly need a social media/user-generated content communication strategy. This is particularly important in the travel sector, where customers are on the move and service is a critical point of differentiation.

- *Make use of video-sharing networks.* YouTube, Vimeo and other video-sharing networks provide opportunities to demonstrate a service or show people enjoying a service. They also allow the service provider to target niche audiences and show how the service applies to them.

  Social Media and Digital Marketing

  For example, the KLM YouTube Channel provides videos on destinations for travellers, behind-the-scenes videos for plane enthusiasts, videos aimed at children, music and games videos for the youth market as well as corporate responsibility spots, videos of events and advertisements. All of these can bring the service and the brand alive in the minds of the customer. Video networks can be accessed on mobiles, tablets, interactive TVs and computers, thereby increasing the opportunities for making a service more tangible.

Hotels are now responding to consumers' comments on Facebook pages and on review sites such as Tripadvisor. Many service organizations have set up their own community sites on Facebook where they can interact with customers and potential customers.

Social media has also become mobile with the more recent growth of Twitter. Some travel companies are already active in this space – for example, KLM will deal with customer complaints on Twitter in 'real time'. With the advent of more mobile tablet PCs like the iPad and high-quality cameras in mobile devices, it will become easier for customers to visually report/record service incidents/failures and comment on them.

SERVICE SPOTLIGHT

John Lewis, a UK Department Store chain, launched its Facebook, Twitter and YouTube channels in October 2010. Since then, its Facebook *likes* have grown to 850,000 (2015). Twitter followers have come to number 224,000 in the same period. Customers have used these social media outlets to form their own community, which is backed by a customer service function ready to answer any questions they have.

The UK corporate website also features 'always on' content promoting in-store events to customers around the country, allowing customers to choose their charity of the month and welcoming guest editors on key topics. Staff ('partners' in John Lewis's speak) have also held 'surgeries' on specific topics like new product launches and 'how tos'.

The retailer also launched a competition called 'Guess the gift' in support of the TV advert whereby various children were filmed for johnlewis.com describing one of the top John Lewis Christmas products. Participating customers were asked to guess the identity of the gift and, if they guessed correctly, were awarded that same product as a prize. The competition was promoted across all channels including Facebook, You Tube and Twitter with a very high rate of entries and customer engagement.

The multi-channel approach was extended with the launch of an iPhone app in December 2011, giving customers access to 250,000 John Lewis products while on the move. Since launch, the app has been downloaded onto over 225,000 smartphones.

MANAGE SERVICE PROMISES

In manufacturing physical goods, the departments that make promises and those that deliver them can operate independently. Goods can be fully designed and produced, and then turned over to marketing for promotion and sale. In services, however, the sales and marketing departments make promises about what other employees in the organization will fulfil. Because what employees do cannot be standardized to the same extent as physical goods, greater coordination and management of promises are required. This coordination can be accomplished by creating a strong service brand and by coordinating all of the company's marketing communications.

CREATING A STRONG SERVICE BRAND

Branding plays a special role in service companies:

> *Strong brands enable customers to better visualize and understand intangible products. They reduce customers' perceived monetary, social, or safety risk in buying services, which are difficult to evaluate prior to purchase. Strong brands are the surrogates when the company offers no fabric to touch, no trousers to try on, no watermelons or apples to scrutinize, no automobile to test.*[10]

In contrast to branding in product situations, where each individual product has its own brand, the primary brand in service is frequently the company itself. The focus of brand creation is on raising the awareness, meaning and equity of the company among key target audiences. For example, companies like KLM, Radisson, DHL and Vodafone all focus communication and information on their companies rather than individual services that the company offers. Therefore, the brand becomes the company's method of integrating marketing communication.

1 The *company's presented brand* is that part of the brand image that the company controls and disseminates through all of its activities. Advertising, the brand name itself, websites, employees, facilities and all other types of information dissemination must be coordinated and controlled.
2 The brand is also influenced by *word of mouth and other external publicity* about the company over which the company has no power. This may include online review sites as well as press reports, comments from pressure groups, etc. These sources of communication are potent because they are perceived by customers to be credible and unbiased, but they can have either positive or negative effects on the service brand. McDonald's is frequently criticized in the press or by pressure groups for its environmental record or in relation to its impact on obesity.
3 *Customer experience with the company* – the actual interactions with company employees and other firm manifestations – is another element that shapes the brand and is likely to be more powerful than any marketing messages. No matter how effective and unified advertising is for a service, actual experiences disproportionately provide meaning to customers.

These three inputs lead to *brand awareness*, the customer's recall and recognition of the brand, and *brand perceptions*, the elements and activities that customers associate with the brand. Brand perceptions largely emanate from customer experience, but are also shaped by the company's presented brand and word of mouth/ external publicity. The higher and more positive the brand awareness and brand perceptions, the stronger the brand image and the higher the *brand equity* a company has. Brand equity is the value of customer goodwill and positive attitudes that a company builds up over time. Higher brand equity is usually associated with higher sales and greater customer brand loyalty.

Figure 16.3 is a service-branding model that shows the relationships among the main elements in creating a strong service brand.[11]

Figure 16.3   A service branding model

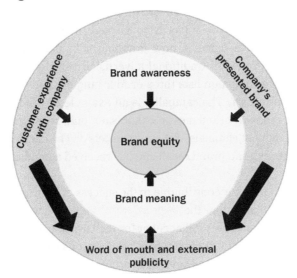

Source: Adapted from L.L. Berry (2000) 'Cultivating Service Brand Equity', *Journal of the Academy of Marketing Science*, 28 (Winter 2000), pp. 128–37.

COORDINATE EXTERNAL COMMUNICATION

For any organization, one of the most important yet challenging aspects of managing brand image involves coordinating all the external communication vehicles that send information to customers. This task has become far more challenging in recent years, because a notable trend is the proliferation of new media. Not only are traditional communication vehicles such as advertising, websites, sales promotion, public relations, direct marketing and personal selling proliferating, but many forms of new media are now available to marketers. As demonstrated in the Santander campaign set out at the start of this chapter, advertising, sponsorship, use of social media, YouTube and events all add to the tools available and may increase the complexity of coordinating a common brand message across all communication channels. However, the main communication channels are as follows:

Websites are the company's own online communication to customers. A disconnect often exists between the look, feel and content of a company's website and its advertising, usually because different parts of the company (or different advertising vendors) are responsible for creating these vehicles. When websites are coordinated in theme, content and promises – as they are in DHL advertising – a company is better able to match service delivery with promises because the promises themselves are consistent. It is important that usability testing is undertaken on a website. This involves observing representative users performing tasks such as product or information searches on a site. For a site to be successful, it must enable the user to complete a task, such as identify the opening hours of a gym, and do so in a timely and user-friendly manner. If a website is difficult to use or is unclear, people will leave and search a competitor's site.

Search Engine Optimization involves achieving the highest position in search engines' listing of results for a specific combination of keywords entered by search engine users. The higher a company ranks in the search engine results pages, the more visitors its website is likely to attract. To improve a website's ranking, it is important to understand how Google and other search engines compile their listing using software processes called spiders or robots to crawl around sites that are registered with that search engine. The main influencing factors are the keywords on the page and the website's metadata, including title page tags as well as links to the site from other web pages. The benefits of focusing on search engine optimization is that it has a highly targeted impact, as it puts an organization's service in front of people who are searching for that service.

Traditional Advertising is any paid form of non-personal presentation and promotion of a company's offerings by an identified sponsor. Traditional advertising vehicles include television, radio, newspapers, magazines and outdoor signage. Because advertising is paid, marketers control the creative appeals, placement and timing. Internet advertising is now grabbing a bigger share of companies' advertising budgets and should be synchronized with traditional advertising vehicles. MasterCard's highly successful worldwide 'Priceless' advertising campaign lists three or four tangible items and their prices followed by a key customer benefit that is 'priceless'. The campaign is an example of solid synchronization because it is 'extraordinarily flexible, and carries a brand message that is not only relevant globally but also adapts well to different media, different payment channels, different markets'.[12] The campaign, now seen in 96 countries and 47 languages, has generated strong brand recall and has received a number of the advertising industry's prestigious awards.

Online Advertising: A major factor contributing to the success of Internet advertising is the availability of approaches that are more popular than the banner advertisement which dominated the medium for years. Banner advertisements[13] still account for the largest category of Internet advertisements, but their effectiveness as a marketing tool is being seriously questioned. Click-through rates, the most common measure of effectiveness, have dropped from 10 per cent to 0.025 per cent over the years. Analysts suggest the following reasons for the drop:

- *Banner clutter.* As spending increased, so did the number of advertisements, which reduced the novelty and created sites filled with banners that often led to no value. Just as with other advertising clutter, users learned to stop paying attention.
- *Boring banners.* Although the potential to create fun and interactive banner advertisements existed, many advertisers simply created me-too banners that were low on content and creativity.
- *Built-in banners.* Once advertisers started using animation and other colourful attention-getting devices, the advertisements became intrusive, interfering with the users' surfing stream and with the time they spent on sites. Some advertisements took so long to download that they delayed and derailed users' interactions on the Web.

Advertisers had to face the fact that their hopes for banner advertisements were not being fulfilled, at least as measured simply by click-through rates. Improved advertising approaches have been developed in the last few years, with the most significant being search-based advertising, or paid search advertising. In this form of advertising, which currently represents the largest share of online spending among all online advertisement formats, advertisers pay only when qualified leads are delivered to their websites. With AdWords, a pay-per-click advertising service offered by Google, advertisers buy the rights to words and terms related to their business. When a consumer searches Google using one of those keywords, the advertiser's Uniform Resource Locator (URL), along with its name and description, appears in a coloured box beside the search results. The advertiser pays only when a user clicks on the advertisement. Marketers recognize that managing their media planning and buying strategy as a whole, rather than as segregated channels, maximizes campaign effectiveness. For this reason, more and more advertisers are adding online advertising to their traditional advertising buys. Today, online advertising accounts for a small percentage of total advertising expenditures, largely because the medium is not as costly as television or print. In the future, as consumers spend more time on the Web, Internet advertising will become even more important than before.

Social Media Advertising: Because social networks gather such a large amount of user information, social media advertising is able to target an audience more precisely than many other media channels. Facebook can not only target audiences based on location, language, age and other common demographics, it can also target people based on their interests and behaviours. The advertisements will appear on the right hand side of a user's Facebook page. Twitter distinguishes between three kinds of Twitter Ads: *Promoted Tweets* are messages that appear directly in the timelines of targeted Twitter users;

Promoted Accounts invite targeted Twitter users to follow a brand; *Promoted Trends* give users' stories the top position the trending topic list for 24 hours. Twitter targeting is especially valuable in reaching people based on the size and relevance of their networks.

Mobile apps: The average person has 26 mobile apps stored on his or her smartphone. These generally combine fun and social elements with rewards, discounts and ways of buying or reserving a service. They can create high visibility and build brand recognition as smartphone users check their devices many times a day. They create a direct marketing channel that potentially can build engagement and customer loyalty. They can be as a relevant for a small coffee shop or a hair salon as they can be for a major multinational corporation. However, to be successful mobile apps need to have features that the user values, while at the same time being well branded and easy to use. It can be a way of staying closer to customers, simply by being at their fingertips at all times.

Sales promotion includes short-term incentives such as coupons, premiums, discounts and other activities that stimulate customer purchases and stretch media spending. The fast-food industry, including McDonald's, Burger King and Wendy's, offers premiums like action figures that link the chains' offerings to current movies and television shows.

Public relations covers the activities that build a favourable company image through publicity, relations with the news media and community events. Sir Richard Branson, founder of Virgin Atlantic Airways, is a master at obtaining publicity for his airline. When launching the airline, he claimed, 'I knew that the only way of competing with British Airways and the others was to get out there and use myself to promote it'.[14] In the years since the airline was launched, his publicity-winning stunts have included recording the fastest time across the Atlantic Ocean in a speedboat, flying a hot-air balloon across the Atlantic Ocean and from Japan to Canada, dressing up in everything from a stewardess's uniform to a bikini on Virgin flights, and being photographed in his bath. Sir Branson has his own online blog, Twitter feed, Facebook and Google Plus accounts to communicate his thoughts and maintain his high profile. All of these have links to the Virgin group website.

SERVICE SPOTLIGHT

IKEA, the home furniture store, sought media coverage in the UK by launching a pop-up Breakfast in Bed Café, where tables were replaced with beds and sleeping was encouraged. In this experiential activation, customers could book a slot at the IKEA Breakfast in Bed Café, either in the morning for breakfast, or in the afternoon for tea and a 'siesta'. The café was set up with IKEA furnishings and the dining room was specifically designed to resemble a homely eatery. As well as providing a breakfast menu, which comprised toast, tea, fresh juice and an array of traditional Swedish treats, the Breakfast in Bed Café also offered a 'pillow menu' to ensure optimum comfort. Once fed, guests were served sleep-inducing teas as chilled out music filled the room and IKEA's sleep specialists gave out tips to get a great night's sleep. With these tips in mind, guests could then enjoy a power nap in one of nine beds. Despite its short run-time and so little marketing prior to the event, this activation generated a large amount of buzz, with hundreds of comments and shares, and thousands of likes on social media.

Direct marketing involves the use of mail, telephone, email and text messaging to communicate directly with specific consumers to obtain a direct response. It can be delivered in the form of a campaign for a particular service or in the form of a newsletter. Direct marketing by email has registered significant growth as the physical costs are substantially less than direct mail or telephone. It also enables the opportunity for direct click-through from the e-mail to a website. However, response rates to any of these forms of direct marketing can be low unless customers have opted in to receive the service provider's newsletters and regular updates. Where customers have not opted in to receive such direct marketing, the campaigns may be considered negatively as spam emails, junk mail or nuisance phone calls. There may also be significant difficulties in obtaining an accurate and up-to-date mailing list of e-mail addresses.

⭐ **SERVICE SPOTLIGHT**

American Express is a service company that uses direct marketing extensively and ensures that it integrates well with all its other messages, including interactive messages from employees. As the executive vice president of global advertising at American Express states clearly:

> *Service brands are not created solely in advertising. In fact, much of a brand's equity stems from the direct consumer experiences with the brand. We partner with a relationship marketing company to help us manage consumer experiences with our brand across all products and services – Card, Travel, Financial Services, and Relationship Services – via all direct channels, including phone, Internet, and mail.*[15]

Michael Bronner, the founder of the relationship marketing company that American Express uses, emphasizes the need for coordinating external and interactive marketing communications:

> *The client [such as American Express] may spend millions on TV advertising but lose when the customer is working his way through layer upon layer of voice response options on the customer service line.*[16]

Viral Marketing is the seeding of interesting content on websites, blogs or by e-mail that people will want to see and pass on through their online networks and friends. It requires a video clip, a TV advertisement, a song or a picture that is seen as being sufficiently funny, clever or shocking to make it compulsive viewing. A good example is the video that launched the Domino's Pizza app. It translates a users' stomach rumbles into a personalized recommendation of a specific pizza to satisfy their hunger. The Tummy Translator app uses what Domino's calls 'Gastro-Acoustic-Enterology' and is designed to help drive sales as well as showing the range of options on its menu.

Personal selling is face-to-face presentation by a representative from the firm to make sales and build customer relationships. One way that personal selling and advertising are integrated in business-to-business companies is through the development of advertising materials that salespeople distribute to customers. This approach not only creates an integrated message to customers, but also keeps salespeople fully informed of the promises the company is making.

MANAGE CUSTOMER EXPECTATIONS

Accurately promising when and how service will be delivered is one of the most important ways to close the communication gap. Among the most effective strategies to manage customer expectations are to make realistic promises; to offer service guarantees, options and tiered-value offerings; and to communicate criteria customers can use to assess service.

MAKE REALISTIC PROMISES

The expectations that customers bring to the service affect their evaluations of its quality: the higher the expectation, the better the delivered service must be to be perceived as high quality. Therefore, promising reliability in advertising is appropriate only when reliability is actually delivered. It is essential for a firm's marketing or sales department to understand the actual levels of service delivery (percentage of times the service is provided correctly, or percentage and number of problems that arise) before making promises about reliability. To be appropriate and effective, communications about service quality must accurately reflect what customers will actually receive in service encounters.

Probably the simplest and most important point to remember is to promise what is possible. Many companies hope to create the perception that they provide high-quality service by claiming it in marketing communications, but this strategy can backfire when the actual service does not live up to the promises raised in advertising. In line with the strategies we discuss in the next section, all service communications should promise only what is possible and not attempt to make services more attractive than they actually are.

OFFER SERVICE GUARANTEES

As discussed in Chapter 15, service guarantees are formal promises to customers about aspects of the service that they will receive. Although many services carry implicit service satisfaction guarantees, their true benefits – an increase in the likelihood of a customer choosing or remaining with the company – come only when the customer knows that guarantees exist and trusts that the company will stand behind them.

OFFER CHOICES

One way to set proper expectations is to give customers options for aspects of service that are meaningful, such as time and cost. A lawyer charging 100 euros per hour, for example, might offer clients the choice between a price increase of 10 euros per hour or a reduction in the number of minutes comprising the hour (such as 50 minutes). With the choice, clients can select the aspect of the trade-off (time or money) that is most meaningful to them. Making the choice solidifies the client's expectations of service.

This strategy is effective in business-to-business situations, particularly in terms of speed versus quality. Customers who are time-conscious often want reports, proposals or other written documents quickly. When asked to provide a 10-page proposal for a project within three days, an architectural firm responded that it could provide either a two-page proposal in three days or a 10-page proposal in a week. Its customer selected the latter option, recognizing that the deadline could be extended. In most business-to-business services, speed is often essential but threatens performance. If customers understand the trade-off and are asked to make a choice, they are likely to be more satisfied because their service expectations for each option become more realistic.

CREATE TIERED-VALUE SERVICE OFFERINGS

Product companies are accustomed to offering different versions of their products with prices commensurate with the value customers perceive. Cars with different configurations of features carry price tags that match not their cost but their perceived value to the customer. This same type of formal bundling and pricing can be accomplished in services, with the extra benefit of managing expectations.

Credit card companies offer tiered-value service offerings. American Express has multiple levels of credit card services based on the type of service provided: the traditional green card offers basic service features, the gold card additional benefits and the platinum card still more. Two advantages of tiered offerings are (1) the practice puts the burden of choosing the service level on the customer, thereby familiarizing the customer with specific service expectations, and (2) the company can identify which customers are willing to pay more for higher service levels.

The opportunity to set expectations accurately is present at the time of purchase: when customers make the decision is the moment they can be reminded of the terms of the agreement if they request support that is above the level in the contract.

COMMUNICATE THE CRITERIA AND LEVELS OF SERVICE EFFECTIVENESS

At times companies can establish the criteria by which customers assess service. Consider a business customer who is purchasing market research services for the first time. Because market research is an expert service, it is high in credence properties that are hard for customers to judge. Moreover, the effectiveness of this type of service differs depending on the objectives the client brings to the service. In this situation a service provider can teach the customer the criteria by which to evaluate the service. The provider that teaches the customer in a credible manner will have an advantage in shaping the evaluation process.

As an example, consider research company A, which communicates the following criteria to the customer: (1) a low price signals low quality, (2) reputation of the firm is critical, and (3) person-to-person interviews are the only type of customer feedback that will provide accurate information. A customer who accepts these criteria will evaluate all other suppliers using them. If research company B had talked to the customer first, consider these (very different!) criteria and their impact on the buyer: (1) market research companies with good reputations are charging for their reputation, not their skill, (2) telephone interviews have been found to work as well as person-to-person interviews, and (3) price does not indicate quality level.

The same approach can be used with service *levels* rather than evaluative criteria. For example, if research company B provides four-day turnaround on the results of its data analysis, the company has just set the customer's expectation level for all other suppliers.

MANAGE CUSTOMER EDUCATION

As discussed in Chapter 12, customers must perform their roles properly for many services to be effective. If customers forget to perform their roles, or perform them improperly, disappointment may result. For this reason, communication to customers can take the form of customer education.

PREPARE CUSTOMERS FOR THE SERVICE PROCESS

On a return trip from Singapore on Singapore Airlines, a customer neglected to heed the airline's warning that return flights must be confirmed 24 hours in advance. On arriving at the airport to return home, they found that their seat had been given to another customer who had conformed to the airline's request for confirmation. Depending on the perspective taken, you could argue that either the company or the customer was right in this situation. Whose responsibility is it to make sure that customers perform their roles properly?

Companies can avoid such situations by preparing customers for the service process, and companies may need to prepare the customer often, even every step of the way, for the subsequent actions the customer needs to take. A business-to-business example will help illustrate this strategy.

Customers of management consulting services purchase intangible benefits: marketing effectiveness, motivated workforces, culture change. The very fact that companies purchase these services usually indicates that they do not know how to perform them on their own. Many clients will also not know what to look for along the way to judge progress. In management consulting and other complex service situations, the effective provider prepares the customer for the service process and creates structure for the customer. At the beginning of the engagement, the management consulting firm establishes checkpoints throughout the process, at which times progress will be evaluated, and leads the customer to establish objectives for project completion. Because customers do not know what that progress will look like, the consulting firm takes the lead in setting goals or criteria to be examined at those times.

A similar approach is effective with individual service customers. Do you remember registration at the beginning of your first university semester or term? How aware were you of the steps in the process and what to do after each one? It is unlikely that directions, even in great detail, made you feel confident and competent in the new service experience. You may have required step-by-step – 'next call this telephone number or go to page B' – guidance.

As these examples show, whenever a customer is inexperienced or a service process is new or unique, education about what to expect is essential.

CONFIRM PERFORMANCE TO STANDARDS AND EXPECTATIONS

Service providers sometimes provide service, even explicitly requested service, yet fail to communicate to the customer that it has been accomplished. These providers stop short of getting credit for their actions when they do not reinforce actions with communication about their having fulfilled the request. This situation may happen under one or more of the following conditions:

- The customer cannot evaluate the effectiveness of a service.
- The decision-maker in the service purchase is a person different from the users of the service.
- The service is invisible.
- The provider depends on others to perform some of the actions to fulfil customer expectations.

When customers cannot evaluate service effectiveness, usually because they are inexperienced or the service is technical, the provider may fail to communicate specific actions that address client concerns because the actions seem too complex for the customer to comprehend. In this situation, the service provider can improve perceptions by translating the actions into customer-friendly terms. A personal injury lawyer who aids a client with the medical and financial implications of an accident needs to be able to tell the client in plain language that he or she has performed the necessary actions.

When the decision-maker in service purchases is different from the users of the service, a wide discrepancy in satisfaction may exist between decision-makers and users. An example is in the purchase of information technology products and services in a company. The decision-maker – the manager of information technology or someone in a similar position – makes the purchase decisions and understands the service promises. If users are not involved in the purchase process, they may not know what has been promised and may be dissatisfied.

Customers are not always aware of everything that is done behind the scenes to serve them well. Most services have invisible support processes. For instance, doctors frequently request diagnostic tests to rule out possible causes for illness. When these tests come back negative, doctors may neglect to inform patients. Many hairstyling firms have guarantees that ensure customer satisfaction with haircuts, permanents and colour treatments. However, only a few of them actively communicate these guarantees in advertising because they assume customers know about them. The firm that explicitly communicates the guarantee may be selected over others by a customer who is uncertain about the quality of the service. Making customers aware of standards or efforts to improve service that are not readily apparent can improve service quality perceptions.

CLARIFY EXPECTATIONS AFTER THE SALE

When service involves a handover between sales and operations, as it does in most companies, clarifying expectations with customers helps the service delivery arm of the company to align with customer expectations. Salespeople are motivated and compensated to raise customer expectations – at least to the point of making the sale – rather than to communicate realistically what the company can provide. In these situations, service providers can avoid future disappointment by clarifying what was promised as soon as the handover is made.

TEACH CUSTOMERS TO AVOID PEAK DEMAND PERIODS AND SEEK SLOW DEMAND PERIODS

Few customers want to face queues or delays in receiving services. In the words of two researchers: 'At best, waiting takes their time, and at worst, they may experience a range of unpleasant reactions – feeling trapped, tired, bored, angry, or demeaned'.[17] In a bank setting, researchers tested three strategies for dealing with customer waits: (1) giving customers prior notice of busy times, (2) having employees apologies for the delays, and (3) assigning all visible employees to serving customers. Only the first strategy focuses on educating customers; the other two involve managing employees. Researchers expected – and confirmed – that customers warned of a wait in line tended to minimize the negative effects of waiting to justify their decision to seek service at peak times. In general, customers given a card listing the branch's busiest and slowest times were more satisfied with the banking service. The other two strategies, apology and all tellers serving, showed no effects on satisfaction.[18] Educating customers to avoid peak times benefits both customers (through faster service) and companies (by easing the problem of over-demand).

MANAGE INTERNAL MARKETING COMMUNICATION

The fifth major category of strategies necessary to match service delivery with promises involves managing internal marketing communications. Internal marketing communications can be both vertical and horizontal. *Vertical communications* are either downward, from management to employees, or upward, from employees to management. *Horizontal communications* are those across functional boundaries in an organization.

CREATE EFFECTIVE VERTICAL COMMUNICATIONS

Companies that give customer-contact employees adequate information, tools and skills allow them to perform successful interactive marketing. Some of these skills come through training and other human resource efforts discussed in Chapter 11, but some are provided through *downward communication*. Among the most important forms of downward communication are company newsletters and magazines, corporate television networks, email, briefings, videotapes and internal promotional campaigns, and recognition programmes. One of the keys to successful downward communication is keeping employees informed of everything that is being conveyed to customers through external marketing. Employees should see company advertising before it is aired or published and should be familiar with the website, mailings and direct selling approaches being used. If these vertical communications are not present, both customers and employees suffer – customers will not receive the same messages from employees that they hear in company external marketing, and employees will feel uninformed and 'in the dark' about what their company is doing. In such circumstances, customers come asking for services that have been marketed externally but not internally, making the employees feel uninformed, left out and helpless.[19]

Sell the Brand Inside the Company. Having knowledge about what the company is doing in marketing communications is one aspect of internal marketing, but it is not enough. It is important to market the company's brand and brand message to employees so that they can deliver the brand values to customers. There are three principles for selling the brand internally:[20] choose the right moment to educate and inspire employees, link internal and external marketing, and bring the brand alive for employees.

Choosing the right moment is essential, because employees don't have the capacity, or the willingness, to absorb too many change initiatives, and the company therefore has to be selective in identifying opportunities when it can create enthusiasm for the brand. This may be at a time when new services are launched, when a company acquires another company, after refurbishment or when new geographical markets are being entered. When the Savoy hotel reopened after a major refurbishment, Fairmont Hotels (the parent company), spent a large amount of time and effort on communicating the Savoy brand values to the staff.

Linking internal and external marketing means that employees need to hear the same message from management that customers hear. If customers hear that serving them is most important but employees are told that cost savings matter more, employees will be confused and unable to deliver the brand values. One of the best ways to link the two types of communication is to create advertising that targets both customers and employees. Bringing the brand alive to employees involves creating a strong emotional connection between employees and the company. Employees in retailers such as Abercrombie and Fitch are encouraged to dress in A&F branded clothing at work and at home.

SERVICE SPOTLIGHT

Bodyshop, the cosmetic retail chain, has an internal communicator network. In every department, there is a 'Communicator' who is responsible for ensuring that upward, downward and horizontal communications happen in that area. This is supplemented in the individual retail stores with 'Public Relations Officers' who perform a similar role, ensuring that communication happens both internally with staff as well as within the local community through the media and local organizations.

CREATE EFFECTIVE UPWARD COMMUNICATION

Upward communication is also necessary in closing the gap between service promises and service delivery. Employees are at the front line of service, and they – more than anyone else in the organization – know what can and cannot be delivered. They know when service breakdowns are occurring and, very often, why they are happening. Having open communication channels from employees to management can prevent service problems from happening and minimize them when they do take place.

CREATE EFFECTIVE HORIZONTAL COMMUNICATIONS

Horizontal communication – communication across functional boundaries in an organization – facilitates coordinated efforts for service delivery. This task is difficult because functions typically differ in goals, philosophies, outlooks and views of the customer, but the payoff is high. Coordination between marketing and operations can result in communication that accurately reflects service delivery, thus reducing the gap between customer expectations and actual service delivery. Integration of effort between marketing and human resources can improve the ability of each employee to become a better marketer. Coordination between finance and marketing can create prices that accurately reflect the customer's evaluation of a service. In service firms, all these functions need to be integrated to produce consistent messages and to narrow the service gaps.

One important strategy for effective horizontal communications is to open channels of communication between the marketing department and operations personnel. For example, when a company creates advertising that depicts the service encounter, it is essential that the advertising accurately reflects what customers will experience in actual service encounters. Exaggeration puts service quality perceptions at risk, especially when the firm is consistently unable to deliver to the level of service portrayed in the advertising. Coordination and communication between advertising and service providers are pivotal in delivering service that meets expectations.

Featuring actual employees doing their jobs or explaining the services they provide, a strategy we mentioned earlier in this chapter, is one way to coordinate advertising portrayals and the reality of the service encounter. To create this type of advertising, the advertising department or agency interacts directly with service employees, facilitating horizontal communications. Similar benefits can be achieved if employees are included in the advertising process in other ways, such as by being shown advertising in its pre-test forms.

Another important strategy for horizontal communications involves opening channels of communication between sales and operations. Mechanisms for achieving this goal can be formal or informal and can include annual planning meetings, retreats, team meetings or workshops in which departments clarify service issues. In these sessions the departments can interact to understand the goals, capabilities and constraints of the other. Some companies hold 'gap workshops' at which employees from both functions meet for a day or two to try to understand the difficulties in matching promises made through selling with delivery accomplished by operations personnel.[21]

Likewise, involving the operations staff in face-to-face meetings with external customers allows operations personnel to understand the salesperson's role and the needs and desires of customers more readily. Rather than filtering customers' needs through the sales force, operations employees can witness at first hand the pressures and demands of customers. A frequent and desirable outcome of this strategy is the operations staff giving better service to the internal customer – the salesperson as they become aware of their own roles in satisfying both external and internal customers.

ALIGN BACK-OFFICE AND SUPPORT PERSONNEL WITH EXTERNAL CUSTOMERS THROUGH INTERACTION OR MEASUREMENT

As companies become increasingly customer focused, front-line personnel develop improved skills in discerning what customers require. As they become more knowledgeable about, and empathetic toward, external customers, they also experience intrinsic rewards for satisfying customers. Back-office or support personnel, who typically do not interact directly with external customers, miss out on this bonding and, as a consequence, fail to gain the skills and rewards associated with it.

Interaction: Companies are creating ways to facilitate the interaction between back-office and support personnel and external customers. Scottish and Southern Energy, a utilities provider, facilitates such interaction by regularly getting support staff (such as finance and human resource personnel) to handle customers' calls in the company's call centres.

When actual interaction is difficult or impossible, some companies videotape customers during the purchase and consumption process in their service facilities to vividly portray customers' needs and requirements and to show all personnel the support that front-line people need in order to deliver to meet customer expectations.

Measurement: When company measurement systems are established, employees are sometimes judged on the basis of how they perform for the next internal customer in the chain. Although this approach provides feedback in terms of how well the employees are serving the internal customer, it lacks the motivation and reward that come from seeing their efforts affect the end-customer.

CREATE CROSS-FUNCTIONAL TEAMS

Another approach to improving horizontal communications to better serve customers is to involve employees in cross-functional teams to align their jobs with end-customer requirements. For example, if a team of telecommunications service representatives is working to improve interaction with customers, back-office people such as computer technicians or training personnel can become part of the team. The team then learns the requirements and, together, sets goals for achieving them, an approach that directly creates communications across the functions.

The cross-functional team approach can best be explained by the example of an advertising agency. The individual in an advertising agency who typically interacts directly with the client is the account executive (often called a 'suit' by the creative staff). In the traditional agency, the account executive visits the client, uncovers client expectations, elicits a brief, and then interacts with the various departments in the agency (art, copywriting, production, traffic and media buying) that will perform the work. All functions are specialized and, in the extreme case, get direction for their portion of the work right from the account executive. In a cross-functional team, representatives from all functional areas meet with the account executive, and even with the client, collectively discuss the account and approaches to address this particular client's needs. Each team member brings his or her function's perspective and opens communication. All members can then understand the constraints and schedules of the other groups.

SUMMARY

Discrepancies between service delivery and external communications have a strong effect on customer perceptions of service quality. In this chapter we discussed the role of, and need for, integrated services marketing communications in minimizing these discrepancies. We described external, interactive and internal marketing communications based on the service triangle and emphasized the need to coordinate all three of its dimensions to deliver service that meets customer expectations. We also discussed the factors that lead to challenges in services marketing communications, including service intangibility; management of service promises; and management of customer expectations, customer education, and internal marketing communication.

We then offered strategies to address each of these service communications challenges. To address service intangibility, we described specific strategies such as the use of vivid imagery and tangible icons in communications, as well as ways to maximize the use of word-of-mouth communication. To manage service promises, we delineated the need for a strong service brand and coordinated external communications. To manage customer expectations, we suggested the need for making realistic promises, extending service guarantees, offering choices, creating tiered-value service offerings and communicating the criteria and levels of service effectiveness. To manage customer education, we emphasized the need to prepare customers for the service process, to make performance conform to standards and expectations, to clarify expectations after the sale and to teach customers how to avoid peak demand periods. Finally to manage internal communication, we discussed internal branding in addition to effective vertical communication, horizontal communication, aligning teams and support staff.

KEY CONCEPTS

EXERCISES

1 Explore each area of the DHL website (ww.dhl.com) and make a list of the types of information you find based on the three categories of marketing communication (external, interactive, internal) discussed in this chapter. What additional information do you find useful on the site?

2 Find five effective service advertisements in newspapers and magazines. Using the criteria given in this chapter, identify why they are effective. Then critique them and discuss ways in which they could be improved.

3 Examine the contents of Sir Richard Branson's blog site (www.virgin.com/richard-branson). How does this strengthen or weaken the Virgin brand?

DISCUSSION QUESTIONS

1 Which of the key reasons for provider gap 4 discussed at the beginning of this chapter is the easiest to address in a company? Which is the hardest to address? Why?

2 Review the five general strategies for achieving integrated services marketing communications. Would all these strategies be relevant in goods firms? Which would be most critical in goods firms? Which would be most critical in services firms? Are there any differences between those most critical in goods firms and those most critical in services firms?

3 What are the most effective Internet advertisements that you have seen? Why are they effective?

4 Using the section on managing customer expectations, put yourself in the position of your lecturer, who must reduce the amount of 'service' provided to the students in your class. Give an example of each strategy in this context. Which of the strategies would work best with you (the student) in managing your expectations? Why?

5 Why are social media channels like Facebook and YouTube so important in service firms? Are they important in product firms?

6 What other strategies can you suggest for taking advantage of online social media channels?

7 In which form of internal marketing communication – vertical or horizontal – would you invest if you had to choose between them as CEO of an organization? Why?

8 What other strategies can you add to the four offered in the section on customer education? What types of education do you expect from service firms? Give an example of a firm from which you have received adequate customer education. What firm has not provided you with adequate customer education?

9 Discuss the proposition that the interaction between companies and customers in online social media results in customer expectations being raised about service employees being more open and flexible during a service encounter in the physical environment.

FURTHER READING

Chaffey D. Ellis-Chadwick, F., Mayer, R. and Johnston, K. (2009). *Internet marketing: strategy, implementation and practice*, 4th edn, Pearson Education.

Colliander, J. and Dahlén, M. (2011). Following the fashionable friend: The power of social media-weighing publicity effectiveness of blogs versus online magazines. *Journal of Advertising Research*, 51(1), 313–20.

de Chernatony, L., Drury, S. and Segal-Horn, S. (2003). Building a services brand: stages, people and orientation. *The Service Industries Journal*, 23(3), 1–21.

Mangold, W. G. and Faulds, D. J. (2009). Social media: The new hybrid element of the promotion mix. *Business horizons*, 52(4), 357–65.

Miles, S. J. and Mangold, W. G. (2014). Employee voice: Untapped resource or social media time bomb? *Business Horizons*, 57(3), 401–11.

Pescher, C., Reichhart, P. and Spann, M. (2014). Consumer decision-making processes in mobile viral marketing campaigns. *Journal of interactive marketing*, 28(1), 43–54.

Punjaisri, K. and Wilson A. M. (2011). Internal branding process: key mechanisms, outcomes and moderating factors. *European Journal of Marketing*, 45(9/10), 1521–37.

Punjaisri, K., Wilson, A. and Evanschitsky, H. (2009). Internal branding: an enabler of employees' brand-supporting behaviours. *Journal of Service Management*, 20(2), 209–26.

CHAPTER 17

Pricing of Services

LEARNING OBJECTIVES

This chapter's objectives are to:

1 Discuss three major ways that service prices are perceived differently from goods prices by customers.
2 Articulate the key ways that pricing of services differs from pricing of goods from a company's perspective.
3 Demonstrate what value means to customers and the role that price plays in value.
4 Describe strategies that companies use to price services.
5 Give examples of pricing strategy in action.

OPENING EXAMPLE
Airberlin Restructures their Airfares

No frills airlines traditionally price their services as a basic flight plus costs for discretionary add-ons such as seat reservations, airport check-in, hold baggage, priority boarding, premium or emergency exit seat reservations, snacks and drinks, credit card payments, and even separate fees for taking babies on board. Often, what seems like a cheap flight when fares are advertised turns into an expensive proposition after all these add-ons are included.

In May 2015, airberlin launched a new structure of bundled airfares aimed at improving transparency and addressing the needs of different market segments. The separate pricing bundles, showing what is included (✓) and what is excluded (X), are set out below:

	JustFly	FlyDeal	FlyClassic	FlyFlex+
	The affordable package for spontaneous short breaks with little baggage.	The solid package with a generous free baggage allowance for price-conscious travellers.	The traditional package with a number of comfort options to ensure you enjoy your trip to the full.	The flexible package with many exclusive benefits for a relaxing flight, and spontaneous itinerary changes at any time.
Snacks and Drinks	✓	✓	✓	✓
Cabin Baggage	≤8 kg	≤8 kg	≤8 kg	≤8 kg
Checked Baggage	€	23 kg	23 kg	2 × 23 kg
Ability to make Changes to the Booking	X	X	For a fee	✓
Cancellation	X	X	X	✓
Seat Reservation	€	€	✓	✓
Extra Large Seat Emergency Exit	€	€	€	✓
Check in the evening before a flight	€	€	✓	✓
Priority Check in	X	X	X	✓
Security Fast Lane	X	X	X	✓
Top bonus miles for European Flight	250	750	1500	2000

In many ways, the price bundling approach being adopted by airberlin is reminiscent of the original economy, premium economy, business and first class options offered by the full service airlines. For airberlin, the main aim is to align itself more closely to the needs of its customers.

Source: www.airberlin.com

According to one of the leading experts on pricing, most service organizations use a 'naive and unsophisticated approach to pricing without regard to underlying shifts in demand, the rate that supply can be expanded, prices of available substitutes, consideration of the price–volume relationship, or the availability of future substitutes'.[1] What makes the pricing of services more difficult than pricing of goods? What approaches work well in the context of services?

This chapter builds on three key differences between customer evaluation of pricing for services and goods: (1) customers often have inaccurate or limited reference prices for services, (2) price is a key signal of quality in services, and (3) monetary price is not the only price relevant to service customers. As we demonstrate, these three differences can have a profound impact on the strategies companies use to set and administer prices for services.

This chapter also discusses common pricing structures, including cost-based, competition-based, and demand-based pricing. One of the most important aspects of demand-based pricing is perceived value, which must be understood by service providers so that they price in line with offerings and customer expectations. For that reason we also describe how customers define value, and discuss pricing strategies in the context of value.

THREE KEY WAYS THAT SERVICE PRICES ARE DIFFERENT FOR CONSUMERS

What role does price play in consumer decisions about services? How important is price to potential buyers, compared with other factors and service features? Service companies must understand how pricing works, but first they must understand how customers perceive prices and price changes. In the next three subsections, we describe what we know about the ways that customers perceive the cost of services, and each is central to effective pricing.

CUSTOMER KNOWLEDGE OF SERVICE PRICES

To what extent do customers use price as a criterion in selecting services? How much do consumers know about the costs of services? Before you answer these questions, take the services pricing quiz in Figure 17.1. Were you able to fill in a price for each of the services listed? If you were able to answer the questions on the basis of memory, you have internal *reference prices* for the services. A reference price is a price point

Figure 17.1 What do you know about the prices of services?

What do the following services cost in your town or city?

	Price?
Dental check-up	
A grocery home delivery	
Legal help with a divorce	
Laundering a dress or suit	
Rental of a car for one day	
One hour of house-cleaning	
Room at an ibis hotel	
Haircut	
Repairing a leaking tap	

in memory for a good or a service; it can consist of the price last paid, the price most frequently paid or the average of all prices customers have paid for similar offerings.[2]

To see how accurate your reference prices for services are, you can compare them with the actual price of these services from the providers in your town or city. If you are like many consumers, you feel quite uncertain about your knowledge of the prices of services, and the reference prices you hold in memory for services are not generally as accurate as those you hold for goods. There are many reasons for this difference.

SERVICE VARIABILITY LIMITS KNOWLEDGE

Because services are not created on a factory assembly line, service firms have great flexibility in the configurations of services they offer. Firms can conceivably offer an infinite variety of combinations and permutations, leading to complex and complicated pricing structures. How did you answer the questions about prices for a dental check-up? If you are like most consumers, you probably wanted more information before you offered a reference price. You probably wanted to know what type of check-up the dentist is providing. Does it include X-rays and other diagnostic tests? What types of tests? How long does it take? What is its purpose? If the check-up is undertaken simply as a regular semi-annual consultation, you may expect to pay less than if it is occasioned by some problem that you are having with your teeth or to advise you on elements of cosmetic dentistry. The point we want to illustrate here is that a high degree of variability often exists across providers of services. Not every dentist defines a check-up the same way.

PROVIDERS ARE UNWILLING TO ESTIMATE PRICES

Another reason customers lack accurate reference prices for services is that many providers are unable or unwilling to estimate price in advance. For example, car servicing and legal services providers are rarely willing – or even able – to estimate a price in advance. The fundamental reason is that they do not know themselves what the services will involve until they have fully examined the car or the client's situation, or until the process of service delivery (such as mechanical repairs or a court trial) unfolds. In a business-to-business context, companies will obtain bids or estimates for complex services such as consulting or construction, but this type of price estimation is typically not undertaken with end-consumers; therefore, they often buy without advance knowledge about the final price of the service.

INDIVIDUAL CUSTOMER NEEDS VARY

Another factor that results in the inaccuracy of reference prices is that individual customer needs vary. Some hairstylists' service prices vary across customers on the basis of hair length, type of haircut and whether a conditioning treatment and styling are included. Therefore, if you were to ask a friend how much he or she spent on a haircut from a particular stylist, chances are that your cut from the same stylist may cost a different price. In a similar vein, a service as simple as a hotel room will have prices that vary greatly: by size of room, time of year, type of room availability and individual versus group rate. These two examples are for very simple services. Now consider a service purchase as idiosyncratic as cosmetic surgery from a dentist or help from a lawyer. In these and many other services, customer differences in need will play a strong role in the price of the service.

COLLECTION OF PRICE INFORMATION IS OVERWHELMING IN SERVICES

Still another reason customers lack accurate reference prices for services is that customers feel overwhelmed with the information they need to gather. With most goods, retail stores display the products by category to allow customers to compare and contrast the prices of different brands and sizes. Rarely is there a similar display of services in a single outlet. If customers want to compare prices (of dry-cleaning, for example), they must call or drive to individual outlets, or search various websites.

The fact that consumers often possess inaccurate reference prices for services has several important managerial implications. Promotional pricing (as in couponing or special pricing) may be less meaningful for services, for which price anchors typically do not exist. Perhaps that is why price is not featured in service advertising as much as it is featured in advertising for goods. Promotional pricing may also create problems if the promotional price (such as a 30-euro cut and blow dry special from a salon) is the only one customers see in advertising, for it could become the customer's anchor price, making the regular price of 50 euros for a future purchase seem high by comparison.

The absence of accurate reference prices also suggests that advertising actual prices for services the customer is not used to purchasing may reduce uncertainty and overcome a customer's inflated price expectations for some services. For example, a marketing research firm's advertisements citing the price for a simple study (such as 7,500 euros) would be informative to business customers who are not familiar with the costs of research studies and therefore would be guessing at the cost. By featuring price in advertising, the company overcomes the fear of high cost by giving readers a price anchor.

PRICES ARE NOT VISIBLE

One requirement for the existence of customer reference prices is *price visibility* – the price cannot be hidden or implicit. In many services, particularly financial services, most customers know about only the rate of return and not the costs they pay in the form of fund management and insurance fees.

For all the reasons discussed here, many customers do not see the price at all until *after* they receive certain services. Of course, in situations of urgency, such as in the case of accident or illness, customers must make the decision to purchase without respect to cost. And if cost is not known to the customer before purchase, it cannot be used as a key criterion for purchase, as it often is for goods. Price is likely to be an important criterion in *repurchase*, however. Furthermore, monetary price in repurchase may be an even more important criterion than in initial purchase.

THE ROLE OF NON-MONETARY COSTS

Economists have long recognized that monetary price is not the only sacrifice consumers make to obtain products and services. Demand, therefore, is not just a function of monetary price but is influenced by other costs as well. Non-monetary costs represent other sources of sacrifice perceived by consumers when buying and using a service (see Figure 17.2). Time costs, search costs and psychological costs often enter into the evaluation of whether to buy or rebuy a service, and may at times be more important concerns than monetary price. Customers will trade money for these other costs.

- *Time costs.* Most services require direct participation of the consumer and thus consume real time: time waiting as well as time when the customer interacts with the service provider. Consider the investment you make to exercise, see a doctor or get through the crowds to watch a concert or a football game. Not only are you paying money to receive these services, but you are also expending time. Time becomes a sacrifice made to receive service in multiple ways. First, because service providers cannot completely control the number of customers or the length of time it will take for each customer to be served, customers are likely to expend time waiting to receive the service. Waiting time for a service is frequently longer and less predictable than waiting time to buy goods. Second, customers often have to wait for an available appointment from a service provider. Virtually everyone has expended waiting time to receive services.

SERVICE SPOTLIGHT

At Disneyland Paris, the waiting time for popular rides (such as *Big Thunder Mountain, Crush's Coaster* and *Ratatouille: The Adventure*) is often in excess of 60 minutes. Combined with shorter waits on other attractions on an average day, a family visiting the park may spend 4 to 5 hours waiting and only 30 to 40 minutes on the actual rides.

- *Search costs.* Search costs – The effort invested to identify and select among services you desire – your search costs – are often higher for services than for physical goods. Prices for services are rarely displayed on shelves of service establishments for customers to examine as they shop, so these prices are often known only when a customer has decided to experience the service. As an example, how well did you estimate the costs of an hour of house-cleaning in the price quiz? As a student, it is unlikely that you regularly purchase house-cleaning, and you probably have not seen the price of an hour of cleaning displayed in any retail store. Another factor that increases search costs is that each service establishment typically offers only one 'brand' of a service (with the exception of brokers in insurance or financial services), so a customer must initiate contact with several different companies to get information across sellers. Price comparisons for some services (travel and hotels, for example) have been facilitated through the Internet.
- *Convenience costs.* There are also convenience (or, perhaps more accurately, inconvenience) costs of services. If customers have to travel to a service, they incur a cost, and the cost becomes greater when travel is difficult, as it is for elderly persons. Further, if service hours do not coincide with customers' available time, they must arrange their schedules to correspond to the company's schedule. And if consumers have to expend effort and time to prepare to receive a service (such as removing furniture before getting a carpet laid), they make additional sacrifices.
- *Psychological costs.* Often the most painful non-monetary costs are the psychological costs incurred in receiving some services. Fear of not understanding (insurance), fear of rejection (bank loans), fear of outcomes (medical treatment or surgery) – all these fears constitute psychological costs that customers experience as sacrifices when purchasing and using services. New services, even those that create positive change, bring about psychological costs that consumers factor into the purchase of services. When banks first introduced ATMs, customer resistance was significant, particularly to the idea of putting money into a machine: customers felt uncomfortable with the idea of letting go of their cheque and bank cards. And most customers also rejected voicemail when it was first developed.

NON-MONETARY COST PRIORITIES

Everybody will have different cost priorities. Some people will wait longer or travel further to get their car serviced, to save money. Others will be more concerned about convenience and will seek the nearest car service centre, no matter what the price. Quality may be more important to others and they will travel further for a car service centre that they perceive as employing better mechanics.

Figure 17.2   Monetary and non-monetary costs

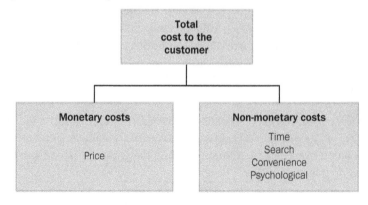

REDUCING NON-MONETARY COSTS

The managerial implications of these other sources of sacrifice are compelling. First, a firm may be able to increase monetary price by reducing time and other costs. For example, a services marketer can reduce the perceptions of time and convenience costs when use of the service is embedded in other activities (such as when a convenience store provides utility bill payment services, sells stamps and serves coffee along with selling products). Second, customers may be willing to pay to avoid the other costs. Many customers willingly pay extra to have items delivered to their home – including restaurant meals – rather than transporting the services and products themselves. Some customers also pay a premium for fast check-in and checkout when hiring cars, for reduced waiting time in a professional's office (as in so-called 'executive appointments' where, for a premium price, a busy executive comes early in the morning and does not have to wait) and to avoid doing the work themselves (such as paying one and one-half times the price per litre to avoid having to refuel a rental car before returning it). If time or other costs are pivotal for a given service, the company's advertising can emphasize these savings rather than monetary savings.

Many other services save time, thus actually allowing the customer to 'buy' time. Household cleaning services, lawn care, babysitting, online shopping, home banking, home delivery of groceries, decorating and carpet cleaning – all these services represent net gains in the discretionary time of consumers and can be marketed that way. Services that allow the customer to buy time are likely to have monetary value for busy consumers.

PRICE AS AN INDICATOR OF SERVICE QUALITY

One of the intriguing aspects of pricing is that buyers are likely to use price as an indicator of both service costs and service quality – price is at once an attraction variable and a repellent.[3] Customers' use of price as an indicator of quality depends on several factors, one of which is the other information available to them. When service cues to quality are readily accessible, when brand names provide evidence of a company's reputation or when the level of advertising communicates the company's belief in the brand, customers may prefer to use those cues instead of price. In other situations, however, such as when quality is hard to detect or when quality or price varies a great deal within a class of services, consumers may believe that price is the best indicator of quality. Many of these conditions typify situations that consumers face when purchasing services.[4] Another factor that increases the dependence on price as a quality indicator is the risk associated with the service purchase. In high-risk situations, many of which involve credence services such as restaurants or management consulting, the customer will look to price as a surrogate for quality.

Because customers depend on price as a cue to quality and because price sets expectations of quality, service prices must be determined carefully. In addition to setting prices to cover costs or match competitors, companies must select the price points that convey the appropriate quality signal. Pricing too low can lead to inaccurate inferences about the quality of the service. Pricing too high can set expectations that may be difficult to match in service delivery.

APPROACHES TO PRICING SERVICES

Rather than repeat the basics of pricing that are common across products and services and are set out in many standard marketing textbooks, we want to emphasize in this chapter the way that services prices and pricing differ from the customer's and the company's perspective. We discuss these differences in the context of the three pricing structures typically used to set prices: (1) cost-based, (2) competition-based, and (3) demand-based pricing. These categories are the same bases on which goods prices are set, but adaptations must be made in services. The figure shows the three structures interrelating because companies need to consider each of the three to some extent in setting prices. In the following sections we describe in general

Figure 17.3   Three basic marketing price structures and challenges associated with their use for services

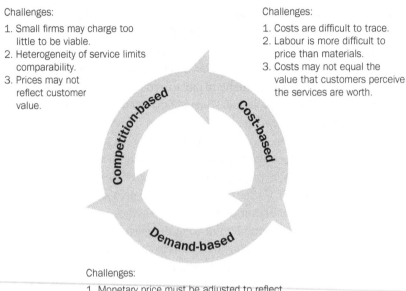

Challenges:
1. Small firms may charge too little to be viable.
2. Heterogeneity of service limits comparability.
3. Prices may not reflect customer value.

Challenges:
1. Costs are difficult to trace.
2. Labour is more difficult to price than materials.
3. Costs may not equal the value that customers perceive the services are worth.

Challenges:
1. Monetary price must be adjusted to reflect the value of non-monetary costs.
2. Information on service costs is less available to customers; hence, price may not be a central factor.

each basis for pricing and discuss challenges that occur when the approach is used in services pricing. Figure 17.3 summarizes those challenges.

COST-BASED PRICING

In cost-based pricing, a company determines expenses from raw materials and labour, adds amounts or percentages for overhead and profit, and thereby arrives at the price. This method is widely used by industries such as utilities, contracting, wholesaling and advertising. The basic formula for cost-based pricing is

$$\text{Price} = \text{Direct costs} + \text{Overhead costs} + \text{Profit margin}$$

Direct costs involve materials and labour that are associated with delivering the service, overhead costs are a share of fixed costs, and the profit margin is a percentage of full costs (direct + overhead).

SPECIAL CHALLENGES IN COST-BASED PRICING FOR SERVICES

One of the major difficulties in cost-based pricing for services involves defining the units in which a service is purchased. Thus the price per unit – a well-understood concept in pricing of manufactured goods – is a vague entity. For this reason many services are sold in terms of input units rather than units of measured output. For example, most professional services (such as consulting, engineering, architecture, psychotherapy and tutoring) are sold by the hour.

What is unique about services when using cost-based approaches to pricing? First, costs are difficult to trace or calculate in services businesses, particularly where multiple services are provided by the firm.[5] Consider how difficult it must be for a bank to allocate teller time accurately across its current, savings and money market accounts in order to decide what to charge for the services. Second, a major component of cost is employee time rather than materials, and the value of people's time, particularly non-professional time, is not easy to calculate or estimate.

An added difficulty is that actual service costs may under-represent the value of the service to the customer. A local tailor charges 10 euros for taking in a seam on a 350-euro ladies' suit jacket and an equal

10 euros for taking in a seam on a pair of 30-euro trousers. The tailor's rationale is that both jobs require the same amount of time. What she neglects to see is that the customer would pay a higher price – and might even be happier about the alterations – for the expensive suit jacket, and that 10 euros is too high a price for the trousers.

EXAMPLES OF COST-BASED PRICING STRATEGIES USED IN SERVICES

Cost-plus pricing is a commonly used approach in which component costs are calculated and a mark-up added. In product pricing, this approach is quite simple; in service industries, however, it is complicated because the tracking and identification of costs are difficult. The approach is typically used in industries in which cost must be estimated in advance, such as construction, engineering and advertising. In construction or engineering, bids are solicited by clients on the basis of the description of the service desired. Using their knowledge of the costs of the components of the service (including the raw materials such as stone and timber), labour (including both professional and unskilled) and margin, the company estimates and presents to the client a price for the finished service. A contingency amount – to cover the possibility that costs may be higher than estimated – is also stated because in large projects specifications can change as the service is provided.

Fee for service is the pricing strategy used by professionals; it represents the cost of the time involved in providing the service. Consultants, psychologists, accountants and lawyers, among other professionals, charge for their services on an hourly basis. Virtually all psychologists and lawyers have a set hourly rate they charge to their clients, and most structure their time in increments of an hour.

One of the most difficult aspects of this approach is that record-keeping is tedious for professionals. Lawyers and accountants must keep track of the time they spend for a given client, often down to 10-minute increments. For this reason the method has been criticized because it does not promote efficiency and sometimes ignores the expertise of the lawyers (those who are very experienced can accomplish much more than novices in a given time period, yet billings do not always reflect this). Clients often fear padding of their legal bills, and they frequently audit them. Despite these concerns, the hourly bill dominates the industry, with the majority of revenues billed this way.[6]

COMPETITION-BASED PRICING

The competition-based pricing approach focuses on the prices charged by other firms in the same industry or market. Competition-based pricing does not always imply charging the identical rate others charge but rather using others' prices as an anchor for the firm's price. This approach is used predominantly in two situations: (1) when services are standard across providers, such as in the dry-cleaning industry, and (2) in oligopolies characterized by few large service providers, such as in the airline or rental car industry. Difficulties involved in provision of services sometimes make competition-based pricing less simple than it is in goods industries.

SPECIAL CHALLENGES IN COMPETITION-BASED PRICING FOR SERVICES

Small firms may charge too little and not make margins high enough to remain in business. Many family-owned service establishments – dry-cleaning, retail and fast food outlets, among others – cannot deliver services at the low prices charged by chain operations.

Further, the heterogeneity of services across and within providers makes this approach complicated. Bank services illustrate the wide disparity in service prices. Customers buying current accounts, money orders or foreign currency, to name a few services, find that prices are rarely similar across providers. For example, there are likely to be major differences in overdraft charges between banks, and the commission and exchange rates quoted for foreign currency transactions can also differ significantly. Banks claim that they set fees high enough to cover the costs of these services. The wide disparity in prices probably reflects banks' difficulty in determining prices as well as their belief that financial customers do not shop around nor discern the differences (if any) among offerings from different providers. A banking expert makes the point that 'It's not like buying a litre of milk . . . . Prices aren't standardized'.[7] Only in very standardized services (such as dry-cleaning) are prices likely to be remembered and compared.

EXAMPLES OF COMPETITION-BASED PRICING IN SERVICES INDUSTRIES

Price signalling occurs in markets with a high concentration of sellers. In this type of market, any price offered by one company will be matched by competitors to avoid giving a low-cost seller a distinct advantage. The airline industry exemplifies price signalling in services. When any competitor drops the price of routes, others match the lowered price almost immediately.

Going-rate pricing involves charging the most prevalent price in the market.

⭐ SERVICE SPOTLIGHT

Rental car pricing is an illustration of this technique (and an illustration of price signalling, because the rental car market is dominated by a small number of large companies). For years, the prices set by one company (Hertz) have been followed by the other companies. When Hertz instituted a new pricing plan that involved 'no mileage charges, ever', other rental car companies imitated the policy. They then had to raise other factors such as base rates, size and type of car, daily or weekly rates and drop-off charges to continue to make profits. Prices in different geographic markets, even cities, depend on the going rate in that location, and customers often pay different rates in contiguous cities in the same country.

DEMAND-BASED PRICING

The two approaches to pricing just described are based on the company and its competitors rather than on customers. Neither approach takes into consideration that customers may lack reference prices, may be sensitive to non-monetary prices and may judge quality on the basis of price. All these factors can be accounted for in a company's pricing decisions. The third major approach to pricing, *demand-based pricing*, involves setting prices consistent with customer perceptions of value: prices are based on what customers will pay for the services provided.

SPECIAL CHALLENGES IN DEMAND-BASED PRICING FOR SERVICES

One of the major ways that pricing of services differs from pricing of goods in demand-based pricing is that non-monetary costs and benefits must be factored into the calculation of perceived value to the customer. When services require time, inconvenience and psychological and search costs, the monetary price must be adjusted to compensate. And when services save time, inconvenience and psychological and search costs, the customer is willing to pay a higher monetary price. The challenge is to determine the value to customers of each of the non-monetary aspects involved.

Another way services and goods differ with respect to this form of pricing is that information on service costs may be less available to customers, making monetary price not as salient a factor in initial service selection as it is in goods purchasing.

FOUR MEANINGS OF PERCEIVED VALUE

One of the most appropriate ways that companies price their services is basing the price on the perceived value of the service to customers. Among the questions a services marketer needs to ask are the following: what do consumers mean by *value*? How can we quantify perceived monetary value so that we can set appropriate prices for our services? Is the meaning of value similar across consumers and services? How can value perceptions be influenced? To understand demand-based pricing approaches, we must fully understand what value means to customers.

This is not a simple task. When consumers discuss value, they use the term in many different ways and talk about myriad attributes or components. What constitutes value, even in a single service category, appears to be highly personal and idiosyncratic. As shown in Figure 17.4, customers define value in four ways: (1) value is low price; (2) value is whatever I want in a product or service; (3) value is the quality I get for the price I pay; and (4) value is what I get for what I give.[8] Let us take a look at each of these definitions more carefully.[9]

Figure 17.4   Four customer definitions of value

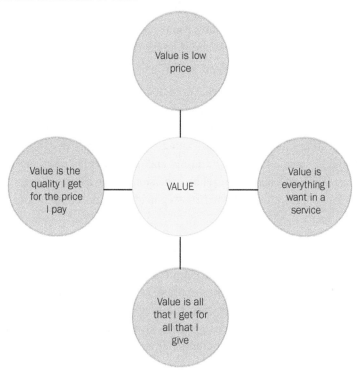

Value is Low Price.   Some consumers equate value with low price, indicating that what they have to give up in terms of money is most salient in their perceptions of value, as typified in these representative comments from customers:

- *For dry cleaning:* 'Value means the lowest price.'
- *For carpet steam-cleaning:* 'Value is price – which one is on sale.'
- *For a fast-food restaurant:* 'When I can use coupons, I feel that the service is a value.'
- *For airline travel:* 'Value is when airline tickets are discounted.'

Value is whatever I Want in a Product or Service.   Rather than focusing on the money given up, some consumers emphasize the benefits they receive from a service or product as the most important component of value. In this value definition price is far less important than the quality or features that match what the consumer wants. In the telecommunications industry, for example, business customers strongly value the reliability of the systems and are willing to pay for the safety and confidentiality of the connections. Service customers describe this definition of value as follows:

- *For an MBA degree:* 'Value is the very best education I can get.'
- *For dental services:* 'Value is high quality.'
- *For a social club:* 'Value is what makes me look good to my friends and family.'
- *For a rock concert or music festival:* 'Value is the best performance.'

Value is the Quality I Get for the Price I Pay.   Other consumers see value as a trade-off between the money they give up and the quality they receive.

* *For a hotel for a vacation:* 'Value is price first and quality second.'
* *For a hotel for business travel:* 'Value is the lowest price for a quality brand.'
* *For a computer services contract:* 'Value is the same as quality. No – value is affordable quality.'

Value is What I Get for What I Give.   Finally, some consumers consider all the benefits they receive as well as all sacrifice components (money, time, effort) when describing value.

* *For a housekeeping service:* 'Value is how many rooms I can get cleaned for what the price is.'
* *For a hairstylist:* 'Value is what I pay in cost and time for the look I get.'
* *For executive education:* 'Value is getting a good educational experience in the shortest time possible.'

The four consumer expressions of value can be captured in one overall definition consistent with the concept of utility in economics: *perceived value is the consumer's overall assessment of the utility of a service based on perceptions of what is received and what is given.* Although what is received varies across consumers (some may want volume, others high quality, still others convenience), as does what is given (some are concerned only with money expended, others with time and effort), value represents a trade-off of the give and get components. Customers will make a purchase decision on the basis of perceived value, not solely to minimize the price paid. These definitions are the first step in identifying the elements that must be quantified in setting prices for services.

INCORPORATING PERCEIVED VALUE INTO SERVICE PRICING

The buyer's perception of total value prompts the willingness to pay a particular price for a service. To translate the customer's value perceptions into an appropriate price for a specific service offering, the marketer must answer a number of questions. What benefits does the service provide? How important is each of these benefits? How much is it worth to the customer to receive a particular benefit from a service? At what price will the service be economically acceptable to potential buyers? In what context is the customer purchasing the service?

The most important thing a company must do – and often a difficult thing – is to estimate the value to customers of the company's services. Value may be perceived differently by consumers because of idiosyncratic tastes, knowledge about the service, buying power and ability to pay. In this type of pricing, what the consumers value – not what they pay – forms the basis for pricing. Therefore its effectiveness rests solely on accurately determining what the market perceives the service to be worth.

When the services are for the end-consumer, most often service providers will decide that they cannot afford to give each individual exactly the bundle of attributes he or she values. They will, however, attempt to find one or more bundles that address segments of the market. On the other hand, when services are sold to businesses (or, in the case of high-end services, to end-customers), the company can understand and deliver different bundles to each customer.

One of the most complex and difficult tasks of services marketers is setting prices internationally. If services marketers price on the basis of perceived value and if perceived value and willingness to pay differ across countries (which they often do), then service firms may provide essentially the same service but charge different prices in different countries. Here, as in pricing domestically, the challenge is to determine the perceived value, not just to different customers but to customers in different parts of the world.

PRICING STRATEGIES THAT LINK TO THE FOUR VALUE DEFINITIONS

In this section we describe the approaches to services pricing that are particularly suited to each of the four value definitions.

PRICING STRATEGIES WHEN THE CUSTOMER MEANS 'VALUE IS LOW PRICE'

When monetary price is the most important determinant of value to a customer, the company focuses mainly on price. This focus does not mean that the quality level and intrinsic attributes are always irrelevant, just that monetary price dominates in importance. To establish a service price in this definition of value, the marketer must understand to what extent customers know the objective prices of services in this category, how they interpret various prices and how much is too much of a perceived sacrifice. These factors are best understood when the service provider also knows the relative monetary value of the purchase, the frequency of past price changes and the range of acceptable prices for the service. Some of the specific pricing approaches appropriate when customers define value as low price include discounting, odd pricing, synchro-pricing and penetration pricing (Figure 17.5).

Figure 17.5   Pricing strategies when the customer defines value as low price

Value is low price
- Discounting
- Odd pricing
- Synchro-pricing
- Dynamic pricing
- Penetration pricing

DISCOUNTING

Service providers offer discounts or price cuts to communicate to price sensitive buyers that they are receiving value. Airlines such as British Airways, easyJet and Ryanair advertise short periods of two to three months when ticket prices within Europe will be discounted. Ryanair occasionally advertises free seats where the passenger only pays taxes and administration charges for a flight. These attract customers to try their flights and help fill planes during off-peak periods. It also brings traffic to the company's website which may result in flights other than the free ones being booked.

ODD PRICING

Odd pricing is the practice of pricing services just below the exact Euro amount to make buyers perceive that they are getting a lower price. Dry-cleaners charge 2.98 euros for a shirt rather than 3.00 euros, health clubs have membership fees priced at 33.90 euros per month rather than 34 euros, and haircuts are 19.50 euros rather than 20.00 euros. Odd prices suggest discounting and bargains and are appealing to customers for whom value means low price.

SYNCHRO-PRICING

Synchro-pricing is the use of price to manage demand for a service by capitalizing on customer sensitivity to prices. Certain services, such as tax preparation, passenger transportation, long-distance telephone, hotels and theatres, have demand that fluctuates over time as well as constrained supply at peak times. For companies in these and other industries, setting a price that provides a profit over time can be difficult. Pricing can, however, play a role in smoothing demand and synchronizing demand and supply. Time, place, quantity and incentive differentials have all been used effectively by service firms, as discussed in Chapter 14.

Place differentials are used for services in which customers have a sensitivity to location. The front row at concerts, centre court in tennis or basketball, beach-side rooms in hotels – all these represent place differentials that are meaningful to customers and that therefore command higher prices.

Time differentials involve price variations that depend on when the service is consumed. Off-peak rail fares, airline tickets that include a Saturday night stay, and health spas in the off-season are time differentials that reflect slow periods of service. By offering lower prices for underused time periods, a service company can smooth demand and also gain incremental revenue.

Quantity differentials are usually price decreases given for volume purchasing. This pricing structure allows a service company to predict future demand for its services. Customers who buy a booklet of coupons for a tanning salon or facial, a quantity of tokens for toll roads or ferries, or packages of advertising spots on radio or television are all responding to price incentives achieved by committing to future services. Corporate discounts for airlines, hotels and rental cars exemplify quantity discounts in the business context; by offering lower prices, the service provider locks in future business.

Differentials **as incentives** are lower prices for new or existing clients in the hope of encouraging them to become regular users or more frequent users. Some professionals – lawyers, dentists and, even, some chiropractors – offer free consultations at the front end, usually to overcome fear and uncertainty about high service prices. Other companies stimulate use by offering regular customers discounts or premiums during slow periods.

DYNAMIC PRICING

Dynamic pricing is a form of technology-led synchro-pricing frequently used as part of a revenue management/ yield management model (discussed in Chapter 14). It involves the buying and selling of goods and services in markets in which prices move quickly in response to supply and demand fluctuations. Dynamic pricing is estimated to account for more than 40 per cent of total online transactions. For example, airlines adjust their fares for a particular flight frequently, sometimes several times a day, as the flight's departure date nears, to reflect customer demand and the time remaining until the departure date. In addition to dynamic pricing being undertaken by the service provider directly, dynamic prices can also be offered through third-party sites such as comparison websites (aggregators), group buying sites or on auction sites.

Comparison websites or *aggregators* are website portals or search utilities that enable clients to gain several quotes or prices via an electronic e-quote form. In the insurance sector, they include websites such as comparethemarket.com, gocompare.com and confused.com; in flights and travel, they include sites such as skyscanner.net, trivago.com, trainline.com and expedia.com; in restaurants they include 5pm.co.uk; and in utilities, uswitch.com and moneysupermarket.com. These aggregators conclude agreements with a number of suppliers to provide a comparative quote to potential customers based on pre-determined list of specified needs as disclosed by them. These prices also change.

★ SERVICE SPOTLIGHT

Online flight aggregator skyscanner.net was born out of one of its founders' difficulties in finding cheap flights to ski resorts. In 2002, convinced they could do better, he and a group of other IT professionals developed the concept at weekends while continuing to work as contractors. By 2014 the Edinburgh-based flight comparison website achieved a turnover of £93 million. The company now receives more than 35 million monthly visitors from some 230 countries with particularly strong growth in Russia, Italy, Spain and China. In addition, their mobile search apps have been installed on 35 million devices. The company's technology searches millions of Internet sites for flights and then compares and contrasts each offering for their relative advantages, such as cost, time and date of departure and destination. It also books the flight. The site is now available in 30 languages and the company has offices in the UK, Singapore, Beijing, Shenzhen, Miami, Barcelona, Sofia and Budapest. The service has recently expanded to include hotels and car rental.

Group buying sites work on the concept that the greater the number of people who want to buy a service, the lower the price will be for everyone. Groupon is an example of a site that operates in 18 countries within Europe. Each day, Groupon features a variety of service offers from spa treatments to restaurants in major cities. By promising service businesses a minimum number of customers (a form of collective buying power), they can offer discounts. If the minimum number of customers for a particular deal is reached, then the customer gets the service at the discounted rate. If not enough people sign up, then the specific deal is cancelled for all customers. On some sites, the greater the number of people who want to buy the service, the lower the price will be for everyone. Sellers generally group the prices of the product being sold based on the number of buyers. For example, for 5 to 10 buyers, the price for each buyer is 100 euros; for 10–20 buyers, the price for each buyer is 95 euros, and so on. Word of mouth is critical, because interested buyers are encouraged to enlist their friends and relatives to get a cheaper price for the whole group. Sellers motivate this action by placing an 'Invite Your Friend' icon right next to the service or price information. Advantages of this form of dynamic pricing are that the price decreases as a greater number of people bid, and the exact service and its specifications are known to buyers when bidding.

Online auction sites such as eBay are generally used for auctioning products rather than services. However, eBay has seen some growth in auctions of vacations, hotel stays and holiday property rentals. Priceyourmeal.com is a UK website that allows customers to bid for meal packages at particular restaurants (i.e. a meal for four including wine) – the highest bid at the end of the auction period gets the meal package at that price. Online auctions of this type represent dynamic pricing because customers pay what they are willing and compete with each other on the service they desire.

PENETRATION PRICING

Penetration pricing is a strategy in which new services are introduced at low prices to stimulate trial and widespread use. The strategy is appropriate when (1) sales volume of the service is very sensitive to price, even in the early stages of introduction; (2) it is possible to achieve economies in unit costs by operating at large volumes; (3) a service faces threats of strong potential competition very soon after introduction; and (4) there is no class of buyers willing to pay a higher price to obtain the service.[10] Penetration pricing can lead to problems when companies then select a 'regular' increased price. Care must be taken not to penetrate with so low a price that customers feel the regular price is outside the range of acceptable prices.

PRICING STRATEGIES WHEN THE CUSTOMER MEANS 'VALUE IS EVERYTHING I WANT IN A SERVICE.'

When the customer is concerned principally with the 'get' components of a service, monetary price is not of primary concern. The more desirable intrinsic attributes a given service possesses, the more highly valued the service is likely to be and the higher the price the marketer can set. Figure 17.6 shows appropriate pricing strategies.

Figure 17.6   Pricing strategies when the customer defines value as everything wanted in a service

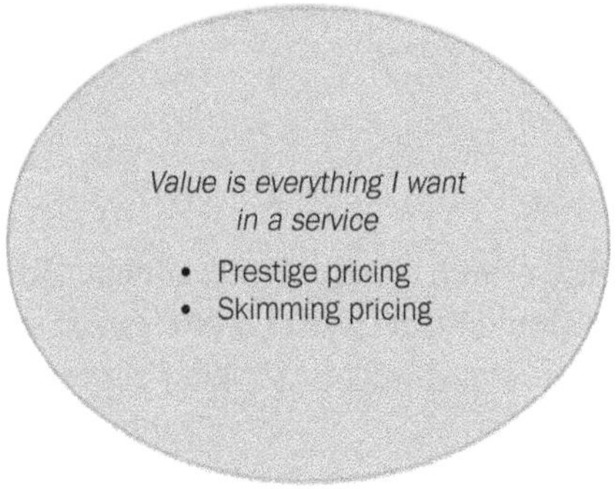

*Value is everything I want
in a service*

• Prestige pricing
• Skimming pricing

PRESTIGE PRICING

Prestige pricing is a special form of demand-based pricing by service marketers who offer high-quality or status services. For certain services – restaurants, health clubs, airlines and hotels – a higher price is charged for the luxury end of the business. Some customers of service companies who use this approach may actually value the high price because it represents prestige or a quality image. Others prefer purchasing at the high end because they are given preference in seating or accommodation and are entitled to other special benefits. In prestige pricing, demand may actually increase as price increases because the costlier service has more value in reflecting quality or prestige.

SKIMMING PRICING

Skimming pricing, a strategy in which new services are introduced at high prices with large promotional expenditures, is an effective approach when services are major improvements over past services. In this situation customers are more concerned about obtaining the service than about the cost of the service, allowing service providers to skim the customers most willing to pay the highest prices.

PRICING STRATEGIES WHEN THE CUSTOMER MEANS 'VALUE IS THE QUALITY I GET FOR THE PRICE I PAY.'

Some customers primarily consider both quality and monetary price. The task of the marketer is to understand what *quality* means to the customer (or segments of customers) and then to match quality level with price level. Specific strategies are shown in Figure 17.7.

Figure 17.7   Pricing strategies when the customer defines value as quality for the price paid

Value is the quality I get for the price I pay

- Value pricing
- Market segmentation pricing

VALUE PRICING

The widely used term *value pricing* has come to mean 'giving more for less'. In current usage it involves assembling a bundle of services that are desirable to a wide group of customers and then pricing them lower than they would cost separately.

 SERVICE SPOTLIGHT

Subway offers value pricing with their three-euro lunch saver menu. This includes a 15 cm sub sandwich and a drink. Rivals Burger King, McDonald's and other fast-food restaurants have similar product ranges. The terminology used may vary from 'meal deals' to 'king savers' but they all represent a bundled offering at a low price.

MARKET SEGMENTATION PRICING

With market segmentation pricing, a service marketer charges different prices to groups of customers for what are perceived to be different quality levels of service, even though there may not be corresponding differences in the costs of providing the service to each of these groups. This form of pricing is based on the premise that segments show different price elasticities of demand and desire different quality levels.

Services marketers often price by *client category*, based on the recognition that some groups find it difficult to pay a recommended price. Health clubs will typically offer student memberships, recognizing that this segment of customers has limited ability to pay full price. In addition to the lower price, student memberships may also carry with them reduced hours of use, particularly in peak times. The same line of reasoning leads to memberships for retired people who are less able to pay full price but are willing to patronize the clubs during daytime hours when most full-price members are working.

Companies also use market segmentation by *service version*, recognizing that not all segments want the basic level of service at the lowest price. When they can identify a bundle of attributes that are desirable enough for another segment of customers, they can charge a higher price for that bundle. Companies can configure service bundles that reflect price and service points appealing to different groups in the market. Hotels, for example, offer standard rooms at a basic rate but then combine amenities and tangibles related to the room to attract customers willing to pay more for the executive floor, spa baths, additional beds and sitting areas.

PRICING STRATEGIES WHEN THE CUSTOMER MEANS 'VALUE IS ALL THAT I GET FOR ALL THAT I GIVE.'

Some customers define value as including not just the benefits they receive but also the time, money, and effort they put into a service. Figure 17.8 illustrates the pricing strategies described in this definition of value.

Figure 17.8   Pricing strategies when the customer defines value as all that is received for all that is given

Value is all that I get for all that I give
- Price framing
- Price bundling
- Complementary pricing
- Results-based pricing

PRICE FRAMING

Because many customers do not possess accurate reference prices for services, services marketers are more likely than product marketers to organize price information (price framing) for customers so they know how to view it. Customers naturally look for price anchors as well as familiar services against which to judge focal services.

⭐ **SERVICE SPOTLIGHT**

Sky satellite television in the UK has various packages putting together channels into a 'original bundle at 28 euros', a 'variety bundle at 42 euros' and a 'family bundle at 50 euros'. They are then charged an additional fee if they want movie or sports packages. By organizing price information in this way, consumers find it easier to select the optimum package for their household.[11]

PRICE BUNDLING

Some services are consumed more effectively in conjunction with other services; other services accompany the products they support (such as extended service warranties, training and expedited delivery). When customers find value in a package of services that are interrelated, price bundling is an appropriate strategy. Bundling, which means pricing and selling grouped rather than individual services, has benefits to both customers and service companies. As an example, a health club customer may be able to contract for aerobics classes at 10 euros per month, weight machines at 15 euros and the swimming pool at 15 euros – or the group of three services for 27 euros (a price incentive of 13 euros per month). Customers find that bundling simplifies their purchase and payment, and companies find that the approach stimulates demand for the firm's service line, thereby achieving cost economies for the operations as a whole while increasing net contributions.[12] Bundling also allows the customer to pay less than when purchasing each of the services individually, which contributes to perceptions of value.

The effectiveness of price bundling depends on how well the service firm understands the bundles of value that customers or segments perceive, and on the complementarity of demand for these services. Effectiveness also depends on the right choice of services from the firm's point of view. Because the firm's objective is to increase overall sales, the services selected for bundling should be those with a relatively small sales volume without the bundling to minimize revenue loss from discounting a service that already has a high sales volume.

COMPLEMENTARY PRICING

Services that are highly interrelated can be leveraged by using complementary pricing. This pricing includes three related strategies – captive pricing, two-part pricing and loss leadership.[13] In captive pricing, the firm offers a base service or product and then provides the supplies or peripheral services needed to continue using the service. In this situation the company could offload some part of the price for the basic service to the peripherals. For example, photocopier rental services often drop the price for installation to a very low level, then compensate by charging enough for the ink, paper and maintenance contracts to make up for the loss in revenue. With service firms, this strategy is often called *two-part pricing* because the service price is broken into a fixed fee plus variable usage fees (also found in telephone services and health clubs). *Loss leadership* is the term typically used in retail stores when providers place a familiar service on special, largely to draw the customer to the store and then reveal other levels of service available at higher prices.

RESULTS-BASED PRICING

In service industries in which outcome is very important but uncertainty is high, the most relevant aspect of value is the *result* of the service. In personal injury lawsuits, for example, clients value the settlement they receive at the conclusion of the service. From tax accountants, clients most value cost savings. From universities and colleges, students most value getting a job upon graduation. In these and other situations, an appropriate value-based pricing strategy is to price on the basis of results or outcome of the service.

The most prevalent form of results-based pricing is a practice called *contingency pricing* used by lawyers. Contingency pricing is the major way that personal injury and certain consumer cases are billed. In this approach, lawyers do not receive fees or payment until the case is settled, when they are paid a percentage of the money that the client receives. Therefore, only an outcome in the client's favour is compensated. From the client's point of view, the pricing makes sense, in part because most clients in these cases are unfamiliar with and possibly intimidated by law firms. Their biggest fears are high fees for a case that may take years to settle. By using contingency pricing, clients are ensured that they pay no fees until they receive a settlement.

In these and other instances of contingency pricing, the economic value of the service is hard to determine before the service, and providers develop a price that allows them to share the risks and rewards of delivering value to the buyer. Partial contingency pricing, now being used in commercial law cases, is a version in which the client pays a lower fee than usual but offers a bonus if the settlement exceeds a certain level. Results-based pricing is demonstrated clearly in the online 'pay-per-click' advertising industry today. Rather than buying media with estimated audiences, companies that buy advertisements on Google pay only for users who actually respond to their ads by clicking on them.

SUMMARY

This chapter began with three key differences between customer evaluation of pricing for services and goods: (1) customers often have inaccurate or limited reference prices for services, (2) price is a key signal to quality in services, and (3) monetary price is not the only relevant price to service customers. These three differences can have a profound impact on the strategies that companies use to set and administer prices for services. The chapter next discussed common pricing structures, including cost-based, competition-based and demand-based pricing. Central to the discussion were the specific challenges in each of these structures and the services pricing techniques that have emerged in practice.

Finally, the chapter defined customer perceptions of value and suggested appropriate pricing strategies that match each customer definition. The four value definitions include (1) value is low price, (2) value is whatever I want in a product or service, (3) value is the quality I get for the price I pay, and (4) value is all that I get for all that I give.

KEY CONCEPTS

Aggregators	390	Online auction sites	391
Comparison websites	390	Penetration pricing	389
Competition-based pricing	379	Perceived value	386
Complementary pricing	394	Prestige pricing	392
Cost-based pricing	379	Price bundling	394
Demand-based pricing	379	Price framing	393
Discounting	389	Reference prices	379
Dynamic pricing	390	Results-based pricing	394
Group buying sites	390	Skimming pricing	392
Market segmentation pricing	393	Synchro-pricing	389
Non-monetary costs	381	Value pricing	392
Odd pricing	389		

EXERCISES

1 List five services for which you have no reference price. Now put yourself in the role of the service provider for two of those services and develop pricing strategies. Be sure to include in your description which of the value definitions you believe customers will possess and what types of strategies would be appropriate given those definitions.

2 In the next week, find three price lists for services (such as from a restaurant, drycleaner or hairstylist). In each case, identify what the pricing base is and what strategy is being used. How effective is each one?

3 Consider that you are the owner of a new health club and can prepare a value/price package that is appealing to students. Describe your approach. How does it differ from existing offerings?

DISCUSSION QUESTIONS

1 Which approach to pricing (cost-based, competition-based or demand-based) is the most fair to customers? Why?

2 Is it possible to use all three approaches simultaneously when pricing services? If you answer yes, describe a service that is priced this way.

3 For what consumer services do you have reference prices? What makes these services different from others for which you lack reference prices?

4 Name three services you purchase in which price is a signal of quality. Do you believe that there are true differences across services that are priced high and those that are priced low? Why or why not?

5 Describe the non-monetary costs involved in the following services: getting a car loan, belonging to a health club, attending an executive education class, and getting dental braces.

6 Consider the specific pricing strategies for each of the four customer value definitions. Which of these strategies could be adapted and used with another value definition?

7 What are the implications of comparison websites or aggregators for a service organization trying to differentiate its offering?

8 Why are auction sites such as eBay more suited to products rather than services?

FURTHER READING

Bilotkach, V., Gaggero, A. A. and Piga, C. A. (2015). Airline pricing under different market conditions: Evidence from European Low-Cost Carriers. *Tourism Management*, 47, 152–63.

Docters, R., Reopel, M., Sun, J.-M. and Tanny, S. (2004). Capturing the unique value of services: why pricing services is different. *Journal of Business Strategy*, 25(2), 23–28.

Indounas, K.A. (2009). Succesful industrial service pricing. *Journal of Business and Industrial Marketing*, 24(2), 86–97.

Indounas, K.A. and Avlonitis, G.J. (2009). Pricing objectives and their antecedents in the services sector. *Journal of Service Management*, 20(3), 342–74.

Lin, C.-H., Sher, P.J. and Shih, H.-Y. (2005). Past progress and future directions in conceptualizing customer perceived value. *International Journal of Service Industry Management*, 16(4), 318–36.

Schlereth, C. and Skiera, B. (2012). Measurement of consumer preferences for bucket pricing plans with different service attributes. *International Journal of Research in Marketing*, 29(2), 167–80.

Xia, L., Monroe, K.B. and Cox, J.L. (2004). The price is unfair! A conceptual framework of price fairness perceptions. *Journal of Marketing*, 68, 1–15.

PART 6

Service and the Bottom Line

CHAPTER 18 The Financial Impact of Service Quality

In this final section of the text, we discuss one of the most important questions about service that managers have been debating for many years: is excellent service profitable to an organization? We pull together research and company experience to answer this question. We present our own model of how the relationship works and consider some alternative models that have been used. Our model shows how service quality has offensive effects (gaining new customers) and defensive effects (retaining customers).

We also discuss several important performance models in this chapter including customer equity which compares investments in service with expenditures on other marketing activities. The balanced scorecard is an approach that includes multiple company factors including financial, customer, operational and innovative measures. The balanced scorecard allows a company to measure performance from the customer's perspective (Chapter 9), from the employee's perspective (Chapter 11) and from an innovation and new service perspective (Chapter 8). Thus, in Chapter 18 we synthesize the measurement issues that underlie the provision of service and offer a way for companies to demonstrate that service is accountable financially. We also present an approach called strategic performance mapping that helps companies integrate all elements of their balanced scorecards. These models help companies understand more accurately their benefits from investments in service excellence.

CHAPTER 18

The Financial Impact of Service Quality

CHAPTER OUTLINE

LEARNING OBJECTIVES

This chapter's objectives are to:

1 Examine the direct effects of service on profits.
2 Consider the effect of service on getting new customers.
3 Evaluate the role of service in keeping customers.
4 Discuss what is known about the key service drivers of overall service quality, customer retention and profitability.
5 Discuss the balanced performance scorecard that allows for strategic focus on measurements other than financials.

OPENING EXAMPLE
Zappos – The Value of Investing in Service Quality

Zappos, the world's biggest online shoe retailer, sells shoes internationally from its base in Las Vegas, Nevada, in the USA. The success of the company is partly attributed to its loyal customers: 75 per cent of Zappos orders come as repeat business. This loyalty is engendered by the organization's obsessive focus on service quality. Customer focus is reflected in its consumer-friendly, highly intuitive website and fast, free shipping (in both directions). Service is evidenced by the company's vast model selection, including special sizes, and its more than 2.9 million items in stock.

Whilst the majority of orders are placed directly on the Internet, calls are also made to the Zappos call centre which is staffed 24 hours per day. The call centre operators are there to solve customer problems, even if that means helping a customer to find a non-stocked item by searching competitors' websites. Call-takers are encouraged to take as much time as necessary to assist customers with their orders, answer their questions and troubleshoot their problems. In 2009, one call lasted 5 hours and 20 minutes with a woman who was interested in buying a special pair of shoes. Zappos employees are held accountable for 'wowing' customers with outstanding service. They routinely send handwritten thank-you notes to customers and have been known to also send bouquets of flowers or boxes of chocolates in sympathy or in celebration.

This focus on the customer and service quality resulted in significant financial returns. In the ten years between its launch in 1999 and 2009, company value soared as Zappos went from start-up to being bought by Amazon for around 1 billion euros.[1]

Virtually all companies hunger for evidence and tools to ascertain and monitor the payoff and payback of new investments in service. Many managers still see service and service quality as costs rather than as contributors to profits, partly because of the difficulty involved in tracing the link between service and financial returns. Determining the financial impact of service parallels the age-old search for the connection between advertising and sales. Service quality's results – like advertising's results – are cumulative, and therefore, evidence of the link may not come immediately or even quickly after investments, and, like advertising, service quality is one of many variables – among them pricing, advertising, efficiency and image – that simultaneously influence profits. Furthermore, spending on service per se does not guarantee results, because strategy and execution must both also be considered.

In recent years, however, researchers and company executives have sought to understand the relationship between service and profits, and have found strong evidence to support the relationship. For example, a study examined the comparative benefits of revenue expansion and cost reduction on return on quality. The research addressed a common strategic dilemma faced by executives: whether to reduce costs through the use of quality programmes such as Six Sigma that focus on efficiencies and cost-cutting, or to build revenues through improvements to customer service, customer satisfaction and customer retention.[2] Using managers' reports as well as secondary data on firm profitability and stock returns, the study investigated whether the highest return on quality was generated from cost-cutting, revenue expansion or a combination of the two approaches. The results suggest that firms that adopt primarily a revenue expansion emphasis perform better and have higher return on quality than firms that emphasize either cost reduction or both revenue expansion and cost reduction together.[3]

Executives are also realizing that the link between service and profits is neither straightforward nor simple. Service quality affects many economic factors in a company, some of them leading to profits through variables not traditionally in the domain of marketing. For example, the traditional total quality management approach expresses the financial impact of service quality in lowered costs or increased productivity. These relationships involve operational issues that concern marketing only in the sense that marketing research is used to identify service improvements that customers notice and value.

More recently, other types of evidence have become available on which to examine the relationship between service and profitability. The overall goal of this chapter is to synthesize that recent evidence and to identify relationships between service and profits. This chapter is divided into seven sections, parallelling the chapter's objectives. In each section we assess the evidence and identify what is currently known about the topics. The chapter is organized using a conceptual framework linking all the variables in the topics.

SERVICE AND PROFITABILITY: THE DIRECT RELATIONSHIP

Figure 18.1 shows the underlying question at the heart of this chapter. The executives of leading service companies such as British Airways and Disney were willing to trust their intuitive sense that better service would lead to improved financial success. Without formal documentation of the financial payoff, they have committed significant resources over the years to improving service and were richly rewarded for their leaps of faith. However, executives in other companies are sometimes reluctant to invest in service, waiting for solid evidence of its financial soundness.

Figure 18.1   The direct relationship between service and profits?

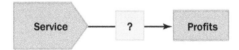

PROFITS AND SERVICE

A review by Gupta and Zeithaml[4] of two decades of studies examining the links among customer satisfaction, service quality, and firm performance resulted in several important recurring findings across studies. Some studies explicitly consider the impact of service quality on financial performance, while others subsume service quality as a driver of customer satisfaction and therefore focus on the impact of overall customer satisfaction on financial performance. As discussed in Chapter 4, customer satisfaction is a broader concept than service quality, but service quality is almost always an important driver of customer satisfaction across all types of industries. Therefore, the results of the review of both concepts are relevant in this chapter. Because so many studies were examined in the review, only a subset are mentioned here, but the complete list of sources can be found-in the published review itself.

Studies that were reviewed used a variety of metrics for financial performance: profit, stock price, Tobin's q (ratio of the market value of a firm divided by the replacement cost of its tangible assets), return on assets (ROA), return on investment (ROI), abnormal earnings, and cash flows. Here is what the authors concluded:

GENERALIZATION 1: IMPROVEMENT IN CUSTOMER SATISFACTION HAS A SIGNIFICANT AND POSITIVE IMPACT ON FIRMS' FINANCIAL PERFORMANCE

Many studies have shown a strong link between customer satisfaction and firm profitability. For example, one comprehensive study by Anderson, Fornell, and Mazvancheryl[5] using 200 of the *Fortune* 500 firms across

40 industries showed that a 1 per cent change in ACSI (as measured by the American Customer Satisfaction Index on a 0–100 scale) is associated with 1.016 per cent change in shareholder value as measured by Tobin's q. This implies that a 1 per cent improvement in satisfaction for these firms will lead to an increase in firm's value of approximately 190 million euros. Supporting this finding, a similar study by Gruca and Rego[6] found that a 1-point increase in ACSI results in an increase of around 38 million euros in a firm's net operational cash flow next year and a decrease of 4 per cent in cash flow variability.

In a service-industry study using data from almost 8,000 customers of a national hotel chain, researchers found that return on investment in service quality (e.g. cleanliness) was almost 45 per cent. Another study showed that a 1-point improvement in satisfaction (on a 7-point scale) increased ROA by 0.59 per cent.

Collectively, these studies show a strong and positive impact of customer satisfaction on firm performance. They further provide a rough benchmark about the size of the impact: a 1 per cent change in ACSI can lead to a 160 to 190 million euros' improvement in firm value. In sum, these results provide a strong guideline to firms about how much they should spend on improving customer satisfaction.

GENERALIZATION 2: THE LINK BETWEEN SATISFACTION AND FIRM PERFORMANCE IS ASYMMETRIC

An *asymmetric relationship* means that increases in customer satisfaction do not always have the same impact on firm performance as decreases in customer satisfaction. For example, a study by Anderson and Mittal[7] found that a 1 per cent increase in satisfaction led to 2.37 per cent increase in ROI, whereas a 1 per cent drop in satisfaction reduced ROI by 5.08 per cent. Another study by Nayyar[8] found that positive news about customer service led to an increase in compounded annualized rate (CAR) of about 0.46 per cent, whereas reports of reductions in customer service were met with declines in CAR of about half or 0.22 per cent. Also, Anderson and Mittal[9] found that the impact on ROI of a drop in satisfaction was twice that of an increase in satisfaction. In contrast, another study found that negative news of customer service had only half the impact on CAR that positive news produces.

GENERALIZATION 3: THE STRENGTH OF THE SATISFACTION-PROFITABILITY LINK VARIES ACROSS INDUSTRIES AS WELL AS ACROSS FIRMS WITHIN AN INDUSTRY

The strength of the relationships among customer satisfaction, service quality, and profitability is not consistent across industries. In a study by Ittner and Larcker,[10] the impact was found to be stronger in service industries than in durable and non-durable manufacturing firms. In that study the ACSI had a positive but insignificant impact on market value of durable and non-durable manufacturing firms, and a positive and significant impact on the market value of transportation, utility and communication firms. The effect was strongly negative for retailers. Anderson and Mittal[11] also found that trade-offs between customer satisfaction and productivity (e.g., labour productivity) were more likely for services than for goods. Specifically, a simultaneous 1 per cent increase in both customer satisfaction and productivity is likely to increase ROI by 0.365 per cent for goods, but only 0.22 per cent for services.

In addition to the differences found in the studies cited, Anderson and Mittal's study[12] found that, while a 1 per cent change in satisfaction had an *average* impact of 1.016 per cent on shareholder value (Tobin's q), the impact ranged from 2.8 per cent for department stores to –0.3 per cent for discount stores. Anderson and Mittal's[13] study again found that industry characteristics explain 35 per cent of the variance in cash flow growth and 54 per cent of the variance in cash flow variability. They also found that the influence of customer satisfaction on cash flow growth is greatest for low-involvement, routinized and frequently purchased products (e.g., beer and fast food).

While this summary represents a considerable improvement over what we knew in the past, companies are very eager to learn more. This general information about the relationships among customer satisfaction, service quality, and financial performance will help them understand that investing in customer satisfaction and service quality is beneficial. Thus, indications are that the investments are worthwhile and that not investing can be harmful to firms.

Although some companies continued to approach the relationship at a broad level, others have focused more specifically on particular elements of the relationship: for example, the relationship between service quality and either customer acquisition or retention.

OFFENSIVE MARKETING EFFECTS OF SERVICE: ATTRACTING MORE AND BETTER CUSTOMERS

Service quality can help companies attract more and better customers to the business through offensive marketing.[14] Offensive effects (shown in Figure 18.2) involve market share, reputation and price premiums. When service is good, a company gains a positive reputation and through that reputation a higher market share and the ability to charge more than its competitors for services. These benefits were documented in a multi-year, multi-company study called PIMS (profit impact of marketing strategy). The PIMS research shows that companies offering superior service achieve higher than normal market share growth and that service quality influences profits through increased market share and premium prices as well as lowered costs and less rework.[15] The study found that businesses rated in the top fifth of competitors on relative service quality average an 8 per cent price premium over their competitors.[16]

Figure 18.2   Offensive marketing effects of service on profits

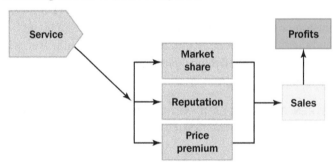

To document the impact of service on market share, a group of researchers described their version of the path between quality and market share, claiming that satisfied customers spread positive word of mouth, which leads to the attraction of new customers and then to higher market share. They claim that advertising service excellence without sufficient quality to back up the communications will not increase market share.[17]

DEFENSIVE MARKETING EFFECTS OF SERVICE: CUSTOMER RETENTION

When it comes to keeping the customers a firm already has – an approach called defensive marketing[18] – researchers and consulting firms have often documented and quantified the financial impact of existing customers. In Chapter 7 we explained that customer defection, or 'customer churn', is widespread in service businesses. Customer defection is costly to companies because new customers must replace lost customers, and replacement comes at a high cost. Getting new customers is expensive; it involves advertising, promotion and sales costs as well as start-up operating expenses. New customers are often unprofitable for a period of time after acquisition. In the insurance industry, for example, the insurer does not typically recover selling costs until the third or fourth year of the relationship. Capturing customers from other companies is also an expensive proposition: a greater degree of service improvement is necessary to make a customer switch from a competitor than to retain a current customer.

In general, the longer a customer remains with a company, the more profitable the relationship is for the organization: 'Served correctly, customers generate increasingly more profits each year they stay with a company. Across a wide range of businesses, the pattern is the same: the longer a company keeps a customer, the more money it stands to make.'[19] The money a company makes from retention comes from four sources (shown in Figure 18.3): costs, volume of purchases, price premium and word-of-mouth communication. This section provides research evidence for many of the sources.

Figure 18.3 Defensive marketing effects of service on profits

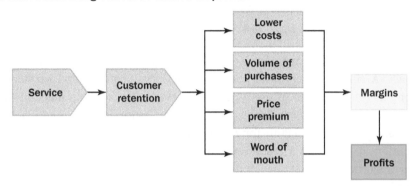

LOWER COSTS

Attracting a new customer is five times as costly as retaining an existing one. Consultants who have focused on these relationships assert that customer defections have a stronger effect on a company's profits than market share, scale, unit costs and many other factors usually associated with competitive advantage.[20] They also claim that, depending on the industry, companies can increase profits from 25 to 85 per cent by retaining just 5 per cent more of their customers.

Consider the following facts about the role of service quality in lowering costs:

- 'Our costs of not doing things right the first time were from 25 to 30 per cent of our revenue' (David F. Colicchio, regional quality manager, Hewlett-Packard Company).[21]
- Bain and Company, a consulting organization specializing in retention research, estimates that in the life insurance business, a 5 per cent annual increase in customer retention lowers a company's costs per policy by 18 per cent.

VOLUME OF PURCHASES

Customers who are satisfied with a company's services are likely to increase the amount of money they spend with that company or the types of services offered. A customer satisfied with a broker's services, for example, will likely invest more money when it becomes available. Similarly, a customer satisfied with a bank's current account services is likely to open a savings account with the same bank and to use the bank's loan services as well.

PRICE PREMIUM

Evidence suggests that a customer who notices and values the services provided by a company will pay a price premium for those services. Most of the service quality leaders in industry command higher prices than their competitors: DHL collects more for overnight delivery than the national postal services, Hertz rental cars cost more than Budget cars, and staying at the Ritz-Carlton is a more expensive undertaking than staying at the Sofitel.

WORD-OF-MOUTH COMMUNICATION

In Chapter 2 we described the valuable role of word-of-mouth communications in purchasing service. Because word-of-mouth communication is considered more credible than other sources of information, the best type of promotion for a service may well come from other customers who advocate the services provided by the company. Word-of-mouth communication brings new customers to the firm, and the financial value of this form of advocacy can be calibrated by the company in terms of the promotional costs it saves as well as the streams of revenues from new customers.

Managers of service firms are only beginning to understand the topics discussed in this chapter. For each of the sections on the service quality/profitability relationship in this chapter, there are answers that managers and researchers most want to know.[22]

1 *What is a loyal customer?* Customer loyalty can be viewed as the way customers feel or as the way they act. A simple definition is possible with some products and services: customers are loyal as long as they continue to use a good or service. For washing machines or long-distance telephone service, customers are deemed loyal if they continue to use the machine or telephone service. Defining customer loyalty for other products and services is more problematic. What is the definition of loyalty to a restaurant: always eat there, eat there more times than at other restaurants or eat there at least once during a given period? These questions highlight the growing popularity of the concept of 'share of wallet' that company managers are very interested in. 'Share of wallet' means what percentage of the spending in a particular service category is made on a given service provider. The other way to define loyalty is in terms of the customer's sense of belonging or commitment to the product. Some companies have been noted for their 'apostles', customers who care so much about the company that they stay in contact to provide suggestions for improvement and constantly preach to others the benefits of the company. Is this the best way to define loyalty?

2 *What is the role of service in defensive marketing?* Quality products at appropriate prices are important elements in the retention equation, but both these marketing variables can be imitated. Service plays a critical role – if not the critical role – in retaining customers. Providing consistently good service is not as easy to duplicate and therefore is likely to be the cementing force in customer relationships. Exactly how important is service in defensive marketing? How does service compare in effectiveness to other retention strategies such as price? To date, no studies have incorporated all or most factors to examine their relative importance in keeping customers. Many companies actually have survey data that could answer this question but either have not analysed the data for this purpose or have not reported their findings.

3 *What levels of service provision are needed to retain customers?* How much spending on service quality is enough to retain customers? Initial investigations into this question have been argued but have not been confirmed. One consultant, for example, proposed that when satisfaction rose above a certain threshold, repurchase loyalty would climb rapidly. When satisfaction fell below a different threshold, customer loyalty would decline equally rapidly. Between these thresholds, he believed that loyalty was relatively flat. The material discussed in Chapter 3 offered a different prediction. The zone of tolerance described in that chapter captures the range within which a company is meeting expectations. This framework suggests that firms operating within the zone of tolerance should continue to improve service, even to the point of reaching the desired service level. This hypothesis implies an upward-sloping (rather than flat) relationship with the zone of tolerance.

4 *What aspects of service are most important for customer retention?* The only studies that have examined specific aspects of service and their impact on customer retention have been early studies looking at customer complaint management. A decade ago such a study was appropriate because service was often equated with customer service, the after-sale function that dealt with dissatisfied

customers. But today, most companies realize that service is multifaceted and want to identify the specific aspects of service provision that will lead to keeping customers.

5 *How can defection-prone customers be identified?* Companies find it difficult to create and execute strategies responsive enough to detect customer defections. Systems must be developed to isolate potential defecting customers, evaluate them and retain them if it is in the best interest of the company. One author and consultant advises that companies focus on three groups of customers who may be candidates for defection: (a) customers who close their accounts and shift business to a competitor, (b) customers who shift some of their business to another firm, and (c) customers who actually buy more but whose purchases represent a smaller share of their total expenditures. The first of these groups is easiest to identify, and the third group is the most difficult. Among the other customers who would be vulnerable are any customer with a negative service experience, new customers and customers of companies in very competitive markets. Developing early warning systems of such customers is a pivotal requirement for companies.

Although research has come a long way in the last decade, researchers and companies must continue working on these questions for a more complete understanding of the impact of service on defensive marketing.

CUSTOMER PERCEPTIONS OF SERVICE QUALITY AND PURCHASE INTENTIONS

In Chapter 4, we highlighted the links among customer satisfaction, service quality and increased purchases. Here we provide more research and empirical evidence supporting these relationships.

 SERVICE SPOTLIGHT

With revenues in excess of €11bn and customers in more than 80 countries, the Finnish company Stora Enso is one of the world's leading paper, packaging and wood products producers. The company is keen to build their competitive differentiation by focusing on criteria like service quality, product quality, delivery reliability and new product development. Its operations and processes have become fundamental to establishing new best practices focused on improving customer satisfaction. The implementation of these practices has resulted in significant improvements in the company's net promoter score (NPS – see chapter 4). In the period 2010–2011, an additional 7 million euros of sales revenue was obtained from customers who had previously been detractors about the company (awarding a NPS of 6 or below) but had moved to become passives(NPS – 7–8) or promoters (NPS score 9–0).[23]

Figure 18.4 shows this service quality/customer intention relationship.

Evidence also shows that customer satisfaction and service quality perceptions affect consumer intentions to behave in other positive ways – praising the firm, preferring the company over others, increasing volume of purchases or agreeably paying a price premium. Most of the early evidence looked only at overall benefits in terms of purchase intention rather than examining specific types of behavioural intentions. One study, using information from a Swedish customer satisfaction barometer, found that stated repurchase intention is strongly related to stated satisfaction across virtually all product categories.[24]

Studies have found relationships between service quality and more specific behavioural intentions. One study involving university students found strong links between service quality and other behavioural

FIGURE 18.4   The effects of service

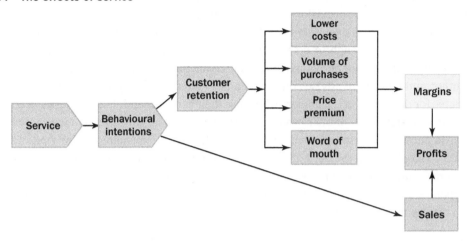

intentions of strategic importance to a university, including behaviour such as saying positive things about the school, and planning to recommend the school to employers as a place from which to recruit.[25] Another comprehensive study examined a battery comprising 13 specific behavioural intentions likely to result from perceived service quality. The overall measure was significantly correlated with customer perceptions of service quality.[26]

Individual companies have also monitored the impact of service quality on selected behavioural intentions. Toyota found that intent to repurchase a Toyota automobile increased from a base of 37 to 45 per cent with a positive sales experience, from 37 to 79 per cent with a positive service experience, and from 37 to 91 per cent with both positive sales and service experiences.[27]

Table 18.1 shows a list of the questions that businesses still need to know more about this topic and the others in this chapter.

THE KEY DRIVERS OF SERVICE QUALITY, CUSTOMER RETENTION AND PROFITS

Understanding the relationship between overall service quality and profitability is important, but it is perhaps more useful to managers to identify specific drivers of service quality that most relate to profitability (shown in Figure 18.5). Doing so will help firms understand what aspects of service quality to change to influence the relationship, and therefore where to invest resources.

Figure 18.5   The key drivers of service quality, customer retention and profits

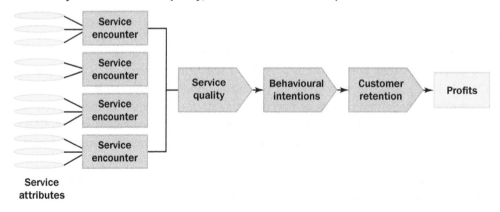

Table 18.1   Service quality and the economic worth of customers: businesses still need to know more

Topic	Key research questions
Service quality and profitability: the direct relationship	1. What methodologies need to be developed to allow companies to capture the effect of service quality on profit? 2. What measures are necessary to examine the relationship in a consistent, valid and reliable manner? 3. Does the relationship between service quality and profitability vary by industry, country, category of business (e.g. in services companies versus goods companies, in industrial versus packaged goods companies) or other variables? 4. What are the moderating factors of the relationship between service quality and profitability? 5. What is the optimal spending level on service in order to affect profitability?
Offensive effects of service quality	1. What is the optimal amount of spending on service quality to obtain offensive effects on reputation? 2. To obtain offensive effects, are expenditures on advertising or service quality itself more effective? 3. In what ways can companies signal high service quality to customers to obtain offensive effects?
Defensive effects of service quality	1. What is a loyal customer? 2. What is the role of service in defensive marketing? 3. How does service compare in effectiveness to other retention strategies such as price? 4. What levels of service provision are needed to retain customers? 5. How can the effects of word-of-mouth communication from retained customers be quantified? 6. What aspects of service are most important for customer retention? 7. How can defection-prone customers be identified?
Perceptions of service quality, behavioural intentions and profits	1. What is the relationship between customer purchase intentions and initial purchase behaviour in services? 2. What is the relationship between behavioural intentions and repurchase in services? 3. Does the degree of association between service quality and behaviour change at different quality levels?
Identifying the key drivers of service quality, customer retention and profits	1. What service encounters are most responsible for perceptions of service quality? 2. What are the key drivers in each service encounter? 3. Where should investments be made to affect service quality, purchase, retention and profits? 4. Are key drivers of service quality the same as key drivers of behavioural intentions, customer retention and profits?

Most evidence for this issue has come from examining the aspects of service (such as empathy, responsiveness and tangibles) on overall service quality, customer satisfaction and purchase intentions rather than on financial outcomes such as retention or profitability. As you have discovered in this text, service is multifaceted, consisting of a wide variety of customer-perceived dimensions including reliability, responsiveness and empathy, and resulting from innumerable company strategies such as technology and process improvement. In research exploring the relative importance of service dimensions on overall service quality or customer satisfaction, the bulk of the support confirms that reliability is most critical; but other research has demonstrated the importance of customization and other factors. Because the dimensions and attributes are delivered in many cases with totally different internal strategies, resources must be allocated where they are most needed, and study in this topic could provide direction.

Some companies and researchers have viewed the effect of specific service encounters on overall service quality or customer satisfaction and the effect of specific behaviours within service encounters.

⭐ **SERVICE SPOTLIGHT**

Marriott Hotels conducted extensive customer research to determine what service elements contribute most to customer loyalty. They found that four of the top five factors came into play in the first ten minutes of the guest's stay – those that involved the early encounters of arriving, checking in and entering the hotel rooms. Other companies have found that mistakes or problems that occur in early service encounters are particularly critical, because a failure at early points results in greater risk for dissatisfaction in each ensuing encounter.

CUSTOMER EQUITY AND RETURN ON MARKETING[28]

Although the marketing concept has articulated a customer-centred view since the 1960s, marketing has only recently decreased its emphasis on short-term transactions and increased its focus on long-term customer relationships. Much of this refocus stems from the changing nature of the world's leading economies, which have undergone a century-long shift from the goods sector to the service sector.

Because service often tends to be more relationship based, this structural shift in the economy has resulted in more attention to relationships and therefore more attention to customers. This customer-centred view is starting to be reflected in the concepts and metrics that drive marketing management, including such metrics as customer value and voice of the customer. For example, the concept of brand equity, a fundamentally product-centred concept, is now being challenged by the customer-centred concept of *customer equity*.

CUSTOMER EQUITY IS THE TOTAL OF THE DISCOUNTED LIFETIME VALUES SUMMED OVER ALL THE FIRM'S CUSTOMERS.

In other words, customer equity is obtained by summing up the customer lifetime values of the firm's customers. In fast-moving and dynamic industries that involve customer relationships, products come and go but customers remain. Customers and customer equity may be more central to many firms than brands and brand equity, although current management practices and metrics do not yet fully reflect this shift. The shift from product-centred thinking to customer-centred thinking implies the need for an accompanying shift from product-based metrics to customer-based metrics.

USING CUSTOMER EQUITY IN A STRATEGIC FRAMEWORK

Consider the issues facing a typical marketing manager or marketing-oriented CEO: how do I manage my brand? How will my customers react to changes in service and service quality? Should I raise price? What is the best way to enhance the relationships with my current customers? Where should I focus my efforts? Determining customer lifetime value, or customer equity, is the first step, but the more important step is to evaluate and test ideas and strategies using lifetime value as the measuring stick. At a very basic level, strategies for building customer relationships can affect five basic factors: retention rate, referrals, increased sales, reduced direct costs and reduced marketing costs.

Rust, Zeithaml and Lemon have developed an approach based on customer equity that can help business executives answer their questions. The model that represents this approach is shown in Figure 18.6. In this context, customer equity is a new approach to marketing and corporate strategy that finally puts the customer – and, more important, strategies that grow the value of the customer – at the heart of the organization. The researchers identify the drivers of customer equity – value equity, brand equity and relationship equity – and explain how these drivers work, independently and together, to grow customer equity. Service strategies are prominent in both value equity and relationship equity. Within each of these drivers are specific, incisive actions ('levers') that the firm can take to enhance its overall customer equity.

Figure 18.6   The customer equity model

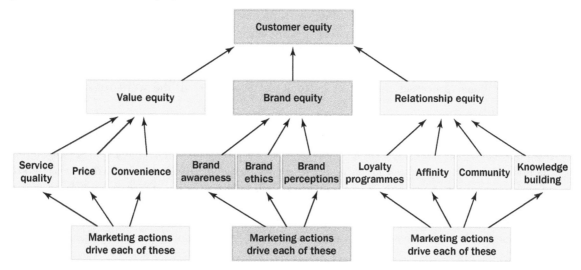

Sources: Adapted from R.T. Rust, K.N. Lemon and V.A. Zeithaml (2004) 'Return on marketing: using customer equity to focus marketing strategy', *Journal of Marketing*, 68, no. 1 (January 2004), pp. 109–27; R. Rust, V. Zeithaml and K. Lemon (2000) *Driving Customer Equity*, New York: Free Press, 2000.

WHY IS CUSTOMER EQUITY IMPORTANT?

For most firms, customer equity – the total of the discounted lifetime values of all the firm's customers – is certain to be the most important determinant of the long-term value of the firm. Although customer equity will not be responsible for the entire value of the firm (consider, for example, physical assets, intellectual property, research and development competencies, etc.), the firm's current customers provide the most reliable source of future revenues and profits – and provide a focal point for marketing strategy.

Although it may seem obvious that customer equity is key to long-term success, understanding how to grow and manage customer equity is much more complex. Growing customer equity is of utmost importance, and doing it well can lead to significant competitive advantage.

CALCULATING RETURN ON MARKETING USING CUSTOMER EQUITY

At the beginning of this chapter, we told you about an approach called return on quality that was developed to help companies understand where they could get the biggest impact from quality investments. A more general form of that approach is called return on marketing, which enables companies to look at all competing marketing strategy options and trade them off on the basis of projected financial return. This approach allows companies not just to examine the impact of service on financial return but also compare the impact of service with the impact of branding, price changes and all other marketing strategies. Using the customer equity model, firms can analyse the drivers that have the greatest impact, compare the drivers' performance with that of competitors' drivers, and project return on investment from improvements in the drivers. The framework enables 'what-if' evaluation of marketing return on investment, which can include such criteria as return on quality, return on advertising, return on loyalty programmes and, even, return on corporate citizenship, given a particular shift in customer perceptions. This approach enables firms to focus marketing efforts on strategic initiatives that generate the greatest return.

COMPANY PERFORMANCE MEASUREMENT: THE BALANCED PERFORMANCE SCORECARD

Traditionally, organizations have measured their performance almost completely on the basis of financial indicators such as profit, sales and return on investment. This short-term approach leads companies to emphasize financials to the exclusion of other performance indicators. Today's corporate strategists recognize the limitations of evaluating corporate performance on financials alone, contending that these income-based financial figures measure yesterday's decisions rather than indicate future performance. This recognition came when many companies' strong financial records deteriorated because of unnoticed declines in operational processes, quality or customer satisfaction.[29] In the words of one observer of corporate strategy:

> *Financial measures emphasize profitability of inert assets over any other mission of the company. They do not recognize the emerging leverage of the soft stuff – skilled people and employment of information – as the new keys to high performance and near-perfect customer satisfaction . . . . If the only mission a measurement system conveys is financial discipline, an organization is directionless.*[30]

For this reason, companies began to recognize that balanced scorecards – strategic measurement systems that captured other areas of performance – were needed. The developers of balanced scorecards defined them as follows:

> *a set of measures that gives top managers a fast but comprehensive view of the business . . . [that] complements the financial measures with operational measures of customer satisfaction, internal processes, and the organization's innovation and improvement activities – operational measures that are the drivers of future financial performance.*[31]

Having a firm handle on what had been viewed as 'soft' measures became the way to help organizations identify customer problems, improve processes and achieve company objectives. Balanced scorecards have become extremely popular. One recent report indicates that more than one-half of the largest companies worldwide use them.

As shown in Figure 18.7, the balanced scorecard captures three perspectives in addition to the financial perspective: customer, operational and learning. The balanced scorecard brings together, in a single management report, many of the previously separated elements of a company's competitive agenda and forces senior managers to consider all the important measures together. The scorecard has been facilitated by recent developments in software that allow companies to create balanced scorecards, automating and integrating measurements from all parts of the company.

Methods for measuring financial performance are the most developed and established in corporations, having been created more than 400 years ago. In contrast, efforts to measure market share, quality, innovation, human resources and customer satisfaction have only recently been created. Companies can improve their performance by developing this discipline in their measurement of all four categories.

SERVICE SPOTLIGHT

The French-owned EDF Group uses an adapted balanced scorecard approach to link overall objectives to continuous improvement to create a strategy-linked culture throughout the whole of its organization. The scorecard they use reflects the Group's strategic vision in the form of five ambitions, with associated performance measures. The five ambitions are to meet shareholder expectations, care for customers, be a positive point of reference (corporate reputation), be safe and responsible and maximize staff satisfaction. These ambitions do not in themselves follow the traditional balanced scorecard template but they are seen as the issues that are critical to an energy provider. The balanced scorecard is EDF Group's corporate-wide strategic reference framework for decisions at local and operational levels including decisions relating to service delivery.

Figure 18.7   Sample measurements for the balanced scorecard

Financial measures

Price premium
Volume increases
Value of customer referrals
Value of cross-sales
Long-term value of customer

Customer perspective

Service perceptions
Service expectations
Perceived value
Behavioural intentions:
   Percentage of loyalty
   Percentage of intent to
   switch
   Number of customer
   referrals
   Number of cross-sales
   Number of defections

Operation perspective

Right first time (percentage of hits)
Right on time (percentage of hits)
Responsiveness (percentage on time)
Transaction time (hours, days)
Throughput time
Reduction in waste
Process quality

**Innovation and learning
perspective**

Number of new products
Return on innovation
Employee skills
Time to market
Time spent talking to customers

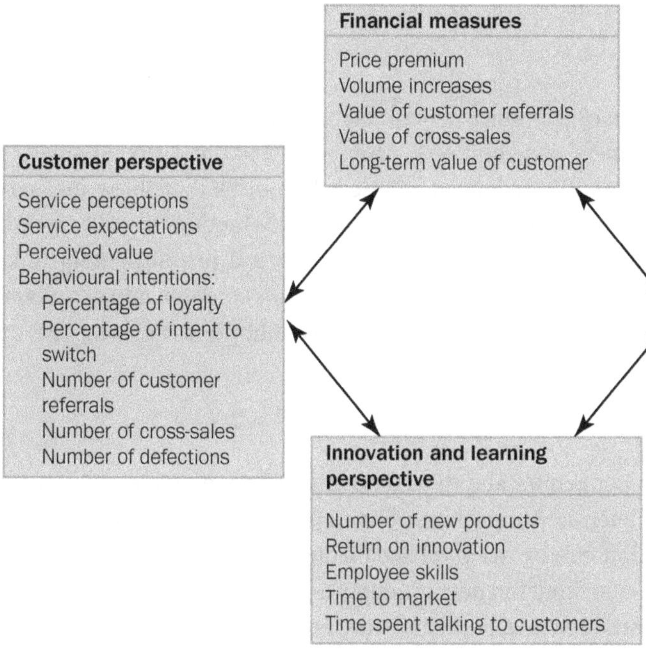

Sources: Adapted from *Harvard Business Review,* an excerpt from J.R.S. Kaplan and D.P. Norton (1992) 'The balanced scorecard measures that drive performance', *Harvard Business Review* (January–February 1992).

CHANGES TO FINANCIAL MEASUREMENT

One way that service leaders are changing financial measurement is to calibrate the defensive effect of retaining and losing customers. The monetary value of retaining customers can be projected through the use of average revenues over the lifetimes of customers. The number of customer defections can then be translated into lost revenue to the firm and become a critical company performance standard:

> *Ultimately, defections should be a key performance measure for senior management and a fundamental component of incentive systems. Managers should know the company's defection rate, what happens to profits when the rate moves up or down and why defections occur.*

Companies can also measure actual increases or decreases in revenue from retention or defection of customers by capturing the value of a loyal customer, including expected cash flows over a customer's lifetime or lifetime customer value (as described in Chapter 7). Other possible financial measures (as shown in Figure 18.7) include the value of price premiums, volume increases, customer referrals and cross-sales.

CUSTOMER PERCEPTUAL MEASURES

Customer perceptual measures are leading indicators of financial performance. As we discussed in this chapter, customers who are not happy with the company will defect and will tell others about their dissatisfaction. As we also discussed, perceptual measures reflect customer beliefs and feelings about the company and its products and services, and can predict how the customer will behave in the future. Overall forms of the measurements we discussed in Chapters 5 and 6 (shown in the customer perspective box of Figure 18.7) are measures that can be included in this category. Among the measures that are valuable to track are overall service perceptions and expectations, customer satisfaction, perceptual measures of value and behavioural intention measures such as loyalty and intent to switch. A company that notices a decline in these numbers should be concerned that the decline will translate into less profit for the company.

OPERATIONAL MEASURES

Operational measures involve the translation of customer perceptual measures into the standards or actions that must be set internally to meet customers' expectations. Although virtually all companies count or calculate operational measures in some form, the balanced scorecard requires that these measures stem from the business processes that have the greatest effect on customer satisfaction. In other words, these measures are not independent of customer perceptual measures but instead are intricately linked with them. In Chapter 9 we called these customer-linked operational measures *customer-defined standards* – operational standards determined through customer expectations and calibrated the way the customer views and expresses them.

INNOVATION AND LEARNING

The final area of measurement involves a company's ability to innovate, improve and learn – by launching new products, creating more value for customers and improving operating efficiencies. This measurement area is most difficult to capture quantitatively but can be accomplished using performance-to-goal percentages. For example, a company can set a goal of launching ten new products a year, then measure what percentage of that goal it does achieve. If four new products are launched, its percentage for the year is 40 per cent, which can then be compared with subsequent years.

EFFECTIVE NON-FINANCIAL PERFORMANCE MEASUREMENTS

According to field research conducted in 60 companies and survey responses from 297 senior executives, many companies do not identify and act on the correct non-financial measures.[32] One example involves a bank that surveyed satisfaction only from customers who physically entered the branches, a policy that caused some branch managers to offer free food and drinks in order to increase their scores. According to the authors of the study, companies make four major mistakes:

1 *Not linking measures to strategy.* Companies can easily identify hundreds of non-financial measures to track, but they also need to use analysis that identifies the most important drivers of their strategy. Successful organizations use value-driver maps, tools that lay out the cause-and-effect relationships between drivers and strategic success. Figure 18.8 shows the causal model developed by a successful fast-food chain to understand the key drivers of shareholder value. The factors on the right were identified as most important in leading to the concepts on the left, and the sequence of concepts from top to bottom show the relationships among company strategies (such as selection and staffing) and intermediate results (such as employee and customer satisfaction) that result in financial results (such as sustained profitability and shareholder value). The study found that fewer than 30 per cent of the firms surveyed used this causal modelling approach.

2 *Not validating the links.* Only 21 per cent of companies in the study verify that the non-financial measures lead to financial performance. Instead, many firms decide what they are going to measure in each category and never link the categories. Many managers believed that the relationships were self-evident instead of conducting analysis to validate the linkages. This chapter's strategy insight shows

one way that companies can create this type of linkage. In general, it is critical that companies pull together all their data and examine the relationships among the categories.

3 *Not setting the right performance targets.* Companies sometimes aim too high in setting improvement targets. Targeting 100 per cent customer satisfaction might seem to be a desirable goal, but many companies expend far too many resources to gain too little improvement in satisfaction. The study's authors found that a telecommunications company aiming for 100 per cent customer satisfaction was wasting resources because customers who were 100 per cent satisfied spent no more money than those who were 80 per cent satisfied.[33]

Figure 18.8   The measures that matter most: a causal model for a fast-food company shows the critical drivers of performance and the concepts that lead to shareholder value

Source: Adapted from C.D. Ittner and D.F. Larcker (2003) 'Coming up short on nonfinancial performance measurement', *Harvard Business Review* (November 2003), pp. 88–95.

4   *Measuring incorrectly.* Companies need to use metrics with statistical validity and reliability. Organizations cannot measure such a complex phenomenon as customer satisfaction with one or two simple measures, nor can they use inconsistent methodologies to measure the same concept. Another problem that companies may encounter is trying to use quantitative metrics to capture qualitative results for important factors such as leadership and innovation.

Creating a balanced scorecard in and of itself does not improve performance. Companies will not reap the benefits of techniques such as the balanced scorecard unless they effectively address how to measure non-financial performance.

SUMMARY

Each of the five sections in this chapter assessed the evidence and identified what is currently known about the relationship between service and profitability. The chapter used a conceptual framework to link all the variables in these topics: (1) the direct relationship between service and profits; (2) offensive effects of service quality, the ability to obtain new customers; (3) defensive effects of service quality, the ability to retain existing customers; (4) the relationship between service quality and purchase intentions; and (5) key drivers of service quality, customer retention and profits. Considerable progress has been made in the investigation of service quality, profitability and the economic worth of customers, but managers are still lacking many of the answers that would help them make informed decisions about service quality investments. The chapter concluded with a discussion of the balanced scorecard, which offers a strategic approach for measuring all aspects of a company's performance.

KEY CONCEPTS

Balanced scorecard	412	Service quality/customer intention relationship	407
Defensive marketing	404	Service quality/profitability relationship	406
Offensive marketing	404		

EXERCISES

1   Use a Web search engine to locate three software companies that make balanced scorecard software. What are their current offerings? How can these software firms help individual companies understand the concepts and relationships discussed in this chapter? Which of the three companies would you select based on the information you have found?

2   Interview a local firm to find out what it knows about its key drivers of financial performance. What are the key service drivers of the firm? Does the company know whether these service drivers relate to profit?

3   Select a service industry (such as fast food) or a company (such as McDonald's) that you are familiar with, either as a customer or as an employee, and create a balanced scorecard. Describe the operational, customer, financial and learning measures that could be used to capture performance.

DISCUSSION QUESTIONS

1 Why has it been difficult for executives to understand the relationship between service improvements and profitability in their companies?

2 To this day, many companies believe that service is a cost rather than a revenue producer. Why might they hold this view? How would you argue the opposite view?

3 What is the difference between offensive and defensive marketing? How does service affect each of these?

4 If the costs of retaining an existing customer are lower than the costs of attracting a new customer, why do many insurance companies offer lower prices to new customers?

5 Discuss the proposition that 100 per cent customer satisfaction is a goal that is not ever achievable nor profitable.

6 What are the main sources of profit in defensive marketing?

7 What are the main sources of profit in offensive marketing?

8 How will the balanced scorecard help you understand and document the information presented in this chapter? Which of the five sections that discuss different aspects of the relationship between service quality and profits can it illuminate?

FURTHER READING

Fornell, C., Mithas, S., Morgeson, F. and Krishnan, M.S. (2006). Customer satisfaction and stock prices: high returns, low risk. *Journal of Marketing*, 70(1), 3–14.

Jääskeläinen, A., Laihonen, H. and Lönnqvist, A. (2014). Distinctive features of service performance measurement. *International Journal of Operations & Production Management*, 34(12), 1466–86.

Kaplan, R. S. (2012). The balanced scorecard: comments on balanced scorecard commentaries. *Journal of Accounting & Organizational Change*, 8(4), 539-45.

Kaplan, R. S. and Norton, D.P. (1996). *Balanced Scorecard: Translating Strategy into Action*. Cambridge: Harvard Business School Press.

Meyer, M.W. (2003). *Rethinking Performance Measurement: Beyond the Balanced Scorecard*. Cambridge: Cambridge University Press.

Neely, A. (2002). *Business Performance Measurement: Theory and Practice*. Cambridge: Cambridge University Press.

Raithel, S., Sarstedt, M., Scharf, S. and Schwaiger, M. (2012). On the value relevance of customer satisfaction. Multiple drivers and multiple markets. *Journal of the Academy of Marketing Science*, 40(4), 509–25.

Wilson, A.M. (2000). The use of performance information in the management of service delivery. *Marketing Intelligence and Planning*, 18(3), 127–34.

CASE
SECTION

CASE 1   DISNEY'S MAGIC BANDS: ENHANCING CUSTOMER EXPERIENCE

This case was written by Vasudha M, Amity Research Centers Headquarters, Bangalore.
© 2014, Amity Research Centers Headquarters, Bangalore.

More than a year after Walt Disney World's announcement about the MyMagic+, the full rollout of the MagicBand was due in the summer of 2014. The MagicBands which were selectively tested among guests staying at Walt Disney World resort hotels were also being offered to annual pass holders. The MagicBand, which was tied to the new FastPass+ system, was equipped with RFID technology allowing Walt Disney World guests 'to simply tap Mickey Mouse-emblazoned readers' in order to gain admission to the theme parks, to hotel rooms, and to check in for rides, shows, parades, fireworks, and other attractions.

The official rollout of MyMagic+ and FastPass+ was scheduled during Walt Disney World's press event scheduled during the month of April/May 2014. Disney planned to include highly personalised attractions and character interactions in the future thus improving the overall Disney park experience. While there were concerns regarding the privacy of information that customers divulged to Disney and the efficiency of the MagicBands, Disney was confident that this technology driven new Consumer Experience Management tool would drive revenues in the months to come.

"Our goal from the beginning has been to enhance the guest experience and make it even more immersive, seamless and personal than ever before."[1]

– Tom Staggs, Chairman, Walt Disney Parks and Resorts

"It's a complete game changer... The implications for big data and for personalization are extraordinary. It could radically change interaction between customers and the company."[2]

– Douglas Quinby, Vice President, Research, PhoCusWright[3]

DISNEY'S PARKS & RESORTS: AN OVERVIEW

The Walt Disney Company (Disney), which included a number of subsidiaries and affiliates, was a leading family entertainment and media enterprise. The diversified enterprise that operated across the world consisted of five business segments namely, 'media networks, parks and resorts, studio entertainment, consumer products and interactive media'. Walt Disney opened Disneyland on July 17th 1955, ushering in a new era of family entertainment. Disneyland was a unique entertainment destination which was focused on storytelling and providing immersive experiences. More than half a century later, Walt Disney Parks and Resorts (WDP&R) had gained the status of one of the world's leading providers of travel and leisure experiences to families. WDP&R's core business consisted of five vacation destinations including 11 theme parks and 44 resorts in the three continents of North America, Europe and Asia. Disney had a sixth destination under construction in Shanghai.[4]

The operating income of Disney's theme park division had witnessed an increase of 16%, amounting to $671 million, in the quarter ending December 2013. Sales at the division also grew by 6% to reach $3.6 billion. In the Fiscal year 2014, income for the theme park division increased by 17% to $2.2 billion. Disney's pricing strategy for its park entry tickets was designed to promote the sales of multiday park passes. Multiday park passes lowered per-day costs, with a three-day pass amounting to $91.34 per day while a five-day pass was $60.80 per day. In total, the park entrance fee along with hotel and meals expenses resulted in a hugely expensive Disney vacation for a family. But single-day tickets were even more expensive having increased by 41% since 2005. While the price of the four- day pass had only increased by about $40 from 2004 to 2013. Disney claimed that an increase of up to $20 did not deter customers from visiting a Disney property given the popularity that the theme parks enjoyed among children.[5]

MYMAGIC+ MAGIC BANDS: ENHANCING CUSTOMER EXPERIENCE

MyMagic+[6] reshaped the Walt Disney World Resort vacation experience by making it more customised, more magical and more convenient for guests to create lasting memories along with their families and friends. From April 2014, guests visiting the resort using the MyMagic+ could register online at the My Disney Experience website and reserve access to some of their favorite attractions with FastPass+.[7] MyMagic+ also gave guests the option to purchase MagicBands on site.[8] The cost of the project was expected to be between $800 million and $1 billion. MyMagic+ aimed to make the experience at Disney

parks 'less daunting and more amenable'. Tom Staggs (Tom), the Chairman of Walt Disney Parks and Resorts, felt, "If we can enhance the experience, more people will spend more of their leisure time with us."[9]

The secure all-in-one devices, the MagicBands and cards allowed guests to access the plans and vacation choices booked by them via the My Disney Experience effortlessly. The My Disney Experience site helped guests to make day-by-day plans and also manage their vacation details. MagicBands were 'colorful, waterproof wristbands, resembling a watch or bracelet'. The bands could be quickly and easily swiped to a sensor called a touch point (**Exhibit IV**). Both MagicBands and cards facilitated guests to travel lighter throughout their vacation. The card or MagicBand could be used by guests as a key to the Disney Resort hotel room, as an entry ticket to theme and water parks, to check in at FastPass+ entrances, to connect the Disney PhotoPass images to their user's account and to link their food and merchandise purchases to their Disney Resort hotel room (in case the guest was staying at the hotel).[10]

The bands were available in adult and child sizes and were equipped with both Bluetooth and RF technology which enabled long-range and short-range reading. The bands were delivered at the home of the buyer ahead of the park visit. The Fastpass tickets which were in use before the introduction of My Magic+ caused a lot of separation of family groups. Hence for visitors, Fastpass strategies were 'a major part of their daily planning'. With the MagicBand, visitors could pre-arrange for attractions through E-tickets and for events such as character meetings, parades and fireworks shows. According to Tom, "When we decrease people's anxiety, they have more fun at the park." The band was specifically designed to reduce the time spent in strategising while increasing the time they spent enjoying the park.[11]

In case a band was stolen or lost, it could be disconnected from the user's account remotely. Purchases were limited to $50 and for purchases above this limit a pin code was to be entered, thus helping in elimination of fraudulent activities. A band could also be programmed to not allow purchases at all as well, or could be set with a spending limit.[12]

The long-range Bluetooth reading would help in keeping track of traffic flowing past particular locations in the park. But tracking of individual bands was a complicated issue which brought in the 'tricky privacy question'. Hence this was left to the user, where he/ she could opt-in for this feature. Opting in had the benefits of increased personalisation. When an attraction recognised a particular visitor and that it was the adult or child's birthday, it was possible to greet and wish them using their name and also to customise the ride according to their special wishes as a birthday treat. For instance, the ride could also offer as a special gift, a 'Small World doll' that the child had created online. This feature also opened up the possibility of rides like 'Pirates of the Caribbean' to have personalised conversations with visitors in the future. Tom added, "The things that people are requesting to reserve are not just big rides...but reserved seating for fireworks and the parade." Once this was done visitors arrived just in time with reserved seating and thus avoided congestion at the entry points. This also allowed Disney to time the starting of events in particular locations of the park thus controlling traffic flow at these points efficiently.[13]

The RF device of each user was unique and allowed authentication of the user as well as the benefits associated with the visitor. When a visitor used his/ her RF device at a touch point, Disney recorded the transaction. These interactions provided Disney information such as the waiting time for different rides, waiting time at restaurants and other attractions. The focus was to better understand guest behavior and make improvements to the overall guest experience.[14]

Guests had the option of not participating in MyMagic+ or not registering on the My Disney Experience website thus not providing any personal information. Whereas guests who chose to participate in MyMagic+ and register on My Disney Experience would be able to use the FastPass+ service and make dining reservations online. This would enable them to enjoy the convenience of having their tickets, FastPass+ selections, Resort room key and other advanced features in one place. Guests participating in MyMagic+ also had the option of using a card instead of a MagicBand. They could also decide whether they wished to use the band to make purchases at select Resort locations.[15]

The embedded microchip in the band allowed the wearer to use it as an admission ticket, room key as well as wallet. In addition to keeping track

of FastPass+ reservations allowing visitors to pre-book rides and attractions, the bands also allowed quick and easy payments at restaurants and shops. The bands also synched the photos that Disney took of the visitors. The bands helped select character 'meet and greets' and book a spot on the parade route. Disney had tested the bands among the guests staying at the park's hotels and in March 2014 the bands were also offered to Disney World's Annual passholders. The MagicBand was very convenient when a visitor wished to pay for the many products available in the park. The guest's credit card information was on file, so in order to buy something the guest just had to swipe the band, enter his/ her pin number for verification and the sale was completed. There was no need to carry a wallet or cash or credit cards.[16]

This tracking ability of the RF devices made the devices very crucial for the $14.1 billion theme park and resort business at Disney. The information collected through the bands along with the information provided by visitors voluntarily on the related My Disney Experience app and website helped Disney to make decisions regarding the number of staff to man the rides, menu at restaurants, souvenirs to be stocked and the number of employees in Disney costumes to be available on its grounds at a given time. Intelligence collected on customer preferences would also be used to design e-mails or text messages sent to guests. It would help Disney to decide whether to include information such as restaurant menu changes, reservation availability in attractions such as the 'Space Mountain' or the 'Twilight Zone Tower of Terror'. The goal was to offer 'a more immersive, more seamless, and more personal experience'. The company also felt that the probability of visitors, who had their entire Disney World schedules planned in advance using the MyMagic+ system, moving to attractions provided by competition was much lesser than those who had not. The company claimed that the MagicBands also made it 'so easy to spend'.[17]

MYMAGIC+: A WINNING FORMULA FOR DISNEY?

Disney said that it had plans to share information about guests' experiences at the Resort with other members of the Walt Disney Family of Companies. But the guest could always choose to opt out of receiving marketing messages from the company. Information regarding specific park experience of visitors collected automatically when the MagicBand was read by long-range readers would not be shared with Walt Disney Family of Companies unless the visitor gave permission for the company to do so. Only information collected automatically when the MagicBand was read by long-range readers would be shared with third parties for their marketing uses, if the visitor gave permission for the company to do so. Guests who participated in MyMagic+ were allowed to have a role in how information collected about their experience would be used for marketing purposes. They could also opt out of receiving any marketing communications from Disney. Guests were also given the option of requesting for information regarding offers and tips during their visit to Disney World. The company also gave the assurance that the information collected in connection with MyMagic+ would not be used to target children under the age of 13.[18] In spite of these assurances, the MyMagic+ project moved Disney 'deeper into the hotly debated terrain of personal data collection'.[19]

Disney offered another convenient feature called Ticket Tag at the entrance of most of its theme parks and water parks. Ticket Tag helped in facilitating easy re-entry into parks and in preventing fraud. To use Ticket Tag, one had to place a finger on a biometric reader. The reader took an image of the finger and converted it into a unique numerical value while discarding the image. When Ticket Tag was used for re-entry or to visit some other Park, the numerical value was recalled. Ticket Tag did not store fingerprints. If a guest did not wish to use Ticket Tag, he/she could use a photo ID that matched the name used for purchase of the ticket. The security, integrity and confidentiality of information collected from its visitors were very important to Disney. The company had implemented measures to protect this information from unauthorised access. Disney also reviewed its security procedures frequently to ensure that it did not miss out on relevant new technology and methods.[20]

Personal information about the user 'does not sit on the band'. Hence there were no security issues even when the band was misplaced or lost. Disney bands also could not 'track' the location of a guest as they moved about the theme park.[21]

Despite such concerns regarding the safety and privacy of the information disclosed by the customers to the company and the tracking power of the devices, Disney's Chief Financial Officer, Jay Rasulo was upbeat about the initiative. He commented during a November 2014 investor call, "When you make [the logistics] easier, people tend to spend more time on entertainment and more time on consumables – be that food and beverage, merchandise, etc. We do expect this to be a growingly positive impact on our business in the years to come."[22]

Duncan Dickson, who taught theme-park management at the University of Central Florida said, "Because it is a reservation system, it is a game changer. Now you can plan your vacation and your ride sequence well ahead of your trip." He also added that Disney would have, "… some very robust data to use in understanding guest behavior and desires. It is a marketing dream." An industry analyst[23] said, "Disney could theoretically tailor the visitor's experience more effectively. MM+ is not solely for the benefit of Disney. Its intention is to simplify and enhance the visitor's experience. So while technology of this sort certainly benefits the business side, ultimately the consumer is the intended beneficiary. Data security is going to be paramount in its success." Tom assured those concerned with safety and privacy involving the usage of the tracking system, "These bands don't track people through the park; they are not GPS bands. We designed this with privacy in mind from the get go. Walt Disney World Parks and Resort's vision is simple, it's to be the most trusted provider of shared family travel and leisure experiences throughout the world. The key word there is trusted. We won't betray that trust."[24]

This ambitious $1 billion rollout took over a year and was planned to increase profitability at Disney World by making its 30 million guests happier. The implementation of this multifaceted system included complex aspects such as training its 70,000 employees, installing RF readers in 28,000 hotel room doors and encouraging guests to wear data-collecting electronic wristbands. Disney started to market MyMagic+ via national TV ads and 'quirky online videos' as it prepared for the peak summer season.[25]

On March 31st 2014, Disney allowed all visitors to use the system which was one of its most important initiatives. Theme parks had emerged as a growth business even during the economic recession. Hence Disney felt the need to use technology to augment its offerings while younger consumers were also clamouring for latest technology driven initiatives. Tom revealed that about 3.5 million visitors had participated in tests for the new system. He claimed that early feedback was 'fantastic'.[26]

The findings showed that the MyMagic+ system reduced the time taken at the park entry by 25%. It also helped Disney to take in 3,000 additional guests per day during the peak Christmas season at the Magic Kingdom Park. Usage of the new FastPass reservation system increased by 40% compared to the usage of the old one. The FastPass+ reduced the time guests spent in standing in queues and increased the number of experiences they were able to enjoy. Investors eagerly awaited proof for the profitability of the $1 billion investment in MyMagic+. Disney's parks business had fared well with operating profit increasing by 17% in 2013 to $2.33 billion. In spite of this, the spending on the project had made a dent on its margins at the flagship property.[27] MyMagic+ aimed to increase the utilisation rates of attractions and entertainment in addition to increased personalisation. Guest satisfaction along with how much time visitors spend in the parks were key indicators of whether customers would come back.[28]

Steve Brown (Steve), Chief Operating Officer for Lo-Q[29] commented, "If Disney can drive more value from existing infrastructure by layering on technology, that is extremely powerful. They can't just compete by building new rides; it's already a theme-park arms race out there." Disney anticipated that MagicBands would grow into a big business of its own. The company had plans to facilitate this by introducing collectible versions of MagicBand accessories and charms.[30]

A guest, Jayne Townsley (Jayne) wrote on StitchKingdom.com, "Although I know this type of technology is making its way into every facet of life, it still makes me feel a bit creeped out." So there was the danger of some customers like Jayne, totally rejecting this new initiative. Disney was fully cognizant of the privacy concerns involved especially those concerning children. The plan

was introduced during a sensitive period when the federal government was involved in strengthening online privacy protections. Hence experts felt that it could turn out to be troublesome for Disney, which was already considered by some consumers as being 'too controlling'. But Disney was committed to MyMagic+ and felt that it was essential. The company was set on aggressively building new technology into its parks while not changing 'the sense of nostalgia' the whole experience was built on. Disney also did not want to risk 'becoming irrelevant to future generations'. From a business point of view, MyMagic+ was expected to be transformational. This prompted Steve to comment, "When Disney makes a move, it moves the culture."[31] With the MyMagic+ system in its initial stage of introduction, industry analysts were waiting with bated breath to see the impact of the project on the entertainment giant's fortunes.

ENDNOTES

1 Staggs Tom, "MyMagic+ Now Available to Walt Disney World Resort Hotel and Day Guests", http://disneyparks.disney.go.com/blog/2014/04/mymagic-now-available-to-walt-disney-world-resort-hotel-and-day- guests/, April 2nd 2014.

2 Palmeri Christopher, "Disney Bets $1 Billion on Technology to Track Theme-Park Visitors", http://www.businessweek.com/articles/2014-03-07/disney-bets-1-billion-on-technology-to-track-theme-park-visitors, March 7th 2014.

3 A travel consulting firm.

4 "Company Overview", http://thewaltdisney company.com/about-disney/company-overview

5 Bachman Justin, "Disney's Magic Kingdom Nears $100 Tickets, and the Crowds Keep Coming", http://www.businessweek.com/articles/2014-02-25/disneys-magic-kingdom-nears-100-tickets-and-the-crowds-keep-coming, February 25th 2014.

6 MyMagic+ consists of the following features: My Disney Experience mobile application and website, Disney's MagicBand is a new waterproof RFID ticketing system, Disney FastPass+ service which allows guests to reserve access to experiences, PhotoPass Memory Maker allows guests to take unlimited photos while in the park,

then download them within 45 days of picture taking.

7 Disney's Fastpass is a virtual queuing system created by the Walt Disney Company. First introduced in late 1999 (though the idea of a ride reservation system was first introduced in world fairs), Fastpass allows guests to avoid long lines at the attractions on which the system is installed, freeing them to enjoy other attractions during their wait. The service is available at no additional charge to all park guests. FastPass+ enables visitors to skip the lines at an expanded number of attractions, including certain character greetings and other events.

8 Momdjian Cynthia, "Disney News This Week: MyMagic+ at Walt Disney World Resort, 'Maleficent' Banner, Disney's 'The Lion King' Australia Cast Sings 'Circle of Life'", https://thewaltdisneycompany.com/blog/disney-news-week-mymagic-walt-disney-world-resort-maleficent-banner-disneys-lion-king-australia, April 4th 2014.

9 Barnes Brooks, "At Disney Parks, a Bracelet Meant to Build Loyalty (and Sales)", http://www.nytimes.com/2013/01/07/business/media/at-disney-parks-a-bracelet-meant-to-build-loyalty-and- sales.html?_r=1&, January 7th 2013.

10 "Your Key to a More Carefree Visit", https://disneyworld.disney.go.com/plan/my-disney-experience/bands-cards/

11 Panzarino Matthew, "Disney gets into wearable tech with the MagicBand", http://thenextweb.com/insider/2013/05/29/disney-goes-into-wearable-tech-with-the-magic-band/, May 29th 2013.

12 "Disney gets into wearable tech with the MagicBand", op.cit.

13 ibid.

14 "My Disney Experience – Frequently Asked Questions", https://disneyworld.disney.go.com/faq/my-disney-experience/privacy-policy/

15 ibid.

16 Gambacorta Krista, "Putting Disney MagicBands to the test", http://www.foxnews.com/travel/2014/03/21/putting-disney-magicbands-to-test/, March 21st 2014.

17 "Disney Bets $1 Billion on Technology to Track Theme-Park Visitors", op.cit.

18 "My Disney Experience – Frequently Asked Questions", op.cit.

19 "At Disney Parks, a Bracelet Meant to Build Loyalty (and Sales)", op.cit.

20 "My Disney Experience – Frequently Asked Questions", op.cit.

21 "Putting Disney MagicBands to the test", op.cit.

22 "Disney Bets $1 Billion on Technology to Track Theme-Park Visitors", op.cit.

23 James Crompton, at IBISWorld.

24 Sekula Sarah, "Disney gets personal with new MyMagic+ system http://www.usatoday.com/story/dispatches/2014/01/27/disney-mymagic-vacation-planning/4582957/, February 25th 2014

25 Barnes Brooks, "A Billion-Dollar Bracelet Is the Key to a Disney Park", http://www.nytimes.com/2014/04/02/business/billion-dollar-bracelet-is-key-to-magical-kingdom.html?_r=0, April 1st 2014.

26 "A Billion-Dollar Bracelet Is the Key to a Disney Park", op.cit.

27 "A Billion-Dollar Bracelet Is the Key to a Disney Park", op.cit.

28 Schaal Dennis, "Disney's 'magic' bracelets are driving more people to its parks", http://qz.com/174644/disneys-magic-bracelets-are-driving-more-people-to-its-parks/, February 6th 2014.

29 A British company which provided line management and ticketing systems at theme parks and zoos.

30 "At Disney Parks, a Bracelet Meant to Build Loyalty (and Sales)", op.cit.

31 ibid.

This case was written by Dr. Suchitra Mohanty, Amity Research Centers Headquarter, Bangalore. © 2015, Amity Research Centers Headquarter, Bangalore.

"Ryanair changed air travel in Europe forever - now we want to change the world of online travel and we're going to do that through Ryanair Labs, a state-of-the-art digital innovation hub based at our new Dublin offices. We're seeking to hire the best of the best to reimagine the online travel sector. Whether you write code or copy we want free thinkers, creatives and people who can not only imagine, but build amazing experiences."[1]

– Robin Kiely, Head of Communications, Ryanair

Smart devices like smartphone, digital television and digital watch etc. and smart platforms like social media, analytics and cloud computing etc. had encouraged businesses to connect with the customers in a more effective manner in the 21st century.[2] Even the consumers were deeply engaged with their favourite brands and wanted to get innovative offers to assist them in their everyday life, travel and work etc.[3] Analysts also justified that quick adoption of technology, changing behavior of the consumers and increasing competition in the markets were some of the key factors that had driven the adoption of digital strategy as the core element in the company's business strategies.[4]

In 2013, like many companies, Ryanair, the pioneer in Europe's ultra-low cost and no-frill air travel had also decided to revamp its digital strategy. Analysts highlighted that Ryanair had signaled two profit warnings in 2013.[5] Intense competition from the rivals (both in price and capacity) coupled with gloomy economic situation in Europe were some of the key factors identified by the company for the profit warning of Ryanair.[6] However, Ryanair's shareholders cautioned that poor customer service was one of the prime reasons for the profit warning of the company.[7]

The airline had identified three prime areas for improvement i.e. its own website, mobile platform and social media presence to shake off its tainted image pertaining to customer service.[8] Ryanair revamped its website Ryanair.com and unveiled a customer friendly website with hassle free online booking.[9] The European LCC major had overhauled its digital strategy by taking various other initiatives like airing advertisements in TV in Europe, creating Twitter account @Ryanair Twitter and introducing Ryanair mobile apps, etc.[10] In 2014, the no-frill airline had also introduced 'Ryanair Labs', a digital innovation platform, to kick off its 'online travel revolution'. The company was also planning to hire around 200 IT personnel to build a 'world class online travel platform'.[11] The new digital strategy might help Ryanair to throw a tough competition to its rival particularly easyJet.[12] However, the new web addresses of Ryanair without proper redirects led the search for Ryanair flight to display error pages in Google. Amidst this scenario, the industry analysts were perplexed at whether Ryanair would be able to sustain its leadership by capitalizing its digital marketing strategies in the wake of intense competition in the aviation industry.

DIGITAL WAVE IN THE AVIATION SECTOR

Increasing penetration of web based companies like Google Inc., Amazon Inc. and Facebook etc. had boosted the expectation of the consumers to connect with the brand in a digital manner. According to Nielsen Research, consumers wanted everything in digital. Digital companies (Google, Amazon and facebook etc.) had set exceptional customer experience by leveraging technologies. The traditional non-web based companies were also trying to follow suit through digital transformation.[13]

Digital Transformation implied the efficient use of the advanced technology to enhance the performance and reach of the business entities.[14] Like many sectors, the Aviation sector was also trying to capitalize on the digital media for their business. Shashank Nigam, CEO, SimpliFlying[15] reiterated that, "Today, airline brands are shaped by management direction as well as the goodwill of social advocates. If you're not where your customers are, you're going to lose a lot of business."[16]

Digitalization in the Aviation sector was initiated way back in the 1950s.[17] During that period, Airlines had invested heavily on the Information and Communication Technologies (ICTs) mainly to handle the inventories in an accurate manner for providing effective communication to the travelers, travel agencies and the distributors around the world. In 1960s, SABRE Computer Reservation System (CRS) was introduced by the American Airlines. By 1970s, SABRE CRS had offered technical support like generating flight plans for the aircraft, tracking the spare parts, scheduling crews etc. Soon after the deregulation in the aviation sector, SABRE CRS also helped the airline to quickly change their routes as well as fares according to the demand.[18]

During the mid-1980s, CRSs were further developed as comprehensive Global Distribution Systems (GDSs) that offered a wide range of travel related packages such as car rental and hotel reservations along with the flight booking. During this period, internet was also becoming popular among the people. In the early 1990s GDS effectively acted as travel supermarkets that offered comprehensive information for the whole range of travel products such as accommodation, car rental and schedule for non-air transport etc. In the mid-1990s, with the onset of technological revolution, internet emerged as a significant game changer in the aviation sector. Internet facilitated the airlines to increase competitiveness by minimizing the distribution cost.[19]

In the early 2000s, a number of LCCs entered the aviation sectors in Europe and the US. The LCCs introduced their own distribution system and availed the technology of the internet to communicate with their customers effectively. Even the new LCCs such as easyJet and Ryanair had tried to utilize the internet technology in different stages of flight operation such as flight ticket booking, online promotions and electronic ticket etc. According to the 'Airlines IT Trends survey, conducted in 2001, the Internet Protocol (IP) systems became popular among the airlines. Airlines surged on the new technological solutions to connect with the customers and to reduce their operational costs.[20] By 2008 almost 90% of the airlines in the world used their own websites to sell flight tickets.[21]

Soon, digitalization became a key component for almost all the airlines in the world. In 2011, Emirates joined Facebook to create an 'emotional' attachment with its customers.[22] American Airlines and Air France allowed the customers to select the flight through the Facebook pages and redirected them (customers) to the company website for the final purchase of the tickets. British Airways used Facebook as its marketing platform and introduced 'Perfect Day' application that facilitated the customers to create as well as share their travel itineraries.[23] Virgin America was the first airline to participate in the 'Promoted Tweet' programme of Twitter.[24] In 2013, the Malaysia Airlines had opted Adobe solutions to revamp its digital strategies. "We selected five solutions from Adobe Marketing Cloud, including Adobe Target, Adobe Social, Adobe Media Optimizer, Adobe Analytics and Adobe Experience Manager. We'll also be deploying managed services for Experience Manager. The solution provided us with the most intuitive, easy-to-use user interface along with deep analytic power and robust delivery", said Dean Dacko, Chief Marketing Officer, Malaysia Airlines.[25]

Like the full service carriers, the LCCs were also trying to reap the benefits from the digital strategy. On September 20th 2013,[26] in Ryanair's annual shareholders meeting, Michael O'Leary, CEO, Ryanair, had announced the company's decision to overhaul its marketing strategy by diverting more funds into various digital media.[27]

RYANAIR: GOING DIGITAL

Ryanair, Europe's favourite airline started its maiden journey in 1985,[28] flying between Waterford (Ireland) and Gatwick (London) with one plane. Low-cost and no-frill business strategy of the company created a revolution in the global aviation industry and Ryanair successfully cemented its position as the leading LCC in Europe.[29] The global recession had further compelled people to opt for low cost carriers that acted as a driving factor for the robust growth of the Irish airline.[30]

In 2000,[31] Ryanair launched its website Ryanair.com. Within three months of its launch, the no-frill-low-cost airline received around 50,000 bookings every week through the website. In 2001, Ryanair was recognized as the largest travel website in Europe. Around 96% of the airline's tickets were distributed through the website.[32]

However, Ryanair's attitude towards customers was described as uncaring and insensible,[33] which was very much evident when O'Leary, quoted, "People say the customer is always right, but you know what - they're not. Sometimes they are wrong and they need to be told so."[34] Besides, the company was criticized by experts for releasing various inappropriate and misleading advertisements.[35]

In 2010, the company had worked upon its own website 'Ryanair.com' instead of venturing into other social media sites likes Twitter and Facebook. Stephen McNamara, Spokesman, Ryanair emphasized that, "we don't have people sitting around to answer questions. With social media you get any and every query and a lot of rubbish, like people asking if they can bring a 10kg bag, which of course you can. The information is there on our site."[36]

Ryanair's clever tricks i.e. charges for excess baggage, charges for credit card use, fine for failing to show the printout of boarding pass etc. enabled the airline to become the most profitable carrier in the world. However, the airline shocked the entire aviation sector with its two[37] profit warnings in 2013.[38]

On March 31st 2014, the Irish airline had reported almost 8% fall in its net profit, which sent a strong warning signal for the company to introspect its business strategy.[39] Intense price-cutting competition from the rivals and Europe's gloomy economic scenario were some of the key factors highlighted by Ryanair for the poor performance of the company.[40] However, Ryanair was countenanced with rising criticism over its poor customer service from both the customers and shareholders. While maintaining a strong growth momentum, it seemed the company had failed to strike a balance between customer services and brand image.[41] The company was also rated as the worst customer service provider among the 100 biggest brands in UK, revealed a British Magazine 'Which?'[42]

Soon, Ryanair had planned to revamp its digital strategy to shed its tarnished image for poor customer service. The company had identified three prime areas for improvement i.e. its own website, mobile platform and social media presence to shake off its tainted image. "Our primary focus this winter will be to significantly invest in, and improve, the Ryanair.com website, our mobile platform and our interaction with passengers using social media', mentioned O'Leary. The makeover plan was supported by a new digital marketing strategy that focused more on mobile and various social media platforms.[43] To improve the perception of customers towards the brand, Ryanair had set up a team to reply to the e-mails of the customers. It had also planned to eliminate the charges for heavy luggage. "We should try to eliminate things that unnecessarily piss people off. A lot of those customer services elements don't cost a lot of money… It's something we are committed to addressing over the coming year," highlighted O'Leary.[44]

In 2013, Ryanair revamped its website and unveiled a customer friendly website with hassle free online booking. The new website had removed many additional options offered by the company that ultimately reduced the number of clicks by the users from 17 to five for online booking. The company also introduced 'My Ryanair' feature that allowed the customers to create individual profile and store personal information. Customers need not re-enter these information while booking further on the site. The airline also encouraged the passengers to use various social media to 'share the fare' of Ryanair with their family and friends.[45]

Since inception, the budget airline had always allocated a smaller amount for marketing. Analysts pointed out that Ryanair, which had once ignored marketing as the core element of its business, had now created a new post of chief marketing officer to overhaul its brand image. The Irish airline also hired Kenny Jacobs (Jacobs), the former marketing executive 'Moneysupermarket.com' as its mentor and Chief Marketing Officer for improving its tarnished brand image.[46] Jacobs mentioned that the prime objective of Ryanair in 2014 was to improve the brand perception, loyalty and customer service of the European LCC major with the help of various digital strategies.[47] The budget airline had also increased its marketing expenditure by almost three times from €12million[48] to €36 million in 2015.[49]

Dare[50] was the first ad agency signed up by Ryanair in more than 25 years of its long journey. Till then the low cost airline depended only on its in-house publicity.[51] In April 2014, the company had launched its brand advertisement campaign.[52] The ad campaign entitled 'Low Fares. Made Simple' was launched to send a specific message across Europe that Ryanair offered low prices along with improved customer service. (http://www.youtube.com/watch?v=LehpLu4TyZA). "We have the best product in the airline industry with the lowest fares and biggest choice of routes. We have made significant improvements to our customer service and this campaign is designed to increase awareness of the new improved Ryanair. It was a pleasure working on this project with Dare as the lead creative agency, TAG in support, and Mediacom", emphasized Jacobs. The new advertisements on Ryanair's new web look, Free Second Cabin Bag Allowance and Allocated Seating were unveiled in Ireland, the UK, Italy and Spain via TV, radio and print media etc.[53] Sean Thompson, Chief Creative Officer, Dare led the advertisement campaign of Ryanair. 'Destination Anywhere' was the tagline of television advertisement in UK and Ireland. "For Dare to work with Ryanair on their first ever pan-European advertising has been a real privilege especially as the brand is at such an important time in its evolution. Creatively it was important that we tackle people's negative perceptions of Ryanair head-on but do it with a charm and wit that people would expect of the brand", explained Dare's Sean Thompson.[54]

Ryanair also launched Ryanair Labs, a digital and IT innovation hub in Dublin, Swords.[55] It also launched Labs.Ryanair.com website for the digital Labs.[56] The airline was planning to hire around 200 IT staff to build up a world class sophisticated online travel platform. "Strategy, architecture, design and content will all be done here in Dublin and the work will be used by millions of people. We're proud to pay well to make sure we get and keep the best people and Ryanair Labs will offer the perks and culture of a start-up without the downsides. We're hiring a range of digital and IT roles and those interested in starting an online travel revolution can apply through Labs.Ryanair.com," said Robin Kiely, Head of Communications, Ryanair.[57]

John Hurley[58] (Hurley) was taken aboard by the low-cost airline as the chief technology officer. Hurley would oversee the digital technology strategy of Ryanair. He would also look after the digital innovation labs of the airline. "We are pleased to appoint John Hurley as chief technology officer, who will head up our Ryanair Labs team, as we continue to implement our programme of digital and customer improvements," added O'Leary.[59]

Further as people were gradually shifting towards mobile devices from the desktops, the company unveiled a new, advanced version of mobile app that provided scannable digital boarding pass to the customers. The app was available in smartphones such as iPhone and Android phones. Ryanair was the first Irish airline to offer customer friendly digital boarding pass.[60] The budget airline also created its Twitter account @Ryanair Twitter and LinkedIn account.[61]

OPPORTUNITIES AND CHALLENGES

"The biggest change is going to come in all things digital. So what data we get on customers, how we use it to make the experience better, how we personalize and retarget, what we do on CRM, mobile and content. All of those things over the next two years will become the bigger levers of, not new growth, but improved customer retention… I'll be honest, Ryanair wasn't aware enough of the change in consumer behaviour in moving to mobile. It wasn't a strategic decision to take our time, we've missed it and we're now catching up… So imagine if we hold on to the low fares, keep adding the destinations and have a great website that works on mobile alongside our app. If we then improve the in-flight service as well, then the opportunity is huge," opined Jacobs.[62]

In order to improve the customer experience Ryanair signed a new payment partnership with PayPal in August 2014. "Ryanair revolutionized low fare air travel in Europe. As the pioneer of faster, safer online payments, PayPal is delighted to help Ryanair develop its customer experience by making it even easier and quicker for travellers to book and pay for their flights online. With our 152 million active accounts across the world, we're also making it easier for businesses such as Ryanair to expand their international sales", highlighted Louise Phelan, Vice President, PayPal, Global Operations Europe, Middle East and Africa.[63]

Besides ease of payment through PayPal, ticket booking through the new website was also made simpler, "You can book a flight on the Ryanair app in less than 100 seconds, and it's going to be the way I think people increasingly will check the Ryanair flights, check pricing and make bookings", emphasized O'Leary. The mobile app also helped the customers to book tickets online in the entire 1,600 routes of Ryanair via their 'My Ryanair' profile. The app also offered various associated services such as online hotel booking, pay for car hire, insurance, check live flight times etc. to the users. The app was offered in English, Spanish and Italian languages. Jacobs highlighted that the company "worked hard to develop a product we're proud of and will make travelling with Ryanair even better. Our customers can expect regular app updates that will make it an even more useful travel tool… Our 'Always Getting Better' programme has delivered better services, more choice and enhanced in- flight and digital experiences," said Jacobs.[64] The company was also planning to offer the mobile app in various other languages.[65]

However, critics said that Ryanair might face difficulty in its mobile app initiative. Around 10%[66] of the airports in which Ryanair operated, lacked of mobile-check-in services. Besides the company would not take any responsibility if the mobile would run out of battery and Ryanair would charge £15 for providing a print out of boarding pass at the airport.[67]

Analysts had cautioned that the new-look of the website might also have a negative impact on

Ryanair. For most of the online businesses retaining the top slot on the first page of Google search results was very important. Due to certain changes in the search criteria, Moneysupermarket.com, a price comparison site, experienced a double-digit fall in its share price when it failed to retain its lead position in Google search results.[68] After the introduction of the company's new look website in April, 2014, Ryanair too was vanished from the 'country destination flight searches' on Google. Ryanair was also not featured in top 100 results on Google search for various destinations in Europe. Earlier Ryanair used to appear in the first slot during web search for places such as Romania and Belgium.[69] Sam Silverwood-Cope (Silverwood-Cope), Director, Intelligent Positioning pointed out that Ryanair had skipped some basic precautions and added that, "They've ignored the legacy of the old Ryanair. com. It's quite startling. They are doing it just before their busiest time of the year."[70] Further the new web addresses of Ryanair without proper redirects led the search for Ryanair flight to display error pages in Google. "Unless redirects get put in pretty soon, the position is going to get worse and worse," cautioned Silverwood-Cope.[71] However, Ryanair was convinced that the flight search problem was a temporary one.[72]

In September 2014, Ryanair had agreed to collaborate with Amadeus, a travel technology firm. The collaboration would facilitate Ryanair to sell its tickets through the GDS system of Amadeus. Besides, the deal would help the travel agents to sell the Ryanair tickets without difficulty and would enable the business travelers to book the ticket easily.[73] O'Leary admitted that, "I am the person who for 10 years said over my dead body will we go back on GDSs. So I have to start by apologizing for yet another thing I've got wrong at Ryanair over the last 10 years. It's a sign of the change and evolution that's going on. We expect to appeal to more and more of the bigger businesses and corporate."[74] However, Shaun Smith[75] forecasted that the sudden change in the strategy of the company (from the culture of money saving to satisfying the customer) might be beneficial for Ryanair in the short term, but the organizational overarhaul and brand building would take a longer time. He further added that, "What you then end up with is almost a dissonance within the organization... a classic 'stuck in the middle' strategy where you become neither one thing nor another," highlighted Smith.[76] Further, the new digital strategy of the company was considered as a wise decision of Ryanair particularly in the era of social media and smart gadgets, to get closer to the customers by offering better flying experience.[77] "We're building the best digital travel team on the planet. We have the resources to do it. We have the desire to do it. We have forty million people a month already visiting our web site. This is serious,"[78] emphasized Ryanair.

ENDNOTES

1 "Ryanair Labs open but needs 200 staff", http://www.businessworld.ie/livenews.htm?a=3184708, July 7th 2014, © 2015, Amity Research Centers HQ, Bangalore. All rights reserved.

2 "The U.S. Digital Consumer Report", http://www.nielsen.com/gh/en/insights/reports/2014/the-us-digital-consumer-report.html, February 10th 2014.

3 Bridwell Lisa, "Digital transformation: Helping build loyalty", http://dellworld.com/digital-transformation/.

4 Deloitte, "The digital transformation of customer services Our point of View", http://www2.deloitte.com/content/dam/Deloitte/nl/Documents/consumer-business/deloitte-nl-the-digital-transformation-of-customer-services.pdf.

5 "Ryanair profit drop for the first time in five years", http://www.bbc.com/news/business-27465993, May 19th 2014.

6 Pratley Nils, "Ryanair profit warning-could this mean take-off for sharp pricing?", http://www.theguardian.com/business/2013/sep/04/ryanair-profit-warning-pricing-takeoff, September 4th 2013.

7 Vizard Sarah, "Ryanair overhauls digital strategy to focus on mobile and social media", http://www.marketingweek.co.uk/old-in-depth-digital/ryanair-overhauls-digital-strategy-to-focus-on-mobile-and-social-media/4007999., September 20th 2013.

8 ibid.

9 Paris Natalie, "Ryanair unveils simpler website", http://www.telegraph.co.uk/travel/travelnews/10460167/Ryanair-unveils-simpler-website.html, November 19th 2013.

10 "Ryanair overhauls digital strategy to focus on mobile and social media", op.cit.

11 "Ryanair Labs open but needs 200 staff", http://www.businessworld.ie/livenews.htm?a= 3184708, July 7th 2014.

12 Lundgren Kari and Doyle Dara, "Ryanair Updates its Digital Strategy to Take on a Stronger EasyJet", http://skift.com/2013/09/20/ryanair-updates-its-digital-strategy-to-take-on-a-stronger-easyjet/, September 20th 2013.

13 "Digital transformation: Helping build loyalty", op.cit.

14 "Digital Transformation: A Roadmap for Billion-Dollar Organisations", http://www.capgemini.com/resource-file-access/resource/pdf/Digital_Transformation_A_Road-Map_for_Billion-Dollar_Organizations.pdf, October 2012.

15 Founded by Shashank Nigam, Simpliflying was one of the leading strategy firms offered constancies in Aviation Marketing around the Globe.

16 "Trends that transform how airlines are marketing their brands", http://webintravel.com/trends-transform-airlines-marketing-brands/, July 24th 2014.

17 Buhalis Dimitrios, "eAirlines: Strategic and tactical use of ICTs in the airline industry", http://epubs.surrey.ac.uk/1120/1/fulltext.pdf, August 6th 2003.

18 ibid.

19 ibid.

20 "eAirlines: Strategic and tactical use of ICTs in the airline industry", op.cit.

21 SITA, "Airline Distribution", www.sita.aero/file/526/Airline_distribution_positioning_paper.pdf, 2009.

22 Shearman Sarah, "Emirates targets rival airlines with Facebook Strategy", http://www.marketingmagazine.co.uk/article/1105265/emirates-targets-rival-airlines-facebook-strategy, November 22nd 2011.

23 ibid.

24 "Tweets at 35, 000 Feet: How Virgin America Uses Promoted Tweets", http://mashable.com/2010/04/13/virgin-america-promoted-tweets/, April 13th 2013.

25 Kumar Avanti, "Malaysia Airlines decides on Adobe to drive 'critical digital business refresh'",

http://www.computerworld.com.my/resource/cloud-computing/malaysia-airlines-decides-on-adobe-to-drive-critical-digital-business-refresh/, February 11th 2014.

26 Lundgren Kari and Wall Robert", "The Revolution at Ryanair: The Customer Finally Matters", http://skift.com/2013/09/18/the-revolution-at-ryanair-the-customer-finally-matters/, September 18th 2013.

27 "Ryanair overhauls digital strategy to focus on mobile and social media", op.cit.

28 Lunn Emma, "How does Ryanair make so much of money?", https://uk.finance.yahoo.com/news/how-does-ryanair-money-29102012.html, February 27th 2014.

29 "How does Ryanair make so much of money?", op.cit.

30 "Ryanair shares plunge after warning over profits", http://www.bbc.com/news/business-24800604, November 4th 2013.

31 "Ryanair website", http://www.airflights.to/Airlines/Europe/Ireland/RyanAir-flights/Ryanair-website/Ryanair-website.php5

32 Dhalla Manpreet, "Ryanair", http://www.marketbusting.com/casestudies/Ryanair%20Report.pdf.

33 Humphries Conor, "Ryanair Is Finally Changing Polices That 'Unnecessarily Piss People Off'", http://www.businessinsider.com/ryanair-trying-to-improve-customer-service-2013-9?IR=T, September 20th 2013

34 "Michael O'Leary's most memorable quotes", http://www.telegraph.co.uk/travel/travelnews/9522319/Michael-OLearys-most-memorable-quotes.html, September 5th 2012.

35 Ganusauskaite Ruta, "Improving 'Ryanair' Brand Image in Europe", http://archive.ism.lt/bitstream/handle/1/314/ETD2014-06_R%C5%ABta%20Ganusauskait%C4%97_publikuoti.pdf?sequence=1, January 2014.

36 Poulsen Heidi Mariegaard and Fowler Alice Host, "A Comparative Analysis of the Social Media Marketing Approaches of Ryanair and easyJet", http://pure.au.dk/portal/files/45322350/Comp._Ryanair_and_easyJet_without_app.pdf, May 3rd 2012.

37 "Ryanair profit drop for the first time in five years", http://www.bbc.com/news/business-27465993, May 19th 2014.

38 Wallop Harry, "Ryanair profits warning could refocus airline on good service", http://www.telegraph.co.uk/finance/newsbysector/transport/10294619/Ryanair-profits-warning-could-refocus-airline-on-good-service.html, September 8th 2013.

39 "Ryanair overhauls digital strategy to focus on mobile and social media", op. cit.

40 Pratley Nils, "Ryanair profit warning-could this mean take-off for sharp pricing?", http://www.theguardian.com/business/2013/sep/04/ryanair-profit-warning-pricing-takeoff, September 4th 2013.

41 "Ryanair overhauls digital strategy to focus on mobile and social media", op. cit.

42 ibid.

43 "Ryanair overhauls digital strategy to focus on mobile and social media", op. cit.

44 ibid.

45 "Ryanair unveils simpler website", op.cit.

46 "Ryanair hires Moneysupermarket executive to boost image", http://www.reuters.com/article/2014/01/17/ryanair-image-idUSL5N0KR2QA20140117, January 17th 2014.

47 "Ryanair's new marketing man: We want to make it better for customers", http://businessetc.thejournal.ie/kenny-jacobs-marketing-ryanair-dmx-dublin-1343054-Mar2014/#comments, March 3rd 2014.

48 CAPA, "Ryanair slips into loss in 3Q FY2014 on average fare weakness, but hints at a more stable outlook", http://centreforaviation.com/analysis/ryanair-slips-into-loss-in-3q-fy2014-on-average-fare-weakness-but-hints-at-a-more-stable-outlook-150823, February 4th 2014.

49 Eleftherious-Smith Loulla-Mae, "Ryanair CMO Kenny Jacobs: 'I have the best marketing job in Europe'", http://www.marketingmagazine.co.uk/article/1295223/ryanair-cmo-kenny-jacobs-i-best-marketing-job-europe, May 21st 2014.

50 Dare was one of the leading ad companies based in UK focused on brand behavior.

51 McCabe Sarah, "Ryanair's daring new ad strategy", http://www.independent.ie/business/media/ryanairs-daring-new-ad-strategy-30193127.html, April 17th 2014.

52 "Ryanair Lunches First Pan European Brand Advertising Campaign", http://corporate.ryanair.

com/news/news/140410-ryanair-launches-first-pan-european-brand-advertising-campaign/?market=en, April 10th 2014.

53 ibid.

54 "Ryanair's daring new ad strategy", op.cit.

55 "Ryanair Labs open but needs 200 staff", op.cit.

56 Garcia Marisa, "Ryanair Is Launching a Digital Innovation Hub for Online Travel", http://skift.com/2014/07/07/ryanair-is-launching-a-digital-innovation-hub-for-online-travel/, July 7th 2014.

57 "Ryanair Labs open but needs 200 staff", op.cit.

58 John Hurley was the former VP, engineering and product operations, Houghton Mifflin Harcourt.

59 Benjamin Kim, "Ryanair hires John Hurley as CTO to spearhead digital push", http://www.brandrepublic.com/news/1308647/ryanair-hires-cto-spearhead-digital-push/, August 21st 2014.

60 Hade Emma Jane, "New Ryanair app heralds flight revolution - O'Leary", http://www.herald.ie/news/new-ryanair-app-heralds-flight-revolution-oleary-30430896.html, July 15th 2014.

61 Eleftheriou-Smith Loulla-Mae, "Ryanair revamps digital strategy with creation of Twitter account", http://www.marketingmagazine.co.uk/article/1212986/ryanair-revamps-digital-strategy-creation-twitter-account, September 23rd 2013.

62 Moth David, "Ryanair CMO: Digital is key for improving our customer experience", https://econsultancy.com/blog/64796-ryanair-cmo-digital-is-key-for-improving-our-customer-experience#i.1e62g4edsxddv1, May 7th 2014.

63 "Ryanair Launches Paypal Partnership", http://corporate.ryanair.com/news/news/140818-ryanair-launches-paypal-partnership/?market=en, August 17th 2014.

64 "New Ryanair app heralds flight revolution - O'Leary", op.cit.

65 "Ryanair goes paperless! Budget airline launches app that stores boarding passes on your smartphone (but you'll still be charged €15 if you run out of battery)", http://www.dailymail.co.uk/travel/article-2691793/Ryanair-launches-app-stores-boarding-passes-smartphone-youll-charged-15-euros-run-battery.html, July 15th 2014.

66 ibid.

67 Smith Oliver, "Ryanair launches Mobile Boarding Passes", http://www.telegraph.co.uk/travel/travelnews/10965845/Ryanair-launches-mobile-boarding-passes.html, July 14th 2014.

68 Cookson Robert and Wild Jane, "Ryanair website tumbles down Google rankings", http://www.ft.com/intl/cms/s/0/8a741a36-c63c-11e3-9839-00144feabdc0.html#axzz3DNSf22Vo, April 17th 2014.

69 Topham Gwyn, "Ryanair drops out of top Google flight search results after website overhaul", http://www.theguardian.com/business/2014/apr/17/ryanair-website-drops-out-top-google-flight-search-results, April 17th 2014.

70 ibid.

71 ibid.

72 ibid.

73 Topham Gwyn, "Ryanair tie-up with Amadeus paves way for codeshare deals with national carriers", http://www.theguardian.com/business/2014/sep/24/ryanair-amadeus-deal-flight-sharing, September 24th 2014

74 ibid.

75 Shaun Smith was a leading Brand Consultant. He was also the founder of Smith + Co Consultancy in UK.

76 Wild Jane, "O'Leary Rings The Changes In Ryanair Remodelling", http://jamaica-gleaner.com/gleaner/20140528/business/business8.html, May 28th 2014.

77 O'Flaherty Amy, "Ryanair Presentation", http://prezi.com/kos8koinarv_/ryanair-presentation/, March 24th 2014.

78 "Ryanair Labs", http://labs.ryanair.com/.

This case was written by Professor Dr Monali Hota, léseg School of Management. © 2008, léseg School of Management.

GROUNDED IN HISTORY

In 1971, entrepreneurs Jerry Baldwin, Gordon Bowker, and Zev Siegl launched the first Starbucks in Seattle's Pike Place Market. At that time, a bitter price war had thrown the American coffee market into turmoil. Trying to maintain profit margins, producers of the major brands had begun using cheaper beans, resulting in what many consumers believed was a dramatic decline in coffee quality.

The Starbucks entrepreneurs brewed the idea of opening a retail store dedicated to selling only the finest coffee brewing equipment to brew only the highest-quality, whole-bean coffee. They believed that such a store could satisfy the few coffee enthusiasts who had to order coffee from Europe and convert other coffee drinkers to the gourmet coffee experience. To differentiate its coffee from the bland, dishwater-like store brands, Starbucks scoured the globe for a special type of coffee bean – the high-altitude Arabica bean, as will be discussed later.

Despite early success, Starbucks remained a small-time Seattle operation until the company hired Howard Schultz as its marketing director in 1982. In 1983, Shultz, while travelling in Italy, visited a coffeehouse and realised that Starbuck's future was not in retailing coffee beans and equipment that were springing up. Further, although more people were developing tastes for gourmet coffee, many people did not have the time or equipment to brew specialty coffees properly. By brewing the coffee in its coffee houses, Starbucks could use the proper equipment and well-trained employees to produce the best possible coffee in an environment that enhanced the coffee-drinking experience. And offering the coffee by the cup made the experience convenient for the busy Seattle businesspeople who were Starbucks' prime customers.

In 1987, Schultz became president of Starbucks and began to reshape its image as a prelude to rapid growth. He updated the company's logo from an earthen brown colour to green. He worked to shape Starbucks' coffeehouses to be a blend of Italian elegance and American informality. He carefully designed the store to "enhance the quality of everything the customers see, hear, touch, smell or taste." He wanted the store to be a "personal treat" for the customers, providing a refreshing break in the day or a place to relax in the night. To achieve this goal, Schultz and his managers invested in employee training and a strong employee benefit program so that they could attract and retain skilled employees who would enhance the customer's experience.

By the late 1990s, Schultz's strategy was paying off handsomely. In 1993, the American coffee market had been worth about $13.5 billion, with specialty coffees, like those Starbucks sold, accounting for only about $1 billion. By 1999, the U.S. coffee market had mushroomed to over

$18 billion, with specialty coffees capturing $7.5 billion. In 1996 alone, Starbucks added a store a day and almost matched that by adding 325 in 1997. By the end of 1997, it had added 30,000 employees since Shultz joined the company and was hiring 500 employees a week. Sales had almost doubled from $700 million in just 1996 to over $1.3 billion by 1998. A typical Starbucks customer visited his or her favourite store 18 times a month.

The story of how Schultz and Co. transformed a pedestrian commodity into an upscale consumer accessory has a fairy-tale quality. Starbucks has grown from 17 coffee shops in Seattle in 1987, to nearly 6000 outlets in 28 countries by 2002. Sales have climbed an average of 20 percent annually since the company went public in 1992, to reach $2.6 billion in 2001. Profits in the same period have bounded ahead an average of 30 per cent per year, hitting $181.2 million in 2001. And the momentum continues.

Moreover; the Starbucks name and image has connected with millions of customers around the globe. It was one of the fastest growing brands in a Business Week survey of the top 100 global brands published in August 2002. Starbucks is also considered the last great growth story on Wall Street, as its stock including four splits, has soared more than 2200 per cent from 1992 to 2002, surpassing Wal-Mart, General Electric, PepsiCo, Coca-Cola, Microsoft and IBM in total return.

STARBUCKS – THE CORE

Walk past a Starbucks Coffee shop any morning of the week, and you'll find a line of people waiting to pay about $3 for a cup of coffee. What makes Starbucks a brand that fosters such tremendous loyalty? The primary reason is that Starbucks sets out to provide great coffee drinks in a warm, comforting environment staffed by good, friendly people.

FABULOUS COFFEE

Starbucks uses Arabica beans to make its coffee, but not just any Arabica bean. The Starbucks' Arabica beans are grown above 10,000 feet in altitude by a carefully selected group of growers in countries like Sumatra, Kenya, Ethopia and Costa Rica. The company has focused on Arabica beans, rather than the cheaper robusta beans, because consumers can brew the Arabica beans at higher temperatures, thus producing a richer coffee flavour.

FRIENDLY BARISTAS

Starbucks has invested in a strong employee benefit program that helps the company to attract and retain skilled employees. According to the CEO Erin Smith, Starbucks offers better pay, benefits and training than comparable companies, while it encourages promotion from within. Further, Starbucks has a policy of giving health insurance and modest stock options to part-time workers making barely more than minimum wage, which is considered a pioneering initiative in the restaurant business. All this has added up to a cheery army of baristas who have significantly enhanced the customer's Starbucks' experience.

FAMILIAR CLUSTERS

Starbucks follows a 'place' principle of blanketing an area with stores, that is, of creating clusters of stores in potential areas such as big cities, affluent areas and shopping malls. This can cut sales at existing outlets as individual stores will poach on each other's sales. As Chairman Howard Schultz says, "we probably self-cannibalise our stores at a rate of 30 percent a year". However, clustering stores increases total revenues and market share, Orin Smith, the company's CEO argues, as the strategy works because of Starbucks' size. The company is large enough to absorb losses at existing stores as new ones open up, and soon overall sales grow beyond what they would have with just one store. Meanwhile, it's cheaper to deliver to and manage stores located close together. And thus by clustering, Starbucks can quickly dominate a local market.

BEYOND COFFEE

Starbucks, in the early 2000s, realised that it had to cope with some predictable challenges of being a mature company in the United States, such as the need to attract the next generation of customers, and the need to curb growing employee discontent over long work hours. Starbucks managed to sidestep these issues somewhat, by aggressively expanding to new and emerging international markets, especially traditional tea-drinking areas, such as United Kingdom, Japan and China. However, the challenges on the home front still had to be dealt with, especially the tough task of attracting the next generation of customers.

Younger coffee drinkers already feel uncomfortable in the stores, due to a multitude of reasons. Firstly, many young people can't afford to buy coffee at Starbucks and don't feel wanted in a place that sells designer coffee at $3 a cup. Secondly, these youngsters have the perception that the only peers they see at Starbucks outlets are those working behind the counter. Then, there are those who just find the whole Starbucks scene a bit pretentious.

Therefore Starbucks has created many innovative offerings beyond the core of coffee to entice new customers, to retain the loyalty of current customers, and thereby ultimately to maintain and continue its 20 percent annual revenue growth.

FOOD AND MORE

Starbucks initial efforts to move beyond coffee have been through sales of food and other non- coffee items, but it has stumbled somewhat. In the late 90s, Schultz thought that offering $8 sandwiches, desserts and CDs in his stores and selling packaged coffee in supermarkets would significantly boost sales. The speciality business has accounted for about 16 percent of sales by 2002, but growth has been less than expected at 19 percent compared to the 38 percent growth rate of fiscal 2000. That suggests that while coffee can command high prices in a slump, food – at least at Starbucks cannot.

For Howard Behar, the head of North American operations, one of the most important goals is to improve that record. For instance, in 2002, the company ran a test programme of serving hot breakfasts in 20 Seattle stores and may move to expand supermarket sales of whole beans. The Associated Press has recently revealed that Starbucks is expanding its efforts to sell hot breakfast sandwiches in stores, indicating that the test programme may have worked. The hot sandwiches have been tested in Washington, DC and Portland, OR, as well as in selected other stores. Starbucks will be increasing the number of stores that sell the sandwiches from 250 to 600 over the course of this year, expanding into San Francisco stores in early April and Chicago in the fall.

STARBUCKS CARDS

What's more important for the bottom line, though, is that Starbucks has proven to be highly innovative in the way it sells its main course: coffee. In 2001 Starbucks installed automatic espresso machines to speed up service, and also started offering prepaid Starbucks cards in November the same year. These cards were priced from $5 to $500, which clerks swiped through a reader to deduct a sale, and this reduced transaction times by 50 percent.

The Starbucks Card has been more successful than insiders and analysts ever expected. Starbucks attributed its significant December 2001 same-store sales growth to the card. In fiscal 2002, Starbucks activated more than six million new cards worth $70 million. That is, six million customers paid in advance for their coffee in that year. The Starbucks Card has rapidly become the preferred payment method for Starbucks most frequent customers. The Card's popularity is fuelled by several special features that make it a convenient and secure payment method. By visiting Starbucks.com, customers can register their cards, which will allow them to be replaced if they are lost or stolen. Additionally, cards can be automatically reloaded online or at any Starbucks location that accepts the Card. Latest reports say that the Starbucks Card has in fact, had $1 billion loaded onto more than 58 million cards from November 2001 to July 2005.

So successful has been the original Starbucks Card that it has led Starbucks to create and launch the Starbucks Card Duetto Visa in October 2003. Issued by Bank One in the US, the Duetto card combines credit and prepaid features into a rewarding and seamless cardholder payment experience. Just like a credit card customers can use the card at any Visa merchant. The Duetto Card also seems to be one of Starbucks' latest success stories going by industry reports. Robert Kenley, Director CardsConsult Limited, says that "Whilst there are many prepaid products available from banks around the world in travel, youth and T&E segments, there is one bank- issued retail prepaid card program that has reached critical mass: the *Starbucks Duetto* card." Further, Business Week named the Duetto Card as one of the best products of 2003, though Starbucks and Chase which bought Bank One in 2004 are unwilling to share sales statistics.

STARBUCKS EXPRESS

In October 2001, Starbucks launched Starbucks Express, its boldest experiment yet, which blends java, web technology, and faster service. Customers could pre-order and prepay for beverages and pastries via phone or on the Starbucks Express website. They just made the call or clicked on their mouse before arriving at the store, and their beverage would be waiting – with their name printed on the cup. Starbucks Express was launched as a pilot program in 12 stores in the Seattle area; and the enthusiastic consumer response made the company extend this to around 60 stores in the Denver area. The company was supposed to decide in January 2003 on a national launch; however, it announced that it would be ending both the test and the service in February of the same year. A note on the Starbucks Express website stopped short of calling the test a failure, and thanked the consumers for their enthusiastic participation in the program, as well as the insights gained from them.

HIGH-SPEED WIRELESS INTERNET

And Starbucks is bent on even more fundamental store changes. On 21 August 2002, it announced expansion of a high-speed wireless internet service to about 1200 Starbucks locations in North America and Europe. Partners in the project - which Starbucks calls the world's largest Wi-Fi network – include Mobile International, a wireless subsidiary of Deutsche Telekom, and Hewlett Packard. Customers will sit in a store and check e-mail, surf the web, or download multimedia presentations without looking for connections and tripping over cords. They will start with 24 hours of free wireless broadband before choosing from a variety of monthly subscription plans.

According to Howard Schultz, chairman and chief global strategist, "this service is a natural extension of the Starbucks coffeehouse experience, which has always been about making connections with the people and things that are important to us over a cup of coffee." Starbucks decided to add wireless access to its outlets after learning through surveys that 90 percent of its 14 million customers are frequent Internet users, and this has paid off in a big way. Wi-Fi is now available at 4000 Starbucks locations, and is considered a driver of outlet sales according to company spokespersons.

STARBUCKS – WHAT'S BREWING NEXT?

Starbucks mission statement in its quest for international expansion is "to be a global company, making a difference in peoples' lives by leveraging our brand and the coffee experience to foster human connections." This mission has been more than met by the company as it continues to expand and grow internationally with strong profits, albeit, with both successes and failures along the way. Today, Starbucks has a presence in 34 countries worldwide and generated $6.4 billion in revenue and net earnings of $494 million in fiscal 2005, to reach a stronghold of 10,868 stores worldwide (with 7,699 in the US) by end January 2006. For fiscal 2006, Starbucks expects to achieve even greater heights by opening around 1,800 new stores globally, and by targeting total net revenue growth of roughly 20%.

In fact, adding new products and services to keep alive the excitement around the core of coffee, seems to have now become a way of life at Starbucks. Late last year, Starbucks has tested yet another project designed to keep customers in the store for a longer time – the Hear Music media bar – in several American cities. This is a concept where consumers can listen to songs, burn a CD or create a customised mix of music, by paying $8.99 for seven songs and then 99 cents per song thereafter.

FURTHER READING

1. Kotler Philip, Gary Armstrong, Starbucks: Brewing a Worldwide Experience, Principles of Marketing, 10th Edition, Pearson.

2. Ghauri Pervez, Philip Cateora, Starbucks: Going Global Fast, International Marketing, 2nd Edition, McGrawHill.

3. Coffee and a Hotspot, http://www.utmb.edu/oto/HowTo.dir/Wireless-network/Starbucks-wireless.htm, November 9, 2002.

4. Dennis Duffy, Environment that Encourages Loyalty, http://www.dmcny.org/mc/page.do?sitePageId=26320.

5. Fred Minnick, Gift Cards are Big Business, http://www.selfserviceworld.com/article.php?id=4347&prc=273&page=56, February 27, 2006.

6. Starbucks Coffee Company, Bank One and Visa Team Up to Develop the Next Evolution of the Starbucks Card, http://usa.visa.com/about_visa/newsroom/press_releases/nr149.html, February 21, 2003.

7. Robert Kenley, Should we believe the hype about prepaid cards? The Wise Marketer, December 2005.

8. Starbucks Express Keeps Rolling, http://www.thestreet.com/stocks/retail/10235150.html, July 27, 2005.

9. Jeff Goldman, Starbucks on the Move, http://www.thefeaturearchives.com/topic/Wi- Fi/Starbucks_On_The_Move.html, May 28, 2002.

10. Nicole Weston, Starbucks Serves Up Hot Breakfast Sandwiches, http://www.slashfood.com/2006/03/04/starbucks-serves-up-hot-breakfast-sandwiches/, March 4, 2006.

11. Pamela S. Schindler, Starbucks, Bank One and Visa Launch Starbucks Duetto Visa – A Case Study, Marketing Research, 1st edition, 2004.

12. QSR's Continue to Catch-on to Card Payments, ISO&AGENT, Volume 2, Issue 7, November 16, 2005.

INTRODUCTION

On a hot rainy day in Paris, France, in early August 2012, Emilie Marchal was wriggling on her chair, impatient for the meeting to end, so that she can start working on her new project. The newly hired marketing manager at Uniqlo Europe, one of the world leaders in the apparel industry, just joined the European headquarters 18 months ago, as a fresh alumnus in marketing management.

Today, after an intensive training period as a store manager in London and Paris, Emilie was getting her first project with some strategic marketing challenge. She will be in charge of the European expansion of Uniqlo in Southern Europe, i.e. the opening of one new store in Milan (Italy).

This early morning kick-off meeting gathered only four people : Emilie, Sophie Marin, Head of Marketing & Promotion, Tom Dickson, Senior Merchandise Planner and Masaki Uemura, Head of Uniqlo France. Mr Uemura started the meeting with a brief overview of Uniqlo strategy of expansion. As he explained: *'Uniqlo is now at a turning point in its development. The company plans to open 200 new stores worldwide per year in Asia, Europe and the Americas[1]. Uniqlo is already considered as the market leader in the apparel sector in Asia and Eastern Asia. But the competition gets tougher, as European competitors such as Inditex (Zara) or*

H&M enter the market at a very fast pace. We have to accelerate the development of the western and particularly southern European markets in the next 3 years to come'.

Next, Sophie Marin went through a slide presentation, reviewing the key industry characteristics of the apparel market and competitors' positions in Europe (cf. Appendix 1). She declared: *'In fact, the European market is the most difficult and most competitive in the world. Europe has traditionally been the birthplace of fashion apparel since the 18th century. Originally, the knowledge flow and trend creation in the apparel industry has been a one-way traffic: from Europe or the USA to Japan.[2] European consumers are known to be the most sophisticated and demanding in the world as they are very educated to fashion codes and brands. Even if we have opened stores in U-K, France and Russia; Uniqlo is not yet established in the other European countries, compared to Zara or H&M.*

Time is now for Uniqlo to move on quickly and enter those markets in order to expand globally. The brand cannot rely anymore on its historical Japanese market, which is shrinking at the moment.[3] The objective is to become the N°1 in the fashion business by 2020.[4]

Southern Europe is the next key focal point. Still, we have to define how to penetrate the Italian market effectively. For this Italian expansion, we must avoid the initial mistakes we made when we entered the UK market. We must also consider, on a long term basis, the financial and commercial viability of the current global flagship concept.

Indeed Japan still represents 80% of our sales result.[5] Our domestic expansion has been historically based on small tiny stores in sub-urban cities of Japan. The global expansion via global flagships in major international centers is forcing us to eventually reconsider our positioning in Japan, from the 'old, low-cost' Uniqlo to a global apparel brand.

Looking at Emilie, Sophie Marin said *'Emilie, you have an opportunity to be part Uniqlo's global development by helping us enter new markets. For this, I would like you to prepare a report suggesting plans for our next expansion in Milan, Italy.*

When designing your future strategy and recommendations for the Italian expansion, think disruptively.

Don't forget to remember that if you want to really differentiate your brand, you shall not just look at your obvious competitors in your narrow little market. Uniqlo, for example, thinks that its competitors are not the other fashion brands such as Zara or Gap. For us, the benchmark could be Decathlon for its technical advance in terms of active apparel, Apple for its focus on design, or even Monoprix for its proximity with its clients. In fact, we don't think we have any real competitor in the fashion-retailing industry at the moment.[6]

And also use your experience as a Uniqlo consumer as well'.

For your report, you shall work on the following points:

1. **Global Positioning Definition**: First, identify Uniqlo differentiation factors and brand identity. Then, suggest the future global positioning, by analyzing the possible differences in Uniqlo perceived image, on the domestic and foreign markets. Recommend potential ways of enhancement to define the future brand platform.

2. **Experiential Retail Policy**: In order to implement the new positioning on the Italian market, please determine which location and retail format would be the best to select. Define an innovative and experiential retail concept for the different store formats. Keep in mind your store concept must meet the following requirements: enhance the shopping experience, immerse the customer in the brand universe and unify the global brand image.

3. **Innovative Promotional Campaigns**: You must communicate the new concept to Italian customers. To go beyond the current storytelling around Uniqlo *"Japaneseness"*, you must develop alternative and ground-breaking actions to enhance brand awareness in the Italian market and prepare store openings.

UNIQLO – COMPANY BACKGROUND

OVERVIEW

Uniqlo is part of the holding company Fast Retailing, based in Japan. Everything started in 1949 when Hitoshi Yanai opened a multi-brand store for men's apparel, called Ogori Shoji in Ube (West Japan)[7]. The small family business became rapidly profitable, due to the rise in the Japanese economy after WW2, and turned to a P.L.C. in 1963.

In 1972, Tadashi Yanai joined the family business, after a master in economics & politics and a first work experience. In 1984, the company opened a unisex casual clothing store in Hiroshima, under the name Unique Clothing Warehouse. The shortened Uniqlo name was soon adopted. This warehouse-style shop offered understated garments, in line with Tadashi Yanai's simple and rational vision of the apparel world, remote from the traditional tailor offerings. The chain quickly grew in size, and in 1991 the name of the parent company was changed from Ogori Shoji to Fast Retailing.

By 1994, there were more than 100 Uniqlo stores in Japan. In 1998, the first Tokyo store was opened, in the very hype Harajuku district. By 2001, the number of outlets in Japan exceeded 500.

The early noughties also saw the success of Uniqlo in selling fashion blockbusters: first, the fleece fever in 1999/2000 with 35 million pieces sold in Japan, followed by the sensational success of the Heat-Tech in 2003 with a record sales of more than 64 million pieces sold in the domestic market.[8] From 2001, the company began to expand abroad by opening stores in Shanghai and London. In 2006, Uniqlo opened its first American megastore in Soho, Manhattan (NYC), and in 2009 the first French flagship was launched in Paris. In November 2012, Uniqlo now has 851 retail locations in Japan and 347 in overseas markets.[9]

In 2012, Uniqlo is now one of the largest apparel chains in the world, the leading fashion chain in Asia and the largest apparel retailer in Japan.[10] It is the first Japanese company in the apparel industry to have such a huge success on a global scale.

THE SPA BUSINESS MODEL IN THE FASHION INDUSTRY

The Specialty Store Retailer of Private Label Apparel business model appeared in the mid-eighties in the USA, when GAP, the American brand, entitled itself as a SPA business model company. Three successive generations of SPA firms can be distinguished.[11]

FIRST GENERATION OF SPA BRANDS: PRODUCTION - ORIGINATED MODEL

This first version of the SPA model characterizes companies that have integrated all stages of the clothes-making business, from *'design and production to final sales'*.[12] This integration strategy led to the progressive globalization of the fashion apparel manufacturing system under the total control of corporate headquarters, enabled by the technical innovation in Information Technology and computerization. SPA companies partner with local factories for production, by establishing secured contracts with regional producers, to reduce costs and benefit from partners' expertise.

The American GAP and the Italian Benetton are widely recognized as the most representative of this first chronological sequence of the SPA business model. *'These companies offered standardized basic and good quality apparel items, at an affordable price. They moved from a very retail-oriented view at their beginning towards a production-focused perspective'*.[13] Considering Uniqlo, the Japanese firm established during the 80's early contracts with regional apparel producers in China and Hong-Kong. It can then be considered as a classical version of SPA.

SECOND GENERATION: RETAILING – ORIGINATED MODEL

In the 90's, the European apparel brands focused on enhancing the fashion elements in their value chain, beyond the total integration strategy. The business value shifted from the initial standardization of items or "off-the-peg" to an "off-the-catwalks" vision. The idea was to quickly adapt the creations of couture designers to street fashion garments, at an affordable price.

That was the starting point of what is known recognized as the 'Fast-Fashion industry'. In this most-advanced version of SPA, strategic competitiveness drives from reduced production timelines and the ability to lead fashion trends. Retail digitalization is required to accurately estimate market demand and trends.

The most typical representatives of this business model are the Inditex Group (Spain) and its Zara brand, H&M's (Sweden) and Next (U-K). Quickly, those firms also focused on reaching a global scale, by aggressively penetrating foreign markets and developing international retail networks.

THE NOUGHTIES: SPA 3RD G

During the last decade, all the fashion brands were all focused *'on speeding up their access to a critical mass in street fashion'*.[14] Their key concerns were to create new trends at a very fast pace, to catch consumers' signals with precision, and to fill up the market as quickly as possible.

In this context, the development of efficient retail systems is crucial both for production and sales. Hence the strategic advantage derives from the ability to set up pertinent networks (alliances, cross-sector collaborations) and to optimize outsourcing. H&M, Next or Forever[21] are current representatives of this generation of SPA companies.

UNIQLO FASHION FUNCTIONALISM CONCEPT

In the early 90's, Uniqlo product development policy seemed similar to its European counterparts:

- The company set up design centers both in Tokyo and NYC, to get an enhanced vision of the global trends,
- The firm initiated an increased digitalization of its infrastructure to process more efficiently store information and established POS[15] systems to collect sales data. The firm implemented IT to get a more flexible production and develop mass customization.

However, Uniqlo vision of Fashion was very different from its fast-fashion competitors and led to '*a new fashion paradigm: the Fashion Functionalism*'.[16] Since the beginning, Uniqlo has been involved in creating specific apparels, combining both design and function. The offering consists of basic, good quality items, both rational and functional. Indeed, the production management team has always consisted of '*sports and outdoor wear experts. Uniqlo products are fashionable and function-centered (high-tech driven) items at an affordable price*'.[17]

The proposal made by Uniqlo is then fairly different from:

- Sports brands interested in developing high-tech products with a lessened consideration for product's trendiness (and often at very expensive prices),
- Fast-fashion actors focused on the latest trends at the expense of product quality, durability and textile functions.

The focus on product quality and durability motivated an innovation strategy based on an active collaboration with textile experts, amongst which the Japanese group Toray Industries. This approach resulted in a conjoint product development of 'functional and fashionable garments', around two conceptual axes: enhancing functions for comfort (skin, ventilation, warmth, texture…) and improving protection (preserving moisture, blocking UV). The first success was the Fleece, offered at the very affordable price of ¥1,900 in 50 different colors in 1999: 35 million pieces were sold in Japan during the winter.

This sales record convinced Uniqlo top-management that it was possible to create new business venues by re-categorizing the market '*under this fashion functionalism frame: from the traditional apparel categories (jackets, trousers, dress…) to a new vision of function-based categories delivering top performance and preserving comfort in use*'.[18]

The Fleece success was renewed with the Heat-Tech, preserving heat, in 2003: more than 64 million units were sold in the domestic market. It was quickly followed by the Airism or the Silky Dry sensations, all made of artificial fibers.

The constant refinement of the following generations of hit-products (e.g.: 2004 Heat-Tech

with an anti-microbial treatment; 2005 Heat-Tech with a moisturizing function; 2007 Heat-Tech with all the functions and in more than 50 colors) confirms the Kaizen orientation of the company.

With the design of basic garments for '*undifferentiated mass customers with unchanging wants*', the collaboration enabled both companies to focus on their '*key assignment*': what is fundamentally needed from apparel functions (Uniqlo) and what is technologically possible from corporate resources (Toray Industries). In this vision, the focus is placed on '*the primary elements of the product (warmth, freshness…) and then on the secondary items (blocking UV…) and art elements (color matching, cutting, design)*'. In this '*Mass-user innovation system*', the stores and the IT system are competitive tools to '*constantly communicate and collaborate with mass-users to develop mega-hit products, all designed with the active voice of the customer*'.[19]

THE APPAREL CLOTHING MARKET IN EUROPE

THE MARKET

According to the 2012 Xerfi Global report,[20] the clothing retail business is a very competitive and atomistic business, yet profitable. Demand is sustained by the importance of fashion in modern lifestyles and changing consumer habits in emerging countries. Still, and even if all actors mostly rely on their domestic market, those are mature markets, with limited growth opportunities. In order to expand their business opportunities, all the groups currently internationalize their market presence, especially in emerging countries.

In this respect, some actors have been quicker than Fast-Retailing Co, Ltd and its Uniqlo brand (cf. Appendix 1). In 2011, the Spanish Inditex and the Swedish H&M are far ahead of the Japanese apparel group, in terms of current net sales (Inditex: €13.79 bn ; H&M: €14.26 bn *vs.* Fast-Retailing[21]: €5.26 bn). Inditex overtakes its closest competitors in terms of global market presence with 5,527 stores in 82 different markets (H&M: 2,472 stores in 44 markets; Fast-Retailing: 2,258 stores in 40 countries). Both Inditex and H&M groups exhibit a positive growth evolution in 2011 (respectively + 4% for Inditex and + 1.5% for H&M).

On a corporate brand comparison basis, H&M (H&M AB Group) is the market leader with 2,352 stores in 43 countries, accounting for more than 85% of its parent group's sales results (€11.5 bn). H&M is followed by Zara (Inditex), which represents 63.8% of Inditex global sales (€8.79 bn), with its 1,608 stores in 74 different countries worldwide.

Considering Fast-Retailing's mainstay operation, i-e. the specialty retailer Uniqlo, in 2011, Uniqlo stood for 84.4% of the global sales results (€4.5 bn) with 852 stores in 9 different countries.

Finally, the Gap, one of Uniqlo closest competitor, according to its latest financial report, had a negative evolution this year (−4%).[22] In terms of business perspectives, the apparel market is predicted to polarize in two strategic groups:

- The high-end segment, to benefit from a financially more stable customer base and reduce risks. Brands adopting this strategy will be forced to ensure their market presence worldwide and adopt pertinent differentiation strategies,
- The low-end segment, due to the economic crisis: demand is expected to explode and competition will be tougher, with potential new entrants such as hard & online discounters, and large department stores getting on the segment. Consequently, companies must quickly move on one segment or the other: intermediate positions will probably lead to future failure.

Turnover for the European clothing retail market represents €197 bn. Italy is part of the five big fashion market (UK, Italy, Germany, France, Spain), accounting for more than 75% of clothing sales in the zone. Italy is the fourth market (16%), after the UK (23%), Germany (15.1%) and France (12%).

Compared to the average European consumption, Italy is the biggest clothing consumer in terms of volume per capita, with an average Italian spending 43.3% more for clothing than the average EU consumer. Italians are more interested in fashion and spend more on clothing than other western consumers: the share of clothing expenditures in total household consumption accounts for 7.5% *vs.* an EU average 5.1%.

The Italian clothing market is about €26.39 bn, with an annual growth rate of +1% since 2008. The structure of the retail clothing market is slightly different from other western European countries, as the independent stores still dominate retail chains in the Italian market *(for more details on the Italian apparel market, its structure and the competitive landscape, please refer to Appendix 2).*

In terms of market presence, Benetton is by far the most established chain in Italy with 1,000 stores all over the country, 66 in Lombardia and 15 inside Milano city. Others retailers are far beyond.

COMPETITORS' POSITIONS

In the industry, the following factors are considered as useful for defining the apparel makers' market position: the price positioning, the business orientation (functional *vs.* ephemeral fashion), and the brand core business (sports *vs.* fashion).

Table 1   Distribution Channels' relative weight by main EU clothing markets[24]

Distribution Channel	UK	Germany	Italy	France	Spain
Independent Stores	+	++	++++	++	+++
Specialty Stores	+++	+++	+++	+++	+++++
Department Stores	++	++	+	+	+
Hyper & Supermarkets	+	++	++	++	+
Direct Sales	++	+	-	+	-

Table 2   Retail Clothing Chains in Italy[25]

	Nb of Stores Italy	Nb of stores Lombardia	Nb of stores Milano
Benetton	1,000	66	15
Zara	88	11	7
H&M	87	23	9
The Gap Inc	10	2	1

Some other criteria can be used to define the brand positioning, such as:

- The timeframe from product R&D to display (slow *vs.* rapid),
- The collection cycles /year and the length/ deepness of product ranges,
- The brand style: casual, sporty, trendy, sophisticated, classical, business…..
- The core focus of the company: style-oriented (trying to satisfy each and every ephemeral fad), innovation-oriented (in terms of fabrics and apparel functions), lifestyle brands (developing brand extension to offer a wider brand experience).

Of course, those differentiation criteria are not exclusive and can be mixed by any apparel brand to create its own identity.

UNIQLO GOING GLOBAL

REPLICATING THE DOMESTIC RETAIL STRATEGY ABROAD: THE INITIAL FAILURE

At first, Uniqlo was a casual chain on the back streets of Hiroshima. Uniqlo was perceived in Japan as a retailer of low-priced goods. The brand has been traditionally under-represented in the main Japanese urban centers such as Tokyo, Osaka or Nagoya. Its stores were mainly located in regional, secondary sub-urban areas, with a typical sales floor of 500 sq. meters.[26]

More recently, Uniqlo has started opening larger stores in the main Japanese cities.[27] To date, Uniqlo has 851 stores in its domestic market. It is Japan's largest apparel retailer, with a 5.5% share of the 1.05 trillion euros Japanese market. 129 shops are large-scale stores which represent 20% of total sales and Uniqlo has 3 global flagship stores in Japan: Shinsaibashi, Ginza and Shinjuku in Tokyo.[28]

Since the Global Quality Declaration of 2004 (See Appendix 6), Uniqlo has worked on changing the domestic brand image, shifting from the previous price positioning to a top-quality clothing made from functional materials and superior fabrics.

For Japanese consumers, Uniqlo is the only company that offers clothing made with luxury materials at reasonable prices, e.g. cashmere jumpers at only €69.99. This is of course made possible by the mass- production scale of the company. It is also a company that is able to create demand by developing clothes with innovative and unique functionalities at prices that everyone can afford, such as the Heat-Tech or the Airism (cf. Appendix 5, Visuals 1 and 2).

Uniqlo products are considered as an "investment" on the domestic market: the garments are top- quality a-temporal items, designed to last in one's wardrobe, they can adapt to any style and can be worn in many circumstances (work/leisure….). Due to its strong and historical establishment on the domestic market, Uniqlo is perceived as a proximity brand, very close to its local customers.

The first overseas expansion was initiated in 2001 by the entering of the British market, followed in 2005 by the opening of the first Chinese stores. 10 years later, this initial expansion is internally recognized as a complete disaster, as the initial branches opened in London and in China were closed down within a two-year frame.[29]

For the U-K expansion, the problems have been multiple. The initial choice of replication outside Japan was totally wrong, according to Uniqlo managers. The stores were, like in Japan, located in secondary zones and suburban malls: not attractive at all for British consumers. Plus, the assortment was terrible: very basic products, unisex line-up, and medium quality: again, not attractive for the 'educated' British consumers. Finally, the UK staff was not trained enough to Uniqlo culture, values and objectives: the sales results were very deceptive.

This situation was worsened by the total absence of promotional campaigns on the brand, the store openings and the products. As a result, there was no impact at all and no reaction on the consumer side.

PREPARING FOR GLOBAL SUCCESS: AN INTEGRATED MARKETING APPROACH

Decision was then made to step back, close some stores and re-launch the expansion in overseas markets, this time with more preparation. The marketing strategy was reviewed and adapted to ensure international retail success

REFINING UNIQLO VALUES AND EXPRESSING THE NO-SEGMENT STRATEGY

According to Naoki Takizawa,[30] *'Uniqlo is not Fashion, it is about creating basic items that everybody can wear'*. For Nicola Formichetti, Uniqlo Artistic Director, Uniqlo clothes are basic elements that can be adapted to *'any sauce, like plain rice'*.[31] In the Uniqlo vision, there is no abstract notion: clothes are seen as simple and essential items, that help the customer feel comfortable, well dressed, with style, every day. In fact, Uniqlo doesn't want to dictate style nor trends. It doesn't want to turn customers into shop window models. The brand philosophy is more a mindset focusing on change, diversity and challenging conventional wisdom, which considers fashion garments as a toolkit with elements or pieces of information, full of details, to help the customer develop his/her own style.

Another key factor lays in the vision of the market itself. While the fast-fashion actors divide the market into different groups according to socio-demographic factors (gender, age) or fashion tribes (sporty *vs.* classic *vs.* trendy…), Uniqlo targets undifferentiated mass consumers by offering basic quality goods that everybody needs in his wardrobe.

Its products are made for all, beyond everything that could classify people. Uniqlo offers fashion items that transcend each social category or group.

The focus is placed on practical clothes, with a superior quality, a good design and functionality. This disruptive cross-generational approach is currently seen as the way to go in marketing, and has also been adopted by many brands such as Nike or Louis Vuitton.

For Uniqlo, the core idea is to enable the customer to mix western fashion with a Japanese twist. The influence of the Japanese culture lays both in the sense given to details and the opportunity given to the client to create or recreate his original style.

PRODUCT POLICY

For fashion experts, in terms of product cycles, Uniqlo is not considered as a fast-fashion company, but rather as it a slow-fashion firm: compared to other actors, Uniqlo offers a limited number of basic garments. Consequently, the company wants to develop top-quality items: each prototype is modified repeatedly before going into production. Samples are checked very frequently to minimize the number of defective items, and on-site manufacturing controls are important to solve problems before moving to mass-production. Fabrics are carefully selected and Uniqlo conducts close examination to ensure uniform colors.

Uniqlo also deploys 250 *takumi*, or expert textile artisans, in all its Chinese partners' production factories to resolve problems, offer instructions on technology, and to pass on the Japanese textile expertise to new generations of Chinese technicians. Uniqlo constantly works on improving product quality and on infusing new technology from Toray Industries in its items.

As the range of offered garments is quite basic and limited, Uniqlo must offer a huge variety in terms of colors, fabrics and style (from simple to elaborate) so that everyone can find something pleasing him/her in the stores.

RETAIL POLICY: THE UNIQLO STORE EXPERIENCE

In line with the current customer expectations for hedonic consumption, Uniqlo has selected an experiential approach to conquer western markets. The Uniqlo Experience relies primarily on Experiential Retailing to actively engage and immerse the consumer in the brand universe.

Experiential Retailing can be defined as a '*retail strategy that transforms products and services into a total consumption experience, satisfying emotional or expressive (hedonic) desires as well as rational or functional (utilitarian) needs of the consumer*' (Kim *et al.* 2007).[32] This in-store experience is made possible through the use of elaborated store environments, technology, interactive facets, highly - trained staff and entertainment.

According to Tadashi Yanai, '*Stores are parts of the Uniqlo Experience. The Uniqlo Experience is made of parts and finished products. Clothes are parts and products are finished when clients wear the clothes. It is then very important to present those parts in a systematic way to convey the brand philosophy. The customer should enjoy each and every step guiding his choice through the huge variety of products offered, the top-quality level of in-store service, and the unique store atmosphere*'.[33]

Therefore, stores have been considered as the primary promotional media to convey the brand identity and values in overseas markets. For this, a distinctive retailscape has been designed, in which environmental cues (technology, design, sensory marketing and premium customer service) and innovative in-store events play an important role to enhance the customer shopping experience.

UNIQLO STORE ENVIRONMENT

In an experiential perspective, Uniqlo has chosen to enter western markets through flagship stores. Those super-large stores (89,000 sq. ft., 3 levels in Soho Manhattan; 30,000 sq. ft., 3 levels in Paris Haussmann) are currently located on the best high-streets worldwide, such as the 5th avenue in Manhattan, rue Scribe close to the Galeries Lafayette Haussmann in Paris, or Oxford street in London.

Uniqlo megastores' environment is unique and very different from its fast-fashion competitors. Designed in collaboration with the design company Wonderwall, their atmosphere intends to reinforce Uniqlo cultural Japanese roots, while expressing the Japanese cool and futuristic side of the brand.[34] They also aim at conveying the other brand facets: *functionality, emotion and beauty.*

As Japan is often considered by western consumers as a leading nation for High Technology, a strong emphasis has first been placed on the use of in-store interactive HT to reinforce the 'Japanese cool side' of Uniqlo, e.g.: promotional messages displayed by red LED-lights, image walls, color-changing LED-illuminated star risers, hundreds of LCD monitors throughout the space, and image-changing LED panels in the glass elevator cabs, plus rotating mannequins to give the stores a futuristic look (cf. Appendix 8, visuals 6 to 8). This HT touch must make people think "Here, it's Tokyo!".

In addition, some minimalistic hints of typical Japanese style can be found in the megastores: sleek modern design, industrial chic and softer elements such as *tatami* to express the ultra-contemporary cool aspect of Japan (cf. Appendix 8, visuals 6 to 8).

Via the unique collaboration Uniqlo has with Japanese music labels, designers and major manga authors for its UT t-shirt lines, the Japanese Pop culture touch is also represented on the sales floor.

Capitalizing on the brand cultural heritage, Uniqlo cashiers give tickets using their two hands, like in Japan (cf. Appendix 8, Visual 13). Still, some other Japanese traditions such as the salespeople yelling promotions in-store have been abandoned for foreign markets, due to cultural factors.

In-store atmospherics are mainly based on the visual and sound sensory variables. The visual dimension is considered crucial for Uniqlo differentiation. Indeed, the merchandising and display are used to expose and ultimately sell the wide range and colorful image of the brand. The store walls are massive, beautiful and vibrant colorama of products, visually expressing Uniqlo multicolored aspect and its textile expertise, while eliciting consumer positive emotions.

Besides from color, the visual display is used to differentiate Uniqlo from its sometimes messy fast-fashion competitors. Each and every Uniqlo store must be very clean, without any dirty area, and nicely organized, which is a real difference. Another objective is to limit to a minimum the number of damaged products on the store surface to positively impact on consumer perceptions. In order to also reinforce consumer functional benefits, Uniqlo merchandising is very attractive and clear, similarly to what can be found in supermarkets. As Uniqlo sells basic clothes, it must be easy for the consumer to shop in the stores.

In this view, products are always placed in the same location. This is to foster repeated purchase without any change or distraction for the consumer. As one can find routine products in supermarkets, the Uniqlo consumer can find his daily wardrobe in Uniqlo stores.

Accordingly, the layout must be very clear, with apparent signage on prices, products' fabrics and functionality. Mannequins and walls are also a way to help the customer to easily spot where the product is.

To ultimately enhance the experience, the in-store music will be selected so that it won't disturb the shopping. The playlist is intended to be non-recognizable by the consumer, different and more abstract than the generic pop/club music fast-fashion retailers use to play in their high-street stores. The airy music played aims at relaxing the customer during the shopping at Uniqlo while surprising him or her, thus reinforcing hedonistic reactions.

In order to deliver a consistent store experience, a great emphasis has also been placed on a premium level of service in Uniqlo stores. Based on the Japanese sense of hospitality, the Uniqlo in-store service policy is a basis for brand differentiation – compared to competitors.

That's why the company places such a great emphasis on the selection and training of the sales teams. Indeed, the salespeople are part of the brand image and can greatly influence the consumer experience, by conveying the right message, and adopting appropriate behaviors.

They are here to sell but also to assist the customer during the shopping experience: they must always be available, for any customer enquiries, nice and polite, approachable and attentive to foster customer loyalty: 'they must be the reason to come back', according to Uniqlo managers. To enhance the experience and offer a premium level of service, in each and every Uniqlo shop worldwide, a dedicated salesperson welcomes the customer when he/she enters or leaves the store.

Furthermore, the customer is also offered free alteration when he/she purchases a pair of trousers, done in-store within one hour. The brand doesn't want to compromise on hospitality and customer service, despite its affordable prices, and thereby focuses on customer comfort and pleasure.

INNOVATIVE IN-STORE ANIMATIONS

To boost customer shopping experience, Uniqlo also uses innovative in-store animations.

First, to drive in-store traffic, reinforce the brand futuristic universe, and promote specific products, some events are focused on interactive in-store games using innovative technologies such as:

- *The Mickey Touch Wall Party* for the launching of the 2011 UTGP t-shirt lines: customers were encouraged to act and create in-store, through a drawing app in a massive multitouch wall - in order to give their interpretation of the current t-shirt theme (Mickey in 2011). The multitouch wall also enabled interactive customer battles on the screen. Shopwindow-encapsuled screens broadcasted the on-going creations; the best ones being broadcasted on Uniqlo wat.tv event channel. This event focused on the playful, hedonic and aesthetic dimensions in the offered experience.
- *The 2012 Heat-Tech Game*: the concept is to convert customers' energy through an innovative floor surface that transforms footsteps to energy at the entrance of the flagship store. Alongside the kinetic pads that power digital screens through the shop floor, 'heat spots' popped up in high- streets, where passersby can interact with them through a custom-made game, converting their social energy to redeem a piece of the Heat-Tech product. This original event was backed-up by online actions: it was also possible to convert energy on Uniqlo Facebook page or through the mobile app, and all the social media conversations on the event were showcased on the in-store screens.
- *The Happy Machine Event*: the Happy Machine is placed in-store, for a limited time (usually 3 days, twice a year), filled by Uniqlo products at heavily discounted prices. It drops different items at different times of the day (12:00 AM; 3:00 and 6:00 PM) (cf. Appendix 8, Visual 12). During the event, the first customers in the queue can receive free items (scarf; limited edition bag) or be given free breakfast. It has sometimes

been coupled with street marketing, for which the street teams aim at making people happy with balloons, performances, and random acts of happiness; thus insisting on surprising and eliciting customer positive emotions to reinforce brand linking.

Second, other actions intend to emphasize the cultural roots of the brand through:

- Special in-store events to promote the unique Manga t-shirts line (One Piece, Naruto, Bleach…). Those events are temporarily immersing customers in the manga universe, welcoming autograph sessions with manga authors or game creators, and staging parades of manga heroes. Of course, the customer can be portrayed with them, eat Japanese food or win Japanese products trough specific games in the flagship store. Manga and Japan fans are usually delighted by those unique events and end up purchasing their favorite hero exclusive t-shirts.
- To emphasize its involvement in arts and music, Uniqlo also organizes acoustic live sessions in its flagships to commemorate the bi-annual release of the Uniqlo-Music Labels collaboration t-shirts: e.g. Scandal live concert at Uniqlo Ginza in 2012.
- When opening new flagships or for specific fashion events, such as the London Fashion Week, Uniqlo sets up VIP parties celebrating fashion, technology, art, design and Japanese culture through interactive experiences and artistic performances in flagships or pop-up stores. During the time of the event, limited edition items can be purchased by mass-customers, reinforcing the brand innovativeness and uniqueness.

Finally, in order to always surprise the customer, Uniqlo also systematizes the constant change of its store layout and shop windows. Taken all in one, this experiential approach has been very pertinent: nearly 500 people were queuing outside the Soho store and more than 800 people in Paris the day the flagships opened. At the moment, Uniqlo has 9 flagship stores worldwide (New York Soho and 5th Avenue, Paris, London, Shanghai, Osaka, Taipei, Seoul, Tokyo), all of them being very profitable.

DEDICATED PROMOTIONAL CAMPAIGNS

The latest international campaigns recently moved from expressing the Japanese roots of Uniqlo to insisting on emotions and inclusivity for all, through the new motto: Made for All (cf. Appendix 4). This new campaign was developed to better reach overseas consumers.

To ensure that the message is equally understood anywhere in the world and will engage the consumer to interact with the brand, a growing emphasis has been placed on very creative campaigns, including dance, music, color and digital marketing rather than traditional methods of advertising.

Since the 2007 Uniqlock break-through campaign (27,000 widgets circulating in 76 countries, 68 million views of the widget and the website in 209 countries[35]), the brand has been digitally very active: e.g. the 2008 Uniqlo Jump Campaign was distributed via Flickr, Youtube and a blog site, ahead from the official campaign site; the 2009 Lucky Switch widget generated 3 million clicks and clicks and 4,000 blog badges were installed.

In order to deepen the user's brand experience, encourage user's participation and creativity, Uniqlo has developed innovative digital campaigns such as the Uniqlo Explorer microsite that offers an *'infinite voyage in the company's products'*,[36] or the Uniqlo Grid which allows users to manipulate, on a collaborative and interactive basis, the Uniqlo logo on a dedicated microsite.[37] More recently the Uniqlooks campaign was launched; enabling customers all over the world to share their Uniqlo style on Facebook, with the most liked photos posted on Uniqlo website and used in-store to showcase the items. Following the Uniqlock success, the brand has also developed specific apps such as Uniqlo calendar and Uniqlo wake-up, in-between branded entertainment and utility in order to build brand awareness worldwide.

FROM TOKYO TO THE WORLD

Since the opening of the NY store in 2006, the strategy of expansion for foreign markets has been based on 3 different steps:

- First, a modification of the original Uniqlo style, i-e. unisex clothes, to better meet western tastes, especially for the woman collection: more colors, a larger mix of classic and seasonal items. It was also decided to infuse more fashion in the collection, through collaborations with fashion designers such as Jil Sander or Undercover, or the Uniqlo Innovation Project to attract the more sophisticated western consumer and express the brand innovation (cf. Appendix 5, Visuals 3 to 5). The brand logo was revised too to better express the Japanese roots of the brand (cf. Appendix 3).

- Second, the opening of temporary pop-up stores to test market reactions, such as the Colette corner and Marais pop-up (Paris) or rented containers filled with garments disposed on IKEA tables (Soho Manhattan). The idea was to develop Uniqlo brand experience by heightening customers' awareness for Uniqlo typical products, and favor WOM from opinion leaders before the establishment of real flagships.
- Third, the development of specific promotional campaigns to express the brand values and proximity with the local market:
  - The first step relies on a teasing approach with the appearance of Uniqlo logo on 'typically national' goods, such as the yellow cab in New York or the paper bread bag in Paris. This to create buzz and elicit customer's attention around one question: *What is Uniqlo?*
  - The second *step* aims at informing on the company and its products by setting-up product pile-ups in pop-up stores, installing billboards all around the targeted city, and insisting on hit- products (cashmere, denim, Japanese t-shirts) and price in the ads to create customer's excitement,
  - The third step is to launch the People advertising campaign, using national celebrities to personify Uniqlo brand values. In 2006, the baseline was From Tokyo to the World (or Paris, NY etc…) and the basic promise was 'Uniqlo is very close to your everyday life',
  - The final step is the opening of the flagship, with an in-store private party welcoming local VIPs and fashion experts.

DECISION TIME

Despite the success of the global flagship stores, Uniqlo has several challenges to face at the moment.

The first challenge relates to retail formats. Besides the flagships, Uniqlo has opened traditional stores in the U-K, France and the USA. Those stores are smaller, less experiential than the flagships, and often located in shopping malls. The merchandising is classical, with nicely arranged colorama walls. Yet, there is no infusion of technology within the stores, their atmosphere is quite cold and not really differentiating. Western customers are actually not attracted to these stores and Uniqlo must sometimes develop temporary discounts to create traffic[38]. What is even more alarming is that the sales and profit objectives are sometimes not reached for those more traditional stores (cf. Appendix 8, Visuals 9 to 11).

The second challenge is linked to financial questions. In the industry, debates are currently going on. The focus is placed on the profitability of flagships, compared to traditional stores. Experts question the viability of the super-large experiential stores strategy for apparel brands. It is then crucial for companies to carefully select their store formats when entering a new market abroad. The retail costs will vary according to the store format and location:

- In urban city centers such as the Opéra district in Paris, entrance fees for best locations may vary from 1 to 10 million euros, with monthly rents from €2,000 to 3,000/sq. meter,
- In urban shopping malls such as Paris la Défense, a good location can cost up to 2 million euros and €1,500 monthly rents/sq. meter.
- In newly created shopping malls such as So'Ouest in Levallois Perret, the entrance fees are very low (approx. €100,000). The monthly rent can vary from €350 to 600/sq. meter accordingly to the commercial surface (the biggest, the least expensive). It is more expensive for Fashion (€350 to 600/sq. m) than for Furniture stores (€300 to 400/sq. m). Contributions of €130/year must be expected, including the Tradesmen Association.

The final challenge deals with Uniqlo blurry brand positioning.

In Japan, the brand familiarity is very high, yet Uniqlo is still perceived as a low-cost apparel maker by some customers. It is also considered as an apparel brand that develops made for all garments. Because of the financial crisis, Uniqlo core customers buy less, and they look for value more.

Some experts[39] even state that Uniqlo global communication policy, too much centered on overseas sales and promotions, has no meaning for the Japanese consumers, that are still the brand's biggest consumers: in 2011, Uniqlo Japan net sales were about 600 M¥ *vs.* only 93.7 M¥ for overseas markets[40]

At the same time, the image of Uniqlo outside the domestic is that of 'a cool brand from Japan', with a modish, up-market touch and a futuristic image, appealing to design-conscious and trendy urban consumers in big cities. However, the brand awareness overseas is very low, due to the limited number of stores. Western consumers do always associate Uniqlo with good quality basic items. They don't really perceive the innovative and stylish elements of the brand. The company has to find future ways to appeal simultaneously to its historical Japanese customers and western clients to become what Yanai stated: '*the brand that represents Japan globally*' and '*the global brand that represents what clothing is*'.[41]

ENDNOTES

1   Fast Retailing Annual Report 2011, p 11.
2   Choi Eugene K. (2011), The rise of Uniqlo: Leading Paradigm Change in fashion business and distribution in Japan, ESKA/ Entreprises et Histoire, 64/3, pp. 85-101.
3   Warc News, Uniqlo seeks global brand status, July 17, 2012, available at: http://www.warc.com/Content/News/N30115_Uniqlo_seeks_global_brand_status.content?CID=N30115&ID=6f76cb4f-01ac-46b3-92ec-687d66c5aee1&q=uniqlo&qr=.
4   Fast Retailing Annual Report 2011, p 34.
5   Fast-Retailing, Performance by Group Operation, available at: http://www.fastretailing.com/eng/ir/financial/group.html, retrieved on 01/14/2013.
6   Based on the author's interview with Uniqlo France Head of Marketing and Communication, July 2012.
7   Fast Retailing Annual Report 2011, pp. 86–87.
8   Choi Eugene K. (2011), The rise of Uniqlo: Leading Paradigm Change in fashion business and distribution in Japan, ESKA/ Entreprises et Histoire, 64/3, pp. 85–101.
9   Fast–Retailing, Sales and Stores Numbers, available at: http://www.fastretailing.com/eng/about/business/pdf/sales_storenumbers.pdf, retrieved on 01/14/2013.
10 Fast Retailing Annual Report 2011, pp. 34–35.
11 Choi (2011), cf. ibid.
12 Fast Retailing Annual Report 2011, p. 28.
13 Choi (2011), cf. ibid.
14 Choi (2011), cf. ibid.
15 POS: Point of Sales
16 Choi (2011), cf. ibid.
17 Choi (2011), cf. ibid.
18 Choi (2011), cf. ibid.
19 Choi (2011), cf. ibid.
20 Xerfi Global (2012), Report 2XDIS01, Clothing Retail Chains in Europe, Market Analysis, 2012-2017 Trends, Corporate Strategies.
21 Fast–Retailing, Sales and Stores Numbers, cf. ibid.
22 The Gap Inc., 2011 Annual Report, p.20, available at: http://investors.gapinc.com/phoenix.zhtml?c=111302&p=irol-reportsAnnual, retrieved on 01/14/2013.
23 Xerfi Global (2012), cf. ibid.
24 Xerfi Global (2012), cf. ibid.
25 Xerfi Global (2012), cf. ibid.
26 Fast Retailing Annual Report 2011; Fast-Retailing, Performance by Group Operation, cf. ibid.
27 Michiyo Nakamoto, Japan's king of casual smartens up, Financial Times, July 15, 2012, available at: http://www.ft.com/intl/cms/s/2/afae506a-cb51-11e1-b896-00144feabdc0.html.
28 Fast Retailing Annual Report, 2011.
29 Uniqlo internal documents and authors' interview with Head of Uniqlo France, July 2012.
30 Naoki Takizawa is the principal designer of the IPJ (Innovation Project) line for Uniqlo. He previously worked as a designer for the Issey Miyake Haute Couture brand.
31 Uniqlo Made for All Promotional Leaflet, 2011.
32 Kim, Y., Sullivan, P., and Forney, J. C. (2007). Experiential Retailing. New York, NY: Fairchild Publications.

33 From Masamishi Katayama's interview in Uniqlo Made for All Promotional Leaflet, 2011, France.

34 Chainstore Age, February/March 2012, p. 40; Drugstorenews.com, June 25 2012, p. 88; http://visual-merchandising-elodie.blogspot.fr/2010/02/flagship-uniqlo-paris-2150-metres.html.

35 Tessa Thorniley (2011), Uniqlo thrives on digital marketing, Market Leader, Quarter 2, available at: www.warc.com.

36 Patrick Burgoyne (2008), Uniqlo Reborn, Creative Review: Advertising, Design and Visual Culture, available at: http://www.creativereview.co.uk/cr-blog/2008/january/uniqlo-reborn.

37 Bill Sansom (2008), Case Study Uniqlo, Contagious Magazine, 16, available at: http://www.contagiousmagazine.com/resources/Uniqlo.pdf.

38 e.g. the price cut on the ultralight down jackets from September 28, 2012 to October 7, 2012, at La Défense store.

39 Tessa Thorniley (2011), How Uniqlo used digital marketing to build a global brand, Warc Exclusive, available on www.warc.com.

40 Fast Retailing Annual Report 2011, p. 64.

41 James Topham (2011), Fast Retailing plans to ramp up overseas openings of its Uniqlo stores to 200 to 300 shops a year, as Japan's largest clothing seller aims to leap frog foreign rivals and other global mass-market apparel giants, Reuters, available at: http://in.reuters.com/article/2011/09/14/idINIndia-59324920110914.

CASE 5   EMPLOYER BRANDING AT McDONALD'S: REDEFINING McJOBS

This case was written by Syeda Maseeha Qumer, under the direction of Debapratim Purkayastha, IBS Hyderabad. © 2014, IBS Center for Management Research

"What it did brilliantly was make an assessment of the large gap between external perceptions and the internal reality of work at McDonald's. They then worked hard to redefine the meaning of 'McJob' by putting forward irrefutable evidence about the quality of jobs they offer."[1]

– Andy Dolby, managing director of Barkers Resourcing[*], in November 2008.

In early 2009, when an outlet of the world's leading fast food chain, McDonald's Corporation (McDonald's), in western Ireland put up a "Now Hiring" banner on its site, it received more than 500 applications. These included applications from bankers, architects, and accountants.[2] Analysts viewed this as a sign of the troubled times with a recessionary trend setting in. But industry observers also pointed out that it was an indication that the company had been largely successful in bridging the gap between external perceptions of work at McDonald's and the internal reality through effective employer branding initiatives.

Since the 1980s, the word 'McJobs' had been used as slang to describe a low-prestige, low-benefit, no-future job in the service or retail sector, particularly in fast food restaurants and retail stores. Though the term had been coined to describe jobs at McDonald's, it later came to refer to any low-status job where

little training was required and workers' activities were strictly regulated. Because of its common usage, the term appeared in the online version of the Oxford English Dictionary (OED) in March 2001 and the Merriam-Webster Collegiate Dictionary in 2003. The OED described McJobs as "an unstimulating, low-paid job with few prospects, esp. one created by the expansion of the service sector."[3]

McDonald's objected to this definition of 'McJobs' and said it was not only inaccurate but was also demeaning to the thousands of people working in the service sector. Realizing the need to change these negative perceptions about McJobs and to reinforce its employer brand, McDonald's initiated a series of initiatives such as advertising campaigns, promotions, creation of career sites, and projecting the opinions of employees. Since 2005, the company came out with various campaigns in the UK in its endeavor to redefine the word McJobs. David Fairhurst (Fairhurst), senior vice president people (UK and Northern Europe), was entrusted with this responsibility. Regarding the challenge, Fairhurst had said, "But bridging the divide between people's perceptions of the McJob and the positive employment experience of people actually working for the brand is not going to be easy. While our employees tell me that they find the comments made about 'people like them' upsetting and demeaning, if we argue our case too stridently, we risk the old Shakespearian dilemma of seeming to be "protesting too much". We intend, instead, to acknowledge the McJob and all it has come to represent, and respectfully offer objective evidence that might challenge people's preconceptions."[4]

BACKGROUND NOTE

Headquartered in Oak Brook, Illinois, McDonald's is one of the largest fast food restaurant chains in the world with about 31,967 restaurants serving more than 58 million people in 118 countries as of 2008. The group's principal activity includes operating

___
[*] Barkers Resourcing is a UK-based HR consultancy company

and franchising restaurant businesses under the McDonald's brand. All McDonald's restaurants are either operated by the company, or by franchisees or affiliates operating under joint venture agreements between the group and local businesses. As of 2008, out of the 31,967 McDonald's restaurants, 25,465 were operated by franchisees (including 18,402 operated by conventional franchisees, 2,926 operated by developmental licensees and 4,137 operated by foreign affiliated markets) and 6,502 were operated by the company. For the year ended 2008, McDonald's recorded revenues of US$ 23.5 billion with a 6.9% increase in global comparable sales[5] *(See Exhibit I)*.

One of the biggest markets for McDonald's in Europe was the UK. McDonald's opened its first UK restaurant in Woolwich in 1974. As of 2008, McDonald's operated about 1,200 restaurants in the UK. Though the UK had only 4% of the total number of McDonald's restaurants worldwide, it contributed to 7% of McDonald's global profits.[6] The UK business model was different from those in other countries as less than 30% of the McDonald's restaurants in the country were franchised while the majority of them were owned by the company.

One of the core factors responsible for the success of McDonald's was its assembly line system used to prepare food. At McDonald's everything was process specific and was produced in an assembly-line fashion that allowed the management to serve high volumes of customers in a short time while keeping product quality consistent and cost low. By applying the procedure of assembly line in food preparation, McDonald's ensured standard quality of production, efficiency, and customer satisfaction.

McDonald's was a large scale employer. As of 2008, it employed around 400,000 people at its restaurants, divisional, regional, and local-country offices worldwide. Each McDonald's restaurant was an independent business entity with the restaurant management responsible for accounting, operations, inventory control, training, and human resources management. The employees who worked for the company were salaried office staff, working in either the corporate or regional departments. It was reported that in the US, about three-fourth of the employees at McDonald's restaurants were part-time workers and many of them were young people who had had no previous training or work experience.

On an average, each McDonald's restaurant employed about 65 workers most of whom were hired as crew members. Crew members constituted the entry-level position and were responsible for preparing food, serving customers, and setting up equipment or unloading trucks of supplies. A crew member could be promoted to crew trainer, crew chief, or swing manager. Crew trainers and crew chiefs were responsible for checking the work of crew members and monitoring new workers at their jobs. Swing managers were hourly workers who could run a shift on their own. Their tasks involved cash dealings, attending to customer complaints, and making adjustments in the number and distribution of workers. Each McDonald's restaurant employed four to five salaried managers whose responsibility was to manage the restaurant's operations, crew, and business performance.

At McDonald's restaurants, most employees were paid by the hour including training squad members, dining area hostesses, party entertainers, administrative assistants, security co-coordinators, maintenance staff, night closers, floor managers, and shift running floor managers. Promotion within the restaurant followed a specific series of steps with an employee being promoted several times within a restaurant before reaching the managerial level.

According to McDonald's, employees were its biggest assets as it believed that employee satisfaction ensured customer satisfaction. The company offered various benefits program for its employees including a Profit Sharing and Savings Plan and McDESOP.* McDonald's offered both full and part-time career opportunities to its employees so that they could balance work with family and educational commitments. In September 2006, McDonald's UK launched "Our Lounge," an online learning website which helped McDonald's staff in procuring qualifications such as GCSEs and A-levels, apprenticeships, and degrees in Math and English. Analysts felt that the launch of such initiatives motivated the workforce to perform better. In 2006, McDonald's became one of the first companies in

---

* McDESOP allows McDonald's executives, staff, and restaurant managers to participate in profit sharing contributions and shares released under the employee stock option (ESOP), based on their compensation.

the UK to be given the Awarding Body status by the Qualifications and Curriculum Authority (QCA). With this, it could award qualifications such as GCSEs and A-levels to its employees.

McDonald's said that to help its employees grow and develop it invested in training and development programs. For instance, in 2007, McDonald's in the UK invested about £14 million investment in staff development, which included basic skills training for employees who had left school with no qualifications.[7] It provided career opportunities for its employees by recognizing team and individual performances. The fast food chain had a career progression program to help a first job employee to progress through merit-based promotions to a senior position. It was reported that over 40% of McDonald's managers had started as hourly-paid staff members in the restaurants. For instance, 21 of their 50 senior management team had started their careers on the restaurant floor including Chief Restaurant Officer Jeff Stratton, the COO of McDonald's US business, Janice Fields, and two of their three US Division presidents.

The company was recognized for its employment practices in many countries, including in the US, Australia, Austria, Brazil, Sweden, and the UK (See Exhibit II for HR practices at McDonald's and Exhibit III for rewards and recognition achieved by McDonald's).

ORIGIN OF THE TERM 'McJOBS'

In 1977, McDonald's launched an advertising campaign using its icon Ronald McDonald (a red-haired clown character) to create a 'McLanguage' specifically associated with McDonald's. 'McLanguage' involved formulation of words by combining the 'Mc' prefix with a variety of nouns and adjectives. In McDonald's television advertisements, Ronald McDonald taught children how to add the Mc-prefix before different words to formulate 'Mc' words such as 'McShakes,', 'McPrice,' 'McFries,' and 'McBest.' The campaign worked and as a result, many new Mc- words began appearing in the press, including 'McHospital,' 'McStory,' 'McTelevision,' 'McArt,' 'McLawyers,' and 'McJobs.' McDonald's also coined 'Mc' words for many of its own products and services like McChicken, Chicken McNuggets,

Egg McMuffin, McHappy Day, McFortune Cookie, McFeast, McCola, McPizza, McSnack, etc. It obtained trademark registrations for all of these. The 'Mc' language was not limited to the fast food area alone. McDonald's obtained registrations for the use of 'Mc' words in other areas as well. For example, for children's clothing it used McKids, for tours and travels, McStop, for job programs McJobs, and for ground shuttle transportation, McShuttle. It called the hotels present at its offices in Illinois McLodge.

People soon started to use the term "McJobs" as slang for temporary low paying jobs in the retail or service sector which offered minimal benefits and no scope for growth or promotion. They were sometimes also referred to as "dead-end jobs" or "burger flipping" jobs. These jobs were common in the service industry, particularly at fast food restaurants and supermarkets. In 2005, according to the ONS Labor Market Survey[*], 82% of people were engaged in such jobs in the UK.

McJobs were meant for new entrants in the labor market with negligible work skills, particularly youngsters. Individuals working in such jobs were paid low and were governed by strict working rules, analysts said. It was reported that in the UK, the number of people doing this kind of a job had gradually increased as many middle-class jobs had been outsourced to second and third-world countries where labor costs were cheaper. According to a study, about two-thirds of high-school students in America worked in such part-time jobs.

Though the term McJobs was initially used to refer to only jobs at McDonald's, it later began to be used for any low-status job where workers were usually inexperienced, expendable, and exploited by the employers. Analysts felt that McJob was just a job to fill a lack, and certainly not the ultimate goal of any worker. McJobs involved a series of simple tasks in which the emphasis was on performing the job efficiently. The tasks at these jobs were simplified and streamlined like operating a machine, counting change, greeting customers with courtesy, cooperating with fellow workers, and accepting orders from supervisors. Employees performed the

---

* The ONS (Office for National Statistics) Labor Market Survey provides information on the labor market within the UK.

same tasks hour after hour and day after day like robots. The workers were poorly paid and were offered no benefits. There were no paid sick days, health insurance, or retirement plans for McJob holders. The working schedules were inflexible and the working hours were too long as these restaurants closed very late. McJobs provided little opportunity for career advancement and lack of job security was common in such jobs. Analysts felt that for youngsters, the financial component associated with the job was more important than the experience and skills gained from the job. They were of the view that these jobs offered no job satisfaction as they offered low wages with no promotions.

The term 'McJob' was used as early as in 1986 by sociologist Amitai Etzioni in an article in *The Washington Post* article titled "McJobs are Bad for Kids", on August 24, 1986, that outlined the disadvantages of low-paying, robotic jobs at fast-food restaurants. Later, the term was popularized by Canadian novelist Douglas Coupland in his 1991 novel *Generation X: Tales for an Accelerated Culture* where the term 'McJobs' appeared as a margin definition[*] to describe "a low-pay, low- prestige, low-dignity, low benefit, no-future job in the service sector. Frequently considered a satisfying career choice by people who have never held one." The term 'McJobs' also appeared in the 1994 novel *Interface* by Neal Stephenson and George Jewsbury to describe jobs that were briefly held and underpaid. In the 1999 in the British film *Human Traffic*, the term McJob was used to refer to a character's work in a burger outlet. Gradually, the term got associated with low-prestige, low-dignity, low-benefit, no-future jobs in the service sector. The term 'McJobs' closely resembled McDonald's training program for mentally and physically challenged people- McJOBS.[†]

---

* The word McJob was used in the following context in the novel: "Dag...was bored and cranky after eight hours of working his McJob" ('Low pay, low prestige, low benefits, low future').

† In May 1984, the term "McJOBS" was first registered as a trademark by McDonald's in US for a program meant to train handicapped persons as restaurant employees. The trademark lapsed in February 1992, but following the publication of *Generation X: Tales for an Accelerated Culture* in October 1992, McDonald's again restored the trademark.

Over the years, because of its increased everyday usage in English language, OED entered the term as a dictionary definition for low-paid jobs. The meaning of the term appeared in the online version of the OED in 2001[*]. Later in November 2003, the term entered the Merriam-Webster's Collegiate Dictionary which defined it as "low-paying and dead-end work".

Talking about his experience of working for a McJob, Kerry who had worked for McDonald's in the UK said, "I'm afraid for me the McJob myth was true. I worked at McDonald's for three months before beginning university and ended up ill with exhaustion at the end of those three months. I would often be running the till, drive thru, and cleaning the shop alone during 12-hour shifts. They often 'forgot' to give me breaks. My shifts were so long that I often failed to see my family and friends for days at a time even though when I started I was told I would only work for 20 hours a week. I can safely say that working at McDonald's was the worst job I have ever had."[8]

To McDonald's consternation, some experts in the field too held similar views. For instance, in the *The Employer Brand: Bringing the Best of Brand Management to People at Work* (2005), Simon Barrow and Richard Moseley, consultants at People in Business Ltd[§], wrote, "There appears to be a huge gulf between the happy, smiley, family orientation of the external brand personality; the tired, McJob drudgery of its front-line employees; and the faceless, corporate machine that appears to exist behind the façade."[9]

TACKLING THE 'McJOB' ISSUE

McDonald's complained about the definition of the term 'McJobs' after it was recorded in the OED. The company claimed that the meaning of the term as described in the dictionaries was offensive to McDonald's employees all over the world and that it brought negative publicity to the brand. Commenting

---

* The term appeared in the dictionary as: McJob, n. colloq. and depreciative (orig. US). An unstimulating, low-paid job with few prospects, esp. one created by the expansion of the service sector.

† People in Business Ltd is a UK-based employer brand consulting firm.

on the inaccuracy of the definition, Fairhurst said, "We believe that it is out of date, out of touch with reality, and most importantly, it is insulting to those talented, committed, hard-working people who serve the public every day."[10] McDonald's even thought of taking legal action against the dictionary publishers but later backed off.

Analysts felt that McJobs which were basically entry-level positions, deserved respect as they were the stepping stones to success. Many workers who had started as crew members at McDonald's had gone on to become managers and CEOs. For instance, the company reported that 1,200 owners of McDonald's restaurants had started as crew members and 20 of its top 50 managers had begun work as regular crew members.[11]

But officials at the OED pointed out that lexicographers simply recorded linguistic usage rather than judging it and included words of common usage in society. They felt that there were many such terms similar to McJobs used in the dictionary and that changing their definition or removing them from the dictionary would not stop people from using them. According to a spokeswoman from the OED, "We monitor changes in the language and reflect these in our definitions, according to the evidence we find."[12]

Analysts felt that the meaning of a word was derived from the way it was being used in the language and since the word McJobs was commonly used to describe low-status jobs, it had found a place in the OED. Whether the word 'McJob' was pejorative, derogatory, or offensive to McDonald's was irrelevant, they said. They felt that the definition of McJobs could not be changed until people started perceiving these jobs differently. Stefan Stern, a columnist with the *Financial Times*, wrote, "I think they've finally had enough of feeling tarred or slurred with this phrase McJob. But I think they're misunderstanding something about language really: We use words and they mean what we want them to mean and it's not really for companies to dictate to us what a word means. They've made a good case for the fact that they've improved conditions in the stores and the staff get trained and have careers and so on. But it's like fighting with the weather or the tide, trying to change the way people speak."[13]

Analysts felt that lexicographers had their own methods of determining the meanings of words appearing in the dictionary and would not succumb to pressure from external sources while deciding on how a particular word would be defined. Analysts said that dictionaries did not tell people how to use words, but only described how people used them. Supporting OED, Stephen Smoliar of The Rehearsal Studio* said, "People do not take the O.E.D. definition for 'McJob' as the meaning of the word because the O.E.D. has sanctioned it; the O.E.D. published the definition because that is consistent with how people are using the word. If McDonald's wants that definition changed, they should be paying closer attention to what the English-speaking public thinks about them."[14] Analysts felt that the description of such jobs would change only when the conditions and prospects associated with the jobs changed.

In 2003, McDonald's former CEO Jim Cantalupo (Cantalupo) wrote an open letter to the publisher of the Merriam-Webster's dictionary dismissing the term as "an inaccurate description of restaurant employment" and called it "a slap in the face to the 12 million" industry's staff. In the letter, he pointed out to the benefits gained by teenagers and unskilled workers by starting out at McDonald's, and wrote that "more than 1,000 of the men and women who own and operate McDonald's restaurants today got their start by serving customers behind the counter."[15] Explaining the advantages youngsters derived by taking up a McJob, Cantalupo said, "Young people learn what it takes to succeed. They learn how to interact with customers, how to prepare food properly, the importance of cleanliness, the value of showing up on time, and what it means to work as an integral member of a team."[16] The letter was sent to media organizations, and was also published in the edition of an industry trade organization. But officials at Merriam-Webster said they stood by the aptness of their definition which reflected the way the term had been described for at least 17 years.

---

* The Rehearsal Studio is the name of the blog maintained by Stephen Smoliar, a concerts examiner from San Francisco.

REDEFINING MCJOBS

McDonald's decided to redefine the meaning of McJobs. In order to change the perception of McJobs and to redefine McDonald's image as an employer, the fast food chain began concentrating on employer branding. Employer branding is concerned with the engagement and retention of employees in an organization. Officials at McDonald's felt that employer branding was a powerful tool that could be used to engage employees and by doing this, McDonald's could break the misconceptions associated with McJobs. The management decided to come out with certain initiatives that would position McDonald's as an employer brand of choice in the market. Commenting on the importance of employer branding, Farirhurst said, "At the end of the day, if your employer brand is not authentic to the organization's values, it's worth very little. Your customers won't buy into it, the public won't buy into it, and crucially, your employees won't buy into it."[17]

In late 2005, when Fairhurst joined McDonald's, he felt that the description of McJobs was not appropriate. It was, in fact, rather insulting.[18] He wanted to redefine the image of McDonald's as an employer brand in order to represent the core values of McDonald's including culture, systems, attitudes, and employee relationship. He felt that the misconception associated with McJobs had damaged the employer brand image of McDonald's and that a change in image would be possible only through effective employer branding strategies. Fairhurst said, "Jeff Bezos, the founder of Amazon, once said: "Your brand is what people say about you when you leave the room." But having worked at McDonald's for a year now, I can tell Mr Bezos that this is one brand where people have no such inhibitions – they say what they think about us whether we are in the room or not. But Bezos' definition serves as a powerful reminder that a brand is something that can't be wholly controlled by an organization. A brand has a life of its own in people's minds and it will be shaped and influenced along the way by what others have to say too."[19]

As part of its employer branding strategy, McDonald's organized campaigns to showcase the experience and benefits of working at McDonald's restaurants. To change the opinion about McJobs and overturn the misconceptions associated with them, Fairhurst decided to launch a series of advertising campaigns. Talking about his plans, Fairhurst said, "With such a weight of prejudice to overcome, our approach was to deploy a series of counter-intuitive and fact-based proof points as evidence that would encourage people to reconsider their opinions."[20]

"MY FIRST JOB" CAMPAIGN

In September 2005, McDonald's launched a television campaign to promote the advantages of a McJob and to enhance its image as an employer brand. The campaign, titled "My First Job" was designed to position McDonald's as a preferred place of employment and McJobs as stepping stones to a successful career. The commercial created by Leo Burnett Worldwide, Inc. was McDonald's first employer-brand advertising attempt to communicate a brand message about McDonald's as a global employer. The advertisements featured 15 people whose first jobs were as crew members at McDonald's including celebrities such as Olympic gold medalist Carl Lewis and singer Macy Gray. The ads described their experiences of working at McDonald's and how these restaurants had given the required start to their careers.

Many such advertisements followed in which McDonald's showed how its employees who started at a lower level were able to achieve higher positions in the company. For instance, one of the advertisements aired by McDonald's showed how Jim Skinner, who worked as a regular restaurant employee at McDonald's, had gone on to become the CEO of the company.

In January 2006, McDonald's launched the innovative, UK-first family contract, which allowed family members working in the same McDonald's restaurant to swap shifts without prior managerial permission. To prove its credentials as an employer brand, McDonald's conducted employee surveys to convey the experiences of employees working at McDonald's. Regarding the surveys, Fairhurst said, "I'm always interested to know what people say about McDonald's. My job also means that I really like to know what people think about the brand as an employer. What kind of people do you think we employ? Are they well trained and treated with respect? Do they feel valued? Does each person feel that they have a satisfying job? Are they proud to work for McDonald's?"[21]

McDONALD'S PEOPLE PROJECT

During this time, McDonald's Ireland ad agency Cawley Nea/TBWA launched the 'People Project' in Ireland to change the negative perception about McDonald's as an employer. The aim of this employer branding initiative was, according to McDonald's, to address the false impression about it as an employer. It said the project involved redefining its position as an employer by projecting its real employer brand image. The objective of the campaign was to build employee morale by providing training, flexibility, and opportunities to its employees.

The Cawley Nea/TBWA planning team carried out an in-depth strategic analysis to understand the perceptions about McDonald's as an employer from internal as well as external sources and key opinion leaders. As part of the project, the planning team talked to people about their views on McDonald's as an employer. The external sources of study were young people who took up part-time jobs at McDonald's and their parents. The planning team spoke to teenagers to understand the essence of a first-time job and to their parents to understand their take on such jobs. The internal sources comprised McDonald's store managers and crew members. The team spoke to them to understand what opportunities a part-time job at McDonald's offered and their experiences as a McDonald's employee. The team worked closely with McDonald's Human Resource and marketing departments all through the project. The key opinion leaders who were interviewed during the course of the project were Career Guidance Counselors (to understand the importance of a part-time job in the development of a teenager), Human Resource professionals (to understand the importance given to candidates with part time work experience while recruiting), and University professors (to know their views about health and obesity).

The perspectives from these sources helped the team gain insights into McDonald's employer brand. With the help of this strategic analysis, McDonald's developed a 'Hierarchy of Needs' structure to understand what it was like to work at McDonald's from the perspective of parents and influencers as well as young adults. The hierarchical structure was conceptualized by gathering opinions about working at McDonald's from teenagers who worked in its stores, their parents, McDonald's store managers and crew members, and other influencers. Through this 'Hierarchy of Needs', the team was able to gain first-hand information on what it was like to be a McDonald's employee for young adults as well as their parents (*See Exhibit IV for 'Hierarchy of Needs' structure*).

As part of the 'The People Project' initiative, McDonald's launched 'McPassport – your passport to a better future' campaign. The idea behind the "McPassport' initiative was to value the skills and training received by crew members and to enable them to travel to other countries to share their experiences of working at McDonald's with employees in those countries. The McPassport Program provided employees with an opportunity to work in a McDonald's restaurant anywhere in the world. Besides the McPassport initiative, a new logo and identity representing the diversity of experience and cultures at McDonald's was also created. The employees' uniforms were changed to casual T-shirts to make them feel more at home.

To dispel apprehensions towards McDonald's crew members, TV commercials were launched featuring employees. The main purpose of this advertising campaign was to change the views of people on jobs at McDonald's and to encourage them to speak positively about the benefits of working there. Cawley Nea/TBWA presented the McDonald's People Project to the UK, French, and Australian McDonald's teams so that they could apply a similar strategy in their local environments. The campaign was successful in getting the target audience to re-evaluate the possibility of building a career at McDonald's and in raising the status of McDonald's employees. McDonald's 'People Project' won the CIPD/Watson Wyatt HR Excellence Awards 2007[*] for

---

[*] CIPD/Watson Wyatt HR Excellence Awards are the premier awards in Ireland which recognize excellence and achievement in the field of human resource management.

creating an impact on the employer brand image of McDonald's.

"NOT BAD FOR A McJOB" CAMPAIGN

In April 2006, McDonald's UK started a nationwide poster campaign highlighting the positive business practices of the company and the advantages of working at McDonald's *(See Exhibit V for employment benefits offered to McDonald's employees in the UK)*. The poster campaign which used the slogan "Not bad for a McJob" was rolled out in 1,225 McDonalds's restaurants in Britain. A total of 18 poster ads were created to support the campaign *(See Exhibit VI for some of these poster ads)*. The poster ads illustrated the benefits the workers could derive by working at McDonald's. Talking about the purpose of the campaign, Fairhurst said, "Our reputation is extremely important and the simple fact is our employer reputation isn't justified and this campaign tackles the McJob perception head on."[22]

These posters were also displayed on electronic hoardings at Piccadilly Circus in London's West End. This was the first time that a company had used the iconic London site for employer brand advertising. Talking about the campaign, Jez Langhorn, reputation manager for McDonald's, said, "We think the adverts are humble, disruptive, and tongue in cheek. We are putting the facts about the company forward in the advertising. We are letting people know that half our executive team started out in our restaurants and that graduates can soon earn £45,000 and drive a company car. The McDonald's employer brand is all about career opportunities."[23]

The "Not bad for a McJob" campaign was backed by Brighter Futures independent research study* carried out by Adrian Furnham (Furnham), Professor of Psychology at University College London in June 2006. According to the study, working at McDonald's had a positive impact on the development of young people in terms of their skills, personal growth,

and career opportunities. The study proved that the advantages of working in a McDonald's store were both personal and practical and that McJobs boosted the confidence, communication skills, and career prospects of young people. Talking about the analysis of the study, Furnham said, "The youngsters we spoke to started work viewing a McJob like most other people. But there is an amazing change in perception once they start. They are happy, motivated, and the work gives them confidence and self-esteem. The evidence indicates that these types of jobs are positive for young people."[24]

As per the Bight Futures study, 90% of people working at McJobs showed high levels of engagement, 85% said the job was better than they had expected, 83% had seen a positive change in themselves since starting work, and 74% were looking at a long-term career at McDonald's.

Commenting on the study, Fairhurst said, "We've known for years the jobs we offer are good for young people. If we'd based an advertising campaign around it, people would quite rightly have challenged us to prove it – now we can. This report is saying is that our jobs transform young people in a positive way – that's not bad for a McJob."[25]

McDonald's believed that the "Not Bad for a McJob" campaign would help in wiping out the image associated with McJobs and dispel the myth that working for McDonald's was derogatory.[26]

"CHANGE THE DEFINITION" PETITION CAMPAIGN

In March 2007, McDonald's launched a petition campaign to get the dictionary definition of a McJob changed. The petition aimed at garnering public opinion about the change in definition was circulated across McDonald's restaurants in 40 British cities for signatures from supporters. As part of the campaign, vans with digital display plied across these cities showing films describing the experiences of McDonald's employees and the importance of 'McJobs' to them. The petition was supported by the fact that half of McDonald's executive team had started working in restaurants, and 80% of McDonald's restaurant management and one in five franchisees had started out as hourly paid

---

* Brighter Futures, a student-led society in the UK, carried out an independent study on 475 people including young McDonald's employees, their working friends, parents, managers, and teachers.

crew members. The petition was further supported by the fact that the 'McJob' tag had become outdated as McDonald's name appeared in the *Financial Times* Best Workplaces rankings in 2007.

To gather online support for the campaign, McDonald's launched a website called change the definition.com to get people to sign up and support the petition. The campaign was backed by high profile figures from the worlds of business, education, and retail such as the former chief of the Confederation of British Industry Sir Digby Jones (Jones), British Chambers of Commerce director general David Frost, British Retail Consortium director general Kevin Hawkins, and City & Guilds director general Chris Humphries. Supporting the campaign, Jones said, "Service sector employees … should be respected and valued, not written off."[27] In May 2007, Conservative party Member of Parliament Clive Betts (Bettts) along with 35 other MPs co-signed an Early Day Motion in the Commons in Britain's parliament condemning the pejorative use of McJob to describe service sector jobs. According to Betts, "It would be helpful if the dictionary took the lead on this. It's not a proper and true reflection of the service industry today."[28]

As part of the campaign, a survey was carried out which reported that more than two thirds (69%) of the 1,000 adults questioned agreed that the OED definition represented an outdated picture of work in the service sector, while 61% said they would be insulted if their work was described as a McJob.[29] Talking about the petition campaign, Fairhurst said, "I hope our campaign will underline the value of the service sector and jobs like ours to individuals and the UK economy. It is insulting to talented, hardworking people who serve the public every day in the UK. It's time the dictionary definition of McJob was changed to reflect a job that is stimulating, rewarding, and offers opportunities for career progression and skills that last a lifetime."[30]

During the campaign, the UK branch of McDonald's collected over 105,000 signatures to petition publishers of the dictionary regarding the description of the 'McJob' term. McDonald's employees, customers, suppliers, and the general public added close to 1,000 signatures a day. In October 2007, the petition was presented to senior executives in charge of the OED.

'MY McJOB' CAMPAIGN

In April 2008, McDonald's UK redesigned its staff uniforms to give its employees a modern and professional look and to narrow the gap between the perceptions and reality of work at McDonald's. The uniforms, designed by famous British fashion designer Bruce Oldfield, reportedly made the staff feel good about working in a fast food chain. On designing new uniforms for McDonald's employees, Oldfield said that the uniforms created "a new, contemporary look for McDonald's employees that match the modern style of the company's new restaurants."[31]

In August 2008, McDonald's launched a recruitment campaign called the 'My McJob' campaign to support the increase in the demand for jobs because of the economic recession. As part of the campaign, McDonald's created posters of its employees talking about the career benefits and job opportunities available at the chain. The posters were rolled out in its 1,200 restaurants in UK as well as in print and online and were expected to be noticed by about 2 million people each day. Talking about the campaign, Fairhurst said, "In 2006, we reclaimed the term 'McJob' with our iconic 'Not Bad for a McJob' campaign. Over the past two years, we have received considerable support from our employees, our customers, and business leaders. We feel the time is now right to take another step forward and start celebrating the McJobs we offer. This campaign is an important milestone in the evolution of McDonald's recruitment advertising – signalling a more confident and assertive attitude toward the McJob term."[32]

CAMPAIGNS IN OTHER COUNTRIES

McDonald's US too launched advertising campaigns to depict the advantages of working at McJobs. In the US, in order to get rid of the dead-end job perception of McJobs, McDonald's started an advertising campaign in 2007. The campaign designed by Omnicom Media Group's DDB, Chicago, highlighted the career opportunities available within the company on its website www.mcdonald.com/careers. The site featured banner ads with profiles of workers, ranging from crew member to restaurant manager. Public petition campaigns were also started in the US for a change in the definition of the term in the Merriam-Webster Dictionary.

In a bid to reflect the career growth of employees working at McDonald's, the fast food chain aired US and Hispanic ads featuring employees who had climbed up the corporate ladder at McDonald's and attained successful positions in the company. A 30-second commercial featuring Karen King (Karen), east division president of McDonald's USA, who started her career at McDonald's in 1975, was aired to emphasize career opportunities at the fast-food chain. Talking about the growth prospects at McDonald's, Karen said, "In 1975, I began as a swing manager in Georgia. Now I oversee 5,200 restaurants between Maine and Florida. I truly believe that with hard work, anyone at McDonald's has the chance to excel. One of the things that is important about this campaign is I want employees to have that same sense of pride that I do and to understand they have the opportunities that I have."[33]

The ads also featured the success story of Ofelia Melenerz, who started her career as an intern at McDonald's and later went on to become the Vice President of QSC (Quality, Service & Cleanliness) in the Southwest region. Talking about the commercials involving employees, Bill Lamar, chief marketing officer, McDonald's USA, said, "This campaign underscores the intense pride that we feel for our employees at all levels throughout the organization. Karen's story is just one example of many. We are proud of the opportunity that we offer at McDonald's and of those employees that strive for excellence every day they're on the job."[34] The company reported that at its restaurants in the US, 30% of its franchise owners, 50% of its corporate staff, and 70% of restaurant managers had started as crew and 40% of McDonald's top management had started behind the counter.[35]

In 2008, to enhance its employer brand image, McDonald's used Web 2.0 technologies to promote employee engagement. Channel M* was used as an internal blog system for US and Canadian employees. This allowed staff at McDonald's locations to stay in

* Channel M is a regional television channel based in Manchester, UK.

touch with each other by facilitating communication between stores and headquarters. Analysts felt that this sharing of information between management and staff helped cut across hierarchy and led to a motivated and satisfied workforce.

In April 2007, as part of its employee branding initiatives, McDonald's Singapore launched the "i-stories" campaign featuring inspirational stories about McDonald's employees and highlighting their career path within the company. The "i-stories" were publicized at McDonald's recruitment drives. According to Eunice Lee, Director of Human Resource and Development, McDonald's Restaurants, Singapore, "Indeed, it reinforced what we have always believed – that our employees are our brand ambassadors, our true stars in employee branding."[36]

RESULTS

The sustained campaign of McDonald's forced OED to analyze the situation. In 2007, in order to prove that the interpretation of the term McJob was correct in the dictionary, OED invited the public to submit opinions on the definition of a McJob. According to a representative from OED John Simpson, "We're analyzing the situation at the moment and evidence for the usage of the word. It's a continuing process."[37]

McDonald's, on the other hand, tried to shed its 'McJob' tag by launching various campaigns. The initiatives by McDonald's led to a public debate on the issue and many influential people backed its claim. According to former McDonald's employee and Labor MP Ian Austin, "It is about time the myth of the 'McJob' label was challenged. Having begun my working life at McDonald's in Dudley High Street, I can vouch for the fact that customer service sector work like this is categorically not the dead end job it is made out to be. In fact, I learnt things then that have helped me throughout my working life."[38]

In 2006, McDonald's conducted an independent survey in UK in which 85% of its hourly-paid employees took part. The survey reported that among those employees, 91% of employees claimed that they were treated with respect, 81% were satisfied with their jobs, 80% felt valued as employees, and 74% were proud to say that they worked for McDonald's. The company quoted a crew member from McDonald's UK saying "When I first came to England I couldn't get a job anywhere – no one wanted me as I didn't have experience and only spoke a little English. Then I came to McDonald's and they gave me a chance. I've worked hard to prove they were right and now I'm being trained up as a manager. I am so proud."[39]

Analysts felt that the petition campaign might help McDonald's in altering the definition of 'McJobs.' The campaign projected McDonald's as good employers who offered fair wages, flexible hours, training, and career opportunities to their employees. Commenting on the support received for the campaign, Fairhurst said, "The heavyweight support our petition has already attracted shows we have struck a chord, and are not alone in our belief that the current definition of 'McJob' is inaccurate and out of date."[40]

In August 2008, McDonald's created 4,000 jobs in the UK in response to the increase in the demand for jobs due to economic recession. The new McJobs program aimed to boost McDonald's workforce by 6% at a time when many employers were cutting jobs because of the economic downturn. There were speculations that the demand for McJobs might rise even more in the future and analysts sensed that it was the right opportunity for McDonald's to remove the misconceptions associated with McJobs.[41]

In 2009, research conducted by Leeds Metropolitan University revealed that "McJobs" were an important means of social mobility as thousands of staff who had joined as crew members at McDonald's with not very high qualifications had gone on to carve out a successful career for themselves at the company. According to the report, half the workforce had left the company with better qualifications than they had had when they had joined. Describing the report, Fairhurst said, "This report challenges the view that "McJobs" are a dead end. By investing in staff through training and providing qualifications, large organizations such as McDonald's get enthusiastic staff, who when they leave the organization, do so with love and go on to have successful careers. And it's not just an ethical project – the company benefits from having an engaged, well-qualified workforce who continue to be advocates and customers even when they have left our employment."[42]

According to sources from the company, McDonald's success as an employer brand could be measured by its impact on the absence, recruitment, and retention of employees. Commenting on the employee turnover ratio at McDonald's, Fairhurst said, "Our staff turnover is now at an all-time low, and hourly-paid crew turnover has fallen by over 20% in the past two years. Absenteeism is less than 1% and we have seen a 33% reduction in the number of new starters leaving within 90 days of starting. Similarly, average tenure for restaurant mangers has reached an all time high and is now approaching 11 years. In addition to improved retention and absenteeism rates, employee satisfaction is also on the rise."[43]

THE OTHER VIEW

But some observers felt that McDonald's was using the McJobs issue to promote its brand. According to a marketing expert, "McDonald's have been clever in a tactical sense. They have taken the opportunity to win public sympathy and support, and show they are good employers at the same time."[44] They wondered why McDonald's had taken such a long time to respond even though the term 'McJob' had appeared in the dictionary in 2001. They felt that the 'sudden commotion' created by McDonald's over the meaning of the term was some PR strategy to gain free publicity. By organizing advertising and petition campaigns, McDonald's could boast about its work culture, they said. Moreover, the definition of the term in the dictionary would not affect its business as customers would be more concerned about quality and price rather than the company's employer brand image. According to Stefan Stern, "I don't think people stop on the doorstep and go 'aw now I was gonna get a hamburger but all those McJobs in there, I feel awful, I'm going to go and get a pizza instead.' If they're so confident that they offer good jobs, well let them get on with doing that you know, and if we still use a phrase like McJobs outside, well, that doesn't really affect the bottom line as a business."[45]

LOOKING AHEAD

According to analysts, the biggest challenge for McDonald's would be to attract new talent as derogatory comments that were still being made about McJobs would discourage prospective employees from working in such jobs. Bridging the divide between people's perceptions of the McJob and the real employment experience of people actually working for the brand would be a constant challenge for McDonald's, they said. Commenting on the opportunities that the company would provide to its employees, Fairhurst said, "We will try to provide the opportunity for people to prove themselves and progress, set up flexible working patterns that fit our peoples' lifestyles, and create an engaging, structured, and fun environment. We want to give people skills and self-confidence that will last a lifetime. Which may not be the sun, moon, and stars promised by some other organizations, but it's not bad for a McJob."[46] According to Larry Light, global chief marketing officer of McDonald's, the ultimate success of its various employer branding initiatives

would be when a parent had this to say to his/her child, "I want your first job to be at McDonald's."[47]

McDonald's planned to offer new learning and development and career progression opportunities to employees in order to boost its employer brand. Commenting on the employer branding efforts of McDonald's, Fairhurst said, "Over the past few years, we've worked extremely hard to close this gap and have had a good deal of success, but we know this isn't something that happens overnight. You have to be honest, open, and transparent and make clear the values you stand for in order to change people's misconceptions in the longer term."[48]

EXHIBIT I: KEY FINANCIALS OF MCDONALD'S CORPORATION (2004–2008)

US Dollars in millions, except per share data	2008	2007	2006	2005	2004
Company-operated sales	16,561	16,611	15,402	14,018	13,055
Franchised revenues	6,961	6,176	5,493	5,099	4,834
Total revenues	23,522	22,787	20,895	19,117	17,889
Operating income	6,443	3,879	4,433	3,984	3,554
Net income	4,313	2,395	3,544	2,602	2,279

Source: Adapted from McDonald's 2008 Annual Report

EXHIBIT II: HR PRACTICES AT MCDONALD'S CORPORATION

McDonald's is one of the largest employers in the world with about 400,000 people working at its restaurants worldwide as of 2008. McDonald's considers its employees as one of the biggest assets of the company and the company believes that employee satisfaction ensures customer satisfaction. To satisfy its employees, McDonald's provided them opportunities to grow in the organization and offered training programs to all staff levels. It continuously invested in staff recruitment and training. McDonald's invested in development programs which included basic skills training for employees who had left school with no qualifications. In 2009, McDonald's provided apprenticeships to 6,000 of its 72,000 UK employees

and planned to increase the number to 10,000 per year by 2010. The company aimed to roll out the apprenticeship scheme across all its outlets in the UK which would make McDonald's the largest apprenticeship provider in the UK.

McDonald's provided career opportunities for its employees by recognizing team and individual performances. The fast food chain had a career progression program to help a first job employee to progress through merit-based promotions to a senior position. It rewards the best-performing employees by giving away awards such as "housekeeping performer of the month," "crew member of the month" and "supervisor of the month." Besides competitive pay, McDonald's offered medical coverage to full- and part-time employees working at company-owned units. It increased retirement savings of its workers through a 401(k) plan available to both hourly workers as well as managers. It promoted diversity among its employees and helped them in leveraging their talents and strengths.

Work-life balance was one of the key elements of the Employee Value Proposition at McDonald's. Workers could swap shifts, choose their working hours, fulfill their study commitments, and even choose to work with friends and family members. In the UK, McDonald's offered its employees a flexible working scheme that enabled any two employees to exchange shifts without prior notice. The scheme was popular among students, parents of young children,

and carers who preferred flexibility in working hours. The company's hourly paid staff enjoyed benefits such as free meal allowance, paid holidays (4 weeks per annum), service awards (at completion of 3, 5, 10, 15, 20 and 25 years of service), employment discount card, free life insurance (value dependent upon service) etc. As a result, the employee turnover at McDonald's generally ranged between 10% and 20% as against the industry average of 33%. McDonald's placed more emphasis on Job progression in order to encourage and motivate employees and to improve their morale in the workplace. Because of its employee friendly practices, McDonald's workforce grew significantly over the years.

Compiled from various sources

EXHIBIT III: EMPLOYER AWARDS AND RECOGNITION

Year	Award
1997	*ComputerWorld Magazine* recognized McDonald's As One Of The Top In Training.
1998	McDonald's was named the most admired company in the food services category by the *Fortune*.
2000	*Fortune* recognized McDonald's as among America's 50 Best Companies for minorities to work. In 2000, McDonald's received the prestigious Best Employer Award in Brazil.
2001	*Working Mother* named McDonald's one of the 100 Best Employers for Working Mothers in the US. In 2001, *Latina style magazine* named it one of the Top 50 Best Companies for Hispanic Women to Work for in the US.
2007	McDonald's UK won the "Best Place to Work in Hospitality" Award by *Caterer and Hotelkeeper magazine*.
2008	McDonald's Corporation in UK won the following awards: – "The Times Top 50 Places Where Women Want to Work" award – "Top 50 Great Places to Work" award, the most prestigious employment award in the UK. – "Best Place to Work in Hospitality 2008" award in the category 'restaurants with 11+ sites'. Britain's Top Employers 2008 award. – "Times Top 100 Graduate Employers" award – "Investors in People" award. – McDonald's Canada was named as one of Canada's 10 Most Admired Corporate Cultures.
2009	In February 2009, McDonald's Singapore won "HRM Awards for Best Employer Branding and Innovation in Recruitment." McDonald's Canada was chosen as one of Canada's 50 Best Employers.

*The list is not exhaustive. Compiled from various sources
Source: http://iapiadvertisingeffectiveness.ie/cases/cases06/mcdonalds.pdf

EXHIBIT IV:

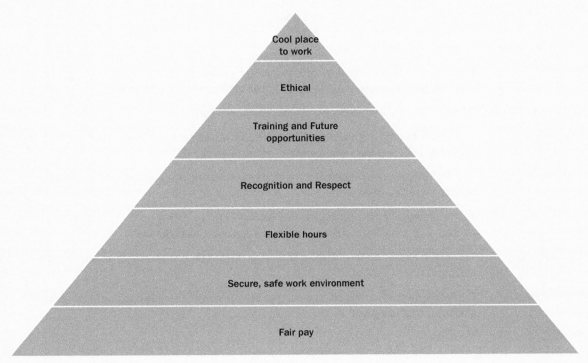

EXHIBIT V: EMPLOYEE BENEFITS AND REWARDS AT MCDONALD'S UK

CREW MEMBERS	TRAINEE BUSINESS MANAGERS
28 days paid holiday per annum.	Six weeks' holiday per annum.
Free private health care after three years of service.	Annual performance related pay review.
Stakeholder Pension Scheme	Life assurance cover.
Restaurant performance related bonuses.	Optional contributory pension scheme.
Argos vouchers awarded at service milestones.	Private healthcare for the employee, his/her spouse and any dependent children up to 21 years of age, after six months' service.
Employees could pay up to £110 per pay period in exchange for childcare vouchers, which is taken from gross salary, therefore saving on tax & National Insurance (NI) payments.	Company car or cash alternative after six months as a Business Manager.
Regional employee of the quarter award.	Home telephone bill assistance up to
Annual pay reviews.	£300 per annum for restaurant managers.
Over 80 great discounts at theme parks, on short breaks.	A paid sabbatical leave of eight weeks for every 10 years of service.

Source: http://www.mcdcareers.co.uk/html/
rewardsCrewMember.htm

EXHIBIT VI: "NOT BAD FOR A McJOB" POSTER ADS

McOpportunities	This poster highlighted that workers were given two pay reviews in the first year of their job. It read "McOpportunity – two pay reviews in your first year. Not bad for a McJob"
McValued	The McValued poster ad highlighted the Investors in People status awarded to the company. The company claimed that it spent £14 million on training its people in 2005 to become the first employer to achieve the prestigious British certification "Investor in People."
McBenefits	"McBenefits", featured McDonald's' employee health care card.
McProspects	This ad emphasized the advantages of working for McDonald's. The poster read "McProspects – over half our Executive Team started in our restaurants."
McFlexible	The "McFlexible" poster underlined the flexibility of working hours at McDonald's offered to parents as well as students.
McPackage	The "McPackage" poster highlighted how McDonald's' pay package of £45,000 per annum was on a par with a middle-rung doctor in Britain's National Health Service.
McDiscounts	The "McDiscounts" poster showed discounts on items offered to newly joined employees at McDonald's.
McRespected	The "McRespected" poster pointed out that the company had made it to the Times' top 100 graduate employers' list.

Source: Compiled from various sources.

END NOTES

1   "Brand Aid," *People Management*, November 13, 2008

2   David Sharrock, "Ireland's Dream is Over as Bankers Chase McJobs," www.business.timesonline.co.uk, April 8, 2009

3   Allen Butler, "McDonald's to Battle Oxford Dictionary Over "McJobs"," www.associatedcontent.com, March 22, 2007

4   Ruth Mortimer, "The US Follows the UK's Lead on McJobs," www.brandstrategy.wordpress.com, May 16, 2007

5   McDonald's Corporation, 2008 Annual Report.

6   www.mcdonalds.co.uk/static/pdf/aboutus/education/mcd_finance.pdf.

7   Karen Dempsey, "McDonald's Shows How HR Can Raise its Game," www.personneltoday.com, May 29, 2007

8   Denise Winterman, "The Flip Side of a McJob," www.news.bbc.co.uk, June 8, 2006

9   Ruth Mortimer, "The US Follows the UK's...," www.brandstrategy.wordpress.com, May 16, 2007

10 Stefan Stern and Jenny Wiggins, "McDonald's Seeks toRedefine 'McJob'," www.ft.com, March 19, 2007

11 James K. Glassman, "Even Workers with "McJobs" Deserve Respect," www.aei.org, June 7, 2005

12 Stefan Stern and Jenny Wiggins, "McDonald's Seeks to Redefine 'McJob'," www.ft.com, March 19, 2007

13 "Redefining McJobs . . . or Not," www.marketplace.publicradio.org, March 20, 2007

14 Mike Nizza, "A Redefining Moment for McDonald's," www.thelede.blogs.nytimes.com, May 24, 2007

15 "McDonald's Anger over McJob Entry," www.news.bbc.co.uk, November 9, 2003

16 Heide B. Malhotra, "Debunking the 'McJob' Steroetype," www.epoch-archive.com, December 20–26, 2007

17 "Employer Branding: Biting Through the Candy Floss," www.hrzone.co.uk, October 16, 2008

18 Sarah Woods, "McDonald's Unveils Campaign to Lose Low-Paid McJob Tag," www.brandrepublic.com, April 20, 2006

19 Ruth Mortimer, "The US Follows the UK's…," www.brandstrategy.wordpress.com, May 16, 2007

20 "Employer Branding: Biting Through the Candy Floss," www.hrzone.co.uk, October 16, 2008

21 Ruth Mortimer, "The US Follows the UK's…," www.brandstrategy.wordpress.com, May 16, 2007

22 Mark Sweney, "Fast Food Giant Says No to 'McJobs'," www.guardian.co.uk, April 20, 2006

23 "Sell Yourself as Candidates' First Choice," www.auroravoice.com, August 5, 2007

24 Denise Winterman, "The Flip Side of a McJob," www.news.bbc.co.uk, June 8, 2006

25 *Ibid.*

26 Sarah Woods, "McDonald's Unveils Campaign…," www.brandrepublic.com, April 20, 2006

27 Christopher Thompson, "Can McDonald's Alter the Dictionary?" www.time.com, June 5, 2007

28 *Ibid.*

29 "Burger Chain Hits Back at 'McJob' Tag," www.telegraph.co.uk, May 24, 2007

30 *Ibid.*

31 http://www.mcdonalds.co.uk/about-us/latest-news/latest-news.shtml.

32 Greg Pitcher, "McDonald's to Create 4,000 Jobs across the UK," www.personneltoday.com, August 6, 2008

33 "Fast Food Business Seeks Employees Who Seek Careers, not 'McJobs'," www.connpost.com, November 15, 2007

34 "New McDonald's(R) Marketing Campaign Features Southwest Region VP Ofelia Melendrez," www.hispanicprwire.com, May 21, 2007

35 "Fast Food Business Seeks Employees…," www.connpost.com, November 15, 2007.

36 Lisa Cheong, "Professional of the Year 2007: Employer Branding," www.humanresourcesonline.net, September 12, 2008

37 Christopher Thompson, "Can McDonald's Alter the Dictionary?" www.time.com, June 5, 2007

38 "Not Bad for a McJob?" www.management-issues.com, June 8, 2006

39 Ruth Mortimer, "The US Follows the UK's…," www.brandstrategy.wordpress.com, May 16, 2007

40 Simon Pritchett, "Sign the Petition, Change the Definition," www.people1st.co.uk, August 2007

41 http://www.mcdonalds.co.uk/about-us/latest-news/latest-news.shtml.

42 Rosa Prince, "Thousands Signing Up for McJobs during Credit Crisis," www.telegraph.co.uk, March 24, 2009

43 "Employer Branding: Biting Through the Candy Floss," www.hrzone.co.uk, October 16, 2008

44 "Burger Chain Hits Back at 'McJob' Tag," www.telegraph.co.uk, May 24, 2007

45 "Redefining McJobs … or Not," www.marketplace.publicradio.org, March 20, 2007

46 Ruth Mortimer, "The US Follows the UK's…," www.brandstrategy.wordpress.com, May 16, 2007

47 Gregg Cebrzynski, "McD Promotes Job Opportunities in New TV Campaign," Nation's Restaurant News, May 13, 2009

48 "Employer Branding: Biting Through the Candy Floss," www.hrzone.co.uk, October 16, 2008

© 2014, Singapore Management University

Our strength lies beyond our surroundings and high value location - it lies in our core values that guide us to treat each and every one with honour as kin, as family. In our family, you will find the tranquility, sincerity, and something greater - our special kind of hospitality, hospitality from the heart. We are saying: "Our Shangri-La"... These powerful messages are well understood and our people take pride being with us... We hired the right people for the right departments, and I strongly believe that Shangri-La Bosphorus Istanbul will become one of the best luxury-grade hotels in the world.

– Sinan Yilmaz, general manager
Shangri-La Bosphorus

On a fine afternoon of May 11, 2013, the Shangri-La Bosphorus opened its doors in Istanbul for the first time in a glittering official opening ceremony that was attended by many dignitaries, including the Prime Minister of Turkey. Sinan Yilmaz, the general manager of the hotel, was relieved to note that the grand inaugural reception was going off smoothly, and would offer an excellent opportunity to showcase the hospitality and service culture that the Shangri-La hotels were renowned for.

The Hong Kong-based Shangri-La Hotels and Resorts was Asia Pacific's leading luxury hotel group and globally regarded as one of the finest hotel ownership and management companies. The Group had opened its first deluxe hotel in Singapore in 1971, and over the next 40 years or so had grown into a chain that included 82 hotels and resorts throughout Asia Pacific, North America and the Middle East, with an inventory of over 34,000 rooms. In 2009, Shangri-La ventured into Europe, opening the first Shangri-La hotel in Paris. The Turkish property was the Group's second foray into the European market. Similar to the premier addresses that it occupied elsewhere in the world, the Shangri-La Bosphorus Hotel too was ideally located in the financial and entertainment district of Istanbul, yielding spectacular views of the Bosphorus Strait. The architecture of the property and its spacious, well-furnished rooms were in keeping with what a Shangri-La customer had come to expect.

Looking around the grand inauguration reception, Yilmaz recalled the many challenges that he and his team had faced in launching the hotel, which had also led to several delays in its opening date. Despite the successful opening, he realized that the coming months were not going to be easy. The Shangri-La brand was not very well known in the highly competitive Turkish and neighbouring markets. Internally, Yilmaz had found recruiting, particularly of the front line staff, to be difficult as the applicants' expectations were not necessarily commensurate with the experience or competency expected of a Shangri-La employee. How could he now ensure that the employees he had painstakingly recruited from the many thousands who had applied were able to meet the exacting standards of customer service that the Shangri-La Group prided itself on? What else did he need to focus on to ensure the sustained and viable growth of the Shangri-La Bosphorus Hotel for it to become recognized as the best hotel in Istanbul? What would it take for him and his team to break-even in the shortest possible time to make this venture a financial success for the Shangri-La Group and its partner?

SHANGRI-LA GROUP

The Shangri-La Hotels origin could be traced back to 1949, when the Kuok Group, which was the parent company for these hotels, was established. However, it was only about twenty years later that the Hong Kong-based Group first ventured into the hotel industry, and set up the first Shangri-La Hotel in Singapore in 1971. In 1982, the Shangri-La International Hotel Management Limited was founded. Over the rest of the 1980s, the Group established three more hotels – one in Bangkok, Thailand; and the other two in Hangzhou and Beijing in China. This was then followed by a period of rapid expansion.

In 1991, Shangri-La International Hotel Management Limited took over the management of all owned properties. In 1993, Shangri-La Asia Limited, which was the property and hotel management company, went public on the Hong Kong Stock Exchange. By 2013, the group had businesses in three main segments: hotel ownership and management of the same; hotel management and related services to group-owned hotels and hotels owned by third parties; and rentals received from the leasing of office properties, commercial properties and serviced apartments/residences.

By December 31, 2012, the Shangri-La Group ("Group") had 81 hotels and resorts throughout Asia Pacific, North America, the Middle East, and Europe, with an inventory of over 34,000 rooms. Shangri-La Hotels and Resorts had come to be regarded as Asia Pacific's leading luxury hotel group, and were renowned for its superior customer service. This was encapsulated in its simple, yet clear, vision of "To be the first choice for guests, colleagues, shareholders and business partners". The mission statement too was well aligned to the vision, and it proposed, "To delight our guests every time by creating engaging experiences straight from our heart."

The Shangri-La Hotels & Resorts had four distinct brands. The first was the Shangri-La Hotels, which were five-star luxury hotels located in premier city addresses. The second, Shangri-La Resorts, was focused towards offering travellers and families a relaxing and engaging vacation in some of the world's most exotic destinations. Traders Hotels were four-star hotels aimed at the business traveller, while Kerry Hotels, with contemporary and functional designs, was the latest five-star brand introduced in 2011.

For the year ending December 31, 2012, Shangri-La Asia Ltd reported an increase in sales of 8% over the previous year to US$2 billion. Net profits went up by 42% over the same period to US$359 million. The Group had an extensive presence in Asia, particularly mainland China, which as a region performed relatively better than the economies of Europe and North America, and enabled its owned hotels to post year on year improvement in operating results. There had also been a large increase in the profit after tax received from its investment properties – which included offices, serviced apartments and some retail shop space – that went up by 31.6% over 2011 figures to US$81.5 million (refer to **Exhibit 1** for further details on the financial performance). The weighted average room yields, or revenue per available room ("RevPAR"[1]) for the Group's owned hotels registered a 6% increase in 2012 over the previous year (refer to **Exhibit 2** for further details on the RevPAR across different countries).

Until the early 2000s, the Shangri-La chain had chosen to focus on its core market in the Asia- Pacific region. 2003 was its first foray out of this market, when it opened hotels in Sydney and Dubai (refer to **Exhibit 3** for key milestones).

THE LUXURY HOTEL INDUSTRY IN ISTANBUL, TURKEY

TURKEY

Located between south-eastern Europe and south-western Asia, the Republic of Turkey (Turkey) was the 17th most populated country in the world, with an estimated 80 million residents as of July 2013.[2] Istanbul was the most populated city with around 10 million residents, followed by the capital Ankara with 3.8 million inhabitants. Turkey was a largely free-market economy increasingly driven by its industry and service sectors, although its traditional agriculture sector still accounted for about 25% of employment.[3] Turkey benefited from its membership in the European Union customs, which made it an attractive platform for export-oriented manufacturers.

However, it was tourism that was the key reason for foreign visitor inflow to Turkey, as compared to business travel (refer to **Exhibit 4** for further details on visitor inflow to Turkey). Renowned for its natural beauty and great historical significance, often referred to as the 'cradle of cultures and civilizations', Turkey was a very popular tourist destination that had witnessed a steady increase in foreign arrivals over the past decade. The United Nations World Tourism Organization's Tourism Highlights 2012 Edition had ranked Turkey as the sixth most popular tourist destination in the world, attracting a total of 31.8 million foreign visitors in 2012.[4] This influx had a natural corollary in the rapid increase in the number of hotels and other services that came up to meet the growing demand from this segment. The hotel supply, particularly in Istanbul, began rapidly expanding (refer to **Exhibit 5** for further details of the existing and new hotels planned in Turkey). As at 2011, it was estimated that Turkey had 276,000 hotel rooms, with 583,000 hotel beds and around 64.6% occupancy rate.[5]

There were however some concerns that traffic to Turkey could be adversely affected due to the weak economic conditions in the Eurozone, which was a major source of inbound tourists to Turkey (as at 2010, the three largest source markets of tourists to Turkey were from Germany at 4.8 million, followed by Russia at 3.4 million and the UK at 1.9 million[6]). Also, regional political instability was likely to discourage visitors. Moreover, there were concerns that the number of upmarket hotels in the four- and five-star range had increased to the point where overcapacity could become an issue.[7]

ISTANBUL

Istanbul was the only city in the world that spanned over two continents. The Bosphorus Strait ran through the city, and divided the city such that the western part was in Europe, and the eastern part in Asia. Istanbul was one of the most historical places in the world, with a history that spanned the rise and fall of some of the world's greatest empires, including the Byzantine, the Roman and the Ottoman Empires. The scenic beauty of the region, along with its pleasant climate and interesting shopping options

were some of the driving factors that made this city a very popular destination for visitors.

In a report published in November 2011 on the Istanbul hotel industry, STR Global, a leading provider of market data to the hotel industry averred,

The Istanbul hotel market experienced positive growth in both average daily rate (ADR) and revenue per available room year-to-September 2011. The trend is encouraging, as new supply has grown by an additional 1,868 daily rooms (+5.9%) since 2010. Istanbul was ready to welcome an increase in tourism arrivals with an attractive exchange rate against the major currencies and a growing new hotel supply of branded hotels. It was one of the top 10 destinations for Conference and Incentive events in 2010, and became the third- fastest growing tourist destination in the world in terms of visitor number (+30%) in 2010, according to a MasterCard Worldwide report published in July 2011.

– Market researcher STR Global, as quoted in Hotel News Resource[8]

The future for the hotel industry in Istanbul appeared bright, with market research predicting that the city would continue to remain attractive for both the tourist and business traveller. In 2012, Istanbul registered a 16% increase in inbound arrivals over the previous year, and room demand rose by 8.9%, while supply increased at just 4.6%.[9] Thus, Istanbul was perceived as an incredibly attractive market for hotel investors, and there were more than 5,000 hotel rooms that were already in the development pipeline.[10] There was however, some concern that the volatility in the global environment, and the expected 9.3% increase in room supply by year end 2011, could present challenges for the market.[11]

SHANGRI-LA BOSPHORUS

Optimistic about the Istanbul hotel industry's future, the Shangri-La Group decided to enter this market, and develop the Shangri-La Bosphorus Hotel. The Shangri-La Bosphorus was to have 169 rooms, with the smallest room starting at 452 square feet. There would also be 17 luxury suites, with an area ranging from 861 to 4,000 square feet. The hotel itself was to be equipped with over 1,000 pieces of original art, and each room would contain luxurious amenities. Its location was considered incomparable, as it was beside the Bosphorus waters, in the heart of the tourist, shopping and business area and most rooms would have a view of the river.

Shangri-La's positioning statement (refer to **Exhibit 6** for further details) was communicated as,

> *To the affluent guests, Shangri-La Bosphorus, Istanbul, conveniently located on the Bosphorus, is an elegant sanctuary offering caring and attentive Shangri-La Hospitality from the heart.*

This was translated into the three very clear corporate objectives stated earlier: to be the first choice for guests, colleagues, shareholders and business partners; to be the market leader in terms of Revenue per Available Room ("RevPAR"); and to be recognized as the best hotel in Istanbul.

CHALLENGES DURING THE PRE-LAUNCH STAGE

When Yilmaz first arrived in Turkey in August 23, 2011, he realized that it was highly unlikely that the project would be completed as planned in November 2012, as the construction was far from being completed. He said,

> *When I joined, I realized that the three key challenges pre-opening were focusing and dealing with the projects during the construction stage, getting the Human Relations team in place, and working closely with the local partner.*

RECRUITING THE 'RIGHT' TALENT

In June 2010, a report by the global Deloitte Research team, 'Hospitality 2015' stated that an average hotelier spent 33% of revenue on labour costs, but continued to be plagued by employee turnover that was as high as 31% in the industry.[12] Recognizing this challenge, and accepting that getting the right talent was critical in order to deliver the exceptional service that the Shangri-La was renowned for, Yilmaz focused on recruitment. He commented,

> *I wanted to give an opportunity to the local people here, as I believe that they would know the market. We used the emotional appeal while recruiting, as the Turks are known for their national pride, as well as their emotional attachment to everything, be it personal or business.*

Putting together his senior leadership team was the first step. While Yilmaz managed to recruit most of his Executive Committee by mid-2012, he did not have any success in recruiting a local for the key position of Director Sales and & Marketing. It was finally decided to relocate Stanley Tan, an experienced Shangri-La hand, from Shangri-La Tokyo to take over this position in July 2012.

The next key decision taken was that the new hotel would create its own website to aid its recruitment. This was quite novel, as in the past no hotel in Turkey had recruited in such a manner. Yilmaz believed that by doing so, there was far more confidentiality in the process, and it also avoided the 'mass recruitment' fairs that were popular. The recruitment drive was very successful, bringing in a large number of applicants.[13] Over 15,000 applications were received for the approximately 300 positions across the hotel. Each one of these applicants was screened, and around 5,500 were interviewed.

Yilmaz elaborated,

> *As a GM, I interviewed around 3,700 applicants - from senior executives, all the way to a steward - because our main purpose was to find the right person for the right position. This was also a way for us to reveal our Shangri-La core culture, to show that we are humble, and that we give everyone equal opportunities. And of course, every General Manager has a way to interview. My strengths were that I spoke the language and knew the culture.*

Tan too joined in the recruitment drive, and like Yilmaz, interviewed scores of potential applicants. Commenting on the process, Tan remarked,

> *Everybody was sending their friend's resume to me. So even if it was a person I had interviewed and rejected, this person too would probably send me somebody else's resume to consider.*

And, so that was a bit of a cultural shock for me. I've never experienced something like that. I've probably seen half of all the hoteliers in this market. So while that was good, it was also time consuming.

Yet, on interviewing the applicants, it was found that most thought that given Shangri-La's ultra-luxury-hotel status, they could expect a much higher salary than what they were currently making at a competitor. Moreover, most of the applicants were very young and did not have the necessary experience or maturity needed for the job, and had reached the position they had by moving around the hospitality industry every other year. In addition, as Istanbul had in the last few years enjoyed a phenomenal growth in its hospitality industry, most applicants, even those in a managerial position, had not experienced any economic downturn. Thus, they had not learnt sales strategies, and their idea of sales tactics was limited to increasing the number of sales calls and corporate entertainment.

Yilmaz concluded,

We had to really look for those needles in the haystack - those who had the right attitude and the ability to fit in our hotel.

TRAINING THE TALENT

All applicants selected had to attend a one-week orientation before they started on the job. There were considerable challenges faced in training these new employees. To begin with, there was not enough space to put all the people together. To manage this issue, many separate training schedules for smaller-sized groups were set up, and batches of trainers were brought in from the other Group hotels. The training was not only about teaching the policies and procedures of core modules such as "delighting the customer", but was also an opportunity to bring together the new employees into a team.

Yilmaz commented,

In our orientation programmes, we used a lot of emotion to talk about the Shangri-La brand, the Shangri-La culture, our core values, why

we are here, why our brand is different from the others... Through this, we inspire our people to do a great job, a better job. Rather than making them act like robots, we encourage them to act as role models. We always tell them that we are a family, and we share something powerful: our genuine care and respect for others. This belief shapes us, it shapes the way we treat all people - with selfless sincerity and thoughtful courtesy, understanding needs and sharing feelings. It shapes the way we transform our gracious and enchanting Asian manner to authentic experiences, straight from the heart.

There was also important training conducted on using the Shangri-La operating systems. This was conducted for all staff 3 to 4 months before the launch.

DELAYS IN THE PROJECT: CHALLENGES IN SALES AND MARKETING

There were several delays in the opening of the hotel. While originally scheduled for November 2012, it was then postponed to February 2013, again to the beginning of March 2013, and finally to May 2013. During this period of time, there was a push to complete the outstanding projects at a frenetic pace.

The most critical project outstanding was the construction of the hotel building itself. The architectural plans for the hotel remained fluid for some time, and were only crystallized about a year prior to opening. Even then, changes had to be made along the way. Tan commented,

I think the first and most important point is to just settle the basic information or facts about the hotel – such as the room types and how many restaurants and functions rooms would there be. Because it is with this very primary information about the hotel that I would fill up all the templates, such as the one on our new hotel brief. Once I had the new hotel brief, I could also start sending out information to the advertising agencies and everybody in the Shangri-La group, and all our sales force around the world can help talk about and promote the hotel... But the plans kept changing.

Undoubtedly the frequent changes in the opening date also had a number of implications in terms of sales and marketing, as the pre-opening media buzz and publicity could not be gained. Yilmaz elaborated:

Because of the delays in the project getting completed, our hotel's restaurants, health clubs and spas could not be promoted in time, as we could hardly invite journalists to come wearing a hard hat! Even as late as the beginning of May, when clients came for inspection, they could not visualize our finished product. Many weddings and social events could not be confirmed as a result. The inability to predict an official opening date in advance also had a domino effect on our Start Sell date, website launch, media and digital marketing efforts, which was a real challenge to us. There was also a lack of selling tools. Unlike other pre-opening hotels, we did not have any high quality 3D renderings.

It was decided to commission a local design firm to come up with a few renderings, although this was an expensive and time consuming proposition. Moreover, a local photographer was employed to take a few photographs of a show room some months before the opening, and these were then used for promotion purposes.

But all was not rough. As Yilmaz commented,

It really helped us that Istanbul had been growing as a tourist city, and our hotel location as well as the Shangri-La name worked a lot in our favour. We made trips to the US, South America (Brazil), London, Barcelona, the Middle East – as these were important markets for us. We also registered ourselves in the luxury travel market... I then went to travel and hospitality schools, and had a great response as I promised them future opportunities in terms of practical training, etc. All this not only spread publicity, but also projected the image of the Shangri-La.

The time was also gainfully used in doing considerable research to come up with a story for the hotel – which entailed finding out more about Istanbul, and what was fascinating about the city.

Travel agents and Destination Management Companies that included tour operators were invited to view the renderings and see how the hotel would look like, despite it being under construction. These were people who had heard of the Shangri-La brand, and so bookings were made, even though there was uncertainty whether the hotel would be opened on schedule. Tan explained,

Hoteliers talk to each other, and everybody in this market had very high regard for the Shangri-La brand. All of them know it is Asian, with the best location in the city, that somehow that it's going to be really luxurious, and have service that is indisputable. So despite being aware of some of our 'hardware' challenges, such as the lack of an outdoor pool, many people booked with us. I was also very lucky because all our sales people take great pride in their work, and they have the contacts. They are very popular but yet they are humble people who treat the guests with courtesy and respect. The clients liked that and actually booked with us - ensuring that we had some occupancy when we opened our doors.

RECOGNIZING THE COMPETITION ... AND PRICING ACCORDINGLY

When the Shangri-La was to be launched in Istanbul, the city already had around 20 to 25 five-star hotels. As a well-established hotel in the market for 21 years, Çıragan Palace Kempinski ("Kempinski") had a high reputation in the local and international market, and was, by far, the market leader. The other strong brand in the market was the Ritz Carlton, which had been operating since 2001, and targeted the same luxury market segment as the Kempinski.

But it was in 2008 that the Kempinski ceased to be the preferred hotel for any luxury business in all segments, when the Four Seasons Bosphorus opened, and became its main competitor. The two hotels shared the same key selling points in terms of the location on the Bosphorus and strong brand name in the luxury market. Moreover, as both hotels had the capacity to cater to the same segments (transient, groups and social events); the Four Seasons took away a lot of Kempinski's business volume.

Later in the same year, in November 2008, the Park Hyatt Istanbul – Macka Palas opened, as a new, luxury and boutique hotel in the market. It was positioned as an elegant and classy hotel with the best room product in the city, complemented by a friendly and service oriented team. The Park Hyatt did take some corporate business away from the top producing accounts of the Kempinski, but was not perceived to be at the same level of competition as the Four Seasons. Another new brand, which also opened in 2008, was the W hotel. Although the brand was not well known in the local market, the trendy style of the hotel made it an attractive spot, especially for the younger crowd. The W's initial room rate was targeted to be in line with the above mentioned hotels, and they started off with high rates - however it was unable to sustain this strategy as it could not attract occupancy. Thereafter the hotel dropped its rates, and became very flexible in its pricing. Finally, another well-known boutique hotel was the local brand SOFA Hotel, which had 82 rooms, and was considered to be in direct competition to the W Hotel and Park Hyatt Hotel.

Elaborating on the competitor analysis, Tan explained,

> If you are not on the Bosphorus, there's no way you can be considered a luxury hotel. So regardless of how good these hotels are – and you have many good hotels here - Park Hyatt, Ritz Carlton, Movenpick, the Swissotel, the Conrad... - and they are all five-star hotels – but their rates will be in the range of 200-300 Euros. It is only on the Bosphorus that you can charge a rate like 500-600 Euros, which these two hotels, the Four Seasons and the Kempinski, are enjoying. So, we are on the Bosphorus too, and we are trying to emulate their rates, and hopefully we'll be successful.

The pre-opening days were thus a good time to assess where the Shangri-La Bosphorus should be positioned vis-à-vis the competition. Because of its location by the Bosphorus, hotels such as the Kempinski and the Four Seasons, which were also along the Bosphorus, were included. The other two hotels that were considered primary competitors were the Ritz Carlton and the Park Hyatt. Shangri-La typically shared a number of its global clientele with all four of these perceived competitors. Moreover, these hotels were part of the American Express Fine Hotels and Resorts programme. They also participated in the Virtuoso programme. Virtuoso was the industry's leading luxury travel network and a by-invitation-only organization. Using its marketing funds and brand name, Shangri-La Bosphorus successfully became part of the exclusive Preview programme from Virtuoso - which brought it considerable recognition. A detailed study of each of these hotels was conducted to understand where and how best the Shangri-La could position itself (refer to **Exhibit 7** for further details).

Based on the above analysis, and its own internal anticipated revenue model, a rate chart with six clear tiers was prepared. This chart also took into account the anticipated seasonal flow of guests (refer to **Exhibit 8** for details on the rate chart for Shangri-La and two key competitors). However, when these rates were publicly announced, it was found that there was some resistance from the market in terms of this price point expectation, as that part of the world was largely unfamiliar with the Shangri-La brand, and it was believed that the price charged for a new yet untested hotel should be far lower than that of its competitors.

But it was of utmost importance for Shangri-La to become profitable and capture a "fair share" of the market, which could also be described as its "piece of the pie" in the market. This was measured by the RevPAR (Yield) Index, which was the hotel's RevPAR divided by the segment's RevPAR, multiplied by 100.[14] Based on the projections made for 2014, Yilmaz concluded that of all its competitors, the Four Seasons would be ranked highest in terms of the hotel's revenue share of the market, where the market represented the aggregate of the hotel and its competitors (refer to **Exhibit 9** for further details).

A SPECTACULAR LAUNCH – BUT WHAT NEXT?

Yilmaz concluded,

> *Why should people come to us? What is different from other hotels? I say that every division of this hotel has to prepare its selling points. It could be the view, the location, the fact that it's the first Asian hotel, our different uniforms, the Shangri-La hospitality, the way we greet the people at the airport and escort them directly to the room... this is the uniqueness. So marketing for us is beyond the price, and its key is our people. We need to show that we are humble and friendly, that the Shangri-La experience is about the core values - but this must be from the heart.*

Satisfied that the inauguration had gone off exceedingly well, and generated an estimated US$1 million in exposure, Yilmaz thought about the days ahead. On-going retention and development of his hand-picked employees to deliver the consistent Shangri-La service quality was a key factor that played in his mind. He also realized that the brand awareness for the newest Shangri-La hotel had to be enhanced. So far, attention had been on advertisements that appeared in the print media or on its website, but the power of digital marketing had already been tapped on in other group hotels, and it was clear that the focus would also need to include online platforms and social media (refer to **Exhibit 10** for further details on the proposed media plan). What other forms of advertising could he use to improve publicity?

What else did he need to focus on to drive the growth of the Shangri-La Bosphorus Hotel, such that the unfamiliar brand of Shangri-La in Turkey and the neighbouring markets would become the top choice for travellers to Istanbul? How could his team identify and engage influencers in this new region to drive business? How should he position Shangri-La Bosphorus against the Four Seasons and the Kempinski, despite it lacking an outdoor pool and larger grounds? Should he emphasize the views, or the only authentic Chinese dining experience to be found in Istanbul? Or should he focus on the warm, embracing Shangri-La "service from the heart" hospitality? If so, how would he convey this to potential customers, particularly from countries outside Asia, who had not previously experienced it?

Over and above positioning itself well, the financial viability of the Bosphorus project was of key importance to the Shangri-La Group and its partners. How should he make it possible for the Shangri-La Group to break-even in the shortest possible time? As Yilmaz surveyed the ballroom savouring the success of the inauguration, he approached Tan to organize a meeting of his team the next morning to discuss these issues.

ENDNOTES

1 Revenue per Available Room (RevPAR) was the total guest room revenue divided by the total number of available rooms.

2 CIA World Factbook, *Turkey*, downloaded from https://www.cia.gov/library/publications/the-world-factbook/geos/tu.html, accessed September 2013.

3 Ibid.

4 TendersInfo - News (Mumbai, India), Turkey: Turkey's tourism fastest growing in the Mediterranean, September 4, 2013, http://infoweb. newsbank.com/... multi=TN98, accessed September 2013.

5 Business Monitor International, Turkey Tourism Report Q4 2012, October 1, 2012, accessed from Ebscohost, SMU Library, http://ehis.ebscohost.com/eds/detail..., accessed September 2013.

6 Ibid.

7 Ibid.

8 Hotel News Resource, Istanbul Hotel Industry Enjoys 9% ADR Growth in Euro-terms, November 10, 2011, http://www.hotelnewsresource.com/article59366.html, accessed September 2013.

9 Elizabeth Bains, Ambitious Targets set for Tourism, *MEED: Middle East Economic Digest, 6/7/2013 Turkey & The Middle East*, July 2013, downloaded from SMU Library, accessed October 2013.

10 Ibid.

11 Hotel News Resource, Istanbul Hotel Industry Enjoys 9% ADR Growth in Euro-terms, November 10, 2011, http://www.hotelnewsresource.com/article59366.html, accessed September 2013.

12 Deloitte, *Deloitte Hospitality 2015: Seven key trends to shape future success*, June 2010, http://www.deloitte.com/view/en_GB/uk/industries/.html, accessed October 2013.

13 According to the World Bank report, as at 2011, Turkey had an unemployment rate of around 9.8%. Source: World Bank, *Unemployment*, October 2013, http://data.worldbank.org/indicator/SL.UEM.TOTL.ZS, accessed October 2013.

14 If a hotel was capturing its fair market share, the index would be 100; if capturing less than its fair market share, the index would be less than 100; and if capturing more than its fair market share, the index would be greater than 100.

15 Hotel News Now, *Hotel Industry Terms to Know*, May 24, 2013, http://www.hotelnewsnow.com/Article/3229/Hotel-Industry-Terms-to-Know#E-F, accessed December 2013.

EXHIBIT 1: FINANCIAL HIGHLIGHTS OF SHANGRI-LA ASIA LTD (IN US$ MILLION)

	Year ending December 31, 2012	Year ending December 31, 2012	Year ending December 31, 2012
Sales	2,057	1,912	1,575
Cost of Sales	(881)	(840)	(679)
Gross Profit	1,176	1,072	896
Operating Profit	302	239	51
Net Finance Costs	(79)	(44)	(24)
Profit before Income Tax	484	361	298
Income Tax expense	(102)	(77)	(37)
Net Profit	382	284	261

Note 1: On an unconsolidated basis and consistent with 2011, room revenues accounted for over 50% while food and beverage revenues accounted for over 43% of the total revenues from hotel operation. Both room revenues and food and beverage revenues increased 8% to US$1,274.1 million and US$1,103.4 million, respectively over 2011.

Note 2: Net profit attributable to equity holders of the Company from hotel operation, property rental from investment properties and hotel management increased by US$9.9 million, US$19.6 million and US$10.3 million, respectively.

Source: Shangri-La Group, Consolidated Income Statement 2012 and 2010, http://www.brandequity.com.my/web/images/stories/pdfstore/communications/companyannualreports/Shangri%20La%20Hotels%20Malaysia%20Berhad%20Part1.pdf; and http://pg.jrj.com.cn/acc/HK_DISC/stock_time/2011/04/26/001194522-0.PDF, accessed September 2013.

EXHIBIT 2: SHANGRI-LA ASIA LTD - WEIGHTED AVERAGE ROOM YIELDS ("REVPAR")

	2012 Weighted Average			2011 Weighted Average		
	Occupancy (%)	Transient Room Rate (US$)	RevPAR (US$)	Occupancy (%)	Transient Room Rate (US$)	RevPAR (US$)
Hong Kong	80	336	264	80	327	258
Mainland China	59	166	95	62	155	94
Singapore	75	257	198	73	250	193
Malaysia	73	145	106	70	138	97
The Philippines	71	201	148	71	184	131

EXHIBIT 2: SHANGRI-LA ASIA LTD - WEIGHTED AVERAGE ROOM YIELDS ("REVPAR") (*CONTINUED*)

	2012 Weighted Average			2011 Weighted Average		
	Occupancy (%)	Transient Room Rate (US$)	RevPAR (US$)	Occupancy (%)	Transient Room Rate (US$)	RevPAR (US$)
Japan	70	521	355	56	493	273
Thailand	60	152	90	46	155	68
France	82	1,289	982	55	1,296	623
Australia	77	237	181	73	172	122
Other countries	64	200	128	67	183	121
Subsidiaries and associates	64	196	125	65	182	117

Source: Shangri-La Asia Ltd Group, Annual Report 2012, http://quote.morningstar.com/stock-filing/Annual- Report/2012/12/31/t. aspx?t=PINX:SHALY&ft=&d=5e3b6ec0d6e999a2ec7763891bea89ae, accessed September 2013.

EXHIBIT 3: KEY MILESTONE EVENTS OF SHANGRI-LA ASIA LTD – 1940 TO 2011

1940s	
1949	Parent company, the Kuok Group, is established
1970s	
1971	Shangri-La Hotel, Singapore, opens under the management of Western International Hotels
1979	Kuok Hotels is formed to manage three properties: Shangri-La's Rasa Sayang Resort and Spa, Penang-Golden Sands Resort, Malaysia, and The Fijian, Yanuca Island, Fiji
1980s	
1982	Shangri-La International Hotel Management Ltd. is founded
1984	Shangri-La International Hotel Management Ltd. assumes management of Shangri-La Hotel, Singapore
1984	First hotel in China opens in Hangzhou
1986	Shangri-La Hotel, Bangkok opens (the first Shangri-La hotel in Thailand)
1989	First Traders hotel opens in Beijing
1990s	
1991	Shangri-La International Hotel Management Ltd. assumes management of all owned properties
1992	Shangri-La enters the Philippines with Edsa Shangri-La, Manila
1993	Shangri-La Asia Limited goes public
1994	Shangri-La enters Indonesia with Shangri-La Hotel, Jakarta
1997	Golden Circle guest loyalty programme is introduced
1997	Shangri-La Asia Limited buys Shangri-La International Hotel Management Ltd.
2000s	
2003	Shangri-La enters Australia with Shangri-La Hotel, Sydney
2003	Shangri-La enters the Middle Eastern market with Shangri-La Hotel, Dubai

2004	Shangri-La Academy opens near Beijing
2005	First CHI, The Spa, opens in Bangkok, Thailand
2005	Shangri-La enters India with Shangri-La's Eros Hotel, New Delhi
2009	Shangri-La enters North America with Shangri-La Hotel, Vancouver
2009	Shangri-La Hotel, Tokyo, opens the first Shangri-La hotel in Japan
2010s	
2010	Shangri-La launches new global brand campaign "It's In Our Nature" 2010 Golden Circle Loyalty Programme introduces Golden Circle Awards 2010 Shangri-La enters the European market with Shangri-La Hotel, Paris
2011	Introduction of Kerry Hotels brand with the opening of Kerry Hotel Pudong, Shanghai

Source: Shangri-La Group (2012), Company Milestones, http://www.shangri-la.com/corporate/about-us/milestones/, accessed September 2013.

EXHIBIT 4: VISITOR INFLOW TO TURKEY – 2009 TO 2016

	2009	2010	2011	2012	2013	2014	2015	2016
Arrivals (in '000s)	27,093	28,637	31,462	31,982	33,736	36,180	38,826	41,537
Tourists (in '000s)	25,913	27,392	30,098	30,595	32,275	34,616	37,151	39,747
Percentage change (year-on-year)	3.7	5.7	9.9	1.7	5.5	7.3	7.3	7.0
Tourist arrivals by purpose of trip ('000)								
	2009	2010	2011	2012	2013	2014	2015	2016
Leisure	20,072	21,173	23,189	23,559	24,811	26,554	28,441	30,375
Business	2,607	2,718	2,922	2,959	3,086	3,262	3,453	3,648
Other	4,414	4,745	5,352	5,463	5,840	6,364	6,932	7,514

Note: Business Monitor International forecast Regional data was used to estimate the number of tourists. Proportions of UNWTO data were used to estimate historical data. Source: UNWTO, Turkstat
Source: Business Monitor International, Turkey Tourism Report. Q4 2012, October 1, 2012, accessed from Ebscohost, SMU Library, http://ehis.ebscohost.com/eds/detail?, accessed September 2013.

EXHIBIT 5: THE HOTEL OPERATORS IN TURKEY AS AT FOURTH QUARTER 2012

The major international hotel operators in Turkey's prime accommodation centres were Hilton Worldwide, Maritim, Iberotel, Radisson, Mövenpick, InterContinental Hotels Group (IHG), Marriott and Sheraton. The largest operators in the domestic sector were Dedeman Hotels & Resorts International, Taksim International and the Doğuş Tourism Group.

Some of the new hotel developments that took place over 2012 were as follows:
• In August 2012, Marriott opened its ninth hotel in Turkey, under a franchise agreement with Polat Holding. This was the 212-rooms Renaissance Istanbul Bosphorus Hotel.
• In mid-2012, Swissôtel Hotels & Resorts announced plans to operate two new properties in southwest Turkey near the city of Bodrum, on the Aegean Sea. The group already operated three hotels in Turkey.

(Continued)

EXHIBIT 5: THE HOTEL OPERATORS IN TURKEY AS AT FOURTH QUARTER 2012 (*CONTINUED*)

- In May, Hilton Worldwide opened its first dual-branded property in Turkey, the 187-room Hilton Bursa Convention Center & Spa and the budget 107-room Hampton by Hilton Bursa.
- In the second quarter of 2012, Rotana signed an agreement with Rhossos Tourism and Hospitality to manage the 300-room Rhossos Rotana Resort and Serviced Apartments. This would be Rotana's first hotel in Turkey, due to open in 2014 in the southern port city of Iskenderun.
- US luxury hotel management company Viceroy Hotel Group would enter Europe in Istanbul, to operate the 58-unit Viceroy Istanbul, a five-star urban resort, expected to open in late 2013.
- In early 2012, Rezidor opened its third hotel in Istanbul, the 195-rooms Radisson Blu Hotel Istanbul Asia.
- The Dubai-based Jumeirah Group signed a management agreement with Istanbul-based Demsa Group to operate the Pera Palace Hotel. From the beginning of May 2012, the 115-room hotel became the Pera Palace Hotel Jumeirah.
- In early 2012, Dedeman Hotels & Resorts signed a management agreement with Apeas Engineering and Consultation for 10 Dedeman Park hotels, which would open over the next five years in Turkey, Kazakhstan and Russia.
- It was reported in February 2012 that Hong Kong-based group Mandarin Oriental would make its debut in Turkey, managing the Mandarin Oriental, Bodrum, which is expected to open in 2014 on the Bodrum peninsula on the Aegean coast. The resort would be owned and developed by Astas Real Estate and Tourism.
- After considerable expansion by Hilton Worldwide in Turkey in 2011, the group announced further hotels in the country over the next few years. By the end of 2013, Hilton expected to have 33 hotels in operation in Turkey.
- At the start of 2012, Starwood Hotels & Resorts' Le Méridien brand made its debut in Turkey with the opening of the 259-room Le Méridien Istanbul Etiler on the city's European side, overlooking the Bosphorus. Starwood Hotels & Resorts also signed an agreement with Serka Turizm, an affiliate of Istanbul-based construction group Adali Holding, for a new hotel in Turkey, on the banks of the River Seyhan, in Adana.
- In December 2011, Morgans Hotel Group signed a management agreement for Mondrian Istanbul, which is expected to open in 2012.
- The US-based Wyndham Hotel Group signed a franchise agreement with Reisler Deri Sanayi Ve Ticaret Limited Siketi for its second hotel, Wyndham Istanbul Kalamis Marina, due to open in 2012 in Istanbul. It was further reported that the Group was planning to open its first hotel in Turkey, the Wyndham Petek Istanbul, in autumn 2012.

Source: Business Monitor International, Turkey Tourism Report. Q4 2012, October 1, 2012, accessed from Ebscohost, SMU Library, http://ehis.ebscohost.com/eds/detail?, accessed September 2013.

EXHIBIT 6: THE POSITIONING STATEMENT OF THE SHANGRI-LA BOSPHORUS

To the affluent guests, Shangri-La Bosphorus, Istanbul, conveniently located on the Bosphorus, is an elegant sanctuary offering caring and attentive Shangri-La Hospitality from the heart.

Shangri-La Bosphorus, Istanbul : What it Means	Asian, unique, CHI Spa, Chinese restaurant, luxury brand, progressive, quality, oriental, authentic, delicious cuisine, luxurious amenities, kids-friendly, exclusive, urban resort/resort city, joint management
Luxurious	To be 'pampered', 'best quality', uncompromising standards, right of guests to be 'demanding'. Luxury hotel, competitive with Four Seasons, Kempinski, Park Hyatt, Ritz-Carlton, etc.
Conveniently located	Efficient, saves time, central, accessible, ease of travel, hassle- free
Elegant	Stylish, ambience, elegant
Sanctuary	Heaven, comfort, safe, peaceful, cosy, 'wolf', hideaway
Caring	Warm, family, one- stop shop, kind
Attentive	High technology, treated like a king, professional staff, personalised service, anticipation of needs, smile, proactive, organised, disciplined, anticipative
Shangri-La Hospitality	Staff with positive attitude, making guests feel recognized, making guests feel like a king, smile, beautiful and handsome staff, skilful, pleasant, our core values
Istanbul	Vibrant, busy, with iconic Bosphorus, excitable, active, contrastive, 'hectic', hilly, lively

(Continued)

EXHIBIT 6: THE POSITIONING STATEMENT OF THE SHANGRI-LA BOSPHORUS

There was a strong five-point strategy to achieve the above objectives:

• Constantly provide the most memorable experience to guests who enjoy a comfortable haven in the hustle and bustle of the busy Bosphorus and city (consistent level of quality in service, amenities and culinary offerings)
• Use effective tools to maximise revenue and increase profit
• Treat partners with courtesy and respect to ensure a win-win partnership
• Ensure colleagues are given proper training and career development in a fair environment
• Practice team work and helpful coordination among departments to ensure success in operations

Source: Company data.

EXHIBIT 7: SHANGRI-LA'S COMPETITOR ANALYSIS

	Four Seasons Bosphorus (166 rooms)	Çıragan Palace Kempinski (313 rooms)	Park Hyatt Istanbul – Maçka Palas (90 rooms)	Ritz Carlton (244 rooms)
Location	Located on the shores of the Bosphorus	Located on the shores of the Bosphorus	No view of the Bosphorus	Bosphorus view rooms
	Further from the business district and old city		Located within the famous shopping & entertainment district, steps away from trendy cafes, bars and restaurants, close to the business district. Often traffic congestion around the hotel. Noisy	Located in the congress valley, close to Dolmabahçe Palace and Taksim square. Noisy. Located on a hill, so difficult to walk to
Brand Image and Customer base	Strong brand image and strong in the US market. As the second Four Seasons hotel in Istanbul, benefited from the existing hotel's database	Strong international image	Business opportunities through the owning company	Strong in the US market. Business opportunities through the owning company
Building	Landmark building	Landmark Ottoman Palace building	Historical building blending history with contemporary luxury. Entrance not well located, and on the side street	High rise multi-purpose building
Rooms	Most of the rooms do not have Bosphorus view	Rooms overlooking the park, and some are worn down	Rain shower, light therapy and heated floors. Low number of rooms. Many different room shapes due to it being a historical building	Rooms without balcony / terrace

EXHIBIT 7: SHANGRI-LA'S COMPETITOR ANALYSIS (*CONTINUED*)

Facilities	Outdoor banquet facilities and some meeting rooms with Bosphorus view		Innovative lobby featuring a wine lounge Limited meeting facilities	Small lobby Lobby lounge, some meeting rooms, foyer area with Bosphorus view Bar with large collection of malt whiskies and premium cigars
	Famous for local and international weddings and social functions	Famous for local and international weddings and social functions		Exclusive privileges in the Club Lounge
	Private dock	Private dock and heli-pad	Limited car parking space	Small car park not run by the hotel
	Heated outdoor pool with whirlpool overlooking the Bosphorus	Outdoors swimming pool		Very limited outdoor facilities (no outdoor pool)
	Spacious spa with indoor pool		Spacious spa rooms with extensive facilities including Turkish 'hammam'	Spa with indoor swimming pool
Membership and loyalty programmes	Member of Virtuoso, Amex Fine Hotels and Signature	Member of Virtuoso, LHW and Signature	Member of Virtuoso and Signature	Member of Virtuoso
	No loyalty programme	Loyalty Programme - Global Hotel Alliance	Loyalty programme (Gold Passport & Meeting Dividends)	Loyalty Programme - Ritz Carlton Rewards

Source: Company data.

EXHIBIT 8: ROOM TYPES/BAR RATES OF SHANGRI-LA BOSPHORUS, FOUR SEASONS HOTEL ISTANBUL AND CIRAGAN PALACE KEMPINSKI, ISTANBUL (IN EUROS)

Shangri-La Hotel Bosphorus			
	Size (in square metres)	**Lowest Price**	**Highest Price**
Deluxe Room	42–60	350	600
Deluxe City View Room	42–60	390	640
Deluxe Bosphorus View Room	42–60	440	690
Premier Bosphorus View Room	42–60	500	850
Grand Premier Bosphorus	42–60	700	1.350
Executive Suite	80	1.000	3.000
Executive Bosphorus Suite	100	1.500	3.500

Bosphorus Duplex Suite	100	2.500	4.500
Deluxe Bosphorus Suite	110	4.000	6.000
Barbaros Suite	180	8.000	8.000
Shangri-La Suite	366	25.000	25.000

Low Season:	January, February, December
Shoulder Season:	March, November
High Season:	April, May, June, July, August

Note: Although July and August were low season months for Istanbul, these two months could be considered more as a high season for the hotels located on the Bosphorus. If these months overlapped with the fasting period in Ramadan, the business level would go down; however the *Eid* period would reach its peak, especially with business from the Middle East.

Four Seasons Hotel Istanbul at the Bosphorus			
	Size (in square metres)	Lowest Price	Highest Price
Superior Room	38–45	350	510
Courtyard Room	38–45	380	540
Deluxe Room	38–45	490	650
Palace Courtyard	40–55	460	680
Palace Bosphorus Room	40–55		
Junior Suite	60–65	1.000	1.400
Palace Roof Suite	60–65	1.400	1.600
One Bedroom Bosphorus Suite	80	2.250	3.500
One Bedroom Bosphorus Palace Suite	80	5.000	6.000
Two Bedroom Bosphorus Palace Suite	170	6.500	7.500
Atik Pasha Suite	350	25.000	25.000
1 Bedroom Bosphorus View Palace Suite	97		
3 Bedroom Corner Palace Suite	196		
2 Bedroom Corner Palace Suite	138		
Presidential (Pasha) Suite	156		
Sultan Suite	458		

(*Continued*)

Ciragan Palace Kempinski, Istanbul			
	Size (in square metres)	Lowest	Highest
Park View Room	32	340	540
Superior Bosphorus View	32	425	680
Deluxe Bosphorus View	65	600	1.250
Grand Deluxe Bosphorus View	50	800	1.450
Studio Suite	54	800	1.550
1 Bedroom Park View Palace Suite	52–72	750	2.000
Lale or Superior Bosphorus Suite	111–139	1.350	2.400
One Bedroom Suite	66	1.400	2.500
2 Bedroom Park View Palace Suite	152	1.350	3.850
Vezir Suite	72	2.500	5.500

Source: Company data.

EXHIBIT 9: PROJECTED ADR AND REVPAR FOR SHANGRI-LA'S KEY COMPETITORS IN 2014

	Four Seasons	Kempinski	Ritz Carlton	Park Hyatt
Number of rooms	170	313	244	90
Available Room Nights	62,050	114,245	89,060	32,850
Room Nights Used	46,750	88,742	72,673	23,196
Occupancy Percentage	75%	78%	82%	71%
Room Revenue (*in Euro*)	26,086,500	42,862,386	19,767,056	5,729,412
Market Penetration Index*	97%	100%	105%	91%
Average Daily Rate* (*in Euro*)	558	483	272	247
Average Rate Index*	134%	116%	65%	59%
Revenue per Available Room (*in Euro*)*	420	375	222	174
Revenue Generator Index (RGI)*	130%	116%	69%	54%
RGI ranking	1 of 4	2 of 4	3 of 4	4 of 4

* Terms used by the hotel industry:[15]
- **MPI - Market Penetration Index** measured the hotel's occupancy results versus the average occupancy of its competitors.
- **ADR - Average Daily Rate** was a measure of the average rate paid for rooms sold, calculated by dividing room revenue by rooms sold.
- **ARI - Average Rate Index** measured the Average Room Rate (ARR) versus the average ARR of competitors.
- **RevPAR - Revenue per available room** was the total guest room revenue divided by the total number of available rooms. This differed from ADR because it was affected by the amount of unoccupied available rooms, while ADR only showed the average rate of rooms actually sold. Occupancy × ADR = RevPAR
- **RGI - Revenue Generator Index** reflected the hotel's revenue share of the market, where the market represented the aggregate of the hotel and its competitors. RGI should be above 100 (Index base 100).

Source: Company data.

EXHIBIT 10: SHANGRI-LA'S PROPOSED MEDIA PLAN – JUNE–DECEMBER 2013

Market Focus	Nature/Type	Title	Circulation	Frequency	Format
Offline (66%)					
Global	Luxury Lifestyle	F.T. - How To Spend It (WW)	337,700	30 times a year	Full Page 4C
Global	Inflight TV Billboard	CX Billboard in Short Feature		Monthly	5-sec
Global	Inflight TV Billboard	SIA TV Billboard (After Language Menu) All Aircrafts	100% flights	Monthly	5-sec
Global	Design	Monocle	72,000	Monthly	Full Page 4C
Hong Kong	Lifestyle Magazine	SCMP Post Magazine	73,342	Weekly	Full Page 4C
Russia	Travel	Conde Nast Traveller	70,000	Monthly	Full Page 4C
UK	British Airways, First Class	First Life	19,500	Bi - Monthly	Full Page 4C
Germany	Inflight - Lufthansa Airlines	Lufthansa - Exclusive	301,144	Monthly	Full Page 4C
Germany	Inflight TV Billboard	Lufthansa - TV Prog Opener	-	Monthly	5-sec
UK	Travel	Conde Nast Traveller UK	80,898	Monthly	Full Page 4C
US	Travel	Departures	875,000	Monthly	Full Page 4C
US	Travel	Travel & Leisure	871,513	Monthly	Full Page 4C
Turkey	Local Magazine	The Guide Istanbul	25,000	Bi-monthly	Full Page 4C
Turkey	Local Magazine	Capital	13,000	Monthly	Full Page 4C
Turkey	Local Magazine	Robb Report	7,411	Monthly	Full Page 4C
Turkey	Local Magazine	Alem	14,000	Weekly	Full Page 4C
Turkey	Inflight TV Billboard	THY Airshow (Turkish Airlines)	149 Aircrafts	-	10-sec
Turkey	Inflight TV Billboard	Sun Express Airshow	19 Aircrafts	-	10-sec
Middle East	Travel Trade	TTG MENA Luxury	6,000	Quarterly	Full Page 4C
UAE	Travel	Ultra Travel	65,000	7 times a year	Full Page 4C - Page 3
Middle East	Travel	Kanoo Travel	22,953	Monthly	Full Page 4C
Middle East	Lifestyle magazine	Sayidaty	138,907	Weekly	Full Page 4C
Middle East	Lifestyle magazine	Zahrat Al Khaleej	198,375	Weekly	Full Page 4C
Middle East	Lifestyle magazine	Laha	135,515	Weekly	Full Page 4C

EXHIBIT 10: SHANGRI-LA'S PROPOSED MEDIA PLAN – JUNE–DECEMBER 2013 (*CONTINUED*)

Market Focus	Nature/Type	Title	Circulation	Frequency	Format
Online (34%)					
Europe	News	BBC / Homepage, Travel, News, Business, ROS	1,573,500	Daily	Video LREC / LREC
Europe	News	BBC / iPad	398,955	Daily	Half Page
Europe	News	FT / Business Position: C-Suites	406,566	Daily	Video LREC / LREC
Europe	News	HowToSpendIt / iPad	374,000	Daily	Video LREC / LREC
USA	News	CNN / Homepage, Run of Businesss	420,000	Daily	Video LREC / LREC
Turkey, Russia, Middle East, Asia	Business / Travel	Google / Run of Business and Travel	11,666,667	Daily	Banners
Turkey, Russia, Middle East, Asia	Business / Travel	Tribal Fusion / Run of Business and Travel	8,641,975	Daily	Banners/ Video LREC
Middle East, Saudi Arabia	Business / Travel	Tribal Fusion / Run of Business and Travel	8,641,975	Daily	Banners/ Video LREC

Source: Company data.

CASE 7   LIVERPOOL VICTORIA (LV): ACHIEVING BUSINESS TURN-AROUND THROUGH EMPLOYEE ENGAGEMENT

This case was written by Luke Fletcher under the direction of Professor Katie Truss, Kent Business School, University of Kent. © 2013, University of Kent

Back in the summer of 2006, the General Insurance (GI) division of Liverpool Victoria (as the company was known then) was in crisis, with huge financial losses of £22 million a year, customer attrition running at a rate of 10,000 a month. Internally, staff morale was at an all-time low, with turnover as high as 60% in some areas. The company was obliged to make redundancies whilst at the same time trying to cope with an outdated and under-resourced technological infrastructure. A radical transformation was needed to prevent the GI business from total collapse.

The transformation started swiftly from September 2006 and was tackled on several fronts. However, the company recognized that key to it all was people. It quickly became apparent, through initial plans and actions, that this was going to involve more than just developing employees' customer service skills, and would encompass a total turn-around to create an engaged workforce that was willing to go the extra mile for their customers, their colleagues and the company.

This case study tells the story of this transformation from an employee engagement perspective from when it began in the autumn of 2006, to where it is now in the spring of 2012. From interviews with key people involved (Peter Horton – GI Chief Operating Officer, Karen Sharpe – Head of Internal Communications and GI Engagement; and Nicola Dunning – Regional Manager and GI Engage Champion) as well as from a focus group with a range of frontline staff, this case study outlines

the key problems, solutions, and challenges along the way, as well as plans for the future. It is by no means the full and complete picture, but it gives a concise and comprehensive narrative that aims to provide evidence that employee engagement can be a useful way of leveraging competitive advantage and achieving business success.

THE BACKGROUND

In 1843 Liverpool Victoria was established with the aim of "making financial security and peace of mind available to more than just the privileged few" (www.lv.com). Starting from humble beginnings as a burial society, it gradually acquired other mutuals and societies to become LV= the UK's largest 'friendly society' (mutual) with over 5,500 employees in 17 locations across the UK, over 4 million customers and members, and an underlying profit of

£99.4 million in 2011 (LV= Annual Report, 2012).

Currently, there are two financial product ranges: a) General Insurance – that covers motor, home, pet, travel, and breakdown cover; and b) Life and Pensions – that covers income protection, mortgage payment protection, retirement products, and life and critical illness cover.

By 2006, the Life and Pensions Division had been financially stable over several years, generating an underlying profit of £30-40 million. In contrast, the General Insurance (GI) division had declined dramatically over the previous few years and achieved a loss of £22 million in 2006. With such a dip in financial performance, Liverpool Victoria knew they had to make some radical changes to the GI division, and so sought out a new senior management team that could turn its fortunes around.

During this time, a newly-formed insurance company, ABC Insurance, led by John O'Roarke was seeking capital to establish itself in the marketplace. During negotiations for investment, Liverpool Victoria offered to acquire ABC Insurance, so that they could secure the talent of its reputable executive team. This team had a vast pool of experience, having been key figures in founding and developing the successful rival firm, Churchill Insurance. Following negotiations, on 4th September 2006, Liverpool Victoria appointed their new GI Managing Director (John O'Roarke) and senior management team of the GI division (Steve Castle, - Finance Director; Phil Bunker – Broker Director, Paul Cassidy- Corporate Director, and Peter Horton – Chief Operating Officer).

Coming into the company with fresh eyes, the team could see the complexity and challenge of the task they faced. Turning the GI Division around would require interventions on several fronts: a) pricing and selling distributions of the product portfolio; b) dealing with potential fraud more effectively and efficiently; c) growing the business in lean and inorganic ways; and d) developing the expertise, customer service skills, and initiative of employees. It is this last area that is the focus of this case study. In order to deliver on the core plan, relevant expertise was brought in during the Autumn/Winter of 2006. These people included key communication and marketing specialists who were recruited externally, such as Karen Sharpe (Head of Internal Communications and GI Engagement) and Guy Hedger (Director of Marketing), as well as existing customer service managers, such as Nicola Dunning (Regional Manager and GI Engage Champion) and Peter Sinden (Director of Sales & Service).

THE PROBLEMS

The most critical issue for the new team was the regular monthly loss of 10,000 customers who were dissatisfied with the service they were being given, with the products they were being offered, and with Liverpool Victoria as a company. Moreover, there was a more deeply-rooted cultural issue that was holding Liverpool Victoria back:

> "The culture was un-dynamic, matriarchal and old-fashioned: the message was 'we'll care for you no matter how good or bad you are at your job'. So, people were not using their initiative, they were just doing the bare

minimum, and were not 'involved' in what they were doing" (Karen Sharpe, Head of Internal Communications and GI Engagement).

In consequence, people were loath to challenge poor decisions or take personal responsibility for improving performance. Customer Service Representatives noted that people did not feel empowered to discuss problems with line managers. Because performance was not being monitored and handled in a clear, standardized, and transparent way, there were ambiguous expectations of what 'good' performance looked like. Therefore, many employees felt unable to improve as they did not fully understand what they could or could not do. For example, although team leaders would monitor their direct reports' customer service calls, there were no universally acceptable or independent assessments of customer service performance. There was also a climate of hierarchical fear:

> "There was a fear culture that people didn't want to put their head above the parapet, they didn't want to speak up, and they didn't want to change anything because they were fearful of the consequences." (Nicola Dunning, Regional Manager and GI Engage Champion)

Several people commented that, at the time, senior managers adopted an 'ivory tower' mentality, rarely spending time being visible and accessible to their employees. There were no mechanisms for incentivizing and rewarding employees for exceptional or improved performance. These cultural barriers were a major challenge to overcome, as some deeply- held attitudes and habitual patterns of behaviour had to be dismantled.

Linked with this, the outdated technological infrastructure (e.g. telephone system and email system) were no longer fit for purpose and were preventing staff from delivering excellent customer service. An example comes from Mandy, a Customer Service Representative, who explained how staff at the time were expected to deal with customer queries: "We used to have a system where you would spend ages finding the question and then it would only be a one-line answer which didn't help you; and Team Leaders often came from other departments and didn't know our systems."

In addition, many crucial functions (such as Claims and HR) were outsourced in order to reduce costs. This meant that many job roles within the company became deskilled and unappealing to staff. This, as Peter Horton (GI Chief Operating Officer) reflects, "*watered down the overall skill-base within the company with the result that many of the good people were leaving*".

THE SOLUTION

From the outset, the new senior management team saw that it was the employees who held the power to make the business prosper or fail:

> "*Ultimately, it's the people that are going to make the difference for the company. If you focus on and invest in your people, they will look after your customers, who will then stay with you longer and will buy more products from you, and they become fans and so tell more people about you, which then reduce your marketing costs, and improves your profitability.*" (Peter Horton, GI Chief Operating Officer)

Peter Horton (GI Chief Operating Officer) and his colleagues recognized that in order to turn the GI division into a profitable business they had to focus on involving, empowering, and energizing their staff to go the extra mile. In this most general sense, LV = 's aim for employee engagement was, and still is, to ensure that: "*… people understand what we're trying to achieve as an organization and how they fit into that. It's about them feeling involved in the organization and it's about us meeting the aspirations that they have for themselves.*" (Karen Sharpe, Head of Internal Communications and GI Engagement).

Although LV= did not have a formalized 'Employee Engagement' strategy, senior managers had a clear, shared understanding of what it meant and what they wanted to achieve:

> "*Employee engagement is about great communication with our people and making sure that we are listening and we understand what their journey is and what their life is like on a daily basis - it's their surroundings, it's the way they get rewarded and respected, and how they can get job enrichment.*" (Peter Horton, GI Chief Operating Officer)

> "*Employee engagement means low attrition and sickness, and high customer satisfaction and staff motivation.*" (Nicola Dunning, Regional Manager & GI Engage Champion)

For LV = , employee engagement involves a broad range of initiatives that demonstrate concern for and appreciation of their staff, with an ultimate focus on customer service:

> "*It's quite broad, and I'll be honest that everything I do is centred around my people in the hope that in return my customers will be looked after.*" (Nicola Dunning, Regional Manager and GI Engage Champion)

The engagement transformation programme was multi-faceted and evolved from 2006 in three main stages: 1) The first 18 months from summer 2006 to winter 2007 when a new 'LV = ' culture was created; 2) The two-year period from January 2008 to December 2009 when the 'LV = ' culture was developed and 'lived' out; and 3) The period from January 2010 to Spring 2012 when initiatives were embedded and the 'LV = ' culture strengthened.

This six-year evolution was important because Peter Horton (GI Chief Operating Officer) and his team knew that a quick management fix or a severe short-term cost-cutting programme would not create a sustainable business that yielded long-term benefits to all stakeholders. Rather, they understood that an ambitious long-term cultural transformation was needed which would involve several intensive stages of activity.

THE TRANSFORMATION

2006 TO 2007: LV =: CREATING A NEW 'ENGAGED' CULTURE

The first year of the transformation heralded a new and dramatic shift in the way the GI Division operated. In order to effectively and efficiently embed a culture around the principles of engagement and empowerment, the management style of the executive team had to reflect these principles. However, it was also important for the senior managers to set a clear direction for the future, and so initiatives that took place during this initial 12-month period were carefully guided and directed by key decision-makers such as Peter Horton (GI Chief Operating Officer), and senior managers such as Karen Sharpe (Head of Internal Communications and GI Engagement). This top-down approach was needed during the first phase in order to achieve consistency and direction.

The senior managers not only articulated a clear purpose and vision for change, but also took the risk of enabling and empowering key line managers to take the lead on embedding a new and 'engaged' culture. This early phase of empowerment was vital in setting the tone for how the business would operate in future. Nicola Dunning, Regional Manager and GI Engage Champion, commented on the senior managers' actions at the time:

> "It was really with their direction and their willingness to take calculated risks, their backgrounds in making really successful businesses, and the fact that they allowed people to take opportunities to get involved that made the real difference - they really did truly empower people. They could have just told us exactly what they wanted to do and done things faster because they knew what they were doing. But, if they did those things then they would have lost a lot of people, and the cost of recruitment would have outweighed the value."

Peter Horton (GI Chief Operating Officer) also realized that the lack of powerful and ambitious vision was holding the company back from engaging its staff successfully. One of the first actions taken was to communicate a clear, challenging, yet attainable vision, and a company-wide re-branding. These were led by Guy Hedger, GI's Marketing Director, and John O'Roarke, GI Managing Director.

At the time, although the Division's largest insurance area was motor insurance; the company was only ranked 12th in the UK. John O'Roarke determined that the new vision was: **"To be a top 5 motor insurer in the UK by 2012"**. However, it was not only this vision that inspired employees, but also the linked re-branding that acted as the catalyst for change.

The aim for the new brand was to visualize the core essence of the new culture, whilst reflecting the well-established beliefs around Liverpool Victoria's status as a friendly society. The company wanted to achieve an immediate visceral and emotional impact on all stakeholders (i.e. management, employees, and customers) whereby they would all personally identify with and be motivated by the same basic principles. As Karen Sharpe (Head of Internal Communications and GI Engagement) remarked: *"the brand was to be vibrant, energetic, modern and fun. We wanted the internal culture to follow the external brand"*. And so LV= was born; a logo that exuded passion, love and warmth, with the image of a heart being used to reflect those emotions:

The rebranding re-invigorated and re-aligned employees around a desire to deliver the best customer experience. As Lee, a Customer Service Representative, said: *"On the phone, I want to be able to do everything I can for the customer and make sure that their experience is the best it can possibly be. That's just plays straight into our brand and what we want as a company."*

It was how the brand was executed that was particularly important, specifically the creation and establishment of a set of ideal values and behaviours. The overarching ethos of LV= was eloquently reflected by the principle of **'Sharp with a Heart'**. This meant being competitive, performance-driven, and efficient (i.e. 'sharp') whilst also being trustworthy, caring, and personal (i.e. 'with a heart'). In order to achieve this aim, four core values were developed that were to be upheld by all employees:

1) ***Know your stuff*** – keeping up-to-date on product and market knowledge ('finger on the pulse'), and seeking the most suitable solutions for customers ('find solutions').
2) ***Don't wait to be asked*** – being proactive and taking personal initiative in order to deliver what's best for the customer ('delivery'); as well as making suggestions for improvements and raising concerns ('courage')
3) ***Make it feel special*** – delivering a caring, compassionate, and trust-based service

('customer focus'), as well as providing leadership and mentoring to other staff ('leadership').

4) **Treat people like family** - being helpful, friendly, and supportive ('support') as well as sharing information, knowledge and experiences ('communication').

These values were felt to be particularly powerful as they enabled all employees to develop a shared identity and mind-set. However, employees needed training and development on what they meant in everyday working life:

> "The branding and values were critical and they underpinned everything that we did, and they really brought alive what we were about and what we wanted to achieve. It was really about educating our people about what the values actually meant and how they were brought alive. For example, treating people like family doesn't mean being nice to people all the time, sometimes it's about telling people what they don't want to hear." (Nicola Dunning, Regional Manager and GI Engage Champion)

In line with the vision of 'Sharp with a Heart', five core areas of LV = 's people management practices were dramatically changed in the wake of the re-branding: a) Top-down communication; b) Recruitment; c) Training and Development; d) Performance Management; and e) Reward and Recognition.

A NEW APPROACH TO TOP-DOWN COMMUNICATION

Karen Sharpe (Head of Internal Communications and GI Engagement) comments that in order to prevent many people who were used to the 'old' culture and behaviours from becoming disengaged and disgruntled, it was imperative that those implementing the changes were 'genuine, open and honest' and communicated with employees in interesting and charismatic ways. Three main mechanisms were developed:

INTERNAL MAGAZINE

The GI Heartbeat quarterly magazine is a colourful, exciting and energizing read. Packed full of fun and entertaining photographs of LV= people and LV= social events, it is delivered in a way that is more like a high-end gossip magazine than a traditional corporate newsletter:

Thus, it is not simply used to inform employees of updates and changes in the company, but rather it has a much wider appeal that includes: a) Celebrating individual and team successes, both inside work and outside volunteering activities; b) Dedicated 'one-on-one' pages discussing specific roles and teams so that everyone knows who people are and what they do; c) Personal update/discussion pages with senior management figures, such as Peter Horton (GI Chief Operating Officer); d) News-in-brief sections detailing wider market stories, changes, and updates; and e) Introductions to new people management initiatives such as Hall of Fame.

The Heartbeat magazine has been well-received by GI staff:

> "With Heartbeat you do get people from different departments that you vaguely know on there and it's like, 'Oh well done for them, they've done this', and it backs up what you're doing. And other people do notice it - it's not like that stuff just gets whacked on there just for us." (Chloe – Customer Service Representative)

INTRANET

As part of a wider need to integrate all people management practices and communication, an intranet was created to provide an interactive and personal way of centralizing all resources and information. This helped ensure that people management practices maintained consistency and unity rather than becoming separate and disparate activities. Each department has its own dedicated and regularly updated section that all employees can easily access. Furthermore, employees can keep informed of department and company performance via a graphical performance tracker widget, and keep up-to-date with news and information regarding other departments.

CORPORATE EVENTS

John O'Roarke (GI Managing Director) and other senior managers made a firm and long-term commitment to be as visible, approachable, and communicative as possible with all employees. One way of doing this was by holding a variety of corporate events at different times of the year. At a formal level, this involved holding an annual update roadshow at each of the main LV= sites, whereby senior managers would deliver annual reviews of company performance, highlights/successes during the year, and updates for the coming year. At a more informal level, this involved holding bi-annual social events which would be more about employees and managers (at all levels) getting together outside the work environment to celebrate successes. And, at a more personal level, this would be an individual senior manager visiting a site per month, and having informal discussions with a range of frontline staff regarding issues, concerns, and improvements.

Peter Horton (GI Chief Operating Officer) remarks that he often asks, 'If you were the boss today, what would change?' This open style of communication helps people see the company from the managers' perspective and feel involved. Mandy, a Customer Service Representative, commented:

> *"The new management team came in and communicated with you directly, so you could see performance going up and up, and how much better we were doing, and how much more known we were. And it showed that they had to change things. If we were not seeing how well we were doing and if they didn't tell us everything, then we'd be thinking, 'Oh no not another change'!".*

A NEW APPROACH TO RECRUITMENT

Recruitment practices were realigned to better identify those with the 'can-do' attitude, who would most likely fit with the new 'LV = ':

> *"The ideal employee is somebody who is conscientious, reliable, turns up to work on time, interacts with their team, wants the best for the customer, will make suggestions for improvements, people that will question and escalate issues, and wants to develop their skills." (Nicola Dunning, Regional Manager and GI Engage Champion)*

This involved training managers more effectively in recruitment processes, and LV = 's preferences. Training was reinforced by tools and guides in a dedicated recruitment section on the company's intranet, for example, template interview sheets and guides on behavioural style interviews.

The development of 'recruiting for attitude' has had a positive impact on staff morale and on building a supportive culture:

> *"They've done a good job at employing the right people. The people you work with are personable, and there's nobody above me that you are afraid to speak to. You don't feel awkward. They're so supportive here." (Jolene – Customer Service Representative)*

The induction process was overhauled to include a welcome presentation from an Executive Team member, and a buddy system was implemented to help newcomers get integrated within the company quickly. This helped retain good performers, and also helped embed LV = 's values and behaviours early on in the individual's life with LV=.

A NEW APPROACH TO TRAINING AND DEVELOPMENT

Training and development was seen as key to increasing motivation to develop a career within LV = , as well as enabling all employees to deliver the highest possible customer service. Building and harnessing the confidence, aspirations, and talents of employees was critical. This involved a wide range of initiatives that included:

- **LEON** – an online learning tool that allowed employees to 'dip in and out' of learning new skills and knowledge whenever they wanted. A vast array of topics was covered by LEON from technical areas such as data protection, to psychological areas such as confidence and resilience. Some learning modules, which are key to the business, must be completed by all employees every year (e.g. data protection, customer complaints etc.).
- **EVOLUTION** – a comprehensive online collection of information and updates regarding each and every General Insurance product/service.

- *Role Progression Paths* – Both vertical (e.g. moving from Customer Service Representative to Team Leader to management) and lateral (e.g. moving from sales and service to claims and motor insurance to home insurance) progression paths were introduced and actively encouraged throughout the division. If the individual is willing, then they will be encouraged and supported to progress in a way that suits them.

- *Line Trainers and Buddying Courses* – It was recognized that some high-performing employees could help other employees learn the skills needed to become competent at certain jobs, and help newcomers become integrated within the LV= culture.

Therefore, 'train-the-trainer' type programmes were developed, and they helped to create role models within the organization that other employees could aspire to.

These training and development activities have been an important factor in engaging employees:

> "It's nice to feel that you're wanted, and you're thought about. There's always been something more to learn, this job is really as fulfilling as you want it to be; you have the opportunity. It's not forced on anybody either. Also, it's nice to be able to see other people progressing and moving around in different roles. When they have that attitude you realize that you can do that yourself". (Chloe and Lee –Customer Service Representatives)

A NEW APPROACH TO PERFORMANCE MANAGEMENT

Given the company's dire financial situation, performance management was a crucial area to change. Firstly, a training initiative was developed for Team Leaders and managers that standardized and make clear the expectations for performance and for customer service, and clarified a fair and transparent route for dealing with poor performance or customer service. Secondly, Peter Horton (GI Chief Operating Officer) introduced monthly one-to- one's between each employee and their line manager, as well as monthly team meetings, with the aim of outlining expectations, reviewing performance, and giving constructive feedback on how to improve. A new appraisal system was introduced to ensure a centralized approach so that everyone understood what support/actions would be taken if their performance was below the standard required.

The approach to performance management reflected the 'Sharp with a Heart' principle – staff knew that they could get help, support, and personal encouragement before any disciplinary actions were taken (unless it was a severe issue). Moreover, Nicola Dunning (Regional Manager and GI Engage Champion) points out that although each employee has a personal performance plan with certain metrics to meet, employees should not be working in a state of fear. It was recognized that the 'fear factor' was one reason why people had previously been prevented from delivering excellent customer service:

> "Very soon into the new relationship the culture was changing. It was more of a coaching process and there wasn't the fear. If you did something wrong but to the best intentions, then we were not going to "beat you up", instead we would let you know how you could have possibly done it differently." (Nicola Dunning, Regional Manager and GI Engage Champion)

A NEW APPROACH TO REWARD AND RECOGNITION

Reward and recognition were seen as the factors that would really promote the values and behaviours in everyday working life. By investing in a fully integrated online system (My Recognition), LV= now has a comprehensive reward and recognition system that enables every employee to:

- *Submit ideas and suggestions* for improving customer service, business practices, or the employee experience. These ideas and suggestions are reviewed regularly, usually monthly, by the relevant department who assess them for potential implementation. Those who submit reasonable suggestions get an e-card and a formal thank-you, even if they are not implemented. Those that are implemented receive rewards with a monetary value. This mechanism provides a continuous loop of improvement and feedback that allows the business to save costs and time by harnessing the knowledge and insight of its own workforce rather than hiring expensive consultants. Perhaps more significantly, it empowers employees to challenge the status quo, and engages them with the purpose of making LV= a better business. Moreover, LV= try, wherever possible, to include the individual(s) who have come up with the initial improvement idea in the planning and implementation of that improvement. This has proven highly successful, and they often have 30+ projects on the go with 50+ employees involved at any one time.

- ***Recognize and say thank-you*** to other co-workers and managers who have helped them or have shown exemplary behaviour. This is usually through an e-card, but if it is particularly significant they can nominate that person for a small financial reward. Nicola Dunning (Regional Manager and GI Engage Champion) reflects that a thank- you goes a very long way to encourage both the recipient and giver to go the extra mile.
- Personalize their own rewards by choosing from a range of products/services such as drinks, shop vouchers, or one-off experiences like zorbing or riding in a sports car.

This helps to make the process much more flexible, and reinforces the idea that it is the individual who matters at LV=.

Although getting a thank-you is a fundamental cornerstone of this approach, it is through a formal monthly review process carried out by a team of managers that more significant rewards (usually a number of points that can be exchanged for personalized rewards) are given out. This review considers both the quantity and quality of improvement suggestions, recognition notes, and feedback from line managers/co-workers. This ensures that people are rewarded according to the merit of their efforts, rather than the output alone. Such merit is measured according to the LV = 's values and behaviours. This is an explicit form of positive reinforcement, and makes employees think regularly and actively about how they behave and what specific actions they can take to do better:

"My Recognition highlights the good behaviours and makes you think, 'Yes, that is something I've done well'. It makes you want to do more because otherwise you would think 'I'd just get on with it, come in and go home'. But you have the morale of your team to consider too and you also think well I got praise for doing it last month, so I'll do it again this month" (Chloe – Customer Service Representative)

Overall, the period September 2006 to December 2007 saw rapid and profound changes to many core people management practices, and so this was a time of excitement but also of stress. Transformational change is psychologically unsettling and, as Peter Horton (GI Chief Operating Officer) reflects, it was a real challenge knowing when to implement different changes and how best to manage the overall cultural shift. It was not until the period of 2008 to 2009 that these practices, described above, were fully implemented and embedded because everyone needed some time to adjust and cope with the changes.

2008 – 2009: BEING SHARP WITH A HEART: LIVING BY THE LV= VALUES EVERYDAY

During this period of time, the focus was firmly fixed on getting everyone in the business to understand the LV= brand and values and apply them to their everyday lives. The new approaches to people management and communication were finalized and embedded within this 2008-2009 period. The executive team had to deliver on their promises – they had to be seen to leading by example and by progressing with changes they had proposed. A collection of initiatives that complemented the new people management practices were developed. These extended the principle of engagement by giving all employees the opportunity to voice their opinion and their concerns, and to feel empowered to get involved and to represent LV= in external activities and events. This was not just to help increase staff morale, but also to raise the standard of customer service and the profile of LV= in the marketplace.

'WHY ON EARTHS?' AND TREATING CUSTOMERS FAIRLY

To get employees to take ownership and responsibility for the service they provided, and to voice their concerns regarding customer service processes and systems, two mechanisms were created. The first was called: 'Why on Earths?' – if an employee ever thought, 'Why am I doing this like this, why can't I do it another way that's better?' when dealing with a customer, then they can raise it straight away with a line manager. The issue and how it was or could be changed would be fed up to the Business Improvement Team (who also review improvement suggestions via My Recognition) who would examine it in more detail and give a reasoned judgement for future changes/ actions. This, according to Nicola Dunning (Regional Manager and GI Engage Champion), has saved the company a great deal of money through operational savings, and has had a positive impact on employees too.

The other mechanism introduced was, 'Treat Customers Fairly'. As well as being an FSA (Financial Services Authority) requirement, this involves employees highlighting specific situations where they feel the customer may not have been treated fairly, or needed to be treated in a different way from the company's normal procedure. In these situations, employees are encouraged to use their own judgement on how best to deal with customers, and to seek support if the issue is particularly sensitive or problematic. These are then examined by Regional Managers, such as Nicola Dunning, who make changes to the firm's customer service policies and practices if necessary, and ensures that if the employee has handled the situation particularly well, they are appropriately recognized and rewarded. An example of this is described by Nicola: *"A Customer Service Representative took a call for an elderly couple who had had a crash. Regardless of the call handling times, he got Google maps up, located a pub near to them, and phoned the pub to ask whether they could pick them up. The couple was looked after and their car was recovered. So, instead of the adviser thinking, 'I need to get on with the next call because of my average handling time', he thought,*

'I need to help this customer'" (Nicola Dunning, *Regional Manager and GI Engage Champion*)

EXTERNAL AWARDS

Winning external awards has become something that the GI division is very good at. In the space of four years, they have won over 20 prestigious industry awards from institutions such as Which?, Defaqto, Institute of Customer Service, Chartered Management Institute and the 2012 General Insurer of the Year at the prestigious British Insurance Awards. This is a particularly admirable achievement, bearing in mind that it was as recently as 2009 that Peter Horton (GI Chief Operating Officer) felt that the GI division was ready to compete with leading businesses, and began to submit entries for various customer service and insurance industry awards. Winning these awards is good for LV = 's external reputation, but it is also a key way to galvanize and engage employees as highlighted by Lee and Chloe, Customer Service Representatives:

> *"It reinforces the idea that you're doing a good job and it's nice to get that stamp of approval from an external organization. And it gives a bit of competition because it shows where we're coming in comparison with other companies and it does make you think, 'right we're going to stay on top of this', but what is nice is I don't have to go out of my way to do anything- I just have to do my job to my best"* (Lee and Chloe – Customer Service Representatives)

Winning external awards is an external validation and stamp of approval not just for the company but also for individual staff members who can see that it is not just LV= that appreciate their efforts, but the wider industry as well.

'ENGAGE' SURVEY AND ACTION PLANNING

An annual employee survey, known as 'Engage', was launched in 2007 and is conducted at the beginning of November each year by an external consultancy. This survey provides an important overview of how people are feeling and gives a guide to what is working well as well areas where improvement is needed. As with most employee attitude surveys, the questionnaire covers a whole range of factors from how the employee feels about training opportunities, line management behaviours, and attitudes towards the values and vision of the company. One section covers how the employee feels towards the company as a whole, such as feeling proud to work there, and whether the company encourages them to behave in certain ways, such as going the 'extra mile'. This dual focus on attitude and behaviour with regard to engagement is also reflected by LV = :

"We needed to look at employee engagement holistically. We can see engaged people by what they do – they're going to sell more and our customers will be more satisfied; they're going to be more involved in internal activities such as social events, reading internal magazines, suggesting improvements; and they're going to get involved in volunteering. And so it becomes a virtuous cycle of involvement and engagement." (Karen Sharpe, Head of Internal Communications and GI Engagement)

The survey provides another mechanism to gain vital feedback from employees that further allows the company to embed their values and to develop a trust-based relationship with their staff. For example, LV= incentivizes completion of the survey by giving £1 to charity for every survey completed, reinforcing their commitment to social responsibility and mutuality. They also present the survey results in an open and non-defensive way by communicating head-line results at all-employee events, in internal magazines and bulletins, and departmental results in a dedicated section on the intranet.

LV= have committed to act on the results of the survey by setting up an action planning and review committee for each department, who set specific and time-bounded deliverables based on the three lowest scoring sections of the survey for each department. These actions are communicated directly to employees via the intranet, and employees can hold the committee to account if actions have not been implemented.

Lastly, LV= is committed to ensuring anonymity for individuals by only looking at data at the departmental level rather than drilling down to individual managers and their direct reports. This

helps to encourage participation (completion rates are consistently above 90%), trust, and a positive attitude towards giving feedback to the company, whether it be positive or negative:

"With the Engage Survey, it allows people that don't really like to say anything in team meetings etc. a chance to say what you want and it doesn't come back on them. You can just put it out there and they will bring it up in meetings afterwards and will act on it. It's so good because you can be honest." (Mandy – Customer Service Representative)

Looking at the Engage Survey results since 2007, the most significant changes have been in relation to recognition and reward (145% improvement between 2007 and 2011); image and competitiveness (82% improvement between 2007 and 2011); and talent management (58% improvement between 2007 and 2011). There has been a 30% improvement in employee engagement from a score of 64% in 2007 (much lower than the average of 70% for financial service businesses) to a score of 83% in 2011 (much higher than the average of 71% for financial service businesses that year). These positive changes in employee attitudes reflect the tremendous efforts that went into improving the key people management practices of reward and recognition, recruitment, and training and development, as well as the entire rebranding exercise.

VOLUNTEERING AND CORPORATE SOCIAL RESPONSIBILITY (CSR) ACTIVITIES

Since 2009, volunteering and CSR have become increasingly valued as a way of living the LV= values, and for engaging and involving employees at the regional, rather than head office, level. The central aim has been to move volunteering and CSR away *"from being something that the company just 'does' and then writes about it in the annual report, into something that's an organic part of how we work"* *(Phil Francis, Engagement Manager)*. Budgets for volunteering and CSR activities were increased and devolved so that each office site has ownership and responsibility. Thus, each site's workforce could choose which charity to support, typically opting for local or grassroots charities/initiatives.

This meant that a whole range of activities were implemented that went beyond fundraising to actually giving time and resources to help charities and social enterprises. Examples include sponsored walks/marathons, painting/decorating facilities, organizing events, and helping in international aid projects. This has benefitted not only the local communities in which employees live and work, but also fostered a sense of pride, achievement, and community within LV= itself:

> *"It's nice to know that we're doing our bit and it's that real positive, 'I did that' as well. It's a nice thing to be associated with, it makes you feel good to work for LV = , and it creates that good opinion of LV= in the community. Someone I know did one of those away days and he came back to work so happy and so positive, and that helps with morale for the team too." (Chloe and Jolene – Customer Service Representatives)*

A core focus during the period January 2008 - December 2009 was on embedding the new values, ethos and way of working. However, this spirit was still quite fragile, and a major challenge was to keep building and fortifying a sense of mutual trust and communication between senior management and the rest of the workforce. In overcoming this challenge, Peter Horton (GI Chief Operating Officer) reflects that: *"Every time we were doing what we said we were going to do, we went out and told people, 'This is what we said we would do, and this is what we have done'. And so, over a period of time, we got to a tipping point where people said, 'We believe you now!'"*

2010 – 2012: TO BE BRITAIN'S BEST LOVED INSURER: STRENGTHENING THE LV= CULTURE

Once the trust had been built and the major transformational changes had been completed, there was time to take stock of what had been achieved and where LV= were heading in the marketplace. It was apparent that a renewed vision was needed for the whole of LV = , and that some initiatives could be further expanded to be of greatest value for the GI business.

NEW VISION

By the end of 2010, the GI Division had realized their initial vision, established by John O'Roarke in 2006, to become a top 5 motor insurer in the UK. Therefore, a new vision was needed that not only fitted with the ideals of the embedded LV= culture that had now also been carried over to the Life Division, but would still engage and inspire employees from the entire LV= organization in the long-term. In line with the emphasis on two-way communication and empowering leadership, all employees were invited, during the annual Roadshows that took place at the end of 2010, to vote on their choice (out of three) for the new vision. The winner, by a landslide, was **"To be Britain's Best Loved Insurer"**.

Karen Sharpe (Head of Internal Communications and GI Engagement) remarks how this particular option was the only one to highlight a holistic view that reflected the good that LV= does for the community. By allowing employees to have a say in the overall vision of the company, LV= not only reinforced its principles of engagement, but also embedded its values much more deeply across the whole organization:

> *"It was our choice. Management gave us that choice and I'm glad they did because it let us take part and let us become part of the business, not just be those people that make the calls, we also make the decisions. At LV= it feels different - you feel part of the process and part of company." (Lee – Customer Service Representative)*

Employees felt that the vision provided a continuous desire for betterment, as there was no specified end outcome, such as being a market leader or achieving certain profitability. This may at first glance seem problematic because, without a specific milestone, there is no definite measure of success. However, the vision is very much an aspiration for the future that will continue to inspire and engage employees with the organization for a long period of time, and each area of the business does in fact assess their success against a range of internal measures relating to customer service, financial performance and employee engagement:

> *"'To be' feels like the business is always pushing forwards – it instils a, 'what are we going to do next?' attitude, where we are always looking for new solutions" (Chloe, Customer Service Representative)*

EXPANSION OF INITIATIVES

Although the range of people management practices had been implemented and embedded successfully, it was recognized that they could be strengthened further.

An online discussion forum, 'Ask the Exec', was set up on the intranet site where John O'Roarke and his GI Executive team could regularly, quarterly, answer in person any queries, concerns or issues that employees had. This has been a useful way of addressing rumours or concerns within the workplace regarding changes in the company strategy, the marketplace, or internal infrastructures (and the questions are submitted anonymously, encouraging maximum openness).

Reward and recognition were further strengthened by a 'Hall of Fame' initiative, whereby Peter Horton (GI Chief Operating Officer) would choose three or four employees each month who had really gone the extra mile for their customers and for LV=. These employees would receive an additional financial reward and a personal thank you from Peter, and attend an annual celebration dinner.

Lastly, as volunteering and CSR activities were beginning to flourish, funding was increased so that employees from each site could nominate a charity to which a mini-bus could be donated, and the company would match-fund any initiative that an employee personally fund-raised for. This aimed to show appreciation for the efforts of their employees in making 'LV= the best loved', and to demonstrate that the employment relationship was one of mutual reciprocation.

THE OUTCOMES AND THE FUTURE

The outcomes of the transformation have been extremely positive and have far outweighed the huge investment of time, effort, and finances. Moreover, considering the difficult economic climate and competitive market environment during this time, LV= has been a shining example of how businesses can still thrive under adverse conditions. Comparing key performance metrics between 2006 and 2011, it is clearly demonstrated that developing a culture around the principles of employee engagement has been critical in producing a highly profitable, reputable, and service-orientated business.

In addition to examining performance metrics, it is also important to consider the impact on the employees themselves because, at the heart of this transformation, were LV = 's people.

GI Division of LV=	2006	2011
Motor Insurer ranking	12th in UK	4th in UK
Profitability	£22 million loss	£72 million profit
New GI Sales (Motor & Home)	170,000 policies	833,000 policies
Average customer query resolution time	48 hours	3.5 minutes
Sales Turnover	£0.35 billion	>£1.00 billion
Staff Absence/Sickness	6%	<3%
Staff Turnover	30–60%	15–20%

Sources: LV= Annual Reports 2006 to 2012; LV= presentations for external awards

For Jolene, who has started recently with LV = , feeling a significant part of the company made her more confident in her ability to deliver excellent customer service:

> "All these regular activities make you feel that you're constantly involved in the business, and that makes you feel more confident, and it shows when you're on the phone to customers.
>
> And not sounding confident on the phones is possibly the worst thing you could do!" (Jolene, Customer Service Representative)

For Chloe, who is hoping to be promoted within the company, it was about LV= taking an interest in her aspirations and in helping her to achieve those that made her want to go the extra mile:

> "It's really encouraging because they're interested in you and you get a lot of help and support. It kind of works both ways. It's that give and take. That for me drives me and makes me think right what else can I do. They're already going the extra mile (for you) so that makes you want to put in extra effort and go the extra mile as well." (Chloe – Customer Service Representative)

For Mandy, who has been with LV= since before the transformation, the impact of the changes on the morale and personal development of her colleagues made her feel more empowered to voice her own concerns and to use her initiative:

> "Back then (prior to 2006) people would come and go, but now a lot of people are here for the long haul and progress to be team leaders and managers. People are a lot more positive and happier, and the atmosphere is better. You used to think that if you had a problem you would just sit there and not go to your manager, but now you can and you want to improve things." (Mandy –Customer Service Representative)

For Lee, who started just after the rebranding, it was the whole package that ranged from motivational incentives to having the right tools, to being able to make improvement suggestions that enabled him to deliver the best possible service to customers:

> "We want everybody to be happy and comfortable and to have the tools that they need. And it's only when you have those core foundations in place that you can then help anybody else. So, it's everything together that makes us strong (in terms of delivering the best possible customer service) because we have all these different things and they all go hand-in-hand". (Lee – Customer Service Representative)

The transformation has had a deep and positive long-term positive impact on the workforce. Despite this, it is acknowledged that LV= cannot afford to rest easy. The effects of the economic crisis, significant market competition, and regulatory changes, are proving a major challenge for the coming years:

> "My main worry now is cost control because we've taken market share quite rapidly and the market is getting increasingly challenging. So we've got to be leaner, and we may not be able to fulfil all of our promises because they're too expensive. But if we've made a guarantee then we stick by that wherever possible to keep our integrity". (Nicola Dunning, Regional Manager and GI Engage Champion)

LV= recognizes that it will need to continue to invest in their staff even through these times:

> "It's really important to look after our people during this time so that they help you through these current economic and market challenges." (Peter Horton, GI Chief Operating Officer)

These investments, for the GI Division, include developing a new leadership initiative that aims to profile what a 'great' manager looks like, and identifying personal development goals for each team leader/manager. This will include training modules, 360 degree feedback, and regular self-assessments. Another major initiative will be a collection of innovative and flexible work practices. This will build on the 'Best Loved' vision, and ensure that every worker is enabled to do their best. These work practices will comprise homeworking, more part-time and alternative shift patterns, and

EXHIBIT 1: KEY ACCOUNTING INFORMATION FOR LV= GROUP AND GI DIVISION FROM 2006 TO 2011

	2006	2007	2008	2009	2010	2011
New Policies Sold (in 000s)						
GI Motor Insurance	106	171	379	327	470	708
GI Home Insurance	64	67	84	91	107	133
Financial Information (in £ million)						
GI Turnover	351	347	446	811	1,180	1,450
GI Pre-tax Profit (loss)	(22)	(46)	(30)	7	31	72
LV= Group Underlying Profit	(20)	50	2	44	91	99
Return of Investment (in %)						
LV= Group vs Market	11.2/11.4	5.7/5.8	17.8/16.3	15.4/13.4	15.4/12.5	5.7/6.1

Sources: LV= Annual Reports 2006–2011

enhanced online and social media communication technologies. These will not only allow employees to have more control over their work and their work-life balance, but also will enable customers to have better quality and coverage of service.

The path to employee engagement for LV= has not yet come to an end. Instead, employee engagement is an on-going process that needs to be sustained and renewed in order for it to keep momentum and to still reap benefits.

At 14:00 on 27 May 2008 Claude Brunet, the chief operating officer of AXA, smiled and gave a thumbs-up to the information technology team. The AXA Forum, a 24-hour global online forum, had just gone live for 120,000 employees. Regional forums, each sponsored by the CEO of a local subsidiary, were already receiving feedback about the group's new brand signature, which had been revealed a week earlier. As incoming messages flowed onto a hub screen over his head, Brunet reflected on how AXA had prepared itself for this moment.

CONSOLIDATING THE BUSINESS

2001 had been one of the worst years in history for the insurance industry and for AXA. In 2002, during his third year as chairman of the AXA management board, Henri de Castries had launched a consolidation plan. After an initial cost-cutting period, the new operational model would emphasize the benefits of organic growth, set technical profitability as the main priority, and promote a culture of excellence through the pursuit of service quality. AXA was to stick to its financial protection business (refer to Exhibit 1) rather than move into bancassurance[*], strive to recover profitability a in a core business lines rather than sell non-performing activities; and focus on key markets rather than spread itself across the markets.

By the end of the 2004, the AXA Group had considerably improved its key performance indicators – a key challenge. Revenues amounted to €72 billion in: life savings (65 per cent); property and casualty (25 per cent); asset management (4 per cent); and others. Its assets under management equaled €870 billion and its net income was 2.5 billion. To earn these levels, the company had persuaded 50 million customers, mainly in Europe, North America and the Asia Pacific, to place their trust in AXA, its employees and distributors.

AMBITION 2012

Then in May 2005, de Castries opened the annual corporate meeting with big news: 'The time has come to aim at a new frontier: Ambition 2012. It will double revenues and triple underlying earnings from now to 2012'.

Having set this remarkable target, he came quickly to the heart of the matter: 'We must get everybody on board with a bold ambition: making AXA the preferred company in financial protection'. He also stressed: 'We want to be recognized by our customers as a close and qualified company for the excellence of our

---

[*]   AXA rejected the business model based upon the combination of a large insurance company with a large universal bank. But, its multi-distribution approach integrated partnerships whereby its insurance products could be sold through a bank sales channel.

Exhibit 1   AXA's business: financial protection

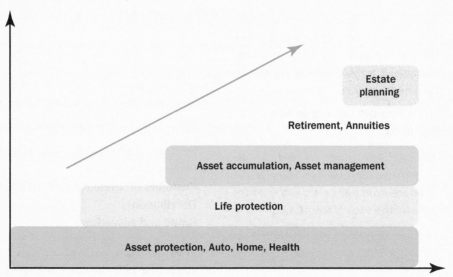

Exhibit 2   Becoming the preferred company

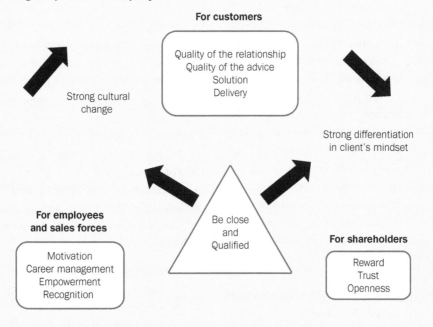

products, services and distribution. We must deliver the signature of our brand: *Be Life Confident.*'

Apart from its signature, the brand was then communicated through the value proposition 'close and qualified' and included its main customer need – Financial Protection – in its logo.

Although these brand attributes had been introduce in 2003, they had never before received so much attention in a presidential address. De Castries proclaimed the brand would provide a significant competitive advantage, based on external support from *Be Life Confident* and internal support through 'close and qualified' (Exhibit 2).

The following month, a crowd of guests gathered in a reception hall beneath the glass pyramid of the Louvre Museum, Claude Bébéar , AXA's founder, and de Castries were hosting AXA's 20th anniversary. Bébéar reminisced:

> "Back in 1985, I became convinced that a single brand name would provide unity and, therefore, greater strength. It would motivate the teams. It played a fundamental part in shaping AXA."

But de Castries was not content to leave it at nostalgia. He responded:

> "Your decision has since proved to be visionary... Today, Be Life Confident is the state of mind we want our customers to be in. It is what motivates each of use at AXA!"

WHAT ABOUT MARKETING?

Despite its generally decentralized structure, AXA managed its brand centrally, under the guidance of the Communications, Brand and Sustainable Development department, which reported to Claude Brunet. Brunet, a former top automobile executive, had joined AXA in 2001. He became chief operating officer and joined the management board in 2003.

Brunet identified two critical brand management challenges. First, AXA needed to confer more emotion to a brand often perceived as cold. Brand tracking survey indicated it represented 'qualified' (expertise) more than 'close' (trust). Most customers thought AXA was more 'self-centered' than 'customer-centred'. Benchmark studies suggested competitors had similar reputations. Secont, the CEOs of the local subsidiaries demanded some new initiatives that could support their differentiation strategies. To resolve both issues, Brunet determined that AXA needed to translate *Be Life Confident* into operational terms.

But in the meantime, he also had to address an internal challenge. Despite its claims to be pursuing a customer orientation, the AX Group did not include 'marketing' in its organization chart. The debate about the need for a fully dedicated marketing function at group level persisted for months. Brunet believed, 'We need to promote innovation throughout the AXA Group while offering all business units a common approach. Local and central levels should form a complete whole'. He emphasized that 'Marketing should no longer stand as a service provider or, at best, as an advisor. It must become a strategic driver

of differentiation and growth... an authentic partner for our local CEOs'.

A (BRAND) NEW STRUCTURE

The debate ended on 1 January 2007, with the launch of AXA Group's marketing department. It reported to Brunet and comprised five pillars:

1. Strategic marketing and customer insight
2. Offer and innovation
3. Customer programmes and quality service
4. Distribution
5. Brand and advertising

A marketing board, which consisted of the heads of marketing and the group's largest subsidiaries, supported the new head of AXA Group marketing. Brunet made the rule plain: 'Marketing won't be a private enclosure for those with "marketing" on their business card'. The first marketing board meeting confirmed the willingness to act as an open forum. The directors of the AXA Group's strategic planning and IT departments both took part as full members. The marketing board quickly determined that AXA Way[*], the company's process improvement methodology, would be applied to customer programmes and service quality. Local structures aligned according to the new model. A CMO (chief marketing officer) would soon report directly to the CEO of each subsidiary.

Although the marketing board saw a need for consolidating the 'close' and 'qualified' attributes, both we well perceived. As Brunet pointed out, the real issue lay elsewhere:

> "Be Life Confident *is the item our marketing people challenge most. It has gathered limited influence and provides insufficient support to the subsidiaries. Plus, its overall fit with 'preferred company' is not evident."*

The wording may have been part of the problem, but the concept also suggested some isolation of brand management, which had been stuck in an

---

[*] See J. Weaks, J.-P. Balliot, and S. Weeks (2009) AXA Way@ The Pursuit of Excellent through Quality Service. IMD Case no. IMD-4-0310, 2009.

'ivory tower' offering limited applicable tools and objectives.

THE AXA BRAND SPIRIT

As marketing emerged and found its way, the AXA Group continued to focus on its progress toward Ambition 2012. According to Brunet:

> *"By the end of 2006, a lot of ground had already been covered. Preference, customer focus, employee engagement and executive leadership were no longer mere buzz words, yet we were still trying to connect all the dots!"*

In May 2007 de Castries asked for feedback from his top managers, who indicated that the corporate mindset was still not customer oriented and employee engagement was insufficient. They also suggested that there were some gaps in executive leadership:

1. 'Most of the time, we don't recognize our customers when they call. They need to explain who they are and business we have with them!'
2. 'We do not demonstrate enough that we value our own people'.
3. 'We must take on greater responsibility for walking the talk'.

Thanking them for their openness, de Castries noted, 'We cannot drive change and not empower people. We cannot drive change and not be exemplary ourselves'. He assigned Brunet the task of investigating ongoing brand issues and providing regular feedback to the management board. The plan was for a final decision to be communicated to top managers in May 2008, followed by full employee involvement thereafter.

In response, Brunet established an AXA brand spirit taskforce: four CEOs and two heads of marketing from different subsidiaries joined forces with three group-level senior executives (marketing, human resources and communications). An external consultant would advise them. During the kick-off meeting, Brunet cautioned the task force that: 'Reinforcing the brand will not result in a declaration of intent'. Their goal, he directed, would be to 'first investigate what could be AXA's most compelling difference. Then, we will determine the "spirit" of the brand before focusing on how to prove, express and communicate our difference' (refer to Exhibit 3).

To gather input, the task force interview 30 top executives, including all six members of the management board. The interviewees cited financial strength and innovation capability as essential to the AXA Group's credibility. But few of them considered these features capable of differentiating AXA for end consumers. They also named the shift toward a customer culture as the company's biggest single challenge – and opportunity. Delivering a positive consumer experience and evolving from a financial to a service business, from a product provider to a solution provider, would be the key.

In terms of the brand communications, these respondents considered 'Financial Protection' too difficult to grasp and 'close and qualified' too general. *Be Life Confident* may not have done much harm, but it did not do much good either. These interviewees could cite a host of local consumer-centric developments, but they still felt that a company-wide link could facilitate and coordinate these initiatives. The link needed to be inspirational enough to induce change and participation, but realistic enough to avoid the damaged of unmet promised. The goal was to earn trust, not just promise or announce it.

Exhibit 3   The AXA brand spirit

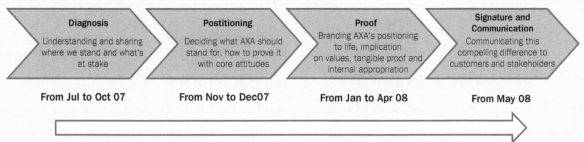

Diagnosis	Postitioning	Proof	Signature and Communication
Understanding and sharing where we stand and what's at stake	Deciding what AXA should stand for, how to prove it with core attitudes	Branding AXA's positioning to life, implication on values, tangible proof and internal appropriation	Communicating this compelling difference to customers and stakeholders
From Jul to Oct 07	**From Nov to Dec07**	**From Jan to Apr 08**	**From May 08**

THE VOICE OF THE CUSTOMER

By the end of 2006, one year after the announcement of Ambition 2012, AXA had 51.9 million customers – 600,000 more than at the end of 2005. But Brunet as concerned about the nature of this net count, because the company had still lost 3.8 million existing customers even though it had gained 4.4 million new ones. The poor quality of service reportedly accounted for at least 10 per cent of the value lost when these customers left.

In an annual customer survey, AXA measured satisfaction according to opinions expression after 'moments of truth' such as policy purchases, claim payments and policy surrenders. The rate of net positive opinions had increased between 2004 and 2006 (refer to Exhibit 4) and reached 79 in 2997, just missing its target of 80. (The target was 82 for 2008). In 2007 only 53 per cent of customers would have 'definitely' recommended AXA to their family and friends; another 31 per cent would 'probably' have recommended it.

Furthermore, brand tracking surveys identified customers' main expectations: trust, quality of service, value for money and attention to needs. The order of these demands varied from one country to another, but all four items systematically appeared at the top of the surveys. In the summer of 2007 Brunet commissioned a new survey to ask 18,000 consumers from nine countries their opinions of the brand, their personal needs and their expectations.

THE VOICE OF THE EMPLOYEE

Any mention of Ambition 2012 was accompanied by a single image: a virtuous circle connecting customer centricity and employee engagement as reinforcing components (refer to Exhibit 4). In other words, Ambition 2012 required the engagement of AXA's employees, 'our most valuable asset', as de Castries put it. According to Brunet:

> *"Engagement measures AXA's ability to speak to the hearts and the minds. It is a combination of satisfaction, motivation, confidence and involvement."*

A high engagement score meant employees would support corporate goals and values because of their sense of belonging and attachment. To assess this engagement, AXA conducted annual employee surveys. Engagement scores had increased (refer to Exhibit 4) and reached 73 in 2007, but Brunet considered this level insufficient, in relation to external benchmarks. The AXA Group aimed to reach 80 by 2009 to put it among the best multinational corporations.

The surveys revealed that 'recognition' and 'development' demanded the most focus. Passport 2012 – a human resources tool designed to give staff a better understanding of their personal contribution to Ambition 2012 –promoted exchanges between employees and managers about these very topics.

Exhibit 4   Customer centricity and employee engagement

**Customer   Employee
centricity   engagement**

Customer satisfaction	
2004	71.0
2005	75.7
2006	78.5
2007	79.2

Employee engagement	
2005	75.7
2006	78.5
2007	79.2

Furthermore, Brunet noted, 'The brand issues under scrutiny could definitely impact employee engagement. Aren't AXA employees our 'brand ambassadors?' It is essential to get and take into account their input'. Therefore, he inserted a few additional questions into the 2007 edition of the employee survey. Specifically, employees could select the most relevant items from a list of 12 differentiating core attitudes; the list was identical to one incorporate in the latest consumer survey:

- Available
- Attentive
- Constructive
- Fair
- Inventive
- Passionate
- Performing
- Proactive
- Reassuring
- Reliable
- Resourceful
- Simple

The 85,000 employee responses put 'available', 'attentive', and 'reliable' at the top of the list (refer to Exhibit 5). It seemed like a good omen to Brunet:

> *"What do consumers expect from AXA? The latest survey shows they want us to be available, attentive and reliable. What do employees think? Precisely the same: the degree of convergence is truly impressive!"*

COMPETITIVE REVIEW

To differentiate itself from competitors, AXA needed to understand their offerings. Therefore, it performed reviewers of 50 local competitors. Their brand messages were, of course, widely divergent, but on two main dimensions – 'rational versus emotional' and 'protecting versus empowering' – they suggested a cross-country pattern. Each brand positioned itself in some way on the four quadrants. A brand that claimed to be 'reliable' represented a rational focus, whereas one that promoted itself as 'trustworthy' pursued an emotional reputation. No single competitor achieved a well-balanced positioning on both dimensions.

An external consulting company performed a global competitive review of international competitors, include each brand's positioning, signature, territory, posture, keywords and differentiation. The review analyzed institutional and commercial communications at both global and local levels. Although 'one player struck a rather good balance … it still failed to convince since it didn't offer any tangible proof to back up its statements.'

FINDING A POSITION

The analyses had confirmed what Brunet fear: the AXA brand did not stand out from its competitors. It also indicated a low overall level of trust in the sector. Consumers were still waiting for insurers to meet their fundamental demands; they believed all providers, including AXA, made promises they did not keep. The clichés that swarmed financial advertising had lost any persuasive power – consumers had tired of attractive, healthy-looking older people walking well-behaved Labradors on sunny beaches.

So customers' expectations were plain, and yet the AXA Group was not delivered. Wasn't this scenario a clarion call for a repositioning effort? The task force came to the difficult conclusion that

Exhibit 5   Brand image in 2007 employee scope

Which would make you proud of AXA **tomorrow**		If you were a customer what would make you choose AXA **tomorrow**	
Reliable	34%	Available	51%
Attentive	34%	Attentive	39%
Available	34%	Reliable	38%

AXA had to stop pretending it could fulfil everyone's expectations. It needed to exit the 'land of promises' and settle into a 'land of proof'. The team demanded a genuine commitment to 'continuously work to prove AXA is worth trusting'. They argued that if the company upheld it with strong dedication, this commitment could make big difference in the end.

THE PROOF

In March 2008 the CEOs of all AXA's business units were invited to discuss whether the AXA Group values matched its new brand spirit. The values expressed the underlying personality of the AXA Group; the attitudes translated this personality to the customer. Did the three new core attitudes and five existing AXA Group values (refer to Exhibit 6) connect? The CEOs determined that they were comfortable with the current set of values and argued that any adaptation would unnecessarily confuse their teams.

The task force therefore proceeded to translate the core attitudes into benefits for the customer. The 'translation' went like this:

- Available: We are there when our customers need us and we listen to them, truly.
- Attentive: We treat our customers with empathy and consideration, provide personalized advice throughout their lives, and reward their loyalty.

- Reliable: We say what we do and do what we say; we deliver and keep our customers informed, so they can trust us.

The core attitudes were also translated into a set of specific customer-facing behaviours that employees were to display during any contact with a customer. The task force believed these recommendations would help employees act consistently and foster value appropriation throughout the AXA Group. The local customer programs would concentrate on three customer-facing streams:

1. Welcome on board
2. Communicate clearly
3. Develop and reward loyalty

Each stream would clarify the benefit attached to a core attitude, and the business units would deploy their programmes throughout their customer' 'journeys' with the company.

The proof was a new challenge. For example, product marketing needed to evaluate and demonstrate the potential of the products. A standard benefit could not constitute proof by itself; however, a particular commitment embedded within a product offer could provide proof that AXA was worth trusting. As an example, in France the company offered taxi vouchers for young drivers, which enabled them to call a taxi, free of charge, rather than drive under the influence of alcohol. Other local

Exhibit 6   Positioning, core attitudes and values

marketing plans had to adopt similar ideas in their move from the land of promised to the land of proof.

THE SIGNATURE

The new brand signature would be disclosed at the May 2008 corporate meeting. Minimal information was leaking behind the scenes. The signature would state a strong ambition. It would commit AXA to redefine, for the better, the benefits people should expect from insurance. Its communication would be anchored in the reality of its customers' lives rather than in some wonderland. It would be a motto to be used both externally and in-house. Only a small inner circle knew the signature would also attempt to boost brand recognition by including a 'switch' the red diagonal line from the local. The switch, designed to represent a symbol of change at AXA, would facilitate message customization.

Brunet heightened the anticipation with his corporate teasing; 'Besides the wording, what matters is the way in which we will coordinate our actions to give the signature meaning'.

A QUESTION OF LEADERSHIP

Concluding his opening address to the 2008 corporate meeting, de Castries made plain the he expected his audience to allow all AXA employees to be available, attentive, and reliable:

> *"The attitude employees want to display to the customers are the very ones they expect from their managers. We should, at the end of each business day, ask ourselves, 'Have I been available, attentive and reliable to my staff?' I am convinced each of use, including myself, can progress on this!"*

De Castries then broadened his last remarks by addressing the management style that prevailed at the AXA Group. Recent human resource surveys had revealed that either aggressive or defensive tactics were far more widespread than constructive methods. The challenge ahead demanded a significant rebalance, in favour of more constructive, cooperative executive leadership. The AXA Group needed to move from a culture in which managers seemed like experts and task providers to a situation in which they acted as competent coaches.

A slide appeared on the screen with a quote from Gandhi: 'We must become the change we want to see'. De Castries explained:

> *"As we reposition our brand, we have a unique opportunity to accept to change ourselves. If we don't adopt our leadership, the repositioning will not fully succeed, since it will reflect a culture of the past rather than wheat we want it to become."*

REDEFINING STANDARDS

The following morning, the meeting session went live on the Executive Web, available to some 5000 managers throughout the AXA Group. The brand signature would be revealed internally within a few minutes.

AXA Music, a new musical signature, burst into allegro fortissimo. The stage curtain opened on a wide screen. The brand film started. A voice-over read the announcement text as it appeared on the screen, scrolling slowly down and then back up to the first line. With the concluding line, 'This is what people must think. AXA, redefining/standards'. The voice-over stopped.

De Castries and Brunet walked onto the stage to open the exchange. They began by acknowledging that the timing of the launch of 'redefining/standards' was a challenge in itself. The AXA Group was not completely ready; material proof was still being collected! And the whole industry, including AXA, was going through very rough times. But waiting for the perfect time, they argued, would only be an excuse for delaying.

Would the challenge take AXA out of its 'comfort zone?' Of course! But that might be the best receipt for success. They noted the risk that the resolute-sounding wording of the signature might sound arrogant, if taken out of context. But its true intention would soon become clear to everyone.

So, far from being arrogant, AXA was recognizing that it had not performed as well as it ought to for its customers. Its commitment to redefine, improve and then be judged on material proof was a sign of its openness. De Castries insisted that this was 'neither complacency nor arrogance'.

There would be no external 'big bang'; the local launches would be scheduled according to each subsidiary's aptitude to deliver its proofs. Some subsidiaries would begin very soon; most would do it in a few months. The most urgent task, said Brunet, was to get all employees on board. The soon-to-be-launched forum would be an ideal initial opportunity for each CEO to do so.

THE FORUM

The second day of operation of the worldwide online forum started with the Asia Pacific forum. The previous day had attracted high attendance.

Participation would likely exceed 50,000 members. The forum had thus already demonstrated the concern that most AXA people felt. Though corporate correctness had crept into some comments, most of the exchanges had been genuine. Enthusiasm and expectation had been voiced … as had criticism and incredulity. A fair amount of additional explanation and exchange clearly would be necessary, and the road ahead looked steeper for some subsidiaries than for others.

Brunet knew that AXA had taken only the first step on its journey to the land of proof. Would the new signature achieve the dramatic differentiation that AXA wanted? Would AXA and its employees be up to the challenge? And if they were, could they ultimately convince customers?

Endnotes

CHAPTER 1

1   Source: www.forbes.com – *The Forbes Global 2000* (published April 2014).

2   C.H. Lovelock, 'Classifying services to gain strategic marketing insights', *Journal of Marketing*, 47 (Summer 1983), pp. 9–20.

3   J.B. Quinn, J.J. Baruch and P.C. Paquette, 'Technology in services', *Scientific American*, 257, no. 6 (December 1987), pp. 50–8.

4   C.H. Lovelock, 'Classifying services to gain strategic marketing insights', *Journal of Marketing*, 47 (Summer 1983), pp. 9–20.

5   S.L. Vargo and R.F. Lusch, 'Evolving to a new dominant logic for marketing', *Journal of Marketing*, 68 (January 2004), pp. 1–17.

6   S.L. Vargo and R.F. Lusch, 'Service dominant logic: continuing the evolution', *Journal of the Academy of Marketing Science*, 36,1 (2008), pp. 1–10.

7   C. Grönroos, 'Value co-creation in service logic: A critical analysis', *Marketing Theory*, 11/3 (2011), pp. 279–301.

8   E. Gummesson and F. Polese, 'B2B is not an island', *Journal of Business and Industrial Marketing*, 24, nos 5/6 (2009), pp. 337–50.

9   R.H.K. Vietor, *Contrived Competition* (Cambridge, MA: Harvard University Press, 1994).

10 M. Sawhney, S. Balasubramanian and V.V. Krishnan, 'Creating growth with services', *Sloan Management Review* (Winter 2004), pp. 34–43.

11 J.A. Alexander and M.W. Hordes, *S-Business: Reinventing the Services Organization* (New York: SelectBooks, 2003); R. Oliva and R. Kallenberg, 'Managing the transition from products to services', *International Journal of Service Industry Management* 14, no. 2 (2003), pp. 160–72.

12 J. Pine and J. Gilmore, *The Experience Economy* (Boston: Harvard Business School Press, 1999).

13 L. Berry, *Discovering the Soul of Service* (New York: Free Press, 1999).

14 R.T. Rust, C. Moorman, and P.R. Dickson, 'Getting return on quality: revenue expansion, cost reduction, or both?' *Journal of Marketing* 66 (October 2002), pp. 7–24.

15 J.L. Heskett, T.O. Jones, G.W. Loveman, W.E. Sasser Jr and L.A. Schlesinger, 'Putting the service–profit chain to work', *Harvard Business Review* (March–April 1994), pp. 164–74.

16 E.W. Anderson and V. Mittal, 'Strengthening the satisfaction –profit chain', *Journal of Service Research* 3, no. 2 (November 2000), pp. 107–20.

17 L.P. Willcocks and R. Plant, 'Getting from bricks to clicks', *Sloan Management Review* (Spring 2001), pp. 50–9.

18 G. Eysenbach, E.R. Sa and T.L. Diepgen, 'Shopping around the Internet today and tomorrow: towards the millennium of cybermedicine', *British Medical Journal* 319 (1999), p. 1294.

19 M.J. Bitner, S.W. Brown and M.L. Meuter, 'Technology infusion in service encounters', *Journal of the Academy of Marketing Science* 28 (Winter 2000), pp. 138–49.

20 M.J. Bitner, 'Self-service technologies: what do customers expect?', *Marketing Management* (Spring 2001), pp. 10–11.

21 R. Hallowell, 'Service in e-commerce: findings from exploratory research', Harvard Business School, Module Note, N9-800-418, 31 May 2000.

22 A. Parasuraman and C.L. Colby, *Techno-Ready Marketing: How and Why Your Customers Adopt Technology* (New York: Free Press, 2001).

23 Discussion of these issues is found in many services marketing publications. The discussion here is based on V.A. Zeithaml, A. Parasuraman and L.L. Berry, 'Problems and strategies in services marketing', *Journal of Marketing* 49 (Spring 1985), pp. 33–46.

24 For research supporting the idea of goods–services continua, see D. Iacobucci, 'An empirical examination of some basic tenets in services: goods–services continua', in *Advances in Services Marketing and Management*, eds T.A. Swartz, D.E. Bowen and S.W. Brown (Greenwich, CT: JAI Press, 1992), vol. 1, pp. 23–52.

25 S.L. Vargo and R.F. Lusch, 'The four service marketing myths', *Journal of Service Research* 6 (May 2004), pp. 324–35.

26 C. Lovelock and E. Gummesson, 'Whither services marketing? In search of a new paradigm and fresh perspectives', *Journal of Services Research* 7 (August 2004), pp. 20–41.

27 E.J. McCarthy and W.D. Perrault Jr, *Basic Marketing: A Global Managerial Approach* (Burr Ridge, IL: Richard D. Irwin, 1993).

28 B.H. Booms and M.J. Bitner, 'Marketing strategies and organizational structures for service firms', in *Marketing of Services*, eds J.H. Donnelly and W.R. George (Chicago: American Marketing Association, 1981), pp. 47–51.

29 E. Langeard, J. Bateson, C. Lovelock and P. Eiglier, *Marketing of Services: New Insights from Consumers and Managers* (Cambridge, MA: Marketing Sciences Institute, 1981).

30 Ibid.

CHAPTER 2

1   P. Nelson, 'Information and consumer behaviour', *Journal of Political Economy* 78, no. 20 (1970), pp. 311–29.

2   M.R. Darby and E. Karni, 'Free competition and the optimal amount of fraud', *Journal of Law and Economics* 16 (April 1973), pp. 67–86.

3   T.S. Robertson, *Innovative Behavior and Communication* (New York: Holt, Rinehart & Winston, 1971).

4   M. Laroche, G.H.G. McDougall, J. Bergeron and Z. Yang, 'Exploring how intangibility affects perceived risk', *Journal of Service Research* 6, no. 4 (May 2004), pp. 373–89; K.B. Murray and J.L. Schlacter, 'The impact of services versus goods on consumers' assessment of perceived risk and variability', *Journal of the Academy of Marketing Science* 18 (Winter 1990), pp. 51–65; M. Laroche, J. Bergeron and C. Goutaland, 'How intangibility affects perceived risk: the moderating role of knowledge and involvement', *Journal of Services Marketing* 17, no. 2 (2003), pp. 122–40.

5   M. Laroche et al., 'Exploring how intangibility affects perceived risk'.

6   R.F. Lusch, S.W. Brown and G.J. Brunswick, 'A general framework for explaining internal vs. external exchange', *Journal of the Academy of Marketing Science* 10 (Spring 1992), pp. 119–34.

7   M.L. Meuter, A.L. Ostrom, R.I. Roundtree and M.J. Bitner, 'Self-service technologies: understanding customer satisfaction with technology-based service encounters', *Journal of Marketing* 64 (July 2000), pp. 50–64; M.J. Bitner, 'Self-service technologies: what do customers expect?', *Marketing Management* (Spring 2001), pp. 10–11.

8   J.H. Gilmore and B.J. Pine II, 'The experience is the marketing', report from Strategic Horizons LLP (2002).

9   See, for example, B.J. Pine II and J.H. Gilmore, *The Experience Economy* (Boston, MA: Harvard Business School Press, 1999); B.H. Schmitt, *Experiential Marketing* (New York: Free Press, 1999); B.H. Schmitt, *Customer Experience Management* (Hoboken, NJ: John Wiley & Sons, 2003).

10 S.J. Grove and R.P. Fisk, 'Service theater: an analytical framework for services marketing', in *Services Marketing*, 4th edn, ed. C. Lovelock (Englewood Cliffs, NJ: Prentice Hall, 2001), pp. 83–92.

11 S.J. Grove, R.P. Fisk and M.J. Bitner, 'Dramatizing the service experience: a managerial approach', in *Advances in Services Marketing and Management*, vol. 1, eds T.A. Swartz, D.E. Bowen and S.W. Brown (Greenwich, CT: JAI Press, 1992), pp. 91–121.

12 Grove, Fisk and Bitner, 'Dramatizing the service experience'.

13 Grove and Fisk, 'Service theater'.

14 Ibid.

15 Grove, Fisk and Bitner, 'Dramatizing the service experience'.

16 Ibid.

17 Ibid.

18 M.R. Solomon, C. Surprenant, J.A. Czepiel and E.G. Gutman, 'A role theory perspective on dyadic interactions: the service encounter', *Journal of Marketing* 49 (Winter 1985), pp. 99–111.

19 Ibid.

20 R.F. Abelson, 'Script processing in attitude formation and decision making', in *Cognition and Social Behavior*, eds J.S. Carroll and J.S. Payne (Hillsdale, NJ: Erlbaum, 1976).

21 R.A. Smith and M.J. Houston, 'Script-based evaluations of satisfaction with services', in *Emerging Perspectives on Services Marketing*, eds L. Berry, G.L. Shostack and G. Upah (Chicago, IL: American Marketing Association, 1982), pp. 59–62.

22 J.E.G. Bateson and M.K.M. Hui, 'Crowding in the service environment', in *Creativity in Services Marketing: What's New, What Works, What's Developing*, eds M. Venkatesan, D.M. Schmalensee and C. Marshall (Chicago, IL: American Marketing Association, 1986), pp. 85–8.

23 J. Baker, 'The role of the environment in marketing services: the consumer perspective', in *The Services Challenge: Integrating for Competitive Advantage*, eds J.A. Czepiel, C.A. Congram and J. Shanahan (Chicago, IL: American Marketing Association, 1987), pp. 79–84.

24 C.L. Martin and C.A. Pranter, 'Compatibility management: customer-to-customer relationships in service environments', *Journal of Services Marketing* 3 (Summer 1989), pp. 43–53.

25 Ibid.

26 N. Bendapudi and R.P. Leone, 'Psychological implications of customer participation in coproduction', *Journal of Marketing* 67 (January 2003), pp.14–28.

27 L.A. Bettencourt, A.L. Ostrom, S.W. Brown and R.I. Roundtree, 'Client co-production in knowledge-intensive business services', *California Management Review* 44, no. 4 (Summer 2002), pp. 100–28.

28 S. Dellande, M.C. Gilly and J.L. Graham, 'Gaining compliance and losing weight: the role of the service provider in health care services', *Journal of Marketing* 68 (July 2004), pp. 78–91; M.L. Meuter, M.J. Bitner, A.L. Ostrom and S.W. Brown, 'Choosing among alternative service delivery modes: an investigation of customer trials of self-service technologies', *Journal of Marketing* (2005), pp. 61–83.

29 C.K. Prahalad and V. Ramaswamy, 'The new frontier of experience innovation', *Sloan Management Review* (Summer 2003), pp. 12–18.

30 A.F. Firat and A. Venkatesh, 'Liberatory postmodernism and the reenchantment of consumption', *Journal of Consumer Research* 22, no. 3 (December 1995), pp. 239–67.

31 M.P. Gardner, 'Mood states and consumer behavior: a critical review', *Journal of Consumer Research* 12 (December 1985), pp. 281–300.

32 Ibid., p. 288.

33 S.S. Tomkins, 'Affect as amplification: some modifications in theory', in *Emotion: Theory, Research, and Experience*, eds R. Plutchik and H. Kellerman (New York: Academic Press, 1980), pp. 141–64.

34 L.L. Berry, L.P. Carbone and S.H. Haeckel, 'Managing the total customer experience', *Sloan Management Review* (Spring 2002), pp. 85–9.

35 V.S. Folkes and V.M. Patrick, 'The positivity effect in perceptions of services: seen one, seen them all?', *Journal of Consumer Research* 30 (June 2003), pp. 125–37.

36 B.D. Keillor, G.T.M. Hult and D. Kandemir, 'A study of the service encounter in eight countries', *Journal of International Marketing* 12, no. 1 (2004), pp. 9–35.

37 D.E. Murphy, 'New East Europe retailers told to put on a happy face', *Los Angeles Times*, 26 November 1994, pp. A1, A18.

38 E. Arnould, L. Price and G. Zinkhan, *Consumers*, 2nd edn (New York: McGraw-Hill, 2004).

39 For excellent coverage of buyer behaviour in organizations, see M.D. Hutt and T.W. Speh, *Business Marketing Management*, 8th edn (Mason, OH: South-Western, 2004), ch. 3.

40 Ibid., pp. 68–9.

41 Ibid., pp. 62–7.

CHAPTER 3

1 The model on which this chapter is based is taken from V.A. Zeithaml, L.L. Berry and A. Parasuraman, 'The nature and determinants of customer expectations of service', *Journal of the Academy of Marketing Science* 21, no. 1 (1993), pp. 1–12.

2 R.B. Woodruff, E.R. Cadotte and R.L. Jenkins, 'Expectations and norms in models of consumer satisfaction', *Journal of Marketing Research* 24 (August 1987), pp. 305–14.

3 J.A. Miller, 'Studying satisfaction, modifying models, eliciting expectations, posing problems, and making meaningful measurements', in *Conceptualization and Measurement of Consumer Satisfaction and Dissatisfaction*, ed. H.K. Hunt (Bloomington, IN: Indiana University School of Business, 1977), pp. 72–91.

4 W.H. Davidow and B. Uttal, 'Service companies: focus or falter', *Harvard Business Review* (July–August 1989), pp. 77–85.

5 A. Parasuraman, L.L. Berry and V.A. Zeithaml, 'Understanding customer expectations of service', *Sloan Management Review* 32 (Spring 1991), p. 42.

6 L.L. Berry, A. Parasuraman and V.A. Zeithaml, 'Ten lessons for improving service quality', Marketing Science Institute, Report No. 93–104 (May 1993).

7 D. Bowen, 'Leadership aspects and reward systems of customer satisfaction', speech given at CTM Customer Satisfaction Conference, Los Angeles, 17 March 1989.

8 D.L. Davis, J.G. Guiltinan and W.H. Jones, 'Service characteristics, consumer research, and the classification of retail services', *Journal of Retailing* 55 (Fall 1979), pp. 3–21; and W.R. George and L.L. Berry, 'Guidelines for the advertising of services', *Business Horizons* 24 (May–June 1981), pp. 52–6.

9 E.R. Cadotte, R.B. Woodruff and R.L. Jenkins, 'Expectations and norms in models of consumer satisfaction', *Journal of Marketing Research* 14 (August 1987), pp. 353–64.

10 Parasuraman, Berry and Zeithaml, 'Understanding customer expectations', p. 40.

11 Davidow and Uttal, 'Service companies'.

12 W. Boulding, A. Kalra, R. Staelin and V.A. Zeithaml, 'A dynamic process model of service quality: from expectations to behavioral intentions', *Journal of Marketing Research* 30 (February 1993), pp. 7–27.

13 R.T. Rust and R.L. Oliver, 'Should we delight the customer?', *Journal of the Academy of Marketing Science* 28 (Winter 2000), pp. 86–94.

14 T.S. Gross, *Positively Outrageous Service* (New York: Warner Books, 1994).

15 J. Clemmer, 'The three rings of perceived value', *Canadian Manager* (Summer 1990), pp. 30–2.

16 Rust and Oliver, 'Should we delight the customer?'.

17 Parasuraman, Berry and Zeithaml, 'Understanding customer expectations', p. 41.

18 See http://corporate.ritzcarlton.com.

CHAPTER 4

1 For more discussion of the debate on the distinctions between quality and satisfaction, see A. Parasuraman, V.A. Zeithaml and L.L. Berry, 'Reassessment of expectations as a comparison standard in measuring service quality: implications for future research', *Journal of Marketing* 58 (January 1994), pp. 111–24; R.L. Oliver, 'A conceptual model of service quality and service satisfaction: compatible goals, different concepts', in *Advances in Services Marketing and Management*, vol. 2, eds T.A. Swartz, D.E. Bowen and S.W. Brown (Greenwich, CT: JAI Press, 1994), pp. 65–85; M.J. Bitner and A.R. Hubbert, 'Encounter satisfaction vs. overall satisfaction vs. quality: the customer's voice', in *Service Quality: New Directions in Theory and Practice*, eds R.T. Rust and R.L. Oliver (Newbury Park, CA: Sage, 1993), pp. 71–93; D.K. Iacobucci, A. Grayson and A.L. Ostrom, 'The calculus of service quality and customer satisfaction: theory and empirical differentiation and integration', in *Advances in Services Marketing and Management*, vol. 3, eds T.A. Swartz, D.E. Bowen and S.W. Brown (Greenwich, CT: JAI Press, 1994), pp. 1–67; P.A. Dabholkar, C.D. Shepherd and D.I. Thorpe, 'A comprehensive framework for service quality: an investigation of critical conceptual and measurement issues through a longitudinal study', *Journal of Retailing* 7, no. 2 (Summer 2000), pp. 139–73; and J.J. Cronin Jr, M.K. Brady and G.T.M. Hult, 'Assessing the effects of quality, value, and customer satisfaction on consumer behavioral intentions in service environments', *Journal of Retailing* 7 (Summer 2000), pp. 193–218.

2   See in particular, Parasuraman, Zeithaml and Berry, 'Reassessment of expectations'; Oliver, 'A conceptual model of service quality'; and M.K. Brady and J.J. Cronin Jr, 'Some new thoughts on conceptualizing perceived service quality: a hierarchical approach', *Journal of Marketing* 65 (July 2001), pp. 34–49.

3   A. Parasuraman, V.A. Zeithaml and L.L. Berry, 'SERVQUAL: a multiple-item scale for measuring consumer perceptions of service quality', *Journal of Retailing* 64 (Spring 1988), pp. 12–40.

4   Parasuraman, Zeithaml, and Berry, 'Reassessment of expectations'.

5   Oliver, 'A conceptual model of service quality'.

6   See V. Mittal, P. Kumar and M. Tsiros, 'Attribute-level performance, satisfaction, and behavioral intentions over time', *Journal of Marketing* 63 (April 1999), pp. 88–101; L.L. Olsen and M.D. Johnson, 'Service equity, satisfaction, and loyalty: from transaction-specific to cumulative evaluations', *Journal of Service Research* 5 (February 2003), pp. 184–95.

7   Olsen and Johnson, 'Service equity, satisfaction, and loyalty'.

8   R.L. Oliver, *Satisfaction: A Behavioral Perspective on the Consumer* (New York: McGraw-Hill, 1997).

9   For a more detailed discussion of the different types of satisfaction, see E. Arnould, L. Price and G. Zinkhan, *Consumers*, 2nd edn (New York: McGraw-Hill, 2004), pp. 754–96.

10 S. Fournier and D.G. Mick, 'Rediscovering satisfaction', *Journal of Marketing* 63 (October 1999), pp. 5–23.

11 Oliver, *Satisfaction*, ch. 2.

12 A. Ostrom and D. Iacobucci, 'Consumer trade-offs and the evaluation of services', *Journal of Marketing* 59 (January 1995), pp. 17–28.

13 For more on emotions and satisfaction, see Oliver, *Satisfaction*, ch. 11; and L.L. Price, E.J. Arnould and S.L. Deibler, 'Consumers' emotional responses to service encounters', *International Journal of Service Industry Management* 6, no. 3 (1995), pp. 34–63.

14 L.L. Price, E.J. Arnould, and P. Tierney, 'Going to extremes: managing service encounters and assessing provider performance', *Journal of Marketing* 59 (April 1995), pp. 83–97.

15 V. Liljander and T. Strandvik, 'Emotions in service satisfaction', *International Journal of Service Industry Management* 8, no. 2 (1997), pp. 148–69.

16 For more on attributions and satisfaction, see V.S. Folkes, 'Recent attribution research in consumer behavior: a review and new directions', *Journal of Consumer Research* 14 (March 1988), pp. 548–65; and Oliver, *Satisfaction*, ch. 10.

17 A.R. Hubbert, 'Customer co-creation of service outcomes: effects of locus of causality attributions', doctoral dissertation, Arizona State University, Tempe, Arizona (1995).

18 Ibid.

19 For more on fairness and satisfaction, see E.C. Clemmer and B. Schneider, 'Fair service', in *Advances in Services Marketing and Management*, vol. 5, eds T.A. Swartz, D.E. Bowen and S.W. Brown (Greenwich, CT: JAI Press, 1996), pp. 109–26; Oliver, *Satisfaction*, ch. 7; and Olsen and Johnson, 'Service equity, satisfaction, and loyalty'.

20 Fournier and Mick, 'Rediscovering satisfaction'.

21 See, for example: C. Fornell, M.D. Johnson, E.W. Anderson, J. Cha and B.E. Bryant, 'The American Customer Satisfaction Index: nature, purpose, and findings', *Journal of Marketing* 60 (October 1996), pp. 7–18; C. Fornell, 'A national customer satisfaction barometer: the Swedish experience', *Journal of Marketing* 56 no. 1 (1992), pp. 6–21.

22 E.W. Anderson, C. Fornell and D.R. Lehmann, 'Customer satisfaction, market share, and profitability: findings from Sweden', *Journal of Marketing* 58 (July 1994), pp. 53–66.

23 M. Bruhn and M.A. Grund, 'Theory, development and implementation of national customer satisfaction indices: the Swiss index of customer satisfaction (SWICS)', *Total Quality Management* 11, no. 7 (2000), pp. S1017–S1028; A. Meyer and F. Dornach, 'The German customer barometer', (http://www.servicebarometer.com/de/); Norwegian customer satisfaction barometer (www.kundebarometer.com).

24 F.F. Reichheld, 'The one number you need to grow', *Harvard Business Review*, December 2003, pp. 46–53.

25 T.L. Keiningham, B. Cooil, L. Akjoy, T.W. Andreassen and J. Weiner, 'The value of different customer satisfaction and loyalty metrics in predicting customer retention, recommendation and share of wallet', *Managing Service Quality*, 17 no. 4 (2007), pp. 361–84.

26 Adapted from: N. Clark (2010) 'The satisfaction manifesto: secret of good service', *Marketing*, 3 November, p. 29.

27 Brady and Cronin, 'Some new thoughts on conceptualizing perceived service quality'.

28 Ibid.

29 See C. Grönroos, 'A service quality model and its marketing implications', *European Journal of Marketing* 18, no. 4 (1984), pp. 36–44; R.T. Rust and R.L. Oliver, 'Service quality insights and managerial implications from the frontier', in *Service Quality: New Directions in Theory and Practice*, eds R.T. Rust and R.L. Oliver (Thousand Oaks, CA: Sage, 1994), pp. 1–19; M.J. Bitner, 'Managing the evidence of service', in *The Service Quality Handbook*, eds E.E. Scheuing and W.F. Christopher (New York: AMACOM, 1993), pp. 358–70.

30 Parasuraman, Zeithaml and Berry, 'SERVQUAL: a multiple-item scale'. Details on the SERVQUAL scale and the actual items used to assess the dimensions are provided in Chapter 6.

31 Ibid.

32 C. Grönroos, 'A service quality model and its marketing implications', *European Journal of Marketing* 18 (1984), pp. 36–44.

33 R. Rust and R. Oliver, 'Service quality: insights and managerial implications from the frontier', in *Service Quality: New Directions in Theory and Practice*, eds R.T. Rust and R.L. Oliver (Thousand Oaks, CA: Sage, 1994).

34 E.g. J.H. McAlexander, D.O. Kaldenberg and H.F. Koenig, 'Service quality measurement: examination of dental practices sheds more light on the relationships between service quality, satisfaction, and purchase intentions in a health care setting', *Journal of Health Care Marketing* 14 (Fall 1994), pp. 34–40; G.H. McDougall and T.J. Levesque, 'Benefit segmentation using service quality dimensions: an investigation in retail banking', *International Journal of Bank Marketing* 12, no. 2 (1994), pp. 15–23; Brady and Cronin, 'Some new thoughts on conceptualizing perceived service quality'.

35 For a review of what is known about service quality delivery via the Web see, V.A. Zeithaml, A. Parasuraman and A. Malhotra, 'Service quality delivery through websites: a critical review of extant knowledge', *Journal of the Academy of Marketing Science* 30, no. 4 (2002), pp. 362–75.

36 V. Zeithaml, A. Parasuraman and A. Malhotra, 'A conceptual framework for understanding e-service quality: implications for future research and managerial practice', Marketing Science Institute Working Paper, Report No. 00-115 (2001).

37 R. Normann, *Service Management: Strategy and Leadership in the Service Business*, 3rd edn (Chichester: John Wiley & Sons, 2000).

38 'How Marriott makes a great first impression', *The Service Edge* 6, no. 5 (May 1993), p. 5.

39 A.G. Woodside, L.L. Frey and R.T. Daly, 'Linking service quality, customer satisfaction, and behavioral intention', *Journal of Health Care Marketing* 9 (December 1989), pp. 5–17.

40 G.L. Shostack, 'Planning the service encounter', in *The Service Encounter*, eds J.A. Czepiel, M.R. Solomon and C.F. Surprenant (Lexington, MA: Lexington Books, 1985), pp. 243–54.

41 Ibid.

42 For detailed discussions of the critical incident technique, see J.C. Flanagan, 'The critical incident technique', *Psychological Bulletin* 51 (July 1954), pp. 327–58; M.J. Bitner, J.D. Nyquist and B.H. Booms, 'The critical incident as a technique for analyzing the service encounter', in *Services Marketing in a Changing Environment*, eds T.M. Bloch, G.D. Upah and V.A. Zeithaml (Chicago, IL: American Marketing Association, 1985), pp. 48–51; S. Wilson-Pessano, 'Defining professional competence: the critical incident technique 40 years later', paper presentation to the Annual Meeting of the American Educational Research Association, New Orleans (1988); I. Roos, 'Methods of investigating critical incidents', *Journal of Service Research* 4 (February 2002), pp. 193–204; D.D. Gremler, 'The critical incident technique in service research', *Journal of Service Research* 7 (August 2004), pp. 65–89.

43 For a complete discussion of the research on which this section is based, see M.J. Bitner, B.H. Booms and M.S. Tetreault, 'The service encounter: diagnosing favorable and unfavorable incidents', *Journal of Marketing* 54 (January 1990), pp. 71–84; M.J. Bitner, B.H. Booms and L.A. Mohr, 'Critical service encounters: the employee's view', *Journal of Marketing* 58, no. 4 (1994), pp. 95–106; D. Gremler and M.J. Bitner, 'Classifying service encounter satisfaction across industries', in *Marketing Theory and Applications*, eds C.T. Allen et al. (Chicago, IL: American Marketing Association, 1992), pp. 111–18; and D. Gremler, M.J. Bitner and K.R. Evans, 'The internal service encounter', *International Journal of Service Industry Management* 5, no. 2 (1994), pp. 34–56.

44 Bitner, Booms and Mohr, 'Critical service encounters'.

45 Bitner, 'Managing the evidence of service'.

CHAPTER 5

1 The gaps model of service quality that provides the structure for this text was developed by and is fully presented in V.A. Zeithaml, A. Parasuraman and L.L. Berry, *Delivering Quality Service: Balancing Customer Perceptions and Expectations* (New York: Free Press, 1990).

2 Financial Services Authority, 'Review of Complaint Handling in Banking Groups' (2010).

CHAPTER 6

1 A. Wilson, *Marketing Research: An Integrated Approach*, 3rd edn (London: FT Prentice-Hall, 2011).

2 This section is based on a comprehensive assessment of the critical incident technique in D.D. Gremler, 'The critical incident technique in service research', *Journal of Service Research* 7 (August 2004), pp. 65–89.

3 Ibid.

4 F. Buttle, 'SERVQUAL: review, critique, research agenda', *European Journal of Marketing* 30, no.1 (1996), pp. 8–32.

5 C. Grönroos, *Service Management and Marketing*, 3rd edn (Chichester: John Wiley & Son, 2007).

6 J. Cronin and S. Taylor, 'Measuring service quality: a reexamination and extension', *Journal of Marketing* 56 (1992), pp. 55–68.

7 See http://www.slm-leisure.co.uk.

8 E. Day, 'Researchers must enter consumer's world', *Marketing News*, 17 August 1998, p. 17.

9 G. Khermouch, 'Consumers in the mist', *Business Week*, 26 February 2001, pp. 92–3.

10 Wilson, *Marketing Research: An Integrated Approach.*

11 Adapted from A.M. Wilson, 'The use of mystery shopping in the measurement of service delivery', *The Service Industries Journal* 18, no. 3 (1998), pp. 148–63.

12 P.R. Magnusson, J. Mathing and P. Kristensson, 'Managing user involvement in service innovation: experiments with innovating end users', *Journal of Service Research* 6 (November 2003), pp. 111–24.

13 V.A. Zeithaml, A. Parasuraman and L.L. Berry, *Delivering Quality Service: Balancing Customer Perceptions and Expectations* (New York: Free Press, 1990), p. 28.

14 A. Parasuraman, V.A. Zeithaml and L.L. Berry, 'Moving forward in service quality research', Marketing Science Institute Report No. 94–114, (September 1994).

15 R. Johnson, 'A strategy for service – Disney style', *Journal of Business Strategy* (September–October 1991), pp. 38–43.

16 A. Wilson, *Marketing Research: An Integrated Approach*, 3rd edn (London: FT Prentice-Hall, 2011).

17 Ibid.

18 'Baldridge winner co-convenes quality summit', *Executive Report on Customer Satisfaction*, 30 October 1992.

19 M.J. Bitner, B. Booms and L. Mohr, 'Critical service encounters: the employee's viewpoint', *Journal of Marketing* 58 (October 1994), pp. 95–106.

20 Zeithaml, Parasuraman and Berry, *Delivering Quality Service*, p. 64.

21 'Empowerment is the strength of effective suggestion systems', *Total Quality Newsletter*, August 1991.

CHAPTER 7

1 F.E. Webster Jr, 'The changing role of marketing in the corporation', *Journal of Marketing* (October 1992), pp. 1–17.

2 For discussions of relationship marketing and its influence on the marketing of services, consumer goods, strategic alliances, distribution channels and buyer–seller interactions, see *Journal of the Academy of Marketing Science*, Special Issue on Relationship Marketing, 23 (Fall 1995). Some of the early roots of this paradigm shift can be found in C. Grönroos, *Service Management and Marketing* (New York: Lexington Books, 1990); and E. Gummesson, 'The new marketing – developing long-term interactive relationships', *Long Range Planning* 20 (1987), pp. 10–20. For current thinking and excellent reviews of relationship marketing across a spectrum of topics, see J.N. Sheth, *Handbook of Relationship Marketing* (Thousand Oaks, CA: Sage Publications, 2000).

3 L.L. Berry and A. Parasuraman, *Marketing Services* (New York: Free Press, 1991), ch. 8.

4 G. Knisely, 'Comparing marketing management in package goods and service organizations', a series of interviews appearing in *Advertising Age*, 15 January, 19 February, 19 March and 14 May 1979.

5 This discussion is based on M.D. Johnson and F. Selnes, 'Customer portfolio management: toward a dynamic theory of exchange relationships', *Journal of Marketing* 68 (April 2004), pp. 1–17.

6 R.M. Morgan and S.D. Hunt, 'The commitment-trust theory of relationship marketing', *Journal of Marketing* 58 (July 1994), pp. 20–38; N. Bendapudi and L.L. Berry, 'Customers' motivations for maintaining relationships with service providers', *Journal of Retailing* 73 (Spring 1997), pp. 15–37.

7 Johnson and Selnes, 'Customer portfolio management'.

8 Ibid.

9 See also D. Siredeshmukh, J. Singh and B. Sabol, 'Customer trust, value, and loyalty in relational exchanges', *Journal of Marketing* 66 (January 2002), pp. 15–37.

10 See C. Huffman and B. Kahn, 'Variety for sale: mass customization or mass confusion?' *Journal of Retailing* 74 (Winter 1998), pp. 491–513; B.J. Pine and J.H. Gilmore, 'Welcome to the experience economy', *Harvard Business Review* 76 (July–August 1998), pp. 97–105; B.J. Pine, D. Peppers and M. Rodgers, 'Do you want to keep your customers forever?', *Harvard Business Review* 73 (March–April 1995), pp. 103–14.

11 C. Grönroos, *Service Management and Marketing*, 3rd edn (Chichester: John Wiley & Sons, 2007).

12 The three types of relational benefits discussed in this section are drawn from K.P. Gwinner, D.D. Gremler and M.J. Bitner, 'Relational benefits in service industries: the customer's perspective', *Journal of the Academy of Marketing Science* 26 (Spring 1998), pp. 101–14.

13 See M.B. Adelman, A. Ahuvia and C. Goodwin, 'Beyond smiling: social support and service quality', in *Service Quality: New Directions in Theory and Practice*, eds R.T. Rust and R.L. Oliver (Thousand Oaks, CA: Sage Publications, 1994), pp. 139–72; and C. Goodwin, 'Private roles in public encounters: communal relationships in service exchanges', unpublished manuscript, University of Manitoba (1993).

14 E.J. Arnould and L.L. Price, 'River magic: extraordinary experience and the extended service encounter', *Journal of Consumer Research* 20 (June 1993), pp. 24–45.

15 N. Bendapudi and R.P. Leone, 'How to lose your star performer without losing customers, too', *Harvard Business Review* (November 2001), pp. 104–15.

16 F.F. Reichheld and W.E. Sasser Jr, 'Zero defections: quality comes to services', *Harvard Business Review* (September–October 1990), pp. 105–11; and F.F. Reichheld, *The Loyalty Effect* (Boston, MA: Harvard Business School Press, 1996).

17 R. Dhar and R. Glazer, 'Hedging customers', *Harvard Business Review* 81 (May 2003), pp. 86–92.

18 D.D. Gremler and S.W. Brown, 'The loyalty ripple effect: appreciating the full value of customers', *International*

Journal of Service Industry Management 10, no. 3 (1999), pp. 271–91.

19   L.A. Bettencourt, 'Customer voluntary performance: customers as partners in service delivery', *Journal of Retailing* 73 (Fall 1997), pp. 383–406.

20   S.J. Grove and R.P. Fisk, 'The impact of other customers on service experiences: a critical incident examination of "getting along"', *Journal of Retailing* 73 (Spring 1997), pp. 63–85.

21   L.L. Price, E.J. Arnould and A. Hausman, 'Commercial friendships: service provider–client relationship dynamics', in *Frontiers in Services*, eds R.T. Rust and R.L. Oliver (Nashville, TN: Vanderbilt University, 1996).

22   Reichheld and Sasser, 'Zero defections'.

23   Additional frameworks for calculating lifetime customer value that include a variety of other variables can be found in W.J. Reinartz and V. Kumar, 'The impact of customer relationship characteristics on profitable lifetime duration', *Journal of Marketing* 67 (January 2003), pp. 77–99; Dhar and Glazer, 'Hedging customers'; H.K. Stahl, K. Matzler and H.H. Hinterhuber, 'Linking customer lifetime value with shareholder value', *Industrial Marketing Management* 32, no. 4 (2003), pp. 267–79.

24   S. Gupta, D.R. Helmann and J.A. Stuart, 'Valuing customers', *Journal of Marketing Research* 41 (February 2004), pp. 7–18.

25   For more on customer profitability segments and related strategies, see V.A. Zeithaml, R.T. Rust and K.N. Lemon, 'The customer pyramid: creating and serving profitable customers', *California Management Review* 43 (Summer 2001), pp. 118–42.

26   D. Brady, 'Why service stinks', *BusinessWeek*, 23 October 2000, pp. 118–28.

27   Dhar and Glazer, 'Hedging customers'.

28   D. Rosenblum, D. Tomlinson and L. Scott, 'Bottomfeeding for blockbuster businesses', *Harvard Business Review* 81 (March 2003), pp. 52–9.

29   See P.C. Verhoef, K.N. Lemon, A. Parasuraman, A. Roggeveen, M. Tsiros and L.A. Schlesinger, 'Customer experience creation: Determinants, dynamics and management strategies', *Journal of Retailing* 85(1) (2009), pp. 31–41

30   See T.A. Burnham, J.K. Frels and V. Mahajan, 'Consumer switching costs: a typology, antecedents, and consequences', *Journal of the Academy of Marketing Science* 32 (Spring 2003), pp. 109–26; F. Selnes, 'An examination of the effect of product performance on brand reputation, satisfaction, and loyalty', *European Journal of Marketing* 27, no. 9 (2003), pp. 19–35; P. Klemperer, 'The competitiveness of markets with switching costs', *Rand Journal of Economics* 18 (Spring 1987), pp. 138–50.

31   T.L. Huston and R.L. Burgess, 'Social exchange in developing relationships: an overview', in *Social Exchange in Developing Relationships*, eds

R.L. Burgess and T.L. Huston (New York: Academic Press, 1979), pp. 3–28; L. White and V. Yanamandram, 'Why customers stay: reasons and consequences of inertia in financial services', *Managing Service Quality* 14, nos 2/3 (2004), pp. 183–94.

32   See J.P. Guiltinan, 'A classification of switching costs with implications for relationship marketing', in *Marketing Theory and Practice*, eds Terry L. Childers et al. (Chicago, IL: American Marketing Association, 1989), pp. 216–20; Klemperer, P., 'The competitiveness of markets with switching costs', *The RAND Journal of Economics* 18, no. 1 (Spring 1987), pp. 138–50; C. Fornell, 'A national customer satisfaction barometer: the Swedish experience', *Journal of Marketing* 56 (January 1992), pp. 6–21; P.G. Patterson and T. Smith, 'A cross-cultural study of switching barriers and propensity to stay with service providers', *Journal of Retailing* 79 (Summer 2003), pp. 107–20.

33   See Bendapudi and Berry, 'Customers' motivations for maintaining relationships with service providers'; H.S. Bansal, P.G. Irving and S.F. Taylor, 'A three-component model of customer commitment to service providers', *Journal of the Academy of Marketing Science* 32 (Summer 2004), pp. 234–50.

34   Berry and Parasuraman, *Marketing Services*, pp. 136–42.

35   For more information on cautions to be considered in implementing rewards strategies, see L. O'Brien and C. Jones, 'Do rewards really create loyalty?', *Harvard Business Review* (May–June 1995), pp. 75–82; and G.R. Dowling and M. Uncles, 'Do customer loyalty programs really work?', *Sloan Management Review* (Summer 1997), pp. 71–82.

36   D.D. Gremler and S.W. Brown, 'Service loyalty: its nature, importance, and implications', in *Advancing Service Quality: A Global Perspective*, eds B. Edvardsson, S.W. Brown, R. Johnston and E.E. Scheuing (Jamaica, NY: International Service Quality Association, 1996), pp. 171–80; H. Hansen, K. Sandvik and F. Selnes, 'Direct and indirect effects of commitment to a service employee on the intention to stay', *Journal of Service Research* 5 (May 2003), pp. 356–68.

37   C.W. Hart, 'Made to order', *Marketing Management* 5 (Summer 1996), pp. 11–23.

38   R. Brooks, 'Alienating customers isn't always a bad idea', P. Carroll and S. Rose, 'Revisiting customer retention', *Journal of Retail Banking* 15, no. 1 (1993), pp. 5–13.

39   J. Dahl, 'Rental counters reject drivers without good records', *The Wall Street Journal*, 23 October 1992, p. B1.

40   See L.C. Harris and K.L. Reynolds, 'The consequences of dysfunctional customer behavior', *Journal of Service Research* 6 (November 2003), p. 145 for cites; also, see A.A. Grandey, D.N. Dickter and H.P. Sin, 'The customer is *not* always right: customer aggression and emotion regulation of service employees', *Journal of Organizational Behavior* 25 (2004), pp. 397–418.

41 K. Ohnezeit, recruiting supervisor for Enterprise Rent-A-Car, personal communication, 12 February 2004.

42 See Harris and Reynolds, 'The consequences of dysfunctional customer behavior'.

43 S.M. Noble and J. Phillips, 'Relationship hindrance: why would consumers not want a relationship with a retailer?', *Journal of Retailing*, 80, no. 4 (2004), pp. 289–303.

44 For a detailed discussion on relationship ending, see A. Halinen and J. Tähtinen, 'A process theory of relationship ending', *International Journal of Service Industry Management* 13, no. 2 (2002), pp. 163–80.

45 M. Schrage, 'Fire your customers', *The Wall Street Journal*, 16 March 1992, p. A8.

46 S.Vargo,'Toward a transcending conceptualization of relationship', *Journal of Business & Industrial Marketing*, 24(5/6) (2009), pp. 373–379

CHAPTER 8

1 D.H. Henard and D.M. Szymanski, 'Why some new products are more successful than others', *Journal of Marketing Research* (August 2001), pp. 362–75.

2 M.J. Bitner and S.W. Brown, 'The Service Imperative', *Business Horizons 50th Anniversary Issue*, 51 (January–February 2008), pp. 39–46.

3 Sources: M.J. Bitner and S.W. Brown, 'The Service Imperative', *Business Horizons* 50th *Anniversary Issue*, 51 (January–February 2008), pp. 39–46; 'Succeeding through Service Innovation', a white paper published by the University of Cambridge Institute for Manufacturing and IBM, October 2007; and Organisation for Economic Co-operation and Development, 'Promoting Innovation in Services', 2005.

4 Source: European Commission: Enterprise and Industry, *Challenges for EU Support to Innovation in Services*, Pro INNO Europe Paper No. 12, 2009.

5 G.L. Shostack, 'Understanding services through blueprinting', in *Advances in Services Marketing and Management*, vol. 1, eds T.A. Swartz, D.E. Bowen and S.W. Brown (Greenwich, CT: JAI Press, 1992), pp. 75–90, quote from p. 76.

6 For excellent reviews of research and issues in new services development see *Journal of Operations Management* 20 (2002), special issue on New Issues and Opportunities in Service Design Research; A. Johne and C. Story, 'New service development: a review of the literature and annotated bibliography', *European Journal of Marketing* 32, no. 3/4 (1998), pp. 184–251; B. Edvardsson, A. Gustafsson, M.D. Johnson and B. Sanden, *New Service Development and Innovation in the New Economy* (Lund: Studentlitteratur AB, 2000).

7 B. Schneider and D.E. Bowen, 'New services design, development and implementation and the employee', in *Developing New Services*, eds W.R. George and

C. Marshall (Chicago, IL: American Marketing Association, 1984), pp. 82–101.

8 S. Michel, S.W. Brown and A.S. Gallan, 'An expanded and strategic view of discontinuous innovations: deploying a service dominant logic', *Journal of the Academy of Marketing Science* 36 (Winter 2008).

9 For a discussion of these adaptations and related research issues, see M.V. Tatikonda and V.A. Zeithaml, 'Managing the new service development process: synthesis of multidisciplinary literature and directions for future research', in *New Directions in Supply Chain Management: Technology, Strategy, and Implementation*, eds T. Boone and R. Ganeshan (New York: AMACOM, 2002), pp. 200–36; B. Edvardsson et al., *New Service Development and Innovation in the New Economy*.

10 A. Griffin, 'PDMA research on new product development practices: updating trends and benchmarking best practices', *Journal of Product Innovation Management* 14 (1997), pp. 429–58; S. Thomke, 'R&D comes to services: Bank of America's pathbreaking experiments', *Harvard Business Review*, 81 (April 2003), pp. 70–9.

11 R.G. Cooper, 'Stage gate systems for new product success', *Marketing Management* 1, no. 4 (1992), pp. 20–9.

12 M. Iansiti and A. MacCormack, 'Developing products on Internet time', *Harvard Business Review* (September–October 1997), pp. 108–17.

13 A. Khurana and S.R. Rosenthal, 'Integrating the fuzzy front end of new product development', *Sloan Management Review* (Winter 1997), pp. 103–20.

14 Iansiti and MacCormack, 'Developing products on Internet time'.

15 M.E. Porter, *Competitive Strategy* (New York: Free Press, 1980).

16 Khurana and Rosenthal, 'Integrating the fuzzy front end'; see also R.G. Cooper, S.J. Edgett and E.J. Kleinschmidt, *Portfolio Management for New Products* (Reading, MA: Addison-Wesley, 1998).

17 D. Rigby and C. Zook, 'Open-market innovation', *Harvard Business Review* (October 2002), pp. 80–9.

18 D. Leonard and J.F. Rayport, 'Spark innovation through empathic design', *Harvard Business Review* (November–December 1997), pp. 103–13.

19 J. Surowiecki, *The Wisdom of Crowds* (Doubleday Publishing, 2005).

20 R. Cross, A. Hargadon, S. Parise and R.J. Thomas, 'Together we innovate', *The Wall Street Journal*, September 15–16 (2007), p. R6.

21 Shostack, 'Service design'.

22 E.E. Scheuing and E.M. Johnson, 'A proposed model for new service development', *Journal of Services Marketing* 3, no. 2 (1989), pp. 25–34.

23 Shostack, 'Service design', p. 35.

24 Maxey, 'Testing, testing, testing'.

25 The service blueprinting section of the chapter draws from the pioneering works in this area: G.L. Shostack,

'Designing services that deliver', *Harvard Business Review* (January–February 1984), pp. 133–9; G.L. Shostack, 'Service positioning through structural change', *Journal of Marketing* 51 (January 1987), pp. 34–43; J. Kingman-Brundage, 'The ABCs of service system blueprinting', in *Designing a Winning Service Strategy*, eds M.J. Bitner and L.A. Crosby (Chicago, IL: American Marketing Association, 1989), pp. 30–3.

26 Shostack, 'Understanding services through blueprinting', pp. 75–90.

27 These key components are drawn from Kingman-Brundage, 'The ABCs'.

28 S. Flieb and M. Kleinaltenkamp, 'Blueprinting the service company: managing service processes efficiently', *Journal of Business Research* 57 (2004), pp. 392–404.

29 For coverage of the practical benefits of blueprinting, see, E. Gummesson and J. Kingman-Brundage, 'Service design and quality: applying service blueprinting and service mapping to railroad services', in *Quality Management in Services*, eds P. Kunst and J. Lemmink (Assen/Maastricht: Van Gorcum, 1991).

30 Shostack, 'Understanding services through blueprinting'.

31 D. Getz, M. O'Neill and J. Carlsen, 'Service quality evaluation at events through service mapping', *Journal of Travel Research* 39 (May 2001), pp. 380–90.

32 Cooper et al., *Portfolio Management for New Products*.

33 Froehle et al., 'Antecedents of new service development effectiveness'; Henard and Szymanski, 'Why some new products are more successful than others'; Edvardsson et al., *New Service Development and Innovation in the New Economy*.

34 Cooper et al., *Portfolio Management for New Products*.

35 See ibid. for an excellent discussion and coverage of multiple methods for managing product and service portfolios.

36 S.S. Tax and I. Stuart, 'Designing and implementing new services: the challenges of integrating service systems', *Journal of Retailing* 73 (Spring 1977), pp. 105–34.

37 R.G. Cooper, C.J. Easingwood, S. Edgett, E.J. Kleinschmidt, and C. Storey, 'What distinguishes the top performing new products in financial services?', *Journal of Product Innovation Management* 11 (1994), pp. 281–99.

38 B. Edvardsson, L. Haqlund and J. Mattson, 'Analysis, planning, improvisation and control in the development of new services', *International Journal of Service Industry Management* 6, no. 2 (1995) pp. 24–35.

CHAPTER 9

1 T. Levitt, 'Industrialization of service', *Harvard Business Review* (September–October 1976), pp. 63–74.

2 B.S. Lunde and S.L. Marr, 'Customer satisfaction measurement: does it pay off?' (Indianapolis, IN: Walker Customer Satisfaction Measurements, 1990).

3 See 2005 and 2004 National Customer Rage Studies conducted by Customer Care Alliance in collaboration with the Center for Services Leadership at Arizona State University's W.P. Carey School of Business.

4 F. Reichheld, 'e-loyalty', *Harvard Business Review* (July–August 2000), pp. 105–13.

5 D.E. Hansen and P.J. Danaher, 'Inconsistent performance during the service encounter: what's a good start worth?', *Journal of Service Research* 1 (February 1999), pp. 227–35.

6 'Taking the measure of quality', *Service Savvy* (March 1992), p. 3.

7 This discussion about the Four Seasons is based on R. Hallowell, D. Bowen and C. Knoop, 'Four Seasons goes to Paris', *Academy of Management Executive* 16, no. 4 (2002), pp. 7–24.

8 1999 application summary for The Ritz-Carlton Hotel Company, Malcolm Baldrige National Quality Award, 2000.

9 'Taking the measure of quality', p. 3.

CHAPTER 10

1 The term *servicescape* used throughout this chapter, and much of the content of this chapter, are based, with permission, on M.J. Bitner, 'Servicescapes: the impact of physical surroundings on customers and employees', *Journal of Marketing* 56 (April 1992), pp. 57–71. For recent contributions to this topic, see *Servicescapes: The Concept of Place in Contemporary Markets*, ed. J.F. Sherry Jr (Chicago, IL: NTC/Contemporary Publishing, 1998); and M.J. Bitner, 'The servicescape', in *Handbook of Services Marketing and Management*, eds T.A. Swartz and D. Iacobucci (Thousand Oaks, CA: Sage Publications, 2000), pp. 37–50.

2 L.P. Carbone, *Clued In: How to Keep Customers Coming Back Again and Again* (Upper Saddle River, NJ: Prentice Hall, 2004). See also L.L. Berry and N. Bendapudi, 'Clueing in customers', *Harvard Business Review* (February 2003), pp. 100–6.

3 J.H. Gilmore and B.J. Pine II, 'The experience is the marketing', *Strategic Horizons* (2002), an e-Doc; B.J. Pine II and J.H. Gilmore, *The Experience Economy: Work Is Theater and Every Business Is a Stage* (Boston, MA: Harvard Business School Press, 1999); B.H. Schmitt, *Experiential Marketing* (New York: Free Press, 1999).

4 For reviews of environmental psychology, see D. Stokols and I. Altman, *Handbook of Environmental Psychology* (New York: John Wiley, 1987); S. Saegert and G.H. Winkel, 'Environmental psychology', *Annual Review of Psychology* 41 (1990), pp. 441–77; and E. Sundstrom, P.A. Bell, P.L. Busby and C. Asmus, 'Environmental psychology 1989–1994', *Annual Review of Psychology* 47 (1996), pp. 485–512.

5   See M.R. Solomon, 'Dressing for the part: the role of costume in the staging of the servicescape', in *Servicescapes: The Concept of Space in Contemporary Markets*, ed. J.F. Sherry Jr (Chicago, IL: NTC/ Contemporary Publishing, 1998), pp. 81–108; and A. Rafaeli, 'Dress and behavior of customer contact employees: a framework for analysis', in *Advances in Services Marketing and Management*, vol. 2, eds T.A. Swartz, D.E. Bowen and S.W. Brown (Greenwich, CT: JAI Press, 1993), pp. 175–212.

6   See http://www.dezeen.com/20i4/07/18/christopher-jenner-eurostar-london-ticket-hall-redesign/.

7   D. Michaels, 'Business-class warfare: rival airlines scramble to beat BA's reclining bed seats', *The Wall Street Journal*, 16 March 2001, p. B1.

8   Ibid.; and British Airways' website, www.britishairways.com.

9   See www.citizenm.com.

10 Adapted from http://www.creativematch.co.uk/news/

11 Carbone, *Clued In*; Berry and Bendapudi, 'Clueing in customers'; Gilmore and Pine, 'Experience is the marketing'; Pine and Gilmore, *The Experience Economy*; Schmitt, *Experiential Marketing*.

12 A. Mehrabian and J.A. Russell, *An Approach to Environmental Psychology* (Cambridge, MA: Massachusetts Institute of Technology, 1974).

13 R. Donovan and J. Rossiter, 'Store atmosphere: an environmental psychology approach', *Journal of Retailing* 58 (Spring 1982), pp. 34–57.

14 D.J. Bennett and J.D. Bennett, 'Making the scene', in *Social Psychology through Symbolic Interactionism*, eds G. Stone and H. Farberman (Waltham, MA: Ginn-Blaisdell, 1970), pp. 190–6.

15 J.P. Forgas, *Social Episodes* (London: Academic Press, 1979).

16 R.G. Barker, *Ecological Psychology* (Stanford, CA: Stanford University Press, 1968).

17 For a number of excellent papers on this topic spanning a range from toy stores to bridal salons to cybermarketspaces to Japanese retail environments and others, see J.F. Sherry Jr, ed., *Servicescapes: The Concept of Place in Contemporary Markets*.

18 Sherry, 'The soul of the company store: Nike Town Chicago and the emplaced brandscape', in *Servicescapes: The Concept of Place in Contemporary Markets*, ed. J.F. Sherry Jr (Chicago, IL: NTC/ Contemporary Publishing, 1998), pp. 109–46.

19 E.J. Arnould, L.L. Price and P. Tierney, 'The wilderness servicescape: an ironic commercial landscape', in *Servicescapes: The Concept of Place in Contemporary Markets*, ed. J.F. Sherry Jr (Chicago, IL: NTC/ Contemporary Publishing, 1998), pp. 403–38.

20 Adapted from J.F. Sherry Jr, 'The soul of the company store: Nike Town Chicago and the emplaced brandscape', in *Servicescapes: The Concept of Place in Contemporary Markets*, ed. J.F. Sherry Jr (Chicago: NTC/Contemporary Publishing Company, 1998), pp. 109–46. Copyright © 1998 by NTC Business Books. Reprinted by permission of NTC Contemporary Books. The initial quotation is from 'Nike Town Comes to Chicago,' Nike press release, 2 July 1992, as quoted in ibid., p. 109.

21 A. Rapoport, *The Meaning of the Built Environment* (Beverly Hills, CA: Sage Publications, 1982); R.G. Golledge, 'Environmental cognition', in *Handbook of Environmental Psychology*, vol. 1, eds D. Stokols and I. Altman (New York: John Wiley, 1987), pp. 131–74.

22 M.P. Gardner and G. Siomkos, 'Toward a methodology for assessing effects of in-store atmospherics', in *Advances in Consumer Research*, vol. 13, ed. R.J. Lutz (Ann Arbor, MI: Association for Consumer Research, 1986), pp. 27–31.

23 M.J. Bitner, 'Evaluating service encounters: the effects of physical surroundings and employee responses', *Journal of Marketing* 54 (April 1990), pp. 69–82.

24 J.C. Ward, M.J. Bitner and J. Barnes, 'Measuring the prototypicality and meaning of retail environments', *Journal of Retailing* 68 (Summer 1992) pp. 194–220.

25 See, for example, Mehrabian and Russell, *An Approach to Environmental Psychology*; J.A. Russell and U.F. Lanius, 'Adaptation level and the affective appraisal of environments', *Journal of Environmental Psychology* 4, no. 2 (1984), pp. 199–235; J.A. Russell and G. Pratt, 'A description of the affective quality attributed to environments', *Journal of Personality and Social Psychology* 38, no. 2 (1980), pp. 311–22; J.A. Russell and J. Snodgrass, 'Emotion and the environment', in *Handbook of Environmental Psychology*, vol. 1, eds D. Stokols and I. Altman (New York: John Wiley, 1987), pp. 245–81; J.A. Russell, L.M. Ward and G. Pratt, 'Affective quality attributed to environments', *Environment and Behavior* 13 (May 1981), pp. 259–88.

26 See, for example, M.S. Sanders and E.J. McCormick, *Human Factors in Engineering and Design*, 7th edn (New York: McGraw-Hill, 1993); and D.J. Osborne, *Ergonomics at Work*, 2nd edn (New York: John Wiley, 1987).

27 Mehrabian and Russell, *An Approach to Environmental Psychology*; Russell and Snodgrass, 'Emotion and the environment'.

28 A. Mehrabian, 'Individual differences in stimulus screening and arousability', *Journal of Personality* 45, no. 2 (1977), pp. 237–50.

29 For recent research documenting the effects of music on consumers, see J. Baker, D. Grewal and A. Parasuraman, 'The influence of store environment on quality inferences and store image', *Journal of the Academy of Marketing Science* 22 (Fall 1994), pp. 328–39; J.C. Chebat, C. Gelinas-Chebat and P. Filliatrault, 'Interactive effects of musical and visual cues on time perception: an application to waiting lines in banks', *Perceptual and Motor Skills* 77 (1993), pp. 995–1020; L. Dube, J.C. Chebat and S. Morin, 'The effects of background music on consumers' desire to affiliate in buyer–seller interactions', *Psychology and Marketing* 12, no. 4 (1995), pp. 305–19; J.D. Herrington and L.M. Capella, 'Effects of music in service environments: a field study', *Journal of Services Marketing* 10, no. 2 (1996), pp. 26–41; J.D. Herrington and L.M. Capella, 'Practical applications of music in service settings', *Journal of Services Marketing* 8, no. 3 (1994), pp. 50–65; M.K. Hui, L. Dube and J.C. Chebat, 'The impact of music on consumers' reactions to waiting for services', *Journal of Retailing* 73 (Spring 1997), pp. 87–104; A.S. Mattila and J. Wirtz, 'Congruency of scent and music as a driver of in-store evaluations and behavior', *Journal of Retailing* 77 (Summer 2001), pp. 273–89; L. Dube and S. Morin, 'Background music pleasure and store evaluation: intensity effects and psychological mechanisms', *Journal of Business Research* 54 (November 2001), pp. 107–13; J. Bakec, A. Parasuraman, D. Grewal and G.B. Voss, 'The influence of multiple store environment cues as perceived merchandise value and patronage intentions', *Journal of Marketing* 66 (April 2002), pp. 120–41.

30 For recent research documenting the effects of scent on consumer responses, see D.J. Mitchell, B.E. Kahn and S.C. Knasko, 'There's something in the air: effects of congruent and incongruent ambient odor on consumer decision making', *Journal of Consumer Research* 22 (September 1995), pp. 229–38; and E.R. Spangenberg, A.E. Crowley and P.W. Henderson, 'Improving the store environment: do olfactory cues affect evaluations and behaviors?' *Journal of Marketing* 60 (April 1996), pp. 67–80.

31 See www.singaporeair.com.

32 See J.M. Sulek, M.R. Lind and A.S. Marucheck, 'The impact of a customer service intervention and facility design on firm performance', *Management Science* 41, no. 11 (1995), pp. 1763–73; P.A. Titus and P.B. Everett, 'Consumer wayfinding tasks, strategies, and errors: an exploratory field study', *Psychology and Marketing* 13, no. 3 (1996), pp. 265–90; C. Yoo, J. Park and D.J. MacInnis, 'Effects of store characteristics and instore emotional experiences on store attitude', *Journal of Business Research* 42 (1998), pp. 253–63; K.L. Wakefield and J.G. Blodgett, 'The effect of the servicescape on customers' behavioral intentions in leisure service settings', *Journal of Services Marketing* 10, no. 6 (1996), pp. 45–61.

33 T.R.V. Davis, 'The influence of the physical environment in offices', *Academy of Management Review* 9, no. 2 (1984), pp. 271–83.

34 J.C. Ward and J.P. Eaton, 'Service environments: the effect of quality and decorative style on emotions, expectations, and attributions', in *Proceedings of the American Marketing Association Summer Educators' Conference*, eds. R. Achrol and A. Mitchell (Chicago, IL: American Marketing Association 1994), pp. 333–4.

35 This section is adapted from M.J. Bitner, 'Managing the evidence of service', in *The Service Quality Handbook*,
eds E.E. Scheuing and W.F. Christopher (New York: AMACOM, 1993), pp. 358–70.

36 *Sources: Golden Arches East: McDonald's in East Asia*, ed. J.L. Watson (Stanford, CA: Stanford University Press, 1997); 'A unique peak', *Franchise Times* 3, no. 4 (1997), p. 46; C. Walkup, 'McD pins global growth on upgrades to units experience', *Nations's Restaurant News*, August 6 (2007), p. 1

37 F.D. Becker, *Workspace* (New York: Praeger, 1981).

CHAPTER 11

1   S.M. Davis, *Managing Corporate Culture* (Cambridge, MA: Ballinger, 1985).

2   C. Grönroos, *Service Management and Marketing* (Lexington, MA: Lexington Books, 1990), p. 244.

3   See K.N. Kennedy, F.G. Lassk, and J.R. Goolsby, 'Customer mind-set of employees throughout the organization', *Journal of the Academy of Marketing Science*, 30 (Spring 2002), pp. 159–71.

4   R. Hallowell, D. Bowen and C. Knoop, 'Four Seasons goes to Paris', *Academy of Management Executive* 16, no. 4 (2002), pp. 7–24; J.L. Heskett, L.A. Schlesinger and E.W. Sasser Jr, *The Service Profit Chain* (New York: Free Press, 1997); B. Schneider and D.E. Bowen, *Winning the Service Game* (Boston, MA: Harvard Business School Press, 1995).

5   Berry, *Discovering the Soul of Service*, p. 40.

6   Hallowell, Bowen and Knoop, 'Four Seasons goes to Paris'.

7   For an excellent discussion of the complexities involved in creating and sustaining a service culture, see Schneider and Bowen, *Winning the Service Game*, ch. 9. See also M.D. Hartline, J.G. Maxham III and D.O. McKee, 'Corridors of influence in the dissemination of customer-oriented strategy to customer-contact service employees', *Journal of Marketing* 64 (April 2000), pp. 35–50.

8   Adapted from: R. Preston, 'Smiley Culture: Pret A Manger's Secret Ingredients', *Telegraph* 9 March, 2012

9   This quote is most frequently attributed to J. Carlzon of Scandinavian Airline Systems.

10 Adapted from R. Baker, 'Starbucks investment in staff creates brand advocates', *Marketing Week* (6 October 2010).

11 See, for example, H. Rosenbluth, 'Tales from a nonconformist company', *Harvard Business Review* (July–August 1991), pp. 26–36; and L.A. Schlesinger and J.L. Heskett, 'The service-driven service company', *Harvard Business Review* (September–October 1991), pp. 71–81.

12 B. Schneider and D.E. Bowen, 'The service organization: human resources management is crucial', *Organizational Dynamics* 21, (Spring 1993), pp. 39–52.

13 D.E. Bowen, S.W. Gilliland and R. Folger, 'How being fair with employees spills over to customers', *Organizational Dynamics* 27 (Winter 1999), pp. 7–23.

14   See J.L. Heskett, T.O. Jones, G.W. Loveman, W.E. Sasser Jr and L.A. Schlesinger, 'Putting the service–profit chain to work', *Harvard Business Review* (March–April 1994), pp. 164–74; G.W. Loveman, 'Employee satisfaction, customer loyalty, and financial performance', *Journal of Service Research* 1 (August 1998), pp. 18–31; A. Rucci, S.P. Kirn and R.T. Quinn, 'The employee–customer profit chain at Sears', *Harvard Business Review* (January–February 1998), pp. 82–97; and R. Hallowell and L.L. Schlesinger, 'The service–profit chain', in *The Handbook of Services Marketing and Management*, eds T.A. Swartz and D. Iacobucci (Thousand Oaks, CA: Sage Publications, 2000), pp. 203–22.

15   J. Pfeffer, *The Human Equation* (Boston, MA: Harvard Business School Press, 1998); and A.M. Webber, 'Danger: toxic company', *Fast Company* (November 1998), pp. 152–62.

16   M.K. Brady and J.J. Cronin Jr, 'Customer orientation: effects on customer service perceptions and outcome behaviors', *Journal of Service Research* 3 (February 2001), pp. 241–51.

17   L.A. Bettencourt and K. Gwinner, 'Customization of the service experience: the role of the frontline employee', *International Journal of Service Industry Management* 7, no. 2 (1996), pp. 3–20.

18   For research on the influence of front-line employee behaviours on customers, see D.D. Gremler and K.P. Gwinner, 'Customer–employee rapport in service relationships', *Journal of Service Research* 3 (August 2000), pp. 82–104; K. de Ruyter and M.G.M. Wetzels, 'The impact of perceived listening behavior in voice-to-voice service encounters', *Journal of Service Research* 2 (February 2000), pp. 276–84; T.J. Brown, J.C. Mowen, D.T. Donavan and J.W. Licata, 'The customer orientation of service workers: personality trait effects of self- and supervisor performance ratings', *Journal of Marketing Research* 39 (February 2002), pp. 110–19.

19   A. Hochschild, *The Managed Heart: Commercialization of Human Feeling* (Berkeley, CA: University of California Press, 1983).

20   T. Hennig-Thurau, M. Goth, M. Paul and D.D. Gremler, 'Are all smiles created equal? How employee-customer emotional contagion and emotional labor impact service relationships', *Journal of Marketing* 70 (July 2006), pp. 58–73.

21   A. Hochschild, 'Emotional labor in the friendly skies', *Psychology Today* (June 1982), pp. 13–15.

22   For additional discussion on emotional labour strategies, see R. Leidner, 'Emotional labor in service work', *Annals of the American Academy of Political and Social Science* 561, no. 1 (1999), pp. 81–95.

23   Quoted from C.L. Macdonald and C. Sirianni, *Working in the Service Society* (Philadelphia: Temple University Press, 1996), p. 4.

24   Quoted from B.F. Ashforth and R.H. Humphrey, 'Emotional labor in service roles: the influence of identity', *Academy of Management Review* 18 (1993), p. 93.

25   B. Shamir, 'Between service and servility: role conflict in subordinate service roles', *Human Relations* 33(10) (1980), pp. 741–56.

26   M.D. Hartline and O.C. Ferrell, 'The management of customer-contact service employees: an empirical investigation', *Journal of Marketing* 60 (October 1996), pp. 52–70; J. Singh, J.R. Goolsby and G.K. Rhoads, 'Burnout and customer service representatives', *Journal of Marketing Research* 31 (November 1994), pp. 558–69; L.A. Bettencourt and S.W. Brown, 'Role stressors and customer-oriented boundary-spanning behaviors in service organizations', *Journal of the Academy of Marketing Science* 31 (Fall 2003), pp. 394–408.

27   B. Shamir, 'Between service and servility: role conflict in subordinate service roles', *Human Relations* 33, no. 10 (1980), pp. 741–56.

28   E.W. Anderson, C. Fornell and R.T. Rust, 'Customer satisfaction, productivity, and profitability: differences between goods and services', *Marketing Science* 16, no. 2 (1997), pp. 129–45.

29   J. Singh, 'Performance productivity and quality of frontline employees in service organizations', *Journal of Marketing* 64 (April 2000), pp. 15–34.

30   For discussions of internal marketing, see L.L. Berry and A. Parasuraman, 'Marketing to employees', in *Marketing Services*, L.L. Berry and A. Parasuraman (New York: Free Press, 1991), ch. 9; C. Grönroos, 'Managing internal marketing: a prerequisite for successful external marketing', in *Service Management and Marketing*, C. Grönroos (Lexington, MA: Lexington Books, 1990), ch. 10.

31   B. Breen and A. Muoio, 'PeoplePalooza 2001', *Fast Company* (January 2001), cover and feature article.

32   Berry and Parasuraman, 'Marketing to employees', p. 153.

33   This section on hiring for service competencies and service inclination draws from work by B. Schneider and colleagues, specifically, B. Schneider and D. Schechter, 'Development of a personnel selection system for service jobs', in *Service Quality: Multidisciplinary and Multinational Perspectives*, eds S.W. Brown, E. Gummesson, B. Edvardsson and B. Gustavsson (Lexington, MA: Lexington Books, 1991), pp. 217–36.

34   J. Hogan, R. Hogan and C.M. Busch, 'How to measure service orientation', *Journal of Applied Psychology* 69, no. 1 (1984), pp. 167–73. See also Brown et al., 'The customer orientation of service workers'; and D.T. Donovan, T.J. Brown and J.C. Mowen, 'Internal benefits of serviceworker customer orientation: job satisfaction, commitment, and organizational citizenship behaviors', *Journal of Marketing* 68 (January 2004), pp. 128–46.

35   For a detailed description of a model selection system for telephone sales and service people, see Schneider and Schechter, 'Development of a personnel selection system'.

36   R. Normann, 'Getting people to grow', *Service Management* (New York: John Wiley, 1984), pp. 44–50.

37 See www.accor.com/en/recruitment-and-careers/why-choose-accorhotels/training.html

38 J.C. Chebat and P. Kollias, 'The impact of empowerment on customer contact employees' roles in service organizations', *Journal of Service Research* 3 (August 2000), pp. 66–81.

39 C. Argyris, 'Empowerment: the emperor's new clothes', *Harvard Business Review* 76 (May–June 1998), pp. 98–105.

40 D.E. Bowen and E.E. Lawler III, 'The empowerment of service workers: what, why, how, and when', *Sloan Management Review* (Spring 1992), pp. 31–9.

41 Reprinted from 'The empowerment of service workers: what, why, how, and when', by D.E. Bowen and E.E. Lawler, *Sloan Management Review* (Spring 1992), pp. 31–9, by permission of the publisher. Copyright © 1992 by Massachusetts Institute of Technology. All rights reserved.

42 J.H. Gittell, 'Relationships between service providers and their impact on customers', *Journal of Service Research* 4 (May 2002), pp. 299–311.

43 Berry and Parasuraman, 'Marketing to employees', p. 162.

44 A. Sergeant and S. Frenkel, 'When do customer-contact employees satisfy customers?', *Journal of Service Research* 3 (August 2000), pp. 18–34.

45 Reprinted from K. Albrecht, *At America's Service* (Homewood, IL: Dow-Jones-Irwin, 1988), pp. 139–42, as discussed in B. Schneider and D.E. Bowen, *Winning at the Service Game* (Boston, MA: Harvard Business School Press, 1995), pp. 231–2. Copyright © 1988 by Dow-Jones-Irwin. Reprinted by permission of The McGraw-Hill Companies.

46 Scheider and Bowen, *Winning the Service Game*, pp. 230–4.

47 O. Gadiesh and J.L. Gilbert, 'Transforming corneroffice strategy into frontline action', *Harvard Business Review* (May 2001), pp. 73–9.

48 L.L. Berry, 'The employee as customer', *Journal of Retail Banking* 3 (March 1981), pp. 33–40.

49 M.C. Gilly and M. Wolfinbarger, 'Advertising's internal audience', *Journal of Marketing* 62 (January 1998), pp. 69–88.

50 See Schneider and Bowen, *Winning the Service Game*, ch. 6, for an excellent discussion of the complexities and issues involved in creating effective reward systems for service employees.

51 N. Bendapudi and R.P. Leone, 'Managing business-to-business customer relationships following key contact employee turnover in a vendor firm', *Journal of Marketing* 66 (April 2002), pp. 83–101.

52 Ibid.

53 J.R. Katzenbach and J.A. Santamaria, 'Firing up the front line', *Harvard Business Review* (May–June 1999), pp. 107–17.

54 Quoted in D. Stauffer, 'The art of delivering great customer service', *Harvard Management Update* 4, no. 9 (September 1999), pp. 1–3.

CHAPTER 12

1 Sources: www.ikea.com; R. Normann and R. Ramirez, 'From value chain to value constellation: designing interactive strategy', *Harvard Business Review* (July–August 1993), pp. 65–77; B. Edvardsson and B. Enquist, 'The IKEA saga: how service culture drives service strategy', *The Service Industries Journal* 22 (October 2002), pp. 153–86; P.M. Miller, 'IKEA with Chinese characteristics', *The China Business Review* (July–August 2004), pp. 36–8; www.ikea.com (2004).

2 See B. Schneider and D.E. Bowen, *Winning the Service Game* (Boston, MA: Harvard Business School Press, 1995), ch. 4; L.A. Bettencourt, 'Customer voluntary performance: customers as partners in service delivery', *Journal of Retailing* 73, no. 3 (1997), pp. 383–406; P.K. Mills and J.H. Morris, 'Clients as "partial" employees: role development in client participation', *Academy of Management Review* 11, no. 4 (1986), pp. 726–35; C.H. Lovelock and R.F. Young, 'Look to customers to increase productivity', *Harvard Business Review* (Summer 1979), pp. 9–20; A.R. Rodie and S.S. Kleine, 'Customer participation in services production and delivery', in *Handbook of Services Marketing and Management*, eds T.A. Swartz and D. Iacobucci (Thousand Oaks, CA: Sage Publications, 2000), pp. 111–26; C.K. Prahalad and V. Ramaswamy, 'Co-opting customer competence', *Harvard Business Review* (January–February 2000), p. 7; N. Bendapudi and R.P. Leone, 'Psychological implications of customer participation in co-production', *Journal of Marketing* 67 (January 2003), pp. 14–28.

3 S.L. Vargo, and R.F. Lusch, 'Evolving to a new dominant logic for marketing' *Journal of Marketing* 68 (January 2004), pp.1–17; and R.F. Lusch, S.L. Vargo, and M.O. O'Brien, 'Competing through service: insights from service-dominant logic', *Journal of Retailing* 83, no. 1 (2007), pp. 5–18.

4 S.J. Grove, R.P. Fisk and M.J. Bitner, 'Dramatizing the service experience: a managerial approach', in *Advances in Services Marketing and Management*, vol. 1, eds T.A. Swartz, D.E. Bowen and S.W. Brown (Greenwich, CT: JAI Press, 1992), pp. 91–122.

5 For an interesting view of work and business as theatre, see B.J. Pine II and J.H. Gilmore, *The Experience Economy: Work Is Theatre and Every Business a Stage* (Boston, MA: Harvard Business School Press, 1999).

6 See S.J. Grove and R.P. Fisk, 'The impact of other customers on service experiences: a critical incident examination of "Getting Along"', *Journal of Retailing* 73, no. 1 (1997), pp. 63–85; C.I. Martin and C.A. Pranter, 'Compatibility management: customer-to-customer relationships in service environments', *Journal of Services Marketing* 3 (Summer 1989), pp. 5–15.

7 Grove and Fisk, 'The impact of other customers on service experiences'.

8 Ibid.

9   K. Harris and S. Baron, 'Consumer-to-consumer conversations in service settings', *Journal of Service Research* 6 (February 2004), pp. 287–303.

10 See P.K. Mills, R.B. Chase and N. Margulies, 'Motivating the client/employee system as a service production strategy', *Academy of Management Review* 8, no. 2 (1983), pp. 301–10; D.E. Bowen, 'Managing customers as human resources in service organizations', *Human Resource Management* 25, no. 3 (1986), pp. 371–83; and Mills and Morris, 'Clients as "partial" employees'.

11 L.A. Bettencourt, A.L. Ostrom, S.W. Brown and R.I. Rowntree, 'Client co-production in knowledge-intensive business services', *California Management Review*, 44, no. 4 (2002), pp. 100–28.

12 R.B. Chase, 'Where does the customer fit in a service operation?', *Harvard Business Review* (November–December 1978), pp. 137–42.

13 Mills et al., 'Motivating the client/employee system'.

14 M. Adams, 'Tech takes bigger role in air services', *USA Today*, 18 July 2001, p. 1.

15 See D.W. Johnson, R.T. Johnson and K.A. Smith, *Active Learning: Cooperation in the College Classroom* (Edina, MN: Interaction Book Company, 1991).

16 S. Dellande, M.C. Gilly and J.L. Graham, 'Gaining compliance and losing weight: the role of the service provider in health care services', *Journal of Marketing* 68 (July 2004), pp. 78–91.

17 S. Auh, S.J. Bell, C.S. Mcleod and E. Shih, 'Co-production and customer loyalty in financial services', *Journal of Retailing* 83, no. 3 (2007), pp. 359–70

18 S.W. Kelley, S.J. Skinner and J.H. Donnelly Jr, 'Organizational socialization of service customers', *Journal of Business Research* 25 (1992), pp. 197–214.

19 C. Claycomb, C.A. Lengnick-Hall and L.W. Inks, 'The customer as a productive resource: a pilot study and strategic implications', *Journal of Business Strategies* 18 (Spring 2001), pp. 47–69.

20 J.E.G. Bateson, 'The self-service customer – empirical findings', in *Emerging Perspectives in Services Marketing*, eds L.L. Berry, G.L. Shostack and G.D. Upah (Chicago, IL: American Marketing Association, 1983), pp. 50–3.

21 V.S. Folkes, 'Recent attribution research in consumer behavior: a review and new directions', *Journal of Consumer Research* 14 (March 1988), pp. 548–65; and M.J. Bitner, 'Evaluating service encounters: the effects of physical surroundings and employee responses', *Journal of Marketing* 54 (April 1990), pp. 69–82.

22 Bendapudi and Leone, 'Psychological implications of customer participation in co-production'.

23 R.F. Lusch, S.W. Brown and G.J. Brunswick, 'A general framework for explaining internal vs. external exchange', *Journal of the Academy of Marketing Science* 10 (Spring 1992), pp. 119–34.

24 Ibid.

25 See M.J. Bitner, A.L. Ostrom and M.L. Meuter, 'Implementing successful self-service technologies',

Academy of Management Executive 16 (November 2002), pp. 96–109.

26 See P. Dabholkar, 'Consumer evaluations of new technology-based self-service options: an investigation of alternative models of service quality', *International Journal of Research in Marketing* 13 (1), pp. 29–51; F. Davis, 'User acceptance of information technology: system characteristics, user perceptions and behavioral impact', *International Journal of Man-Machine Studies* 38 (1993), pp. 475–87; L.M. Bobbitt and P.A. Dabholkar, 'Integrating attitudinal theories to understand and predict use of technology-based self-service', *International Journal of Service Industry Management* 12, no. 5 (2001), pp. 423–50; J.M. Curran, M.L. Meuter and C.F. Surprenant, 'Intentions to use self-service technologies: a confluence of multiple attitudes', *Journal of Service Research* 5, no. 3 (2003), pp. 209–24.

27 M.L. Meuter, M.J. Bitner, A.L. Ostrom and S.W. Brown, 'Choosing among alternative service delivery modes: an investigation of customer trial of self-service technologies', *Journal of Marketing*, 69 (2005), pp. 61–83.

28 M.L. Meuter, A.L. Ostrom, R.I. Roundtree and M.J. Bitner, 'Self-service technologies: understanding customer satisfaction with technology-based service encounters', *Journal of Marketing* 64 (July 2000), pp. 50–64.

29 Meuter et al., 'Choosing among alternative service delivery modes'; see also Y. Moon and F.X. Frei, 'Exploding the self-service myth', *Harvard Business Review*, 78 (May–June 2000), pp. 26–7; Bitner et al., 'Implementing successful self-service technologies'.

30 A. Parasuraman and C.L. Colby, *Techno-Ready Marketing: How and Why Your Customers Adopt Technology* (New York: Free Press, 2001).

31 Bowen, 'Managing customers as human resources'.

32 Chase, 'Where does the customer fit in a service operation?'

33 See Schneider and Bowen, *Winning the Service Game*, ch. 4. The four job descriptions in this section are adapted from M.R. Bowers, C.L. Martin and A. Luker, 'Trading places, employees as customers, customers as employees', *Journal of Services Marketing* 4 (Spring 1990), pp. 56–69.

34 Bateson, 'The self-service customer'.

35 Meuter et al., 'Choosing among alternative service delivery modes'.

36 Bowen, 'Managing customers as human resources'; and Schneider and Bowen, *Winning the Service Game*, ch. 4; Meuter et al., 'Choosing among alternative service delivery modes'; Dellande et al., 'Gaining compliance and losing weight'.

37 C. Goodwin and R. Radford, 'Models of service delivery: an integrative perspective', in *Advances in Services Marketing and Management*, vol. 1, eds T.A. Swartz, D.E. Bowen and S.W. Brown (Greenwich, CT: JAI Press, 1992), pp. 231–52.

38 S.W. Kelley, J.H. Donnelly Jr and S.J. Skinner, 'Customer participation in service production and delivery', *Journal of Retailing* 66 (Fall 1990), pp. 315–35; and Schneider and Bowen, *Winning the Service Game*, ch. 4.

39 Bowen, 'Managing customers as human resources'.

40 Ibid.; see also L.C. Harris and K.L. Reynolds, 'The consequences of dysfunctional customer behavior', *Journal of Service Research* 6 (November 2003), pp. 144–61.

41 Martin and Pranter, 'Compatibility management'.

CHAPTER 13

1 R. Woodall, C. Colby, A. Parasuraman, 'E-volution to revolution', *Marketing Management*, March/April 2007, pp. 27–38.

2 G. Hamel and J. Sampler, 'The e-corporation', *Fortune*, 7 December 1998, pp. 80–92.

3 D. Clark, 'Safety first', *The Wall Street Journal*, 7 December 1998, p. R14.

4 Ibid.

5 See www.hsbc.com.

6 2013 Nat West/British Franchise Association Survey.

7 See www.thebodyshop.com.

8 See www.dominos.co.uk.

9 See www.prontaprint.com.

10 See www.toniandguy.co.uk.

11 See www.visionexpress.com.

12 A.E. Serwer, 'Trouble in franchise nation', *Fortune*, 6 March 1995, pp. 115–29.

13 2013 Nat West/British Franchise Association Survey.

14 R.S.Toh, P. Raven, and F. DeKay, 'Selling rooms: Hotels vs. third-party websites', *Cornell Hospitality Quarterly* 52.2 (2011): 181–189.

15 See www.fridays.com.

CHAPTER 14

1 C. Lovelock, 'Getting the most out of your productive capacity', in *Product Plus* (Boston, MA: McGraw-Hill, 1994), ch. 16.

2 G. Topham Yodel warns of parcel backlog as Christmas deliveries face delay, *Guardian* (2014), 12 December.

3 Portions of this section are based on C.H. Lovelock, 'Strategies for managing capacity-constrained service organizations', in *Managing Services: Marketing, Operations, and Human Resources*, 2nd edn (Englewood Cliffs, NJ: Prentice Hall, 1992), pp. 154–68.

4 Lovelock, 'Getting the most out of your productive capacity'.

5 M.E. Berge and C.A. Hopperstad, 'Demand driven dispatch: a method for dynamic aircraft capacity assignment, models, and algorithms', *Operations Research* 41 (January–February 1993), pp. 153–68.

6 Lovelock, 'Getting the most out of your productive capacity'.

7 I.C.L. Ng, 'The future of pricing and revenue models' *Journal of Revenue and Pricing Management*, 9(3) (2010): 525–548.

8 S.E. Kimes, 'Yield management: a tool for capacity-constrained service firms', *Journal of Operations Management* 8 (October 1989), pp. 348–63.

9 See www.airberlin.com.

10 N. Templin, 'Your room costs $250 … No! $200 … No', *The Wall Street Journal*, 5 May 1999, p. B1.

11 R. Desiraji and S.M. Shugan, 'Strategic service pricing and yield management', *Journal of Marketing* 63 (January 1999), pp. 44–56; and Fitzsimmons and Fitzsimmons, *Service Management*, ch.13, p. 403.

12 Kimes, 'Yield management'.

13 S.E. Kimes and J. Wirtz, 'Has revenue management become acceptable? Findings from an international study on the perceived fairness of rate fences', *Journal of Service Research* 6 (November 2003), pp. 125–35.

14 F.V. Wangenheim and T. Bayon, 'Behavioral consequences of overbooking service capacity', *Journal of Marketing* 71 (October 2007), pp. 36–47.

15 For research supporting the relationship between longer waits and decreased satisfaction, quality evaluations and patronage intentions see Clemmer and Schneider, 'Toward understanding and controlling customer dissatisfaction'; A.T.H. Pruyn and A. Smidts, 'Customer evaluation of queues: three exploratory studies', *European Advances in Consumer Research* 1 (1993), pp. 371–82; S. Taylor, 'Waiting for service: the relationship between delays and evaluations of service', *Journal of Marketing* 58 (April 1994), pp. 56–69; K.L. Katz, B.M. Larson and R.C. Larson, 'Prescription for the waiting-in-line blues: entertain, enlighten, and engage', *Sloan Management Review* (Winter 1991), pp. 44–53; S. Taylor and J.D. Claxton, 'Delays and the dynamics of service evaluations', *Journal of the Academy of Marketing Science* 22 (Summer 1994), pp. 254–64; D. Grewal, J. Baker, M. Levy and G.B. Voss, 'The effects of wait expectations and store atmosphere on patronage intentions in service-intensive retail stores', *Journal of Retailing* 79 (Winter 2003), pp. 259–68.

16 F. Bielen and N. Demoulin, 'Waiting time influence on the satisfaction-loyalty relationship in services', *Managing Service Quality* 17, no. 2 (2007), pp. 174–93.

17 J.A. Fitzsimmons and M.J. Fitzsimmons, *Service Management*, 3rd edn (New York: Irwin/McGraw-Hill, 2000), ch. 11.

18 R. Zhou and D. Soman, 'Looking back: exploring the psychology of queuing and the effect of the number of people behind', *Journal of Consumer Research* 29 (March 2003), pp. 517–30.

19 Fitzsimmons and Fitzsimmons, *Service Management*, ch. 11.

20 Lovelock, 'Getting the most out of your productive capacity'.

21 For an excellent review of the literature on customer perceptions of and reactions to various aspects of waiting time, see S. Taylor and G. Fullerton, 'Waiting for services: perceptions management of the wait experience', in *Handbook of Services Marketing and Management*, eds T.A. Swartz and D. Iacobucci (Thousands Oaks, CA: Sage Publications, 2000), pp. 171–89.

22 D.A. Maister, 'The psychology of waiting lines', in *The Service Encounter*, eds J.A. Czepiel, M.R. Solomon and C.F. Surprenant (Lexington, MA: Lexington Books, 1985), pp. 113–23.

23 S. Taylor, 'The effects of filled waiting time and service provider control over the delay on evaluations of service', *Journal of the Academy of Marketing Science* 23 (Summer 1995), pp. 38–48.

24 A. Bennett, 'Their business is on the line', *The Wall Street Journal*, 7 December 1990, p. B1.

25 L. Dube-Rioux, B.H. Schmitt and F. Leclerc, 'Consumer's reactions to waiting: when delays affect the perception of service quality', in *Advances in Consumer Research*, vol. 16, ed. T. Srull (Provo, UT: Association for Consumer Research, 1988), pp. 59–63.

26 M.K. Hui, M.V. Thakor and R. Gill, 'The effect of delay type and service stage on consumers' reactions to waiting', *Journal of Consumer Research* 24 (March 1998), pp. 469–79.

27 Taylor and Fullerton, 'Waiting for services'.

28 M.K. Hui and D.K. Tse, 'What to tell consumers in waits of different lengths: an integrative model of service evaluation', *Journal of Marketing* 60 (April 1996), pp. 81–90.

29 J. Baker and M. Cameron, 'The effects of the service environment on affect and consumer perception of waiting time: an integrative review and research propositions', *Journal of the Academy of Marketing Science* 24 (Fall 1996), pp. 338–49.

CHAPTER 15

1 For research that shows different types of service failures, see M.J. Bitner, B.H. Booms and M.S. Tetreault, 'The service encounter: diagnosing favorable and unfavorable incidents', *Journal of Marketing* 54 (January 1990), pp. 71–84; and S.M. Keaveney, 'Customer switching behavior in service industries: an exploratory study', *Journal of Marketing* 59 (April 1995), pp. 71–82.

2 Information provided by TARP Worldwide Inc, based on data from 10 studies (representing responses from more than 8,000 customers) conducted in 2006 and 2007. Companies from the following industries were included: retail (stores, catalogue and online) auto financing and insurance (property/casualty).

3 For research on important outcomes associated with service recovery, see S.S. Tax, S.W. Brown and M. Chandrashekaran, 'Customer evaluations of service complaint experiences: implications for relationship marketing', *Journal of Marketing* 62 (April 1998), pp. 60–76; S.S. Tax and S.W. Brown, 'Recovering and learning from service failure', *Sloan Management Review* (Fall 1998), pp. 75–88; A.K. Smith and R.N. Bolton, 'An experimental investigation of customer reactions to service failure and recovery encounters', *Journal of Service Research* 1 (August 1998), pp. 65–81; S.W. Kelley, K.D. Hoffman and M.A. Davis, 'A typology of retail failures and recoveries', *Journal of Retailing* 69 (Winter 1993), pp. 429–52; R.N. Bolton, 'A dynamic model of the customer's relationship with a continuous service provider: the role of satisfaction', *Marketing Science* 17, no. 1 (1998), pp. 45–65; A.K. Smith and R.N. Bolton, 'The effect of customers' emotional responses to service failures on their recovery effort evaluations and satisfaction judgments', *Journal of the Academy of Marketing Science* 30 (Winter 2002), pp. 5–23.

4 Information is based on data from 10 studies conducted in 2006 and 2007, TARP Worldwide Inc.

5 Ibid: Voorhees, Brady and Horowitz, 'A Voice from the Silent Masses'.

6 2007, 2005 and 2004 National Customer Rage Studies conducted by Customer Care Alliance in collaboration with the Center for Service Leadership at Arizona State University's W.P. Carey School of Business.

7 Aggregated results of 2003–2007 National Customer Rage surveys conducted by Customer Care Alliance.

8 See C.W. Hart, J.L. Heskett and W.E. Sasser Jr, 'The profitable art of service recovery', *Harvard Business Review* 68 (July–August 1990), pp. 148–56; M.A. McCollough and S.G. Bharadwaj, 'The recovery paradox: an examination of consumer satisfaction in relation to disconfirmation, service quality, and attribution based theories', in *Marketing Theory and Applications*, eds C.T. Allen et al. (Chicago, IL: American Marketing Association, 1992), p. 119.

9 C.A. de Matos, J.L. Henrique, and C.A.V. Rossi, 'Service recovery paradox: a meta-analysis', *Journal of Service Research* 10 (August 2007), pp. 60–77.

10 Smith and Bolton, 'An experimental investigation of customer reactions to service failure and recovery encounters'.

11 V.P. Magnini, J.B. Ford, E.P. Markowski and E.D. Honeycutt Jr., 'The service recovery paradox: justifiable theory or smoldering myth?', *Journal of Services Marketing* 21, no. 3 (2007), pp. 213–25; J.G. Maxham III and R.G. Netemeyer, 'A longitudinal study of complaining customers' evaluations of multiple service failures and recovery efforts', *Journal of Marketing* 66 (October 2002), pp. 57–71; M.A. McCullough, L.L. Berry, and M.S. Yadav, 'An empirical investigation of customer satisfaction after service failure and recovery', *Journal of Service Research* 3 (November 2000), pp. 121–37.

12 For research foundations on typologies of customer responses to failures, see R.L. Day and E.L. Landon Jr, 'Towards a theory of consumer complaining behavior',

in *Consumer and Industrial Buying Behavior*, eds A. Woodside, J. Sheth and P. Bennett (Amsterdam: North-Holland, 1977); J. Singh, 'Consumer complaint intentions and behavior: definitional and taxonomical issues', *Journal of Marketing* 52 (January 1988), pp. 93–107; and J. Singh, 'Voice, exit, and negative word-of-mouth behaviors: an investigation across three service categories', *Journal of the Academy of Marketing Science* 18 (Winter 1990), pp. 1–15.

13 Smith and Bolton, 'The effect of customers' emotional responses to service failures'.

14 Ibid.

15 N. Stephens and K.P. Gwinner, 'Why don't some people complain? A cognitive–emotive process model of consumer complaining behavior', *Journal of the Academy of Marketing Science* 26 (Spring 1998), pp. 172–89.

16 Ibid.

17 A.S. Mattila and J. Wirtz, 'Consumer complaining to firms: the determinants of channel choice', *Journal of Services Marketing*, 18, no. 2 (2004), pp. 147–55.

18 Many such websites exist; examples include www.untied.com (for United Airlines experiences), www.starbucked.com (for Starbucks), and www.walmartsucks.com (for Wal-Mart).

19 J.C. Ward and A.L. Ostrom, 'Online complaining via customer-created websites: a protest framing perspective', working paper, W.P. Carey School of Business, Arizona State University (2004).

20 J. Singh, 'A typology of consumer dissatisfaction response styles', *Journal of Retailing* 66 (Spring 1990), pp. 57–99.

21 Source: Adapted from complaint on flightsfromhell.com.

22 J.R. McColl-Kennedy and B.A. Sparks, 'Application of fairness theory to service failures and service recovery', *Journal of Service Research* 5 (February 2003), pp. 251–66; M. Davidow, 'Organizational responses to customer complaints: what works and what doesn't', *Journal of Service Research* 5 (February 2003), pp. 225–50.

23 2007 National Customer Rage Study conducted by Customer Care Alliance.

24 Davidow, 'Organizational responses to customer complaints'.

25 Granier, Kemp and Lawes, 'Customer complaint handling – the multimillion pound sinkhole'.

26 See Tax, Brown and Chandrashekaran, 'Customer evaluations of service complaint experiences'; Tax and Brown, 'Recovering and learning from service failure'.

27 Tax and Brown, 'Recovering and learning from service failure'.

28 Smith and Bolton, 'The effect of customers' emotional responses to service failures'.

29 A.S. Mattila and P.G. Patterson, 'Service recovery and fairness perceptions in collectivist and individualist Contexts', *Journal of Services Research* 6 (May 2004), pp. 336–46; A.S. Mattila and P.G. Patterson, 'The impact of culture on consumers' perceptions of service recovery efforts', *Journal of Retailing* 80 (Fall 2004), pp. 196–206.

30 McCullough, Berry and Yadav, 'An empirical investigation of customer satisfaction after service failure and recovery'.

31 A.S. Mattila, 'The impact of relationship type on customer loyalty in a context of service failures', *Journal of Service Research*, 4 (November 2001), pp. 91–101; see also R.L. Hess Jr, S. Ganesan and N.M. Klein, 'Service failure and recovery: the impact of relationship factors on customer satisfaction', *Journal of the Academy of Marketing Science* 31 (Spring 2003), pp. 127–45; R. Priluck, 'Relationship marketing can mitigate product and service failures', *Journal of Services Marketing* 17, no. 1 (2003), pp. 37–52.

32 H.S. Bansal and S.F. Taylor, 'The service provider switching model (SPSM)', *Journal of Service Research* 2 (November 1999), pp. 200–18.

33 S.M. Keaveney and M. Parthasarathy, 'Customer switching behavior in online services: an exploratory study of the role of selected attitudinal, behavioral, and demographic factors', *Journal of the Academy of Marketing Science* 29, no. 4 (2001), pp. 374–90.

34 I. Roos, 'Switching processes in customer relationships', *Journal of Service Research* 2 (August 1999), pp. 68–85.

35 Keaveney, 'Customer switching behavior in service industries'.

36 A. Parasuraman, V.A. Zeithaml and L.L. Berry, 'SERVQUAL: a multiple-item scale for measuring consumer perceptions of service quality', *Journal of Retailing* 64 (Spring 1988), pp. 64–79.

37 R.B. Chase and D.M. Stewart, 'Make your service failsafe', *Sloan Management Review* (Spring 1994), pp. 35–44.

38 Ibid.

39 F.F. Reichheld and W.E. Sasser Jr, 'Zero defections: quality comes to services', *Harvard Business Review* (September–October 1990), pp. 105–7.

40 Sources: Tax and Brown, 'Recovering and learning from service failure'; O. Harari, 'Thank heaven for complainers', *Management Review* 81 (January 1992), p. 59.

41 Adapted from https://econsultancy.com/blog

42 L.M. Fisher, 'Here comes front-office automation', *Strategy and Business* 13 (Fourth Quarter, 1999), pp. 53–65; and R.A. Shaffer, 'Handling customer service on the web', *Fortune*, 1 March 1999, pp. 204, 208.

43 Davidow, 'Organizational responses to customer complaints'.

44 2007 study conducted by TARP Worldwide Inc.

45 Sources: www.cisco.com (2004); 'The globally networked business', Cisco presentation at 'Activating your firm's service culture' symposium, Arizona State University (1997); R.L. Nolan, 'Cisco Systems architecture: ERP and web-enabled IT', Harvard Business School Case #9-301-099, 2001; 'Ten minutes with John Chambers', *NASDAQ: The International Magazine* 29 (January 2001).

46 L.L. Berry and K. Seiders, 'Serving unfair customers', *Business Horizons* 51 (January/February 2008), pp. 29–37.

47 J. Dunning, A. Pecotich and A. O'Cass, 'What happens when things go wrong? Retail sales explanations and their effects', *Psychology and Marketing* 21, no. 7 (2004), pp. 553–72; McColl-Kennedy and Sparks, 'Application of fairness theory to service failures and service recovery'; Davidow, 'Organizational responses to customer complaints'.

48 Hess, Ganesan and Klein, 'Service failure and recovery: the impact of relationship factors on customer satisfaction'; Priluck, 'Relationship marketing can mitigate product and service failures'.

49 T. DeWitt and M.K. Brady, 'Rethinking service recovery strategies: the effect of rapport on consumer responses to service failure', *Journal of Service Research* 6 (November 2003), pp. 193–207.

50 Hess, Ganesan and Klein, 'Service failure and recovery: the impact of relationship factors on customer satisfaction'.

51 L.L. Berry and A. Parasuraman, *Marketing Services* (New York: Free Press, 1991), p. 52.

52 F.F. Reichheld, 'Learning from customer defections', *Harvard Business Review* (March–April 1996), pp. 56–69.

53 Ibid.

54 A.L. Ostrom and C.W.L. Hart, 'Service guarantees: research and practice', in *Handbook of Services Marketing and Management*, eds T. Swartz and D. Iacobucci (Thousand Oaks, CA: Sage Publications, 2000), pp. 299–316.

55 See ibid.; C.W.L. Hart, 'The power of unconditional guarantees', *Harvard Business Review* (July–August 1988), pp. 54–62; and C.W.L. Hart, *Extraordinary Guarantees* (New York: AMACOM, 1993).

56 See www.landsend.co.uk or www.landsend.de

57 A.L. Ostrom and D. Iacobucci, 'The effect of guarantees on consumers' evaluation of services', *Journal of Services Marketing* 12, no. 5 (1998), pp. 362–78; S.B. Lidén and P. Skålén, 'The effect of service guarantees on service recovery', *International Journal of Service Industry Management* 14, no. 1 (2003), pp. 36–58.

58 Example cited in Ostrom and Hart, 'Service guarantees'.

59 These characteristics are proposed and discussed in C.W.L. Hart, 'The power of unconditional guarantees', *Harvard Business Review* 66 (July–August 1988), pp. 54–62; C.W.L. Hart, *Extraordinary Guarantees* (New York: AMACOM, 1993).

60 J. Wirtz, D. Kum and K.S. Lee, 'Should a firm with a reputation for outstanding service quality offer a service guarantee?', *Journal of Services Marketing* 14, no. 6 (2000), pp. 502–12.

61 J. Wirtz, 'Development of a service guarantee model', *Asia Pacific Journal of Management* 15 (April 1998), pp. 51–75.

62 Ibid.

63 J. Wirtz and D. Kum, 'Consumer cheating on service guarantees', *Journal of the Academy of Marketing Science* 32 (Spring 2004), pp. 159–75.

64 Wirtz, 'Development of a service guarantee model'.

65 Ostrom and Iacobucci, 'The effect of guarantees'.

66 Wirtz, 'Development of a service guarantee model'.

CHAPTER 16

1 Source: adapted from: Parsons, R. (2015) 'Santander bike deal puts engagement first', *Marketing Week*, 5 March page 6.

2 P.G. Lindell, 'You need integrated attitude to develop IMC', *Marketing News*, 26 May 1997, p. 5.

3 B. Mittal, 'The advertising of services: meeting the challenge of Intangibility', *Journal of Service Research* 2 (August 1999), pp. 98–116.

4 H.S. Bansal and P.A. Voyer, 'Word-of-mouth processes within a services purchase decision context', *Journal of Service Research* 3 (November 2000), pp. 166–77.

5 A.S. Mattila, 'The role of narratives in the advertising of experiential services', *Journal of Service Research* 3 (August 2000), pp. 35–45.

6 K.L. Alesandri, 'Strategies that influence memory for advertising communications', in *Information Processing Research in Advertising*, ed. R.J. Harris (Hillsdale, NJ: Erlbaum, 1983).

7 L.L. Berry and T. Clark, 'Four ways to make services more tangible', *Business* (October–December 1986), pp. 53–4.

8 Ibid.

9 W.R. George and L.L. Berry, 'Guidelines for the advertising of services', *Business Horizons* (May–June 1981), pp. 52–6.

10 L.L. Berry, 'Cultivating service brand equity', *Journal of the Academy of Marketing Science 28* (Winter 2000), pp. 128–37.

11 The definitions contained in this section are all from Berry, 'Cultivating service brand equity'.

12 See www.mastercardinternational.com.

13 Sources: K.J. Bannan, 'Seven ways to make online advertising work for you', *Advertising Age*, 11 October 2004, p. 11; R. Bayani, 'Banner ads – still working after all these years?', *Link-up* (November/December 2001), pp. 2, 6.

14 P. Denoyelle and J.-C. Larreche, 'Virgin Atlantic Airways – ten years later', INSEAD Case (1995).

15 D.E. Bell and D.M. Leavitt, 'Bronner Slosberg Humphrey', *Harvard Business School Case 9-598-136* (1998), p. 5.

16 Ibid., p. 4.

17 E.C. Clemmer and B. Schneider, 'Managing customer dissatisfaction with waiting: applying social-psychological theory in a service setting', in *Advances in Services Marketing and Management*, vol. 2, eds T. Schwartz, D.E. Bowen and S.W. Brown (Greenwich, CT: JAI Press, 1993), pp. 213–29.

18 Ibid.

19 L.L. Berry, V.A. Zeithaml and A. Parasuraman, 'Quality counts in services, too', *Business Horizons* (May–June 1985), pp. 44–52.

20 C. Mitchell, 'Selling the brand inside', *Harvard Business Review* 80 (January 2002), pp. 5–11.

21 V.A. Zeithaml, A. Parasuraman and L.L. Berry, *Delivering Quality Service: Balancing Customer Perceptions and Expectations* (New York: Free Press, 1990), p. 120.

CHAPTER 17

1 K. Monroe, 'The pricing of services', *Handbook of Services Marketing*, eds C.A. Congram and M.L. Friedman (New York: AMACOM, 1989), pp. 20–31.

2 Ibid.

3 Ibid.

4 V.A. Zeithaml, 'The acquisition, meaning, and use of price information by consumers of professional services', in *Marketing Theory: Philosophy of Science Perspectives*, eds R. Bush and S. Hunt (Chicago, IL: American Marketing Association, 1982), pp. 237–41.

5 C.H. Lovelock, 'Understanding costs and developing pricing strategies', *Services Marketing* (New York: Prentice Hall, 1991), pp. 236–46.

6 A. Stevens, 'Firms try more lucrative ways of charging for legal services', *The Wall Street Journal*, 25 November 1994, pp. B1ff.

7 J.L. Fix, 'Consumers are snarling over charges', *USA Today*, 2 August 1994, pp. B1–B2.

8 V.A. Zeithaml, 'Consumer perceptions of price, quality, and value: a means-end model and synthesis of evidence', *Journal of Marketing* 52 (July 1988), pp. 2–22.

9 All comments from these four sections are based on those from Zeithaml, 'Consumer perceptions of price, quality, and value', pp. 13–14.

10 Monroe, 'The pricing of services'.

11 See www.sky.com.

12 Monroe, 'The pricing of services'.

13 G.J. Tellis, 'Beyond the many faces of price: an integration of pricing strategies', *Journal of Marketing* 50 (October 1986), pp. 146–60.

CHAPTER 18

1 See www.zappos.com

2 R.T. Rust, C. Moorman and P.R. Dickson, 'Getting return on quality: revenue expansion, cost reduction, or both?', *Journal of Marketing* 66 (October 2002), pp. 7–24.

3 Ibid.

4 S. Gupta and V. Zeithaml, 'Customer metrics and their impact on financial performance', *Marketing Science* 25 (November–December 2006), pp. 718–39.

5 E. Anderson, C. Fornell, and S. Mazvancheryl, 'Customer satisfaction and shareholder value', *Journal of Marketing* 68 (2004), pp. 172–85.

6 T. S.Gruca and L. L. Rego, 'Customer satisfaction, cash flow and shareholder value', *Journal of Marketing* 69 (2005), pp. 115–30.

7 E. Anderson and V. Mittal, 'Strengthening the satisfaction-profit chain', *Journal of Service Research* 3 (2000), pp. 107–20.

8 P. Nayyar, 'Stock market reactions to customer service changes', *Strategic Management Journal* 16, no. 1 (1995), pp. 39–53.

9 E. Anderson and V. Mittal, 'Strengthening the satisfaction-profit chain'.

10 C. Ittner and D. Larcker, 'Are non-financial measures leading indicators of financial performance? An analysis of customer satisfaction', *Journal of Accounting Research*, 36 (3) (1998), pp. 1–35.

11 E. Anderson and V. Mittal, Strengthening the satisfaction-profit chain'.

12 Ibid.

13 Ibid.

14 C. Fornell and B. Wernerfelt, 'Defensive marketing strategy by customer complaint management: a theoretical analysis', *Journal of Marketing Research* 24 (November 1987), pp. 337–46; see also C. Fornell and B. Wernerfelt, 'A model for customer complaint management', *Marketing Science* 7 (Summer 1988), pp. 271–86.

15 B. Gale, 'Monitoring customer satisfaction and market-perceived quality', *American Marketing Association Worth Repeating Series*, no. 922CS01 (Chicago, IL: American Marketing Association, 1992).

16 Ibid.

17 R.E. Kordupleski, R.T. Rust and A.J. Zahorik, 'Why improving quality doesn't improve quality (or whatever happened to marketing?)', *California Management Review* 35 (1993), pp. 82–95.

18 Fornell and Wernerfelt, 'Defensive marketing strategy by customer complaint management', also Fornell and Wernerfelt, 'A model for customer complaint management'.

19 F. Reichheld and E. Sasser, 'Zero defections: quality comes to services', *Harvard Business Review* (September–October 1990), p. 106.

20 Ibid., p. 105.

21 D.F. Colicchio, regional quality manager, Hewlett-Packard Company, personal communication.

22 Reprinted with permission from V.A. Zeithaml, 'Service quality, profitability and the economic worth of customers', *Journal of the Academy of Marketing Science* (January 2000), Copyright © 2000 by the Academy of Marketing Science.

23 See www.storaenso.com.

24 E.W. Anderson and M. Sullivan, 'The antecedents and consequences of customer satisfaction for firms', *Marketing Science* 12 (Spring 1992), pp. 125–43.

25 W. Boulding, R. Staelin, A. Kalra and V.A. Zeithaml, 'Conceptualizing and testing a dynamic process model of service quality', report no. 92–121, Marketing Science Institute (1992).

26 V.A. Zeithaml, L.L. Berry and A. Parasuraman, 'The behavioral consequences of service quality', *Journal of Marketing* 60 (April 1996), pp. 31–46.

27 J.P. McLaughlin, 'Ensuring customer satisfaction is a strategic issue, not just an operational one', paper presented at the AIC Customer Satisfaction Measurement Conference, Chicago, 6–7 December 1993.

28 Sources: R.T. Rust, K.N. Lemon and V.A. Zeithaml, 'Return on marketing: using customer equity to focus marketing strategy', *Journal of Marketing* 68, no. 1 (January 2004), pp. 109; R. Rust, V. Zeithaml and K. Lemon, *Driving Customer Equity* (New York: Free Press, 2000).

29 R.S. Kaplan and D.P. Norton, 'The balanced scorecard – measures that drive performance', *Harvard Business Review* (January–February 1992), pp. 71–9.

30 Kaplan and Norton, 'The balanced scorecard'.

31 S. Silk, 'Automating the balanced scorecard', *Management Accounting* (May 1998), pp. 38–42.

32 The material in this section comes from C.D. Ittner and D.F. Larcker, 'Coming up short on nonfinancial performance measurement', *Harvard Business Review* (November 2003), pp. 88–95.

33 Ibid., p. 92.

Index